T0272029

Telling Stories with Data

The book equips students with the end-to-end skills needed to do data science. That means gathering, cleaning, preparing, and sharing data, then using statistical models to analyse data, writing about the results of those models, drawing conclusions from them, and finally, using the cloud to put a model into production, all done in a reproducible way.

At the moment, there are a lot of books that teach data science, but most of them assume that you already have the data. This book fills that gap by detailing how to go about gathering datasets, cleaning and preparing them, before analysing them. There are also a lot of books that teach statistical modelling, but few of them teach how to communicate the results of the models and how they help us learn about the world. Very few data science textbooks cover ethics, and most of those that do, have a token ethics chapter. Finally, reproducibility is not often emphasised in data science books. This book is based around a straight-forward workflow conducted in an ethical and reproducible way: gather data, prepare data, analyse data, and communicate those findings. This book will achieve the goals by working through extensive case studies in terms of gathering and preparing data and integrating ethics throughout. It is specifically designed around teaching how to write about the data and models, so aspects such as writing are explicitly covered. And finally, the use of GitHub and the open-source statistical language R are built in throughout the book.

Key Features:

- Extensive code examples.
- Ethics integrated throughout.
- Reproducibility integrated throughout.
- Focus on data gathering, messy data, and cleaning data.
- Extensive formative assessment throughout.

CHAPMAN & HALL/CRC DATA SCIENCE SERIES

Reflecting the interdisciplinary nature of the field, this book series brings together researchers, practitioners, and instructors from statistics, computer science, machine learning, and analytics. The series will publish cutting-edge research, industry applications, and textbooks in data science.

The inclusion of concrete examples, applications, and methods is highly encouraged. The scope of the series includes titles in the areas of machine learning, pattern recognition, predictive analytics, business analytics, Big Data, visualization, programming, software, learning analytics, data wrangling, interactive graphics, and reproducible research.

Published Titles

Urban Informatics
Using Big Data to Understand and Serve Communities
Daniel T. O'Brien

Introduction to Environmental Data Science
Jerry Douglas Davis

Hands-On Data Science for Librarians
Sarah Lin and Dorris Scott

Geographic Data Science with R
Visualizing and Analyzing Environmental Change
Michael C. Wimberly

Practitioner's Guide to Data Science
Hui Lin and Ming Li

Data Science and Analytics Strategy
An Emergent Design Approach
Kailash Awati and Alexander Scriven

Telling Stories with Data
With Applications in R
Rohan Alexander

Data Science for Sensory and Consumer Scientists
Thierry Worch, Julien Delarue, Vanessa Rios De Souza and John Ennis

Big Data Analytics
A Guide to Data Science Practitioners Making the Transition to Big Data
Ulrich Matter

Data Science in Practice
Tom Alby

Natural Language Processing in the Real World
Jyotika Singh

For more information about this series, please visit: https://www.routledge.com/Chapman--HallCRC-Data-Science-Series/book-series/CHDSS

Telling Stories with Data

With Applications in R

Rohan Alexander

CRC Press is an imprint of the
Taylor & Francis Group, an **informa** business
A CHAPMAN & HALL BOOK

Designed cover image: © Rohan Alexander

First edition published 2023
by CRC Press
6000 Broken Sound Parkway NW, Suite 300, Boca Raton, FL 33487-2742

and by CRC Press
4 Park Square, Milton Park, Abingdon, Oxon, OX14 4RN

CRC Press is an imprint of Taylor & Francis Group, LLC

Library of Congress Cataloging-in-Publication Data

Names: Alexander, Rohan, author.
Title: Telling stories with data : with applications in R / Rohan
Alexander.
Description: First edition. | Boca Raton : CRC Press, [2023] | Series:
Chapman & Hall/CRC data science series | Includes bibliographical
references and index. | Identifiers: LCCN 2022058452 (print) | LCCN 2022058453 (ebook) |
ISBN 9781032134772 (hbk) | ISBN 9781032133430 (pbk) | ISBN 9781003229407
(ebk)
Subjects: LCSH: Information visualization. | Big data. | R (Computer
program language) | Mathematical statistics.
Classification: LCC QA76.9.I52 A44 2023 (print) | LCC QA76.9.I52 (ebook)
| DDC 001.4/226--dc23/eng/20230127
LC record available at https://lccn.loc.gov/2022058452
LC ebook record available at https://lccn.loc.gov/2022058453

ISBN: 978-1-032-13477-2 (hbk)
ISBN: 978-1-032-13343-0 (pbk)
ISBN: 978-1-003-22940-7 (ebk)

DOI: 10.1201/9781003229407

Typeset in CMR10
by KnowledgeWorks Global Ltd.

Publisher's note: This book has been prepared from camera-ready copy provided by the authors.

For Mum and Dad

Table of contents

Preface

This book will help you tell stories with data. It establishes a foundation on which you can build and share knowledge about an aspect of the world that interests you based on data that you observe. Telling stories in small groups around a fire played a critical role in the development of humans and society (Wiessner 2014). Today our stories, based on data, can influence millions.

In this book we will explore, prod, push, manipulate, knead, and ultimately, try to understand the implications of, data. A variety of features drive the choices in this book.

The motto of the university from which I took my PhD is *naturam primum cognoscere rerum* or roughly "first to learn the nature of things". But the original quote continues *temporis aeterni quoniam*, or roughly "for eternal time". We will do both of these things. I focus on tools, approaches, and workflows that enable you to establish lasting and reproducible knowledge.

When I talk of data in this book, it will typically be related to humans. Humans will be at the center of most of our stories, and we will tell social, cultural, and economic stories. In particular, throughout this book I will draw attention to inequity both in social phenomena and in data. Most data analysis reflects the world as it is. Many of the least well-off face a double burden in this regard: not only are they disadvantaged, but the extent is more difficult to measure. Respecting those whose data are in our dataset is a primary concern, and so is thinking of those who are systematically not in our dataset.

While data are often specific to various contexts and disciplines, the approaches used to understand them tend to be similar. Data are also increasingly global, with resources and opportunities available from a variety of sources. Hence, I draw on examples from many disciplines and geographies.

To become knowledge, our findings must be communicated to, understood, and trusted by other people. Scientific and economic progress can only be made by building on the work of others. And this is only possible if we can understand what they did. Similarly, if we are to create knowledge about the world, then we must enable others to understand precisely what we did, what we found, and how we went about our tasks. As such, in this book I will be particularly prescriptive about communication and reproducibility.

Improving the quality of quantitative work is an enormous challenge, yet it is the challenge of our time. Data are all around us, but there is little enduring knowledge being created. This book hopes to contribute, in some small way, to changing that.

Audience and assumed background

The typical person reading this book has some familiarity with first-year undergraduate statistics, for instance they have run a regression. But it is not targeted at a particular level, instead providing aspects relevant to almost any quantitative course. I have taught from this book at undergraduate, graduate, and professional levels. Everyone has unique needs, but hopefully some aspect of this book speaks to you.

Enthusiasm and interest have taken people far. If you have those, then do not worry about too much else. Some of the most successful students have been those with no quantitative or coding background.

This book covers a lot of ground, but does not go into depth about any particular aspect. As such it especially complements more-detailed books such as: *Data Science: A First Introduction* (Timbers, Campbell, and Lee 2022), *R for Data Science* (Wickham, Çetinkaya-Rundel, and Grolemund [2016] 2023), *An Introduction to Statistical Learning* (James et al. [2013] 2021), and *Statistical Rethinking* (McElreath [2015] 2020). If you are interested in those books, then this might be a good one to start with.

Structure and content

This book is structured around six parts: I) Foundations, II) Communication, III) Acquisition, IV) Preparation, V) Modeling, and VI) Applications.

Part I—Foundations—begins with Chapter 1 which provides an overview of what I am trying to achieve with this book and why you should read it. Chapter 2 goes through three worked examples. The intention of these is that you can experience the full workflow recommended in this book without worrying too much about the specifics of what is happening. That workflow is: plan, simulate, acquire, model, and communicate. It is normal to not initially follow everything in this chapter, but you should go through it, typing out and executing the code yourself. If you only have time to read one chapter of this book, then I recommend that one. Chapter 3 introduces some key tools for reproducibility used in the workflow that I advocate. These are aspects like Quarto, R Projects, Git and GitHub, and using R in practice.

Part II—Communication—considers written and static communication. Chapter 4 details the features that quantitative writing should have and how to write a crisp, quantitative research paper. Static communication in Chapter 5 introduces features like graphs, tables, and maps.

Part III—Acquisition—focuses on turning our world into data. Chapter 6 begins with measurement, and then steps through essential concepts from sampling that govern our approach to data. It then considers datasets that are explicitly provided for us to use as data, for instance censuses and other government statistics. These are typically clean, well-documented, pre-packaged datasets. Chapter 7 covers aspects like using Application Programming Interfaces (APIs), scraping data, getting data from PDFs, and Optical Character Recognition (OCR). The idea is that data are available, but not necessarily designed to be datasets, and that we must go and get them. Finally, Chapter 8 covers aspects where more is expected of us. For instance, we may need to conduct an experiment, run an A/B test, or do some surveys.

Part IV—Preparation—covers how to respectfully transform the original, unedited data into something that can be explored and shared. Chapter 9 begins by detailing some principles to follow when approaching the task of cleaning and preparing data, and then goes through specific steps to take and checks to implement. Chapter 10 focuses on methods of storing and retrieving those datasets, including the use of R data packages and parquet. It then continues onto considerations and steps to take when wanting to disseminate datasets as broadly as possible, while at the same time respecting those whose data they are based on.

Part V—Modeling—begins with exploratory data analysis in Chapter 11. This is the critical process of coming to understand a dataset, but not something that typically finds itself into the final product. The process is an end in itself. In Chapter 12 the use of linear models to explore data is introduced. And Chapter 13 considers generalized linear models, including logistic, Poisson, and negative binomial regression. It also introduces multilevel modeling.

Part VI—Applications—provides three applications of modeling. Chapter 14 focuses on making causal claims from observational data and covers approaches such as difference-in-differences, regression discontinuity, and instrumental variables. Chapter 15 introduces multilevel regression with post-stratification, which is where we use a statistical model to adjust a sample for known biases. Chapter 16 is focused on text-as-data.

Chapter 17 offers some concluding remarks, details some outstanding issues, and suggests some next steps.

Online appendices offer critical aspects that are either a little too unwieldy for the size constraints of the page, or likely to need more frequent updating than is reasonable for a printed book. "R essentials"[1] goes through some essential tasks in R, which is the statistical programming language used in this book. It can be a reference chapter and some students find themselves returning to it as they go through the rest of the book. "Datasets"[2] provides a list of datasets that may be useful for assessment. The core of this book is centered around Quarto, however its predecessor, R Markdown, has not yet been sunsetted and there is a lot of material available for it. As such, "R Markdown"[3] contains R Markdown equivalents of the Quarto-specific aspects in Chapter 3. A set of papers is included in "Papers"[4]. If you write these, you will be conducting original research on a topic that is of interest to you. Although open-ended research may be new to you, the extent to which you are able to: develop your own questions, use quantitative methods to explore them, and communicate your findings, is the measure of the success of this book. "Interactive communication"[5] covers aspects such as websites, web applications, and maps that can be interacted with. "Datasheet"[6] provides an example of a datasheet. "SQL"[7] gives a brief overview of SQL essentials. "Prediction"[8] goes through prediction-focused modeling. "Production"[9] considers how to make model estimates and forecasts more widely available. Finally, "Activities"[10] provides ideas for using this book in class.

[1]https://tellingstorieswithdata.com/20-r_essentials.html
[2]https://tellingstorieswithdata.com/21-datasets.html
[3]https://tellingstorieswithdata.com/22-rmarkdown.html
[4]https://tellingstorieswithdata.com/23-assessment.html
[5]https://tellingstorieswithdata.com/24-interactive_communication.html
[6]https://tellingstorieswithdata.com/25-datasheet.html
[7]https://tellingstorieswithdata.com/26-sql.html
[8]https://tellingstorieswithdata.com/27-prediction.html
[9]https://tellingstorieswithdata.com/28-deploy.html
[10]https://tellingstorieswithdata.com/29-activities.html

Pedagogy and key features

You have to do the work. You should actively go through material and code yourself. S. King (2000) says "[a]mateurs sit and wait for inspiration, the rest of us just get up and go to work". Do not passively read this book. My role is best described by Hamming ([1997] 2020, 2–3):

> I am, as it were, only a coach. I cannot run the mile for you; at best I can discuss styles and criticize yours. You know you must run the mile if the athletics course is to be of benefit to you—hence you must think carefully about what you hear and read in this book if it is to be effective in changing you—which must obviously be the purpose...

This book is structured around a dense, introductory 12-week course. It provides enough material for advanced readers to be challenged, while establishing a core that all readers should master. Typical courses cover most of the material through to Chapter 13, and then pick another chapter that is of particular interest. But it depends on the backgrounds and interests of the students.

From as early as Chapter 2 you will have a workflow—plan, simulate, acquire, model, and communicate—allowing you to tell a convincing story with data. In each subsequent chapter you will add depth to this workflow. This will allow you to speak with increasing sophistication and credibility. This workflow encompasses skills that are typically sought in both academia and industry. These include: communication, ethics, reproducibility, research question development, data collection, data cleaning, data protection and dissemination, exploratory data analysis, statistical modeling, and scaling.

One of the defining aspects of this book is that ethics and inequity concerns are integrated throughout, rather than being clustered in one, easily ignorable, chapter. These are critical, but it can be difficult to immediately see their value, hence their tight integration.

This book is also designed to enable you to build a portfolio of work that you could show to a potential employer. If you want a job in industry, then this is arguably the most important thing that you should be doing. E. Robinson and Nolis (2020, 55) describe how a portfolio is a collection of projects that show what you can do and is something that can help be successful in a job search.

In the novel *The Last Samurai* (DeWitt 2000, 326), a character says:

> [A] scholar should be able to look at any word in a passage and instantly think of another passage where it occurred; ... [so a] text was like a pack of icebergs each word a snowy peak with a huge frozen mass of cross-references beneath the surface.

In an analogous way, this book not only provides text and instruction that is self-contained, but also helps develop the critical masses of knowledge on which expertise is built. No chapter positions itself as the last word, instead they are written in relation to other work.

Each chapter has the following features:

- A list of required materials that you should go through before you read that chapter. To be clear, you should first read that material and then return to this book. Each chapter also contains extensive references. If you are particularly interested in the topic, then you should use these as a starting place for further exploration.
- A summary of the key concepts and skills that are developed in that chapter. Technical chapters additionally contain a list of the software and packages that are used in the chapter. The combination of these features acts as a checklist for your learning, and you should return to them after completing the chapter.
- "Scales" where I provide a small scenario and ask you to work through the workflow advocated in this book. This will probably take 15-30 minutes. Hilary Hahn, the American violinist, publicly documents herself practicing the violin, often scales or similar exercises, almost every day. I recommend you do something similar, and these are designed to enable that.
- A series of short questions that you should complete after going through the required materials, but before going through the chapter, to test your knowledge. After completing the chapter, you should go back through the questions to make sure that you understand each aspect. An answer guide is available on request.
- A tutorial question to further encourage you to actively engage with the material. You could consider forming small groups to discuss your answers to these questions.

Some chapters additionally feature:

- A section called "Oh, you think we have good data on that!" which focuses on a particular setting where it is often assumed that there are unimpeachable and unambiguous data but the reality tends to be quite far from that.
- A section called "Shoulders of giants", which focuses on some of those who created the intellectual foundation on which we build.

Software information and conventions

The software that I primarily use in this book is R (R Core Team 2023). This language was chosen because it is open source, widely used, general enough to cover the entire workflow, yet specific enough to have plenty of well-developed features. I do not assume that you have used R before, and so another reason for selecting R for this book is the community of R users. The community is especially welcoming of newcomers and there is a lot of complementary beginner-friendly material available.

If you do not have a programming language, then R is a great one to start with. Please do go through "R essentials"[11].

[11] https://tellingstorieswithdata.com/20-r_essentials.html

The ability to code is useful well beyond this book. If you have a preferred programming language already, then it would not hurt to also pick up R. That said, if you have a good reason to prefer another open-source programming language (for instance you use Python daily at work) then you may wish to stick with that. However, all examples in this book are in R.

Please download R and RStudio onto your own computer. You can download R for free here[12], and you can download RStudio Desktop for free here[13]. Please also create an account on Posit Cloud here[14]. This will allow you to run R in the cloud. And download Quarto here[15].

Packages are in typewriter text, for instance, `tidyverse`, while functions are also in typewriter text, but include brackets, for instance `filter()`.

About the author

I am an assistant professor at the University of Toronto, jointly appointed in the Faculty of Information and the Department of Statistical Sciences. I am also the assistant director of the Canadian Statistical Sciences Institute (CANSSI) Ontario, a senior fellow at Massey College, a faculty affiliate at the Schwartz Reisman Institute for Technology and Society, and a co-lead of the Data Sciences Institute Thematic Program in Reproducibility. I hold a PhD in Economics from the Australian National University where I focused on economic history and was supervised by John Tang (chair), Martine Mariotti, Tim Hatton, and Zach Ward.

My research investigates how we can develop workflows that improve the trustworthiness of data science. I am particularly interested in the role of testing in data science.

I enjoy teaching and I aim to help students from a wide range of backgrounds learn how to use data to tell convincing stories. I try to develop students that are skilled not only in using statistical methods across various disciplines, but also appreciate their limitations, and think deeply about the broader contexts of their work. I teach in both the Faculty of Information and the Department of Statistical Sciences at both undergraduate and graduate levels. I am a RStudio Certified Tidyverse Trainer.

I am married to Monica Alexander and we have two children. I probably spend too much money on books, and certainly too much time at libraries. If you have any book recommendations of your own, then I would love to hear them.

Acknowledgments

Many people generously gave code, data, examples, guidance, opportunities, thoughts, and time that helped develop this book.

[12]http://cran.utstat.utoronto.ca/
[13]https://rstudio.com/products/rstudio/download/#download
[14]https://posit.cloud
[15]https://quarto.org/docs/get-started/

Thank you to David Grubbs, Curtis Hill, Robin Lloyd-Starkes, and the team at Taylor & Francis for editing and publishing this book, and providing invaluable guidance and support. I am grateful to Erica Orloff who thoroughly edited this book. Thank you to Isabella Ghement, who thoroughly went through an early draft of this book and provided detailed feedback that improved it.

Thank you to Annie Collins, who went through every word in this book, improving many of them, and helped to sharpen my thinking on much of the content covered in it. One of the joys of teaching is the chance to work with talented people like Annie as they start their careers.

Thank you to Emily Riederer, who provided detailed comments on the initial plans for the book. She then returned to the manuscript after it was drafted and went through it in minute detail. Her thoughtful comments greatly improved the book. More broadly her work changed the way I thought about much of the content of this book.

I was fortunate to have many reviewers who read entire chapters, sometimes two, three, or even more. They very much went above and beyond and provided excellent suggestions for improving this book. For this I am indebted to Albert Rapp, Alex Luscombe (who also suggested the Police Violence "Oh, you think..." entry), Ariel Mundo, Benjamin Haibe-Kains, Dan Ryan, Erik Drysdale, Florence Vallée-Dubois, Jack Bailey, Jae Hattrick-Simpers, Jon Khan, Jonathan Keane (who also generously shared their parquet expertise), Lauren Kennedy (who also generously shared code, data, and expertise, to develop my thoughts about MRP), Liam Welsh, Liza Bolton (who also helped develop my ideas around how this book should be taught), Luis Correia, Matt Ratto, Matthias Berger, Michael Moon, Roberto Lentini, Ryan Briggs, and Taylor Wright.

Many people made specific suggestions that greatly improved things. All these people contribute to the spirit of generosity that characterizes the open source programming languages communities this book builds on. I am grateful to them all. A Mahfouz made me realize that that covering Poisson regression was critical. Aaron Miller suggested the FINER framework. Alison Presmanes Hill suggested Wordbank. Chris Warshaw suggested the Democracy Fund Voter Study Group survey data. Christina Wei pointed out many code errors. Claire Battershill directed me toward many books about writing. Ella Kaye suggested, and rightly insisted on, moving to Quarto. Faria Khandaker suggested what became the "R essentials" chapter. Hareem Naveed generously shared her industry experience. Heath Priston provided assistance with Toronto homelessness data. Jessica Gronsbell gave invaluable suggestions around statistical practice. Keli Chiu reinforced the importance of text-as-data. Leslie Root came up with the idea of "Oh, you think we have good data on that!". Michael Chong shaped my approach to EDA. Michael Donnelly, Peter Hepburn, and Léo Raymond-Belzile provided pointers to classic papers that I was unaware of, in political science, sociology, and statistics, respectively. Nick Horton suggested the Hadley Wickham video in Chapter 11. Paul Hodgetts taught me how to make R packages and made the cover art for this book. Radu Craiu ensured sampling was afforded its appropriate place. Sharla Gelfand the approaches I advocate around how to use R. Thomas William Rosenthal made me realize the potential of Shiny. Tom Cardoso and Zane Schwartz were excellent sources of data put together by journalists. Yanbo Tang assisted with Nancy Reid's "Shoulders of giants" entry. Finally, Chris Maddison and Maia Balint suggested the closing poem.

Thank you to my PhD supervisory panel John Tang, Martine Mariotti, Tim Hatton, and Zach Ward. They gave me the freedom to explore the intellectual space that was of interest to me, the support to follow through on those interests, and the guidance to ensure that it all resulted in something tangible. What I learned during those years served as the foundation for this book.

This book has greatly benefited from the notes and teaching materials of others that are freely available online, including: Chris Bail, Scott Cunningham, Andrew Heiss (who independently taught a course with the same name as this book, well before the book was available), Lisa Lendway, Grant McDermott, Nathan Matias, David Mimno, and Ed Rubin. Thank you to these people. The changed norm of academics making their materials freely available online is a great one and one that I hope the free online version of this book, available here[16], helps contribute to.

Thank you to Samantha-Jo Caetano who helped develop some of the assessment items. And also, to Lisa Romkey and Alan Chong, who allowed me to adapt some aspects of their rubric. The catalysts for aspects of the Chapter 4 tutorial were McPhee (2017, 186) and Chelsea Parlett-Pelleriti. The idea behind the "Interactive communication" tutorial was work by Mauricio Vargas Sepúlveda ("Pachá") and Andrew Whitby.

I am grateful for the corrections of: Amy Farrow, Arsh Lakhanpal, Cesar Villarreal Guzman, Chloe Thierstein, Finn Korol-O'Dwyer, Flavia López, Gregory Power, Hong Shi, Jayden Jung, John Hayes, Joyce Xuan, Laura Cline, Lorena Almaraz De La Garza, Matthew Robertson, Michaela Drouillard, Mounica Thanam, Reem Alasadi, Rob Zimmerman, Tayedza Chikumbirike, Wijdan Tariq, Yang Wu, and Yewon Han.

Kelly Lyons provided support, guidance, mentorship, and friendship. Every day she demonstrates what an academic should be, and more broadly, what one should aspire to be as a person.

Greg Wilson provided a structure to think about teaching and suggested the "Scales" style exercises. He was the catalyst for this book, and provided helpful comments on drafts. Every day he demonstrates how to contribute to the intellectual community.

Thank you to Elle Côté for enabling this book to be written by looking after first one, and then two, children during a pandemic.

As at Christmas 2021 this book was a disparate collection of partially completed notes; thank you to Mum and Dad, who dropped everything and came over from the other side of the world for two months to give me the opportunity to rewrite it all and put together a cohesive draft.

Thank you to Marija Taflaga and the ANU Australian Politics Studies Centre at the School of Politics and International Relations for funding a two-week "writing retreat" in Canberra.

Finally, thank you to Monica Alexander. Without you I would not have written a book; I would not have even thought it possible. Many of the best ideas in this book are yours, and those that are not, you made better, by reading everything many times. Thank you for your inestimable help with writing this book, providing the base on which it builds (remember in the library showing me many times how to get certain rows in R!), giving me the time that I needed to write, encouragement when it turned out that writing a book just meant

[16] https://tellingstorieswithdata.com/

endlessly rewriting that which was perfect the day before, reading everything in this book many times, making coffee or cocktails as appropriate, looking after the children, and more.

You can contact me at: rohan.alexander@utoronto.ca.

Rohan Alexander
Toronto, Canada
May 2023

Part I

Foundations

1

Telling stories with data

Prerequisites

- Read *Counting the Countless*, (Keyes 2019)
  - This article discusses the difficulties of turning the world into data.
- Watch *Data Science Ethics in 6 Minutes*, (Register 2020b)
  - This video integrates ethics and data science in a constructive way.
- Read *What is Code?*, (Ford 2015)
  - This article provides an overview of the role of code, and you should focus on the first three sections.

1.1 On telling stories

One of the first things that many parents regularly do when their children are born is read stories to them. In doing so they carry on a tradition that has occurred for millennia. Myths, fables, and fairy tales can be seen and heard all around us. Not only are they entertaining, but they enable us to learn about the world. While *The Very Hungry Caterpillar* by Eric Carle may seem quite far from the world of dealing with data, there are similarities. Both aim to tell a story and impart knowledge.

When using data we try to tell a convincing story. It may be as exciting as predicting elections, as banal as increasing internet advertising click rates, as serious as finding the cause of a disease, or as fun as forecasting basketball games. In any case the key elements are the same. The early twentieth century English author, E. M. Forster, described the aspects common to all novels as: story, people, plot, fantasy, prophecy, pattern, and rhythm (Forster 1927). Similarly, regardless of the setting, there are common concerns when we tell stories with data:

1. What is the dataset? Who generated the dataset and why?
2. What is the process that underpins the dataset? Given that process, what is missing from the dataset or has been poorly measured? Could other datasets have been generated, and if so, how different could they have been to the one that we have?
3. What is the dataset trying to say, and how can we let it say this? What else could it say? How do we decide between these?
4. What are we hoping others will see from this dataset, and how can we convince them of this? How much work must we do to convince them?
5. Who is affected by the processes and outcomes, related to this dataset? To what extent are they represented in the dataset, and have they been involved in the analysis?

In the past, certain elements of telling stories with data were easier. For instance, experimental design has a long and robust tradition within agricultural and medical sciences, physics, and chemistry. Student's t-distribution was identified in the early 1900s by a chemist, William Sealy Gosset, who worked at Guinness, a beer manufacturer (Boland 1984). It would have been relatively straightforward for him to randomly sample the beer and change one aspect at a time.

Many of the fundamentals of the statistical methods that we use today were developed in such settings. In those circumstances, it was typically possible to establish control groups and randomize, and there were fewer ethical concerns. A story told with the resulting data was likely to be fairly convincing.

Unfortunately, little of this applies these days, given the diversity of settings to which statistical methods are applied. On the other hand, we have many advantages. For instance, we have well-developed statistical techniques, easier access to large datasets, and open-source statistical languages such as R. But the difficulty of conducting traditional experiments means that we must also turn to other aspects to tell a convincing story.

1.2 Workflow components

There are five core components to the workflow needed to tell stories with data:

1. **Plan** and sketch an endpoint.
2. **Simulate** and consider that simulated data.
3. **Acquire** and prepare the actual data.
4. **Explore** and understand the actual data.
5. **Share** what was done and what was found.

We begin by **planning and sketching an endpoint** because this ensures that we think carefully about where we want to go. It forces us to deeply consider our situation, acts to keep us focused and efficient, and helps reduce scope creep. In *Alice's Adventures in Wonderland* by Lewis Carroll, Alice asks the Cheshire Cat which way she should go. The Cheshire Cat replies by asking where Alice would like to go. And when Alice replies that she does not mind, so long as she gets somewhere, the Cheshire Cat says then the direction does not matter because one will always get somewhere if one "walks long enough". The issue, in our case, is that we typically cannot afford to walk aimlessly for long. While it may be that the endpoint needs to change, it is important that this is a deliberate, reasoned decision. And that is only possible given an initial objective. There is no need to spend too much time on this to get a lot of value from it. Often ten minutes with paper and pen are enough.

The next step is to **simulate data**, because that forces us into the details. It helps with cleaning and preparing the dataset because it focuses us on the classes in the dataset and the distribution of the values that we expect. For instance, if we were interested in the effect of age-groups on political preferences, then we may expect that our age-group variable would be a factor, with four possible values: "18-29", "30-44", "45-59", "60+". The process of simulation provides us with clear features that our real dataset should satisfy. We could use these features to define tests that would guide our data cleaning and preparation. For instance, we could check our real dataset for age-groups that are not one of those four values. When those tests pass, we could be confident that our age-group variable only contains values that we expect.

Simulating data is also important when we turn to statistical modeling. When we are at that stage, we are concerned with whether the model reflects what is in the dataset. The issue is that if we go straight to modeling the real dataset, then we do not know whether we have a problem with our model. We initially simulate data so that we precisely know the underlying data generation process. We then apply the model to the simulated dataset. If we get out what we put in, then we know that our model is performing appropriately, and can turn to the real dataset. Without that initial application to simulated data, it would be more difficult to have confidence in our model.

Simulation is often cheap—almost free given modern computing resources and statistical programming languages—and fast. It provides "an intimate feeling for the situation", (Hamming [1997] 2020, 239). Start with a simulation that just contains the essentials, get that working, and then complicate it.

Acquiring and preparing the data that we are interested in is an often-overlooked stage of the workflow. This is surprising because it can be one of the most difficult stages and requires many decisions to be made. It is increasingly the subject of research, and it has been found that decisions made during this stage can affect statistical results (Huntington-Klein et al. 2021; Dolatsara et al. 2021).

At this stage of the workflow, it is common to feel a little overwhelmed. Typically, the data we can acquire leave us a little scared. There may be too little of it, in which case we worry about how we are going to be able to make our statistical machinery work. Alternatively, we may have the opposite problem and be worried about how we can even begin to deal with such a large amount of data.

> Perhaps all the dragons in our lives are princesses who are only waiting to see us act, just once, with beauty and courage. Perhaps everything that frightens us is, in its deepest essence, something helpless that wants our love.
>
> Rilke ([1929] 2014)

Developing comfort in this stage of the workflow unlocks the rest of it. The dataset that is needed to tell a convincing story is in there. But, like a sculptor, we need to iteratively remove everything that is not the data that we need, and to then shape that which is.

After we have a dataset, we then want to **explore and understand** certain relationships in that dataset. We typically begin the process with descriptive statistics and then move to statistical models. The use of statistical models to understand the implications of our data is not free of bias, nor are they "truth"; they do what we tell them to do. When telling stories with data, statistical models are tools and approaches that we use to explore our dataset, in the same way that we may use graphs and tables. They are not something that will provide us with a definitive result but will enable us to understand the dataset more clearly in a particular way.

By the time we get to this step in the workflow, to a large extent, the model will reflect the decisions that were made in earlier stages, especially acquisition and cleaning, as much as it reflects any type of underlying data generating process. Sophisticated modelers know that their statistical models are like the bit of the iceberg above the surface: they build on, and are only possible due to, the majority that is underneath, in this case, the data. But when an expert at the whole data science workflow uses modeling, they recognize that the results that are obtained are additionally due to choices about whose data matters, decisions about how to measure and record the data, and other aspects that reflect the world as it is, well before the data are available to their specific workflow.

Finally, we must **share** what we did and what we found, at as high a fidelity as is possible. Talking about knowledge that only you have does not make you knowledgeable, and that includes knowledge that only "past you" has. When communicating, we need to be clear about the decisions that we made, why we made them, our findings, and the weaknesses of our approach. We are aiming to uncover something important so we should write down everything in the first instance, although this written communication may be supplemented with other forms of communication later. There are so many decisions that we need to make in this workflow that we want to be sure that we are open about the entire thing—start to finish. This means much more than just the statistical modeling and creation of the graphs and tables, but everything. Without this, stories based on data lack credibility.

The world is not a rational meritocracy where everything is carefully and judiciously evaluated. Instead, we use shortcuts, hacks, and heuristics, based on our experience. Unclear communication will render even the best work moot, because it will not be thoroughly engaged with. While there is a minimum when it comes to communication, there is no upper limit to how impressive it can be. When it is the culmination of a thought-out workflow, it can even obtain a certain *sprezzatura*, or studied carelessness. Achieving such mastery requires years of work.

1.3 Telling stories with data

A compelling story based on data can likely be told in around ten-to-twenty pages. Anything less than this, and it is likely too light on some of the details. And while it is easy to write much more, often some reflection enables succinctness or for multiple stories to be separated.

It is possible to tell convincing stories even when it is not possible to conduct traditional experiments. These approaches do not rely on "big data"—which is not a cure-all (Meng 2018; Bradley et al. 2021)—but instead on better using the data that are available. Research and independent learning, a blend of theory and application, all combined with practical skills, a sophisticated workflow, and an appreciation for what one does not know, is often enough to create lasting knowledge.

The best stories based on data tend to be multi-disciplinary. They take from whatever field they need to, but almost always draw on statistics, computer science, economics, and engineering (to name a few). As such, an end-to-end workflow requires a blend of skills from these areas. The best way to learn these skills is to use real-world data to conduct research projects where you:

- develop research questions;
- obtain and clean relevant datasets;

- explore the data to answer those questions; and
- communicate in a meaningful way.

The key elements of telling convincing stories with data are:

1. Communication.
2. Reproducibility.
3. Ethics.
4. Questions.
5. Measurement.
6. Data collection.
7. Data cleaning.
8. Exploratory data analysis.
9. Modeling.
10. Scaling.

These elements can be considered within a few different categories including: doing good research (ethics and questions), coming up with credible answers (measurement, collection, cleaning, exploratory data analysis, and modeling), and creating compelling explanations (communication, reproducibility, and scaling). These elements are the foundation on which the workflow is built (Figure 1.1).

This is a lot to master, but **communication** is the most important. Simple analysis, communicated well, is more valuable than complicated analysis communicated poorly. This is because the latter cannot be understood or trusted by others. A lack of clear communication sometimes reflects a failure by the researcher to understand what is going on, or even what they are doing. And so, while the level of the analysis should match the dataset, instrumentation, task, and skillset, when a trade-off is required between clarity and complication, it can be sensible to err on the side of clarity.

Clear communication means writing in plain language with the help of tables, graphs, and models, in a way that brings the audience along with you. It means setting out what was done and why, as well as what was found. The minimum standard is that this is done to an extent such that another person can independently do what you did and find what you found. One challenge is that as you immerse yourself in the data, it can be difficult to remember what it was like when you first came to it. But that is where most of your audience will be coming from. Learning to provide an appropriate level of nuance and detail can be challenging, but is made easier by focusing on writing for the benefit of the audience.

Reproducibility is required to create lasting knowledge about the world. It means that everything that was done—all of it, end-to-end—can be independently redone. Ideally, autonomous end-to-end reproducibility is possible; anyone can get the code, data, and environment to verify everything that was done (Heil et al. 2021). Unrestricted access to code is almost always possible. While that is the default expectation for data also, it is not always reasonable. For instance, studies in psychology may have small, personally identifying samples. One way forward is to openly share simulated data with similar properties, along with defining a process by which the real data could be accessed, given appropriate *bona fides*. Statistical models are commonly subject to an extensive suite of manual checks. Another aspect of reproducibility is that we similarly need to include a broad swathe of automated testing.

Active consideration of **ethics** is needed because the dataset likely concerns humans. This means considering things like: who is in the dataset, who is missing, and why? To what

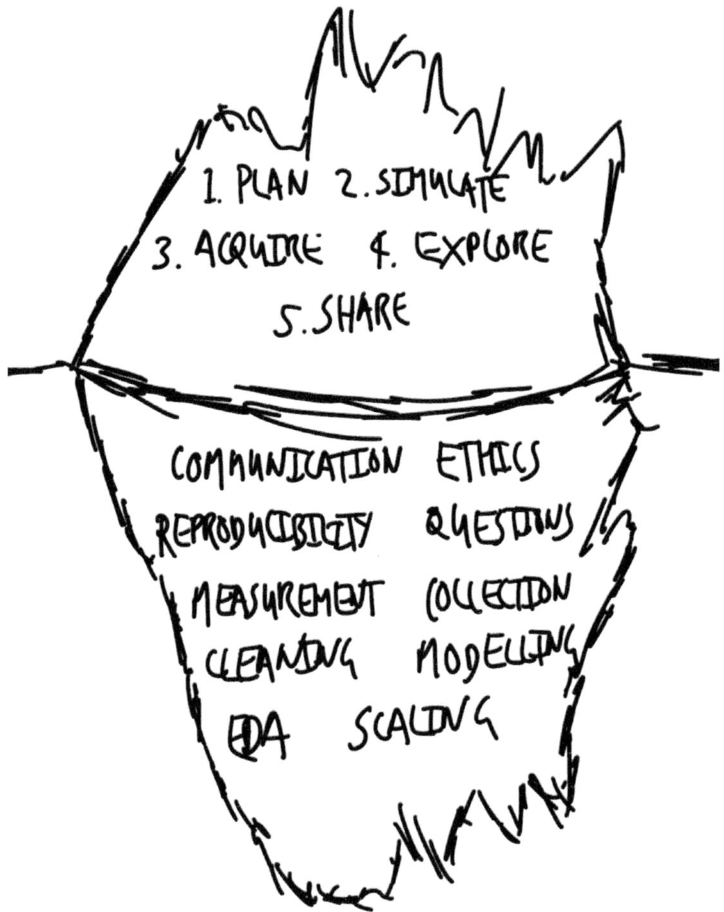

Figure 1.1: The workflow builds on various elements

extent will our story perpetuate the past? And is this something that ought to happen? Even if the dataset does not concern humans, the story is likely being put together by humans, and we affect almost everything else. This means that we have a responsibility to use data ethically, with concern for environmental impact and inequity.

There are many definitions of ethics, but when it comes to telling stories with data, at a minimum it means considering the full context of the dataset (D'Ignazio and Klein 2020). In jurisprudence, a textual approach to law means literally considering the words of the law as they are printed, while a purposive approach means laws are interpreted within a broader context. An ethical approach to telling stories with data means adopting the latter approach, and considering the social, cultural, historical, and political forces that shape our world, and hence our data (Crawford 2021).

Curiosity provides internal motivation to explore a dataset, and associated process, to a proper extent. **Questions** tend to beget questions, and these usually improve and refine as the process of coming to understand a dataset carries on. In contrast to the stock Popperian approach of hypothesis testing often taught, questions are typically developed through a continuous and evolving process (Franklin 2005). Finding an initial question can be challenging. It is especially tough to operationalize research questions into measurable variables that are reasonably available. Selecting an area of interest can help, as can sketching a broad claim with the intent of evolving it into a specific question, and finally, bringing together two different areas.

Developing a comfort and ease in the messiness of real-world data means getting to ask new questions each time the data update. And knowing a dataset in detail tends to surface unexpected groupings or values that you can then work with subject-area experts to understand. Becoming a bit of a "hybrid" by developing a base of knowledge across a variety of areas is especially valuable, as is becoming comfortable with the possibility of initially asking dumb questions.

Measurement and **data collection** are about deciding how our world will become data. They are challenging. The world is so vibrant that it is difficult to reduce it to something that is possible to consistently measure and collect. Take, for instance, someone's height. We can, probably, all agree that we should take our shoes off before we measure height. But our height changes over the course of the day. And measuring someone's height with a tape measure will give different results to using a laser. If we are comparing heights between people or over time, it therefore becomes important to measure at the same time each day, using the same method. But that quickly becomes unfeasible.

Most of the questions we are interested in will use data that are more complicated than height. How do we measure how sad someone is? How do we measure pain? Who decides what we will measure and how we will measure it? There is a certain arrogance required to think that we can reduce the world to a value and then compare these. Ultimately, we must, but it is difficult to consistently define what is to be measured. This process is not value-free. The only way to reasonably come to terms with this brutal reduction is to deeply understand and respect what we are measuring and collecting. What is the central essence, and what can be stripped away?

Pablo Picasso, the twentieth century Spanish painter, has a series of drawings where he depicts the outline of an animal using only one line (Figure 1.2). Despite their simplicity, we recognize which animal is being depicted—the drawing is sufficient to tell the animal is a dog, not a cat. Could this be used to determine whether the dog is sick? Probably not. We would likely want a different depiction. The decision as to which things should be measured, and then of those things that we decide to consider, which features should be measured and collected, and which to ignore, turns on context and purpose.

Figure 1.2: This drawing is clearly a dog, even though it is just one line

Data cleaning and preparation is a critical part of using data. We need to massage the data available to us into a dataset that we can use. This requires making a lot of decisions.

The data cleaning and preparation stage is critical, and worthy of as much attention and care as any other.

Following Kennedy et al. (2022) consider a survey that collected information about a potentially sensitive topic, gender, using four options: "man", "woman", "prefer not to say", and "other", where "other" dissolved into an open textbox. When we come to that dataset, we are likely to find that most responses are either "man" or "woman". We need to decide what to do about "prefer not to say". If we drop it from our dataset, then we are actively ignoring these respondents. If we do not drop it, then it makes our analysis more complicated. Similarly, we need to decide how to deal with the open text responses. Again, we could drop these responses, but this ignores the experiences of some of our respondents. Another option is to merge this with "prefer not to say", but that shows a disregard for our respondents, because they specifically did not choose that option.

There is no easy, nor always-correct, choice in many data cleaning and preparation situations. It depends on context and purpose. Data cleaning and preparation involves making many choices like this, and it is vital to record every step so that others can understand what was done and why. Data never speak for themselves; they are the puppets of the ventriloquists that cleaned and prepared them.

The process of coming to understand the look and feel of a dataset is termed **exploratory data analysis** (EDA). This is an open-ended process. We need to understand the shape of our dataset before we can formally model it. The process of EDA is an iterative one that involves producing summary statistics, graphs, tables, and sometimes even some modeling. It is a process that never formally finishes and requires a variety of skills.

It is difficult to delineate where EDA ends and formal statistical modeling begins, especially when considering how beliefs and understanding develop (Hullman and Gelman 2021). But at its core, it starts with the data, and involves immersing ourselves in it (Cook, Reid, and Tanaka 2021). EDA is not typically explicitly included in our final story. But it has a central role in how we come to understand the story we are telling. It is critical that all the steps taken during EDA are recorded and shared.

Statistical modeling has a long and robust history. Our knowledge of statistics has been built over hundreds of years. Statistics is not a series of dry theorems and proofs but is instead a way of exploring the world. It is analogous to "a knowledge of foreign languages or of algebra: it may prove of use at any time under any circumstances" (Bowley 1901, 4). A statistical model is not a recipe to be naively followed in an if-this-then-that way but is instead a way of understanding data (James et al. [2013] 2021). Modeling is usually required to infer statistical patterns from data. More formally, statistical inference is "the process of using data to infer the distribution that generated the data" (Wasserman 2005, 87).

Statistical significance is not the same as scientific significance, and we are realizing the cost of what has been the dominant paradigm. Using an arbitrary pass/fail statistical test on our data is rarely appropriate. Instead, the proper use for statistical modeling is as a kind of echolocation. We listen to what comes back to us from the model, to help learn about the shape of the world, while recognizing that it is only one representation of the world.

The use of statistical programming languages, such as R, enables us to rapidly **scale** our work. This refers to both inputs and outputs. It is basically just as easy to consider ten observations as 1,000, or even 1,000,000. This enables us to more quickly see the extent to which our stories apply. It is also the case that our outputs can be consumed as easily by one person as by ten, or 100. Using an Application Programming Interface (API) it is even possible for our stories to be considered many thousands of times each second.

1.4 How do our worlds become data?

> There is the famous story by Eddington about some people who went fishing in the sea with a net. Upon examining the size of the fish they had caught, they decided there was a minimum size to the fish in the sea! Their conclusion arose from the tool used and not from reality.
>
> Hamming ([1997] 2020, 177)

To a certain extent we are wasting our time. We have a perfect model of the world—it is the world! But it is too complicated. If we knew perfectly how everything was affected by the uncountable factors that influence it, then we could forecast perfectly a coin toss, a dice roll, and every other seemingly random process each time. But we cannot. Instead, we must simplify things to that which is plausibly measurable, and it is that which we define as data. Our data are a simplification of the messy, complex world from which they were derived.

There are different approximations of "plausibly measurable". Hence, datasets are always the result of choices. We must decide whether they are nonetheless reasonable for the task at hand. We use statistical models to help us think deeply about, explore, and hopefully come to better understand, our data.

Much of statistics is focused on considering, thoroughly, the data that we have. That was appropriate for when our data were agricultural, astronomical, or from the physical sciences. This is not to say that systemic bias cannot exist or have an impact in non-human contexts, but with the rise of data science, partly because of the value of its application to datasets generated by humans, we must also actively consider what is not in our dataset. Who is systematically missing from our dataset? Whose data do not fit nicely into the approach that we are using and are hence being inappropriately simplified? If the process of the world becoming data requires abstraction and simplification, then we need to be clear about when we can reasonably simplify and when it would be inappropriate.

The process of our world becoming data necessarily involves measurement. Paradoxically, often those that do the measurement and are deeply immersed in the details have less trust in the data than those who are removed from it. Even seemingly clear tasks, such as measuring distance, defining boundaries, and counting populations, are surprisingly difficult in practice. Turning our world into data requires many decisions and imposes much error. Among many other considerations, we need to decide what will be measured, how accurately we will do this, and who will be doing the measurement.

i Oh, you think we have good data on that!

An important example of how something seemingly simple quickly becomes difficult is maternal-related deaths. That refers to the number of women who die while pregnant, or soon after a termination, from a cause related to the pregnancy or its management (World Health Organization 2019). It is difficult but critical to turn the tragedy of such a death into cause-specific data because that helps mitigate future deaths. Some countries have well-developed civil registration and vital statistics (CRVS), which collect data about every death. But many countries lack a CRVS, resulting in unrecorded deaths. Even if a death is recorded, defining a cause of death may be difficult, especially when there is a lack of qualified medical personal or equipment. Maternal deaths are particularly difficult because there are typically many causes. Some CRVS systems have a checkbox on the death registration form to specify whether the death should be counted as maternal. But even some developed countries have only recently adopted this. For instance, it was only introduced in the United States in 2003, and even in 2015 Alabama, California, and West Virginia had not adopted the standard question (MacDorman and Declercq 2018). This means there is a risk that maternal deaths are under-reported or misclassified.

We typically use various instruments to turn the world into data. In astronomy, the development of better telescopes, and eventually satellites and probes, enabled new understanding of other worlds. Similarly, we have new instruments for turning our own world into data being developed each day. Where once a census was a generation-defining event, now we have regular surveys, transaction data available by the second, and almost all interactions on the internet become data of some kind. The development of such instruments has enabled exciting new stories.

Our world imperfectly becomes data. If we are to use data nonetheless to learn about the world, then we need to actively seek to understand their imperfections and the implications of those imperfections.

1.5 What is data science and how should we use it to learn about the world?

There is no agreed definition of data science. Wickham, Çetinkaya-Rundel, and Grolemund ([2016] 2023) say it "...allows you to turn raw data into understanding, insight, and knowledge". Similarly, Leek and Peng (2020) contend that it is "...the process of formulating a quantitative question that can be answered with data, collecting and cleaning the data, analyzing the data, and communicating the answer to the question to a relevant audience". Baumer, Kaplan, and Horton (2021) consider it a "...science of extracting meaningful information from data". And Timbers, Campbell, and Lee (2022) define it as "the process of generating insight from data through reproducible and auditable processes". From an earlier age Foster (1968) points clearly to what we now call data science when he says: "(s)tatistics are concerned with the processing and analysis of masses of data and with the development of mathematical methods of extracting information from data. Combine all this activity with computer methods and you have something more than the sum of its parts."

Craiu (2019) argues that the lack of certainty as to what data science is might not matter because "...who can really say what makes someone a poet or a scientist?" He goes on to broadly say that a data scientist is "...someone with a data driven research agenda, who adheres to or aspires to using a principled implementation of statistical methods and uses efficient computation skills."

In any case, alongside specific, technical definitions, there is value in having a simple definition, even if we lose a bit of specificity. Probability is often informally defined as "counting things" (McElreath [2015] 2020, 10). In a similar informal sense, data science can be defined as something like: humans measuring things, typically related to other humans, and using sophisticated averaging to explain and predict. We revisit this in Chapter 17 to provide a more detailed definition.

That may sound a touch cute, but Francis Edgeworth, the nineteenth century statistician and economist, considered statistics to be the science "of those Means which are presented by social phenomena", so it finds itself in good company (Edgeworth 1885). In any case, one feature of this definition is that it does not treat data as *terra nullius*, or nobody's land. Statisticians tend to see data as the result of some process that we can never know, but that we try to use data to come to understand. Many statisticians care deeply about data and measurement, yet there are many cases in statistics where data kind of just appear; they belong to nobody. But that is never actually the case.

Data are generated, and then must be gathered, cleaned, and prepared, and these decisions matter. Every dataset is *sui generis*, or a class by itself, and so when you come to know one dataset well, you just know one dataset, not all datasets.

Much of data science focuses on the "science", but it is important to also focus on the "data". And that is another characteristic of that cutesy definition of data science. A lot of data scientists are generalists, who are interested in a broad range of problems. Often, the thing that unites these is the need to gather, clean, and prepare messy data. And frequently it is the specifics of those data that require the most time, that update most often, and that are worthy of our most full attention.

Jordan (2019) describes being in a medical office and being given some probability, based on prenatal initial screening, that his child, then a fetus, had Down syndrome. By way of background, one can do a test to know for sure, but that test comes with the risk of the fetus not surviving, so this initial screening is done and then parents typically use the probability of Down syndrome from that initial screening to decide whether to do the conclusive test. Jordan (2019) found the probabilities provided by the initial screening were being determined based on a study done a decade earlier in the United Kingdom. The issue was that in the ensuing ten years, imaging technology had improved so the initial screening was not expecting such high-resolution images, and there had been a subsequent (false) increase in Down syndrome diagnoses from the initial screening. The data were the problem.

> **i Shoulders of giants**
>
> Dr Michael Jordan is the Pehong Chen Distinguished Professor at the University of California, Berkeley. After earning a PhD in Cognitive Science from University of California, San Diego, in 1985, he was appointed as an assistant professor at MIT, being promoted to full professor in 1997, and in 1998 he moved to Berkeley. One area of his research is statistical machine learning. For instance, one particularly important paper is Blei, Ng, and Jordan (2003), which defined how text could be grouped together to define topics, and we cover this in Chapter 16.

It is not just the "science" bit that is hard, it is the "data" bit as well. For instance, researchers went back and examined one of the most popular text datasets in computer science, and they found that around 30 per cent of the data were improperly duplicated (Bandy and Vincent 2021). There is an entire field—linguistics—that specializes in these types of datasets, and inappropriate use of data is one of the dangers of any one field being hegemonic. The strength of data science is that it brings together people with a variety of backgrounds and training to the task of learning about some dataset. It is not constrained by what was done in the past. This means that we must go out of our way to show respect for those who do not come from our own tradition, but who are as interested in a dataset as we are. Data science is multi-disciplinary and increasingly critical; hence it must reflect our world. There is a need for a diversity of backgrounds, of approaches, and of disciplines in data science.

Our world is messy, and so are our data. To successfully tell stories with data you need to become comfortable with the fact that the process will be difficult. Hannah Fry, the British mathematician, describes spending six months rewriting code before it solved her problem (Thornhill 2021). You need to learn to stick with it. You also need to accept failure at times, and you do this by developing resilience and having intrinsic motivation. The world of data is about considering possibilities and probabilities, and learning to make trade-offs between them. There is hardly anything that we know for certain, and there is no perfect analysis.

Ultimately, we are all just telling stories with data, but these stories are increasingly among the most important in the world.

1.6 Exercises

Questions

1. According to Register (2020b) data decisions impact (pick one)?
   a. Real people.
   b. No one.
   c. Those in the training set.
   d. Those in the test set.
2. What is data science (in your own words)?
3. According to Keyes (2019) what is data science (pick one)?
   a. The inhumane reduction of humanity down to what can be counted.
   b. The quantitative analysis of large amounts of data for the purpose of decision-making.

   c. Data science is an interdisciplinary field that uses scientific methods, processes, algorithms, and systems to extract knowledge and insights from many structured and unstructured data.
4. Imagine that you have a job in which including race and/or sexuality as predictors improves the performance of your model. When deciding whether to include these in your analysis, what factors would you consider (in your own words)?
5. According to Crawford (2021), as described in this chapter, which of the following forces shape our world, and hence our data (select all that apply)?
   a. Political.
   b. Historical.
   c. Cultural.
   d. Social.
6. Why is ethics a key element of telling convincing stories (in your own words)?
7. Consider the results of a survey that asked about gender. It finds the following counts: "man: 879", "woman: 912", "non-binary: 10" "prefer not to say: 3", and "other: 1". What is the appropriate way to consider "prefer not to say" (pick one)?
   a. Drop them.
   b. Merge it into "other".
   c. Include them.
   d. It depends.

Tutorial

The purpose of this tutorial is to clarify in your mind the difficulty of measurement, even of seemingly simple things, and hence the likelihood of measurement issues in more complicated areas.

Please obtain some seeds for a fast-growing plant such as radishes, mustard greens, or arugula. Plant the seeds and measure how much soil you used. Water them and measure the water you used. Each day take a note of any changes. More generally, measure and record as much as you can. Note your thoughts about the difficulty of measurement. Eventually your seeds will sprout, and you should measure how they grow. We will return to use the data that you gathered.

2

Drinking from a fire hose

Prerequisites

- Read *The mundanity of excellence: An ethnographic report on stratification and Olympic swimmers*, (Chambliss 1989)
  - This paper finds that excellence is not due to some special talent or gift, but instead due to technique, discipline, and attitude.
- Read *Data science as an atomic habit*, (Barrett 2021a)
  - This blog post describes an approach to learning data science that involves making small, consistent, actions.
- Read *This is how AI bias really happens—and why it's so hard to fix*, (Hao 2019)
  - This article highlights some of the ways in which models can perpetuate bias.

Key concepts and skills

- The statistical programming language R enables us to tell interesting stories using data. It is a language like any other, and the path to mastery can be slow.
- The workflow that we use to approach projects is: plan, simulate, acquire, explore, and share.
- The way to learn R is to start with a small project and break down what is required to achieve it into tiny steps, look at other people's code, and draw on that to achieve each step. Complete that project and move onto the next project. With each project you will get a little better.

Software and packages

- Base R (R Core Team 2023)
- Core `tidyverse` (Wickham et al. 2019)
  - `dplyr` (Wickham, François, et al. 2022)
  - `ggplot2` (Wickham 2016)
  - `tidyr` (Wickham, Vaughan, and Girlich 2023)
  - `stringr` (Wickham 2022c)
  - `readr` (Wickham, Hester, and Bryan 2022)
- `janitor` (Firke 2023)
- `knitr` (Xie 2023)
- `lubridate` (Grolemund and Wickham 2011)
- `opendatatoronto` (Gelfand 2022b)

```
library("janitor")
library("knitr")
library("lubridate")
library("opendatatoronto")
library("tidyverse")
```

2.1 Hello, World!

The way to start, is to start. In this chapter we go through three complete examples of the data science workflow advocated in this book. This means we:

$$\text{Plan} \rightarrow \text{Simulate} \rightarrow \text{Acquire} \rightarrow \text{Explore} \rightarrow \text{Share}$$

If you are new to R, then some of the code may be a bit unfamiliar to you. If you are new to statistics, then some of the concepts may be unfamiliar. Do not worry. It will all soon become familiar.

The only way to learn how to tell stories, is to start telling stories yourself. This means that you should try to get these examples working. Do the sketches yourself, type everything out yourself (using Posit Cloud if you are new to R and do not have it locally installed), and execute it all. It is important to realize that it will be challenging at the start. This is normal.

> Whenever you're learning a new tool, for a long time, you're going to suck... But the good news is that is typical; that's something that happens to everyone, and it's only temporary.
>
> Hadley Wickham as quoted by Barrett (2021a).

You will be guided thoroughly here. Hopefully by experiencing the excitement of telling stories with data, you will feel empowered to stick with it.

The first step of the workflow is to plan. We do this because we need to establish an endpoint, even if we later need to update it as we learn more about the situation. We then simulate because this forces us into the details of our plan. In some projects, data acquisition may be as straight-forward as downloading a dataset, but in others the data acquisition may be much of the focus, for instance, if we conduct a survey. We explore the data using various quantitative methods to come to understand it. And finally, we share our understanding, in a way that is focused on the needs of our audience.

To get started, go to Posit Cloud[1] and create an account; the free version is fine for now. We use that initially, rather than the desktop, so that getting started is the same for everyone, but to avoid having to pay you should change to a local installation later. Once you have an account and log in, it should look something like Figure 2.1a.

You will be in "Your Projects". From here you should start a new project: "New Project" → "New RStudio Project" (Figure 2.1b). You can give the project a name by clicking on "Untitled Project" and replacing it.

We will now go through three worked examples: Australian elections, Toronto shelter usage, and neonatal mortality. These examples build increasing complexity, but from the first one,

[1] https://posit.cloud

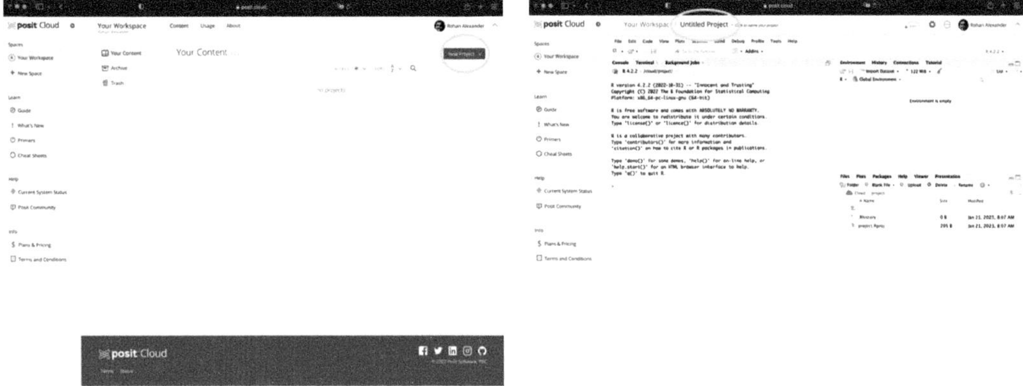

(a) Opening Posit Cloud for the first time

(b) Opening a new RStudio project

Figure 2.1: Getting started with Posit Cloud and a new project

we will be telling a story with data. While we briefly explain many aspects here, almost everything is explained in much more detail in the rest of the book.

2.2 Australian elections

Australia is a parliamentary democracy with 151 seats in the House of Representatives, which is the lower house and that from which government is formed. There are two major parties—"Liberal" and "Labor"—two minor parties—"Nationals" and "Greens"—and many smaller parties and independents. In this example we will create a graph of the number of seats that each party won in the 2022 Federal Election.

2.2.1 Plan

For this example, we need to plan two aspects. The first is what the dataset that we need will look like, and the second is what the final graph will look like.

The basic requirement for the dataset is that it has the name of the seat (sometimes called a "division" in Australia) and the party of the person elected. A quick sketch of the dataset that we would need is Figure 2.2a.

We also need to plan the graph that we are interested in. Given we want to display the number of seats that each party won, a quick sketch of what we might aim for is Figure 2.2b.

2.2.2 Simulate

We now simulate some data, to bring some specificity to our sketches.

To get started, within Posit Cloud, make a new Quarto document: "File" → "New File" → "Quarto document...". Give it a title, such as "Exploring the 2022 Australian Election", add your name as author, and unclick "Use visual markdown editor" (Figure 2.3a). Leave the other options as their default, and then click "Create".

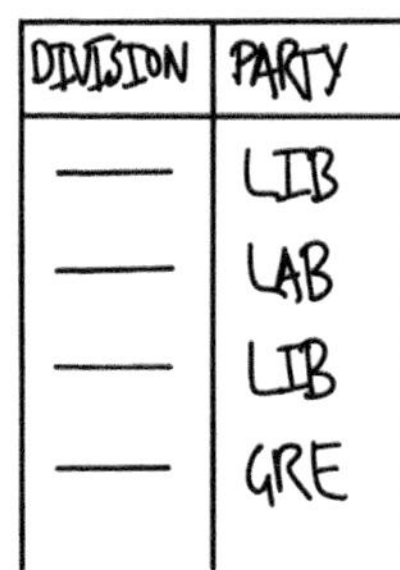

(a) Quick sketch of a dataset that could be useful for analyzing Australian elections

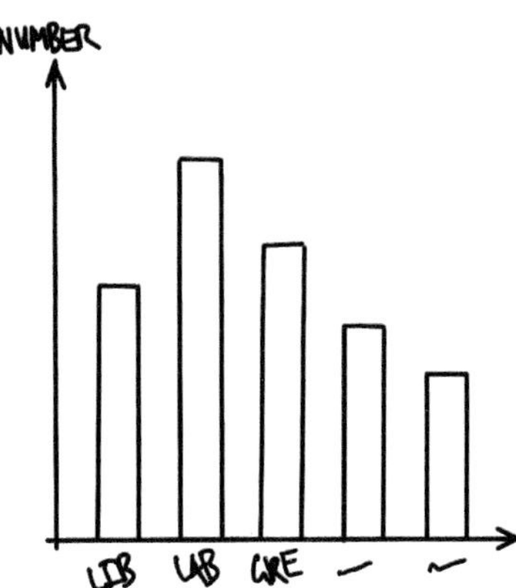

(b) Quick sketch of a possible graph of the number of seats won by each party

Figure 2.2: Sketches of a potential dataset and graph related to an Australian election

You may get a notification along the lines of "Package rmarkdown required…." (Figure 2.3b). If that happens, click "Install". For this example, we will put everything into this one Quarto document. You should save it as "australian_elections.qmd": "File" → "Save As…".

Remove almost all the default content, and then beneath the heading material create a new R code chunk: "Code" → "Insert Chunk". Then add preamble documentation that explains:

- the purpose of the document;
- the author and contact details;
- when the file was written or last updated; and
- prerequisites that the file relies on.

```
#### Preamble ####
# Purpose: Read in data from the 2022 Australian Election and make
# a graph of the number of seats each party won.
# Author: Rohan Alexander
# Email: rohan.alexander@utoronto.ca
# Date: 1 January 2023
# Prerequisites: Know where to get Australian elections data.
```

In R, lines that start with "#" are comments. This means that they are not run as code by R, but are instead designed to be read by humans. Each line of this preamble should start with a "#". Also make it clear that this is the preamble section by surrounding that with "####". The result should look like Figure 2.3c.

After this we need to setup the workspace. This involves installing and loading any packages that will be needed. A package only needs to be installed once for each computer, but needs to be loaded each time it is to be used. In this case we are going to use the `tidyverse` and `janitor`. They will need to be installed because this is the first time they are being used, and then each will need to be loaded.

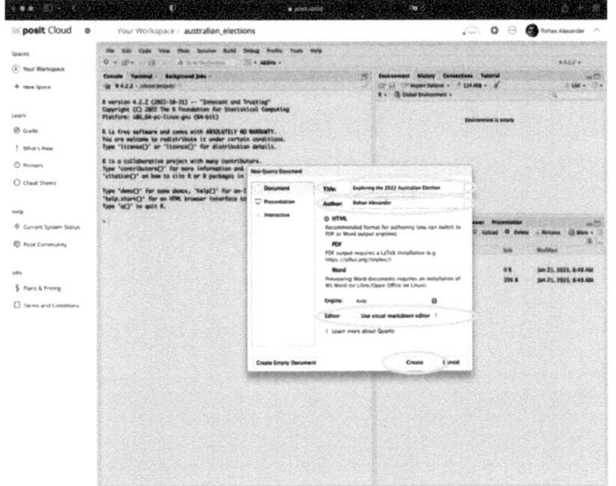

(a) Creating a new Quarto document

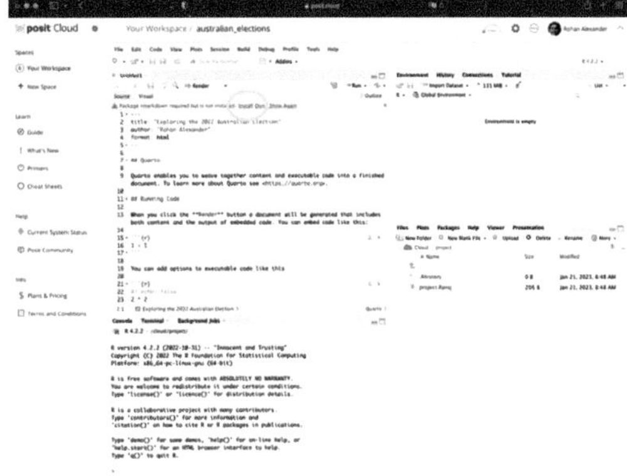

(b) Installing rmarkdown if necessary

(c) After initial setup and with a preamble

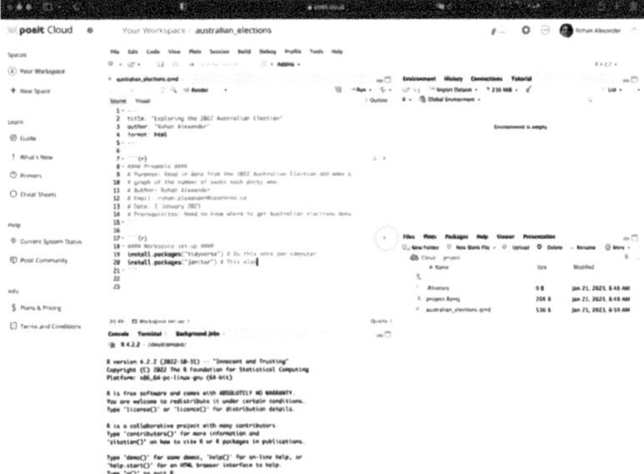

(d) Highlighting the green arrow to run the chunk

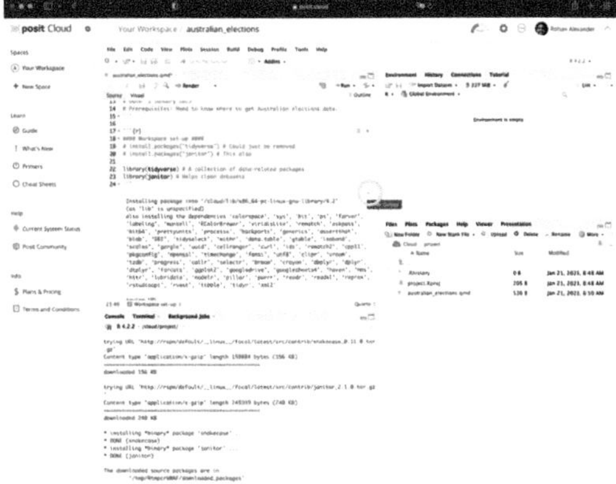

(e) Highlighting the cross to remove the messages

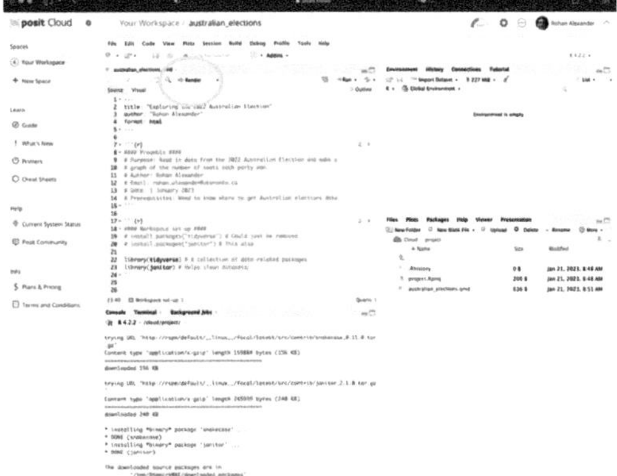

(f) Highlighting the render button

Figure 2.3: Getting started with a Quarto document

> **Shoulders of giants**
>
> Hadley Wickham is Chief Scientist at RStudio. After earning a PhD in Statistics from Iowa State University in 2008 he was appointed as an assistant professor at Rice University, and became Chief Scientist at RStudio, now Posit, in 2013. He developed the `tidyverse` collection of packages, and has published many books including *R for Data Science* (Wickham, Çetinkaya-Rundel, and Grolemund [2016] 2023) and *Advanced R* (Wickham 2019). He was awarded the COPSS Presidents' Award in 2019.

An example of installing the packages follows. Run this code by clicking the small green arrow associated with the R code chunk (Figure 2.3d).

```
#### Workspace setup ####
install.packages("tidyverse")
install.packages("janitor")
```

Now that the packages are installed, they need to be loaded. As that package installation step only needs to be done once per computer, that code can be commented out so that it is not accidentally run, or even just removed. Additionally, we can remove the message that printed when we installed the packages (Figure 2.3e).

```
#### Workspace setup ####
# install.packages("tidyverse")
# install.packages("janitor")

library(tidyverse)
library(janitor)
```

We can render the entire document by clicking "Render" (Figure 2.3f). When you do this, you may be asked to install some packages. If that happens, then you should agree to this. This will result in a HTML document.

For an introduction to the packages that were just installed, each package contains a help file that provides information about them and their functions. It can be accessed by prepending a question mark to the package name and then running that code in the console. For instance `?tidyverse`.

To simulate our data, we need to create a dataset with two variables: "Division" and "Party", and some values for each. In the case of "Division" reasonable values would be a name of one of the 151 Australian divisions. In the case of "Party" reasonable values would be one of the following five: "Liberal", "Labor", "National", "Green", or "Other". Again, this code can be run by clicking the small green arrow associated with the R code chunk.

```
simulated_data <-
  tibble(
    # Use 1 through to 151 to represent each division
    "Division" = 1:151,
    # Randomly pick an option, with replacement, 151 times
    "Party" = sample(
```

```
      x = c("Liberal", "Labor", "National", "Green", "Other"),
      size = 151,
      replace = TRUE
    )
  )

simulated_data
```

```
# A tibble: 151 x 2
   Division Party
      <int> <chr>
 1        1 Liberal
 2        2 Liberal
 3        3 Labor
 4        4 Other
 5        5 National
 6        6 Green
 7        7 National
 8        8 Liberal
 9        9 National
10       10 Green
# i 141 more rows
```

At a certain point, your code will not run and you will want to ask others for help. Do not take a screenshot of a small snippet of the code and expect that someone will be able to help based on that. They, almost surely, cannot. Instead, you need to provide them with your whole script in a way that they can run. We will explain what GitHub is more completely in Chapter 3, but for now, if you need help, then you should naively create a GitHub Gist which will enable you to share your code in a way that is more helpful than taking a screenshot. The first step is to create a free account on GitHub[2] (Figure 2.4a). Thinking about an appropriate username is important because this will become part of your professional profile. It would make sense to have a username that is professional, independent of any course, and ideally related to your real name. Then look for a "+" in the top right, and select "New gist" (Figure 2.4b).

From here you should add all the code to that Gist, not just the final bit that is giving an error. And give it a meaningful filename that includes ".R" at the end, for instance, "australian_elections.R". In Figure 2.4c it will turn out that we have incorrect capitalization, `library(Tidyverse)` instead of `library(tidyverse)`.

Click "Create public gist". We can then share the URL to this Gist with whoever we are asking to help, explain what the problem is, and what we are trying to achieve. It will be easier for them to help, because all the code is available.

2.2.3 Acquire

Now we want to get the actual data. The data we need is from the Australian Electoral Commission (AEC), which is the non-partisan agency that organizes Australian federal elections. We can pass a page of their website to `read_csv()` from `readr`. We do not need to explicitly load `readr` because it is part of the `tidyverse`. The `<-` or "assignment operator"

[2] https://github.com

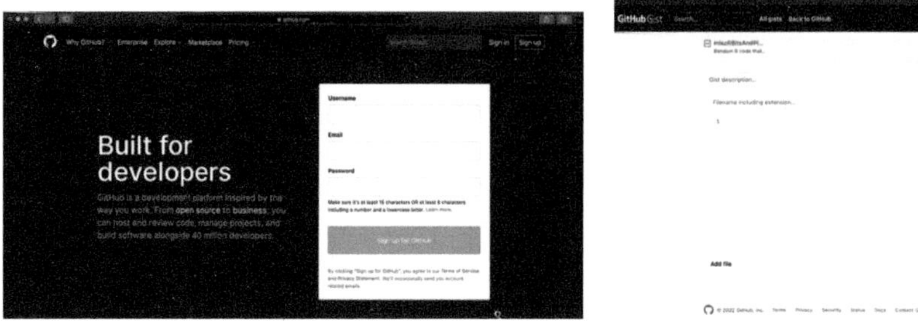

(a) GitHub sign-up screen

(b) New GitHub Gist

(c) Create a public GitHub Gist to share code

Figure 2.4: Creating a Gist to share code when asking for help

allocates the output of `read_csv()` to an object called "raw_elections_data".

```
#### Read in the data ####
raw_elections_data <-
  read_csv(
    file =
      paste0("https://results.aec.gov.au/27966/website/Downloads/",
             "HouseMembersElectedDownload-27966.csv"),
    show_col_types = FALSE,
    skip = 1
  )

# We save the original data in case we lose access
write_csv(
  x = raw_elections_data,
  file = "australian_voting.csv"
)
```

We can take a quick look at the dataset using `head()` which will show the first six rows, and `tail()` which will show the last six rows.

```
head(raw_elections_data)
```

```
# A tibble: 6 x 8
  DivisionID DivisionNm StateAb CandidateID GivenNm    Surname    PartyNm  PartyAb
       <dbl> <chr>      <chr>         <dbl> <chr>      <chr>      <chr>    <chr>
```

```
1         179 Adelaide   SA               36973 Steve      GEORGANAS Austral~ ALP
2         197 Aston      VIC              36704 Alan       TUDGE     Liberal  LP
3         198 Ballarat   VIC              36409 Catherine KING       Austral~ ALP
4         103 Banks      NSW              37018 David      COLEMAN   Liberal  LP
5         180 Barker     SA               37083 Tony       PASIN     Liberal  LP
6         104 Barton     NSW              36820 Linda      BURNEY    Austral~ ALP
```

```
tail(raw_elections_data)
```

```
# A tibble: 6 x 8
  DivisionID DivisionNm StateAb CandidateID GivenNm    Surname  PartyNm  PartyAb
       <dbl> <chr>      <chr>         <dbl> <chr>      <chr>    <chr>    <chr>
1        152 Wentworth  NSW           37451 Allegra    SPENDER  Indepen~ IND
2        153 Werriwa    NSW           36810 Anne Maree STANLEY  Austral~ ALP
3        150 Whitlam    NSW           36811 Stephen    JONES    Austral~ ALP
4        178 Wide Bay   QLD           37506 Llew       O'BRIEN  Liberal~ LNP
5        234 Wills      VIC           36452 Peter      KHALIL   Austral~ ALP
6        316 Wright     QLD           37500 Scott      BUCHHOLZ Liberal~ LNP
```

We need to clean the data so that we can use it. We are trying to make it similar to the dataset that we thought we wanted in the planning stage. While it is fine to move away from the plan, this needs to be a deliberate, reasoned decision. After reading in the dataset that we saved, the first thing that we will do is adjust the names of the variables. We will do this using `clean_names()` from `janitor`.

```
#### Basic cleaning ####
raw_elections_data <-
  read_csv(
    file = "australian_voting.csv",
    show_col_types = FALSE
  )


# Make the names easier to type
cleaned_elections_data <-
  clean_names(raw_elections_data)

# Have a look at the first six rows
head(cleaned_elections_data)
```

```
# A tibble: 6 x 8
  division_id division_nm state_ab candidate_id given_nm  surname   party_nm
        <dbl> <chr>       <chr>           <dbl> <chr>     <chr>     <chr>
1         179 Adelaide    SA              36973 Steve     GEORGANAS Australian ~
2         197 Aston       VIC             36704 Alan      TUDGE     Liberal
3         198 Ballarat    VIC             36409 Catherine KING      Australian ~
4         103 Banks       NSW             37018 David     COLEMAN   Liberal
5         180 Barker      SA              37083 Tony      PASIN     Liberal
6         104 Barton      NSW             36820 Linda     BURNEY    Australian ~
# i 1 more variable: party_ab <chr>
```

The names are faster to type because RStudio will auto-complete them. To do this, we begin typing the name of a variable and then use the "tab" key to complete it.

There are many variables in the dataset, and we are primarily interested in two: "division_nm" and "party_nm". We can choose certain variables of interest with `select()` from `dplyr` which we loaded as part of the `tidyverse`. The "pipe operator", `|>`, pushes the output of one line to be the first input of the function on the next line.

```
cleaned_elections_data <-
  cleaned_elections_data |>
  select(
    division_nm,
    party_nm
  )

head(cleaned_elections_data)
```

```
# A tibble: 6 x 2
  division_nm party_nm
  <chr>       <chr>
1 Adelaide    Australian Labor Party
2 Aston       Liberal
3 Ballarat    Australian Labor Party
4 Banks       Liberal
5 Barker      Liberal
6 Barton      Australian Labor Party
```

Some of the variable names are still not obvious because they are abbreviated. We can look at the names of the columns in this dataset with `names()`. And we can change the names using `rename()` from `dplyr`.

```
names(cleaned_elections_data)
```

```
[1] "division_nm" "party_nm"
```

```
cleaned_elections_data <-
  cleaned_elections_data |>
  rename(
    division = division_nm,
    elected_party = party_nm
  )

head(cleaned_elections_data)
```

```
# A tibble: 6 x 2
  division elected_party
  <chr>    <chr>
1 Adelaide Australian Labor Party
2 Aston    Liberal
3 Ballarat Australian Labor Party
4 Banks    Liberal
5 Barker   Liberal
```

```
6 Barton   Australian Labor Party
```

We could now look at the unique values in the "elected_party" column using `unique()`.

```
cleaned_elections_data$elected_party |>
  unique()
```

```
[1] "Australian Labor Party"
[2] "Liberal"
[3] "Liberal National Party of Queensland"
[4] "The Greens"
[5] "The Nationals"
[6] "Independent"
[7] "Katter's Australian Party (KAP)"
[8] "Centre Alliance"
```

As there is more detail in this than we wanted, we may want to simplify the party names to match what we simulated, using `case_match()` from `dplyr`.

```
cleaned_elections_data <-
  cleaned_elections_data |>
  mutate(
    elected_party =
      case_match(
        elected_party,
        "Australian Labor Party" ~ "Labor",
        "Liberal National Party of Queensland" ~ "Liberal",
        "Liberal" ~ "Liberal",
        "The Nationals" ~ "Nationals",
        "The Greens" ~ "Greens",
        "Independent" ~ "Other",
        "Katter's Australian Party (KAP)" ~ "Other",
        "Centre Alliance" ~ "Other"
      )
  )

head(cleaned_elections_data)
```

```
# A tibble: 6 x 2
  division elected_party
  <chr>    <chr>
1 Adelaide Labor
2 Aston    Liberal
3 Ballarat Labor
4 Banks    Liberal
5 Barker   Liberal
6 Barton   Labor
```

Our data now matches our plan (Figure 2.2a). For every electoral division we have the party of the person that won it.

Having now nicely cleaned the dataset, we should save it, so that we can start with that cleaned dataset in the next stage. We should make sure to save it under a new file name so we are not replacing the raw data, and so that it is easy to identify the cleaned dataset later.

```
write_csv(
  x = cleaned_elections_data,
  file = "cleaned_elections_data.csv"
)
```

2.2.4 Explore

We may like to explore the dataset that we created. One way to better understand a dataset is to make a graph. In particular, here we would like to build the graph that we planned in Figure 2.2b.

First, we read in the dataset that we just created.

```
#### Read in the data ####
cleaned_elections_data <-
  read_csv(
    file = "cleaned_elections_data.csv",
    show_col_types = FALSE
  )
```

We can get a quick count of how many seats each party won using `count()` from `dplyr`.

```
cleaned_elections_data |>
  count(elected_party)
```

```
# A tibble: 5 x 2
  elected_party     n
  <chr>         <int>
1 Greens            4
2 Labor            77
3 Liberal          48
4 Nationals        10
5 Other            12
```

To build the graph that we are interested in, we use `ggplot2` which is part of the `tidyverse`. The key aspect of this package is that we build graphs by adding layers using "+", which we call the "add operator". In particular we will create a bar chart using `geom_bar()` from `ggplot2` (Figure 2.5a).

```
cleaned_elections_data |>
  ggplot(aes(x = elected_party)) + # aes abbreviates "aesthetics"
  geom_bar()

cleaned_elections_data |>
  ggplot(aes(x = elected_party)) +
  geom_bar() +
```

```
theme_minimal() + # Make the theme neater
labs(x = "Party", y = "Number of seats") # Make labels more meaningful
```

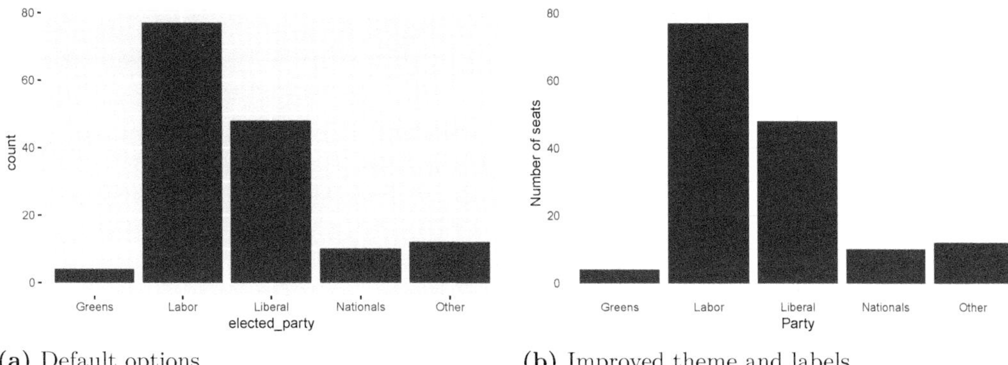

(a) Default options **(b)** Improved theme and labels

Figure 2.5: Number of seats won, by political party, at the 2022 Australian Federal Election

Figure 2.5a accomplishes what we set out to do. But we can make it look a bit nicer by modifying the default options and improving the labels (Figure 2.5b).

2.2.5 Share

To this point we have downloaded some data, cleaned it, and made a graph. We would typically need to communicate what we have done at some length. In this case, we can write a few paragraphs about what we did, why we did it, and what we found to conclude our workflow. An example follows.

Australia is a parliamentary democracy with 151 seats in the House of Representatives, which is the house from which government is formed. There are two major parties—"Liberal" and "Labor"—two minor parties—"Nationals" and "Greens"—and many smaller parties. The 2022 Federal Election occurred on 21 May, and around 15 million votes were cast. We were interested in the number of seats that were won by each party.

We downloaded the results, on a seat-specific basis, from the Australian Electoral Commission website. We cleaned and tidied the dataset using the statistical programming language R (R Core Team 2023) including the `tidyverse` (Wickham et al. 2019) and `janitor` (Firke 2023). We then created a graph of the number of seats that each political party won (Figure 2.5).

We found that the Labor Party won 77 seats, followed by the Liberal Party with 48 seats. The minor parties won the following number of seats: the Nationals won 10 seats and the Greens won 4 seats. Finally, there were 10 Independents elected as well as candidates from smaller parties.

The distribution of seats is skewed toward the two major parties which could reflect relatively stable preferences on the part of Australian voters, or possibly inertia due to the benefits of already being a major party such a national network or funding. A better understanding of the reasons for this distribution are of interest in future work. While the dataset consists of everyone who voted, it worth noting that in Australia some are systematically excluded from voting, and it is much more difficult for some to vote than others.

One aspect to be especially concerned with is making sure that this communication is focused on the needs of the audience and telling a story. Data journalism provides some excellent examples of how analysis needs to be tailored to the audience, for instance, Cardoso (2020) and Bronner (2020).

2.3 Toronto's unhoused population

Toronto has a large unhoused population (City of Toronto 2021). Freezing winters mean it is important there are enough places in shelters. In this example we will make a table of shelter usage in 2021 to compare average use in each month. Our expectation is that there is greater usage in the colder months, for instance, December, compared with warmer months, for instance, July.

2.3.1 Plan

The dataset that we are interested in would need to have the date, the shelter, and the number of beds that were occupied that night. A quick sketch of a dataset that would work is Figure 2.6a. We are interested in creating a table that has the monthly average number of beds occupied each night. The table would probably look something like Figure 2.6b.

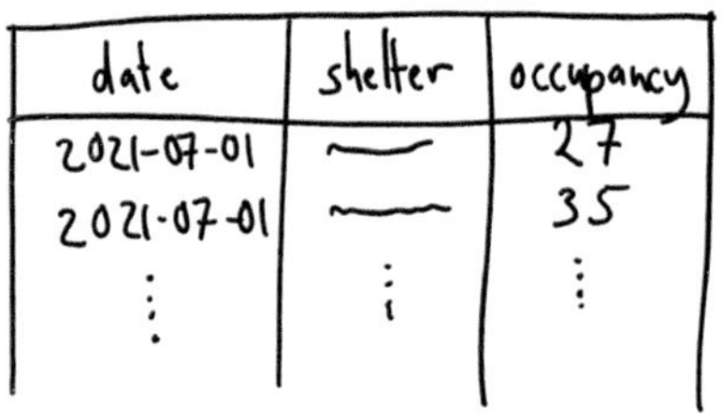

date	shelter	occupancy
2021-07-01	—	27
2021-07-01	—	35
⋮	⋮	⋮

(a) Quick sketch of a dataset

MONTH	AVERAGE OCCUPANCY
JULY	500
AUGUST	475
⋮	⋮
DECEMBER	1000

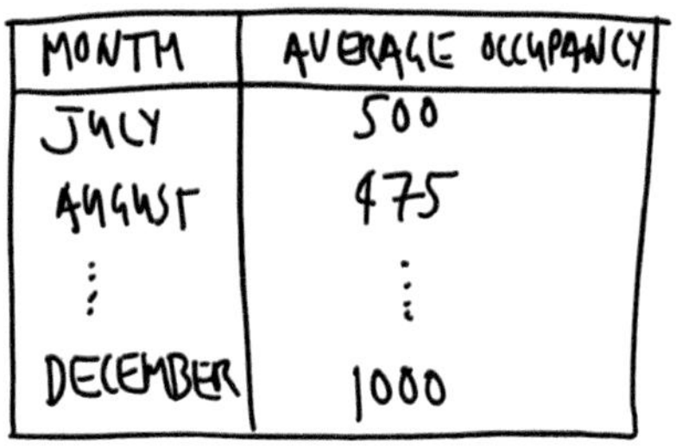

(b) Quick sketch of a table of the average number of beds occupied each month

Figure 2.6: Sketches of a dataset and table related shelter usage in Toronto

2.3.2 Simulate

The next step is to simulate some data that could resemble our dataset. Simulation provides us with an opportunity to think deeply about our data generating process.

In Posit Cloud make a new Quarto document, save it, and make a new R code chunk and add preamble documentation. Then install and/or load the packages that are needed. We will again use the `tidyverse` and `janitor`. As those were installed earlier, they do not need to be installed again. We will also use `lubridate`. That is part of the `tidyverse` and so does not need to be installed independently, but it does need to be loaded. We will also use `opendatatoronto`, and `knitr` and these will need to be installed and loaded.

```
#### Preamble ####
# Purpose: Get data on 2021 shelter usage and make table
# Author: Rohan Alexander
# Email: rohan.alexander@utoronto.ca
# Date: 1 July 2022
# Prerequisites: -

#### Workspace setup ####
install.packages("opendatatoronto")
install.packages("knitr")

library(knitr)
library(janitor)
library(lubridate)
library(opendatatoronto)
library(tidyverse)
```

To add a bit more detail to the earlier example, packages contain code that other people have written. There are a few common ones that you will see regularly in this book, especially the `tidyverse`. To use a package, we must first install it and then we need to load it. A package only needs to be installed once per computer but must be loaded every time. This means the packages that we installed earlier do not need to be reinstalled here.

> **Shoulders of giants**
>
> Dr Robert Gentleman is a co-creator of R. After earning a PhD in Statistics from the University of Washington in 1988, he moved to the University of Auckland. He then went onto various roles including at 23andMe and is now the Executive Director of the Center for Computational Biomedicine at Harvard Medical School.

> **Shoulders of giants**
>
> Dr Ross Ihaka is a co-creator of R. He earned a PhD in Statistics from the University of California, Berkeley, in 1985. He wrote a dissertation titled "Ruaumoko", which is the Māori god of earthquakes. He then moved to the University of Auckland where he remained for his entire career. He was awarded the Pickering Medal in 2008 by the Royal Society of New Zealand Te Apārangi.

Given that people donate their time to make R and the packages that we use, it is important to cite them. To get the information that is needed, we use `citation()`. When run without any arguments, that provides the citation information for R itself, and when run with an argument that is the name of a package, it provides the citation information for that package.

```
citation() # Get the citation information for R
```

```
To cite R in publications use:

  R Core Team (2023). _R: A Language and Environment for Statistical
  Computing_. R Foundation for Statistical Computing, Vienna, Austria.
  <https://www.R-project.org/>.

A BibTeX entry for LaTeX users is

  @Manual{,
    title = {R: A Language and Environment for Statistical Computing},
    author = {{R Core Team}},
    organization = {R Foundation for Statistical Computing},
    address = {Vienna, Austria},
    year = {2023},
    url = {https://www.R-project.org/},
  }

We have invested a lot of time and effort in creating R, please cite it
when using it for data analysis. See also 'citation("pkgname")' for
citing R packages.
```

```
citation("ggplot2") # Get citation information for a package
```

```
To cite ggplot2 in publications, please use

  H. Wickham. ggplot2: Elegant Graphics for Data Analysis.
  Springer-Verlag New York, 2016.

A BibTeX entry for LaTeX users is

  @Book{,
    author = {Hadley Wickham},
    title = {ggplot2: Elegant Graphics for Data Analysis},
    publisher = {Springer-Verlag New York},
    year = {2016},
    isbn = {978-3-319-24277-4},
    url = {https://ggplot2.tidyverse.org},
  }
```

Turning to the simulation, we need three variables: "date", "shelter", and "occupancy". This example will build on the earlier one by adding a seed using `set.seed()`. A seed enables us to always generate the same random data whenever we run the same code. Any integer can be used as the seed. In this case the seed will be 853. If you use that as your seed, then you should get the same random numbers as in this example. If you use a different seed, then you should expect different random numbers. Finally, we use `rep()` to repeat something a certain number of times. For instance, we repeat "Shelter 1" 365 times which accounts for about a year.

```
#### Simulate ####
set.seed(853)

simulated_occupancy_data <-
  tibble(
    date = rep(x = as.Date("2021-01-01") + c(0:364), times = 3),
    # Based on Eddelbuettel: https://stackoverflow.com/a/21502386
    shelter = c(
      rep(x = "Shelter 1", times = 365),
      rep(x = "Shelter 2", times = 365),
      rep(x = "Shelter 3", times = 365)
    ),
    number_occupied =
      rpois(
        n = 365 * 3,
        lambda = 30
      ) # Draw 1,095 times from the Poisson distribution
  )

head(simulated_occupancy_data)
```

```
# A tibble: 6 x 3
  date       shelter   number_occupied
  <date>     <chr>               <int>
1 2021-01-01 Shelter 1              28
2 2021-01-02 Shelter 1              29
3 2021-01-03 Shelter 1              35
4 2021-01-04 Shelter 1              25
5 2021-01-05 Shelter 1              21
6 2021-01-06 Shelter 1              30
```

In this simulation we first create a list of all the dates in 2021. We repeat that list three times. We assume data for three shelters for every day of the year. To simulate the number of beds that are occupied each night, we draw from a Poisson distribution, assuming a mean number of 30 beds occupied per shelter, although this is just an arbitrary choice. By way of background, a Poisson distribution is often used when we have count data, and we return to it in Chapter 13.

2.3.3 Acquire

We use data made available about Toronto shelter usage by the City of Toronto. Shelter usage is measured by a count made each night at 4 a.m. of the number of occupied beds. To access the data, we use `opendatatoronto` and then save our own copy.

```
#### Acquire ####
toronto_shelters <-
  # Each package is associated with a unique id found in the "For
  # Developers" tab of the relevant page from Open Data Toronto
  list_package_resources("21c83b32-d5a8-4106-a54f-010dbe49f6f2") |>
  # Within that package, we are interested in the 2021 dataset
  filter(name ==
    "daily-shelter-overnight-service-occupancy-capacity-2021") |>
  # Having reduced the dataset to one row we can get the resource
  get_resource()

write_csv(
  x = toronto_shelters,
  file = "toronto_shelters.csv"
)

head(toronto_shelters)
```

Not much needs to be done to this to make it similar to the dataset that we were interested in (Figure 2.6a). We need to change the names to make them easier to type using `clean_names()`, and reduce the columns to only those that are relevant using `select()`.

```
toronto_shelters_clean <-
  clean_names(toronto_shelters) |>
  select(occupancy_date, id, occupied_beds)

head(toronto_shelters_clean)
```

```
# A tibble: 6 x 3
  occupancy_date      id occupied_beds
  <date>           <dbl>         <dbl>
1 2021-01-01     7272806            NA
2 2021-01-01     7272807            NA
3 2021-01-01     7272808            NA
4 2021-01-01     7272809            NA
5 2021-01-01     7272810            NA
6 2021-01-01     7272811             6
```

All that remains is to save the cleaned dataset.

```
write_csv(
  x = toronto_shelters_clean,
  file = "cleaned_toronto_shelters.csv"
)
```

2.3.4 Explore

First, we load the dataset that we just created.

```
#### Explore ####
toronto_shelters_clean <-
  read_csv(
    "cleaned_toronto_shelters.csv",
    show_col_types = FALSE
  )
```

The dataset contains daily records for each shelter. We are interested in understanding average usage for each month. To do this, we need to add a month column using `month()` from `lubridate`. By default, `month()` provides the number of the month, and so we include two arguments—"label" and "abbr"—to get the full name of the month. We remove rows that do not have any data for the number of beds using `drop_na()` from `tidyr`, which is part of the `tidyverse`. We will do this here unthinkingly because our focus is on getting started, but this is an important decision and we talk more about missing data in Chapter 6 and Chapter 11. We then create a summary statistic on the basis of monthly groups, using `summarise()` from `dplyr`. We use `kable()` from `knitr` to create Table 2.1.

```
toronto_shelters_clean |>
  mutate(occupancy_month = month(
    occupancy_date,
    label = TRUE,
    abbr = FALSE
  )) |>
  arrange(month(occupancy_date)) |>
  drop_na(occupied_beds) |>
  summarise(number_occupied = mean(occupied_beds),
            .by = occupancy_month) |>
  kable()
```

Table 2.1: Shelter usage in Toronto in 2021

occupancy_month	number_occupied
January	28.55708
February	27.73821
March	27.18521
April	26.31561
May	27.42596
June	28.88300
July	29.67137
August	30.83975
September	31.65405
October	32.32991
November	33.26980
December	33.57806

As with before, this looks fine, and achieves what we set out to do. But we can make some tweaks to the defaults to make it look even better (Table 2.2). In particular we make the column names easier to read, and only show an appropriate number of decimal places.

```
toronto_shelters_clean |>
  mutate(occupancy_month = month(
    occupancy_date,
    label = TRUE,
    abbr = FALSE
  )) |>
  arrange(month(occupancy_date)) |>
  drop_na(occupied_beds) |>
  summarise(number_occupied = mean(occupied_beds),
            .by = occupancy_month) |>
  kable(
    col.names = c("Month", "Average daily number of occupied beds"),
    digits = 1
  )
```

Table 2.2: Shelter usage in Toronto in 2021

Month	Average daily number of occupied beds
January	28.6
February	27.7
March	27.2
April	26.3
May	27.4
June	28.9
July	29.7
August	30.8
September	31.7
October	32.3
November	33.3
December	33.6

2.3.5 Share

We need to write a few brief paragraphs about what we did, why we did it, and what we found to sum up our work. An example follows.

Toronto has a large unhoused population. Freezing winters mean it is critical there are enough places in shelters. We are interested to understand how usage of shelters changes in colder months, compared with warmer months.

We use data provided by the City of Toronto about Toronto shelter bed occupancy. Specifically, at 4 a.m. each night a count is made of the occupied beds. We are interested in averaging this over the month. We cleaned, tidied, and analyzed the dataset using the statistical programming language R (R Core Team 2023) as well as the `tidyverse` (Wickham 2017), `janitor` (Firke 2023), `opendatatoronto` (Gelfand 2022b), `lubridate` (Grolemund and

Wickham 2011), and `knitr` (Xie 2023). We then made a table of the average number of occupied beds each night for each month (Table 2.2).

We found that the daily average number of occupied beds was higher in December 2021 than July 2021, with 34 occupied beds in December, compared with 30 in July (Table 2.2). More generally, there was a steady increase in the daily average number of occupied beds between July and December, with a slight overall increase each month.

The dataset is on the basis of shelters, and so our results may be skewed by changes that are specific to especially large or small shelters. It may be that specific shelters are particularly attractive in colder months. Additionally, we were concerned with counts of the number of occupied beds, but if the supply of beds changes over the season, then an additional statistic of interest would be the proportion occupied.

Although this example is only a few paragraphs, it could be reduced to form an abstract, or increased to form a full report, for instance, by expanding each paragraph into a section. The first paragraph is a general overview, the second focuses on the data, the third on the results, and the fourth is a discussion. Following the example of Hao (2019), that fourth paragraph is a good place to consider areas in which bias may have crept in.

2.4 Neonatal mortality

Neonatal mortality refers to a death that occurs within the first month of life. The neonatal mortality rate (NMR) is the number of neonatal deaths per 1,000 live births (UN IGME 2021). The Third Sustainable Development Goal (SDG) calls for a reduction in NMR to 12. In this example we will create a graph of the estimated NMR for the past 50 years for: Argentina, Australia, Canada, and Kenya.

2.4.1 Plan

For this example, we need to think about what our dataset should look like, and what the graph should look like.

The dataset needs to have variables that specify the country and the year. It also needs to have a variable with the NMR estimate for that year for that country. Roughly, it should look like Figure 2.7a.

We are interested to make a graph with year on the x-axis and estimated NMR on the y-axis. Each country should have its own series. A quick sketch of what we are looking for is Figure 2.7b.

2.4.2 Simulate

We would like to simulate some data that aligns with our plan. In this case we will need three columns: country, year, and NMR.

COUNTRY	YEAR	NMR
ARG	1971	50.0
⋮	1972	48.7
⋮	⋮	⋮
AUS	1971	10.3

(a) Quick sketch of a potentially useful NMR dataset

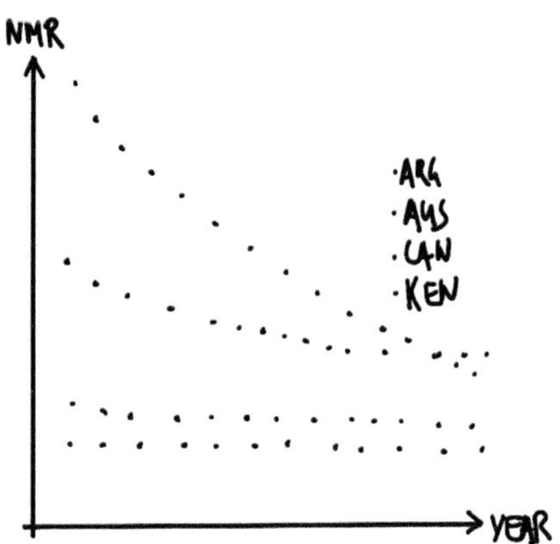

(b) Quick sketch of a graph of NMR by country over time

Figure 2.7: Sketches of a dataset and graph about the neonatal mortality rate (NMR)

Within Posit Cloud, make a new Quarto document and save it. Add preamble documentation and set up the workspace. We will use the `tidyverse`, `janitor`, and `lubridate`.

```
#### Preamble ####
# Purpose: Obtain and prepare data about neonatal mortality for
# four countries for the past fifty years and create a graph.
# Author: Rohan Alexander
# Email: rohan.alexander@utoronto.ca
# Date: 1 July 2022
# Prerequisites: -

#### Workspace setup ####
library(janitor)
library(lubridate)
library(tidyverse)
```

The code contained in packages can change from time to time as the authors update it and release new versions. We can see which version of a package we are using with `packageVersion()`. For instance, we are using version 2.0.0 of the `tidyverse` and version 2.2.0 of `janitor`.

```
packageVersion("tidyverse")
```

```
[1] '2.0.0'
```

```
packageVersion("janitor")
```

```
[1] '2.2.0'
```

To update the version of all of the packages that we have installed, we use `update.packages()`. We can use `tidyverse_update()` to just install the `tidyverse` packages. This does not need to be run, say, every day, but from time to time it is worth updating packages. While many packages take care to ensure backward compatibility, at a certain point this does not become possible. Updating packages could result in old code needing to be rewritten. This is not a big deal when you are getting started and in any case there are tools aimed at loading particular versions that we cover in Chapter 3.

Returning to the simulation, we repeat the name of each country 50 times with `rep()`, and enable the passing of 50 years. Finally, we draw from the uniform distribution with `runif()` to simulate an estimated NMR value for that year for that country.

```
#### Simulate data ####
set.seed(853)

simulated_nmr_data <-
  tibble(
    country =
      c(rep("Argentina", 50), rep("Australia", 50),
        rep("Canada", 50), rep("Kenya", 50)),
    year =
      rep(c(1971:2020), 4),
    nmr =
      runif(n = 200, min = 0, max = 100)
  )

head(simulated_nmr_data)
```

```
# A tibble: 6 x 3
  country    year   nmr
  <chr>     <int> <dbl>
1 Argentina  1971 35.9
2 Argentina  1972 12.0
3 Argentina  1973 48.4
4 Argentina  1974 31.6
5 Argentina  1975  3.74
6 Argentina  1976 40.4
```

While this simulation works, it would be time consuming and error prone if we decided that instead of 50 years, we were interested in simulating, say, 60 years. One way to improve this code is to replace all instances of 50 with a variable.

```
#### Simulate data ####
set.seed(853)

number_of_years <- 50

simulated_nmr_data <-
  tibble(
    country =
      c(rep("Argentina", number_of_years), rep("Australia", number_of_years),
```

```
        rep("Canada", number_of_years), rep("Kenya", number_of_years)),
    year =
      rep(c(1:number_of_years + 1970), 4),
    nmr =
      runif(n = number_of_years * 4, min = 0, max = 100)
  )

head(simulated_nmr_data)
```

```
# A tibble: 6 x 3
  country    year   nmr
  <chr>     <dbl> <dbl>
1 Argentina  1971 35.9
2 Argentina  1972 12.0
3 Argentina  1973 48.4
4 Argentina  1974 31.6
5 Argentina  1975  3.74
6 Argentina  1976 40.4
```

The result will be the same, but now if we want to change from 50 to 60 years, we only have to make the change in one place.

We can have confidence in this simulated dataset because it is relatively straight forward, and we wrote the code for it. But when we turn to the real dataset, it is more difficult to be sure that it is what it claims to be. Even if we trust the data, we need to be able to share that confidence with others. One way forward is to establish some tests of whether our data are as they should be. For instance, we expect:

1. That "country" is exclusively one of these four: "Argentina", "Australia", "Canada", or "Kenya".
2. Conversely, "country" contains all those four countries.
3. That "year" is no smaller than 1971 and no larger than 2020, and is an integer, not a letter or a number with decimal places.
4. That "nmr" is a value somewhere between 0 and 1,000, and is a number.

We can write a series of tests based on these features, that we expect the dataset to pass.

```
simulated_nmr_data$country |>
  unique() == c("Argentina", "Australia", "Canada", "Kenya")

simulated_nmr_data$country |>
  unique() |>
  length() == 4

simulated_nmr_data$year |> min() == 1971
simulated_nmr_data$year |> max() == 2020
simulated_nmr_data$nmr |> min() >= 0
simulated_nmr_data$nmr |> max() <= 1000
simulated_nmr_data$nmr |> class() == "numeric"
```

Having passed these tests, we can have confidence in the simulated dataset. More importantly, we can apply these tests to the real dataset. This enables us to have greater confidence in that dataset and to share that confidence with others.

2.4.3 Acquire

The UN Inter-agency Group for Child Mortality Estimation (IGME) provides[3] NMR estimates that we can download and save.

```
#### Acquire data ####
raw_igme_data <-
  read_csv(
    file =
      "https://childmortality.org/wp-content/uploads/2021/09/UNIGME-2021.csv",
    show_col_types = FALSE
  )

write_csv(x = raw_igme_data, file = "igme.csv")
```

:::

With established data, such as this, it can be useful to read supporting material about the data. In this case, a codebook is available here[4]. After this we can take a quick look at the dataset to get a better sense of it. We might be interested in what the dataset looks like with `head()` and `tail()`, and what the names of the columns are with `names()`.

```
names(raw_igme_data)
```

```
 [1] "Geographic area"        "Indicator"              "Sex"
 [4] "Wealth Quintile"        "Series Name"            "Series Year"
 [7] "Regional group"         "TIME_PERIOD"            "OBS_VALUE"
[10] "COUNTRY_NOTES"          "CONNECTION"             "DEATH_CATEGORY"
[13] "CATEGORY"               "Observation Status"     "Unit of measure"
[16] "Series Category"        "Series Type"            "STD_ERR"
[19] "REF_DATE"               "Age Group of Women"     "Time Since First Birth"
[22] "DEFINITION"             "INTERVAL"               "Series Method"
[25] "LOWER_BOUND"            "UPPER_BOUND"            "STATUS"
[28] "YEAR_TO_ACHIEVE"        "Model Used"
```

We would like to clean up the names and only keep the rows and columns that we are interested in. Based on our plan, we are interested in rows where "Sex" is "Total", "Series Name" is "UN IGME estimate", "Geographic area" is one of "Argentina", "Australia", "Canada", and "Kenya", and the "Indicator" is "Neonatal mortality rate". After this we are interested in just a few columns: "geographic_area", "time_period", and "obs_value".

```
cleaned_igme_data <-
  clean_names(raw_igme_data) |>
  filter(
    sex == "Total",
```

[3] https://childmortality.org/

[4] https://childmortality.org/wp-content/uploads/2021/03/CME-Info_codebook_for_downloads.xlsx

```
      series_name == "UN IGME estimate",
      geographic_area %in% c("Argentina", "Australia", "Canada", "Kenya"),
      indicator == "Neonatal mortality rate"
    ) |>
    select(geographic_area, time_period, obs_value)

  head(cleaned_igme_data)
```

```
# A tibble: 6 x 3
  geographic_area time_period obs_value
  <chr>           <chr>           <dbl>
1 Argentina       1970-06          24.9
2 Argentina       1971-06          24.7
3 Argentina       1972-06          24.6
4 Argentina       1973-06          24.6
5 Argentina       1974-06          24.5
6 Argentina       1975-06          24.1
```

We need to fix two other aspects: the class of "time_period" is character when we need it to be a year, and the name of "obs_value" should be "nmr" to be more informative.

```
  cleaned_igme_data <-
    cleaned_igme_data |>
    mutate(
      time_period = str_remove(time_period, "-06"),
      time_period = as.integer(time_period)
    ) |>
    filter(time_period >= 1971) |>
    rename(nmr = obs_value, year = time_period, country = geographic_area)

  head(cleaned_igme_data)
```

```
# A tibble: 6 x 3
  country    year   nmr
  <chr>     <int> <dbl>
1 Argentina  1971  24.7
2 Argentina  1972  24.6
3 Argentina  1973  24.6
4 Argentina  1974  24.5
5 Argentina  1975  24.1
6 Argentina  1976  23.3
```

Finally, we can check that our dataset passes the tests that we developed based on the simulated dataset.

```
  cleaned_igme_data$country |>
    unique() == c("Argentina", "Australia", "Canada", "Kenya")
```

```
[1] TRUE TRUE TRUE TRUE
```

```
cleaned_igme_data$country |>
  unique() |>
  length() == 4
```

```
[1] TRUE
```

```
cleaned_igme_data$year |> min() == 1971
```

```
[1] TRUE
```

```
cleaned_igme_data$year |> max() == 2020
```

```
[1] TRUE
```

```
cleaned_igme_data$nmr |> min() >= 0
```

```
[1] TRUE
```

```
cleaned_igme_data$nmr |> max() <= 1000
```

```
[1] TRUE
```

```
cleaned_igme_data$nmr |> class() == "numeric"
```

```
[1] TRUE
```

All that remains is to save the nicely cleaned dataset.

```
write_csv(x = cleaned_igme_data, file = "cleaned_igme_data.csv")
```

2.4.4 Explore

We would like to make a graph of estimated NMR using the cleaned dataset. First, we read in the dataset.

```
#### Explore ####
cleaned_igme_data <-
  read_csv(
    file = "cleaned_igme_data.csv",
    show_col_types = FALSE
  )
```

We can now make a graph of how NMR has changed over time and the differences between countries (Figure 2.8).

```
cleaned_igme_data |>
  ggplot(aes(x = year, y = nmr, color = country)) +
```

```
geom_point() +
theme_minimal() +
labs(x = "Year", y = "Neonatal Mortality Rate (NMR)", color = "Country") +
scale_color_brewer(palette = "Set1") +
theme(legend.position = "bottom")
```

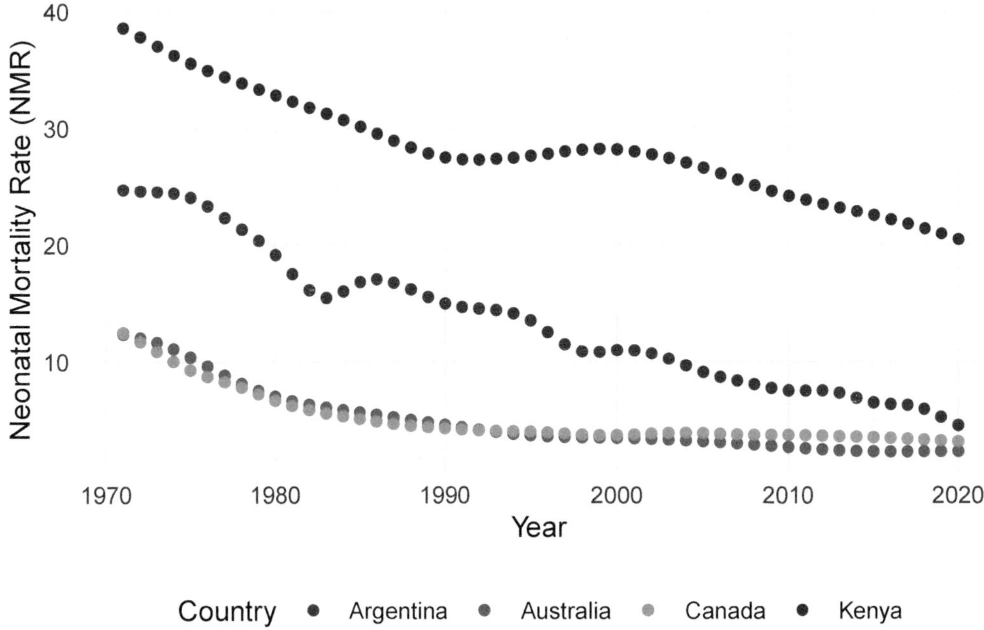

Figure 2.8: Neonatal Mortality Rate (NMR), for Argentina, Australia, Canada, and Kenya (1971-2020)

2.4.5 Share

To this point we downloaded some data, cleaned it, wrote some tests, and made a graph. We would typically need to communicate what we have done at some length. In this case, we will write a few paragraphs about what we did, why we did it, and what we found.

Neonatal mortality refers to a death that occurs within the first month of life. In particular, the neonatal mortality rate (NMR) is the number of neonatal deaths per 1,000 live births. We obtain estimates for NMR for four countries—Argentina, Australia, Canada, and Kenya—over the past 50 years.

The UN Inter-agency Group for Child Mortality Estimation (IGME) provides estimates of the NMR at the website: https://childmortality.org/. We downloaded their estimates then cleaned and tidied the dataset using the statistical programming language R (R Core Team 2023).

We found considerable change in the estimated NMR over time and between the four countries of interest (Figure 2.8). We found that the 1970s tended to be associated with reductions in the estimated NMR. Australia and Canada were estimated to have a low NMR at that point and remained there through 2020, with further slight reductions. The estimates for Argentina and Kenya continued to have substantial reductions through 2020.

Our results suggest considerable improvements in estimated NMR over time. NMR estimates are based on a statistical model and underlying data. The double burden of data is that often high-quality data are less easily available for groups, in this case countries, with worse outcomes. Our conclusions are subject to the model that underpins the estimates and the quality of the underlying data, and we did not independently verify either of these.

2.5 Concluding remarks

We have covered a lot of ground in this chapter, and it is normal to have not followed it all. The best way to proceed is to go through each of the three case studies in your own time. Type all the code out yourself, rather than copy-pasting, and run it bit by bit, even if you do not entirely understand what it is doing. Then try to add your own comments to it.

It is also the case that it is not necessary to fully understand everything in this chapter at this point. Some students find it best to continue going through the next few chapters of this book, and return to this one later.

2.6 Exercises

Scales

1. *(Plan)* Consider the following scenario: *Every day for a year a person records whether they donated \$1, \$2, or \$3.* Please sketch what that dataset could look like, and then sketch a graph that you could build to show all observations.
2. *(Simulate I)* Please further consider the scenario described. Which of the following could be used to simulate the situation (select all that apply)?
    a. `runif(n = 365, min = 1, max = 3) |> floor()`
    b. `runif(n = 365, min = 1, max = 4) |> floor()`
    c. `sample(x = 1:3, size = 365, replace = TRUE)`
    d. `sample(x = 1:3, size = 365, replace = FALSE)`
3. *(Simulate II)* Please write three tests based on this simulation.
4. *(Acquire)* Please identify one possible source of actual data about the amount of money that is donated to charity in a country that you are interested in.
5. *(Explore)* Assume that the `tidyverse` is loaded and the dataset "donations" has the column "amount". Which of the following would result in a bar chart (pick one)?
    a. `donations |> geom_bar(aes(x = amount)) + ggplot()`
    b. `amount |> geom_bar(aes(x = donations)) + ggplot()`

   c. `donations |> ggplot(aes(x = amount)) + geom_bar()`
   d. `amount |> ggplot(aes(x = donations)) + geom_bar()`
6. *(Communicate)* Please write two paragraphs as if you had gathered data from the source you identified, and had built a graph. The exact details contained in the paragraphs do not have to be factual (i.e. you do not actually have to get the data nor create the graphs).

Questions

1. Following Barrett (2021a), please list four atomic habits, related to learning data science, that you could implement.
2. What is not one of the four challenges for mitigating bias mentioned in Hao (2019) (pick one)?
   a. Unknown unknowns.
   b. Imperfect processes.
   c. The definitions of fairness.
   d. Lack of social context.
   e. Disinterest given profit considerations.
3. How does Chambliss (1989) define "excellence" (pick one)?
   a. Prolonged performance at world-class level.
   b. All Olympic medal winners.
   c. Consistent superiority of performance.
   d. All national-level athletes.
4. Think about the following quote from Chambliss (1989, 81) and list three small skills or activities that could help you achieve excellence in data science.

> Excellence is mundane. Superlative performance is really a confluence of dozens of small skills or activities, each one learned or stumbled upon, which have been carefully drilled into habit and then are fitted together in a synthesized whole. There is nothing extraordinary or super-human in any one of those actions; only the fact that they are done consistently and correctly, and all together, produce excellence.

---

5. What is the first sentence in the help file for the `tidyverse`?
6. Use a help file to determine which of the following are arguments for `read_csv()` (select all that apply)?
   a. "all_cols"
   b. "file"
   c. "show_col_types"
   d. "number"
7. We used `rpois()` and `runif()` to draw from the Poisson and Uniform distributions, respectively. Which of the following can be used to draw from the Normal and Binomial distributions (select all that apply)?
   a. `rnormal()` and `rbinom()`
   b. `rnorm()` and `rbinomial()`
   c. `rnormal()` and `rbinomial()`

   d. `rnorm()` and `rbinom()`
8. What is the result of `sample(x = letters, size = 2)` when the seed is set to "853"? What about when the seed is set to "1234" (pick one)?
   a. '"i" "q"' and '"p" "v"'
   b. '"e" "l"' and '"e" "r"'
   c. '"i" "q"' and '"e" "r"'
   d. '"e" "l"' and '"p" "v"'
9. Which function provides the recommended citation to cite R (pick one)?
   a. `cite("R")`.
   b. `cite()`.
   c. `citation("R")`.
   d. `citation()`.
10. How do we get the citation information for `opendatatoronto` (pick one)?
   a. `cite()`
   b. `citation()`
   c. `cite("opendatatoronto")`
   d. `citation("opendatatoronto")`
11. Which function is used to update packages (pick one)?
   a. `update.packages()`
   b. `upgrade.packages()`
   c. `revise.packages()`
   d. `renovate.packages()`
12. What are some features that we might typically expect of a column that claimed to be a year (select all that apply)?
   a. The class is "character".
   b. There are no negative numbers.
   c. There are letters in the column.
   d. Each entry has four digits.
13. Please add a small mistake to the following code. Then add it to a GitHub Gist and submit the URL.

```
midwest |>
  ggplot(aes(x = poptotal, y = popdensity, color = state)) +
  geom_point() +
  scale_x_log10() +
  scale_y_log10()
```

14. Why do we simulate a dataset (write at least three dot points)?

Tutorial

The purpose of this tutorial is to provide an opportunity to do a small self-contained project. We will redo the Australian Elections worked example, but for Canada.

Canada is a parliamentary democracy with 338 seats in the House of Commons, which is the lower house and that from which government is formed. There are two major parties—"Liberal" and "Conservative"—three minor parties—"Bloc Québécois", "New Democratic", and "Green"—and many smaller parties and independents. In this example we will create a graph of the number of seats that each party won in the 2021 Federal Election.

Begin by planning what the dataset that we need will look like, and what the final graph will look like. The basic requirement for the dataset is that it has the name of the seat (sometimes called a "riding" in Canada) and the party of the person elected.

Make a quick sketch of the dataset that we would need. Then make a quick sketch of a graph that we might be interested in.

Put together a Quarto document that simulates some data. Add preamble documentation, then load the packages that are needed: `tidyverse`, and `janitor`. Add numbers for the riding, then use `sample()` to randomly choose one of six options, with replacement, 338 times.

Next we need to get the actual data, from Elections Canada, and the file that we need to download is here[5].

Clean the names, and then select the two columns that are of interest: "electoral_district_name_nom_de_circonscription", and "elected_candidate_candidat_elu". Finally, rename the columns to remove the French and simplify the names.

The column that we need is about the elected candidates. That has the surname of the elected candidate, followed by a comma, followed by their first name, followed by a space, followed by the name of the party in both English and French, separated by a slash. Break-up this column into its pieces using `separate()` from `tidyr` and then use `select()` to just keep party information.

```
cleaned_elections_data <-
  cleaned_elections_data |>
  separate(
    col = elected_candidate,
    into = c("Other", "party"),
    sep = "/"
  ) |>
  select(-Other)
```

Then recode the party names from French to English to match what we simulated.

At this point we can make a nice graph of the number of ridings won by each party in the 2019 Canadian Federal Election.

[5]https://www.elections.ca/res/rep/off/ovr2021app/53/data_donnees/table_tableau11.csv

3

Reproducible workflows

Prerequisites

- Read *What has happened down here is the winds have changed*, (Gelman 2016)
  - A blog post that provides an overview of the replication crisis, and how social science changed in response.
- Read *Good enough practices in scientific computing*, (Wilson et al. 2017)
  - A paper that provides a set of clear, easily adoptable, recommendations for how to do data science, focused on how we use computers.
- Read *How to improve your relationship with your future self*, (Bowers and Voors 2016)
  - A paper that provides a set of clear, easily adoptable, recommendations for how to do data science, focused on analysis.
- Watch *Overcoming barriers to sharing code*, (M. Alexander 2021)
  - This video is a personal reflection on becoming comfortable with sharing code.
- Watch *Make a reprex... Please*, (Gelfand 2021)
  - This video details why creating a reproducible example is so important when asking for help.
- Read *The tidyverse style guide*, (Wickham 2021c)
  - A website documenting a set of recommended best-practices when coding in R.
- Watch *Code smells and feels*, (Bryan 2018b)
  - A video that details things to try to avoid when coding.

Key concepts and skills

- Reproducibility typically begins as something that someone imposes on you. It can be onerous and annoying. This typically lasts until you need to revisit a project after a small break. At that point you typically realize that reproducibility is not just a requirement for data science because it is the only way that we can make genuine progress, but because it helps us help ourselves.
- Reproducibility implies sharing data, code, and environment. This is enhanced by using Quarto, R Projects, and Git and GitHub: Quarto builds documents that integrate normal text and R code; R Projects enable a file structure that is not dependent on a user's personal directory set-up; and Git and GitHub make it easier to share code and data.
- This is not an unimpeachable workflow, but one that is good enough and provides many of the benefits. We will improve various aspects of it through various tools, but improving code structure and comments goes a long way.
- There are always errors that occur, and it is important to recognize that debugging is a skill that improves with practice. But one key aspect of being able to get help is to be able to make a reproducible example others can use.

Software and packages

- Base R (R Core Team 2023)
- `AER` (Kleiber and Zeileis 2008)

- `future` (Bengtsson 2021)
- `gitcreds` (Csárdi 2022)
- `knitr` (Xie 2023)
- `lintr` (Hester et al. 2022)
- `renv` (Ushey 2022)
- `reprex` (Bryan et al. 2022)
- `styler` (Müller and Walthert 2022)
- `tictoc` (Izrailev 2022)
- `tidyverse` (Wickham et al. 2019)
- `tinytex` (Xie 2019)
- `usethis` (Wickham, Bryan, and Barrett 2022)

```
library(AER)
library(future)
library(gitcreds)
library(knitr)
library(lintr)
library(renv)
library(reprex)
library(styler)
library(tictoc)
library(tidyverse)
library(tinytex)
library(usethis)
```

3.1 Introduction

> The number one thing to keep in mind about machine learning is that performance is evaluated on samples from one dataset, but the model is used in production on samples that may not necessarily follow the same characteristics... So when asking the question, "would you rather use a model that was evaluated as 90% accurate, or a human that was evaluated as 80% accurate", the answer depends on whether your data is typical per the evaluation process. Humans are adaptable, models are not. If significant uncertainty is involved, go with the human. They may have inferior pattern recognition capabilities (versus models trained on enormous amounts of data), but they understand what they do, they can reason about it, and they can improvise when faced with novelty.
>
> François Chollet, 20 February 2020.

If science is about systematically building and organizing knowledge in terms of testable explanations and predictions, then data science takes this and focuses on data. This means that building, organizing, and sharing knowledge is a critical aspect. Creating knowledge, once, in a way that only you can do it, does not meet this standard. Hence, there is a need for reproducible data science workflows.

M. Alexander (2019a) defines reproducible research as that which can be exactly redone, given all the materials used. This underscores the importance of providing the code, data, and environment. The minimum expectation is that another person is independently able to use your code, data, and environment to get your results, including figures and tables. Ironically, there are different definitions of reproducibility between disciplines. Barba (2018) surveys a variety of disciplines and concludes that the predominant language usage implies the following definitions:

- Reproducible research is when "[a]uthors provide all the necessary data and the computer codes to run the analysis again, re-creating the results."
- A replication is a study "that arrives at the same scientific findings as another study, collecting new data (possibly with different methods) and completing new analyses."

Regardless of what it is specifically called, Gelman (2016) identifies how large an issue the lack of it is in various social sciences. The problem with work that is not reproducible is that it does not contribute to our stock of knowledge about the world. This is wasteful and potentially even unethical. Since Gelman (2016), a great deal of work has been done in many social sciences and the situation has improved a little, but much work remains. That is also the case in the life sciences (Heil et al. 2021) and computer science (Pineau et al. 2021).

Some of the examples that Gelman (2016) talks about are not that important in the scheme of things. But at the same time, we saw, and continue to see, similar approaches being used in areas with big impacts. For instance, many governments have created "nudge" units that implement public policy (Sunstein and Reisch 2017) even though there is evidence that some of the claims lack credibility (Maier et al. 2022; Szaszi et al. 2022). Governments are increasingly using algorithms that they do not make open (Chouldechova et al. 2018). And Herndon, Ash, and Pollin (2014) document how research in economics that was used by governments to justify austerity policies following the 2007–2008 financial crisis turned out to not be reproducible.

At a minimum, and with few exceptions, we must release our code, datasets, and environment. Without these, it is difficult to know what a finding speaks to (Miyakawa 2020). More banally, we also do not know if there are mistakes or aspects that were inadvertently overlooked (Merali 2010; Hillel 2017; Silver 2020). Increasingly, following Buckheit and Donoho (1995), we consider a paper to be an advertisement, and for the associated code, data, and environment to be the actual work. Steve Jobs, a co-founder of Apple, talked about how the best craftsmen ensure that even the aspects of their work that no one else will ever see are as well finished and high quality as the aspects that are public facing (Isaacson 2011). The same is true in data science, where often one of the distinguishing aspects of high-quality work is that the README and code comments are as polished as, say, the abstract of the associated paper.

Workflows exist within a cultural and social context, which imposes an additional ethical reason for the need for them to be reproducible. For instance, Y. Wang and Kosinski (2018) train a neural network to distinguish between the faces of gay and heterosexual men. (Murphy (2017) provides a summary of the paper, the associated issues, and comments from its authors.) To do this, Y. Wang and Kosinski (2018, 248) needed a dataset of photos of people that were "adult, Caucasian, fully visible, and of a gender that matched the one reported on the user's profile". They verified this using Amazon Mechanical Turk, an online platform that pays workers a small amount of money to complete specific tasks. The instructions provided to the Mechanical Turk workers for this task specify that Barack Obama, the 44th US President, who had a white mother and a black father, should be classified as "Black"; and that Latino is an ethnicity, rather than a race (Mattson 2017). The classification task may seem objective, but, perhaps unthinkingly, echoes the views of Americans with a certain class and background.

This is just one specific concern about one part of the Y. Wang and Kosinski (2018) workflow. Broader concerns are raised by others including Gelman, Mattson, and Simpson (2018). The main issue is that statistical models are specific to the data on which they were trained. And the only reason that we can identify likely issues in the model of Y. Wang and Kosinski (2018) is because, despite not releasing the specific dataset that they used, they were nonetheless open about their procedure. For our work to be credible, it needs to be reproducible by others.

Some of the steps that we can take to make our work more reproducible include:

1. Ensure the entire workflow is documented. This may involve addressing questions such as:
   - How was the original, unedited dataset obtained and is access likely to be persistent and available to others?
   - What specific steps are being taken to transform the original, unedited data into the data that were analyzed, and how can this be made available to others?
   - What analysis has been done, and how clearly can this be shared?
   - How has the final paper or report been built and to what extent can others follow that process themselves?
2. Not worrying about perfect reproducibility initially, but instead focusing on trying to improve with each successive project. For instance, each of the following requirements are increasingly more onerous and there is no need to be concerned about not being able to do the last, until you can do the first:
   - Can you run your entire workflow again?
   - Can another person run your entire workflow again?
   - Can "future-you" run your entire workflow again?
   - Can "future-another-person" run your entire workflow again?
3. Including a detailed discussion about the limitations of the dataset and the approach in the final paper or report.

The workflow that we advocate in this book is:

$$\text{Plan} \rightarrow \text{Simulate} \rightarrow \text{Acquire} \rightarrow \text{Explore} \rightarrow \text{Share}$$

But it can be alternatively considered as: "Think an awful lot, mostly read and write, sometimes code".

There are various tools that we can use at the different stages that will improve the reproducibility of this workflow. This includes Quarto, R Projects, and Git and GitHub.

3.2 Quarto

3.2.1 Getting started

Quarto integrates code and natural language in a way that is called "literate programming" (Knuth 1984). It is the successor to R Markdown, which was a variant of Markdown specifically designed to allow R code chunks to be included. Quarto uses a mark-up language similar to HyperText Markup Language (HTML) or LaTeX, in comparison to a "What You See Is What You Get" (WYSIWYG) language, such as Microsoft Word. This means that all the aspects are consistent, for instance, all top-level headings will look the same. But it means that we must designate or "mark up" how we would like certain aspects to appear. And it is only when we render the document that we get to see what it looks like. A visual editor option can also be used, and this hides the need for the user to do this mark-up themselves.

While it makes sense to use Quarto going forward, there are many resources written for and in R Markdown. For this reason we provide R Markdown equivalents in the "R Markdown" Online Appendix[1].

> **i Shoulders of giants**
>
> Fernando Pérez is an associate professor of statistics at the University of California, Berkeley and a Faculty Scientist, Data Science and Technology Division, at Lawrence Berkeley National Laboratory. He earned a PhD in particle physics from the University of Colorado, Boulder. During his PhD he created iPython, which enables Python to be used interactively, and now underpins Project Jupyter, which inspired similar notebook approaches such as R Markdown and now Quarto. Somers (2018) describes how open-source notebook approaches create virtuous feedback loops that result in dramatically improved scientific computing. And Romer (2018) aligns the features of open-source approaches, such as Jupyter, with the features that enable scientific consensus and progress. In 2017 Pérez was awarded the Association for Computing Machinery (ACM) Software System Award.

One advantage of literate programming is that we get a "live" document in which code executes and then forms part of the document. Another advantage of Quarto is that similar code can compile into a variety of documents, including HTML and PDFs. Quarto also has default options for including a title, author, and date. One disadvantage is that it can take a while for a document to compile because the code needs to run.

We need to download Quarto from here[2]. (Skip this step if you are using Posit Cloud because it is already installed.) We can then create a new Quarto document within RStudio: "File" → "New File" → "Quarto Document...".

After opening a new Quarto document and selecting "Source" view, you will see the default top matter, contained within a pair of three dashes, as well as some examples of text showing a few of the markdown essential commands and R chunks, each of which are discussed further in the following sections.

[1] https://tellingstorieswithdata.com/22-rmarkdown.html
[2] https://quarto.org/docs/get-started/

3.2.2 Top matter

Top matter consists of defining aspects such as the title, author, and date. It is contained within three dashes at the top of a Quarto document. For instance, the following would specify a title, a date that automatically updated to the date the document was rendered, and an author.

```
---
title: "My document"
author: "Rohan Alexander"
date: format(Sys.time(), "%d %B %Y")
format: html
---
```

An abstract is a short summary of the paper, and we could add that to the top matter.

```
---
title: "My document"
author: "Rohan Alexander"
date: format(Sys.time(), "%d %B %Y")
abstract: "This is my abstract."
format: html
---
```

By default, Quarto will create an HTML document, but we can change the output format to produce a PDF. This uses LaTeX in the background and requires the installation of supporting packages. To do this install `tinytex`. But as it is used in the background we should not need to load it.

```
---
title: "My document"
author: "Rohan Alexander"
date: format(Sys.time(), "%d %B %Y")
abstract: "This is my abstract."
format: pdf
---
```

We can include references by specifying a BibTeX file in the top matter and then calling it within the text, as needed.

```
---
title: "My document"
author: "Rohan Alexander"
date: format(Sys.time(), "%d %B %Y")
format: pdf
abstract: "This is my abstract."
bibliography: bibliography.bib
---
```

We would need to make a separate file called "bibliography.bib" and save it next to the Quarto file. In the BibTeX file we need an entry for the item that is to be referenced. For instance, the citation for R can be obtained with `citation()` and this can be added to the "bibliography.bib" file. The citation for a package can be found by including the package name, for instance `citation("tidyverse")`, and again adding the output to the ".bib" file.

It can be helpful to use Google Scholar[3] or doi2bib[4] to get citations for books or articles.

We need to create a unique key that we use to refer to this item in the text. This can be anything, provided it is unique, but meaningful ones can be easier to remember, for instance "citeR".

```
@Manual{citeR,
    title = {R: A Language and Environment for Statistical Computing},
    author = {{R Core Team}},
    organization = {R Foundation for Statistical Computing},
    address = {Vienna, Austria},
    year = {2021},
    url = {https://www.R-project.org/},
  }
@book{tellingstories,
    title = {Telling Stories with Data},
    author = {Rohan Alexander},
    year = {2023},
    publisher = {Chapman and Hall/CRC},
    url = {https://tellingstorieswithdata.com}
  }
```

To cite R in the Quarto document we then include `@citeR`, which would put brackets around the year: R Core Team (2023), or `[@citeR]`, which would put brackets around the whole thing: (R Core Team 2023).

The reference list at the end of the paper is automatically built based on calling the BibTeX file and including references in the paper. At the end of the Quarto document, include a heading "# References" and the actual citations will be included after that. When the Quarto file is rendered, Quarto sees these in the content, goes to the BibTeX file to get the reference details that it needs, builds the reference list, and then adds it at the end of the rendered document.

3.2.3 Essential commands

Quarto uses a variation of Markdown as its underlying syntax. Essential Markdown commands include those for emphasis, headers, lists, links, and images. A reminder of these is included in RStudio: "Help" → "Markdown Quick Reference". It is your choice as to whether you want to use the visual or source editor. But either way, it is good to understand these essentials because it will not always be possible to use a visual editor (for instance if you are quickly looking at a Quarto document in GitHub). As you get more experience it can be useful to use a text editor such as Sublime Text, or an alternative Integrated Development Environment such as VS Code.

- Emphasis: `*italic*`, `**bold**`
- Headers (these go on their own line with a blank line before and after):

```
# First level header

## Second level header
```

[3] https://scholar.google.com
[4] https://www.doi2bib.org

```
### Third level header
```

- Unordered list, with sub-lists:

```
* Item 1
* Item 2
    + Item 2a
    + Item 2b
```

- Ordered list, with sub-lists:

```
1. Item 1
2. Item 2
3. Item 3
    + Item 3a
    + Item 3b
```

- URLs can be added: `[this book](https://www.tellingstorieswithdata.com)` results in this book[5].
- A paragraph is created by leaving a blank line.

```
A paragraph about an idea, nicely spaced from the following paragraph.

A paragraph about another idea, again spaced from the earlier paragraph.
```

Once we have added some aspects, then we may want to see the actual document. To build the document click "Render".

3.2.4 R chunks

We can include code for R and many other languages in code chunks within a Quarto document. When we render the document the code will run and be included in the document.

To create an R chunk, we start with three backticks and then within curly braces we tell Quarto that this is an R chunk. Anything inside this chunk will be considered R code and run as such. We use data from Kleiber and Zeileis (2008) who provide the R package `AER` to accompany their book *Applied Econometrics with R*. We could load the `tidyverse` and install and load `AER` and make a graph of the number of times a survey respondent visited the doctor in the past two weeks.

````
```{r}
library(tidyverse)
library(AER)

data("DoctorVisits", package = "AER")

DoctorVisits |>
  ggplot(aes(x = illness)) +
  geom_histogram(stat = "count")
```
````

The output of that code is Figure 3.1.

[5] https://www.tellingstorieswithdata.com

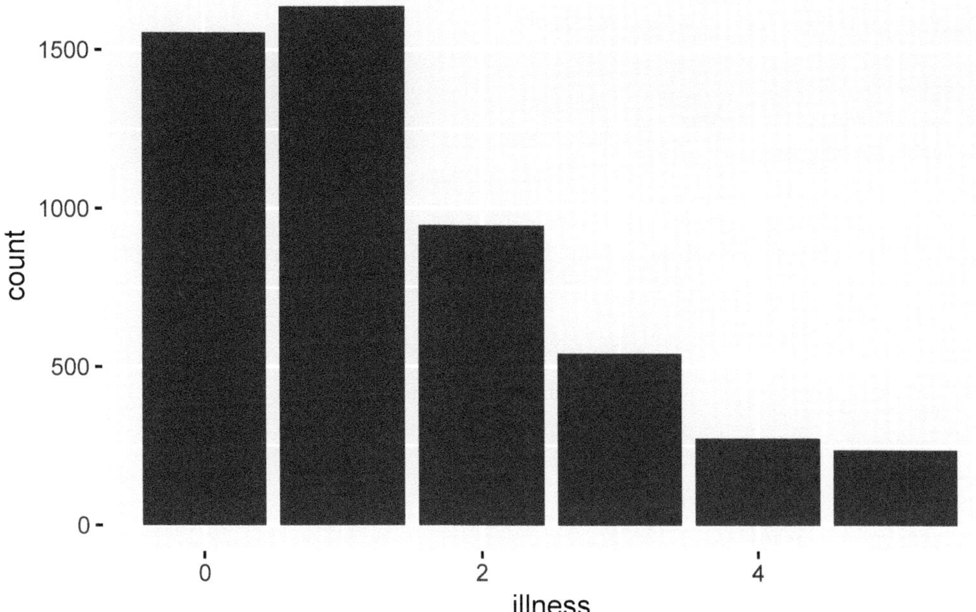

Figure 3.1: Number of illnesses in the past two weeks, based on the 1977–1978 Australian Health Survey

There are various evaluation options that are available in chunks. We include these, each on a new line, by opening the line with the chunk-specific comment delimiter "#|" and then the option. Helpful options include:

- `echo`: This controls whether the code itself is included in the document. For instance, `#| echo: false` would mean the code will be run and its output will show, but the code itself would not be included in the document.
- `include`: This controls whether the output of the code is included in the document. For instance, `#| include: false` would run the code, but would not result in any output, and the code itself would not be included in the document.
- `eval`: This controls whether the code should be included in the document. For instance, `#| eval: false` would mean that the code is not run, and hence there would not be any output to include, but the code itself would be included in the document.
- `warning`: This controls whether warnings should be included in the document. For instance, `#| warning: false` would mean that warnings are not included.
- `message`: This controls whether messages should be included in the document. For instance, `#| message: false` would mean that messages are not included in the document.

For instance, we could include the output, but not the code, and suppress any warnings.

````
```{r}
#| echo: false
#| warning: false

library(tidyverse)
library(AER)
````
````

```
data("DoctorVisits", package = "AER")

DoctorVisits |>
  ggplot(aes(x = visits)) +
  geom_histogram(stat = "count")
```
```

Leave a blank line on either side of an R chunk, otherwise it may not run properly. And use lower case for logical values, i.e. "false" not "FALSE".

````
Most people did not visit a doctor in the past week.

```{r}
#| echo: false
#| warning: false

library(tidyverse)
library(AER)

data("DoctorVisits", package = "AER")

DoctorVisits |>
  ggplot(aes(x = visits)) +
  geom_histogram(stat = "count")
```

There were some people that visited a doctor once, and then...
````

The Quarto document itself must load any datasets that are needed. It is not enough that they are in the environment. This is because the Quarto document evaluates the code in the document when it is rendered, not necessarily the environment.

Often when writing code, we may want to make the same change across multiple lines or change all instances of a particular thing. We achieve this with multiple cursors. If we want a cursor across multiple, consecutive lines, then hold "option" on Mac or "Alt" on PC, while you drag your cursor over the relevant lines. If you want to select all instances of something, then highlight one instance, say a variable name, then use Find/Replace (Command + F on Mac or CTRL + F on PC) and select "All". This will then enable a cursor at all the other instances.

### 3.2.5 Equations

We can include equations by using LaTeX, which is based on the programming language TeX. We invoke math mode in LaTeX by using two dollar signs as opening and closing tags. Then whatever is inside is evaluated as LaTeX mark-up. For instance we can produce the compound interest formula with:

```
$$
A = P\left(1+\frac{r}{n}\right)^{nt}
```
```

```
$$
```

$$A = P\left(1 + \frac{r}{n}\right)^{nt}$$

LaTeX is a comprehensive mark-up language but we will mostly just use it to specify the model of interest. We include some examples here that contain the critical aspects we will draw on starting in Chapter 12.

```
$$
y_i|\mu_i, \sigma \sim \mbox{Normal}(\mu_i, \sigma)
$$
```

$$y_i|\mu_i, \sigma \sim \mbox{Normal}(\mu_i, \sigma)$$

Underscores are used to get subscripts: `y_i` for $y_i$. And we can get a subscript of more than one item by surrounding it with curly braces: `y_{i,c}` for $y_{i,c}$. In this case we wanted math mode within the line, and so we surround these with only one dollar sign as opening and closing tags.

Greek letters are typically preceded by a backslash. Common Greek letters include: `\alpha` for $\alpha$, `\beta` for $\beta$, `\delta` for $\delta$, `\epsilon` for $\epsilon$, `\gamma` for $\gamma$, `\lambda` for $\lambda$, `\mu` for $\mu$, `\phi` for $\phi$, `\pi` for $\pi$, `\Pi` for $\Pi$, `\rho` for $\rho$, `\sigma` for $\sigma$, `\Sigma` for $\Sigma$, `\tau` for $\tau$, and `\theta` for $\theta$.

LaTeX math mode assumes letters are variables and so makes them italic, but sometimes we want a word to appear in normal font because it is not a variable, such as "Normal". In that case we surround it with `\mbox{}`, for instance `\mbox{Normal}` for Normal.

We line up equations across multiple lines using `\begin{aligned}` and `\end{aligned}`. Then the item that is to be lined up is noted by an ampersand.

```
$$
\begin{aligned}
y_i|\lambda_i &\sim \mbox{Poisson}(\lambda_i)\\
\log(\lambda_i) & = \beta_0 + \beta_1 x_i
\end{aligned}
$$
```

$$\begin{aligned}
y_i|\lambda_i &\sim \mbox{Poisson}(\lambda_i)\\
\log(\lambda_i) & = \beta_0 + \beta_1 x_i
\end{aligned}$$

Finally, certain functions are built into LaTeX. For instance, we can appropriately typeset "log" with `\log`.

### 3.2.6 Cross-references

It can be useful to cross-reference figures, tables, and equations. This makes it easier to refer to them in the text. To do this for a figure we refer to the name of the R chunk that creates or contains the figure. For instance, consider the following code.

````
```{r}
#| label: fig-theuniquename
#| fig-cap: Number of illnesses in the past two weeks
#| warning: false

data("DoctorVisits", package = "AER")

DoctorVisits |>
  ggplot(aes(x = illness)) +
  geom_histogram(stat = "count")
```
````

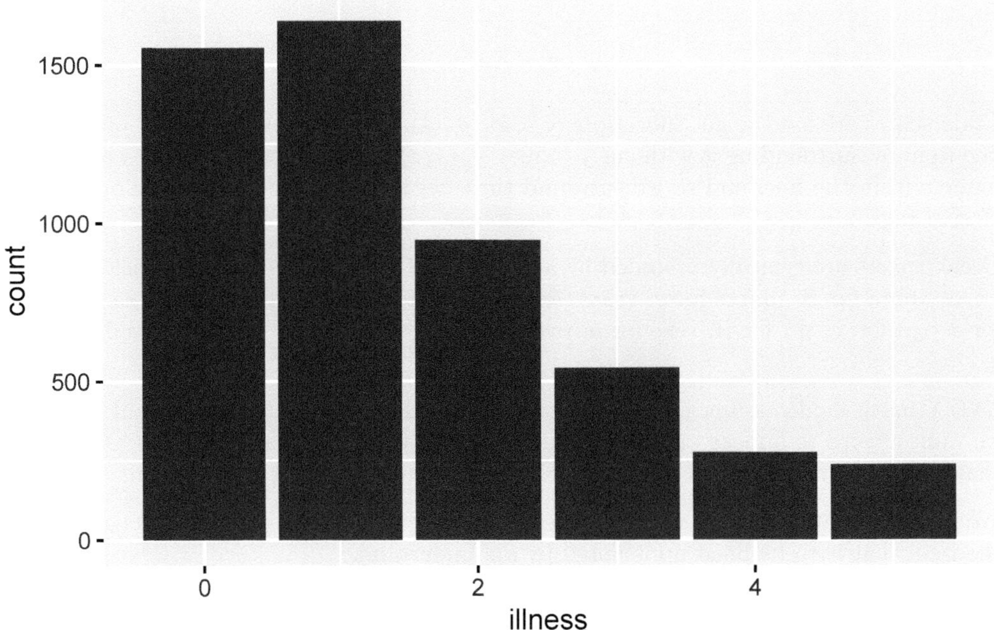

Figure 3.2: Number of illnesses in the past two weeks

Then `(@fig-theuniquename)` would produce: (Figure 3.2) as the label of the R chunk is `fig-theuniquename`. We need to add "fig" to the start of the chunk name so that Quarto knows that this is a figure. We then include a "fig-cap:" in the R chunk that specifies a caption.

We can add `#| layout-ncol: 2` in an R chunk within a Quarto document to have two graphs appear side by side (Figure 3.3). Here Figure 3.3a uses the minimal theme, and Figure 3.3b uses the classic theme. These both cross-reference the same label `#| label: fig-doctorgraphsidebyside` in the R chunk, with an additional option added in the R chunk of `#| fig-subcap: ["Number of illnesses","Number of visits to the doctor"]` which provides the sub-captions. The addition of a letter in-text is accomplished by adding "-1" and "-2" to the end of the label when it is used in-text: `(@fig-doctorgraphsidebyside)`, `@fig-doctorgraphsidebyside-1`, and `@fig-doctorgraphsidebyside-2` for (Figure 3.3), Figure 3.3a, and Figure 3.3b, respectively.

````
```{r}
#| eval: true
#| warning: false
#| label: fig-doctorgraphsidebyside
#| fig-cap: "Two variants of graphs"
#| fig-subcap: ["Illnesses","Visits to the doctor"]
#| layout-ncol: 2

DoctorVisits |>
  ggplot(aes(x = illness)) +
  geom_histogram(stat = "count") +
  theme_minimal()

DoctorVisits |>
  ggplot(aes(x = visits)) +
  geom_histogram(stat = "count") +
  theme_classic()
```
````

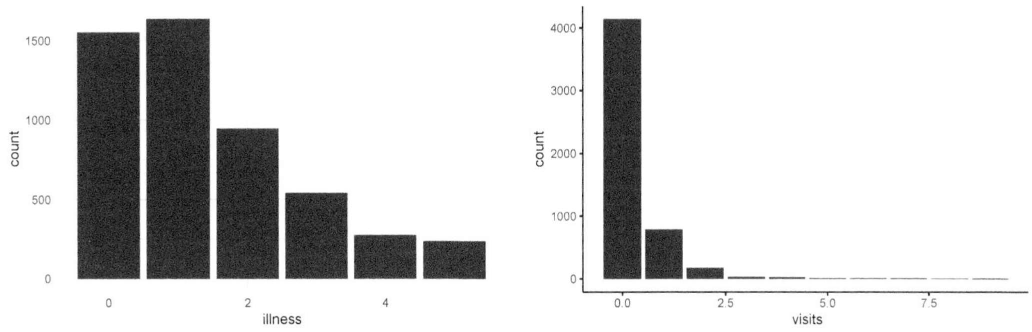

(a) Illnesses

(b) Visits to the doctor

Figure 3.3: Two variants of graphs

We can take a similar approach to cross-reference tables. For instance, `(@tbl-docvisittable)` will produce: (Table 3.1). In this case we specify "tbl" at the start of the label so that Quarto knows that it is a table. And we specify a caption for the table with "tbl-cap:".

````
```{r}
#| label: tbl-docvisittable
#| tbl-cap: "Distribution of the number of doctor visits"

DoctorVisits |>
  count(visits) |>
  kable()
```
````

Table 3.1: Distribution of the number of doctor visits

visits	n
0	4141
1	782
2	174
3	30
4	24
5	9
6	12
7	12
8	5
9	1

Finally, we can also cross-reference equations. To that we need to add a tag such as `{#eq-macroidentity}` which we then reference.

```
$$
Y = C + I + G + (X - M)
$$ {#eq-gdpidentity}
```

For instance, we then use `@eq-gdpidentity` to produce Equation 3.1

$$Y = C + I + G + (X - M) \tag{3.1}$$

Labels should be relatively simple when using cross-references. In general, try to keep the names simple but unique, avoid punctuation, and stick to letters and hyphens. Try not to use underscores, because they can cause an error.

3.3 R Projects and file structure

Projects are widely used in software development and exist to keep all the files (data, analysis, report, etc) associated with a particular project together and related to each other. (This use of "project" in a software development sense, is distinct to a "project", in the project management sense.) An R Project can be created in RStudio. Click "File" → "New Project", then select "Empty project", name the R Project and decide where to save it. For instance, a R Project focused on maternal mortality may be called "maternalmortality". The use of R Projects enables "reliable, polite behavior across different computers or users and over time" (Bryan and Hester 2020). This is because they remove the context of that folder from its broader existence; files exist in relation to the base of the R Project, not the base of the computer.

Once a project has been created, a new file with the extension ".RProj" will appear in that folder. An example of a folder with an R Project, a Quarto document, and an appropriate file structure is available here[6]. That can be downloaded: "Code" → "Download ZIP".

The main advantage of using an R Project is that we can reference files within it in a self-contained way. That means when others want to reproduce our work, they will not need to change all the file references and structure as everything is referenced in relation to the ".Rproj" file. For instance, instead of reading a CSV from, say, `"~/Documents/projects/book/data/"` you can read it from `book/data/`. It may be that someone else does not have a `projects` folder, and so the former would not work for them, while the latter would.

The use of projects is required to meet the minimal level of reproducibility expected of credible work. The use of functions such as `setwd()`, and computer-specific file paths, bind work to a specific computer in a way that is not appropriate.

There are a variety of ways to set up a folder. A variant of Wilson et al. (2017) that is often useful when you are getting started is shown in the example file structure linked above.

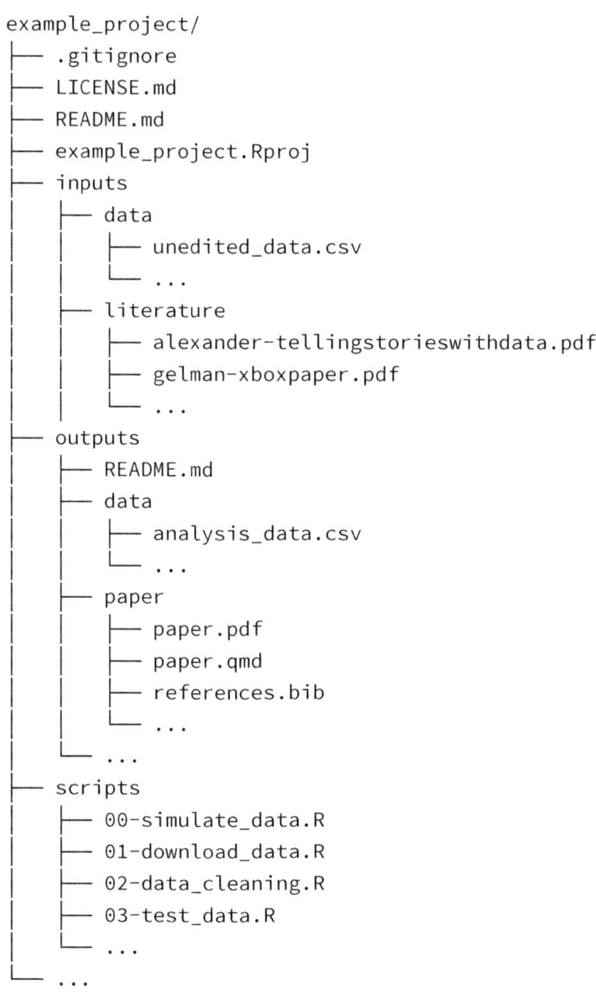

```
example_project/
├── .gitignore
├── LICENSE.md
├── README.md
├── example_project.Rproj
├── inputs
│   ├── data
│   │   ├── unedited_data.csv
│   │   └── ...
│   ├── literature
│   │   ├── alexander-tellingstorieswithdata.pdf
│   │   ├── gelman-xboxpaper.pdf
│   │   └── ...
├── outputs
│   ├── README.md
│   ├── data
│   │   ├── analysis_data.csv
│   │   └── ...
│   ├── paper
│   │   ├── paper.pdf
│   │   ├── paper.qmd
│   │   ├── references.bib
│   │   └── ...
│   └── ...
├── scripts
│   ├── 00-simulate_data.R
│   ├── 01-download_data.R
│   ├── 02-data_cleaning.R
│   ├── 03-test_data.R
│   └── ...
└── ...
```

[6] https://github.com/RohanAlexander/starter_folder

Here we have an `inputs` folder that contains original, unedited data that should not be written over (Wilson et al. 2017) and literature related to the project. An `outputs` folder contains data that we create using R, as well as the paper that we are writing. And a `scripts` folder is what modifies the unedited data and saves it into `outputs`. We will do most of our work in "scripts", and the Quarto file for the paper in `outputs`. Useful other aspects include a `README.md` which will specify overview details about the project, and a LICENSE. An example of what to put in the README is here[7]. Another helpful variant of this project skeleton is provided by Mineault and The Good Research Code Handbook Community (2021).

3.4 Version control

In this book we implement version control through a combination of Git and GitHub. There are a variety of reasons for this including:

1. enhancing the reproducibility of work by making it easier to share code and data;
2. making it easier to share work;
3. improving workflow by encouraging systematic approaches; and
4. making it easier to work in teams.

Git is a version control system with a fascinating history (Brown 2018). The way one often starts doing version control is to have various copies of the one file: "first_go.R", "first_go-fixed.R", "first_go-fixed-with-mons-edits.R". But this soon becomes cumbersome. One often soon turns to dates, for instance: "2022-01-01-analysis.R", "2022-01-02-analysis.R", "2022-01-03-analysis.R", etc. While this keeps a record, it can be difficult to search when we need to go back, because it is hard to remember the date some change was made. In any case, it quickly gets unwieldy for a project that is being regularly worked on.

Instead of this, we use Git so that we can have one version of the file. Git keeps a record of the changes to that file, and a snapshot of that file at a given point in time. We determine when Git takes that snapshot. We additionally include a message saying what changed between this snapshot and the last. In that way, there is only ever one version of the file, and the history can be more easily searched.

One complication is that Git was designed for teams of software developers. As such, while it works, it can be a little ungainly for non-developers. Nonetheless Git has been usefully adapted for data science, even when the only collaborator one may have is one's future self (Bryan 2018a).

GitHub, GitLab, and various other companies offer easier-to-use services that build on Git. While there are tradeoffs, we introduce GitHub here because it is the predominant platform (Eghbal 2020, 21). Git and GitHub are built into Posit Cloud, which provides a nice option if you have issues with local installation. One of the initial challenging aspects of Git is the terminology. Folders are called "repos". Creating a snapshot is called a "commit". One gets used to it eventually, but feeling confused initially is normal. Bryan (2020) is especially useful for setting up and using Git and GitHub.

[7]https://social-science-data-editors.github.io/template_README/

3.4.1 Git

We first need to check whether Git is installed. Open RStudio, go to the Terminal, type the following, and then enter/return.

```
git --version
```

If you get a version number, then you are done (Figure 3.4a).

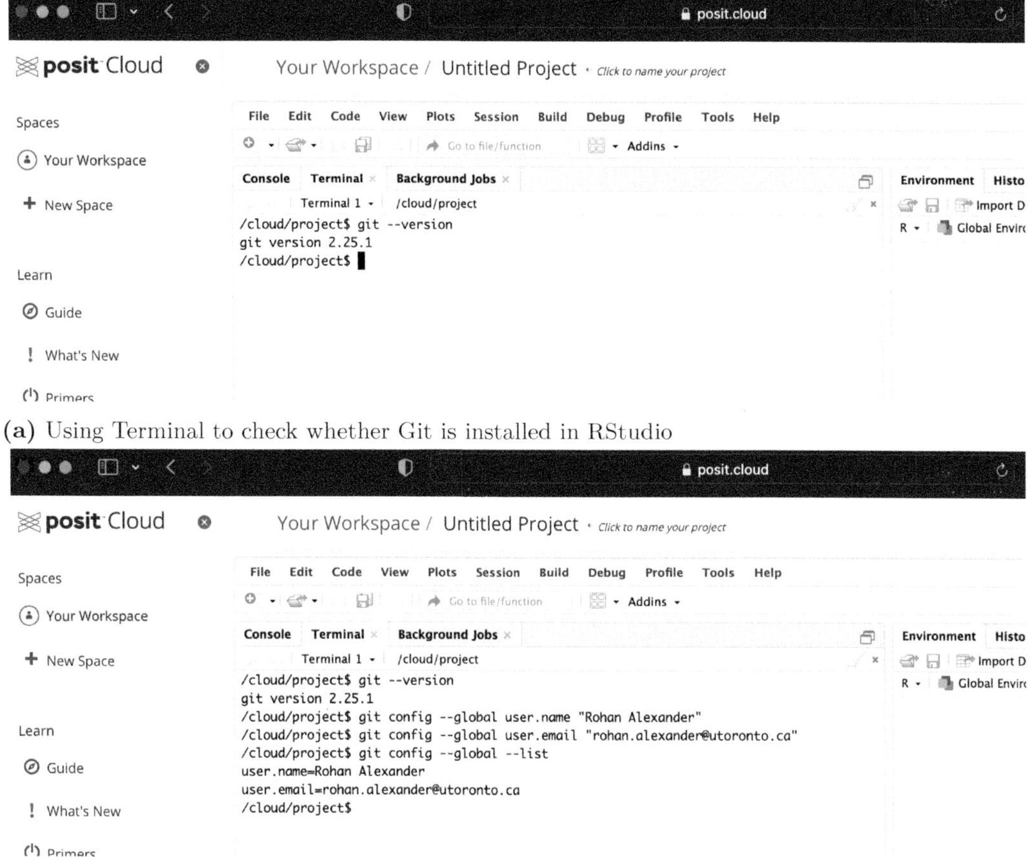

(a) Using Terminal to check whether Git is installed in RStudio

(b) Adding a username and email address to Git in RStudio

Figure 3.4: An overview of the steps involved in setting up Git

Git is pre-installed in Posit Cloud, it should be pre-installed on Mac, and it may be pre-installed on Windows. If you do not get a version number in response, then you need to install it. To do that you should follow the instructions specific to your operating system in Bryan (2020, chap. 5).

After Git is installed we need to tell it a username and email. We need to do this because Git adds this information whenever we take a snapshot, or to use Git's language, whenever we make a commit.

Again, within the Terminal, type the following, replacing the details with yours, and then press "enter/return" after each line.

```
git config --global user.name "Rohan Alexander"
git config --global user.email "rohan.alexander@utoronto.ca"
git config --global --list
```

When this set-up has been done properly, the values that you entered for "user.name" and "user.email" will be returned after the last line (Figure 3.4b).

These details—username and email address—will be public. There are various ways to hide the email address if necessary, and GitHub provides instructions about this. Bryan (2020, chap. 7) provides more detailed instructions about this step, and a trouble-shooting guide.

3.4.2 GitHub

Now that Git is set up, we need to set up GitHub. We created a GitHub account in Chapter 2, which we use again here. After being signed in at `github.com` we first need to make a new folder, which is called a "repo" in Git. Look for a "+" in the top right, and then select "New Repository" (Figure 3.5a).

At this point we can add a sensible name for the repo. Leave it as "public" for now, because it can always be deleted later. And check the box to "Initialize this repository with a README". Change "Add .gitignore" to R. After that, click "Create repository".

This will take us to a screen that is fairly empty, but the details that we need—a URL—are in the green "Clone or Download" button, which we can copy by clicking the clipboard (Figure 3.5b).

Now returning to RStudio, in Posit Cloud, we create a new project using "New Project from Git Repository". It will ask for the URL that we just copied (Figure 3.5c). If you are using a local computer, then this step is accomplished through the menu: "File" → "New Project$dots" → "Version Control" → "Git", then paste in the URL, give the folder a meaningful name, check "Open in new session", then click "Create Project".

At this point, a new folder has been created that we can use. We will want to be able to push it back to GitHub, and for that we will need to use a Personal Access Token (PAT) to link our RStudio Workspace with our GitHub account. We use `usethis` and `gitcreds` to enable this. These are, respectively, a package that automates repetitive tasks, and a package that authenticates with GitHub. To create a PAT, while signed into GitHub in the browser, and after installing and loading `usethis` run `create_github_token()` in your R session. GitHub will open in the browser with various options filled out (Figure 3.5d). It can be useful to give the PAT an informative name by replacing "Note", for instance "PAT for RStudio", then click "Generate token".

We only have one chance to copy this token, and if we make a mistake then we will need to generate a new one. Do not include the PAT in any R script or Quarto document. Instead, after installing and loading `gitcreds`, run `gitcreds_set()`, which will then prompt you to add your PAT in the console.

To use GitHub for a project that we are actively working on we follow this procedure:

1. The first thing to do is almost always to get any changes with "pull". To do this, open the Git pane in RStudio, and click the blue down arrow. This gets any changes to the folder, as it is on GitHub, into our own version of the folder.

(a) Start process of creating a new repository

(b) Copy the URL of the new repository

(c) Adding the project to Posit Cloud

(d) Creating a PAT

(e) Adding files to be committed

(f) Making a commit

Figure 3.5: An overview of the steps involved in setting up GitHub

2. We can then make our changes to our copy of the folder. For instance, we could update the README, and then save it as normal.
3. Once this is done, we need to add, commit, and push. In the Git pane in RStudio, select the files to be added. This adds them to the staging area. Then click "Commit" (Figure 3.5e). A new window will open. Add an informative message about the change that was made, and then click "Commit" in that new window (Figure 3.5f). Finally, click "Push" to send the changes to GitHub.

There are a few common pain-points when it comes to Git and GitHub. We recommend committing and pushing regularly, especially when you are new to version control. This increases the number of snapshots that you could come back to if needed. All commits should have an informative commit message. If you are new to version control, then the expectation of a good commit message is that it contains a short summary of the change, followed by a blank line, and then an explanation of the change including what the change is, and why it is being made. For instance, if your commit adds graphs to a paper, then a commit message could be:

```
Add graphs

Graphs of unemployment and inflation added into Data section.
```

There is some evidence of a relationship between overall quality and commit behavior (Sprint and Conci 2019). As you get more experience ideally the commit messages will act as a kind of journal of the project. But the main thing is to commit regularly.

Git and GitHub were designed for software developers, rather than data scientists. GitHub limits the size of the files it will consider to 100MB, and even 50MB can prompt a warning. Data science projects regularly involve datasets that are larger than this. In Chapter 10 we discuss the use of data deposits, which can be especially useful when a project is completed, but when we are actively working on a project it can be useful to ignore large data files, at least as far as Git and GitHub are concerned. We do this using a ".gitignore" file, in which we list all of the files that we do not want to track using Git. The example folder[8] contains a ".gitignore" file. And it can be helpful to run `git_vaccinate()` from `usethis`, which will add a variety of files to a global ".gitignore" file in case you forget to do it on a project basis. Mac users will find it useful that this will cause ".DS_Store" files to be ignored.

We used the Git pane in RStudio which removed the need to use the Terminal, but it did not remove the need to go to GitHub and set up a new project. Having set up Git and GitHub, we can further improve this aspect of our workflow with `usethis`.

First check that Git is set up with `git_sitrep()` from `usethis`. This should print information about the username and email. We can use `use_git_config()` to update these details if needed.

```
use_git_config(
  user.name = "Rohan Alexander",
  user.email = "rohan.alexander@utoronto.ca"
)
```

[8] https://github.com/RohanAlexander/starter_folder

Rather than starting a new project in GitHub, and then adding it locally, we can now use `use_git()` to initiate it and commit the files. Having committed, we can use `use_github()` to push to GitHub, which will create the folder on GitHub as well.

It is normal to be intimidated by Git and GitHub. Many data scientists only know a little about how to use it, and that is okay. Try to push regularly so that you have a recent snapshot in case you need it.

3.5 Using R in practice

3.5.1 Dealing with errors

> When you are programming, eventually your code will break, when I say eventually, I mean like probably 10 or 20 times a day.
>
> Gelfand (2021)

Everyone who uses R, or any programming language for that matter, has trouble find them at some point. This is normal. Programming is hard. At some point code will not run or will throw an error. This happens to everyone. It is common to get frustrated, but to move forward we develop strategies to work through the issues:

1. If you are getting an error message, then sometimes it will be useful. Try to read it carefully to see if there is anything of use in it.
2. Try to search for the error message. It can be useful to include "tidyverse" or "in R" in the search to help make the results more appropriate. Sometimes Stack Overflow results can be useful.
3. Look at the help file for the function by putting "?" before the function, for instance, `?pivot_wider()`. A common issue is to use a slightly incorrect argument name or format, such as accidentally including a string instead of an object name.
4. Look at where the error is happening and remove or comment out code until the error is resolved, and then slowly add code back again.
5. Check the class of the object with `class()`, for instance, `class(data_set$data_column)`. Ensure that it is what is expected.
6. Restart R: "Session" → "Restart R and Clear Output". Then load everything again.
7. Restart your computer.
8. Search for what you are trying to do, rather than the error, being sure to include "tidyverse" or "in R" in the search to help make the results more appropriate. For instance, "save PDF of graph in R using ggplot". Sometimes there are relevant blog posts or Stack Overflow answers that will help.
9. Make a small, self-contained, reproducible example "reprex" to see if the issue can be isolated and to enable others to help.

More generally, while this is not always possible, it is almost always helpful to take a break and come back the next day.

3.5.2 Reproducible examples

> No one can advise or help you—no one. There is only one thing you should do. Go into yourself.
>
> Rilke ([1929] 2014)

Asking for help is a skill like any other. We get better at it with practice. It is important to try not to say "this doesn't work", "I tried everything", "your code does not work", or "here is the error message, what do I do?". In general, it is not possible to help based on these comments, because there are too many possible issues. You need to make it easy for others to help you. This involves a few steps.

1. Provide a small, self-contained example of your data, and code, and detail what is going wrong.
2. Document what you have tried so far, including which Stack Overflow and Posit Forum posts you looked at, and why they are not what you are after.
3. Be clear about the outcome that you would like.

Begin by creating a minimal REPRoducible EXample—a "reprex". This is code that contains what is needed to reproduce the error, but only what is needed. This means that the code is likely a smaller, simpler version that nonetheless reproduces the error.

Sometimes this process enables one to solve the problem. If it does not, then it gives someone else a fighting chance of being able to help. There is almost no chance that you have got a problem that someone has not addressed before. It is more likely that the main difficulty is trying to communicate what you want to do and what is happening, in a way that allows others to recognize both. Developing tenacity is important.

To develop reproducible examples, `reprex` is especially useful. After installing it we:

1. Load the `reprex` package: `library(reprex)`.
2. Highlight and copy the code that is giving issues.
3. Run `reprex()` in the console.

If the code is self-contained, then it will preview in the viewer. If it is not, then it will error, and you should rewrite the code so that it is self-contained.

If you need data to reproduce the error, then you should use data that is built into R. There are a large number of datasets that are built into R and can be seen using `library(help = "datasets")`. But if possible, you should use a common option such as `mtcars` or `faithful`. Combining a reprex with a GitHub Gist that was introduced in Chapter 2 increases the chances that someone is able to help you.

3.5.3 Mentality

> (Y)ou are a real, valid, *competent* user and programmer no matter what IDE you develop in or what tools you use to make your work work for you
>
> (L)et's break down the gates, there's enough room for everyone
>
> Sharla Gelfand, 10 March 2020.

If you write code, then you are a programmer, regardless of how you do it, what you are using it for, or who you are. But there are a few traits that one tends to notice great programmers have in common.

- **Focused:** Often having an aim to "learn R" or similar tends to be problematic, because there is no real end point to that. It tends to be more efficient to have smaller, more specific goals, such as "make a histogram about the 2022 Australian Election with `ggplot2`". This is something that can be focused on and achieved in a few hours. The issue with goals that are more nebulous, such as "I want to learn R", is that it is easier to get lost on tangents and more difficult to get help. This can be demoralizing and lead to people quitting too early.
- **Curious:** It is almost always useful to "have a go"; that is, if you are not sure, then just try it. In general, the worst that happens is that you waste your time. You can rarely break something irreparably. For instance, if you want to know what happens if you pass a vector instead of a dataframe to `ggplot()` then try it.
- **Pragmatic:** At the same time, it can be useful to stick within reasonable bounds, and make one small change each time. For instance, say you want to run some regressions, and are curious about the possibility of using `rstanarm` instead of `lm()`. A pragmatic way to proceed is to use one aspect from `rstanarm` initially and then make another change next time.
- **Tenacious:** Again, this is a balancing act. Unexpected problems and issues arise with every project. On the one hand, persevering despite these is a good tendency. But on the other hand, sometimes one does need to be prepared to give up on something if it does not seem like a break through is possible. Mentors can be useful as they tend to be a better judge of what is reasonable.
- **Planned:** It is almost always useful to excessively plan what you are going to do. For instance, you may want to make a histogram of some data. You should plan the steps that are needed and even sketch out how each step might be implemented. For instance, the first step is to get the data. What packages might be useful? Where might the data be? What is the back-up plan if the data do not exist there?
- **Done is better than perfect:** We all have various perfectionist tendencies, but it can be useful to initially try to turn them off to a certain extent. Initially just worry about writing code that works. You can always come back and improve aspects of it. But it is important to actually ship. Ugly code that gets the job done is better than beautiful code that is never finished.

3.5.4 Code comments and style

Code must be commented. Comments should focus on why certain code was written and to a lesser extent, why a common alternative was not selected. Indeed, it can be a good idea to write the comments before you write the code, explaining what you want to do and why, and then returning to write the code (Fowler and Beck 2018, 59).

There is no one way to write code, especially in R. However, there are some general guidelines that will make it easier for you even if you are just working on your own. Most projects will evolve over time, and one purpose of code comments is to enable future-you to retrace what was done and why certain decisions were made (Bowers and Voors 2016).

Comments in R scripts can be added by including the # symbol. (The behavior of # is different for lines inside an R chunk in a Quarto document where it acts as a comment, compared with lines outside an R chunk where it sets heading levels.) We do not have to put a comment at the start of the line, it can be midway through. In general, you do not need to comment what every aspect of your code is doing but you should comment parts that are not obvious. For instance, if we read in some value then we may like to comment where it is coming from.

You should try to comment why you are doing something (Wickham 2021c). What are you trying to achieve? You must comment to explain weird things. Like if you are removing some specific row, say row 27, then why are you removing that row? It may seem obvious in the moment, but future-you will not remember.

You should break your code into sections. For instance, setting up the workspace, reading in datasets, manipulating and cleaning the datasets, analyzing the datasets, and finally producing tables and figures. Each of these should be separated with comments explaining what is going on, and sometimes into separate files, depending on the length.

Additionally, at the top of each file it is important to note basic information, such as the purpose of the file, and prerequisites or dependencies, the date, the author and contact information, and finally any red flags or todos.

Your R scripts should have a preamble and a clear demarcation of sections.

```
#### Preamble ####
# Purpose: Brief sentence about what this script does
# Author: Your name
# Date: The date it was written
# Contact: Add your email
# License: Think about how your code may be used
# Pre-requisites:
# - Maybe you need some data or some other script to have been run?


#### Workspace setup ####
# do not keep install.packages lines; comment out if need be
# Load packages
library(tidyverse)

# Read in the unedited data.
raw_data <- read_csv("inputs/data/unedited_data.csv")
```

```
#### Next section ####
...
```

Finally, try not to rely on a user commenting and uncommenting code, or any other manual step, such as directory specification, for code to work. This will preclude the use of automated code checking and testing.

This all takes time. As a rough rule of thumb, you should expect to spend at least as much time commenting and improving your code as you spent writing it. Some examples of nicely commented code include Dolatsara et al. (2021) and Burton, Cruz, and Hahn (2021).

3.5.5 Tests

Tests should be written throughout the code, and you need to write them as we go, not all at the end. This will slow you down. But it will help you to think, and to fix mistakes, which will make your code better and lead to better overall productivity. Code without tests should be viewed with suspicion. There is room for improvement when it comes to testing practices in R packages (Vidoni 2021), let alone R code more generally.

The need for other people, and ideally, automated processes, to run tests on code is one reason that we emphasize reproducibility. That is also why we emphasize smaller aspects such as not hardcoding file-paths, using projects, and not having spaces in file names.

It is difficult to define a complete and general suite of tests, but broadly we want to test:

1) boundary conditions,
2) classes,
3) missing data,
4) the number of observations and variables,
5) duplicates, and
6) regression results.

We do all this initially on our simulated data and then move to the real data. It is possible to write an infinite number of tests but a smaller number of high-quality tests is better than many thoughtless tests.

One type of test is an "assertion". Assertions are written throughout the code to check whether something is true and stop the code from running if not (Irving et al. 2021, 272). For instance, you might assert that a variable should be numeric. If it was tested against this assertion and found to be a character, then the test would fail and the script would stop running. Assertion tests in data science will typically be used in data cleaning and preparation scripts. We have more to say about these in Chapter 9. Unit tests check some complete aspect of code (Irving et al. 2021, 274). We will consider them more in Chapter 12 when we consider modeling.

3.6 Efficiency

Generally in this book we are, and will continue to be, concerned with just getting something done. Not necessarily getting it done in the best or most efficient way, because to a large extent, being worried about that is a waste of time. For the most part one is better off just pushing things into the cloud, letting them run for a reasonable time, and using that time to worry about other aspects of the pipeline. But that eventually becomes unfeasible. At a certain point, and this differs depending on context, efficiency becomes important. Eventually ugly or slow code, and dogmatic insistence on a particular way of doing things, have an effect. And it is at that point that one needs to be open to new approaches to ensure efficiency. There is rarely a most common area for obvious performance gains. Instead, it is important to develop the ability to measure, evaluate, and think.

One of the best ways to improve the efficiency of our code is preparing it in such a way that we can bring in a second pair of eyes. To make the most of their time, it is important that our code easy to read. So we start with "code linting" and "styling". This does not speed up our code, per se, but instead makes it more efficient when another person comes to it, or we revisit it. This enables formal code review and refactoring, which is where we rewrite code to make it better, while not changing what it does (it does the same thing, but in a different way). We then turn to measurement of run time, and introduce parallel processing, where we allow our computer to run code for multiple processes at the same time

3.6.1 Sharing a code environment

We have discussed at length the need to share code, and we have put forward an approach to this using GitHub. And in Chapter 10, we will discuss sharing data. But there is another requirement to enable other people to run our code. In Chapter 2 we discussed how R itself, as well as R packages update from time to time, as new functionality is developed, errors fixed, and other general improvements made. The "R Essentials" Online Appendix[9] describes how one advantage of the `tidyverse` is that it can update faster than base R, because it is more specific. But this could mean that even if we were to share all the code and data that we use, it is possible that the software versions that have become available would cause errors.

The solution to this is to detail the environment that was used. There are a large number of ways to do this, and they can add complexity. We just focus on documenting the version of R and R packages that were used, and making it easier for others to install that exact version. We use `renv` to do this.

Once `renv` is installed and loaded, we use `init()` to get the infrastructure set-up that we will need. We are going to create a file that will record the packages and versions used. We then use `snapshot()` to actually document what we are using. This creates a "lockfile" that records the information.

If we want to see which packages we are using in the R Project, then we can use `dependencies()`. Doing this for the example folder[10] indicates that the following packages are used: `rmarkdown`, `bookdown`, `knitr`, `rmarkdown`, `bookdown`, `knitr`, `palmerpenguins`, `tidyverse`, `renv`, `haven`, `readr`, and `tidyverse`.

We could open the lockfile file—"renv.lock"—to see the exact versions if we wanted. The lockfile also documents all the other packages that were installed and where they were downloaded from. Someone coming to this project from outside could then use `restore()` which would install the exact version of the packages that we used.

[9]https://tellingstorieswithdata.com/20-r_essentials.html
[10]https://github.com/RohanAlexander/starter_folder

3.6.2 Code linting and styling

Being fast is valuable but it is mostly about being able to iterate fast, not necessarily having code that runs fast. Backus (1981, 26) describes how even in 1954 a programmer cost at least as much as a computer, and these days additional computational power is usually much cheaper than a programmer. Performant code is important, but it is also important to use other people's time efficiently.

Linting and styling is the process of checking code, mostly for stylistic issues, and re-arranging code to make it easier to read. (There is another aspect of linting, which is dealing with programming errors, such as forgetting a closing bracket, but here we focus on stylistic issues.) Often the best efficiency gain comes from making it easier for others to read our code, even if this is just ourselves returning to the code after a break. Jane Street, a US proprietary trading firm, places a very strong focus on ensuring their code is readable, as a core part of risk mitigation (Minsky 2011). While we may not all have billions of dollars under the potentially mercurial management of code, we all would likely prefer that our code does not produce errors.

We use `lint()` from `lintr` to lint our code. For instance, consider the following R code (saved as "linting_example.R").

```
SIMULATED_DATA <-
  tibble(
    division = c(1:150, 151),
    party = sample(
      x = c("Liberal"),
      size = 151,
      replace = T
    )
  )
```

```
lint(filename = "linting_example.R")
```

The result is that the file "linting_example.R" is opened and the issues that `lint()` found are printed in "Markers" (Figure 3.6). It is then up to you to deal with the issues.

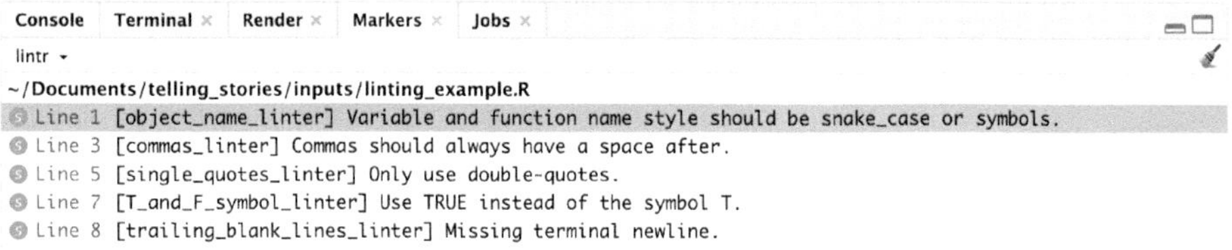

```
Console  Terminal  Render  Markers  Jobs
lintr
~/Documents/telling_stories/inputs/linting_example.R
Line 1 [object_name_linter] Variable and function name style should be snake_case or symbols.
Line 3 [commas_linter] Commas should always have a space after.
Line 5 [single_quotes_linter] Only use double-quotes.
Line 7 [T_and_F_symbol_linter] Use TRUE instead of the symbol T.
Line 8 [trailing_blank_lines_linter] Missing terminal newline.
```

Figure 3.6: Linting results from example R code

Making the recommended changes results in code that is more readable, and consistent with best practice, as defined by Wickham (2021c).

```
simulated_data <-
  tibble(
```

```
    division = c(1:150, 151),
    party = sample(
      x = c("Liberal"),
      size = 151,
      replace = TRUE
    )
  )
```

At first it may seem that some aspects that the linter is identifying, like trailing whitespace and only using double quotes are small and inconsequential. But they distract from being able to fix bigger issues. Further, if we are not able to get small things right, then how could anyone trust that we could get the big things right? Therefore, it is important to have dealt with all the small aspects that a linter identifies.

In addition to `lintr` we also use `styler`. This will automatically adjust style issues, in contrast to the linter, which gave a list of issues to look at. To run this we use `style_file()`.

```
style_file(path = "linting_example.R")
```

This will automatically make changes, such as spacing and indentation. As such this should be done regularly, rather than only once at the end of a project, so as to be able to review the changes and make sure no errors have been introduced.

3.6.3 Code review

Having dealt with all of these aspects of style, we can turn to code review. This is the process of having another person go through and critique the code. Code review is a critical part of writing code, and Irving et al. (2021, 465) describe it as "the most effective way to find bugs". It is especially helpful, although quite daunting, when learning to code because getting feedback is a great way to improve.

Go out of your way to be polite and collegial when reviewing another person's code. Small aspects to do with style, things like spacing and separation, should have been taken care of by a linter and styler, but if not, then make a general recommendation about that. Most of your time as a code reviewer in data science should be spent on aspects such as:

1) Is there an informative README and how could it be improved?
2) Are the file names and variable names consistent, informative, and meaningful?
3) Do the comments allow you to understand why something is being done?
4) Are the tests both appropriate and sufficient? Are there edge cases or corner solutions that are not considered? Similarly, are there unnecessary tests that could be removed?
5) Are there magic numbers that could be changed to variables and explained?
6) Is there duplicated code that could be changed?
7) Are there any outstanding warnings that should be addressed?
8) Are there any especially large functions or pipes that could be separated into smaller ones?
9) Is the structure of the project appropriate?
10) Can we change any of the code to data (Irving et al. 2021, 462)?

For instance, consider some code that looked for the names of prime ministers and presidents. When we first wrote this code we likely added the relevant names directly into the code. But as part of code review, we might instead recommend that this be changed. We might recommend creating a small dataset of relevant names, and then re-writing the code to have it look up that dataset.

Code review ensures that the code can be understood by at least one other person. This is a critical part of building knowledge about the world. At Google, code review is not primarily about finding defects, although that may happen, but is instead about ensuring readability and maintainability as well as education (Sadowski et al. 2018). This is also the case at Jane Street where they use code review to catch bugs, share institutional knowledge, assist with training, and oblige staff to write code that can be read (Minsky 2015).

Finally, code review does not have to, and should not, be an onerous days-consuming process of reading all the code. The best code review is a quick review of just one file, focused on suggesting changes to just a handful of lines. Indeed, it may be better to have a review done by a small team of people rather than one individual. Do not review too much code at any one time. At most a few hundred lines, which should take around an hour, because any more than that has been found to be associated with reduced efficacy (J. Cohen, Teleki, and Brown 2006, 79).

3.6.4 Code refactoring

To refactor code means to rewrite it so that the new code achieves the same outcome as the old code, but the new code does it better. For instance, Chawla (2020) discuss how the code underpinning an important UK Covid model was initially written by epidemiologists, and months later clarified and cleaned up by a team from the Royal Society, Microsoft, and GitHub. This was valuable because it provided more confidence in the model, even though both versions produced the same outputs, given the same inputs.

We typically refer to code refactoring in relation to code that someone else wrote. (Although it may be that we actually wrote the code, and it was just that it was some time ago.) When we start to refactor code, we want to make sure that the rewritten code achieves the same outcomes as the original code. This means that we need a suite of appropriate tests written that we can depend on. If these do not exist, then we may need to create them.

We rewrite code to make it easier for others to understand, which in turn allows more confidence in our conclusions. But before we can do that, we need to understand what the existing code is doing. One way to get started is to go through the code and add extensive comments. These comments are different to normal comments. They are our active process of trying to understand what is each code chunk trying to do and how could this be improved.

Refactoring code is an opportunity to ensure that it satisfies best practice. Trisovic et al. (2022) details some core recommendations based on examining 9,000 R scripts including:

1. Remove `setwd()` and any absolute paths, and ensure that only relative paths, in relation to the ".Rproj" file, are used.
2. Ensure there is a clear order of execution. We have recommended using numbers in filenames to achieve this initially, but eventually more sophisticated approaches, such as `targets` (Landau 2021), could be used instead.
3. Ensure that code can run on a different computer.

For instance, consider the following code:

```
setwd("/Users/rohanalexander/Documents/telling_stories")

library(tidyverse)

d = read_csv("cars.csv")

mtcars =
  mtcars |>
  mutate(K_P_L = mpg / 2.352)

library(datasauRus)

datasaurus_dozen
```

We could change that, starting by creating an R Project which enables us to remove `setwd()`, grouping all the `library()` calls at the top, using "<-" instead of "=", and being consistent with variable names:

```
library(tidyverse)
library(datasauRus)

cars_data <- read_csv("cars.csv")

mpg_to_kpl_conversion_factor <- 2.352

mtcars <-
  mtcars |>
  mutate(kpl = mpg / mpg_to_kpl_conversion_factor)
```

3.6.5 Parallel processing

Sometimes code is slow because the computer needs to do the same thing many times. We may be able to take advantage of this and enable these jobs to be done at the same time using parallel processing. This will be especially useful starting from Chapter 12 for modeling.

After installing and loading `tictoc` we can use `tic()` and `toc()` to time various aspects of our code. This is useful with parallel processing, but also more generally, to help us find out where the largest delays are.

```
tic("First bit of code")
print("Fast code")
```

```
[1] "Fast code"
```

```
toc()
```

```
First bit of code: 0.003 sec elapsed
```

```
tic("Second bit of code")
Sys.sleep(3)
print("Slow code")
```

```
[1] "Slow code"
```

```
toc()
```

```
Second bit of code: 3.008 sec elapsed
```

And so we know that there is something slowing down the code. (In this artificial case it is `Sys.sleep()` causing a delay of three seconds.)

We could use `parallel` which is part of base R to run functions in parallel. We could also use `future` which brings additional features. After installing and loading `future` we use `plan()` to specify whether we want to run things sequentially ("sequential") or in parallel ("multisession"). We then wrap what we want this applied to within `future()`.

To see this in action we will create a dataset and then implement a function on a row-wise basis.

```
simulated_data <-
  tibble(
    random_draws = runif(n = 1000000, min = 0, max = 1000) |> round(),
    more_random_draws = runif(n = 1000000, min = 0, max = 1000) |> round()
  )

plan(sequential)

tic()
simulated_data <-
  simulated_data |>
  rowwise() |>
  mutate(which_is_smaller =
           min(c(random_draws,
                 more_random_draws)))
toc()

plan(multisession)

tic()
simulated_data <-
  future(simulated_data |>
           rowwise() |>
           mutate(which_is_smaller =
                    min(c(
                      random_draws,
                      more_random_draws
                    ))))
toc()
```

The sequential approach takes about 5 seconds, while the multisession approach takes about 0.3 seconds.

3.7 Concluding remarks

In this chapter we have covered a lot of ground and it is normal to be overwhelmed. Come back to the Quarto section as needed. Many people are confused by Git and Github and just know enough to get by. And while there was a lot of material in efficiency, the most important aspect of performant code is making it easier for another person to read it, even if that person is just yourself returning after a break.

3.8 Exercises

Scales

1. *(Plan)* Consider the following scenario: *In a certain country there are only ever four parties that could win a seat in parliament. Whichever candidate has a plurality of votes in the area associated with a given seat wins that seat. The parliament is made up of 175 total seats. An analyst is interested in the number of votes for each party by seat.* Please sketch what that dataset could look like, and then sketch a graph that you could build to show all observations.
2. *(Simulate I)* Please further consider the scenario described, and decide which of the following could be used to simulate the situation (select all that apply)?
   a. `tibble(seat = rep(1:175, each = 4), party = rep(x = 1:4, times = 175), votes = runif(n = 175 * 4, min = 0, max = 1000) |> floor())`
   b. `tibble(seat = rep(1:175, each = 4), party = sample(x = 1:4, size = 175, replace = TRUE), votes = runif(n = 175 * 4, min = 0, max = 1000) |> floor())`
   c. `tibble(seat = rep(1:175, each = 4), party = rep(x = 1:4, times = 175), votes = sample(x = 1:1000, size = 175 * 4))`
   d. `tibble(seat = rep(1:175, each = 4), party = sample(x = 1:4, size = 175, replace = TRUE), votes = sample(x = 1:1000, size = 175 * 4))`
3. *(Simulate II)* Please write three tests based on this simulation.
4. *(Acquire)* Please identify one possible source of actual data about voting in a country of interest to you.
5. *(Explore)* Assume that the `tidyverse` is loaded and the dataset "election_results" has the columns "seat", "party", and "votes", as in the earlier question. Which of the following would result in a count of the number of seats won by each party (pick one)?
   a. `election_results |> slice_max(votes, n = 1, by = seat) |> count(party)`
   b. `election_results |> slice_max(votes, n = 1, by = party) |> count(seat)`
   c. `election_results |> slice_max(votes, n = 1, by = party) |> count(party)`
   d. `election_results |> slice_max(votes, n = 1, by = seat) |> count(seat)`
6. *(Communicate)* Please write two paragraphs as if you had gathered data from that source and built a graph. The exact details contained in the paragraphs do

not have to be factual (i.e. you do not actually have to get the data nor create the graphs).

Questions

1. According to M. Alexander (2019a) research is reproducible if (pick one)?
   a. It is published in peer-reviewed journals.
   b. All of the materials used in the study are provided.
   c. It can be reproduced exactly without the authors providing materials.
   d. It can be reproduced exactly, given all the materials used in the study.
2. Which of the following are components of the project layout recommended by Wilson et al. (2017) (select all that apply)?
   a. requirements.txt
   b. doc
   c. data
   d. LICENSE
   e. CITATION
   f. README
   g. src
   h. results
3. Based on M. Alexander (2021) please write a paragraph about some of the barriers you overcame, or still face, with regard to sharing code that you wrote.
4. According to Wickham (2021c) for naming files, how would the files "00_get_data.R" and "get data.R" be classified (pick one)?
   a. bad; bad.
   b. good; bad.
   c. bad; good.
   d. good; good.
5. Which of the following would result in bold text in Quarto (pick one)?
   a. `**bold**`
   b. `##bold##`
   c. `*bold*`
   d. `#bold#`
6. Which option would hide the warnings in a Quarto R chunk (pick one)?
   a. `echo: false`
   b. `eval: false`
   c. `warning: false`
   d. `message: false`
7. Which options would run the R code chunk and display the results, but not show the code in a Quarto R chunk (pick one)?
   a. `echo: false`
   b. `include: false`
   c. `eval: false`
   d. `warning: false`
   e. `message: false`
8. Why are R Projects important (select all that apply)?
   a. They help with reproducibility.
   b. They make it easier to share code.
   c. They make your workspace more organized.
9. Assuming the packages and datasets have been loaded, what is the mistake in this code: `DoctorVisits |> filter(visits)` (pick one)?

    a. `visits`
    b. `DoctorVisits`
    c. `filter`
    d. `|>`
10. What is a reprex and why is it important to be able to make one (select all that apply)?
    a. A reproducible example that enables your error to be reproduced.
    b. A reproducible example that helps others help you.
    c. A reproducible example during the construction of which you may solve your own problem.
    d. A reproducible example that demonstrates you have actually tried to help yourself.
11. According to Gelfand (2021), what is the key part of "If you need help getting unstuck, the first step is to create a reprex, or reproducible example. The goal of a reprex is to package your problematic code in such a way that other people can run it and feel your pain. Then, hopefully, they can provide a solution and put you out of your misery." (pick one)?
    a. package your problematic code
    b. other people can run it and feel your pain
    c. the first step is to create a reprex
    d. they can provide a solution and put you out of your misery

Tutorial

Code review is an important part of working as a professional (Sadowski et al. 2018). Please put together a small Quarto file that downloads a dataset using `opendatatoronto`, cleans it, and makes a graph. Then exchange it with someone else. Following the advice of Google (2022), please provide them with a review of their code. That should be at least two pages of single-spaced content. Submit the review as a PDF.

Paper

At about this point the *Donaldson* Paper in the "Papers" Online Appendix[11] would be appropriate.

[11]https://tellingstorieswithdata.com/23-assessment.html

Part II

Communication

4

Writing research

Prerequisites

- Read *By Design: Planning Research on Higher Education*, (Light, Singer, and Willett 1990)
  - Focus on Chapter 2 "What are your questions", which provides strategies for developing good research questions.
- Read *On Writing Well*, (any edition is fine) (Zinsser 1976)
  - Focus on Parts I "Principles", and II "Methods", which provide a "how-to" for a particularly effective style of writing.
- Read *Novelist Cormac McCarthy's tips on how to write a great science paper*, (Savage and Yeh 2019)
  - This paper provides specific tips that will improve your writing.
- Read *Publication, publication*, (G. King 2006)
  - This paper details a strategy for moving from a replication to a publishable academic paper.
- Watch *Quantitative Editing*, (Bronner 2021)
  - The video provides strategies for quantitative-based writing based on experience as a quantitative editor at FiveThirtyEight.
- Read *Smoking and carcinoma of the lung*, (Doll and Hill 1950)
  - The paper provides an excellent example of a data section.
- Read one of the following well-written quantitative papers:
  - *Asset prices in an exchange economy*, (R. Lucas 1978)
  - *Individuals, institutions, and innovation in the debates of the French Revolution*, (Barron et al. 2018)
  - *Modeling: optimal marathon performance on the basis of physiological factors*, (Joyner 1991)
  - *On reproducible econometric research*, (Koenker and Zeileis 2009)
  - *Prevented mortality and greenhouse gas emissions from historical and projected nuclear power*, (Kharecha and Hansen 2013)
  - *Seeing like a market*, (Fourcade and Healy 2017)
  - *Simpson's paradox and the hot hand in basketball*, (Wardrop 1995)
  - *Some studies in machine learning using the game of checkers*, (Samuel 1959)
  - *Statistical methods for assessing agreement between two methods of clinical measurement*, (Bland and Altman 1986)
  - *Surgical Skill and Complication Rates after Bariatric Surgery*, (Birkmeyer et al. 2013)
  - *The mundanity of excellence: An ethnographic report on stratification and Olympic swimmers*, (Chambliss 1989)
  - *The probable error of a mean*, (Student 1908)
- Read one of the following articles from *The New Yorker*:
  - *Funny Like a Guy*, Tad Friend, 4 April 2011
  - *Going the Distance*, David Remnick, 19 January 2014

  - *How the First Gravitational Waves Were Found*, Nicola Twilley, 11 February 2016
  - *Happy Feet*, Alexandra Jacobs, 7 September 2009
  - *Levels of the Game*, John McPhee, 31 May 1969
  - *Reporting from Hiroshima*, John Hersey, 23 August 1946
  - *The Catastrophist*, Elizabeth Kolbert, 22 June 2009
  - *The Quiet German*, George Packer, 24 November 2014
  - *The Pursuit of Beauty*, Alec Wilkinson, 1 February 2015
- Read one of the following articles from other publications:
  - *Blades of Glory*, Holly Anderson, Grantland
  - *Born to Run*, Walt Harrington, The Washington Post
  - *Dropped*, Jason Fagone, Grantland
  - *Federer as Religious Experience*, David Foster Wallace, The New York Times Magazine
  - *Generation Why?*, Zadie Smith, The New York Review of Books
  - *One hundred years of arm bars*, David Samuels, Grantland
  - *Out in the Great Alone*, Brian Phillips, ESPN
  - *Pearls Before Breakfast*, Gene Weingarten, The Washington Post
  - *Resurrecting The Champ*, J.R. Moehringer, Los Angeles Times
  - *The Cult of "Jurassic Park"*, Bryan Curtis, Grantland
  - *The House that Hova Built*, Zadie Smith, The New York Times
  - *The Re-Education of Chris Copeland*, Flinder Boyd, SB Nation
  - *The Sea of Crisis*, Brian Phillips, Grantland
  - *The Webb Space Telescope Will Rewrite Cosmic History. If It Works.*, Natalie Wolchover, Quanta Magazine

Key concepts and skills

- Writing is a critical skill—perhaps the most important—of all the skills required to analyze data. The only way to get better at writing is to write, ideally every day.
- When we write, although the benefits typically accrue to ourselves, we must nonetheless write for the reader. This means having one main message that we want to communicate, and thinking about where they are, rather than where we are.
- We want to get to a first draft as quickly as possible. Even if it is horrible, the difference between a first draft existing and not is enormous. At that point we start to rewrite. When doing so we aim to maximize clarity, often by removing unnecessary words.
- We typically begin with some area of interest and then develop research questions, datasets, and analysis in an iterative way. Through this process we come to a better understanding of what we are doing.

Software and packages

- `knitr` (Xie 2023)
- `tidyverse` (Wickham et al. 2019)

```
library(knitr)
library(tidyverse)
```

4.1 Introduction

> If you want to be a writer, you must do two things above all others: read a lot and write a lot. There's no way around these two things that I'm aware of, no shortcut.
>
> S. King (2000, 145)

We predominately tell stories with data by writing them down. Writing allows us to communicate efficiently. It is also a way to work out what we believe and allows us to get feedback on our ideas. Effective papers are tightly written and well-organized, which makes their story flow well. Proper sentence structure, spelling, vocabulary, and grammar are important because they remove distractions and enable each aspect of the story to be clearly articulated.

This chapter is about writing. By the end of it, you will have a better idea of how to write short, detailed, quantitative papers that communicate what you want them to, and do not waste the reader's time. We write for the reader, not for ourselves. Specifically, we write to be useful to the reader. This means clearly communicating something new, true, and important (Graham 2020). That said, the greatest benefit of writing nonetheless often accrues to the writer, even when we write for our audience. This is because the process of writing is a way to work out what we think and how we came to believe it.

Aspects of this chapter can feel a little like a list. It may be that you go through those aspects quickly initially, and then return to them as needed.

4.2 Writing

> The way to do a piece of writing is three or four times over, never once. For me, the hardest part comes first, getting something—anything—out in front of me. Sometimes in a nervous frenzy I just fling words as if I were flinging mud at a wall. Blurt out, heave out, babble out something—anything—as a first draft.
>
> McPhee (2017, 159)

The process of writing is a process of rewriting. The critical task is to get to a first draft as quickly as possible. Until that complete first draft exists, it is useful to try to not to delete, or even revise, anything that was written, regardless of how bad it may seem. Just write. (This advice is directed at less-experienced writers. As you get more experience, you may find that your approach changes.)

One of the most intimidating stages is a blank page, and we deal with this by immediately adding headings such as: "Introduction", "Data", "Model", "Results", and "Discussion". And then adding fields in the top matter for the various bits and pieces that are needed, such as "title", "date", "author", and "abstract". This creates a generic outline, which will play the role of *mise en place* for the paper. By way of background, *mise en place* is a preparatory phase in a professional kitchen when ingredients are sorted, prepared, and arranged for easy access. This ensures that everything that is needed is available without unnecessary delay. Putting together an outline plays the same role when writing quantitative papers, and is akin to placing on the counter, the ingredients that we will use to prepare dinner (McPhee 2017).

Having established this generic outline, we need to develop an understanding of what we are exploring through thinking deeply about our research question. In theory, we develop a research question, answer it, and then do all the writing; but that rarely actually happens (Franklin 2005). Instead, we typically have some idea of the question and the shape of an answer, and these become less vague as we write. This is because it is through the process of writing that we refine our thinking (S. King 2000, 131). Having put down some thoughts about the research question, we can start to add dot points in each of the sections, adding sub-sections with informative sub-headings as needed. We then go back and expand those dot points into paragraphs. While we do this our thinking is influenced by a web of other researchers, but also other aspects such as our circumstances and environment (Latour 1996).

While writing the first draft you should ignore the feeling that you are not good enough, or that it is impossible. Just write. You need words on paper, even if they are bad, and the first draft is when you accomplish this. Remove distractions and focus on writing. Perfectionism is the enemy, and should be set aside. Sometimes this can be accomplished by getting up very early to write, by creating a deadline, or forming a writing group. Creating a sense of urgency can be useful and one option is to not bother with adding proper citations as you go, which could slow you down, and instead just add something like "[TODO: CITE R HERE]". Do similar with graphs and tables. That is, include textual descriptions such as "[TODO: ADD GRAPH THAT SHOWS EACH COUNTRY OVER TIME HERE]" instead of actual graphs and tables. Focus on adding content, even if it is bad. When this is all done, a first draft exists.

This first draft will be poorly written and far from great. But it is by writing a bad first draft that you can get to a good second draft, a great third draft, and eventually excellence (Lamott 1994, 20). That first draft will be too long, it will not make sense, it will contain claims that cannot be supported, and some claims that should not be. If you are not embarrassed by your first draft, then you have not written it quickly enough.

Use the "delete" key extensively, as well as "cut" and "paste", to turn that first draft into a second. Print the draft and using a red pen to move or remove words, sentences, and entire paragraphs, is especially helpful. The process of going from a first draft to a second draft is best done in one sitting, to help with the flow and consistency of the story. One aspect of this first rewrite is enhancing the story that we want to tell. Another aspect is taking out everything that is not the story (S. King 2000, 57).

It can be painful to remove work that seems good even if it does not quite fit into what the draft is becoming. One way to make this less painful is to make a temporary document, perhaps named "debris.qmd", to save these unwanted paragraphs instead of immediately deleting them. Another strategy is to comment out the paragraphs. That way you can still look at the raw file and notice aspects that could be useful.

As you go through what was written in each of the sections try to bring some sense to it with special consideration to how it supports the story that is developing. This revision process is the essence of writing (McPhee 2017, 160). You should also fix the references, and add the real graphs and tables. As part of this rewriting process, the paper's central message tends to develop, and the answers to the research questions tend to become clearer. At this point, aspects such as the introduction can be returned to and, finally, the abstract. Typos and other issues affect the credibility of the work. So these should be fixed as part of the second draft.

At this point the draft is starting to become sensible. The job is to now make it brilliant. Print it and again go through it on paper. Try to remove everything that does not contribute to the story. At about this stage, you may start to get too close to the paper. This is a great opportunity to give it to someone else for their comments. Ask for feedback about what is weak about the story. After addressing these, it can be helpful to go through the paper once more, this time reading it aloud. A paper is never "done" and it is more that at a certain point you either run out of time or become sick of the sight of it.

4.3 Asking questions

Both qualitative and quantitative approaches have their place. In this book we focus on quantitative approaches. Nonetheless qualitative research is important, and often the most interesting work has a little of both. When conducting quantitative analysis, we are subject to issues such as data quality, measurement, and relevance. We are often especially interested in trying to tease out causality. Regardless, we are trying to learn something about the world. Our research questions need to take this all into account.

Broadly, and at the risk of over-simplification, there are two ways to go about research:

1) data-first; or
2) question-first.

But it is not a binary, and often research proceeds by iterating between data and questions, organized around a research puzzle (Gustafsson and Hagström 2017). Light, Singer, and Willett (1990, 39) describe this approach as a spiral of theory → data → theory → data, etc. For instance, a question-first approach could be theory-driven or data-driven, as could a data-first approach. An alternative framing is to compare an inductive, or specific-to-general, approach with a deductive, or general-to-specific, approach to research.

Consider two examples:

1. Mok et al. (2022) examine eight billion unique listening events from 100,000 Spotify users to understand how users explore content. They find a clear relationship between age and behavior, with younger users exploring unknown content less than older users, despite having more diverse consumption. While it is clear that

research questions around discovery and exploration drive this paper, it would not have been possible without access to this dataset. There likely would have been an iterative process where potential research questions and potential datasets were considered, before the ultimate match.

2. Think of wanting to explore the neonatal mortality rate (NMR), which was introduced in Chapter 2. One might be interested in what NMR could look like in Sub-Saharan Africa in 20 years. This would be question-first. But within this, there could be: theory-driven aspects, such as what do we expect based on biological relationships with other quantities; or data-driven aspects such as collecting as much data as possible to make forecasts. An alternative, purely data-driven approach would be having access to the NMR and then working out what is possible.

4.3.1 Data-first

When being data-first, the main issue is working out the questions that can be reasonably answered with the available data. When deciding what these are, it is useful to consider:

1) Theory: Is there a reasonable expectation that there is something causal that could be determined? For instance, Mark Christensen used to joke that if the question involved charting the stock market, then it might be better to hark back to *The Odyssey* and read bull entrails on a fire, because at least that way you would have something to eat at the end of the day. Questions usually need to have some plausible theoretical underpinning to help avoid spurious relationships. One way to develop theory, given data, is to consider "of what is this an instance?" (Rosenau 1999, 7). Following that approach, one tries to generalize beyond the specific setting. For instance, thinking of some particular civil war as an instance of all civil wars. The benefit of this is it focuses attention on the general attributes needed for building theory.
2) Importance: There are plenty of trivial questions that can be answered, but it is important to not waste our time or that of the reader. Having an important question can also help with motivation when we find ourselves in, say, the fourth straight week of cleaning data and debugging code. In industry it can also make it easier to attract talented employees and funding. That said, a balance is needed; the question needs to have a decent chance of being answered. Attacking a generation-defining question might be best broken into chunks.
3) Availability: Is there a reasonable expectation of additional data being available in the future? This could allow us to answer related questions and turn one paper into a research agenda.
4) Iteration: Is this something that could be run multiple times, or is it a once-off analysis? If it is the former, then it becomes possible to start answering specific research questions and then iterate. But if we can only get access to the data once then we need to think about broader questions.

There is a saying, sometimes attributed to Xiao-Li Meng, that all of statistics is a missing data problem. And so paradoxically, another way to ask data-first questions is to think about the data we do not have. For instance, returning to the neonatal and maternal mortality examples discussed earlier one problem is that we do not have complete cause of death data. If we did, then we could count the number of relevant deaths. (Castro et al. (2023) remind us that this simplistic hypothetical would be complicated in reality because there are sometimes causes of death that are not independent of other causes.) Having established some missing data problem, we can take a data-driven approach. We look at the data we do have, and then ask research questions that speak to the extent that we can use that to approximate our hypothetical dataset.

> **i Shoulders of giants**
>
> Xiao-Li Meng is the Whipple V. N. Jones Professor of Statistics at Harvard University. After earning a PhD in Statistics from Harvard University in 1990 he was appointed as an assistant professor at the University of Chicago where he was promoted to professor in 2000. He moved to Harvard in 2001, serving as chair of the statistics department between 2004 and 2012. He has published on a wide range of topics including missing data—Meng (1994) and Meng (2012)—and data quality—Meng (2018). He was awarded the COPSS Presidents' Award in 2001.

One way that some researchers are data-first is that they develop a particular expertise in the data of some geographical or historical circumstance. For instance, they may be especially knowledgeable about, say, the present-day United Kingdom, or late nineteenth century Japan. They then look at the questions that other researchers are asking in other circumstances, and bring their data to that question. For instance, it is common to see a particular question initially asked for the United States, and then a host of researchers answer that same question for the United Kingdom, Canada, Australia, and many other countries.

There are a number of negatives to data-first research, including the fact that it can be especially uncertain. It can also struggle for external validity because there is always a worry about a selection effect.

A variant of data-driven research is model-driven research. Here a researcher becomes an expert on some particular statistical approach and then applies that approach to appropriate contexts.

4.3.2 Question-first

When trying to be question-first, there is the inverse issue of being concerned about data availability. The "FINER framework" is used in medicine to help guide the development of research questions. It recommends asking questions that are: Feasible, Interesting, Novel, Ethical, and Relevant (Hulley et al. 2007). Farrugia et al. (2010) build on FINER with PICOT, which recommends additional considerations: Population, Intervention, Comparison group, Outcome of interest, and Time.

It can feel overwhelming trying to write out a question. One way to go about it is to ask a very specific question. Another is to decide whether we are interested in descriptive, predictive, inferential, or causal analysis. These then lead to different types of questions. For instance:

- descriptive analysis: "What does x look like?";
- predictive analysis: "What will happen to x?";
- inferential: "How can we explain x?"; and
- causal: "What impact does x have on y?".

Each of these have a role to play. Since the credibility revolution (Angrist and Pischke 2010), causal questions answered with a particular approach have been predominant. This has brought some benefit, but not without cost. Descriptive analysis can be just as, indeed sometimes more, illuminating, and is critical (Sen 1980). The nature of the question being asked matters less than being genuinely interested in answering it.

Time will often be constrained, possibly in an interesting way and this can guide the specifics of the research question. If we are interested in the effect of a celebrity's announcements on the stock market, then that can be done by looking at stock prices before and after the announcement. But what if we are interested in the effect of a cancer drug on long term outcomes? If the effect takes 20 years, then we must either wait a while, or we need to look at people who were treated twenty years ago. We then have selection effects and different circumstances compared to if we were to administer the drug today. Often the only reasonable thing to do is to build a statistical model, but that brings other issues.

4.4 Answering questions

The creation of a counterfactual is often crucial when answering questions. A counterfactual is an if-then statement in which the "if" is false. Consider the example of Humpty Dumpty in *Through the Looking-Glass* by Lewis Carroll:

> "What tremendously easy riddles you ask!" Humpty Dumpty growled out. "Of course I don't think so! Why, if ever I did fall off—which there's no chance of—but if I did—" Here he pursed his lips and looked so solemn and grand that Alice could hardly help laughing. "If I did fall," he went on, "The King has promised me—with his very own mouth-to-to-" "To send all his horses and all his men," Alice interrupted, rather unwisely.
>
> Carroll (1871)

Humpty is satisfied with what would happen if he were to fall off, even though he is convinced that this would never happen. It is this comparison group that often determines the answer to a question. For instance, in Chapter 14 we consider the effect of VO2 max on a cyclist's chance of winning a race. If we compare over the general population then it is an important variable. But if we only compare over well-trained athletes, then it is less important, because of selection.

Two aspects of the data to be especially aware of when deciding on a research question are selection bias and measurement bias.

Selection bias occurs when the results depend on who is in the sample. One of the pernicious aspects of selection bias is that we need to know about its existence in order to do anything about it. But many default diagnostics will not identify selection bias. In A/B testing, which we discuss in Chapter 8, A/A testing is a slight variant where we create groups and compare them before imposing a treatment (hence the A/A nomenclature). This effort to check whether the groups are initially the same, can help to identify selection bias. More generally, comparing the properties of the sample, such as age-group, gender, and education, with characteristics of the population can assist as well. But the fundamental problem with selection bias and observational data is that we know people about whom we have data are different in at least one way to those about whom we do not! But we do not know in what other ways they may be different.

Selection bias can pervade many aspects of our analysis. Even a sample that is initially representative may become biased over time. For instance, survey panels, that we discuss in Chapter 6, need to be updated from time to time because the people who do not get anything out of it stop responding.

Another bias to be aware of is measurement bias, which occurs when the results are affected by how the data were collected. A common example of this is if we were to ask respondents their income, then we may get different answers in-person compared with an online survey.

We will typically be interested in using data to answer our question and it is important that we are clear about specifics. For instance, we might be interested in the effect of smoking on life expectancy. In that case, there is some true effect, which we can never know, and that true effect is called the "estimand" (Little and Lewis 2021). Defining the estimand at some point in the paper, ideally in the introduction, is critical (Lundberg, Johnson, and Stewart 2021). This is because it is easy to slightly change some specific aspect of the analysis plan and end up accidentally estimating something different (Kahan et al. 2022). We are looking for a clear description of what the effect represents (Kahan et al. 2023). An "estimator" is a process by which we use the data that we have available to generate an "estimate" of the "estimand". Efron and Morris (1977) provide a discussion of estimators and related concerns.

Bueno de Mesquita and Fowler (2021, 94) describe the relationship between an estimate and an estimand as:

$$\text{Estimate} = \text{Estimand} + \text{Bias} + \text{Noise}$$

Bias refers to issues with an estimator systematically providing estimates that are different from the estimand, while noise refers to non-systematic differences. For instance, consider a standard Normal distribution. We might be interested in understanding the average, which would be our estimand. We know (in a way that we can never with real data) that the estimand is zero. Let us draw ten times from that distribution. One estimator we could use to produce an estimate is: sum the draws and divide by the number of draws. Another is to order the draws and find the middle observation. To be more specific, we will simulate this situation (Table 4.1).

```
set.seed(853)

tibble(
  num_draws = c(
    rep(10, times = 10),
    rep(100, times = 100),
    rep(1000, times = 1000),
    rep(10000, times = 10000)
  ),
  draw = rnorm(
    n = length(num_draws),
    mean = 0,
    sd = 1)
```

```
  ) |>
  summarise(
    estimator_one = sum(draw) / unique(num_draws),
    estimator_two = sort(draw)[round(unique(num_draws) / 2, 0)],
    .by = num_draws
  ) |>
  kable(
    col.names = c("Number of draws", "Estimator one", "Estimator two"),
    digits = 2,
    format.args = list(big.mark = ",")
  )
```

Table 4.1: Comparing two estimators of the average of random draws as the number of draws increases

Number of draws	Estimator one	Estimator two
10	-0.58	-0.82
100	-0.06	-0.07
1,000	0.06	0.04
10,000	-0.01	-0.01

As the number of draws increases, the effect of noise is removed, and our estimates illustrate the bias of our estimators. In this example, we know what the truth is, but when considering real data it can be more difficult to know what to do. Hence the importance of being clear about what the estimand is, before turning to generating estimates.

4.5 Components of a paper

> I had not indeed published anything before I commenced *The Professor*, but in many a crude effort, destroyed almost as soon as composed, I had got over any such taste as I might once have had for ornamented and redundant composition, and come to prefer what was plain and homely.
>
> *The Professor* (Brontë 1857)

We discuss the following components: title, abstract, introduction, data, results, discussion, figures, tables, equations, and technical terms.[1] Throughout the paper try to be as brief and

[1] While there is sometimes a need for a separate literature review section, another approach is to discuss relevant literature throughout the paper as appropriate. For instance, when there is literature relevant to the data then it should be discussed in this section, while literature relevant to the model, results, or discussion should be mentioned as appropriate in those sections.

specific as possible. Most readers will not get past the title. Almost no one will read more than the abstract. Section and sub-section headings, as well as graph and table captions should work on their own, without the surrounding text, because that type of skimming is how many people read papers (Keshav 2007).

4.5.1 Title

A title is the first opportunity that we have to engage our reader in our story. Ideally, we are able to tell our reader exactly what we found. Effective titles are critical because otherwise papers could be ignored by readers. While a title does not have to be "cute", it does need to be meaningful. This means it needs to make the story clear.

One example of a title that is good enough is "On the 2016 Brexit referendum". This title is useful because the reader knows what the paper is about. But it is not particularly informative or enticing. A slightly better title could be "On the Vote Leave outcome in the 2016 Brexit referendum". This variant adds informative specificity. We argue the best title would be something like "Vote Leave outperforms in rural areas in the 2016 Brexit referendum: Evidence from a Bayesian hierarchical model". Here the reader knows the approach of the paper and also the main take-away.

We will consider a few examples of particularly effective titles. Hug et al. (2019) use "National, regional, and global levels and trends in neonatal mortality between 1990 and 2017, with scenario-based projections to 2030: a systematic analysis". Here it is clear what the paper is about and the methods that are used. R. Alexander and Alexander (2021) use "The Increased Effect of Elections and Changing Prime Ministers on Topics Discussed in the Australian Federal Parliament between 1901 and 2018". The main finding is, along with a good deal of information about what the content will be, clear from the title. M. Alexander, Kiang, and Barbieri (2018) use "Trends in Black and White Opioid Mortality in the United States, 1979–2015"; Frei and Welsh (2022) use "How the closure of a US tax loophole may affect investor portfolios". Possibly one of the best titles ever is Bickel, Hammel, and O'Connell (1975) "Sex Bias in Graduate Admissions: Data from Berkeley: Measuring bias is harder than is usually assumed, and the evidence is sometimes contrary to expectation", which we return to in Chapter 14.

A title is often among the last aspects of a paper to be finalized. While getting through the first draft, we typically use a working title that gets the job done. We then refine it over the course of redrafting. The title needs to reflect the final story of the paper, and this is not usually something that we know at the start. We must strike a balance between getting our reader interested enough to read the paper, and conveying enough of the content so as to be useful (Hayot 2014). Two excellent examples are *The History of England from the Accession of James the Second* by Thomas Babington Macaulay, and *A History of the English-Speaking Peoples* by Winston Churchill. Both are clear about what the content is, and, for their target audience, spark interest.

One specific approach is the form: "Exciting content: Specific content", for instance, "Returning to their roots: Examining the performance of Vote Leave in the 2016 Brexit referendum". Kennedy and Gelman (2021) provide a particularly nice example of this approach with "Know your population and know your model: Using model-based regression and post-stratification to generalize findings beyond the observed sample", as does Craiu (2019) with "The Hiring Gambit: In Search of the Twofer Data Scientist". A close variant of this is "A question? And an approach". For instance, Cahill, Weinberger, and Alkema (2020) with "What increase in modern contraceptive use is needed in FP2020 countries to reach 75% demand satisfied by 2030? An assessment using the Accelerated Transition Method and

Family Planning Estimation Model". As you gain experience with this variant, it becomes possible to know when it is appropriate to drop the answer part yet remain effective, such as Briggs (2021) with "Why Does Aid Not Target the Poorest?". Another specific approach is "Specific content then broad content" or the inverse. For instance, "Rurality, elites, and support for Vote Leave in the 2016 Brexit referendum" or "Support for Vote Leave in the 2016 Brexit referendum, rurality and elites". This approach is used by Tolley and Paquet (2021) with "Gender, municipal party politics, and Montreal's first woman mayor".

4.5.2 Abstract

For a ten-to-fifteen-page paper, a good abstract is a three-to-five sentence paragraph. For a longer paper the abstract can be slightly longer. The abstract needs to specify the story of the paper. It must also convey what was done and why it matters. To do so, an abstract typically touches on the context of the work, its objectives, approach, and findings.

More specifically, a good recipe for an abstract is: first sentence: specify the general area of the paper and encourage the reader; second sentence: specify the dataset and methods at a general level; third sentence: specify the headline result; and a fourth sentence about implications.

We see this pattern in a variety of abstracts. For instance, Tolley and Paquet (2021) draw in the reader with their first sentence by mentioning the election of the first woman mayor in 400 years. The second sentence is clear about what is done in the paper. The third sentence tells the reader how it is done i.e. a survey, and the fourth sentence adds some detail. The fifth and final sentence makes the main take-away clear.

> In 2017, Montreal elected Valérie Plante, the first woman mayor in the city's 400-year history. Using this election as a case study, we show how gender did and did not influence the outcome. A survey of Montreal electors suggests that gender was not a salient factor in vote choice. Although gender did not matter much for voters, it did shape the organization of the campaign and party. We argue that Plante's victory can be explained in part by a strategy that showcased a less leader-centric party and a degendered campaign that helped counteract stereotypes about women's unsuitability for positions of political leadership.

Similarly, Beauregard and Sheppard (2021) make the broader environment clear within the first two sentences, and the specific contribution of this paper to that environment. The third and fourth sentences make the data source and main findings clear. The fifth and sixth sentences add specificity that would be of interest to likely readers of this abstract i.e. academic political scientists. In the final sentence, the position of the authors is made clear.

> Previous research on support for gender quotas focuses on attitudes toward gender equality and government intervention as explanations. We argue the

> role of attitudes toward women in understanding support for policies aiming to increase the presence of women in politics is ambivalent—both hostile and benevolent forms of sexism contribute in understanding support, albeit in different ways. Using original data from a survey conducted on a probability-based sample of Australian respondents, our findings demonstrate that hostile sexists are more likely to oppose increasing of women's presence in politics through the adoption of gender quotas. Benevolent sexists, on the other hand, are more likely to support these policies than respondents exhibiting low levels of benevolent sexism. We argue this is because benevolent sexism holds that women are pure and need protection; they do not have what it takes to succeed in politics without the assistance of quotas. Finally, we show that while women are more likely to support quotas, ambivalent sexism has the same relationship with support among both women and men. These findings suggest that aggregate levels of public support for gender quotas do not necessarily represent greater acceptance of gender equality generally.

Another excellent example of an abstract is Sides, Vavreck, and Warshaw (2021). In just five sentences, they make it clear what they do, how they do it, what they find, and why it is important.

> We provide a comprehensive assessment of the influence of television advertising on United States election outcomes from 2000–2018. We expand on previous research by including presidential, Senate, House, gubernatorial, Attorney General, and state Treasurer elections and using both difference-in-differences and border-discontinuity research designs to help identify the causal effect of advertising. We find that televised broadcast campaign advertising matters up and down the ballot, but it has much larger effects in down-ballot elections than in presidential elections. Using survey and voter registration data from multiple election cycles, we also show that the primary mechanism for ad effects is persuasion, not the mobilization of partisans. Our results have implications for the study of campaigns and elections as well as voter decision making and information processing.

Kasy and Teytelboym (2022) provide an excellent example of a more statistical abstract. They clearly identify what they do and why it is important.

> We consider an experimental setting in which a matching of resources to participants has to be chosen repeatedly and returns from the individual chosen matches are unknown but can be learned. Our setting covers two-sided and one-sided matching with (potentially complex) capacity constraints, such as refugee resettlement, social housing allocation, and foster care. We propose a

variant of the Thompson sampling algorithm to solve such adaptive combinatorial allocation problems. We give a tight, prior-independent, finite-sample bound on the expected regret for this algorithm. Although the number of allocations grows exponentially in the number of matches, our bound does not. In simulations based on refugee resettlement data using a Bayesian hierarchical model, we find that the algorithm achieves half of the employment gains (relative to the status quo) that could be obtained in an optimal matching based on perfect knowledge of employment probabilities.

Finally, Briggs (2021) begins with a claim that seems unquestionably true. In the second sentence he then says that it is false! The third sentence specifies the extent of this claim, and the fourth sentence details how he comes to this position, before providing more detail. The final two sentences speak broader implications and importance.

Foreign-aid projects typically have local effects, so they need to be placed close to the poor if they are to reduce poverty. I show that, conditional on local population levels, World Bank (WB) project aid targets richer parts of countries. This relationship holds over time and across world regions. I test five donor-side explanations for pro-rich targeting using a pre-registered conjoint experiment on WB Task Team Leaders (TTLs). TTLs perceive aid-receiving governments as most interested in targeting aid politically and controlling implementation. They also believe that aid works better in poorer or more remote areas, but that implementation in these areas is uniquely difficult. These results speak to debates in distributive politics, international bargaining over aid, and principal-agent issues in international organizations. The results also suggest that tweaks to WB incentive structures to make ease of project implementation less important may encourage aid to flow to poorer parts of countries.

Nature, a scientific journal, provides a guide for constructing an abstract. They recommend a structure that results in an abstract of six parts and adds up to around 200 words:

1) An introductory sentence that is comprehensible to a wide audience.
2) A more detailed background sentence that is relevant to likely readers.
3) A sentence that states the general problem.
4) Sentences that summarize and then explain the main results.
5) A sentence about general context.
6) And finally, a sentence about the broader perspective.

The first sentence of an abstract should not be vacuous. Assuming the reader continued past the title, this first sentence is the next opportunity that we have to implore them to keep reading our paper. And then the second sentence of the abstract, and so on. Work and re-work the abstract until it is so good that you would be fine if that was the only thing that was read; because that will often be the case.

4.5.3 Introduction

An introduction needs to be self-contained and convey everything that a reader needs to know. We are not writing a mystery story. Instead, we want to give away the most important points in the introduction. For a ten-to-fifteen-page paper, an introduction may be two or three paragraphs of main content. Hayot (2014, 90) says the goal of an introduction is to engage the reader, locate them in some discipline and background, and then tell them what happens in the rest of the paper. It should be completely reader-focused.

The introduction should set the scene and give the reader some background. For instance, we typically start a little broader. This provides some context to the paper. We then describe how the paper fits into that context, and give some high-level results, especially focused on the one key result that is the main part of the story. We provide more detail here than we provided in the abstract, but not the full extent. And we broadly discuss next steps in a sentence or two. Finally, we finish the introduction with an additional short final paragraph that highlights the structure of the paper.

As an example (with made-up details):

> The UK Conservative Party has always done well in rural electorates. And the 2016 Brexit vote was no different with a significant difference in support between rural and urban areas. But even by the standard of rural support for conservative issues, support for "Vote Leave" was unusually strong with "Vote Leave" being most heavily supported in the East Midlands and the East of England, while the strongest support for "Remain" was in Greater London.
>
> In this paper we look at why the performance of "Vote Leave" in the 2016 Brexit referendum was so correlated with rurality. We construct a model in which support for "Vote Leave" at a voting area level is explained by the number of farms in the area, the average internet connectivity, and the median age. We find that as the median age of an area increases, the likelihood that an area supported "Vote Leave" decreases by 14 percentage points. Future work could look at the effect of having a Conservative MP which would allow a more nuanced understanding of these effects.
>
> The remainder of this paper is structured as follows: Section 2 discusses the data, Section 3 discusses the model, Section 4 presents the results, and finally Section 5 discusses our findings and some weaknesses.

The introduction needs to be self-contained and tell the reader almost everything that they need to know. A reader should be able to only read the introduction and have an accurate picture of all the major aspects of the whole paper. It would be rare to include graphs or tables in the introduction. An introduction should close by telegraphing the structure of the paper.

4.5.4 Data

Robert Caro, Lyndon Johnson's biographer, describes the importance of conveying "a sense of place" when writing a biography (Caro 2019, 141). He defines this as "the physical setting in which a book's action is occurring: to see it clearly enough, in sufficient detail, so that he feels as if he himself were present while the action is occurring." He provides the following example:

> When Rebekah walked out the front door of that little house, there was nothing—a roadrunner streaking behind some rocks with something long and wet dangling from his beak, perhaps, or a rabbit disappearing around a bush so fast that all she really saw was the flash of a white tail—but otherwise nothing. There was no movement except for the ripple of the leaves in the scattered trees, no sound except for the constant whisper of the wind... If Rebekah climbed, almost in desperation, the hill in the back of the house, what she saw from its crest was more hills, an endless vista of hills, hills on which there was visible not a single house... hills on which nothing moved, empty hills with, above them, empty sky; a hawk circling silently overhead was an event. But most of all, there was nothing human, no one to talk to.
>
> Caro (2019, 146)

How thoroughly we can imagine the circumstances of Johnson's mother, Rebekah Baines Johnson. When writing our papers, we need to achieve that same sense of place, for our data, as Caro provides for the Hill County. We do this by being as explicit as possible. We typically have a whole section about it and this is designed to show the reader, as closely as possible, the actual data that underpin our story.

When writing the data section, we are beginning our answer to the critical question about our claim, which is, how is it possible to know this? (McPhee 2017, 78). An excellent example of a data section is provided by Doll and Hill (1950). They are interested in the effect of smoking between control and treatment groups. After clearly describing their dataset they use tables to display relevant cross-tabs and graphs to contrast groups.

In the data section we need to thoroughly discuss the variables in the dataset that we are using. If there are other datasets that could have been used, but were not, then this should be mentioned and the choice justified. If variables were constructed or combined, then this process and motivation should be explained.

We want the reader to understand what the data that underpin the results look like. This means that we should graph the data that are used in our analysis, or as close to them as possible. And we should also include tables of summary statistics. If the dataset was created from some other source, then it can also help to include an example of that original source. For instance, if the dataset was created from survey responses then the underlying survey questions should be included in an appendix.

Some judgment is required when it comes to the figures and tables in the data section. The reader should have the opportunity to understand the details, but it may be that some are better placed in an appendix. Figures and tables are a critical aspect of convincing people of a story. In a graph we can show the data and then let the reader decide for themselves. And using a table, we can summarize a dataset. At the very least, every variable should be shown in a graph and summarized in a table. If there are too many, then some of these could be relegated to an appendix, with the critical relationships shown in the main body. Figures and tables should be numbered and then cross-referenced in the text, for instance, "Figure 1 shows...", "Table 1 describes...". For every graph and table there should be accompanying text that describes their main aspects, and adds additional detail.

We discuss the components of graphs and tables, including titles and labels, in Chapter 5. But here we will discuss captions, as they are between the text and the graph or table. Captions need to be informative and self-contained. Borkin et al. (2015) use eye-tracking to understand how visualizations are recognized and recalled. They find that captions need to make the central message of the figure clear, and that there should be redundancy. As Cleveland ([1985] 1994, 57) says, the "interplay between graph, caption, and text is a delicate one", however the reader should be able to read only the caption and understand what the graph or table shows. A caption that is two lines long is not necessarily inappropriate. And all aspects of the graph or table should be explained. For instance, consider Figure 4.1a and Figure 4.1b, both from Bowley (1901, 151). They are clear, and self-contained.

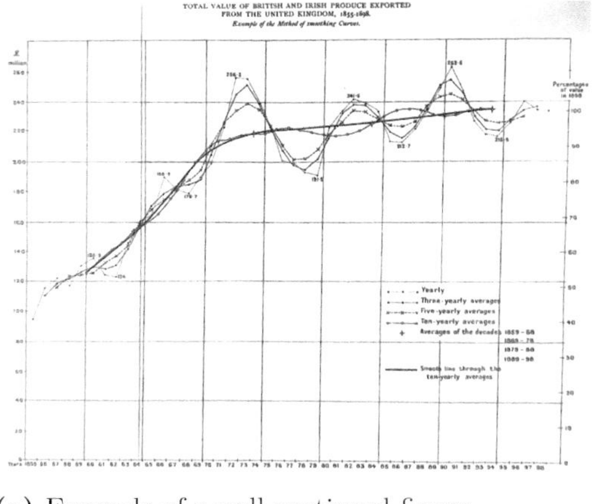

(a) Example of a well-captioned figure

TOTAL DECLARED REAL VALUE OF BRITISH AND IRISH PRODUCE EXPORTED FROM THE UNITED KINGDOM. 1 = £1,000,000.

		Averages.					Averages.		
		Three Yearly.	Five Yearly.	Ten Yearly.			Three Yearly.	Five Yearly.	Ten Yearly.
1855	95.7	...	...	...	1878	192.8	197.4	210.9	218.0
1856	115.8	...	...	...	1879	191.5	194.4	201.4	218.1
1857	122.0	111.2	...	...	1880	223.1	202.5	201.3	220.5
1858	116.6	118.1	...	...	1881	234.0	216.2	208.2	221.6
1859	130.4	123.0	116.1	...	1882	241.5	232.9	216.7	220.1
1860	135.9	127.6	124.1	...	1883	239.8	238.4	226.0	218.6
1861	125.1	130.5	126.0	...	1884	233.0	238.1	234.3	217.9
1862	124.0	128.3	126.4	...	1885	213.1	228.6	232.3	216.9
1863	146.5	131.9	132.4	...	1886	212.7	219.6	228.0	218.1
1864	160.4	143.7	138.4	127.2	1887	221.9	215.6	224.1	220.4
1865	165.8	157.6	144.4	134.3	1888	234.5	223.0	223.0	224.5
1866	188.9	171.7	157.2	141.6	1889	248.9	235.1	226.2	230.2
1867	181.0	178.6	168.7	147.5	1890	263.5	249.0	236.3	234.2
1868	179.7	183.2	175.1	153.8	1891	247.2	253.2	243.2	235.5
1869	190.0	183.6	181.0	159.8	1892	227.1	245.9	244.2	234.1
1870	199.6	189.8	187.8	165.9	1893	218.1	230.8	240.9	231.9
1871	223.1	204.2	194.6	175.7	1894	215.8	220.3	234.3	230.2
1872	256.3	226.3	209.7	188.9	1895	225.9	219.9	226.8	231.4
1873	255.2	244.9	224.8	200.0	1896	240.1	227.3	225.4	234.1
1874	239.6	250.4	234.7	207.9	1897	234.3	233.4	226.8	235.4
1875	223.5	239.4	239.6	213.7	1898	233.4	235.9	229.8	235.3
1876	200.6	221.0	235.1	214.9	1899	255.4*	241 0	237.8	236.1
1877	198.9	207.7	223.7	216.7					

* Not including the newly reckoned value of ships exported.

(b) Example of a well-captioned table

Figure 4.1: Examples of a graph and table from Bowley (1901)

The choice between a table and a graph comes down to how much information is to be conveyed. In general, if there is specific information that should be considered, such as a summary statistic, then a table is a good option. If we are interested in the reader making comparisons and understanding trends, then a graph is a good option (Gelman, Pasarica, and Dodhia 2002).

4.5.5 Model

We often build a statistical model that we will use to explore the data, and it is normal to have a specific section about this. At a minimum you should specify the equations that describe the model being used and explain their components with plain language and cross-references.

The model section typically begins with the model being written out, explained, and justified. Depending on the expected reader, some background may be needed. After specifying the model with appropriate mathematical notation and cross-referencing it, the components of the model should then be defined and explained. Try to define each aspect of the notation. This helps convince the reader that the model was well-chosen and enhances the credibility of the paper. The model's variables should correspond to those that were discussed in the data section, making a clear link between the two sections.

There should be some discussion of how features enter the model and why. Some examples could include:

- Why use age rather than age-groups?
- Why does state/province have a levels effect?
- Why is gender a categorical variable? In general, we are trying to convey a sense that this is the appropriate model for the situation. We want the reader to understand how the aspects that were discussed in the data section assert themselves in the modeling decisions that were made.

The model section should close with some discussion of the assumptions that underpin the model. It should also have a brief discussion of alternative models or variants. You want the strengths and weaknesses to be clear and for the reader to know why this particular model was chosen.

At some point in this section, it is usually appropriate to specify the software that was used to run the model, and to provide some evidence of thought about the circumstances in which the model may not be appropriate. That second point would typically be expanded on in the discussion section. And there should be evidence of model validation and checking, model convergence, and/or diagnostic issues. Again, there is a balance needed here, and some of this content may be more appropriately placed in appendices.

When technical terms are used, they should be briefly explained in plain language for readers who might not be familiar with it. For instance, M. Alexander (2019b) integrates an explanation of the Gini coefficient that brings the reader along.

> To look at the concentration of baby names, let's calculate the Gini coefficient for each country, sex and year. The Gini coefficient measures dispersion or inequality among values of a frequency distribution. It can take any value between 0 and 1. In the case of income distributions, a Gini coefficient of 1 would mean one person has all the income. In this case, a Gini coefficient of 1 would mean that all babies have the same name. In contrast, a Gini coefficient of 0 would mean names are evenly distributed across all babies.

There may be papers that do not include a statistical model. In that case, this "Model" section should be replaced by a broader "Methodology" section. It might describe the simulation that was conducted, or contain more general details about the approach.

4.5.6 Results

Two excellent examples of results sections are provided by Kharecha and Hansen (2013) and Kiang et al. (2021). In the results section, we want to communicate the outcomes of the analysis in a clear way and without too much focus on the discussion of implications. The results section likely requires summary statistics, tables, and graphs. Each of those aspects should be cross-referenced and have text associated with them that details what is seen in each figure. This section should relay results; that is, we are interested in what the results are, rather than what they mean.

This section would also typically include tables of graphs of coefficient estimates based on the modeling. Various features of the estimates should be discussed, and differences between the models explained. It may be that different subsets of the data are considered separately. Again, all graphs and tables need to have text in plain language accompany them. A rough guide is that the amount of text should be at least equal to the amount of space taken up by the tables and graphs. For instance, if a full page is used to display a table of coefficient estimates, then that should be cross-referenced and accompanied by about a full page of text about that table.

4.5.7 Discussion

A discussion section may be the final section of a paper and would typically have four or five sub-sections.

The discussion section would typically begin with a sub-section that comprises a brief summary of what was done in the paper. This would be followed by two or three sub-sections that are devoted to the key things that we learn about the world from this paper. These sub-sections are the main opportunity to justify or detail the implications of the story being told in the paper. Typically, these sub-sections do not see newly introduced graphs or tables, but are instead focused on what we learn from those that were introduced in earlier sections. It may be that some of the results are discussed in relation to what others have found, and differences could be attempted to be reconciled here.

Following these sub-sections of what we learn about the world, we would typically have a sub-section focused on some of the weaknesses of what was done. This could concern aspects such as the data that were used, the approach, and the model. In the case of the model we are especially concerned with those aspects that might affect the findings. This can be especially difficult in the case of machine learning models and J. Smith et al. (2022) provide guidance for aspects to consider. And the final sub-section is typically a few paragraphs that specify what is left to learn, and how future work could proceed.

In general, we would expect this section to take at least 25 per cent of the total paper. This means that in an eight-page paper we would expect at least two pages of discussion.

4.5.8 Brevity, typos, and grammar

Brevity is important. This is partly because we write for the reader, and the reader has other priorities. But it is also because as the writer it forces us to consider what our most important points are, how we can best support them, and where our arguments are weakest. Jean Chrétien, is a former Canadian prime minister. In Chrétien (2007, 105) he wrote that he used to ask "...the officials to summarize their documents in two or three pages and attach the rest of the materials as background information. I soon discovered that this was a problem only for those who didn't really know what they were talking about" .

This experience is not unique to Canada and it is not new. In Hughes and Rutter (2016) Oliver Letwin, the former British cabinet member, describes there being "a huge amount of terrible guff, at huge, colossal, humongous length coming from some departments" and how he asked "for them to be one quarter of the length". He found that the departments were able to accommodate this request without losing anything important. Winston Churchill asked for brevity during the Second World War, saying "the discipline of setting out the real points concisely will prove an aid to clearer thinking." The letter from Szilard and Einstein to FDR that was the catalyst for the Manhattan Project was only two pages!

Zinsser (1976) goes further and describes "the secret of good writing" being "to strip every sentence to its cleanest components." Every sentence should be simplified to its essence. And every word that does not contribute should be removed.

Unnecessary words, typos, and grammatical issues should be removed from papers. These mistakes affect the credibility of claims. If the reader cannot trust you to use a spell-checker, then why should they trust you to use logistic regression? RStudio has a spell-checker built in, but Microsoft Word and Google Docs are useful additional checks. Copy from the Quarto document and paste into Word, then look for the red and green lines, and fix them in the Quarto document.

We are not worried about the n-th degree of grammatical content. Instead, we are interested in grammar and sentence structure that occurs in conversational language use (S. King 2000, 118). The way to develop comfort is by reading a lot and asking others to also read your work. Another useful tactic is to read your writing aloud, which can be useful for detecting odd sentences based on how they sound. One small aspect to check that will regularly come up is that any number from one to ten should be written as words, while 11 and over should be written as numbers.

4.5.9 Rules

A variety of authors have established rules for writing. This famously includes those of Orwell (1946) which were reimagined by The Economist (2013). A further reimagining of rules for writing, focused on telling stories with data, could be:

- Focus on the reader and their needs. Everything else is commentary.
- Establish a structure and then rely on that to tell the story.
- Write a first draft as quickly as possible.
- Rewrite that draft extensively.
- Be concise and direct. Remove as many words as possible.
- Use words precisely. For instance, stock prices rise or fall, rather than improve or worsen.
- Use short sentences where possible.
- Avoid jargon.
- Write as though your work will be on the front page of a newspaper.
- Never claim novelty or that you are the "first to study X"—there is always someone else who got there first.

Fiske and Kuriwaki (2021) have a list of rules for scientific papers and the appendix of Pineau et al. (2021) provides a checklist for machine learning papers. But perhaps the last word should be from Savage and Yeh (2019):

> [T]ry to write the best version of your paper: the one that you like. You can't please an anonymous reader, but you should be able to please yourself. Your paper—you hope—is for posterity.
>
> Savage and Yeh (2019, 442)

4.6 Exercises

Scales

1. *(Plan)* Consider the following scenario: *A child and their parent watch street cars from their apartment window. Every hour, for eight hours, they record the number of streetcars that go past.* Please sketch out what that dataset could look like and then sketch a graph that you could build to show all observations.
2. *(Simulate)* Please further consider the scenario described and simulate the situation. Please include three tests based on the simulated data. Submit a link to a GitHub Gist that contains your code.
3. *(Acquire)* Please describe one possible source of such a dataset.
4. *(Explore)* Please use `ggplot2` to build the graph that you sketched using the simulated data. Submit a link to a GitHub Gist that contains your code.
5. *(Communicate)* Please write two paragraphs about what you did.

Questions

1. According to Chapter 2 of Zinsser (1976), what is the secret to good writing (pick one)?
   a. Correct sentence structure and grammar.
   b. The use of long words, adverbs, and passive voice.
   c. Thorough planning.
   d. Strip every sentence to its cleanest components.
2. According to Chapter 2 of Zinsser (1976), what must a writer constantly ask (pick one)?
   a. What am I trying to say?
   b. Who am I writing for?
   c. How can this be rewritten?
   d. Why does this matter?
3. Which two repeated words, for instance in Chapter 3, characterize the advice of Zinsser (1976) (pick one)?
   a. Rewrite, rewrite.
   b. Remove, remove.
   c. Simplify, simplify.
   d. Less, less.
4. According to G. King (2006), what is the key task of subheadings (pick one)?

a. Enable a reader who randomly falls asleep but keeps turning pages to know where they are.
b. Be broad and sweeping so that a reader is impressed by the importance of the paper.
c. Use acronyms to integrate the paper into the literature.

5. According to G. King (2006), if our standard error was 0.05 then which of the following specificities for a coefficient would be silly (select all that apply)?
   a. 2.7182818
   b. 2.718282
   c. 2.72
   d. 2.7
   e. 2.7183
   f. 2.718
   g. 3
   h. 2.71828
6. What is a key aspect of the re-drafting process (select all that apply)?
   a. Going through it with a red pen to remove unneeded words.
   b. Printing the paper and reading a physical copy.
   c. Cutting and pasting to enhance flow.
   d. Reading it aloud.
   e. Exchanging it with others.
7. What are three features of a good research question (write a paragraph or two)?
8. In your own words, what is a counterfactual (include examples and references and write at least three paragraphs)?
9. What is an estimate (pick one)?
   a. A rule for calculating an estimate of a given quantity based on observed data.
   b. The object of inquiry.
   c. A result given a particular dataset and approach.
10. What is an estimator (pick one)?
    a. A rule for calculating an estimate of a given quantity based on observed data.
    b. The object of inquiry.
    c. A result given a particular dataset and approach.
11. What is an estimand (pick one)?
    a. A rule for calculating an estimate of a given quantity based on observed data.
    b. The object of inquiry.
    c. A result given a particular dataset and approach.
12. Which of the following is the best title (pick one)?
    a. "Problem Set 2"
    b. "Standard errors"
    c. "Standard errors of estimates from small samples"
13. Please write a new title for Fourcade and Healy (2017).
14. Using only the 1,000 most popular words in the English language, according to the XKCD Simple Writer[2], rewrite the abstract of Chambliss (1989) so that it retains its original meaning.

Tutorial

Caro (2019, xii) writes at least 1,000 words almost every day. In this tutorial you will write every day for a week. Please pick one of the papers specified in the prerequisites and

[2]https://xkcd.com/simplewriter/

complete the following tasks:

- Day 1: Transcribe, by writing each word yourself, the entire introduction.
- Day 2: Rewrite the introduction so that it is five lines (or 10 per cent, whichever is less) shorter.
- Day 3: Transcribe, by writing each word yourself, the abstract.
- Day 4: Rewrite a new, four-sentence, abstract for the paper.
- Day 5: Write a second version of your new abstract using only the 1,000 most popular words in the English language as defined here[3].
- Day 6: Detail three points about the way the paper is written that you like
- Day 7: Detail one point about the way the paper is written that you do not like.

Please use Quarto to produce a single PDF for the whole week. Make use of headings and sub-headings to structure your submission. Submit the PDF.

[3]https://xkcd.com/simplewriter/

5

Static communication

Prerequisites

- Read *R for Data Science*, (Wickham, Çetinkaya-Rundel, and Grolemund [2016] 2023)
  - Focus on Chapter 2 "Data visualization", which provides an overview of `ggplot2`.
- Read *Data Visualization: A Practical Introduction*, (Healy 2018)
  - Focus on Chapter 3 "Make a plot", which provides an overview of `ggplot2` with different emphasis.
- Watch *The Glamour of Graphics*, (Chase 2020)
  - This video details ideas for how to improve a plot made with `ggplot2`.
- Read *Testing Statistical Charts: What Makes a Good Graph?*, (Vanderplas, Cook, and Hofmann 2020)
  - This article details best practice for making graphs.
- Read *Data Feminism*, (D'Ignazio and Klein 2020)
  - Focus on Chapter 3 "On Rational, Scientific, Objective Viewpoints from Mythical, Imaginary, Impossible Standpoints", which provides examples of why data needs to be considered within context.
- Read *Historical development of the graphical representation of statistical data*, (Funkhouser 1937)
  - Focus on Chapter 2 "The Origin of the Graphic Method", which discusses how various graphs developed.

Key concepts and skills

- Visualization is one way to get a sense of our data and to communicate this to the reader. Plotting the observations in a dataset is important.
- We need to be comfortable with a variety of graph types, including: bar charts, scatterplots, line plots, and histograms. We can even consider a map to be a type of graph, especially after geocoding our data.
- We should also summarize data using tables. Typical use cases for this include showing part of a dataset, summary statistics, and regression results.

Software and packages

- Base R (R Core Team 2023)
- `carData` (Fox, Weisberg, and Price 2022)
- `datasauRus` (Davies, Locke, and D'Agostino McGowan 2022)
- `ggmap` (Kahle and Wickham 2013)
- `janitor` (Firke 2023)
- `knitr` (Xie 2023)
- `maps` (Becker et al. 2022)
- `mapproj` (McIlroy et al. 2023)
- `modelsummary` (Arel-Bundock 2022)
- `opendatatoronto` (Gelfand 2022b)

- `patchwork` (Pedersen 2022)
- `tidygeocoder` (Cambon and Belanger 2021)
- `tidyverse` (Wickham et al. 2019)
- `troopdata` (Flynn 2022)
- `WDI` (Arel-Bundock 2021)

```
library(carData)
library(datasauRus)
library(ggmap)
library(janitor)
library(knitr)
library(maps)
library(mapproj)
library(modelsummary)
library(opendatatoronto)
library(patchwork)
library(tidygeocoder)
library(tidyverse)
library(troopdata)
library(WDI)
```

5.1 Introduction

When telling stories with data, we would like the data to do much of the work of convincing our reader. The paper is the medium, and the data are the message. To that end, we want to show our reader the data that allowed us to come to our understanding of the story. We use graphs, tables, and maps to help achieve this.

Try to show the observations that underpin our analysis. For instance, if your dataset consists of 2,500 responses to a survey, then at some point in the paper you should have a plot/s that contains each of the 2,500 observations, for every variable of interest. To do this we build graphs using `ggplot2` which is part of the core `tidyverse` and so does not have to be installed or loaded separately. In this chapter we go through a variety of different options including bar charts, scatterplots, line plots, and histograms.

In contrast to the role of graphs, which is to show each observation, the role of tables is typically to show an extract of the dataset or to convey various summary statistics, or regression results. We will build tables primarily using `knitr`. Later we will use `modelsummary` to build tables related to regression output.

Finally, we cover maps as a variant of graphs that are used to show a particular type of data. We will build static maps using `ggmap` after having obtained geocoded data using `tidygeocoder`.

5.2 Graphs

> A world turning to a saner and richer civilization will be a world turning to charts.
>
> Karsten (1923, 684)

Graphs are a critical aspect of compelling data stories. They allow us to see both broad patterns and details (Cleveland [1985] 1994, 5). Graphs enable a familiarity with our data that is hard to get from any other method. Every variable of interest should be graphed.

The most important objective of a graph is to convey as much of the actual data, and its context, as possible. In a way, graphing is an information encoding process where we construct a deliberate representation to convey information to our audience. The audience must decode that representation. The success of our graph depends on how much information is lost in this process so the decoding is a critical aspect (Cleveland [1985] 1994, 221). This means that we must focus on creating effective graphs that are suitable for our specific audience.

To see why graphing the actual data is important, after installing and loading `datasauRus` consider the `datasaurus_dozen` dataset.

```
datasaurus_dozen
```

```
# A tibble: 1,846 x 3
   dataset     x     y
   <chr>   <dbl> <dbl>
 1 dino     55.4  97.2
 2 dino     51.5  96.0
 3 dino     46.2  94.5
 4 dino     42.8  91.4
 5 dino     40.8  88.3
 6 dino     38.7  84.9
 7 dino     35.6  79.9
 8 dino     33.1  77.6
 9 dino     29.0  74.5
10 dino     26.2  71.4
# i 1,836 more rows
```

Table 5.1: Mean and standard deviation for four datasauRus datasets

Dataset	x mean	x sd	y mean	y sd
dino	54.3	16.8	47.8	26.9
away	54.3	16.8	47.8	26.9
star	54.3	16.8	47.8	26.9
bullseye	54.3	16.8	47.8	26.9

The dataset consists of values for "x" and "y", which should be plotted on the x-axis and y-axis, respectively. There are 13 different values in the variable "dataset" including: "dino", "star", "away", and "bullseye". We focus on those four and generate summary statistics for each (Table 5.1).

```
# Based on: https://juliasilge.com/blog/datasaurus-multiclass/
datasaurus_dozen |>
  filter(dataset %in% c("dino", "star", "away", "bullseye")) |>
  summarise(across(c(x, y), list(mean = mean, sd = sd)),
            .by = dataset) |>
  kable(col.names = c("Dataset", "x mean", "x sd", "y mean", "y sd"),
        booktabs = TRUE, digits = 1)
```

Notice that the summary statistics are similar (Table 5.1). Despite this it turns out that the different datasets are actually very different beasts. This becomes clear when we plot the data (Figure 5.1).

```
datasaurus_dozen |>
  filter(dataset %in% c("dino", "star", "away", "bullseye")) |>
  ggplot(aes(x = x, y = y, colour = dataset)) +
  geom_point() +
  theme_minimal() +
  facet_wrap(vars(dataset), nrow = 2, ncol = 2) +
  labs(color = "Dataset")
```

We get a similar lesson—always plot your data—from "Anscombe's Quartet", created by the twentieth century statistician Frank Anscombe. The key takeaway is that it is important to plot the actual data and not rely solely on summary statistics.

```
head(anscombe)
```

```
  x1 x2 x3 x4   y1   y2    y3   y4
1 10 10 10  8 8.04 9.14  7.46 6.58
2  8  8  8  8 6.95 8.14  6.77 5.76
3 13 13 13  8 7.58 8.74 12.74 7.71
4  9  9  9  8 8.81 8.77  7.11 8.84
5 11 11 11  8 8.33 9.26  7.81 8.47
6 14 14 14  8 9.96 8.10  8.84 7.04
```

Anscombe's Quartet consists of eleven observations for four different datasets, with x and y values for each observation. We need to manipulate this dataset with `pivot_longer()` to

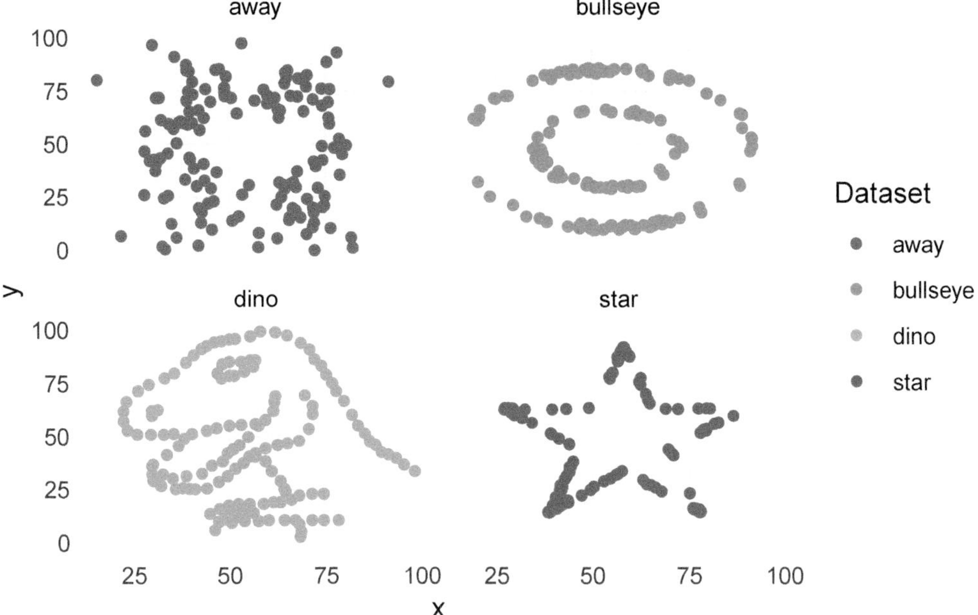

Figure 5.1: Graph of four datasauRus datasets

get it into the "tidy" format discussed in the "R Essentials" Online Appendix[1].

```
# From: https://www.njtierney.com/post/2020/06/01/tidy-anscombe/
# And the pivot_longer() vignette.

tidy_anscombe <-
  anscombe |>
  pivot_longer(
    everything(),
    names_to = c(".value", "set"),
    names_pattern = "(.)(.)"
  )
```

We can first create summary statistics (Table 5.2) and then plot the data (Figure 5.2). This again illustrates the importance of graphing the actual data, rather than relying on summary statistics.

```
tidy_anscombe |>
  summarise(
    across(c(x, y), list(mean = mean, sd = sd)),
    .by = set
    ) |>
  kable(
    col.names = c("Dataset", "x mean", "x sd", "y mean", "y sd"),
    digits = 1, booktabs = TRUE
```

[1] https://tellingstorieswithdata.com/20-r_essentials.html

Table 5.2: Mean and standard deviation for Anscombe's quartet

Dataset	x mean	x sd	y mean	y sd
1	9	3.3	7.5	2
2	9	3.3	7.5	2
3	9	3.3	7.5	2
4	9	3.3	7.5	2

```
)
```

```
tidy_anscombe |>
  ggplot(aes(x = x, y = y, colour = set)) +
  geom_point() +
  geom_smooth(method = lm, se = FALSE) +
  theme_minimal() +
  facet_wrap(vars(set), nrow = 2, ncol = 2) +
  labs(colour = "Dataset") +
  theme(legend.position = "bottom")
```

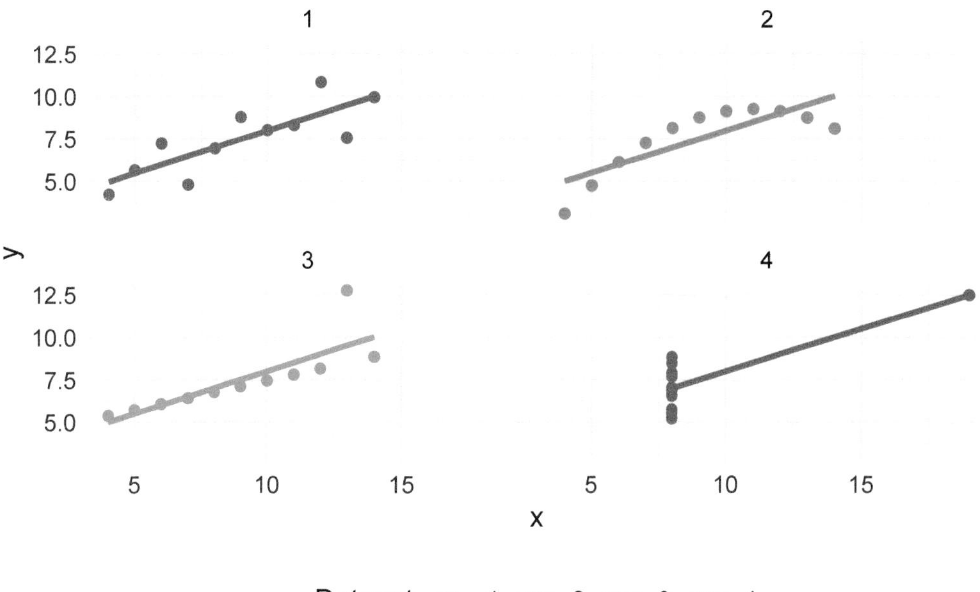

Figure 5.2: Recreation of Anscombe's Quartet

5.2.1 Bar charts

We typically use a bar chart when we have a categorical variable that we want to focus on. We saw an example of this in Chapter 2 when we constructed a graph of the number of occupied beds. The geometric object—a "geom"—that we primarily use is `geom_bar()`, but there are many variants to cater for specific situations. To illustrate the use of bar charts, we use a dataset from the 1997-2001 British Election Panel Study that was put together by Fox and Andersen (2006) and made available with `BEPS`, after installing and loading `carData`.

```
beps <-
  BEPS |>
  as_tibble() |>
  clean_names() |>
  select(age, vote, gender, political_knowledge)
```

The dataset consists of which party the respondent supports, along with various demographic, economic, and political variables. In particular, we have the age of the respondent. We begin by creating age-groups from the ages, and making a bar chart showing the frequency of each age-group using `geom_bar()` (Figure 5.3a).

```
beps <-
  beps |>
  mutate(
    age_group =
      case_when(
        age < 35 ~ "<35",
        age < 50 ~ "35-49",
        age < 65 ~ "50-64",
        age < 80 ~ "65-79",
        age < 100 ~ "80-99"
      ),
    age_group =
      factor(age_group, levels = c("<35", "35-49", "50-64", "65-79", "80-99"))
  )
```

```
beps |>
  ggplot(mapping = aes(x = age_group)) +
  geom_bar() +
  theme_minimal() +
  labs(x = "Age group", y = "Number of observations")

beps |>
  count(age_group) |>
  ggplot(mapping = aes(x = age_group, y = n)) +
  geom_col() +
  theme_minimal() +
  labs(x = "Age group", y = "Number of observations")
```

The default axis label used by `ggplot2` is the name of the relevant variable, so it is often useful to add more detail. We do this using `labs()` by specifying a variable and a name. In the case of Figure 5.3a we have specified labels for the x-axis and y-axis.

By default, `geom_bar()` creates a count of the number of times each age-group appears in the dataset. It does this because the default statistical transformation—a "stat"—for `geom_bar()` is "count", which saves us from having to create that statistic ourselves. But if we had already constructed a count (for instance, with `beps |> count(age_group)`), then we

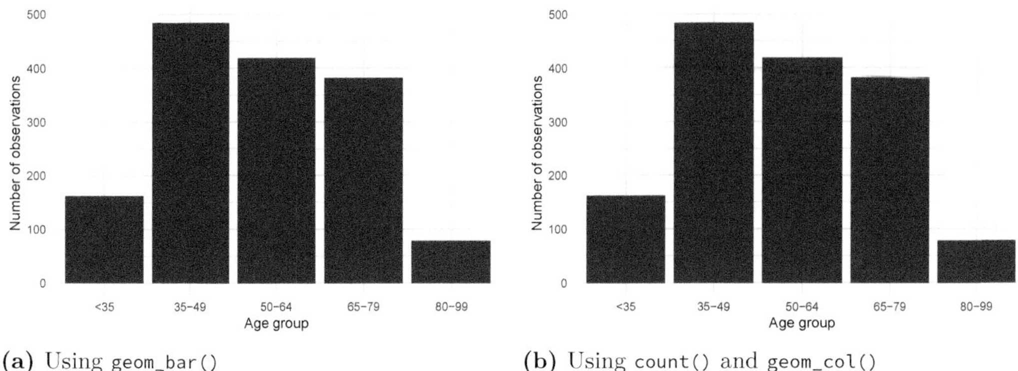

(a) Using `geom_bar()`

(b) Using `count()` and `geom_col()`

Figure 5.3: Distribution of age-groups in the 1997-2001 British Election Panel Study

could specify a variable for the y-axis and then use `geom_col()` (Figure 5.3b).

We may also like to consider various groupings of the data to get a different insight. For instance, we can use color to look at which party the respondent supports, by age-group (Figure 5.4a).

```
beps |>
  ggplot(mapping = aes(x = age_group, fill = vote)) +
  geom_bar() +
  labs(x = "Age group", y = "Number of observations", fill = "Vote") +
  theme(legend.position = "bottom")

beps |>
  ggplot(mapping = aes(x = age_group, fill = vote)) +
  geom_bar(position = "dodge2") +
  labs(x = "Age group", y = "Number of observations", fill = "Vote") +
  theme(legend.position = "bottom")
```

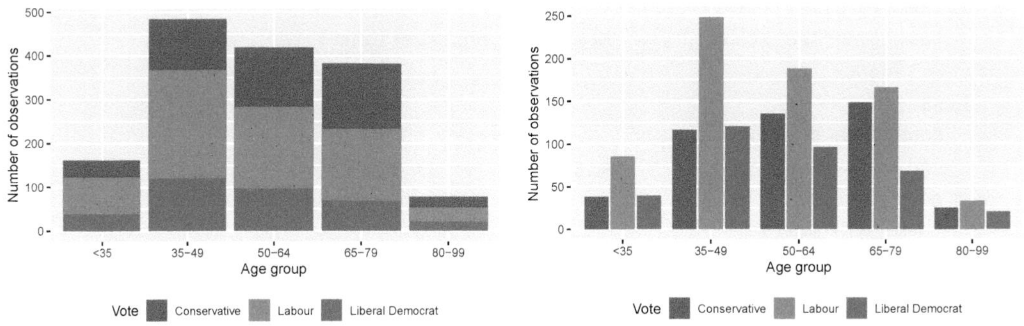

(a) Using `geom_bar()`

(b) Using `geom_bar()` with dodge2

Figure 5.4: Distribution of age-group, and vote preference, in the 1997-2001 British Election Panel Study

By default, these different groups are stacked, but they can be placed side by side with `position = "dodge2"` (Figure 5.4b). (Using "dodge2" rather than "dodge" adds a little space between the bars.)

5.2.1.1 Themes

At this point, we may like to address the general look of the graph. There are various themes that are built into `ggplot2`. These include: `theme_bw()`, `theme_classic()`, `theme_dark()`, and `theme_minimal()`. A full list is available in the `ggplot2` cheat sheet[2]. We can use these themes by adding them as a layer (Figure 5.5). We could also install more themes from other packages, including `ggthemes` (Arnold 2021), and `hrbrthemes` (Rudis 2020). We could even build our own!

```
theme_bw <-
  beps |>
  ggplot(mapping = aes(x = age_group)) +
  geom_bar(position = "dodge") +
  theme_bw()

theme_classic <-
  beps |>
  ggplot(mapping = aes(x = age_group)) +
  geom_bar(position = "dodge") +
  theme_classic()

theme_dark <-
  beps |>
  ggplot(mapping = aes(x = age_group)) +
  geom_bar(position = "dodge") +
  theme_dark()

theme_minimal <-
  beps |>
  ggplot(mapping = aes(x = age_group)) +
  geom_bar(position = "dodge") +
  theme_minimal()

(theme_bw + theme_classic) / (theme_dark + theme_minimal)
```

In Figure 5.5 we use `patchwork` to bring together multiple graphs. To do this, after installing and loading the package, we assign the graph to a variable. We then use "+" to signal which should be next to each other, "/" to signal which should be on top, and use brackets to indicate precedence

5.2.1.2 Facets

We use facets to show variation, based on one or more variables (L. Wilkinson 2005, 219). Facets are especially useful when we have already used color to highlight variation in some other variable. For instance, we may be interested to explain vote, by age and gender (Figure 5.6). We rotate the x-axis with `guides(x = guide_axis(angle = 90))` to avoid overlapping. We also change the position of the legend with `theme(legend.position = "bottom")`.

[2] https://github.com/rstudio/cheatsheets/blob/main/data-visualization.pdf

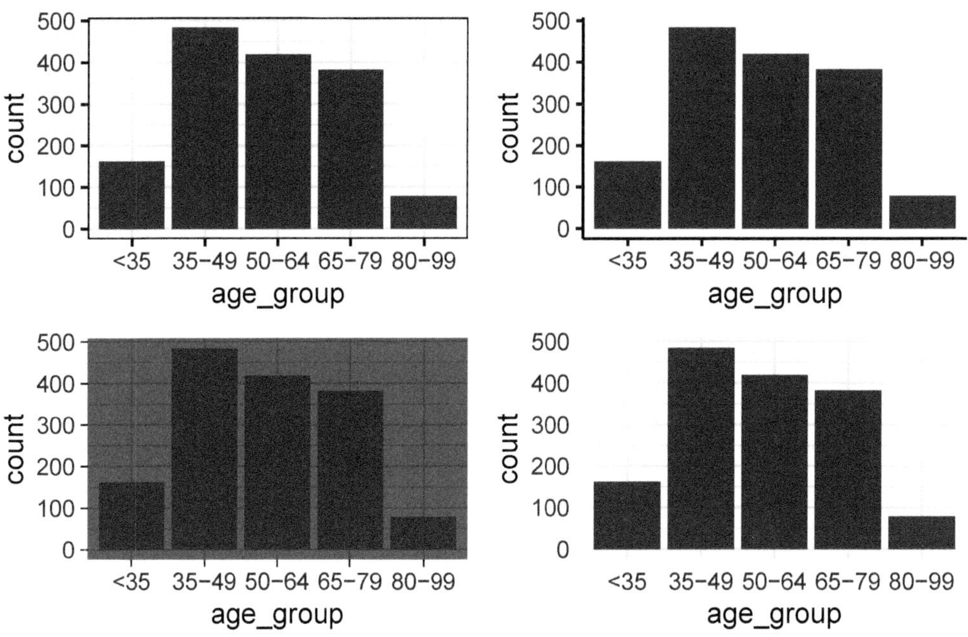

Figure 5.5: Distribution of age-groups, and vote preference, in the 1997-2001 British Election Panel Study, illustrating different themes and the use of `patchwork`

```
beps |>
  ggplot(mapping = aes(x = age_group, fill = gender)) +
  geom_bar() +
  theme_minimal() +
  labs(
    x = "Age-group of respondent",
    y = "Number of respondents",
    fill = "Gender"
  ) +
  facet_wrap(vars(vote)) +
  guides(x = guide_axis(angle = 90)) +
  theme(legend.position = "bottom")
```

We could change `facet_wrap()` to wrap vertically instead of horizontally with `dir = "v"`. Alternatively, we could specify a few rows, say `nrow = 2`, or a number of columns, say `ncol = 2`.

By default, both facets will have the same x-axis and y-axis. We could enable both facets to have different scales with `scales = "free"`, or just the x-axis with `scales = "free_x"`, or just the y-axis with `scales = "free_y"` (Figure 5.7).

```
beps |>
  ggplot(mapping = aes(x = age_group, fill = gender)) +
  geom_bar() +
  theme_minimal() +
  labs(
    x = "Age-group of respondent",
    y = "Number of respondents",
    fill = "Gender"
  ) +
  facet_wrap(vars(vote), scales = "free") +
  guides(x = guide_axis(angle = 90)) +
  theme(legend.position = "bottom")
```

Finally, we can change the labels of the facets using `labeller()` (Figure 5.8).

```
new_labels <-
  c("0" = "No knowledge", "1" = "Low knowledge",
    "2" = "Moderate knowledge", "3" = "High knowledge")

beps |>
  ggplot(mapping = aes(x = age_group, fill = vote)) +
  geom_bar() +
```

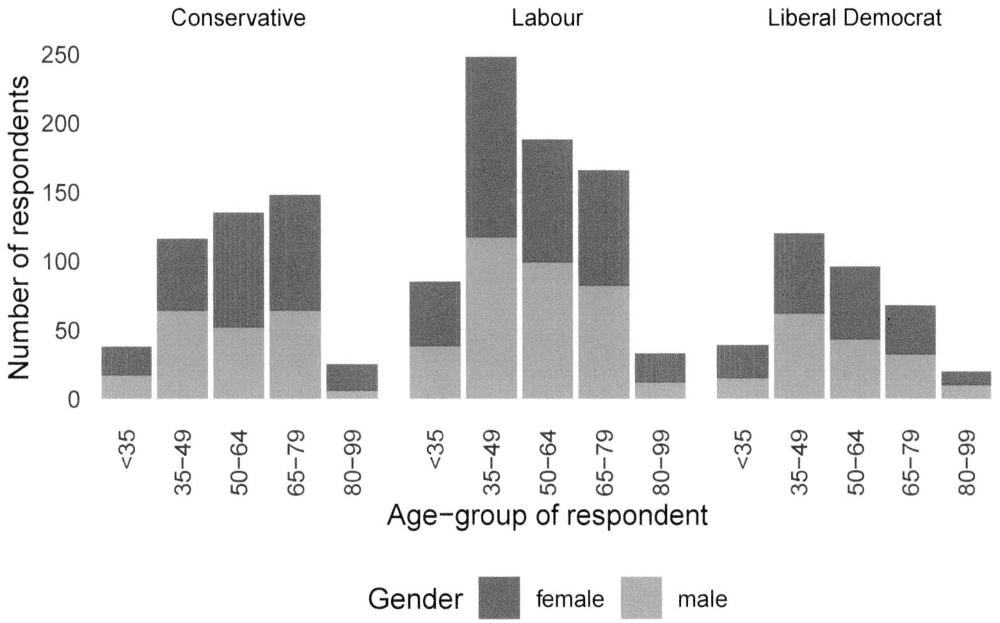

Figure 5.6: Distribution of age-group by gender, and vote preference, in the 1997-2001 British Election Panel Study

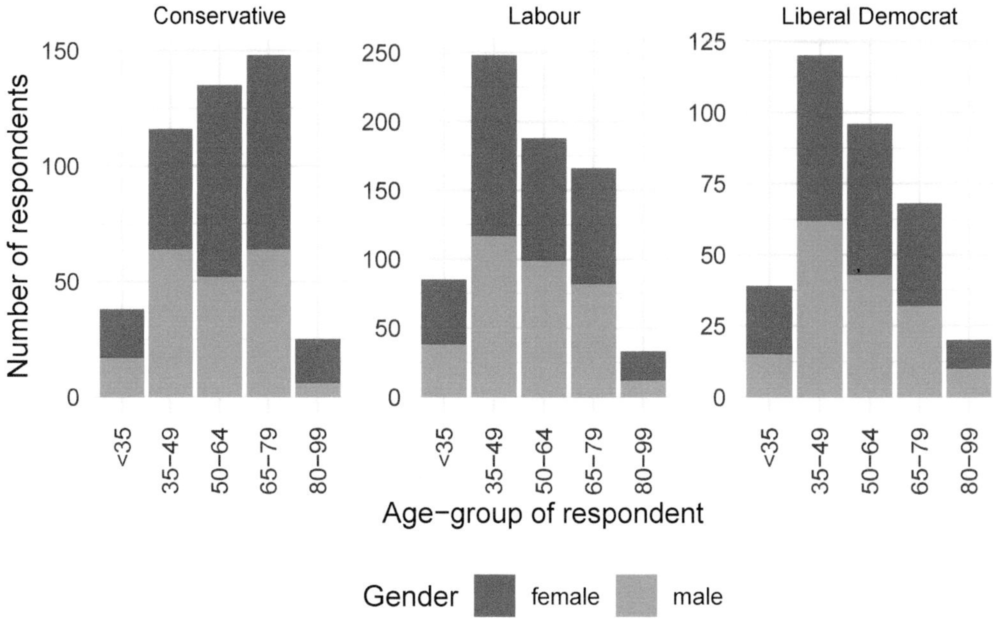

Figure 5.7: Distribution of age-group by gender, and vote preference, in the 1997-2001 British Election Panel Study

```
theme_minimal() +
labs(
  x = "Age-group of respondent",
  y = "Number of respondents",
  fill = "Voted for"
) +
facet_wrap(
  vars(political_knowledge),
  scales = "free",
  labeller = labeller(political_knowledge = new_labels)
) +
guides(x = guide_axis(angle = 90)) +
theme(legend.position = "bottom")
```

We now have three ways to combine multiple graphs: sub-figures, facets, and `patchwork`. They are useful in different circumstances:

- sub-figures—which we covered in Chapter 3—for when we are considering different variables;
- facets for when we are considering a categorical variable; and
- `patchwork` for when we are interested in bringing together entirely different graphs.

5.2.1.3 Colors

We now turn to the colors used in the graph. There are a variety of different ways to change the colors. The many palettes available from `RColorBrewer` (Neuwirth 2022) can be specified using `scale_fill_brewer()`. In the case of `viridis` (Garnier et al. 2021) we

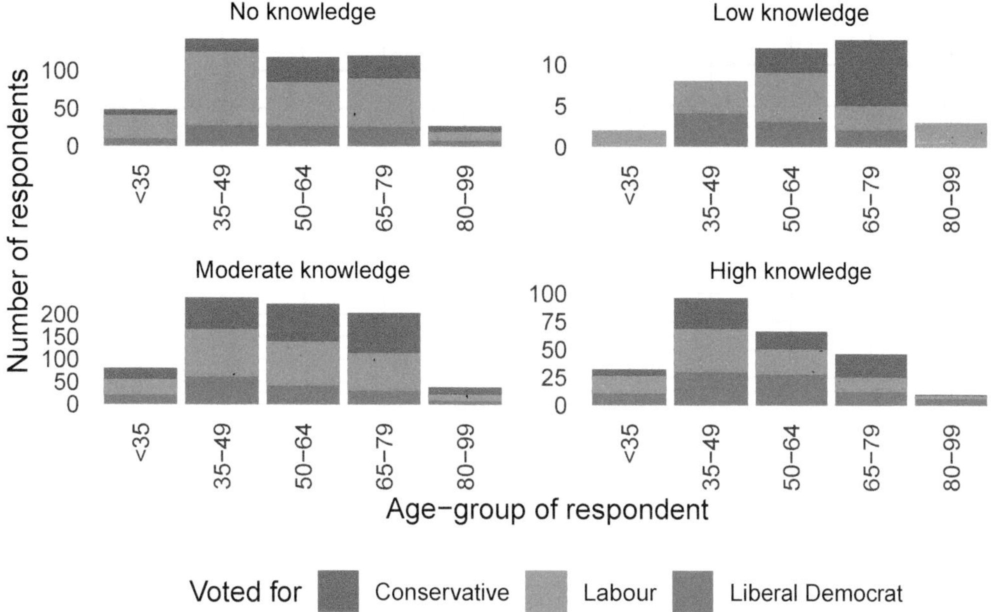

Figure 5.8: Distribution of age-group by political knowledge, and vote preference, in the 1997-2001 British Election Panel Study

can specify the palettes using `scale_fill_viridis_d()`. Additionally, `viridis` is particularly focused on color-blind palettes (Figure 5.9). Neither `RColorBrewer` nor `viridis` need to be explicitly installed or loaded because `ggplot2`, which is part of the `tidyverse`, takes care of that for us.

> **Shoulders of giants**
>
> The name of the "brewer" palette refers to Cindy Brewer (G. Miller 2014). After earning a PhD in Geography from Michigan State University in 1991, she joined San Diego State University as an assistant professor, moving to Pennsylvania State University in 1994, where she was promoted to full professor in 2007. One of her best-known books is *Designing Better Maps: A Guide for GIS Users* (C. Brewer 2015). In 2019 she became only the ninth person to have been awarded the O. M. Miller Cartographic Medal since it was established in 1968.

```
# Panel (a)
beps |>
  ggplot(mapping = aes(x = age_group, fill = vote)) +
  geom_bar() +
  theme_minimal() +
  labs(x = "Age-group", y = "Number", fill = "Voted for") +
  theme(legend.position = "bottom") +
  scale_fill_brewer(palette = "Blues")

# Panel (b)
beps |>
```

```
  ggplot(mapping = aes(x = age_group, fill = vote)) +
  geom_bar() +
  theme_minimal() +
  labs(x = "Age-group", y = "Number", fill = "Voted for") +
  theme(legend.position = "bottom") +
  scale_fill_brewer(palette = "Set1")

# Panel (c)
beps |>
  ggplot(mapping = aes(x = age_group, fill = vote)) +
  geom_bar() +
  theme_minimal() +
  labs(x = "Age-group", y = "Number", fill = "Voted for") +
  theme(legend.position = "bottom") +
  scale_fill_viridis_d()

# Panel (d)
beps |>
  ggplot(mapping = aes(x = age_group, fill = vote)) +
  geom_bar() +
  theme_minimal() +
  labs(x = "Age-group", y = "Number", fill = "Voted for") +
  theme(legend.position = "bottom") +
  scale_fill_viridis_d(option = "magma")
```

In addition to using pre-built palettes, we could build our own palette. That said, color is something to be considered with care. It should be used to increase the amount of information that is communicated (Cleveland [1985] 1994). Color should not be added to graphs unnecessarily—that is to say, it should play some role. Typically, that role is to distinguish different groups, which implies making the colors dissimilar. Color may also be appropriate if there is some relationship between the color and the variable. For instance, if making a graph of the price of mangoes and raspberries, then it could help the reader decode the information if the colors were yellow and red, respectively (Franconeri et al. 2021, 121).

5.2.2 Scatterplots

We are often interested in the relationship between two numeric or continuous variables. We can use scatterplots to show this. A scatterplot may not always be the best choice, but it is rarely a bad one (Weissgerber et al. 2015). Some consider it the most versatile and useful graph option (Friendly and Wainer 2021, 121). To illustrate scatterplots, we install and load `WDI` and then use that to download some economic indicators from the World Bank. In particular, we use `WDIsearch()` to find the unique key that we need to pass to `WDI()` to facilitate the download.

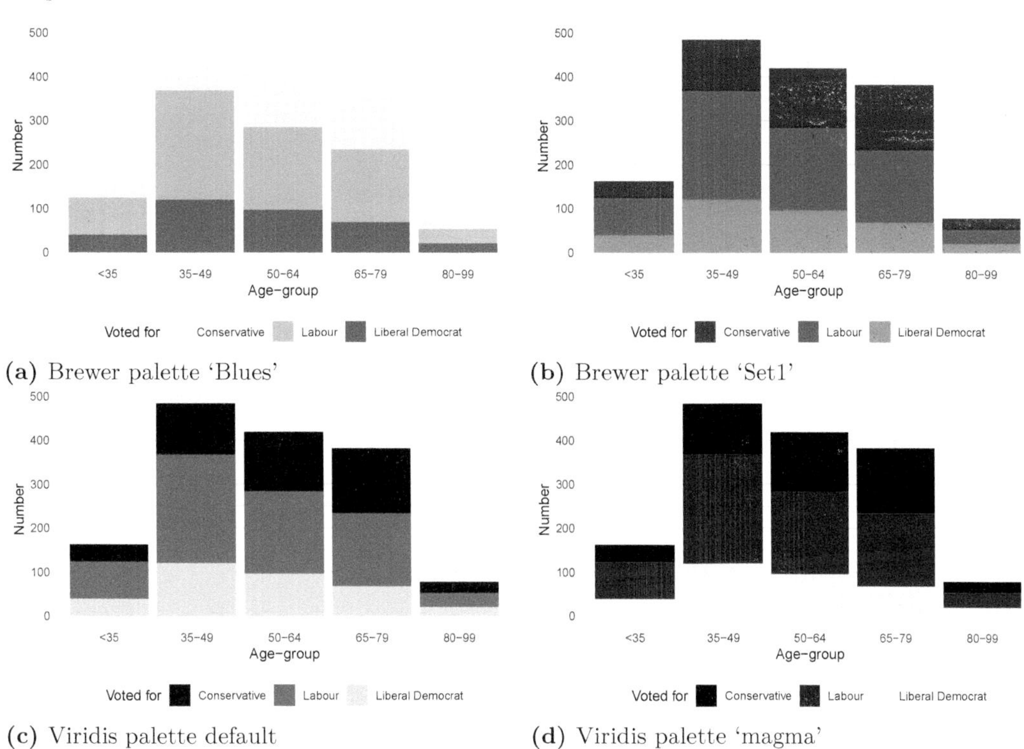

(a) Brewer palette 'Blues'

(b) Brewer palette 'Set1'

(c) Viridis palette default

(d) Viridis palette 'magma'

Figure 5.9: Distribution of age-group and vote preference, in the 1997-2001 British Election Panel Study, illustrating different colors

> **i Oh, you think we have good data on that!**
>
> From OECD (2014, 15) Gross Domestic Product (GDP) "combines in a single figure, and with no double counting, all the output (or production) carried out by all the firms, non-profit institutions, government bodies and households in a given country during a given period, regardless of the type of goods and services produced, provided that the production takes place within the country's economic territory." The modern concept was developed by the twentieth century economist Simon Kuznets and is widely used and reported. There is a certain comfort in having a definitive and concrete single number to describe something as complicated as the economic activity of a country. It is useful and informative that we have such summary statistics. But as with any summary statistic, its strength is also its weakness. A single number necessarily loses information about constituent components, and disaggregated differences can be important (Moyer and Dunn 2020). It highlights short term economic progress over longer term improvements. And "the quantitative definiteness of the estimates makes it easy to forget their dependence upon imperfect data and the consequently wide margins of possible error to which both totals and components are liable" (Kuznets, Epstein, and Jenks 1941, xxvi). Summary measures of economic performance shows only one side of a country's economy. While there are many strengths there are also well-known areas where GDP is weak.

```
WDIsearch("gdp growth")
WDIsearch("inflation")
WDIsearch("population, total")
WDIsearch("Unemployment, total")
```

```
world_bank_data <-
  WDI(
    indicator =
      c("FP.CPI.TOTL.ZG", "NY.GDP.MKTP.KD.ZG", "SP.POP.TOTL","SL.UEM.TOTL.NE.ZS"),
    country = c("AU", "ET", "IN", "US")
  )
```

We may like to change the variable names to be more meaningful, and only keep those that we need.

```
world_bank_data <-
  world_bank_data |>
  rename(
    inflation = FP.CPI.TOTL.ZG,
    gdp_growth = NY.GDP.MKTP.KD.ZG,
    population = SP.POP.TOTL,
    unem_rate = SL.UEM.TOTL.NE.ZS
  ) |>
  select(country, year, inflation, gdp_growth, population, unem_rate)

head(world_bank_data)
```

```
# A tibble: 6 x 6
  country    year inflation gdp_growth population unem_rate
  <chr>     <dbl>     <dbl>      <dbl>      <dbl>     <dbl>
1 Australia  1960     3.73       NA      10276477        NA
2 Australia  1961     2.29        2.48   10483000        NA
3 Australia  1962    -0.319       1.29   10742000        NA
4 Australia  1963     0.641       6.22   10950000        NA
5 Australia  1964     2.87        6.98   11167000        NA
6 Australia  1965     3.41        5.98   11388000        NA
```

To get started we can use `geom_point()` to make a scatterplot showing GDP growth and inflation, by country (Figure 5.10a).

```
# Panel (a)
world_bank_data |>
  ggplot(mapping = aes(x = gdp_growth, y = inflation, color = country)) +
  geom_point()

# Panel (b)
world_bank_data |>
  ggplot(mapping = aes(x = gdp_growth, y = inflation, color = country)) +
  geom_point() +
```

```
  theme_minimal() +
  labs(x = "GDP growth", y = "Inflation", color = "Country")
```

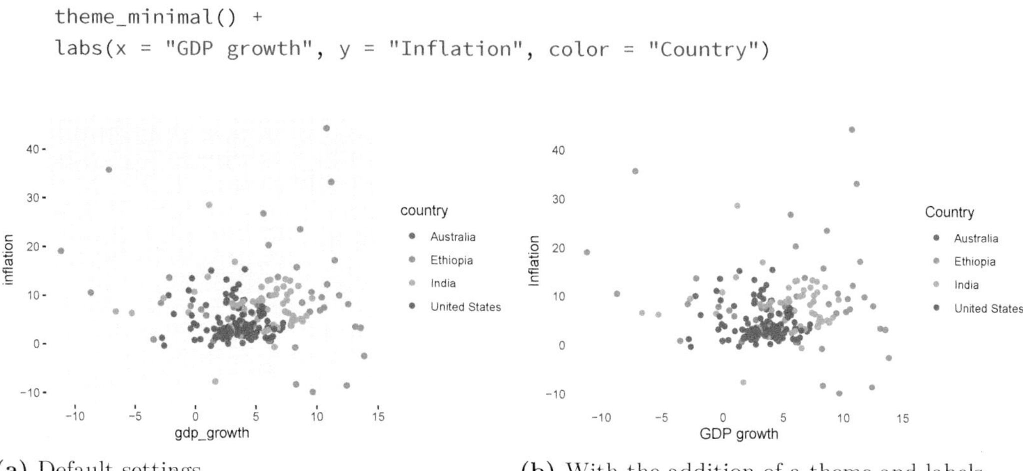

(a) Default settings

(b) With the addition of a theme and labels

Figure 5.10: Relationship between inflation and GDP growth for Australia, Ethiopia, India, and the United States

As with bar charts, we can change the theme, and update the labels (Figure 5.10b).

For scatterplots we use "color" instead of "fill", as we did for bar charts, because they use dots rather than bars. This also then slightly affects how we change the palette (Figure 5.11). That said, with particular types of dots, for instance `shape = 21`, it is possible to have both `fill` and `color` aesthetics.

```
# Panel (a)
world_bank_data |>
  ggplot(aes(x = gdp_growth, y = inflation, color = country)) +
  geom_point() +
  theme_minimal() +
  labs(x = "GDP growth", y = "Inflation", color = "Country") +
  theme(legend.position = "bottom") +
  scale_color_brewer(palette = "Blues")

# Panel (b)
world_bank_data |>
  ggplot(aes(x = gdp_growth, y = inflation, color = country)) +
  geom_point() +
  theme_minimal() +
  labs(x = "GDP growth",  y = "Inflation", color = "Country") +
  theme(legend.position = "bottom") +
  scale_color_brewer(palette = "Set1")

# Panel (c)
world_bank_data |>
  ggplot(aes(x = gdp_growth, y = inflation, color = country)) +
  geom_point() +
  theme_minimal() +
  labs(x = "GDP growth",  y = "Inflation", color = "Country") +
```

```
  theme(legend.position = "bottom") +
  scale_colour_viridis_d()

# Panel (d)
world_bank_data |>
  ggplot(aes(x = gdp_growth, y = inflation, color = country)) +
  geom_point() +
  theme_minimal() +
  labs(x = "GDP growth",  y = "Inflation", color = "Country") +
  theme(legend.position = "bottom") +
  scale_colour_viridis_d(option = "magma")
```

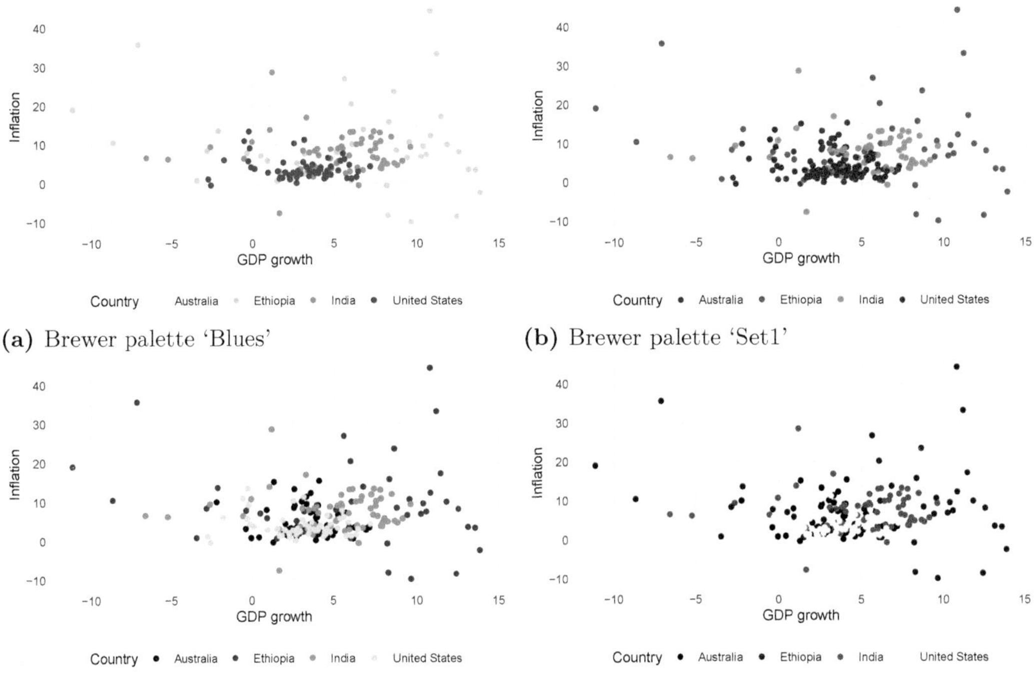

(a) Brewer palette 'Blues'

(b) Brewer palette 'Set1'

(c) Viridis palette default

(d) Viridis palette 'magma'

Figure 5.11: Relationship between inflation and GDP growth for Australia, Ethiopia, India, and the United States

The points of a scatterplot sometimes overlap. We can address this situation in a variety of ways (Figure 5.12):

1) Adding a degree of transparency to our dots with "alpha" (Figure 5.12a). The value for "alpha" can vary between 0, which is fully transparent, and 1, which is completely opaque.
2) Adding a small amount of noise, which slightly moves the points, using `geom_jitter()` (Figure 5.12b). By default, the movement is uniform in both directions, but we can specify which direction movement occurs with "width" or "height". The decision between these two options turns on the degree to which accuracy matters, and the number of points: it is often useful to use `geom_jitter()` when you want to highlight the relative density of points and not necessarily the

exact value of individual points. When using `geom_jitter()` it is a good idea to set a seed, as introduced in Chapter 2, for reproducibility.

```
set.seed(853)

# Panel (a)
world_bank_data |>
  ggplot(aes(x = gdp_growth, y = inflation, color = country )) +
  geom_point(alpha = 0.5) +
  theme_minimal() +
  labs(x = "GDP growth", y = "Inflation", color = "Country")

# Panel (b)
world_bank_data |>
  ggplot(aes(x = gdp_growth, y = inflation, color = country)) +
  geom_jitter(width = 1, height = 1) +
  theme_minimal() +
  labs(x = "GDP growth", y = "Inflation", color = "Country")
```

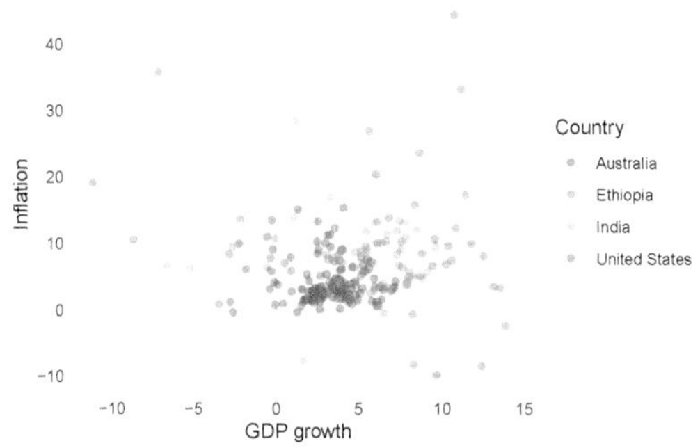

(a) Changing the alpha setting

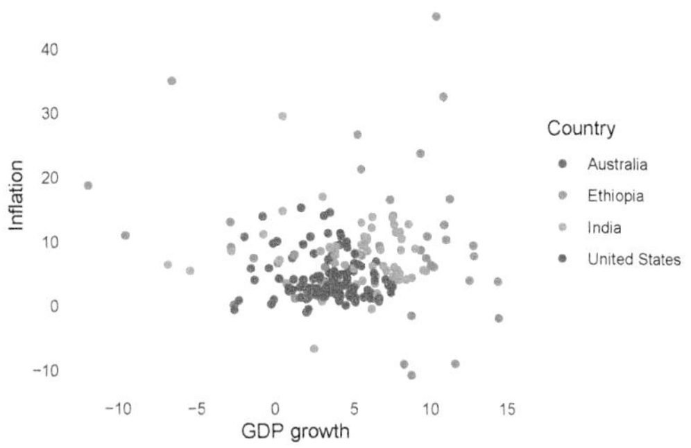

(b) Using jitter

Figure 5.12: Relationship between inflation and GDP growth for Australia, Ethiopia, India, and the United States

We often use scatterplots to illustrate a relationship between two continuous variables. It can be useful to add a "summary" line using `geom_smooth()` (Figure 5.13). We can specify the relationship using "method", change the color with "color", and add or remove standard errors with "se". A commonly used "method" is `lm`, which computes and plots a simple linear regression line similar to using the `lm()` function. Using `geom_smooth()` adds a layer to the graph, and so it inherits aesthetics from `ggplot()`. For instance, that is why we have one line for each country in Figure 5.13a and Figure 5.13b. We could overwrite that by specifying a particular color (Figure 5.13c). There are situation where other types of fitted lines such as splines might be preferred.

```
# Panel (a)
world_bank_data |>
  ggplot(aes(x = gdp_growth, y = inflation, color = country)) +
  geom_jitter() +
  geom_smooth() +
```

```
  theme_minimal() +
  labs(x = "GDP growth", y = "Inflation", color = "Country")

# Panel (b)
world_bank_data |>
  ggplot(aes(x = gdp_growth, y = inflation, color = country)) +
  geom_jitter() +
  geom_smooth(method = lm, se = FALSE) +
  theme_minimal() +
  labs(x = "GDP growth", y = "Inflation", color = "Country")

# Panel (c)
world_bank_data |>
  ggplot(aes(x = gdp_growth, y = inflation, color = country)) +
  geom_jitter() +
  geom_smooth(method = lm, color = "black", se = FALSE) +
  theme_minimal() +
  labs(x = "GDP growth", y = "Inflation", color = "Country")
```

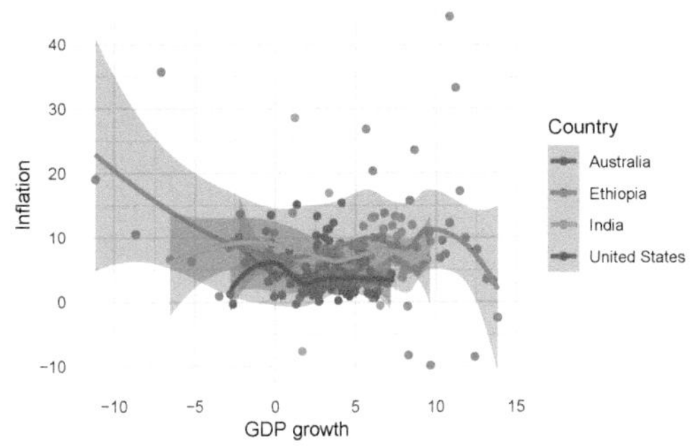

(a) Default line of best fit

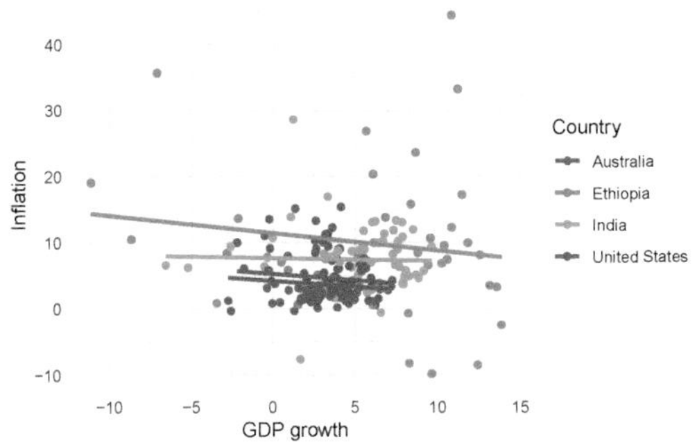

(b) Specifying a linear relationship

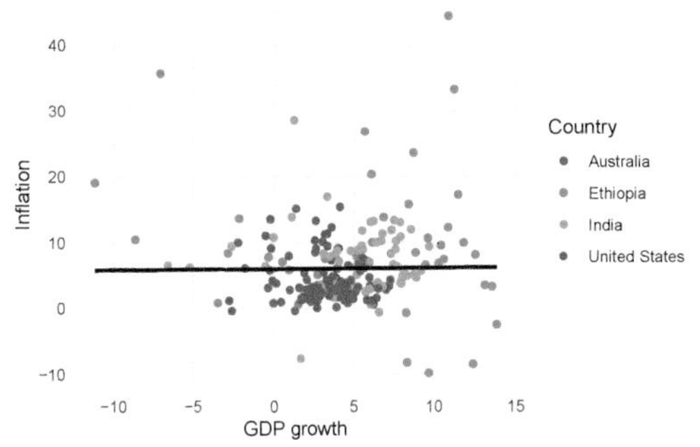

(c) Specifying only one color

Figure 5.13: Relationship between inflation and GDP growth for Australia, Ethiopia, India, and the United States

5.2.3 Line plots

We can use a line plot when we have variables that should be joined together, for instance, an economic time series. We will continue with the dataset from the World Bank and focus on GDP growth in the United States using `geom_line()` (Figure 5.14a). The source of the data can be added to the graph using "caption" within `labs()`.

```
# Panel (a)
world_bank_data |>
  filter(country == "United States") |>
  ggplot(mapping = aes(x = year, y = gdp_growth)) +
  geom_line() +
  theme_minimal() +
  labs(x = "Year", y = "GDP growth", caption = "Data source: World Bank.")

# Panel (b)
world_bank_data |>
  filter(country == "United States") |>
  ggplot(mapping = aes(x = year, y = gdp_growth)) +
  geom_step() +
  theme_minimal() +
  labs(x = "Year",y = "GDP growth", caption = "Data source: World Bank.")
```

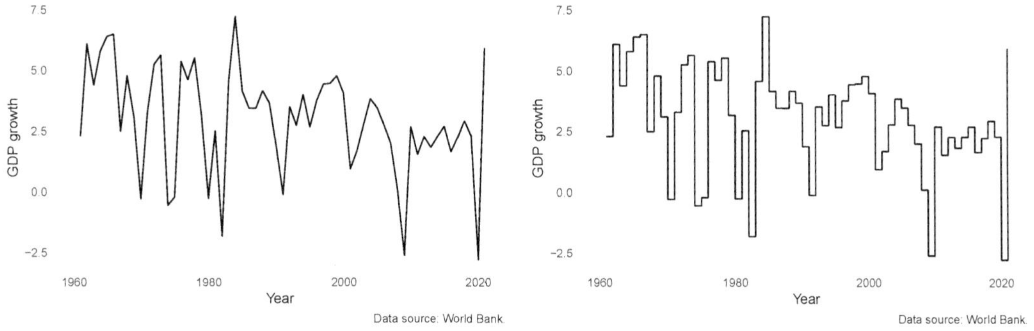

(a) Using a line plot

(b) Using a stairstep line plot

Figure 5.14: United States GDP growth (1961-2020)

We can use `geom_step()`, a slight variant of `geom_line()`, to focus attention on the change from year to year (Figure 5.14b).

The Phillips curve is the name given to plot of the relationship between unemployment and inflation over time. An inverse relationship is sometimes found in the data, for instance in the United Kingdom between 1861 and 1957 (Phillips 1958). We have a variety of ways to investigate this relationship in our data, including:

1) Adding a second line to our graph. For instance, we could add inflation (Figure 5.15a). This requires us to use `pivot_longer()`, which is discussed in the "R Essentials" Online Appendix[3], to ensure that the data are in a tidy format.

[3] https://tellingstorieswithdata.com/20-r_essentials.html

2) Using `geom_path()` to link values in the order they appear in the dataset. In Figure 5.15b we show a Phillips curve for the United States between 1960 and 2020. Figure 5.15b does not appear to show any clear relationship between unemployment and inflation.

```
world_bank_data |>
  filter(country == "United States") |>
  select(-population, -gdp_growth) |>
  pivot_longer(
    cols = c("inflation", "unem_rate"),
    names_to = "series",
    values_to = "value"
  ) |>
  ggplot(mapping = aes(x = year, y = value, color = series)) +
  geom_line() +
  theme_minimal() +
  labs(
    x = "Year", y = "Value", color = "Economic indicator",
    caption = "Data source: World Bank."
  ) +
  scale_color_brewer(palette = "Set1", labels = c("Inflation", "Unemployment")) +
  theme(legend.position = "bottom")

world_bank_data |>
  filter(country == "United States") |>
  ggplot(mapping = aes(x = unem_rate, y = inflation)) +
  geom_path() +
  theme_minimal() +
  labs(
    x = "Unemployment rate", y = "Inflation",
    caption = "Data source: World Bank."
  )
```

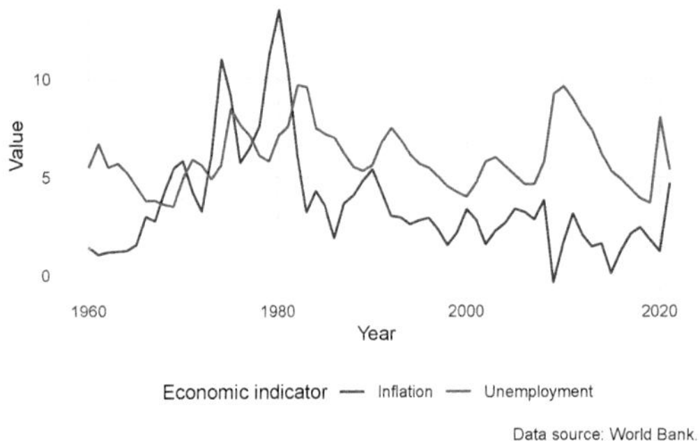

(a) Comparing the two time series over time

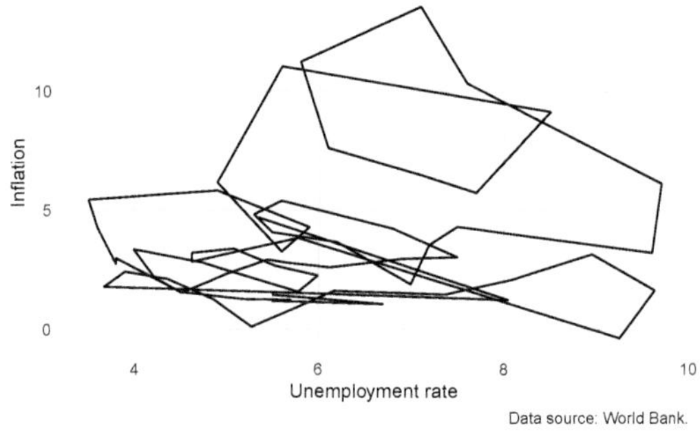

(b) Plotting the two time series against each other

Figure 5.15: Unemployment and inflation for the United States (1960-2020)

5.2.4 Histograms

A histogram is useful to show the shape of the distribution of a continuous variable. The full range of the data values is split into intervals called "bins" and the histogram counts how many observations fall into which bin. In Figure 5.16 we examine the distribution of GDP in Ethiopia.

```
world_bank_data |>
  filter(country == "Ethiopia") |>
  ggplot(aes(x = gdp_growth)) +
  geom_histogram() +
  theme_minimal() +
  labs(
    x = "GDP growth",
    y = "Number of occurrences",
    caption = "Data source: World Bank."
  )
```

The key component that determines the shape of a histogram is the number of bins. This can be specified in one of two ways (Figure 5.17):

1) specifying the number of "bins" to include; or
2) specifying their "binwidth".

```
# Panel (a)
world_bank_data |>
```

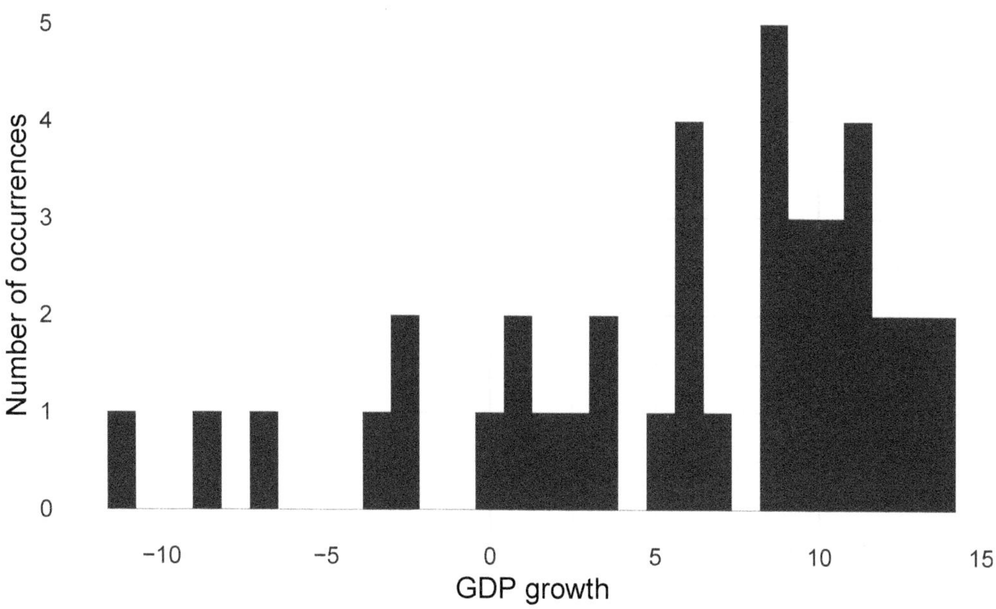

Figure 5.16: Distribution of GDP growth in Ethiopia (1960-2020)

```
  filter(country == "Ethiopia") |>
  ggplot(aes(x = gdp_growth)) +
  geom_histogram(bins = 5) +
  theme_minimal() +
  labs(
    x = "GDP growth",
    y = "Number of occurrences"
  )

# Panel (b)
world_bank_data |>
  filter(country == "Ethiopia") |>
  ggplot(aes(x = gdp_growth)) +
  geom_histogram(bins = 20) +
  theme_minimal() +
  labs(
    x = "GDP growth",
    y = "Number of occurrences"
  )

# Panel (c)
world_bank_data |>
  filter(country == "Ethiopia") |>
  ggplot(aes(x = gdp_growth)) +
  geom_histogram(binwidth = 2) +
  theme_minimal() +
  labs(
    x = "GDP growth",
    y = "Number of occurrences"
  )

# Panel (d)
world_bank_data |>
  filter(country == "Ethiopia") |>
  ggplot(aes(x = gdp_growth)) +
  geom_histogram(binwidth = 5) +
  theme_minimal() +
  labs(
    x = "GDP growth",
    y = "Number of occurrences"
  )
```

Histograms can be thought of as locally averaging data, and the number of bins affects how much of this occurs. When there are only two bins then there is a lot of smoothing, but we lose a lot of accuracy. Too few bins results in more bias, while too many bins results in more variance (Wasserman 2005, 303). Our decision as to the number of bins, or their width, is concerned with trying to balance bias and variance. This will depend on a variety of concerns including the subject matter and the goal (Cleveland [1985] 1994, 135). This is one of the reasons that Denby and Mallows (2009) consider histograms to be especially valuable as exploratory tools.

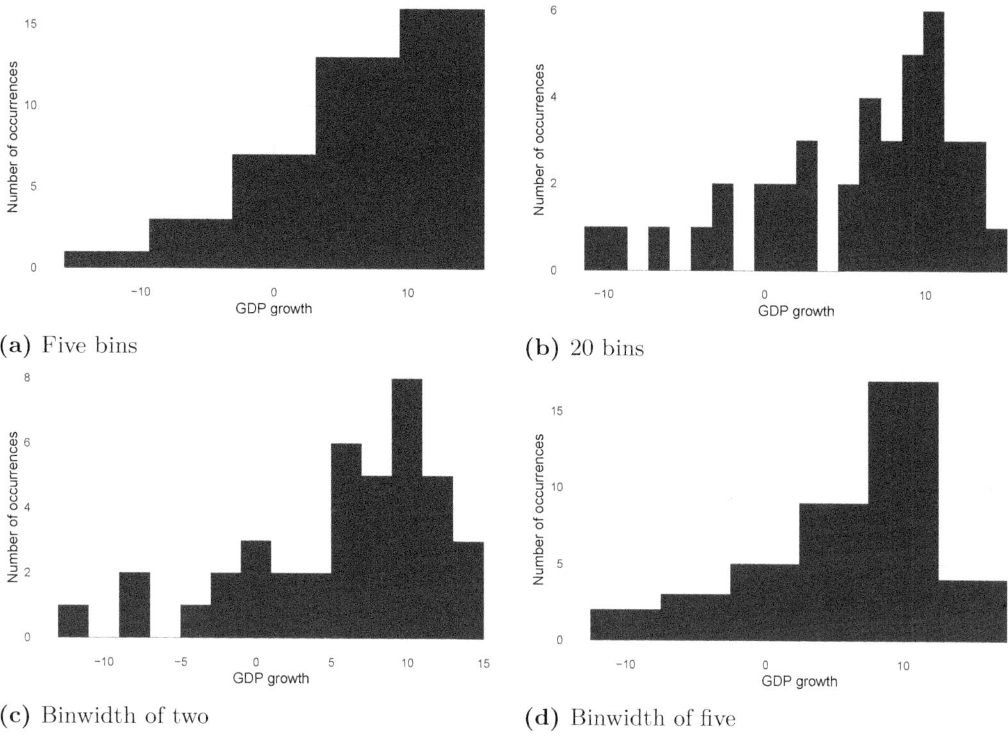

Figure 5.17: Distribution of GDP growth in Ethiopia (1960-2020)

Finally, while we can use "fill" to distinguish between different types of observations, it can get quite messy. It is usually better to:

1. trace the outline of the distribution with `geom_freqpoly()` (Figure 5.18a)
2. build stack of dots with `geom_dotplot()` (Figure 5.18b); or
3. add transparency, especially if the differences are more stark (Figure 5.18c).

```
# Panel (a)
world_bank_data |>
  ggplot(aes(x = gdp_growth, color = country)) +
  geom_freqpoly() +
  theme_minimal() +
  labs(
    x = "GDP growth", y = "Number of occurrences",
    color = "Country",
    caption = "Data source: World Bank."
  ) +
  scale_color_brewer(palette = "Set1")

# Panel (b)
world_bank_data |>
  ggplot(aes(x = gdp_growth, group = country, fill = country)) +
  geom_dotplot(method = "histodot") +
```

```
  theme_minimal() +
  labs(
    x = "GDP growth", y = "Number of occurrences",
    fill = "Country",
    caption = "Data source: World Bank."
  ) +
  scale_color_brewer(palette = "Set1")

# Panel (c)
world_bank_data |>
  filter(country %in% c("India", "United States")) |>
  ggplot(mapping = aes(x = gdp_growth, fill = country)) +
  geom_histogram(alpha = 0.5, position = "identity") +
  theme_minimal() +
  labs(
    x = "GDP growth", y = "Number of occurrences",
    fill = "Country",
    caption = "Data source: World Bank."
  ) +
  scale_color_brewer(palette = "Set1")
```

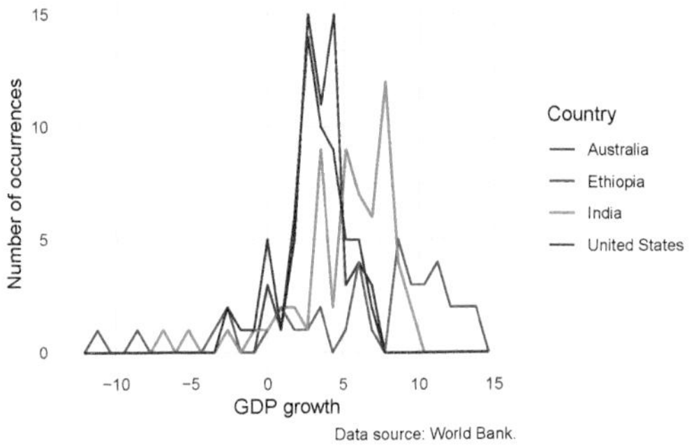

(a) Tracing the outline

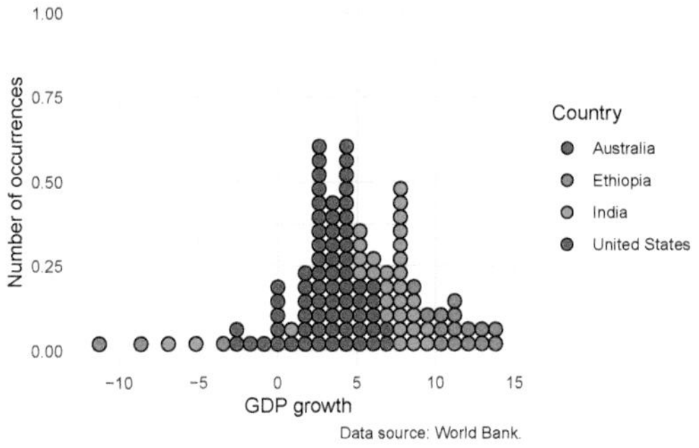

(b) Using dots

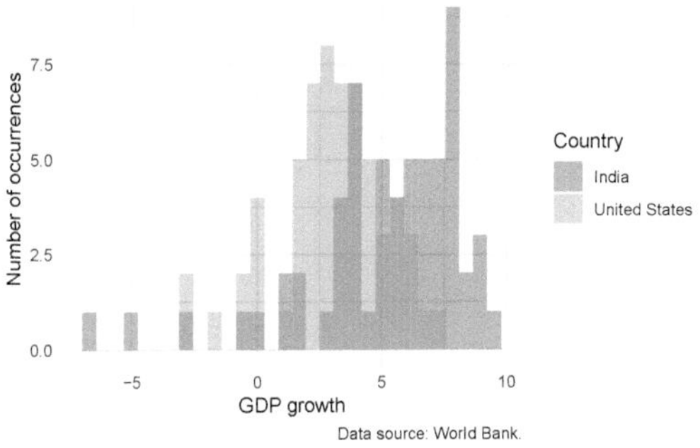

(c) Adding transparency

Figure 5.18: Distribution of GDP growth across various countries (1960-2020)

An interesting alternative to a histogram is the empirical cumulative distribution function (ECDF). The choice between this and a histogram is tends to be audience-specific. It may not appropriate for less-sophisticated audiences, but if the audience is quantitatively comfortable, then it can be a great choice because it does less smoothing than a histogram. We can build an ECDF with `stat_ecdf()`. For instance, Figure 5.19 shows an ECDF equivalent to Figure 5.16.

```
world_bank_data |>
  ggplot(mapping = aes(x = gdp_growth, color = country)) +
  stat_ecdf(geom = "point") +
  theme_minimal() +
  labs(
    x = "GDP growth", y = "Proportion", color = "Country",
    caption = "Data source: World Bank."
  ) +
  theme(legend.position = "bottom")
```

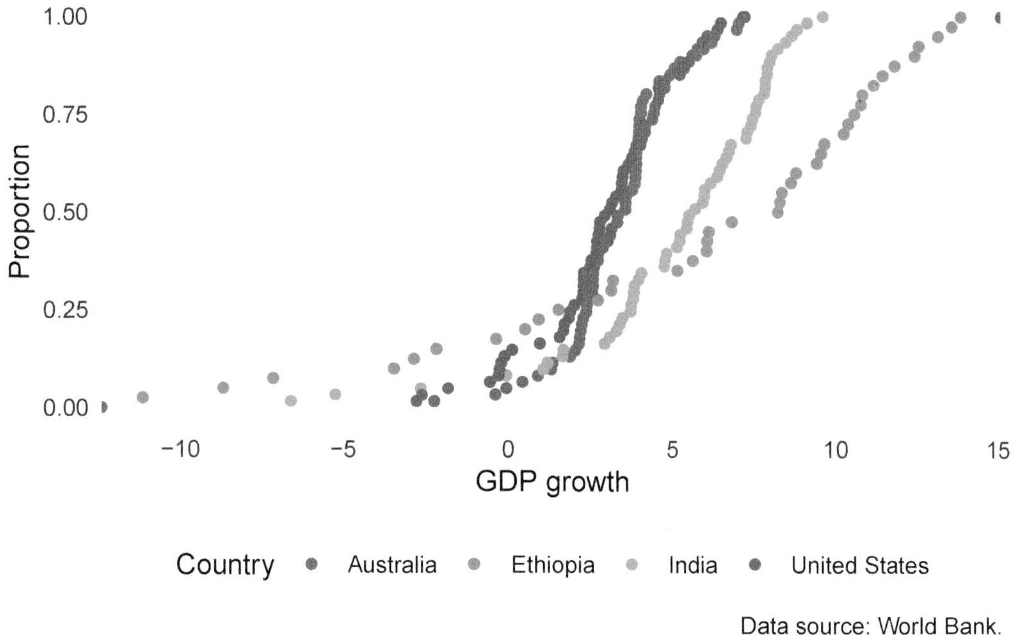

Figure 5.19: Distribution of GDP growth in four countries (1960-2020)

5.2.5 Boxplots

A boxplot typically shows five aspects: 1) the median, 2) the 25th, and 3) 75th percentiles. The fourth and fifth elements differ depending on specifics. One option is the minimum and maximum values. Another option is to determine the difference between the 75th and 25th percentiles, which is the interquartile range. The fourth and fifth elements are then $1.5 \times$ IQR from the 25th and 75th percentiles. That latter approach is used, by default, in `geom_boxplot` from `ggplot2`. Spear (1952, 166) introduced the notion of a chart that focused on the range and various summary statistics including the median and the range, while Tukey (1977) focused on which summary statistics and popularized it (Wickham and Stryjewski 2011).

One reason for using graphs is that they help us understand and embrace how complex our data are, rather than trying to hide and smooth it away (Armstrong 2022). One appropriate use case for boxplots is to compare the summary statistics of many variables at once, such as in Bethlehem et al. (2022). But boxplots alone are rarely the best choice because they hide the distribution of data, rather than show it. The same boxplot can apply to very different distributions. To see this, consider some simulated data from the beta distribution of two types. The first contains draws from two beta distributions: one that is right skewed and another that is left skewed. The second contains draws from a beta distribution with no skew, noting that $\text{Beta}(1, 1)$ is equivalent to $\text{Uniform}(0, 1)$.

```
set.seed(853)

number_of_draws <- 10000

both_left_and_right_skew <-
  c(
    rbeta(number_of_draws / 2, 5, 2),
    rbeta(number_of_draws / 2, 2, 5)
  )

no_skew <-
  rbeta(number_of_draws, 1, 1)

beta_distributions <-
  tibble(
    observation = c(both_left_and_right_skew, no_skew),
    source = c(
      rep("Left and right skew", number_of_draws),
      rep("No skew", number_of_draws)
    )
  )
```

We can first compare the boxplots of the two series (Figure 5.20a). But if we plot the actual data then we can see how different they are (Figure 5.20b).

```
beta_distributions |>
  ggplot(aes(x = source, y = observation)) +
  geom_boxplot() +
  theme_classic()

beta_distributions |>
  ggplot(aes(x = observation, color = source)) +
  geom_freqpoly(binwidth = 0.05) +
  theme_classic() +
  theme(legend.position = "bottom")
```

One way forward, if a boxplot is to be used, is to include the actual data as a layer on top of the boxplot. For instance, in Figure 5.21 we show the distribution of inflation across the four countries. The reason that this works well is that it shows the actual observations, as well as the summary statistics.

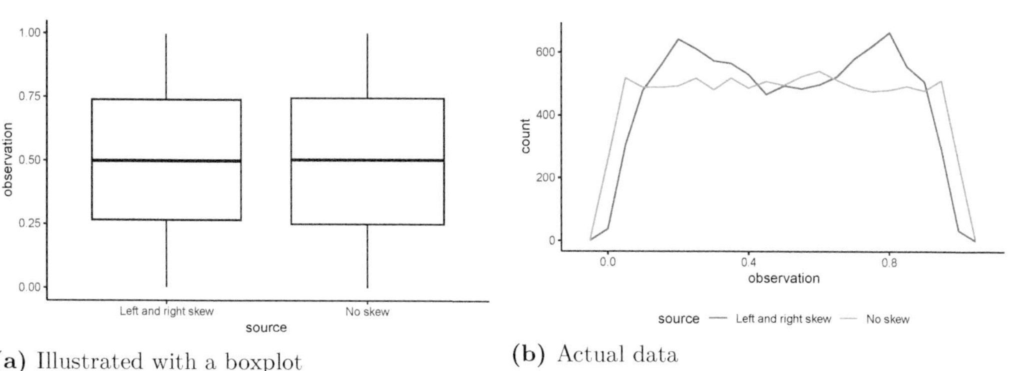

(a) Illustrated with a boxplot

(b) Actual data

Figure 5.20: Data drawn from beta distributions with different parameters

```
world_bank_data |>
  ggplot(mapping = aes(x = country, y = inflation)) +
  geom_boxplot() +
  geom_jitter(alpha = 0.3, width = 0.15, height = 0) +
  theme_minimal() +
  labs(
    x = "Country",
    y = "Inflation",
    caption = "Data source: World Bank."
  ) +
  scale_color_brewer(palette = "Set1")
```

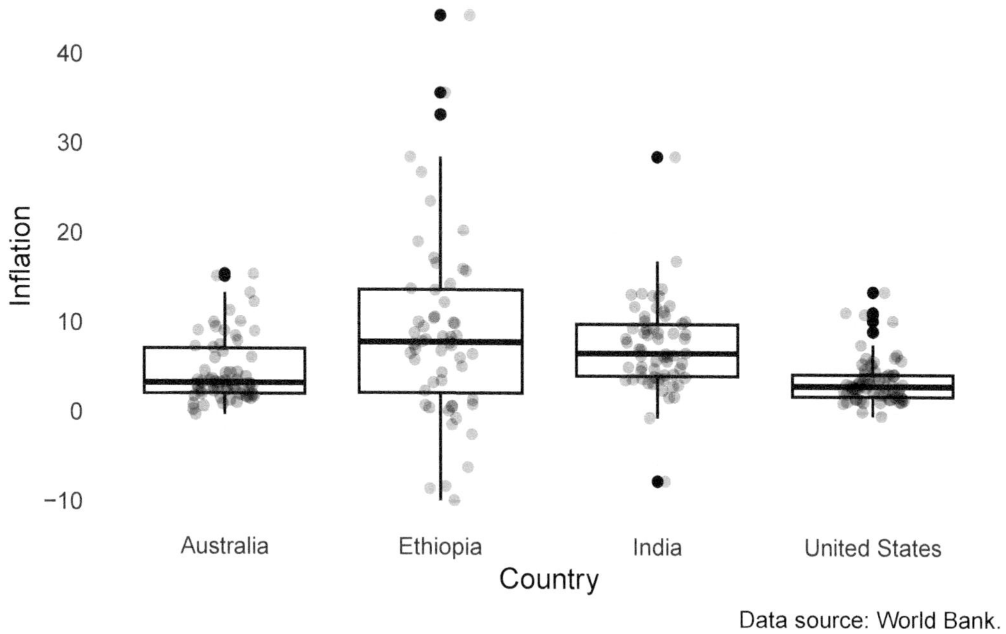

Figure 5.21: Distribution of unemployment data for four countries (1960-2020)

5.3 Tables

Tables are an important part of telling a compelling story. Tables can communicate less information than a graph, but they do so at a high fidelity. They are especially useful to highlight a few specific values (Andersen and Armstrong 2021). In this book, we primarily use tables in three ways:

1. To show an extract of the dataset.
2. To communicate summary statistics.
3. To display regression results.

5.3.1 Showing part of a dataset

We illustrate showing part of a dataset using `kable()` from `knitr`. We use the World Bank dataset that we downloaded earlier and focus on inflation, GDP growth, and population as unemployment data are not available for every year for every country.

```
world_bank_data <-
  world_bank_data |>
  select(-unem_rate)
```

To begin, after installing and loading `knitr`, we can display the first ten rows with the default `kable()` settings.

```
world_bank_data |>
  slice(1:10) |>
  kable()
```

country	year	inflation	gdp_growth	population
Australia	1960	3.7288136	NA	10276477
Australia	1961	2.2875817	2.482656	10483000
Australia	1962	-0.3194888	1.294611	10742000
Australia	1963	0.6410256	6.216107	10950000
Australia	1964	2.8662420	6.980061	11167000
Australia	1965	3.4055728	5.980438	11388000
Australia	1966	3.2934132	2.379040	11651000
Australia	1967	3.4782609	6.304945	11799000
Australia	1968	2.5210084	5.094034	12009000
Australia	1969	3.2786885	7.045584	12263000

To be able to cross-reference a table in the text, we need to add a table caption and label to the R chunk as shown in Section 3.2.6 of Chapter 3. We can also make the column names more informative with "col.names" and specify the number of digits to be displayed (Table 5.3).

```
```{r}
#| label: tbl-gdpfirst
```
```

Table 5.3: A dataset of economic indicators for four countries

Country	Year	Inflation	GDP growth	Population
Australia	1960	3.7	NA	10276477
Australia	1961	2.3	2.5	10483000
Australia	1962	-0.3	1.3	10742000
Australia	1963	0.6	6.2	10950000
Australia	1964	2.9	7.0	11167000
Australia	1965	3.4	6.0	11388000
Australia	1966	3.3	2.4	11651000
Australia	1967	3.5	6.3	11799000
Australia	1968	2.5	5.1	12009000
Australia	1969	3.3	7.0	12263000

```
#| message: false
#| tbl-cap: "A dataset of economic indicators for four countries"

world_bank_data |>
  slice(1:10) |>
  kable(
    col.names = c("Country", "Year", "Inflation", "GDP growth", "Population"),
    digits = 1
  )
```
```
```

5.3.2 Improving the formatting

When producing PDFs, the "booktabs" option makes a host of small changes to the default display and results in tables that look better (Table 5.4). (This should not have an effect for HTML output.) By default a small space will be added every five lines. We can additionally specify "linesep" to stop that.

```
world_bank_data |>
  slice(1:10) |>
  kable(
    col.names = c("Country", "Year", "Inflation", "GDP growth", "Population"),
    digits = 1,
    booktabs = TRUE,
    linesep = ""
  )
```

We can specify the alignment of the columns using a character vector of "l" (left), "c" (center), and "r" (right) (Table 5.5). Additionally, we can change the formatting. For instance, we could specify groupings for numbers that are at least 1,000 using `format.args = list(big.mark = ",")`.

Table 5.4: First ten rows of a dataset of economic indicators for Australia, Ethiopia, India, and the United States

Country	Year	Inflation	GDP growth	Population
Australia	1960	3.7	NA	10276477
Australia	1961	2.3	2.5	10483000
Australia	1962	-0.3	1.3	10742000
Australia	1963	0.6	6.2	10950000
Australia	1964	2.9	7.0	11167000
Australia	1965	3.4	6.0	11388000
Australia	1966	3.3	2.4	11651000
Australia	1967	3.5	6.3	11799000
Australia	1968	2.5	5.1	12009000
Australia	1969	3.3	7.0	12263000

Table 5.5: First ten rows of a dataset of economic indicators for Australia, Ethiopia, India, and the United States

Country	Year	Inflation	GDP growth	Population
Australia	1960	3.7	NA	10,276,477
Australia	1961	2.3	2.5	10,483,000
Australia	1962	-0.3	1.3	10,742,000
Australia	1963	0.6	6.2	10,950,000
Australia	1964	2.9	7.0	11,167,000
Australia	1965	3.4	6.0	11,388,000
Australia	1966	3.3	2.4	11,651,000
Australia	1967	3.5	6.3	11,799,000
Australia	1968	2.5	5.1	12,009,000
Australia	1969	3.3	7.0	12,263,000

```
world_bank_data |>
  slice(1:10) |>
  mutate(year = as.factor(year)) |>
  kable(
    col.names = c("Country", "Year", "Inflation", "GDP growth", "Population"),
    digits = 1,
    booktabs = TRUE,
    linesep = "",
    align = c("l", "l", "c", "c", "r", "r"),
    format.args = list(big.mark = ",")
  )
```

5.3.3 Communicating summary statistics

After installing and loading `modelsummary` we can use `datasummary_skim()` to create tables of summary statistics from our dataset.

Table 5.6: Summary of economic indicator variables for four countries

	Unique (#)	Missing (%)	Mean	SD	Min	Median	Max
year	62	0	1990.5	17.9	1960.0	1990.5	2021.0
inflation	243	2	6.1	6.5	−9.8	4.3	44.4
gdp_growth	224	10	4.2	3.7	−11.1	3.9	13.9

Table 5.7: Summary of categorical economic indicator variables for four countries

country	N	%
Australia	62	25.0
Ethiopia	62	25.0
India	62	25.0
United States	62	25.0

We can use this to get a table such as Table 5.6. That might be useful for exploratory data analysis, which we cover in Chapter 11. (Here we remove population to save space and do not include a histogram of each variable.)

```
world_bank_data |>
  select(-population) |>
  datasummary_skim(histogram = FALSE)
```

By default, `datasummary_skim()` summarizes the numeric variables, but we can ask for the categorical variables (Table 5.7). Additionally we can add cross-references in the same way as `kable()`, that is, include a "tbl-cap" entry and then cross-reference the name of the R chunk.

```
world_bank_data |>
  datasummary_skim(type = "categorical")
```

We can create a table that shows the correlation between variables using `datasummary_correlation()` (Table 5.8).

```
world_bank_data |>
  datasummary_correlation()
```

We typically need a table of descriptive statistics that we could add to our paper (Table 5.9).

Table 5.8: Correlation between the economic indicator variables for four countries (Australia, Ethiopia, India, and the United States)

	year	inflation	gdp_growth	population
year	1	.	.	.
inflation	0.03	1	.	.
gdp_growth	0.11	0.01	1	.
population	0.25	0.06	0.16	1

Table 5.9: Descriptive statistics for the inflation and GDP dataset

	Australia (N=62)		Ethiopia (N=62)	
	Mean	Std. Dev.	Mean	Std. Dev.
year	1990.5	18.0	1990.5	18.0
inflation	4.7	3.8	9.1	10.6
gdp_growth	3.4	1.8	5.9	6.4
population	17351313.1	4407899.0	57185292.0	29328845.8

Data source: World Bank.

This contrasts with Table 5.7 which would likely not be included in the main section of a paper, and is more to help us understand the data. We can add a note about the source of the data using `notes`.

```
datasummary_balance(
  formula = ~country,
  data = world_bank_data |>
    filter(country %in% c("Australia", "Ethiopia")),
  dinm = FALSE,
  notes = "Data source: World Bank."
)
```

5.3.4 Display regression results

We can report regression results using `modelsummary()` from `modelsummary`. For instance, we could display the estimates from a few different models (Table 5.10).

```
first_model <- lm(
  formula = gdp_growth ~ inflation,
  data = world_bank_data
)

second_model <- lm(
  formula = gdp_growth ~ inflation + country,
  data = world_bank_data
)

third_model <- lm(
  formula = gdp_growth ~ inflation + country + population,
  data = world_bank_data
)

modelsummary(list(first_model, second_model, third_model))
```

The number of significant digits can be adjusted with "fmt" (Table 5.11). To help establish credibility you should generally not add as many significant digits as possible (Howes 2022). Instead, you should think carefully about the data-generating process and adjust based on

Table 5.10: Explaining GDP as a function of inflation

	(1)	(2)	(3)
(Intercept)	4.147	3.676	3.611
	(0.343)	(0.484)	(0.482)
inflation	0.006	−0.068	−0.065
	(0.039)	(0.040)	(0.039)
countryEthiopia		2.896	2.716
		(0.740)	(0.740)
countryIndia		1.916	−0.730
		(0.642)	(1.465)
countryUnited States		−0.436	−1.145
		(0.633)	(0.722)
population			0.000
			(0.000)
Num.Obs.	223	223	223
R2	0.000	0.111	0.127
R2 Adj.	−0.004	0.095	0.107
AIC	1217.7	1197.5	1195.4
BIC	1227.9	1217.9	1219.3
Log.Lik.	−605.861	−592.752	−590.704
F	0.024	6.806	
RMSE	3.66	3.45	3.42

that.

```
modelsummary(
  list(first_model, second_model, third_model),
  fmt = 1
)
```

5.4 Maps

In many ways maps can be thought of as another type of graph, where the x-axis is latitude, the y-axis is longitude, and there is some outline or background image. It is possible that they are the oldest and best understood type of chart (Karsten 1923, 1). We can generate a map in a straight-forward manner. That said, it is not to be taken lightly; things quickly get complicated!

The first step is to get some data. There is some geographic data built into `ggplot2` that we can access with `map_data()`. There are additional variables in the `world.cities` dataset from `maps`.

```
france <- map_data(map = "france")
```

Table 5.11: Three models of GDP as a function of inflation

	(1)	(2)	(3)
(Intercept)	4.1	3.7	3.6
	(0.3)	(0.5)	(0.5)
inflation	0.0	−0.1	−0.1
	(0.0)	(0.0)	(0.0)
countryEthiopia		2.9	2.7
		(0.7)	(0.7)
countryIndia		1.9	−0.7
		(0.6)	(1.5)
countryUnited States		−0.4	−1.1
		(0.6)	(0.7)
population			0.0
			(0.0)
Num.Obs.	223	223	223
R2	0.000	0.111	0.127
R2 Adj.	−0.004	0.095	0.107
AIC	1217.7	1197.5	1195.4
BIC	1227.9	1217.9	1219.3
Log.Lik.	−605.861	−592.752	−590.704
F	0.024	6.806	
RMSE	3.66	3.45	3.42

```
head(france)
```

```
      long      lat group order region subregion
1 2.557093 51.09752     1     1   Nord      <NA>
2 2.579995 51.00298     1     2   Nord      <NA>
3 2.609101 50.98545     1     3   Nord      <NA>
4 2.630782 50.95073     1     4   Nord      <NA>
5 2.625894 50.94116     1     5   Nord      <NA>
6 2.597699 50.91967     1     6   Nord      <NA>
```

```
french_cities <-
  world.cities |>
  filter(country.etc == "France")

head(french_cities)
```

```
             name country.etc    pop   lat long capital
1       Abbeville      France  26656 50.12 1.83       0
2         Acheres      France  23219 48.97 2.06       0
3            Agde      France  23477 43.33 3.46       0
4            Agen      France  34742 44.20 0.62       0
5 Aire-sur-la-Lys      France  10470 50.64 2.39       0
6 Aix-en-Provence      France 148622 43.53 5.44       0
```

Using that information you can create a map of France that shows the larger cities (Figure 5.22). Use `geom_polygon()` from `ggplot2` to draw shapes by connecting points within groups. And `coord_map()` adjusts for the fact that we are making a 2D map to represent a world that is 3D.

```
ggplot() +
  geom_polygon(
    data = france,
    aes(x = long, y = lat, group = group),
    fill = "white",
    colour = "grey"
  ) +
  coord_map() +
  geom_point(
    aes(x = french_cities$long, y = french_cities$lat),
    alpha = 0.3,
    color = "black"
  ) +
  theme_minimal() +
  labs(x = "Longitude", y = "Latitude")
```

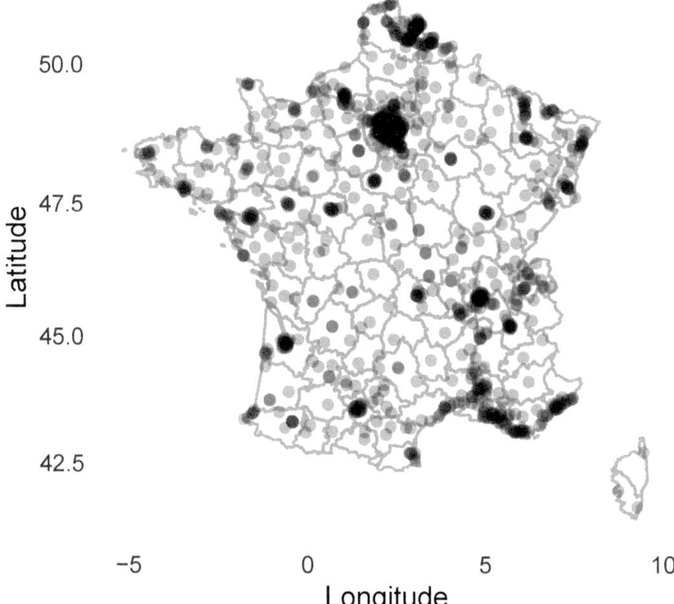

Figure 5.22: Map of France showing the largest cities

As is often the case with R, there are many ways to get started creating static maps. We have seen how they can be built using only `ggplot2`, but `ggmap` brings additional functionality.

There are two essential components to a map:

1) a border or background image (sometimes called a tile); and
2) something of interest within that border, or on top of that tile.

In ggmap, we use an open-source option for our tile, Stamen Maps. And we use plot points based on latitude and longitude.

5.4.1 Australian polling places

In Australia, people have to go to "booths" in order to vote. Because the booths have coordinates (latitude and longitude), we can plot them. One reason we may like to do that is to notice spatial voting patterns.

To get started we need to get a tile. We are going to use ggmap to get a tile from Stamen Maps, which builds on OpenStreetMap[4]. The main argument to this function is to specify a bounding box. A bounding box is the coordinates of the edges that you are interested in. This requires two latitudes and two longitudes.

It can be useful to use Google Maps, or other mapping platform, to find the coordinate values that you need. In this case we have provided it with coordinates such that it will be centered around Australia's capital Canberra.

```
bbox <- c(left = 148.95, bottom = -35.5, right = 149.3, top = -35.1)
```

Once you have defined the bounding box, the function get_stamenmap() will get the tiles in that area (Figure 5.23). The number of tiles that it needs depends on the zoom, and the type of tiles that it gets depends on the type of map. We have used "toner-lite", which is black and white, but there are others including: "terrain", "toner", and "toner-lines". We pass the tiles to ggmap() which will plot it. An internet connection is needed for this to work as get_stamenmap() downloads the tiles.

```
canberra_stamen_map <- get_stamenmap(bbox, zoom = 11, maptype = "toner-lite")

ggmap(canberra_stamen_map)
```

Once we have a map then we can use ggmap() to plot it. Now we want to get some data that we plot on top of our tiles. We will plot the location of the polling place based on its "division". This is available from the Australian Electoral Commission (AEC)[5].

```
booths <-
  read_csv(
    paste0(
      "https://results.aec.gov.au/24310/Website/Downloads/",
      "GeneralPollingPlacesDownload-24310.csv"
    ),
    skip = 1,
    guess_max = 10000
  )
```

This dataset is for the whole of Australia, but as we are only plotting the area around Canberra, we will filter the data to only booths with a geography close to Canberra.

[4]openstreetmap.org
[5]https://results.aec.gov.au/20499/Website/Downloads/HouseTppByPollingPlaceDownload-20499.csv

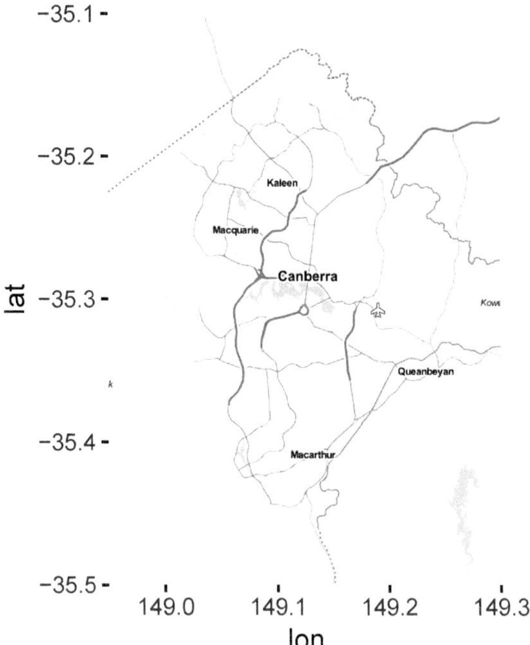

Figure 5.23: Map of Canberra, Australia

```
booths_reduced <-
  booths |>
  filter(State == "ACT") |>
  select(PollingPlaceID, DivisionNm, Latitude, Longitude) |>
  filter(!is.na(Longitude)) |> # Remove rows without geography
  filter(Longitude < 165) # Remove Norfolk Island
```

Now we can use ggmap in the same way as before to plot our underlying tiles, and then build on that using `geom_point()` to add our points of interest.

```
ggmap(canberra_stamen_map, extent = "normal", maprange = FALSE) +
  geom_point(data = booths_reduced,
             aes(x = Longitude, y = Latitude, colour = DivisionNm),
             alpha = 0.7) +
  scale_color_brewer(name = "2019 Division", palette = "Set1") +
  coord_map(
    projection = "mercator",
    xlim = c(attr(map, "bb")$ll.lon, attr(map, "bb")$ur.lon),
    ylim = c(attr(map, "bb")$ll.lat, attr(map, "bb")$ur.lat)
  ) +
  labs(x = "Longitude",
       y = "Latitude") +
  theme_minimal() +
  theme(panel.grid.major = element_blank(),
```

```
    panel.grid.minor = element_blank())
```

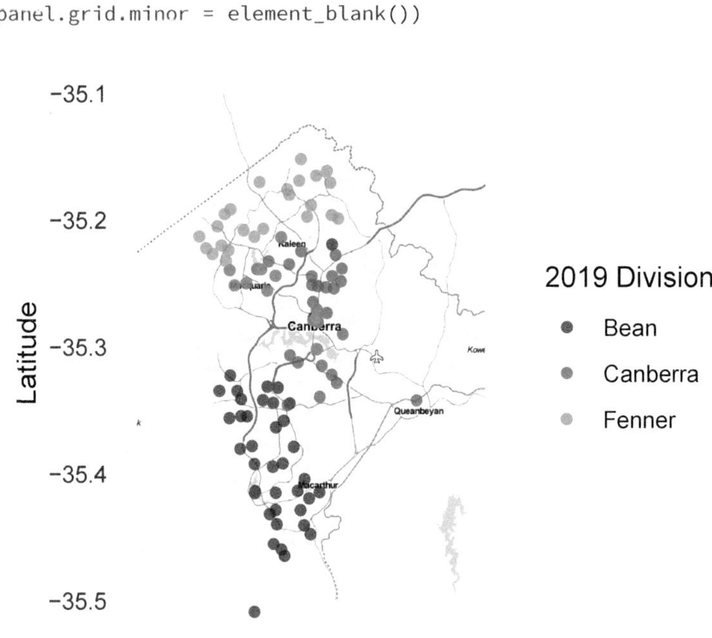

Figure 5.24: Map of Canberra, Australia, with polling places

We may like to save the map so that we do not have to create it every time, and we can do that in the same way as any other graph, using `ggsave()`.

```
ggsave("map.pdf", width = 20, height = 10, units = "cm")
```

Finally, the reason that we used Stamen Maps and OpenStreetMap is because they are open source, but we could have also used Google Maps. This requires you to first register a credit card with Google, and specify a key, but with low usage the service should be free. Using Google Maps—by using `get_googlemap()` within `ggmap`—brings some advantages over `get_stamenmap()`. For instance it will attempt to find a place name rather than needing to specify a bounding box.

5.4.2 United States military bases

To see another example of a static map we will plot some United States military bases after installing and loading `troopdata`. We can access data about United States overseas military bases back to the start of the Cold War using `get_basedata()`.

```
bases <- get_basedata()

head(bases)
```

```
# A tibble: 6 x 9
  countryname ccode iso3c basename               lat    lon  base lilypad fundedsite
```

```
  <chr>         <dbl> <chr> <chr>                <dbl> <dbl> <dbl>   <dbl>      <dbl>
1 Afghanistan    700 AFG   Bagram AB             34.9  69.3     1       0          0
2 Afghanistan    700 AFG   Kandahar Airfield     31.5  65.8     1       0          0
3 Afghanistan    700 AFG   Mazar-e-Sharif        36.7  67.2     1       0          0
4 Afghanistan    700 AFG   Gardez                33.6  69.2     1       0          0
5 Afghanistan    700 AFG   Kabul                 34.5  69.2     1       0          0
6 Afghanistan    700 AFG   Herat                 34.3  62.2     1       0          0
```

We will look at the locations of United States military bases in Germany, Japan, and Australia. The `troopdata` dataset already has the latitude and longitude of each base, and we will use that as our item of interest. The first step is to define a bounding box for each country.

```
# Use: https://data.humdata.org/dataset/bounding-boxes-for-countries
bbox_germany <- c(left = 5.867, bottom = 45.967, right = 15.033, top = 55.133)

bbox_japan <- c(left = 127, bottom = 30, right = 146, top = 45)

bbox_australia <- c(left = 112.467, bottom = -45, right = 155, top = -9.133)
```

Then we need to get the tiles using `get_stamenmap()` from `ggmap`.

```
german_stamen_map <-get_stamenmap(bbox_germany, zoom = 6, maptype = "toner-lite")

japan_stamen_map <- get_stamenmap(bbox_japan, zoom = 6, maptype = "toner-lite")

aus_stamen_map <- get_stamenmap(bbox_australia, zoom = 5, maptype = "toner-lite")
```

And finally, we can bring it all together with maps showing United States military bases in Germany (Figure 5.25a), Japan (Figure 5.25b), and Australia (Figure 5.25c).

```
ggmap(german_stamen_map) +
  geom_point(data = bases, aes(x = lon, y = lat)) +
  labs(x = "Longitude",
       y = "Latitude") +
  theme_minimal()

ggmap(japan_stamen_map) +
  geom_point(data = bases, aes(x = lon, y = lat)) +
  labs(x = "Longitude",
       y = "Latitude") +
  theme_minimal()

ggmap(aus_stamen_map) +
  geom_point(data = bases, aes(x = lon, y = lat)) +
  labs(x = "Longitude",
       y = "Latitude") +
  theme_minimal()
```

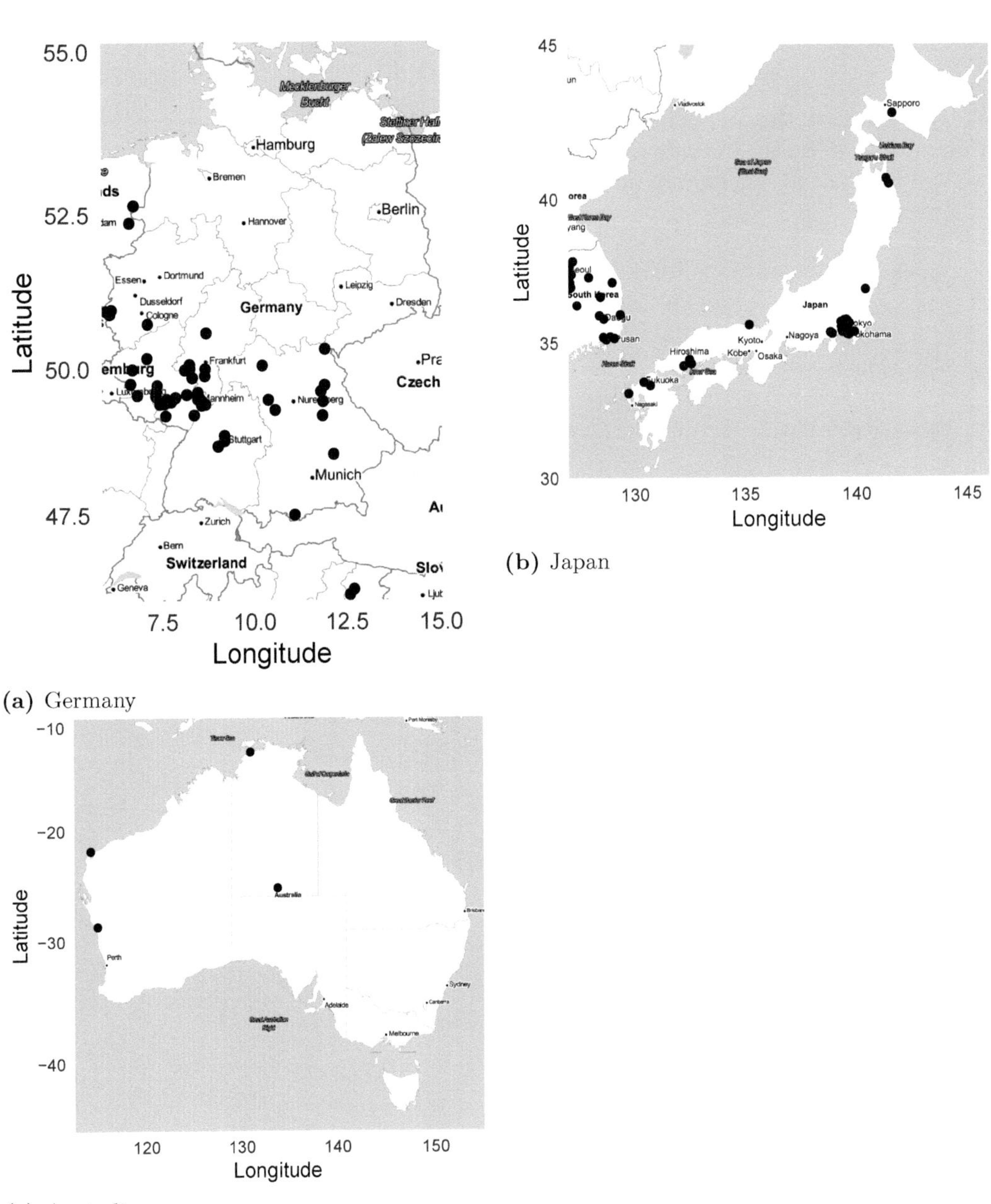

(a) Germany

(b) Japan

(c) Australia

Figure 5.25: Map of United States military bases in various parts of the world

5.4.3 Geocoding

So far we have assumed that we already have geocoded data. This means that we have latitude and longitude coordinates for each place. But sometimes we only have place names, such as "Sydney, Australia", "Toronto, Canada", "Accra, Ghana", and "Guayaquil, Ecuador". Before we can plot them, we need to get the latitude and longitude coordinates for each case. The process of going from names to coordinates is called geocoding.

> **i Oh, you think we have good data on that!**
>
> While you almost surely know where you live, it can be surprisingly difficult to specifically define the boundaries of many places. And this is made especially difficult when different levels of government have different definitions. Bronner (2021) illustrates this in the case of Atlanta, Georgia, where there are (at least) three official different definitions:
>
> 1) the metropolitan statistical area;
> 2) the urbanized area; and
> 3) the census place.
>
> Which definition is used can have a substantial effect on the analysis, or even the data that are available, even though they are all "Atlanta".

There are a range of options to geocode data in R, but `tidygeocoder` is especially useful. We first need a dataframe of locations.

```
place_names <-
  tibble(
    city = c("Sydney", "Toronto", "Accra", "Guayaquil"),
    country = c("Australia", "Canada", "Ghana", "Ecuador")
  )

place_names
```

```
# A tibble: 4 x 2
  city      country
  <chr>     <chr>
1 Sydney    Australia
2 Toronto   Canada
3 Accra     Ghana
4 Guayaquil Ecuador
```

```
place_names <-
  geo(
    city = place_names$city,
    country = place_names$country,
    method = "osm"
  )

place_names
```

```
# A tibble: 4 x 4
```

```
  city      country     lat    long
  <chr>     <chr>     <dbl>   <dbl>
1 Sydney    Australia -33.9  151.
2 Toronto   Canada     43.7  -79.4
3 Accra     Ghana       5.56  -0.201
4 Guayaquil Ecuador    -2.19 -79.9
```

And we can now plot and label these cities (Figure 5.26).

```
world <- map_data(map = "world")

ggplot() +
  geom_polygon(
    data = world,
    aes(x = long, y = lat, group = group),
    fill = "white",
    colour = "grey"
  ) +
  geom_point(
    aes(x = place_names$long, y = place_names$lat),
    color = "black") +
  geom_text(
    aes(x = place_names$long, y = place_names$lat, label = place_names$city),
    nudge_y = -5) +
  theme_minimal() +
  labs(x = "Longitude",
       y = "Latitude")
```

5.5 Concluding remarks

In this chapter we have covered a lot of ground, focused on communicating data. We spent a lot of time on graphs, because of their ability to convey a large amount of information in an efficient way. We then turned to tables because of how they can specifically convey information. Finally, we discussed maps, which allow us to display geographic information. The most important task is to show the observations to the full extent possible.

5.6 Exercises

Scales

1. *(Plan)* Consider the following scenario: *Three friends—Edward, Hugo, and Lucy—each measure the height of 20 of their friends. Each of the three use a slightly different approach to measurement and so make slightly different errors.* Please sketch what that dataset could look like and then sketch a graph that you could build to show all observations.

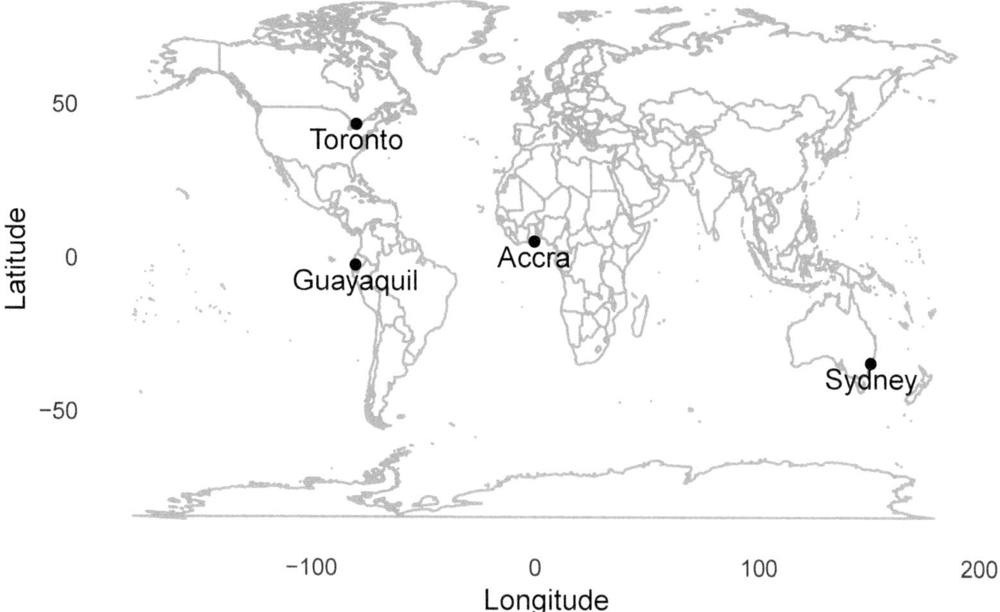

Figure 5.26: Map of Accra, Sydney, Toronto, and Guayaquil after geocoding to obtain their locations

2. *(Simulate)* Please further consider the scenario described and simulate the situation with every variable independent of each other. Please include three tests based on the simulated data.
3. *(Acquire)* Please describe a possible source of such a dataset.
4. *(Explore)* Please use `ggplot2` to build the graph that you sketched using the data that you simulated.
5. *(Communicate)* Please write two paragraphs about what you did.

Questions

1. Assume the `tidyverse` and `datasauRus` are installed and loaded. What would be the outcome of the following code `datasaurus_dozen |> filter(dataset == "v_lines") |> ggplot(aes(x=x, y=y)) + geom_point()`?
   a. Four vertical lines
   b. Five vertical lines
   c. Three vertical lines
   d. Two vertical lines
2. Which theme does not have solid lines along the x and y axes (pick one)?
   a. `theme_minimal()`
   b. `theme_classic()`
   c. `theme_bw()`
3. Assume the `tidyverse` and the `beps` dataset as generated in this chapter have been installed and loaded. Which argument should be added to `geom_bar()` in the following code to make the bars for the different parties be next to each other rather than on top of each other `beps |> ggplot(mapping = aes(x = age, fill = vote)) + geom_bar()`?

a. `position = "side_by_side"`
b. `position = "dodge2"`
c. `position = "adjacent"`
d. `position = "closest"`

4. In the code below, what should be added to `labs()` to change the text of the legend?
   a. `color = "Voted for"`
   b. `legend = "Voted for"`
   c. `scale = "Voted for"`
   d. `fill = "Voted for"`

```
beps |>
  ggplot(mapping = aes(x = age, fill = vote)) +
  geom_bar() +
  theme_minimal() +
  labs(x = "Age of respondent", y = "Number of respondents")
```

5. Based on the help file for `scale_colour_brewer()` which palette diverges?
   a. "Accent"
   b. "RdBu"
   c. "GnBu"
   d. "Set1"
6. Which geom should be used to make a scatter plot?
   a. `geom_smooth()`
   b. `geom_point()`
   c. `geom_bar()`
   d. `geom_dotplot()`
7. Which of these would result in the largest number of bins?
   a. `geom_histogram(binwidth = 5)`
   b. `geom_histogram(binwidth = 2)`
8. Suppose there is a dataset that contains the heights of 100 birds, each from one of three different species. If we are interested in understanding the distribution of these heights, then in a paragraph or two, please explain which type of graph should be used and why.
9. Would this code `data |> ggplot(aes(x = col_one)) |> geom_point()` if we assume the dataset and columns exist (pick one)?
   a. Yes
   b. No
10. Which of the following, if any, are elements of the layered grammar of graphics of Wickham (2010) (select all that apply)?
   a. A default dataset and set of mappings from variables to aesthetics.
   b. One or more layers, with each layer having one geometric object, one statistical transformation, one position adjustment, and optionally, one dataset and set of aesthetic mappings.
   c. Colors that enable the reader to understand the main point.
   d. A coordinate system.
   e. The facet specification.
   f. One scale for each aesthetic mapping used.
11. Which function from `modelsummary` could we use to create a table of descriptive statistics?

a. `datasummary_descriptive()`
b. `datasummary_skim()`
c. `datasummary_crosstab()`
d. `datasummary_balance()`

Tutorial

Please create a graph using `ggplot2` and a map using `ggmap` and add explanatory text to accompany both. Be sure to include cross-references and captions, etc. Each of these should take about pages.

Then, with regard the graph you created, please reflect on Vanderplas, Cook, and Hofmann (2020). Add a few paragraphs about the different options that you considered to make the graph more effective.

And finally, with regard to the map that you created, please reflect on the following quote from Heather Krause, founder of We All Count[6]: "maps only show people who aren't invisible to the makers" as well as Chapter 3 from D'Ignazio and Klein (2020) and add a few paragraphs related to this.

Use Quarto, and include an appropriate title, author, date, and citations. Submit a PDF.

Paper

At about this point the *Mawson* Paper in the "Papers" Online Appendix[7] would be appropriate.

[6]https://weallcount.com
[7]https://tellingstorieswithdata.com/23-assessment.html

Part III

Acquisition

6

Farm data

Prerequisites

- Watch *Introduction to Sampling and Randomization*, (Register 2020a)
  - This video provides an overview of sampling approaches with helpful examples.
- Read *Working-Class Households in Reading*, (Bowley 1913)
  - This historical paper discusses a survey conducted in the United Kingdom in the early 1900s, including a particularly informative discussion of systematic sampling.
- Read *On the Two Different Aspects of the Representative Method*, (Neyman 1934)
  - This paper provides an overview of stratified sampling. You should focus on the following parts: I "Introduction", III "Different Aspects of the Representative Method", V "Conclusion", and Bowley's discussion.
- Read *Guide to the Census of Population*, (Statistics Canada 2017)
  - Focus on Chapter 10 "Data quality assessment". Despite being written by the Canadian government about a particular census, this chapter describes and addresses concerns that are relevant to almost any survey.
- Read *He, she, they: Using sex and gender in survey adjustment*, (Kennedy et al. 2022)
  - This paper describes some of the challenges when considering sex and gender in surveys, and makes suggestions for ways forward.

Key concepts and skills

- Before there is a dataset, there must be measurement, and this brings many challenges and concerns. One dataset that is designed to be complete in certain respects is a census. While not perfect, governments spend a lot of money on censuses and other official statistics, and they are a great foundational data source.
- Even when we cannot obtain such a dataset, we can use sampling to ensure that we can still make sensible claims. There are two varieties of this—probability and non-probability. Both have an important role. Key terminology and concepts include: target population, sampling frame, sample, simple random sampling, systematic sampling, stratified sampling, and cluster sampling.

Key packages and functions

- Base R (R Core Team 2023)
- `cancensus` (von Bergmann, Shkolnik, and Jacobs 2021)
- `canlang` (Timbers 2020) (this package is not on CRAN so install it with: `install.packages("devtools")` then `devtools::install_github("ttimbers/canlang")`)
- `knitr` (Xie 2023)
- `maps` (Becker et al. 2022)
- `tidycensus` (Walker and Herman 2022)
- `tidyverse` (Wickham et al. 2019)

```
library(cancensus)
library(canlang)
library(knitr)
library(maps)
library(tidycensus)
library(tidyverse)
```

6.1 Introduction

As we think of our world, and telling stories about it, one of the most difficult aspects is to reduce the beautiful complexity of it into a dataset that we can use. We need to know what we give up when we do this. And be deliberate and thoughtful as we proceed. Some datasets are so large that one specific data point does not matter—it could be swapped for another without any effect (Crawford 2021, 94). But this is not always reasonable: how different would your life be if you had a different mother?

We are often interested in understanding the implications of some dataset; making forecasts based on it or using that dataset to make claims about broader phenomena. Regardless of how we turn our world into data, we will usually only ever have a sample of the data that we need. Statistics provides formal approaches that we use to keep these issues front of mind and understand the implications. But it does not provide definitive guidance about broader issues, such as considering who profits from the data that were collected, and whose power it reflects.

In this chapter we first discuss measurement, and some of the concerns that it brings. We then turn to censuses, in which we typically try to obtain data about an entire population. We also discuss other government official statistics, and long-standing surveys. We describe datasets of this type as "farmed data". Farmed datasets are typically well put together, thoroughly documented, and the work of collecting, preparing, and cleaning these datasets is mostly done for us. They are also, usually, conducted on a known release cycle. For instance, many countries release unemployment and inflation datasets monthly, GDP quarterly, and a census every five to ten years.

We then introduce statistical notions around sampling to provide a foundation that we will continually return to. Over the past one hundred years or so, statisticians have developed considerable sophistication for thinking about samples, and dealt with many controversies (K. Brewer 2013). In this chapter we consider probability and non-probability sampling and introduce certain key terminology and concepts.

This chapter is about data that are made available for us. Data are not neutral. For instance, archivists are now careful to consider archives not only as a source of fact, but also as part of the production of fact which occurred within a particular context especially constructed by the state (Stoler 2002). Thinking clearly about who is included in the dataset, and who is systematically excluded, is critical. Understanding, capturing, classifying, and naming data is an exercise in building a world and reflects power (Crawford 2021, 121), be that social, historical, financial, or legal.

For instance, we can consider the role of sex and gender in survey research. Sex is based on biological attributes and is assigned at birth, while gender is socially constructed and has both biological and cultural aspects (Lips 2020, 7). We may be interested in the relationship between gender, rather than sex, and some outcome. But the move toward a nuanced concept of gender in official statistics has only happened recently. Surveys that insist on a binary gender variable that is the same as sex, will not reflect those respondents who do not identify as such. Kennedy et al. (2022) provide a variety of aspects to consider when deciding what to do with gender responses, including: ethics, accuracy, practicality, and flexibility. But there is no universal best solution. Ensuring respect for the survey respondent should be the highest priority (Kennedy et al. 2022, 16).

Why do we even need classifications and groupings if it causes such concerns? Scott (1998) positions much of this as an outcome of the state, for its own purposes, wanting to make society legible and considers this a defining feature of modern states. For instance, Scott (1998) sees the use of surnames as arising because of the state's desire for legible lists to use for taxation, property ownership, conscription, and censuses. The state's desire for legibility also required imposing consistency on measurement. The modern form of metrology, which is "the study of how measurements are made, and how data are compared" (Plant and Hanisch 2020), began in the French Revolution when various measurements were standardized. This later further developed as part of Napoleonic state building (Scott 1998, 30). Prévost and Beaud (2015, 154) describe the essence of the change as one where knowledge went from being "singular, local, idiosyncratic... and often couched in literary form" to generalized, standardized, and numeric. That all said, it would be difficult to collect data without categorizable, measurable scales. A further concern is reification, where we forget that these measures must be constructed.

All datasets have shortcomings. In this chapter we develop comfort with "farmed data". We use that term to refer to a dataset that has been developed specifically for the purpose of being used as data.

Even though these farmed datasets are put together for us to use, and can generally be easily obtained, it is nonetheless especially important for us to develop a thorough understanding of their construction. James Mill, the nineteenth century Scottish author, famously wrote *The History of British India* without having set foot in the country. He claimed:

> Whatever is worth seeing or hearing in India, can be expressed in writing. As soon as every thing of importance is expressed in writing, a man who is duly qualified may attain more knowledge of India, in one year, in his closet in England, than he could obtain during the course of the longest life, by the use of his eyes and his ears in India.
>
> Mill (1817, xv)

It may seem remarkable that he was considered an expert and his views had influence. Yet today, many will, say, use inflation statistics without ever having tried to track a few prices, use the responses from political surveys without themselves ever having asked a respondent a question, or use ImageNet without the experience of hand-labeling some of the images. We should always throw ourselves into the details of the data.

6.2 Measurement

Measurement is an old concern. Even Aristotle distinguished between quantities and qualities (Tal 2020). Measurement, and especially, the comparison of measurements, underpins all quantitative analysis. But deciding what to measure, and how to do it, is challenging.

Measurement is trickier than it seems. For instance, in music, David Peterson, Professor of Political Science, Iowa State University, make it clear how difficult it is to define a one-hit wonder. A surprising number of artists that may immediately come to mind, turn out to have at least one or two other songs that did reasonably well in terms of making it onto charts (Molanphy 2012). Should an analysis of all one-term governments include those that did not make it through a full term? How about those that only lasted a month, or even a week? How do we even begin to measure the extent of government transfers when so much of these are in-kind benefits (Garfinkel, Rainwater, and Smeeding 2006)? How can we measure how well represented a person is in a democracy despite that being the fundamental concern (Achen 1978)? And why should the standard definition used by the World Health Organization (WHO) of pregnancy-related and maternal deaths only include those that occur within 42 days of delivery, termination, or abortion when this has a substantial effect on the estimate (Gazeley et al. 2022)?

Philosophy brings more nuance and depth to their definitions of measurement (Tal 2020), but the International Organization Of Legal Metrology (2007, 44) define measurement as the "process of experimentally obtaining one or more quantity values that can reasonably be attributed to a quantity", where a quantity is a "number and reference together". It implies "comparison of quantities, including counting of entities", and "presupposes a description of the quantity commensurate with the intended use of a measurement result, a measurement procedure, and a calibrated measuring system...". This definition of measurement makes clear that we have a variety of concerns including instrumentation and units, and that we are interested in measurements that are valid and reliable.

Instrumentation refers to what we use to conduct the measurement. Thorough consideration of instrumentation is important because it determines what we can measure. For instance, Morange (2016, 63) describes how the invention of microscopes in the sixteenth century led to the observation of capillaries by Marcello Malpighi in 1661, cells by Robert Hooke in 1665, and bacteria by Antonie van Leeuwenhoek in 1677 (Lane 2015). And consider the measurement of time. Again we see the interaction between instrumentation and measurement. With a sundial it was difficult to be much more specific about elapsed time than an hour or so. But the gradual development of more accurate instruments of timekeeping would eventually enable some sports to differentiate competitors to the thousandth of the second, and through GPS, allow navigation that is accurate to within meters.

i Oh, you think we have good data on that!

Knowing the time is a critical measurement. For instance, Formula 1 times laps to the thousandth of a second. And Michael Phelps, an American swimmer, won a gold medal at the Beijing Olympics by only one-hundredth of a second. Timing allows us to distinguish between outcomes even when the event does not happen concurrently. For instance, think back to the discussion of swimmers by Chambliss (1989) and how this would be impossible without knowing how long each event took each swimmer. Timing is also critical in finance where we need market participants to agree on whether an asset is available for sale. But the answer to "What time is it?" can be difficult to answer. The time, according to some individual, can be set to different sources, and so will differ depending on who you ask. Since the 1970s the definitive answer has been to use atomic time. A cesium second is defined by "9192 631 770 cycles of the hyperfine transition frequency in the ground state of cesium 133" (Levine, Tavella, and Milton 2022, 4). But the problem of clock synchronization—how to have all the non-atomic clocks match atomic time and each other—remains. Hopper (2022) provides an overview of how the Network Time Protocol (NTP) of Mills (1991) enables clock synchronization and some of the difficulties that exist for computer networks to discover atomic time. Another measure of time is astronomical time, which is based on the rotation of the Earth. But because the Earth spins inconsistently and other issues, adjustments have been made to ensure atomic and astronomical time match. This has resulted in the inclusions of positive leap seconds, and the possibility of a negative leap second, which have created problems (Levine, Tavella, and Milton 2022). As a result, at some point in the future astronomical and atomic time will be allowed to diverge (Gibney 2022; A. Mitchell 2022b).

A common instrument of measurement is a survey, and we discuss these further in Chapter 8. Another commonly-used instrument is sensors. For instance, climate scientists may be interested in temperature, humidity, or pressure. Much analysis of animal movement, such as Leos-Barajas et al. (2016), uses accelerometers. Sensors placed on satellites may be particularly concerned with images, and such data are available from the Landsat Program. Physicists are very concerned with measurement, and can be constrained not only by their instrumentation, but also storage capacity. For instance, the ATLAS detector at CERN is focused on the collision of particles, but not all of the measurements can be saved because that would result in 80TB per second (Colombo et al. 2016)! And in the case of A/B testing, which we discuss in Chapter 8, extensive use is made of cookies, beacons, system settings, and behavioral patterns. Another aspect of instrumentation is delivery. For instance, if using surveys, then should they be mailed or online? Should they be filled out by the respondent or by an enumerator?

The definition of measurement, provided by metrology, makes it clear that the second fundamental concern is a reference, which we refer to as units. The choice of units is related to both the research question of interest and available instrumentation. For instance, in the Tutorial in Chapter 1 we were concerned with measuring the growth of plants. This would not be well served by using kilometers or miles as a unit. If we were using a ruler, then we may be able to measure millimeters, but with calipers, we might be able to consider tens of micrometers.

6.2.1 Properties of measurements

Valid measurements are those where the quantity that we are measuring is related to the estimand and research question of interest. It speaks to appropriateness. Recall, from Chapter 4, that an estimand is the actual effect, such as the (unknowable) actual effect of smoking on life expectancy. It can be useful to think about estimands as what is actually of interest. This means that we need to ensure that we are measuring relevant aspects of an individual. For instance, the number of cigarettes that they smoked, and the number of years they lived, rather than, say, their opinion about smoking.

For some units, such as a meter or a second, there is a clear definition. And when that definition evolves it is widely agreed on (A. Mitchell 2022a). But for other aspects that we may wish to measure it is less clear and so the validity of the measurement becomes critical. At one point in the fourteenth century attempts were made to measure grace and virtue (Crosby 1997, 14)! More recently, we try to measure intelligence or even the quality of a university. That is not to say there are not people with more or less grace, virtue, and intelligence than others, and there are certainly better and worse universities. But the measurement of these is difficult.

The *U.S. News and World Report* tries to quantify university quality based on aspects such as class size, number of faculty with a PhD, and number of full-time faculty. But an issue with such constructed measures, especially in social settings, is that it changes the incentives of those being measured. For instance, Columbia University increased from 18th in 1988 to 2nd in 2022. But Michael Thaddeus, Professor of Mathematics, Columbia University, showed how there was a difference, in Columbia's favor, between what Columbia reported to *U.S. News and World Report* and what was available through other sources (Hartocollis 2022).

Such concerns are of special importance in psychology because there is no clear measure of many fundamental concepts. Fried, Flake, and Robinaugh (2022) review the measurement of depression and find many concerns including a lack of validity and reliability. This is not to say that we should not try to measure such things, but we should ensure transparency about measurement decisions. For instance, Flake and Fried (2020) recommend answering various clarifying questions whenever measurements have to be constructed. These include questioning the underlying construct of interest, the decision process that led to the measure, what alternatives were considered, the quantification process, and the scale. These questions are especially important when the measure is being constructed for a particular purpose, rather than being adopted from elsewhere. This is because of the concern that the measure will be constructed in a way that provides a pre-ordained outcome.

Reliability draws on the part of the definition of measurement that reads "process of experimentally obtaining...". It implies some degree of consistency and means that multiple measurements of one particular aspect, at one particular time, should be essentially the same. If two enumerators count the number of shops on a street, then we would hope that their counts are the same. And if they were different then we would hope we could understand the reason for the difference. For instance, perhaps one enumerator misunderstood the instructions and incorrectly counted only shops that were open. To consider another example, demographers are often concerned with the migration of people between countries, and economists are often concerned with international trade. It is concerning the number of times that the in-migration or imports data of Country A from Country B do not match the out-migration or exports data of Country B to Country A.

> **i Oh, you think we have good data on that!**
>
> It is common for the pilot of a plane to announce the altitude to their passengers. But the notion and measurement of altitude is deceptively complicated, and underscores the fact that measurement occurs within a broader context (Vanhoenacker 2015). For instance, if we are interested in how many meters there are between the plane and the ground, then should we measure the difference between the ground and where the pilot is sitting, which would be most relevant for the announcement, or to the bottom of the wheels, which would be most relevant for landing? What happens if we go over a mountain? Even if the plane has not descended, such a measure—the number of meters between the plane and the ground—would claim a reduction in altitude and make it hard to vertically separate multiple planes. We may be interested in a comparison to sea level. But sea level changes because of the tide, and is different at different locations. As such, a common measure of altitude is flight level, which is determined by the amount of air pressure. And because air pressure is affected by weather, season, and location, the one flight level may be associated with very different numbers of meters to the ground over the course of a flight. The measures of altitude used by planes serve their purpose of enabling relatively safe air travel.

6.2.2 Measurement error

Measurement error is the difference between the value we observe and the actual value. Sometimes it is possible to verify certain responses. If the difference is consistent between the responses that we can verify and those that we cannot, then we are able to estimate the extent of overall measurement error. For instance, Sakshaug, Yan, and Tourangeau (2010) considered a survey of university alumni and compared replies about a respondent's grades with their university record. They find that the mode of the survey—telephone interview conducted by a human, telephone interview conducted by a computer, or an internet survey—affected the extent of the measurement error.

Such error can be particularly pervasive when an enumerator fills out the survey form on behalf of the respondent. This is especially of concern around race. For instance, Davis (1997, 177) describes how Black people in the United States may limit the extent to which they describe their political and racial belief to white interviewers.

Another example is censored data, which is when we have some partial knowledge of the actual value. Right-censored data is when we know that the actual value is above some observed value, but we do not know by how much. For instance, immediately following the Chernobyl disaster in 1986, the only available instruments to measure radiation had a certain maximum limit. While the radiation was measured as being at that (maximum) level, the implication was that the actual value was much higher.

Right-censored data are often seen in medical studies. For instance, say some experiment is conducted, and then patients are followed for ten years. At the end of that ten-year period all we know is whether a patient lived at least ten years, not the exact length of their life. Left-censored data is the opposite situation. For instance, consider a thermometer that only went down to freezing. Even when the actual temperature was less, the thermometer would still register that as freezing.

A slight variation of censored data is winsorizing data. This occurs when we observe the actual value, but we change it to a less extreme one. For instance, if we were considering age then we may change the age of anyone older than 100 to be 100. We may do this if we are worried that values that were too large would have too significant of an effect.

Truncated data is a slightly different situation in which we do not even record those values. For instance, consider a situation in which we were interested in the relationship between a child's age and height. Our first question might be "what is your age?" and if it turns out the respondent is an adult, then we would not continue to ask height. Truncated data are especially closely related to selection bias. For instance, consider a student who drops a course—their opinion is not measured on course evaluations.

To illustrate the difference between these concepts, consider a situation in which the actual distribution of newborn baby weight has a normal distribution, centered around 3.5kg. Imagine there is some defect with the scale, such that any value less than or equal to 2.75kg is assigned 2.75kg. And imagine there is some rule such that any baby expected to weigh more than 4.25kg is transferred to a different hospital to be born. These three scenarios are illustrated in Figure 6.1. We may also be interested in considering the mean weight, which highlights the bias (Table 6.1).

```
set.seed(853)

newborn_weight <-
  tibble(
    weight = rep(
      x = rnorm(n = 1000, mean = 3.5, sd = 0.5),
      times = 3),
    measurement = rep(
      x = c("Actual", "Censored", "Truncated"),
      each = 1000)
    )

newborn_weight <-
  newborn_weight |>
  mutate(
    weight = case_when(
      weight <= 2.75 & measurement == "Censored" ~ 2.75,
      weight >= 4.25 & measurement == "Truncated" ~ NA_real_,
      TRUE ~ weight
    )
  )

newborn_weight |>
  ggplot(aes(x = weight)) +
  geom_histogram(bins = 50) +
  facet_wrap(vars(measurement)) +
  theme_minimal()
```

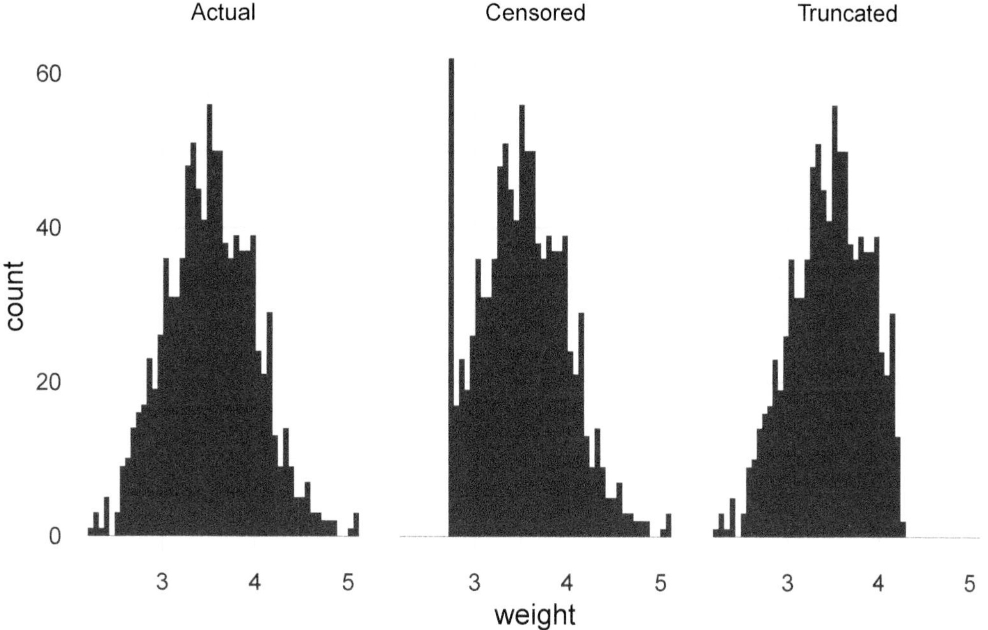

Figure 6.1: Comparison of actual weights with censored and truncated weights

```
newborn_weight |>
  summarise(mean = mean(weight, na.rm = TRUE),
            .by = measurement) |>
  kable(
    col.names = c("Measurement", "Mean"),
    digits = 3
  )
```

Table 6.1: Comparing the means of the different scenarios identifies the bias

Measurement	Mean
Actual	3.521
Censored	3.530
Truncated	3.455

6.2.3 Missing data

Regardless of how good our data acquisition process is, there will be missing data. That is, observations that we know we do not have. But a variable must be measured, or at least thought about and considered, in order to be missing. With insufficient consideration, there is the danger of missing data that we do not even know are missing because the variables were never considered. They are missing in a "dog that did not bark" sense. This is why it is so important to think about the situation, sketch and simulate, and work with subject-matter experts.

Non-response could be considered a variant of measurement error whereby we observe a null, even though there should be an actual value. But it is usually considered in its own right. And there are different extents of non-response: from refusing to even respond to the survey, through to just missing one question. Non-response is a key issue, especially with non-probability samples, because there is usually good reason to consider that people who do not respond are systematically different to those who do. And this serves to limit the extent to which the survey can be used to speak to more than just survey respondents. Gelman et al. (2016) go so far as to say that much of the changes in public opinion that are reported in the lead-up to an election are not people changing their mind, but differential non-response. That is, individual choosing whether to respond to a survey at all depending on the circumstances, not just choosing which survey response to choose. The use of pre-notification and reminders may help address non-response in some circumstances (Koitsalu et al. 2018; Frandell et al. 2021).

Data might be missing because a respondent did not want to respond to one particular question, a particular collection of related questions, or the entire survey, although these are not mutually exclusive nor collectively exhaustive (Newman 2014). In an ideal situation data are Missing Completely At Random (MCAR). This rarely occurs, but if it does, then inference should still be reflective of the broader population. It is more likely that data are Missing At Random (MAR) or Missing Not At Random (MNAR). The extent to which we must worry about that differs. For instance, if we are interested in the effect of gender on political support, then it may be that men are less likely to respond to surveys, but this is not related to who they will support. If that differential response is only due to being a man, and not related to political support, then we may be able to continue, provided we include gender in the regression, or are able to post-stratify based on gender. That said, the likelihood of this independence holding is low, and it is more likely, as in Gelman et al. (2016), that there is a relationship between responding to the survey and political support. In that more likely case, we may have a more significant issue. One approach would be to consider additional explanatory variables. It is tempting to drop incomplete cases, but this may further bias the sample, and requires justification and the support of simulation. Data imputation could be considered, but again may bias the sample. Ideally we could rethink, and improve, the data collection process.

We return to missing data in Chapter 11.

6.3 Censuses and other government data

There are a variety of sources of data that have been produced for the purposes of being used as datasets. One thinks here especially of censuses of population. Whitby (2020, 30–31) describes how the earliest censuses for which we have written record are from China's Yellow River Valley. One motivation for censuses was taxation, and Jones (1953) describes census records from the late third or early fourth century A.D. which enabled a new system of taxation. Detailed records, such as censuses, have also been abused. For instance, Luebke and Milton (1994, 25) set out how the Nazis used censuses and police registration datasets to "locate groups eventually slated for deportation and death". And Bowen (2022, 17) describes how the United States Census Bureau provided information that contributed to the internship of Japanese Americans. President Clinton apologized for this in the 1990s.

Another source of data deliberately put together to be a dataset include official statistics like surveys of economic conditions such as unemployment, inflation, and GDP. Interestingly, Rockoff (2019) describes how these economic statistics were not actually developed by the federal government, even though governments typically eventually took over that role. Censuses and other government-run surveys have the power, and financial resources, of the state behind them, which enables them to be thorough in a way that other datasets cannot be. For instance, the 2020 United States Census is estimated to have cost US$15.6 billion (Hawes 2020). But this similarly brings a specific perspective. Census data, like all data, are not unimpeachable. Common errors include under- and over-enumeration, as well as misreporting (Steckel 1991). There are various measures and approaches used to assess quality (Statistics Canada 2017).

Oh, you think we have good data on that!

Censuses of population are critical, but not unimpeachable. Anderson and Fienberg (1999) describe how the history of the census in the United States is one of undercount, and that even George Washington complained about this in the 1790s. The extent of the undercount was estimated due to the Selective Service registration system used for conscription in World War II. Those records were compared with census records, and it was found that there were about half a million more men recorded for conscription purposes than in the census. This was race-specific, with an average undercount of around 3 per cent, but an undercount of Black men of draft age of around 13 per cent (Anderson and Fienberg 1999, 29). This became a political issue in the 1960s, and race and ethnicity related questions were of special concern in the 1990s. Nobles (2002, 47) discusses how counting by race first requires that race exists, but that this may be biologically difficult to establish. Despite how fundamental race is to the United States census it is not something that is "fixed" and "objective" but instead has influences from class, social, legal, structural, and political aspects (Nobles 2002, 48).

Another similarly large and established source of data are from long-running large surveys. These are conducted on a regular basis, and while not usually directly conducted by the government, they are usually funded, one way or another, by the government. For instance, here we often think of electoral surveys, such as the Canadian Election Study, which has run in association with every federal election since 1965, and similarly the British Election Study which has been associated with every general election since 1964.

More recently there has been a large push toward open data in government. The underlying principle—that the government should make available the data that it has—is undeniable. But the term has become a little contentious because of how it has occurred in practice. Governments only provide data that they want to provide. We may even sometimes see manipulation of data to suit a government's narrative (Kalgin 2014; P. Zhang et al. 2019; Berdine, Geloso, and Powell 2018). One way to get data that the government has, but does not necessarily want to provide, is to submit a Freedom of Information (FOI) request (Walby and Luscombe 2019). For instance, Cardoso (2020) use data from FOI to find evidence of systematic racism in the Canadian prison system.

While farmed datasets have always been useful, they were developed for a time when much analysis was conducted without the use of programming languages. Many R packages have been developed to make it easier to get these datasets into R. Here we cover a few that are especially useful.

6.3.1 Canada

The first census in Canada was conducted in 1666. This was also the first modern census where every individual was recorded by name, although it does not include Aboriginal peoples (Godfrey 1918, 179). There were 3,215 inhabitants that were counted, and the census asked about age, sex, marital status, and occupation (Statistics Canada 2017). In association with Canadian Confederation, in 1867 a decennial census was required so that political representatives could be allocated for the new Parliament. Regular censuses have occurred since then.

We can explore some data on languages spoken in Canada from the 2016 Census using `canlang`. This package is not on CRAN, but can be installed from GitHub with: `install.packages("devtools")` then `devtools::install_github("ttimbers/canlang")`.

After loading `canlang` we can use the `can_lang` dataset. This provides the number of Canadians who use each of 214 languages.

```
can_lang
```

```
# A tibble: 214 x 6
   category            language mother_tongue most_at_home most_at_work lang_known
   <chr>               <chr>            <dbl>        <dbl>        <dbl>      <dbl>
 1 Aboriginal langu~ Aborigi~             590          235           30        665
 2 Non-Official & N~ Afrikaa~           10260         4785           85      23415
 3 Non-Official & N~ Afro-As~            1150          445           10       2775
 4 Non-Official & N~ Akan (T~           13460         5985           25      22150
 5 Non-Official & N~ Albanian           26895        13135          345      31930
 6 Aboriginal langu~ Algonqu~              45           10            0        120
 7 Aboriginal langu~ Algonqu~            1260          370           40       2480
 8 Non-Official & N~ America~            2685         3020         1145      21930
 9 Non-Official & N~ Amharic            22465        12785          200      33670
10 Non-Official & N~ Arabic            419890       223535         5585     629055
# i 204 more rows
```

We can quickly see the top-ten most common languages to have as a mother tongue.

```
can_lang |>
  slice_max(mother_tongue, n = 10) |>
  select(language, mother_tongue)
```

```
# A tibble: 10 x 2
   language                          mother_tongue
   <chr>                                     <dbl>
 1 English                                19460850
 2 French                                  7166700
 3 Mandarin                                 592040
 4 Cantonese                                565270
 5 Punjabi (Panjabi)                        501680
 6 Spanish                                  458850
 7 Tagalog (Pilipino, Filipino)             431385
 8 Arabic                                   419890
 9 German                                   384040
```

```
10 Italian                              375635
```

We could combine two datasets: `region_lang` and `region_data`, to see if the five most common languages differ between the largest region, Toronto, and the smallest, Belleville.

```
region_lang |>
  left_join(region_data, by = "region") |>
  slice_max(c(population)) |>
  slice_max(mother_tongue, n = 5) |>
  select(region, language, mother_tongue, population) |>
  mutate(prop = mother_tongue / population)
```

```
# A tibble: 5 x 5
  region  language            mother_tongue population   prop
  <chr>   <chr>                       <dbl>      <dbl>  <dbl>
1 Toronto English                   3061820    5928040 0.516
2 Toronto Cantonese                  247710    5928040 0.0418
3 Toronto Mandarin                   227085    5928040 0.0383
4 Toronto Punjabi (Panjabi)          171225    5928040 0.0289
5 Toronto Italian                    151415    5928040 0.0255
```

```
region_lang |>
  left_join(region_data, by = "region") |>
  slice_min(c(population)) |>
  slice_max(mother_tongue, n = 5) |>
  select(region, language, mother_tongue, population) |>
  mutate(prop = mother_tongue / population)
```

```
# A tibble: 5 x 5
  region     language mother_tongue population    prop
  <chr>      <chr>            <dbl>      <dbl>   <dbl>
1 Belleville English          93655     103472 0.905
2 Belleville French            2675     103472 0.0259
3 Belleville German             635     103472 0.00614
4 Belleville Dutch              600     103472 0.00580
5 Belleville Spanish            350     103472 0.00338
```

We can see a considerable difference between the proportions, with a little over 50 per cent of those in Toronto having English as their mother tongue, compared with around 90 per cent of those in Belleville.

In general, data from Canadian censuses are not as easily available through the relevant government agency as in other countries, although the Integrated Public Use Microdata Series (IPUMS), which we discuss later, provides access to some. Statistics Canada, which is the government agency that is responsible for the census and other official statistics, freely provides an "Individuals File" from the 2016 census as a Public Use Microdata File (PUMF), but only in response to request. And while it is a 2.7 per cent sample from the 2016 census, this PUMF provides limited detail.

Another way to access data from the Canadian census is to use `cancensus`. It requires an API key, which can be requested by creating an account[1] and then going to "edit profile". The package has a helper function that makes it easier to add the API key to an ".Renviron" file, which we will explain in more detail in Chapter 7.

After installing and loading `cancensus` we can use `get_census()` to get census data. We need to specify a census of interest, and a variety of other arguments. For instance, we could get data from the 2016 census about Ontario, which is the largest Canadian province by population.

```
set_api_key("ADD_YOUR_API_KEY_HERE", install = TRUE)

ontario_population <-
  get_census(
    dataset = "CA16",
    level = "Regions",
    vectors = "v_CA16_1",
    regions = list(PR = c("35"))
  )

ontario_population
```

```
# A tibble: 1 x 9
  GeoUID Type  `Region Name` `Area (sq km)` Population Dwellings Households
  <chr>  <fct> <fct>                  <dbl>      <dbl>     <dbl>      <dbl>
1 35     PR    Ontario              986722.   13448494   5598391    5169174
# i 2 more variables: C_UID <chr>, `v_CA16_1: Age Stats` <dbl>
```

Data for censuses since 1996 are available, and `list_census_datasets()` provides the metadata that we need to provide to `get_census()` to access these. Data are available based on a variety of regions, and `list_census_regions()` provides the metadata that we need. Finally, `list_census_vectors()` provides the metadata about the variables that are available.

6.3.2 United States

6.3.2.1 Census

The requirement for a census is included in the United States Constitution, although births and deaths were legally required to be registered in what became Massachusetts as early as 1639 (Gutman 1958). After installing and loading it we can use `tidycensus` to get started with access to United States census data. As with `cancensus`, we first need to obtain an API key from the Census Bureau API[2] and store it locally using a helper function.

Having set that up, we can use `get_decennial()` to obtain data on variables of interest. As an example, we could gather data about the average household size in 2010 overall, and by owner or renter, for certain states (Figure 6.2).

```
census_api_key("ADD_YOUR_API_KEY_HERE")
```

[1] https://censusmapper.ca/users/sign_up
[2] http://api.census.gov/data/key_signup.html

```
us_ave_household_size_2010 <-
  get_decennial(
    geography = "state",
    variables = c("H012001", "H012002", "H012003"),
    year = 2010
  )

us_ave_household_size_2010 |>
  filter(NAME %in% c("District of Columbia", "Utah", "Massachusetts")) |>
  ggplot(aes(y = NAME, x = value, color = variable)) +
  geom_point() +
  theme_minimal() +
  labs(
    x = "Average household size", y = "State", color = "Household type"
    ) +
  scale_color_brewer(
    palette = "Set1", labels = c("Total", "Owner occupied", "Renter occupied")
    )
```

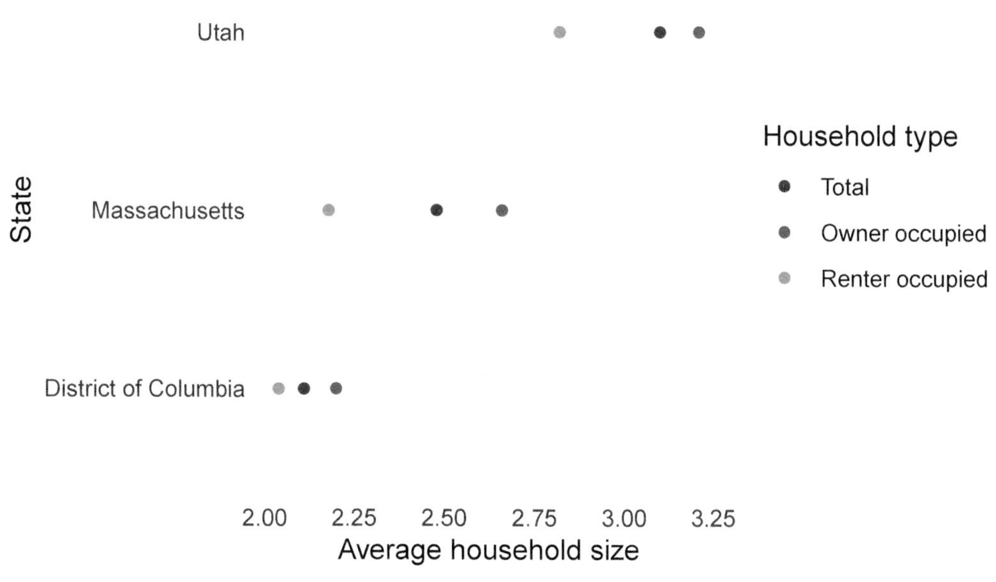

Figure 6.2: Comparing average household size in DC, Utah, and Massachusetts, by household type

Walker (2022) provides further detail about analyzing United States census data with R.

6.3.2.2 American Community Survey

The United States is in the enviable situation where there is usually a better approach than using the census and there is a better way than having to use government statistical agency websites. IPUMS provides access to a wide range of datasets, including international census microdata. In the specific case of the United States, the American Community Survey (ACS) is a survey whose content is comparable to the questions asked on many censuses, but it is available on an annual basis, compared with a census which could be quite out-of-date by the time the data are available. It ends up with millions of responses each year. Although the ACS is smaller than a census, the advantage is that it is available on a more timely basis. We access the ACS through IPUMS.

> **i Shoulders of giants**
>
> Steven Ruggles is Regents Professor of History and Population Studies at the University of Minnesota and is in charge of IPUMS. After earning a PhD in historical demography from the University of Pennsylvania in 1984, he was appointed as an assistant professor at the University of Minnesota, and promoted to full professor in 1995. The initial IPUMS data release was in 1993 (Sobek and Ruggles 1999). Since then it has grown and now includes social and economic data from many countries. Ruggles was awarded a MacArthur Foundation Fellowship in 2022.

Go to IPUMS[3], then "IPUMS USA", and click "Get Data". We are interested in a sample, so go to "SELECT SAMPLE". Un-select "Default sample from each year" and instead select "2019 ACS" and then "SUBMIT SAMPLE SELECTIONS" (Figure 6.3a).

We might be interested in data based on state. We would begin by looking at "HOUSEHOLD" variables and selecting "GEOGRAPHIC" (Figure 6.3b). We add "STATEICP" to our "cart" by clicking the plus, which will then turn into a tick (Figure 6.3c). We might then be interested in data on a "PERSON" basis, for instance, "DEMOGRAPHIC" variables such as "AGE", which we should add to our cart. We also want "SEX" and "EDUC" (both are in "PERSON").

When we are done, we can click "VIEW CART", and then click "CREATE DATA EXTRACT" (Figure 6.3d). At this point there are two aspects that we likely want to change:

1. Change the "DATA FORMAT" from ".dat" to ".dta" (Figure 6.3e).
2. Customize the sample size as we likely do not need three million responses, and could just change it to, say, 500,000 (Figure 6.3f).

Briefly check the dimensions of the request. It should not be much more than around 40MB. If it is then check whether there are variables accidentally selected that are not needed or further reduce the number of observations.

Finally, we want to include a descriptive name for the extract, for instance, "2023-05-15: State, age, sex, education", which specifies the date we made the extract and what is in the extract. After that we can click "SUBMIT EXTRACT".

We will be asked to log in or create an account, and after doing that will be able to submit the request. IPUMS will email when the extract is available, after which we can download it and read it into R in the usual way. We assume the dataset has been saved locally as "usa_00015.dta" (your dataset may have a slightly different filename).

It is critical that we cite this dataset when we use it. For instance we can use the following BibTeX entry for Ruggles et al. (2021).

```
@misc{ipumsusa,
```

[3]https://ipums.org

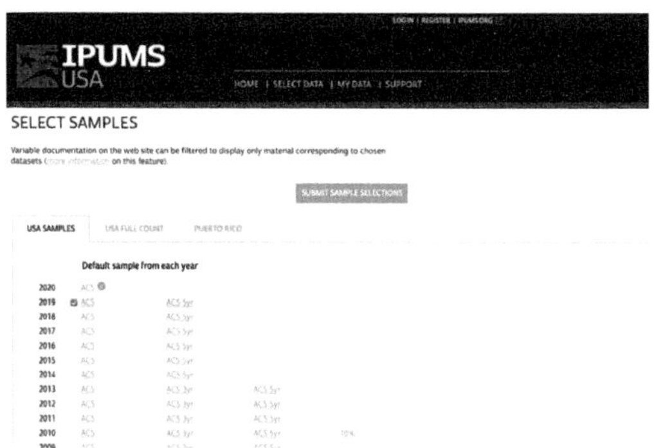

(a) Selecting a sample from IPUMS USA and specifying interest in the 2019 ACS

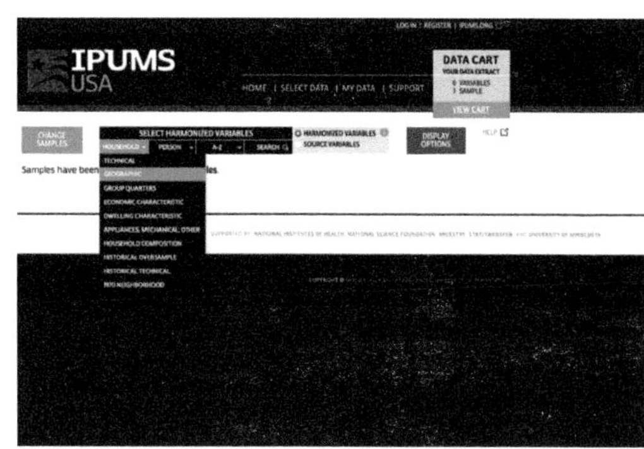

(b) Specifying that we are interested in the state

(c) Adding STATEICP to the cart

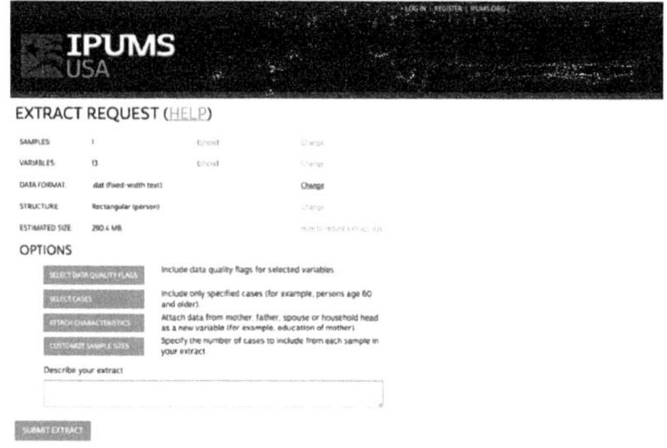

(d) Beginning the checkout process

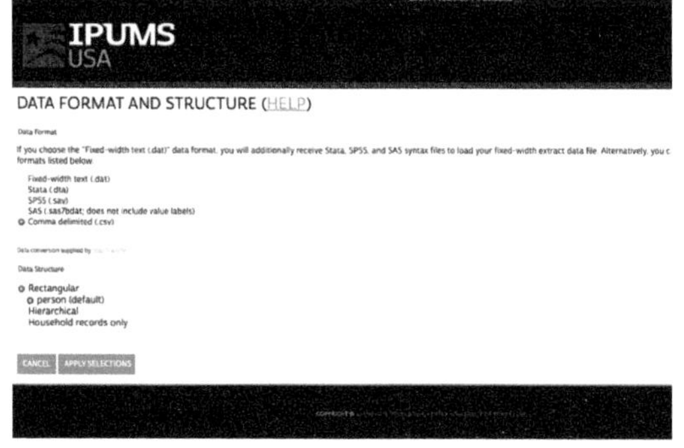

(e) Specifying that we are interested in .dta files

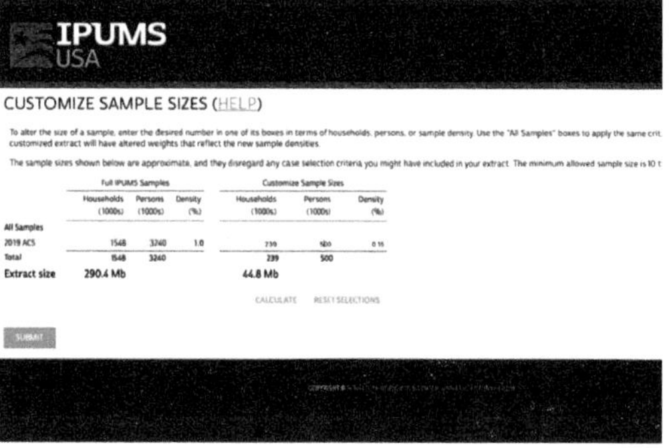

(f) Reducing the sample size from three million responses to half a million

Figure 6.3: An overview of the steps involved in getting data from IPUMS

```
  author        = {Ruggles, Steven and Flood, Sarah and $\dots$},
  year          = 2021,
  title         = {IPUMS USA: Version 11.0},
  publisher     = {Minneapolis, MN: IPUMS},
  doi           = {10.18128/d010.v11.0},
  url           = {https://usa.ipums.org},
  language      = {en},
}
```

We will briefly tidy and prepare this dataset because we will use it in Chapter 15. Our code is based on Mitrovski, Yang, and Wankiewicz (2020).

```
ipums_extract <- read_dta("usa_00015.dta")

ipums_extract <-
  ipums_extract |>
  select(stateicp, sex, age, educd) |>
  to_factor()

ipums_extract
```

```
# A tibble: 500,221 x 4
   stateicp sex    age   educd
 * <fct>    <fct>  <fct> <fct>
 1 alabama  male   77    grade 9
 2 alabama  male   62    1 or more years of college credit, no degree
 3 alabama  male   25    ged or alternative credential
 4 alabama  female 20    1 or more years of college credit, no degree
 5 alabama  male   37    1 or more years of college credit, no degree
 6 alabama  female 19    regular high school diploma
 7 alabama  female 67    regular high school diploma
 8 alabama  female 20    1 or more years of college credit, no degree
 9 alabama  male   66    grade 8
10 alabama  male   58    regular high school diploma
# i 500,211 more rows
```

```
cleaned_ipums <-
  ipums_extract |>
  mutate(age = as.numeric(age)) |>
  filter(age >= 18) |>
  rename(gender = sex) |>
  mutate(
    age_group = case_when(
      age <= 29 ~ "18-29",
      age <= 44 ~ "30-44",
      age <= 59 ~ "45-59",
      age >= 60 ~ "60+",
      TRUE ~ "Trouble"
    ),
    education_level = case_when(
```

```
      educd %in% c(
        "nursery school, preschool", "kindergarten", "grade 1",
        "grade 2", "grade 3", "grade 4", "grade 5", "grade 6",
        "grade 7", "grade 8", "grade 9", "grade 10", "grade 11",
        "12th grade, no diploma", "regular high school diploma",
        "ged or alternative credential", "no schooling completed"
      ) ~ "High school or less",
      educd %in% c(
        "some college, but less than 1 year",
        "1 or more years of college credit, no degree"
      ) ~ "Some post sec",
      educd  %in% c("associate's degree, type not specified",
                    "bachelor's degree") ~ "Post sec +",
      educd %in% c(
        "master's degree",
        "professional degree beyond a bachelor's degree",
        "doctoral degree"
      ) ~ "Grad degree",
      TRUE ~ "Trouble"
    )
  ) |>
  select(gender, age_group, education_level, stateicp) |>
  mutate(across(c(
    gender, stateicp, education_level, age_group),
    as_factor)) |>
  mutate(age_group =
           factor(age_group, levels = c("18-29", "30-44", "45-59", "60+")))

cleaned_ipums
```

```
# A tibble: 407,354 x 4
   gender age_group education_level     stateicp
   <fct>  <fct>     <fct>               <fct>
 1 male   60+       High school or less alabama
 2 male   60+       Some post sec       alabama
 3 male   18-29     High school or less alabama
 4 female 18-29     Some post sec       alabama
 5 male   30-44     Some post sec       alabama
 6 female 18-29     High school or less alabama
 7 female 60+       High school or less alabama
 8 female 18-29     Some post sec       alabama
 9 male   60+       High school or less alabama
10 male   45-59     High school or less alabama
# i 407,344 more rows
```

We will draw on this dataset in Chapter 15, so we will save it.

```
write_csv(x = cleaned_ipums,
          file = "cleaned_ipums.csv")
```

We can also have a look at some of the variables (Figure 6.4).

```
cleaned_ipums |>
  ggplot(mapping = aes(x = age_group, fill = gender)) +
  geom_bar(position = "dodge2") +
  theme_minimal() +
  labs(
    x = "Age-group of respondent",
    y = "Number of respondents",
    fill = "Education"
  ) +
  facet_wrap(vars(education_level)) +
  guides(x = guide_axis(angle = 90)) +
  theme(legend.position = "bottom") +
  scale_fill_brewer(palette = "Set1")
```

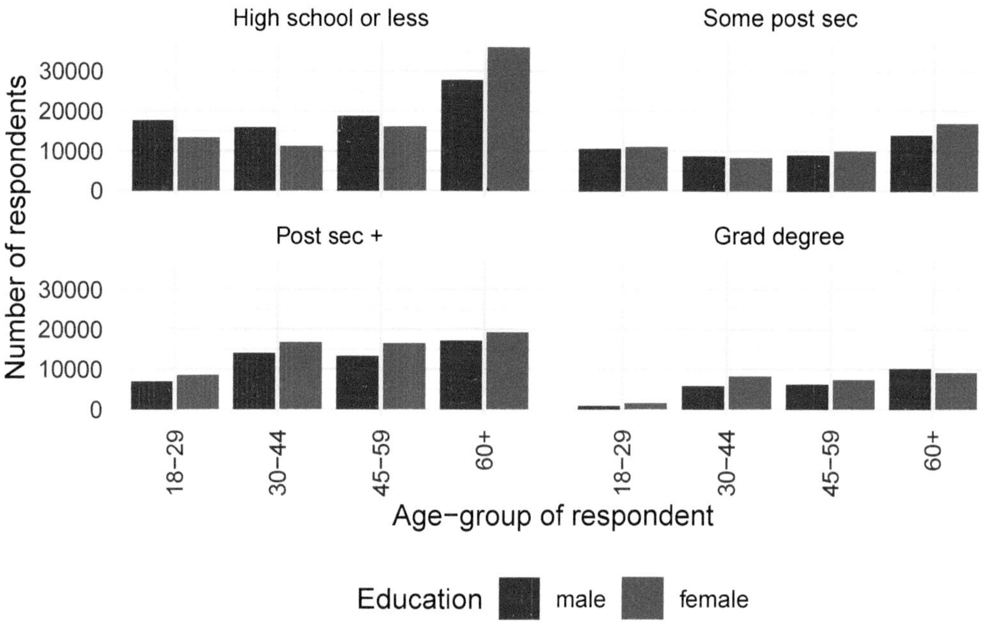

Figure 6.4: Examining counts of the IPUMS ACS sample, by age, gender and education

Full count data—that is the entire census—are available through IPUMS for United States censuses conducted between 1850 and 1940, with the exception of 1890. Most of the 1890 census records were destroyed due to a fire in 1921. One per cent samples are available for all censuses through to 1990. ACS data are available from 2000.

6.4 Sampling essentials

Statistics is at the heart of telling stories with data because it is almost never possible to get all the data that we would like. Statisticians have spent considerable time and effort thinking about the properties that various samples of data will have and how they enable us to speak to implications for the broader population.

Let us say that we have some data. For instance, a particular toddler goes to sleep at 6:00pm every night. We might be interested to know whether that bedtime is common among all toddlers, or if we have an unusual toddler. If we only had one toddler then our ability to use their bedtime to speak about all toddlers would be limited.

One approach would be to talk to friends who also have toddlers. And then talk to friends-of-friends. How many friends, and friends-of-friends, do we have to ask before we can begin to feel comfortable that we can speak about some underlying truth of toddler bedtime?

Wu and Thompson (2020, 3) describe statistics as "the science of how to collect and analyze data and draw statements and conclusions about unknown populations." Here "population" is used in a statistical sense and refers to some infinite group that we can never know exactly, but that we can use the probability distributions of random variables to describe the characteristics of. We discuss probability distributions in more detail in Chapter 12. Fisher ([1925] 1928, 41) goes further and says:

> [t]he idea of an infinite population distributed in a frequency distribution in respect of one or more characters is fundamental to all statistical work. From a limited experience,... we may obtain some idea of the infinite hypothetical population from which our sample is drawn, and so of the probable nature of future samples to which our conclusions are to be applied.

Another way to say this is that statistics involves getting some data and trying to say something sensible based on it even though we can never have all of the data.

Three pieces of critical terminology are:

- "Target population": The collection of all items about which we would like to speak.
- "Sampling frame": A list of all the items from the target population that we could get data about.
- "Sample": The items from the sampling frame that we get data about.

A target population is a finite set of labelled items, of size N. For instance, in theory we could add a label to all the books in the world: "Book 1", "Book 2", "Book 3", ..., "Book N". There is a difference between the use of the term population here, and that of everyday usage. For instance, one sometimes hears those who work with census data say that they do not need to worry about sampling because they have the whole population of the country. This is a conflation of the terms, as what they have is the sample gathered by the census of the population of a country. While the goal of a census is to get every unit—and if this was achieved then sampling error would be less of an issue—there would still be many other issues. Even if a census was done perfectly and we got data about every unit in the target population, there are still issues, for instance due to measurement error, and it being a sample at a particular time. Groves and Lyberg (2010) provide a discussion of the evolution of total survey error.

In the same way that we saw how difficult it can be to define what to measure, it can be difficult to define a target population. For instance, say we have been asked to find out about the consumption habits of university students. How can we define that target population? If someone is a student, but also works full time, then are they in the population? What about mature-aged students, who might have different responsibilities? Some aspects that we might be interested in are formally defined to an extent that is not always commonly realized. For instance, whether an area is classified as urban or rural is often formally defined by a country's statistical agency. But other aspects are less clear. Gelman, Hill, and Vehtari (2020, 24) discuss the difficulty of how we might classify someone as a "smoker". If a 15-year-old has had 100 cigarettes over their lifetime, then we need to treat them differently than if they have had none. But if a 90-year-old has had 100 cigarettes over their lifetime, then are they likely different to a 90-year-old who has had none? At what age, and number of cigarettes, do these answers change?

Consider if we want to speak to the titles of all the books ever written. Our target population is all books ever written. But it is almost impossible for us to imagine that we could get information about the title of a book that was written in the nineteenth century, but that the author locked in their desk and never told anyone about. One sampling frame could be all books in the Library of Congress Online Catalog, another could be the 25 million books that were digitized by Google (Somers 2017). Our sample may be the tens of thousands of books that are available through Project Gutenberg[4], which we will use in later chapters.

To consider another example, consider wanting to speak of the attitudes of all Brazilians who live in Germany. The target population is all Brazilians who live in Germany. One possible source of information would be Facebook and so in that case, the sampling frame might be all Brazilians who live in Germany who have Facebook. And then our sample might be all Brazilians who live in Germany who have Facebook who we can gather data about. The target population and the sampling frame will be different because not all Brazilians who live in Germany will have Facebook. And the sampling frame will be different to the sample because we will likely not be able to gather data about all Brazilians who live in Germany and have Facebook.

6.4.1 Sampling in Dublin and Reading

To be clearer, we consider two examples: a 1798 count of the number of inhabitants of Dublin, Ireland (Whitelaw 1805), and a 1912 count of working-class households in Reading, England (Bowley 1913).

6.4.1.1 Survey of Dublin in 1798

In 1798 the Reverend James Whitelaw conducted a survey of Dublin, Ireland, to count its population. Whitelaw (1805) describes how population estimates at the time varied considerably. For instance, the estimated size of London at the time ranged from 128,570 to 300,000 people. Whitelaw expected that the Lord Mayor of Dublin could compel the person in charge of each house to affix a list of the inhabitants of that house to the door, and then Whitelaw could simply use this.

[4] https://www.gutenberg.org

Instead, he found that the lists were "frequently illegible, and generally short of the actual number by a third, or even one-half". And so instead he recruited assistants, and they went door-to-door making their own counts. The resulting estimates are particularly informative (Figure 6.5). The total population of Dublin in 1798 was estimated at 182,370.

YORK-STREET.																East end, 44, 0 Feet wide. West end, 44, 6 Feet wide.
				UPPER AND MIDDLE CLASS.			SERVANTS OF DITTO.			LOWER CLASS.						
Number of Houses.	Number on Door.	State of Repair.	Stories High.	Males.	Females.	Total.	Males.	Females.	Total.	Males.	Females.	Total.	Total Males.	Total Females.	Grand Total.	NAMES AND OCCUPATIONS OF PROPRIETORS, &c.
AUNGIER-STREET.																
1	1	m	4	0	0	0	0	0	0	8	10	18	8	10	18	Elizabeth Nowlan, Haberdasher, L. H.
2	1	m	4	0	0	0	0	0	0	5	6	11	5	6	11	Lau. Birmingham, Porter-house, L. H.
3	2	n	4	1	4	5	0	1	1	0	0	0	1	5	6	George Shee.
4	3	m	2	0	0	0	0	0	0	3	4	7	3	4	7	I. Woffington, Hair-dresser.
5	4	m	2	0	0	0	0	0	0	5	7	12	5	7	12	John Maxwell, Law Scrivener. Thomas Irwin, Taylor, shop only.
6	5	n	4	1	0	1	1	1	2	0	0	0	2	1	3	P. Marsh.
7	5	n	4	3	0	3	0	1	1	0	0	0	3	1	4	Samuel Montgomery.
8	6	n	4	2	2	4	1	1	2	0	0	0	3	3	6	Mr. Cary.
9	7	n	4	4	3	7	1	2	3	0	0	0	5	5	10	George Lyndon.
10	8	n	3	1	0	1	0	2	2	0	0	0	1	2	3	Charles Fleetwood, Attorney.
11	9	n	4	1	2	3	1	1	2	0	0	0	2	3	5	Mrs. Robnet.
12	10	n	4	3	3	6	3	2	5	0	0	0	6	5	11	William Glascock, Attorney.
13	11	n	4	1	1	2	3	3	6	0	0	0	4	4	8	James Glascock, Attorney.
14	12	n	4	3	3	6	1	2	3	0	0	0	4	5	9	W. Bourne, Attorney.

Figure 6.5: Extract of the results that Whitelaw found in 1798

One aspect worth noticing is that Whitelaw includes information about class. It is difficult to know how that was determined, but it played a large role in the data collection. Whitelaw describes how the houses of "the middle and upper classes always contained some individual who was competent to the task [of making a list]". But that "among the lower class, which forms the great mass of the population of this city, the case was very different". It is difficult to see how Whitelaw could have known that without going into the houses of both upper and lower classes. But it is also difficult to imagine Whitelaw going into the houses of the upper class and counting their number. It may be that different approaches were needed.

Whitelaw attempted to construct a full sample of the inhabitants of Dublin without using much in the way of statistical machinery to guide his choices. We will now consider a second example, conducted in 1912, where they were able to start to use sampling approaches that we still use today.

6.4.1.2 Survey of working-class households in Reading in 1912

A little over one hundred years after Whitelaw (1805), Bowley (1913) was interested in counting the number of working-class households in Reading, England. Bowley selected the sample using the following procedure (Bowley 1913, 672):

> One building in ten was marked throughout the local directory in alphabetical order of streets, making about 1,950 in all. Of those about 300 were marked as shops, factories, institutions and non-residential buildings, and about 300 were found to be indexed among Principal Residents, and were so marked. The remaining 1,350 were working-class houses... [I]t was decided to take only one house in 20, rejecting the incomplete information as to the intermediate tenths. The visitors were instructed never to substitute another house for that

marked, however difficult it proved to get information, or whatever the type of house.

Bowley (1913) says that they were able to obtain information about 622 working-class households. For instance, they were able to estimate how much rent was paid each week (Figure 6.6).

The rates (excluding water) in Reading in 1912 were 8*s*. in the £. The ordinary rent is 20 per cent. more than the rateable value. The number of houses whose rent is over 30*l*. (40*l*. including rates) appears to be about 75 × 21 = 1,600 (approx.).

TABLE II.—*Working-class houses.*

Rent per week.	Number of rooms. 1.	2.	3.	4.	5.	6.	7.	8.	Totals.
2*s*. to 2*s*. 9*d*. ..	1	1	2	—	—	—	—	—	4
3*s*. „ 3*s*. 9*d*.	—	1	13	3	—	—	—	—	17
4*s*. „ 4*s*. 9*d*.....	—	—	2	21	3	1	—	—	27
5*s*. „ 5*s*. 9*d*. ..	—	—	—	70	83	1	—	—	154
6*s*. „ 6*s*. 9*d*.....	—	—	3	28	188	14	—	—	233
7*s*. „ 7*s*. 9*d*.....	—	—	—	2	80	23	3	—	108
8*s*. „ 8*s*. 9*d*.....	—	—	—	—	18	11	4	1	34
9*s*. „ 9*s*. 9*d*.....	—	—	—	—	5	2	4	1	12
10*s*. „ 10*s*. 9*d*.	—	—	—	—	1	4	4	1	10
11*s*. „ 11*s*. 9*d*.	—	—	—	—	—	3	1	1	5
12*s*.	—	—	—	—	—	1	—	—	1
Totals	1	2	20	124	378	60	16	4	605
Median rents*....	—	2/6	3/7	5/6	6/6	7/7	9/1	9/9	6/3
Median rent per room....	—	1/3	1/2	1/4½	1/3½	1/3	1/3½	1/0½	1/3

* The "median" rent is that half-way up the scale when the houses are supposed arranged in order of rent. so that the numbers above and below it are equal. Similarly with the median wage, &c., used below.

Figure 6.6: Extract of the results that Bowley found about rent paid by the working-class in Reading, England

Then, having judged from the census that there were about 18,000 households in Reading, Bowley (1913) applied a multiplier of 21 to the sample, resulting in estimates for Reading overall. The key aspect that ensures the resulting estimates are reasonable is that the sampling was done in a random way. This is why Bowley (1913) was so insistent that the visitors go to the actual house that was selected, and not substitute it for another.

6.4.2 Probabilistic sampling

Having identified a target population and a sampling frame, we need to distinguish between probability and non-probability sampling:

- "Probability sampling": Every unit in the sampling frame has some known chance of being sampled and the specific sample is obtained randomly based on these chances. The chance

of being sampled does not necessarily need to be same for each unit.
- "Non-probability sampling": Units from the sampling frame are sampled based on convenience, quotas, judgement, or other non-random processes.

Often the difference between probability and non-probability sampling is one of degree. For instance, we usually cannot forcibly obtain data, and so there is almost always an aspect of volunteering on the part of a respondent. Even when there are penalties for not providing data, such as the case for completing a census form in many countries, it is difficult for even a government to force people to fill it out completely or truthfully—famously in the 2001 New Zealand census more than one per cent of the population listed their religion as "Jedi" (Taylor 2015). The most important aspect to be clear about with probability sampling is the role of uncertainty. This allows us to make claims about the population, based on our sample, with known amounts of error. The trade-off is that probability sampling is often expensive and difficult.

We will consider four types of probability sampling:

1) simple random;
2) systematic;
3) stratified; and
4) cluster.

To add some more specificity to our discussion, in a way that is also used by Lohr ([1999] 2022, 27), it may help to consider the numbers one to 100 as our target population. With simple random sampling, every unit has the same chance of being included. In this case let us say it is 20 per cent. That means we would expect to have around 20 units in our sample, or around one in five compared with our target population.

```
set.seed(853)

illustrative_sampling <- tibble(
  unit = 1:100,
  simple_random_sampling =
    sample(x = c("In", "Out"),
           size = 100,
           replace = TRUE,
           prob = c(0.2, 0.8))
  )

illustrative_sampling |>
  count(simple_random_sampling)
```

```
# A tibble: 2 x 2
  simple_random_sampling     n
  <chr>                  <int>
1 In                        14
2 Out                       86
```

With systematic sampling, as was used by Bowley (1913), we proceed by selecting some value, and we then sample every fifth unit to obtain a 20 per cent sample. To begin, we randomly pick a starting point from units one to five, say three. And so sampling every fifth unit would mean looking at the third, the eighth, the thirteenth, and so on.

```
set.seed(853)

starting_point <- sample(x = c(1:5), size = 1)

illustrative_sampling <-
  illustrative_sampling |>
  mutate(
    systematic_sampling =
      if_else(unit %in% seq.int(from = starting_point, to = 100, by = 5),
              "In",
              "Out"
              )
    )

illustrative_sampling |>
  count(systematic_sampling)
```

```
# A tibble: 2 x 2
  systematic_sampling     n
  <chr>               <int>
1 In                     20
2 Out                    80
```

When we consider our population, it will typically have some grouping. This may be as straight forward as a country having states, provinces, counties, or statistical districts; a university having faculties and departments; and humans having age-groups. A stratified structure is one in which we can divide the population into mutually exclusive, and collectively exhaustive, sub-populations called "strata".

We use stratification to help with the efficiency of sampling or with the balance of the survey. For instance, the population of the United States is around 335 million, with around 40 million people in California and around half a million people in Wyoming. Even a survey of 10,000 responses would only expect to have 15 responses from Wyoming, which could make inference about Wyoming difficult. We could use stratification to ensure there are, say, 200 responses from each state. We could use random sampling within each state to select the person about whom data will be gathered.

In our case, we will stratify our illustration by considering that our strata are the tens, that is, one to ten is one stratum, 11 to 20 is another, and so on. We will use simple random sampling within these strata to select two units from each.

```
set.seed(853)

picked_in_strata <-
  illustrative_sampling |>
  mutate(strata = (unit - 1) %/% 10) |>
  slice_sample(n = 2, by = strata) |>
  pull(unit)
```

```
illustrative_sampling <-
  illustrative_sampling |>
  mutate(stratified_sampling =
           if_else(unit %in% picked_in_strata, "In", "Out"))

illustrative_sampling |>
  count(stratified_sampling)
```

```
# A tibble: 2 x 2
  stratified_sampling     n
  <chr>               <int>
1 In                     20
2 Out                    80
```

And finally, we can also take advantage of some clusters that may exist in our dataset. Like strata, clusters are collectively exhaustive and mutually exclusive. Our examples from earlier of states, departments, and age-groups remain valid as clusters. However, it is our intention toward these groups that is different. Specifically, with cluster sampling, we do not intend to collect data from every cluster, whereas with stratified sampling we do. With stratified sampling we look at every stratum and conduct simple random sampling within each strata to select the sample. With cluster sampling we select clusters of interest. We can then either sample every unit in those selected clusters or use simple random sampling, within the selected clusters, to select units. That all said, this difference can become less clear in practice, especially after the fact. Rose et al. (2006) gather mortality data for North Darfur, Sudan, in 2005. They find that both cluster and systematic sampling provide similar results, and they point out that systematic sampling requires less training of the survey teams. In general, cluster sampling can be cheaper because of the focus on geographically close locations.

In our case, we will cluster our illustration again based on the tens. We will use simple random sampling to select two clusters for which we will use the entire cluster.

```
set.seed(853)

picked_clusters <-
  sample(x = c(0:9), size = 2)

illustrative_sampling <-
  illustrative_sampling |>
  mutate(
    cluster = (unit - 1) %/% 10,
    cluster_sampling = if_else(cluster %in% picked_clusters, "In", "Out")
    ) |>
  select(-cluster)

illustrative_sampling |>
  count(cluster_sampling)
```

```
# A tibble: 2 x 2
  cluster_sampling     n
```

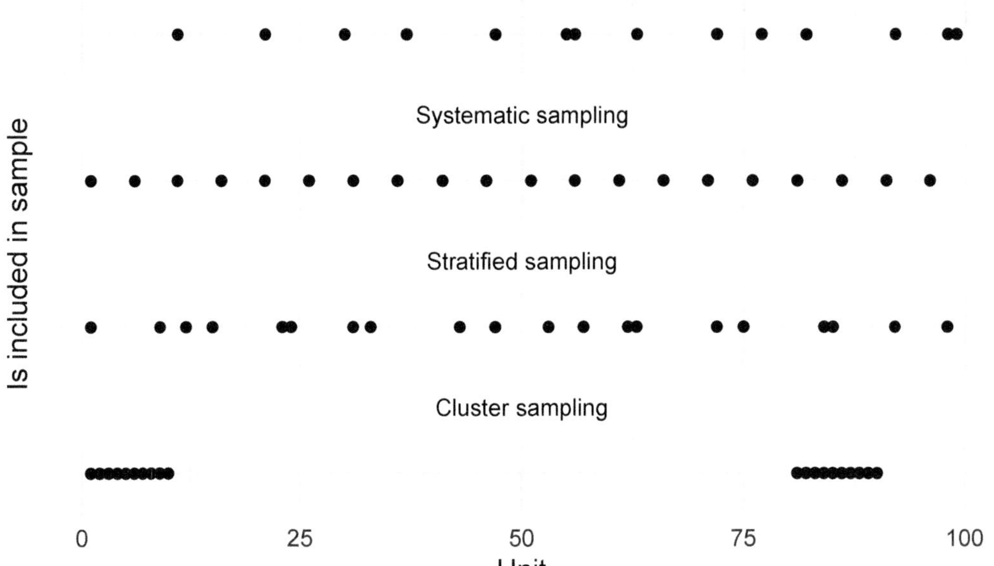

Figure 6.7: Illustrative example of simple random sampling, systematic sampling, stratified sampling, and cluster sampling over the numbers from 1 to 100

```
  <chr>            <int>
1 In                  20
2 Out                 80
```

At this point we can illustrate the differences between our approaches (Figure 6.7). We could also consider it visually, by pretending that we randomly sample using the different methods from different parts of the world (Figure 6.8).

```
new_labels <- c(
  simple_random_sampling = "Simple random sampling",
  systematic_sampling = "Systematic sampling",
  stratified_sampling = "Stratified sampling",
  cluster_sampling = "Cluster sampling"
)

illustrative_sampling_long <-
  illustrative_sampling |>
  pivot_longer(
    cols = names(new_labels), names_to = "sampling_method",
    values_to = "in_sample"
    ) |>
  mutate(sampling_method =
           factor(sampling_method,levels = names(new_labels)))

illustrative_sampling_long |>
  filter(in_sample == "In") |>
```

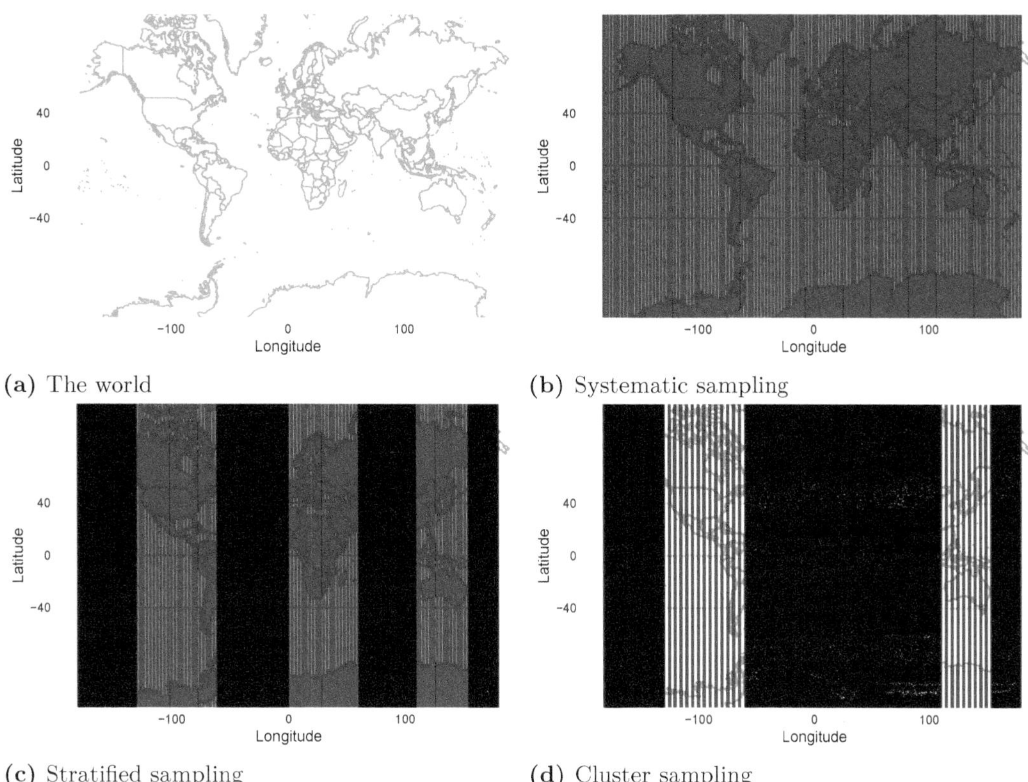

(a) The world

(b) Systematic sampling

(c) Stratified sampling

(d) Cluster sampling

Figure 6.8: Illustrative example of simple random sampling, systematic sampling, stratified sampling, and cluster sampling across different parts of the world

```
ggplot(aes(x = unit, y = in_sample)) +
geom_point() +
facet_wrap(vars(sampling_method), dir = "v", ncol = 1,
           labeller = labeller(sampling_method = new_labels)
           ) +
theme_minimal() +
labs(x = "Unit", y = "Is included in sample") +
theme(axis.text.y = element_blank())
```

Figure 6.7 and Figure 6.8 illustrate the trade-offs between the different methods, and the ways in which they will be differently appropriate. For instance, we see that systematic sampling provides a useful picture of the world in Figure 6.8, but if we were interested only in, say, only land, we would still be left with many samples that were not informative. Stratified sampling and cluster sampling enable us to focus on aspects of interest, but at the cost of a more holistic picture.

A good way to appreciate the differences between these approaches is to consider them in practice. Au (2022) provides a number of examples. One in particular is in the context of counting raptors where Fuller and Mosher (1987) compares simple random sampling, stratified sampling, systematic sampling and cluster sampling, as well as additional considerations.

6.4.2.1 Inference for probability samples

Having established our sample, we typically want to use it to make claims about the population. Neyman (1934, 561) goes further and says that "...the problem of the representative method is *par excellence* the problem of statistical estimation. We are interested in characteristics of a certain population, say π, which it is either impossible or at least very difficult to study in detail, and we try to estimate these characteristics basing our judgment on the sample."

In particular, we would typically be interested to estimate a population mean and variance. We introduced the idea of estimators, estimands, and estimates in Chapter 4. We can construct an estimator to estimate the population mean and variance. For instance, if we were using simple random sampling with a sample of size n, then the sample mean and variance (which we return to in Chapter 12) could be constructed to produce estimates of the population mean and variance:

$$\hat{\mu} = \frac{1}{n} \times \sum_{i=1}^{n} x_i$$

$$\hat{\sigma}^2 = \frac{1}{n-1} \times \sum_{i=1}^{n} (x_i - \hat{\mu})^2$$

We can use the approaches that we have used so far to simulate various types of survey designs. There are also packages that can help, including `DeclareDesign` (G. Blair et al. 2019) and `survey` (Lumley 2020).

Scaling up estimates can be used when we are interested in using a count from our sample to imply some total count for the target population. We saw this in Bowley (1913) where the ratio of the number of households in the sample, compared with the number of households known from the census, was 21 and this information was used to scale up the sample.

Table 6.2: Sum of the numbers in each sample, and implied sum of population

Sampling method	Sum of sample	Implied population sum
Systematic sampling	970	4,850
Stratified sampling	979	4,895
Cluster sampling	910	4,550
Simple random sampling	840	4,200

To consider an example, perhaps we were interested in the sum of the numbers from one to 100. Returning to our example illustrating different ways to sample from these number, we know that our samples are of size 20, and so need to be scaled up five times (Table 6.2).

The actual sum of the population is 5,050.[5] While the specifics are unique to this sample, our estimate of the population sum, based on the scaling, are revealing. The closest is stratified sample, closely followed by systematic sampling. Cluster sampling is a little over 10 per cent off, while simple random sampling is a little further away. To get close to the true sum, it is important that our sampling method gets as many of the higher values as possible. And so stratified and systematic sampling, both of which ensured that we had outcomes from

[5] We can obtain this using a trick attributed to Leonhard Euler, the eighteenth century mathematician, who noticed that the sum of one to any number can be quickly obtained by finding the middle number and then multiplying that by one plus the number. In this case, we have 50×101. Alternatively we can use R: `sum(1:100)`.

the larger numbers did particularly well. The performance of cluster and simple random sampling would depend on the particular clusters, and units, selected. In this case, stratified and systematic sampling ensured that our estimate of the sum of the population would not be too far away from the actual population sum. Here, we might think of implications for the construction and evaluation of measures, such as GDP and other constructions that are summed, and the effect on the total of the different strata based on their size.

This approach has a long history. For instance, Stigler (1986, 163) describes how by 1826 Adolphe Quetelet, the nineteenth century astronomer, had become involved in the statistical bureau, which was planning for a census. Quetelet argued that births and deaths were well known, but migration was not. He proposed an approach based on counts in specific geographies, which could then be scaled up to the whole country. The criticism of the plan focused on the difficulty of selecting appropriate geographies, which we saw also in our example of cluster sampling. The criticism was reasonable, and even today, some 200 years later, something that we should keep front of mind, (Stigler 1986):

> He [Quetelet] was acutely aware of the infinite number of factors that could affect the quantities he wished to measure, and he lacked the information that could tell him which were indeed important. He... was reluctant to group together as homogenous, data that he had reason to believe was not... To be aware of a myriad of potentially important factors, without knowing which are truly important and how their effect may be felt, is often to fear the worst... He [Quetelet] could not bring himself to treat large regions as homogeneous, [and so] he could not think of a single rate as applying to a large area.

We are able to do this scaling up when we know the population total, but if we do not know that, or we have concerns around the precision of that approach then we may use a ratio estimator.

Ratio estimators were used in 1802 by Pierre-Simon Laplace to estimate the total population of France, based on the ratio of the number of registered births, which was known throughout the country, to the number of inhabitants, which was only know for certain communes. He calculated this ratio for the three communes, and then scaled it, based on knowing the number of births across the whole country to produce an estimate of the population of France (Lohr [1999] 2022).

A ratio estimator of some population parameter is the ratio of two means. For instance, imagine that we knew the total number of hours that a toddler slept for a 30-day period, and we want to know how many hours the parents slept over that same period. We may have some information on the number of hours that a toddler sleeps overnight, x, and the number of hours their parents sleep overnight, y, over a 30-day period.

```
set.seed(853)

sleep <-
  tibble(
    toddler_sleep = sample(x = c(2:14), size = 30, replace = TRUE),
```

```
    difference = sample(x = c(0:3), size = 30, replace = TRUE),
    parent_sleep = toddler_sleep - difference
  ) |>
  select(toddler_sleep, parent_sleep, difference)

sleep
```

```
# A tibble: 30 x 3
   toddler_sleep parent_sleep difference
           <int>        <int>      <int>
 1            10            9          1
 2            11           11          0
 3            14           12          2
 4             2            0          2
 5             6            5          1
 6            14           12          2
 7             3            3          0
 8             5            3          2
 9             4            1          3
10             4            3          1
# i 20 more rows
```

The average of each is:

```
sleep |>
  summarise(
    toddler_sleep_average = mean(toddler_sleep),
    parent_sleep_average = mean(parent_sleep)
  ) |>
  kable(
    col.names = c("Toddler sleep average", "Parent sleep average"),
    format.args = list(big.mark = ","),
    digits = 2
  )
```

Toddler sleep average	Parent sleep average
6.17	4.9

The ratio of the proportion of sleep that a parent gets compared with their toddler is:

$$\hat{B} = \frac{\bar{y}}{\bar{x}} = \frac{4.9}{6.16} \approx 0.8.$$

Given the toddler slept 185 hours over that 30-day period, our estimate of the number of hours that the parents slept is $185 \times 0.8 = 148$. This turns out to be almost exactly right, as the sum is 147. In this example, the estimate was not needed because we were able to sum the data, but say some other set of parents only recorded the number of hours that their toddler slept, not how long they slept, then we could use this to estimate how much they had slept.

One variant of the ratio estimator that is commonly used is capture and recapture, which is one of the crown jewels of data gathering. It is commonly used in ecology where we know we can never gather data about all animals. Instead, a sample is captured, marked, and released. The researchers return after some time to capture another sample. Assuming enough time passes that the initially captured animals had time to integrate back into the population, but not so much time has passed that there are insurmountable concerns around births, deaths, and migration, then we can use these values to estimate a population size. The key is what proportion in this second sample have been recaptured. This proportion can be used to estimate the size of the whole population. Interestingly, in the 1990s there was substantial debate about whether to use a capture-recapture model to adjust the 1990 US census due to concerns about methodology. The combination of Breiman (1994) and Gleick (1990) provides an overview of the concerns at the time, those of censuses more generally, and helpful background on capture and recapture methods. More recently we have seen capture and recapture combined with web scraping, which we consider in Chapter 7, for the construction of survey frames (Hyman, Sartore, and Young 2021).

6.4.3 Non-probability samples

While acknowledging that it is a spectrum, much of statistics was developed based on probability sampling. But a considerable amount of modern sampling is done using non-probability sampling. One approach is to use social media and other advertisements to recruit a panel of respondents, possibly in exchange for compensation. This panel is then the group that is sent various surveys as necessary. But think for a moment about the implications of this. For instance, what type of people are likely to respond to such an advertisement? Is the richest person in the world likely to respond? Are especially young or especially old people likely to respond? In some cases, it is possible to do a census. Governments typically do one every five to ten years. But there is a reason that it is generally governments that do them—they are expensive, time-consuming, and surprisingly, they are sometimes not as accurate as we may hope because of how general they need to be.

Non-probability samples have an important role to play because they are typically cheaper and quicker to obtain than probability samples. Beaumont (2020) describes a variety of factors in favor of non-probability samples including declining response rates to probability samples, and increased demand for real-time statistics. Further, as we have discussed, the difference between probability and non-probability samples is sometimes one of degree, rather than dichotomy. Non-probability samples are legitimate and appropriate for some tasks provided one is clear about the trade-offs and ensures transparency (R. Baker et al. 2013). Low response rates mean that true probability samples are rare, and so grappling with the implications of non-probability sampling is important.

Convenience sampling involves gathering data from a sample that is easy to access. For instance, one often asks one's friends and family to fill out a survey as a way of testing it before wide-scale distribution. If we were to analyze such a sample, then we would likely be using convenience sampling.

The main concern with convenience sampling is whether it is able to speak to the broader population. There are also tricky ethical considerations, and typically a lack of anonymity which may further bias the results. On the other hand, it can be useful to cheaply get a quick sense of a situation.

Quota sampling occurs when we have strata, but we do not use random sampling within those strata to select the unit. For instance, if we again stratified the United States based on state, but then instead of ensuring that everyone in Wyoming had the chance to be chosen for that stratum, just picked people at Jackson Hole. There are some advantages to this approach, especially in terms of speed and cost, but the resulting sample may be biased in various ways. That is not to say they are without merit. For instance, the Bank of Canada runs a non-probability survey focused on the method of payment for goods and services. They use quota sampling, and various adjustment methods. This use of non-probability sampling enables them to deliberately focus on hard-to-reach aspects of the population (H. Chen, Felt, and Henry 2018).

As the saying goes, birds of a feather flock together. And we can take advantage of that in our sampling. Although Handcock and Gile (2011) describe various uses before this, and it is notoriously difficult to define attribution in multidisciplinary work, snowball sampling is nicely defined by Goodman (1961). Following Goodman (1961), to conduct snowball sampling, we first draw a random sample from the sampling frame. Each of these is asked to name k others also in the sample population, but not in that initial draw, and these form the "first stage". Each individual in the first stage is then similarly asked to name k others who are also in the sample population, but again not in the random draw or the first stage, and these form the "second stage". We need to have specified the number of stages, s, and also k ahead of time.

Respondent-driven sampling was developed by Heckathorn (1997) to focus on hidden populations, which are those where:

1) there is no sampling frame; and
2) being known to be in the sampling population could have a negative effect.

For instance, we could imagine various countries in which it would be difficult to sample from, say, the gay population or those who have had abortions. Respondent-driven sampling differs from snowball sampling in two ways:

1) In addition to compensation for their own response, as is the case with snowball sampling, respondent-driven sampling typically also involves compensation for recruiting others.
2) Respondents are not asked to provide information about others to the investigator, but instead recruit them into the study. Selection into the sample occurs not from sampling frame, but instead from the networks of those already in the sample (Salganik and Heckathorn 2004).

6.5 Exercises

Scales

1. *(Plan)* Consider the following scenario: *Every day for a year two people—Mark and Lauren—record the amount of snow that fell that day in the two different states they are from.* Please sketch what that dataset could look like and then sketch a graph that you could build to show all observations.
2. *(Simulate)* Please further consider the scenario described and simulate the situation with every variable independent of each other. Please include five tests based on the simulated data. Submit a link to a GitHub Gist that contains your code.
3. *(Acquire)* Please describe a possible source of such a dataset.

4. *(Explore)* Please use `ggplot2` to build the graph that you sketched using the data that you simulated. Submit a link to a GitHub Gist that contains your code.
5. *(Communicate)* Please write two paragraphs about what you did.

Questions

1. In at least two paragraphs, and using your own words, please define measurement error and provide an example from your own experience.
2. Imagine you take a job at a bank and they already have a dataset for you to use. What are some questions that you should explore when deciding whether that data will be useful to you?
3. With reference to Wei Chen et al. (2019) and Martínez (2022), to what extent do you think we can trust government statistics? Please write at least a page and compare at least two governments in your answer.
4. The 2021 census in Canada asked, firstly, "What was this person's sex at birth? Sex refers to sex assigned at birth. Male/Female", and then "What is this person's gender? Refers to current gender which may be different from sex assigned at birth and may be different from what is indicated on legal documents. Male/Female/Or please specify this person's gender (space for a typed or handwritten answer)". With reference to Statistics Canada (2020), please discuss the extent to which you think this is an appropriate way for the census to have proceeded. You are welcome to discuss the case of a different country if you are more familiar with that.
5. How do Kennedy et al. (2022) define ethics (pick one)?
   a. Respecting the perspectives and dignity of individual survey respondents.
   b. Generating estimates of the general population and for subpopulations of interest.
   c. Using more complicated procedures only when they serve some useful function.
6. With reference to Beaumont (2020), do you think that probability surveys will disappear, and why or why not (please write a paragraph or two)?
7. Please use IPUMS to access the 2020 ACS. Making use of the codebook, how many respondents were there in California (STATEICP) that had a Doctoral degree as their highest educational attainment (EDUC) (pick one)?
   a. 4,684
   b. 5,765
   c. 2,007
   d. 732
8. Please use IPUMS to access the 1940 1% sample. Making use of the codebook, how many respondents were there in California (STATEICP) with 5+ years of college as their highest educational attainment (EDUC) (pick one)?
   a. 1,789
   b. 1,056
   c. 532
   d. 904
9. Please name some reasons why you may wish to use cluster sampling (select all that apply)?
   a. Balance in responses.
   b. Administrative convenience.

c. Efficiency in terms of money.
d. Underlying systematic concerns.
e. Estimation of sub-populations.

10. Write R code that considers the numbers 1 to 100, and estimates the mean, based on a cluster sample of 20 numbers. Re-run this code one hundred times, noting the estimate of the mean each time, and then plot the histogram. What do you notice about the graph? Add a paragraph of explanation and discussion.

Tutorial

Pick one of the following options. Use Quarto, and include an appropriate title, author, date, and citations. Submit a PDF. Please write at least two pages.

1. With reference to Dean (2022), please discuss the difference between probability and non-probability sampling.
2. With reference to Daston (2000), please discuss whether GDP and counts of population are invented or discovered?
3. With reference to Meng (2018), please discuss the claim: "When you have one million responses, you do not need to worry about randomization".
4. With reference to Gargiulo (2022), please discuss challenges of measurement in the real world.

7

Gather data

Prerequisites

- Read *Turning History into Data: Data Collection, Measurement, and Inference in HPE*, (Cirone and Spirling 2021)
  - This paper discusses some of the challenges of creating datasets.
- Read *Two Regimes of Prison Data Collection*, (K. Johnson 2021)
  - This paper compares data about prisons from the United States government with data from incarcerated people and the community.
- Read *Atlas of AI*, (Crawford 2021)
  - Focus on Chapter 3 "Data", which discusses the importance of understanding the sources of data.

Key concepts and skills

- Sometimes data are available but they are not necessarily put together for the purposes of being a dataset. We must gather the data.
- It can be cumbersome and annoying to must clean and prepare the datasets that come from these unstructured sources but the resulting structured, tidy data are often especially exciting and useful.
- We can gather data from a variety of sources. This includes APIs, both directly, which may involve semi-structured data, and indirectly through R packages. We can also gather data through reasonable and ethical web scraping. Finally, we may wish to gather data from PDFs.

Software and packages

- Base R (R Core Team 2023)
- `babynames` (Wickham 2021a)
- `gh` (Bryan and Wickham 2021)
- `here` (Müller 2020)
- `httr` (Wickham 2023b)
- `janitor` (Firke 2023)
- `jsonlite` (Ooms 2014)
- `knitr` (Xie 2023)
- `lubridate` (Grolemund and Wickham 2011)
- `pdftools` (Ooms 2022b)
- `purrr` (Wickham and Henry 2022)
- `rvest` (Wickham 2022b)
- `spotifyr` (Thompson et al. 2022)
- `tesseract` (Ooms 2022d)
- `tidyverse` (Wickham et al. 2019)
- `usethis` (Wickham, Bryan, and Barrett 2022)
- `xml2` (Wickham, Hester, and Ooms 2021)

```
library(babynames)
library(gh)
library(here)
library(httr)
library(janitor)
library(jsonlite)
library(knitr)
library(lubridate)
library(pdftools)
library(purrr)
library(rvest)
library(spotifyr)
library(tesseract)
library(tidyverse)
library(usethis)
library(xml2)
```

7.1 Introduction

In this chapter we consider data that we must gather ourselves. This means that although the observations exist, we must parse, pull, clean, and prepare them to get the dataset that we will consider. In contrast to farmed data, discussed in Chapter 6, often these observations are not being made available for the purpose of analysis. This means that we need to be especially concerned with documentation, inclusion and exclusion decisions, missing data, and ethical behavior.

As an example of such a dataset, consider Cummins (2022) who create a dataset using individual-level probate records from England between 1892 and 1992. They find that about one-third of the inheritance of "elites" is concealed. Similarly, Taflaga and Kerby (2019) construct a systematic dataset of job responsibilities based on Australian Ministerial telephone directories. They find substantial differences by gender. Neither wills nor telephone directories were created for the purpose of being included in a dataset. But with a respectful approach they enable insights that we could not get by other means. We term this "data gathering"—the data exist but we need to get them.

Decisions need to be made at the start of a project about the values we want the project to have. For instance, Saulnier et al. (2022) value transparency, reproducibility, fairness, being self-critical, and giving credit. How might that affect the project? Valuing "giving credit" might mean being especially zealous about attribution and licensing. In the case of gathered data we should give special thought to this as the original, unedited data may not be ours.

The results of a data science workflow cannot be better than their underlying data (Bailey 2008). Even the most-sophisticated statistical analysis will struggle to adjust for poorly-gathered data. This means when working in a team, data gathering should be overseen and at least partially conducted by senior members of the team. And when working by yourself, try to give special consideration and care to this stage.

In this chapter we go through a variety of approaches for gathering data. We begin with the use of APIs and semi-structured data, such as JSON and XML. Using an API is typically a situation in which the data provider has specified the conditions under which they are comfortable providing access. An API allows us to write code to gather data. This is valuable because it can be efficient and scales well. Developing comfort with gathering data through APIs enables access to exciting datasets. For instance, Wong (2020) use the Facebook Political Ad API to gather 218,100 of the Trump 2020 campaign ads to better understand the campaign.

We then turn to web scraping, which we may want to use when there are data available on a website. As these data have typically not been put together for the purposes of being a dataset, it is especially important to have deliberate and definite values for the project. Scraping is a critical part of data gathering because there are many data sources where the priorities of the data provider mean they have not implemented an API. For instance, considerable use of web scraping was critical for creating COVID-19 dashboards in the early days of the pandemic (Eisenstein 2022).

Finally, we consider gathering data from PDFs. This enables the construction of interesting datasets, especially those contained in government reports and old books. Indeed, while freedom of information legislation exists in many countries and require the government to make data available, these all too often result in spreadsheets being shared as PDFs, even when they were a CSV to begin with.

Gathering data can require more of us than using farmed data, but it allows us to explore datasets and answer questions that we could not otherwise. Some of the most exciting work in the world uses gathered data, but it is especially important that we approach it with respect.

7.2 APIs

In everyday language, and for our purposes, an Application Programming Interface (API) is a situation in which someone has set up specific files on their computer such that we can follow their instructions to get them. For instance, when we use a gif on Slack, one way it could work in the background is that Slack asks Giphy's server for the appropriate gif, Giphy's server gives that gif to Slack, and then Slack inserts it into the chat. The way in which Slack and Giphy interact is determined by Giphy's API. More strictly, an API is an application that runs on a server that we access using the HTTP protocol.

Here we focus on using APIs for gathering data. In that context an API is a website that is set up for another computer to be able to access it, rather than a person. For instance, we could go to Google Maps[1]. And we could then scroll and click and drag to center the map on, say, Canberra, Australia. Or we could paste this link[2] into the browser. By pasting that link, rather than navigating, we have mimicked how we will use an API: provide a URL and be given something back. In this case the result should be a map like Figure 7.1.

The advantage of using an API is that the data provider usually specifies the data that they are willing to provide, and the terms under which they will provide it. These terms may include aspects such as rate limits (i.e. how often we can ask for data), and what we can

[1] https://www.google.com/maps

[2] https://www.google.com/maps/@-35.2812958,149.1248113,16z

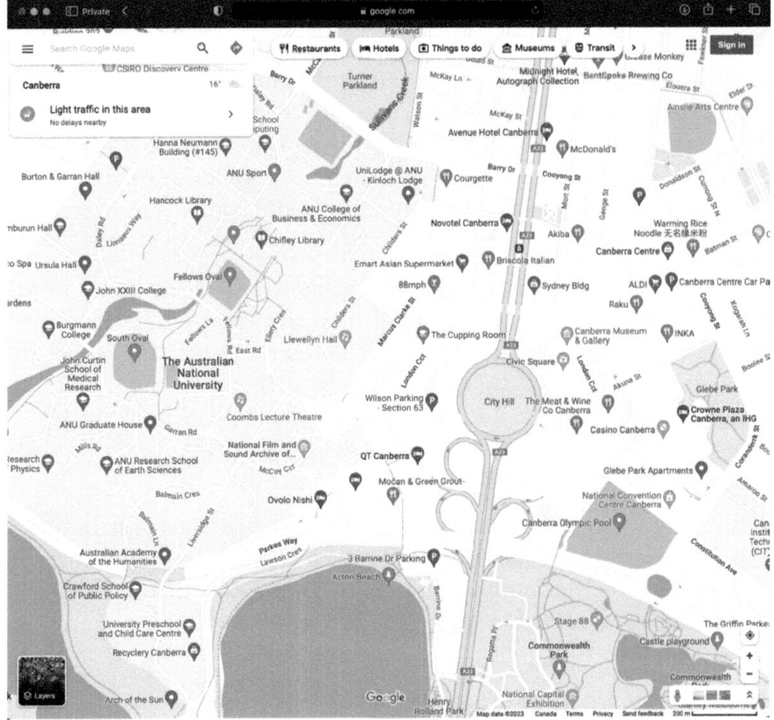

Figure 7.1: Example of an API response from Google Maps, as of 12 February 2023

do with the data, for instance, we might not be allowed to use it for commercial purposes, or to republish it. As the API is being provided specifically for us to use it, it is less likely to be subject to unexpected changes or legal issues. Because of this it is clear that when an API is available, we should try to use it rather than web scraping.

We will now go through a few case studies of using APIs. In the first we deal directly with an API using `httr`. And then we access data from Spotify using `spotifyr`.

7.2.1 arXiv, NASA, and Dataverse

After installing and loading `httr` we use `GET()` to obtain data from an API directly. This will try to get some specific data and the main argument is "url". This is similar to the Google Maps example in Figure 7.1 where the specific information that we were interested in was a map.

7.2.1.1 arXiv

In this case study we will use an API provided by arXiv[3]. arXiv is an online repository for academic papers before they go through peer review. These papers are typically referred to as "pre-prints". We use `GET()` to ask arXiv to obtain some information about a pre-print by providing a URL.

[3] https://arxiv.org/help/api/

```
arxiv <- GET("http://export.arxiv.org/api/query?id_list=2111.09299")

status_code(arxiv)
```

```
[1] 200
```

We can use `status_code()` to check our response. For instance, 200 means a success, while 400 means we received an error from the server. Assuming we received something back from the server, we can use `content()` to display it. In this case we have received XML formatted data. XML is a markup language where entries are identified by tags, which can be nested within other tags. After installing and loading `xml2` we can read XML using `read_xml()`. XML is a semi-formatted structure, and it can be useful to start by having a look at it using `html_structure()`.

```
content(arxiv) |>
  read_xml() |>
  html_structure()
```

We might like to create a dataset based on extracting various aspects of this XML tree. For instance, we might look at "entry", which is the eighth item, and in particular obtain the "title" and the "URL", which are the fourth and ninth items, respectively, within "entry".

```
data_from_arxiv <-
  tibble(
    title = content(arxiv) |>
      read_xml() |>
      xml_child(search = 8) |>
      xml_child(search = 4) |>
      xml_text(),
    link = content(arxiv) |>
      read_xml() |>
      xml_child(search = 8) |>
      xml_child(search = 9) |>
      xml_attr("href")
  )
```

7.2.1.2 NASA Astronomy Picture of the Day

To consider another example, each day, NASA provides the Astronomy Picture of the Day (APOD) through its APOD API[4]. We can use `GET()` to obtain the URL for the photo on particular dates and then display it.

```
NASA_APOD_20190719 <-
  GET("https://api.nasa.gov/planetary/apod?api_key=DEMO_KEY&date=2019-07-19")
```

Examining the returned data using `content()`, we can see that we are provided with various fields, such as date, title, explanation, and a URL.

[4] https://api.nasa.gov

For reasons of space withhold the output here, but it can be seen on the free, online version of this book[5].

```
# APOD July 19, 2019
content(NASA_APOD_20190719)$date
content(NASA_APOD_20190719)$title
content(NASA_APOD_20190719)$explanation
content(NASA_APOD_20190719)$url
```

7.2.1.3 Dataverse

Finally, another common API response in semi-structured form is JSON. JSON is a human-readable way to store data that can be parsed by machines. In contrast to, say, a CSV, where we are used to rows and columns, JSON uses key-value pairs.

```
{
  "firstName": "Rohan",
  "lastName": "Alexander",
  "age": 36,
  "favFoods": {
    "first": "Pizza",
    "second": "Bagels",
    "third": null
  }
}
```

We can parse JSON with `jsonlite`. To consider a specific example, we use a "Dataverse" which is a web application that makes it easier to share datasets. We can use an API to query a demonstration dataverse. For instance, we might be interested in datasets related to politics.

```
politics_datasets <-
  fromJSON("https://demo.dataverse.org/api/search?q=politics")
```

We could look at the dataset using `View(politics_datasets)`, which would allow us to expand the tree based on what we are interested in. We can even get the code that we need to focus on different aspects by hovering on the item and then clicking the icon with the green arrow (Figure 7.2).

This tells us how to obtain the dataset of interest.

```
as_tibble(politics_datasets[["data"]][["items"]])
```

7.2.2 Spotify

Sometimes there is an R package built around an API and allows us to interact with it in ways that are similar what we have seen before. For instance, `spotifyr` is a wrapper around

[5]https://tellingstorieswithdata.com

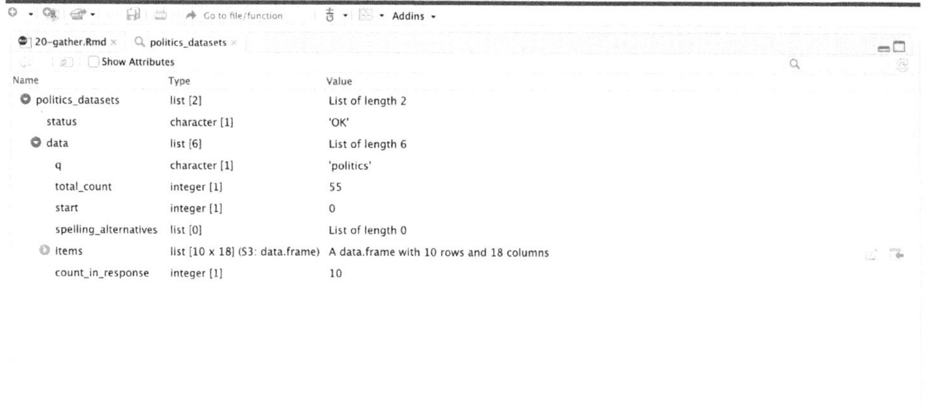

Figure 7.2: Example of hovering over a JSON element, "items", where the icon with a green arrow can be clicked on to get the code that would focus on that element

the Spotify API. When using APIs, even when they are wrapped in an R package, in this case `spotifyr`, it is important to read the terms under which access is provided.

To access the Spotify API, we need a Spotify Developer Account[6]. This is free but will require logging in with a Spotify account and then accepting the Developer Terms (Figure 7.3).

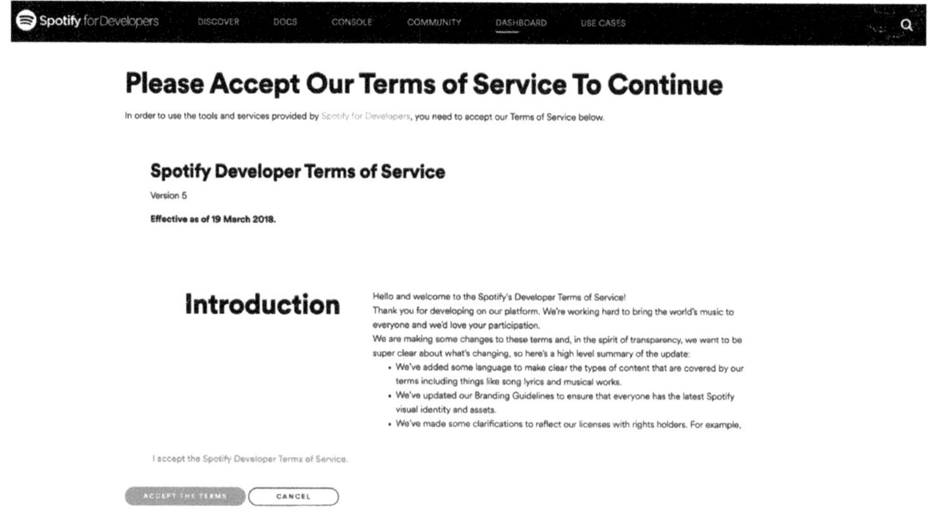

Figure 7.3: Spotify Developer Account Terms agreement page

Continuing with the registration process, in our case, we "do not know" what we are building and so Spotify requires us to use a non-commercial agreement which is fine. To use the Spotify API we need a "Client ID" and a "Client Secret". These are things that we want to keep to ourselves because otherwise anyone with the details could use our developer account as though they were us. One way to keep these details secret with minimum hassle is to keep

[6]https://developer.spotify.com/dashboard/

them in our "System Environment". In this way, when we push to GitHub they should not be included. To do this we will load and use `usethis` to modify our System Environment. In particular, there is a file called ".Renviron" which we will open and then add our "Client ID" and "Client Secret".

```
edit_r_environ()
```

When we run `edit_r_environ()`, a ".Renviron" file will open and we can add our "Spotify Client ID" and "Client Secret". Use the same names, because `spotifyr` will look in our environment for keys with those specific names. Being careful to use single quotes is important here even though we normally use double quotes in this book.

```
SPOTIFY_CLIENT_ID = 'PUT_YOUR_CLIENT_ID_HERE'
SPOTIFY_CLIENT_SECRET = 'PUT_YOUR_SECRET_HERE'
```

Save the ".Renviron" file, and then restart R: "Session" → "Restart R". We can now use our "Spotify Client ID" and "Client Secret" as needed. And functions that require those details as arguments will work without them being explicitly specified again.

To try this out we install and load `spotifyr`. We will get and save some information about Radiohead, the English rock band, using `get_artist_audio_features()`. One of the required arguments is `authorization`, but as that is set, by default, to look at the ".Renviron" file, we do not need to specify it here.

```
radiohead <- get_artist_audio_features("radiohead")
saveRDS(radiohead, "radiohead.rds")
```

```
radiohead <- readRDS("radiohead.rds")
```

There is a variety of information available based on songs. We might be interested to see whether their songs are getting longer over time (Figure 7.4). Following the guidance in Chapter 5 this is a nice opportunity to additionally use a boxplot to communicate summary statistics by album at the same time.

```
radiohead <- as_tibble(radiohead)

radiohead |>
  mutate(album_release_date = ymd(album_release_date)) |>
  ggplot(aes(
    x = album_release_date,
    y = duration_ms,
    group = album_release_date
  )) +
  geom_boxplot() +
  geom_jitter(alpha = 0.5, width = 0.3, height = 0) +
  theme_minimal() +
  labs(
    x = "Album release date",
    y = "Duration of song (ms)"
```

```
)
```

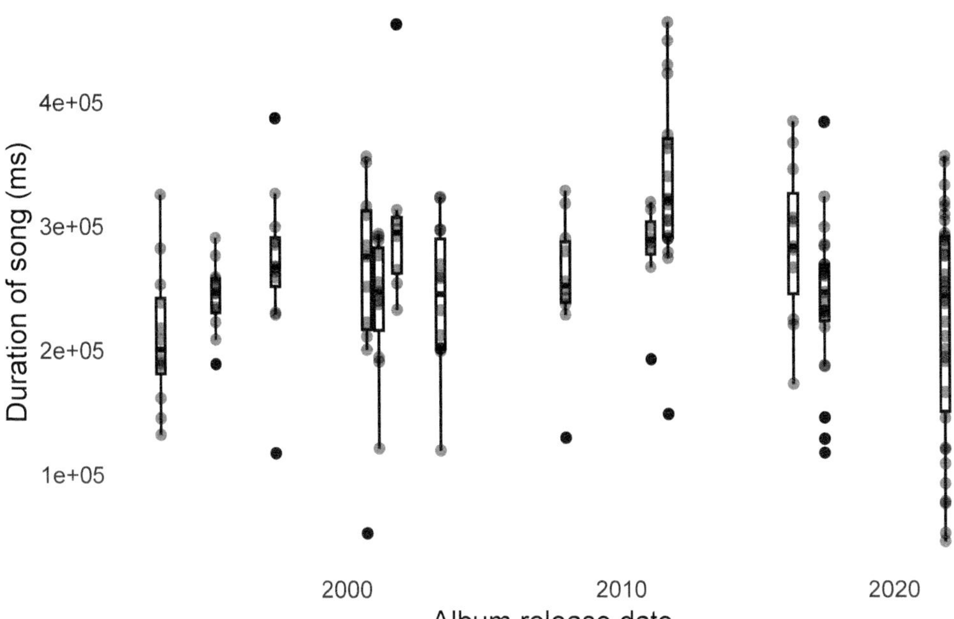

Figure 7.4: Length of each Radiohead song, over time, as gathered from Spotify

One interesting variable provided by Spotify about each song is "valence". The Spotify documentation[7] describes this as a measure between zero and one that signals "the musical positiveness" of the track with higher values being more positive. We might be interested to compare valence over time between a few artists, for instance, Radiohead, the American rock band The National, and the American singer Taylor Swift.

First, we need to gather the data.

```
taylor_swift <- get_artist_audio_features("taylor swift")
the_national <- get_artist_audio_features("the national")

saveRDS(taylor_swift, "taylor_swift.rds")
saveRDS(the_national, "the_national.rds")
```

Then we can bring them together and make the graph (Figure 7.5). This appears to show that while Taylor Swift and Radiohead have largely maintained their level of valence over time, The National has decreased theirs.

```
rbind(taylor_swift, the_national, radiohead) |>
  select(artist_name, album_release_date, valence) |>
  mutate(album_release_date = ymd(album_release_date)) |>
  ggplot(aes( x = album_release_date, y = valence, color = artist_name)) +
```

[7] https://developer.spotify.com/documentation/web-api/reference/#/operations/get-audio-features

```
  geom_point(alpha = 0.3) +
  geom_smooth() +
  theme_minimal() +
  facet_wrap(facets = vars(artist_name), dir = "v") +
  labs(
    x = "Album release date",
    y = "Valence",
    color = "Artist"
  ) +
  scale_color_brewer(palette = "Set1") +
  theme(legend.position = "bottom")
```

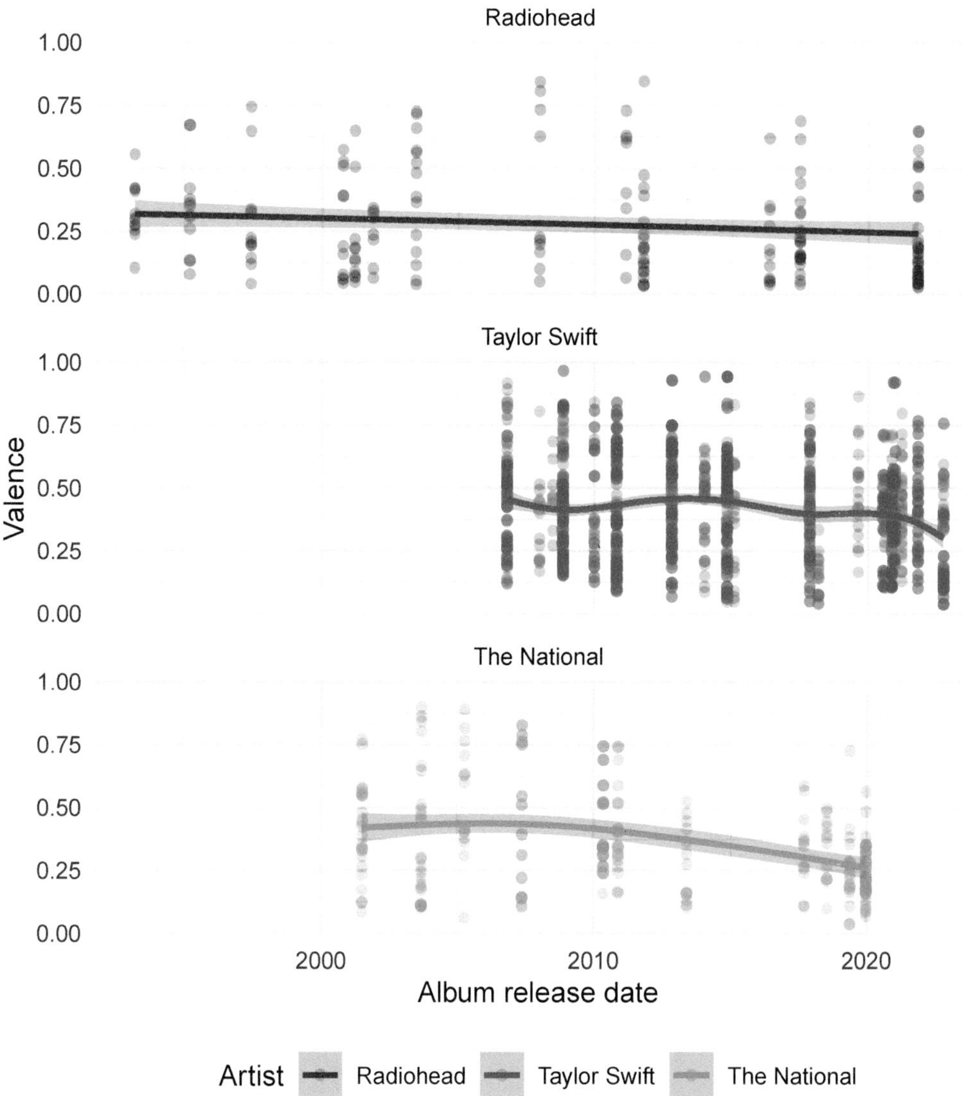

Figure 7.5: Comparing valence, over time, for Radiohead, Taylor Swift, and The National

How amazing that we live in a world where all that information is available with very little effort or cost! And having gathered the data, there is a lot that could be done. For instance, Pavlik (2019) uses an expanded dataset to classify musical genres and The Economist (2022a) looks at how language is associated with music streaming on Spotify. Our ability to gather such data enables us to answer questions that had to be considered experimentally in the past. For instance, Salganik, Dodds, and Watts (2006) had to use experimental data to analyze the social aspect of what makes a hit song, rather than the observational data we can now access.

That said, it is worth thinking about what valence is purporting to measure. Little information is available in the Spotify documentation how it was created. It is doubtful that one number can completely represent how positive is a song. And what about the songs from these artists that are not on Spotify, or even publicly released? This is a nice example of how measurement and sampling pervade all aspects of telling stories with data.

7.3 Web scraping

7.3.1 Principles

Web scraping is a way to get data from websites. Rather than going to a website using a browser and then saving a copy of it, we write code that does it for us. This opens a lot of data to us, but on the other hand, it is not typically data that are being made available for these purposes. This means that it is especially important to be respectful. While generally not illegal, the specifics about the legality of web scraping depend on jurisdictions and what we are doing, and so it is also important to be mindful. Even if our use is not commercially competitive, of particular concern is the conflict between the need for our work to be reproducible with the need to respect terms of service that may disallow data republishing (Luscombe, Dick, and Walby 2021).

Privacy often trumps reproducibility. There is also a considerable difference between data being publicly available on a website and being scraped, cleaned, and prepared into a dataset which is then publicly released. For instance, Kirkegaard and Bjerrekær (2016) scraped publicly available OKCupid profiles and then made the resulting dataset easily available (Hackett 2016). Zimmer (2018) details some of the important considerations that were overlooked including "minimizing harm", "informed consent", and ensuring those in the dataset maintain "privacy and confidentiality". While it is correct to say that OKCupid made data public, they did so in a certain context, and when their data was scraped that context was changed.

Oh, you think we have good data on that!

Police violence is particularly concerning because of the need for trust between the police and society. Without good data it is difficult to hold police departments accountable, or know whether there is an issue, but getting data is difficult (Thomson-DeVeaux, Bronner, and Sharma 2021). The fundamental problem is that there is no way to easily simplify an encounter that results in violence into a dataset. Two popular datasets draw on web scraping:

1) "Mapping Police Violence"; and
2) "Fatal Force Database".

Bor et al. (2018) use "Mapping Police Violence" to examine police killings of Black Americans, especially when unarmed, and find a substantial effect on the mental health of Black Americans. Responses to the paper, such as Nix and Lozada (2020), have special concern with the coding of the dataset, and after re-coding draw different conclusions. An example of a coding difference is the unanswerable question, because it depends on context and usage, of whether to code an individual who was killed with a toy firearm as "armed" or "unarmed". We may want a separate category, but some simplification is necessary for the construction of a quantitative dataset. *The Washington Post* writes many articles using the "Fatal Force Database" (The Washington Post 2023). Jenkins et al. (2022) describes their methodology and the challenges of standardization. Comer and Ingram (2022) compare the datasets and find similarities, but document ways in which the datasets are different.

Web scraping is an invaluable source of data. But they are typically datasets that can be created as a by-product of someone trying to achieve another aim. And web scraping imposes a cost on the website host, and so we should reduce this to the extent possible. For instance, a retailer may have a website with their products and their prices. That has not been created deliberately as a source of data, but we can scrape it to create a dataset. The following principles may be useful to guide web scraping.

1. Avoid it. Try to use an API wherever possible.
2. Abide by their desires. Some websites have a "robots.txt" file that contains information about what they are comfortable with scrapers doing. In general, if it exists, a "robots.txt" file can be accessed by appending "robots.txt" to the base URL. For instance, the "robots.txt" file for https://www.google.com, can be accessed at https://www.google.com/robots.txt. Note if there are folders listed against "Disallow:". These are the folders that the website would not like to be scraped. And also note any instances of "Crawl-delay:". This is the number of seconds the website would like you to wait between visits.
3. Reduce the impact.
    1. Slow down the scraper, for instance, rather than having it visit the website every second, slow it down using `sys.sleep()`. If you only need a few hundred files, then why not just have it visit the website a few times a minute, running in the background overnight?
    2. Consider the timing of when you run the scraper. For instance, if you are scraping a retailer then maybe set the script to run from 10pm through to the morning, when fewer customers are likely using the site. Similarly, if it is

a government website and they have a regular monthly release, then it might be polite to avoid that day.

4. Take only what is needed. For instance, you do not need to scrape the entirety of Wikipedia if all you need is the names of the ten largest cities in Croatia. This reduces the impact on the website, and allows us to more easily justify our actions.
5. Only scrape once. This means you should save everything as you go so that you do not have to re-collect data when the scraper inevitably fails at some point. For instance, you will typically spend a lot of time getting a scraper working on one page, but typically the page structure will change at some point and the scraper will need to be updated. Once you have the data, you should save that original, unedited data separately to the modified data. If you need data over time then you will need to go back, but this is different than needlessly re-scraping a page.
6. Do not republish the pages that were scraped (this contrasts with datasets that you create from it).
7. Take ownership and ask permission if possible. At a minimum all scripts should have contact details in them. Depending on the circumstances, it may be worthwhile asking for permission before you scrape.

7.3.2 HTML/CSS essentials

Web scraping is possible by taking advantage of the underlying structure of a webpage. We use patterns in the HTML/CSS to get the data that we want. To look at the underlying HTML/CSS we can either:

1) open a browser, right-click, and choose something like "Inspect"; or
2) save the website and then open it with a text editor rather than a browser.

HTML/CSS is a markup language based on matching tags. If we want text to be bold, then we would use something like:

```
<b>My bold text</b>
```

Similarly, if we want a list, then we start and end the list as well as indicating each item.

```
<ul>
  <li>Learn webscraping</li>
  <li>Do data science</li>
  <li>Profit</li>
</ul>
```

When scraping we will search for these tags.

To get started, we can pretend that we obtained some HTML from a website, and that we want to get the name from it. We can see that the name is in bold, so we want to focus on that feature and extract it.

```
website_extract <- "<p>Hi, I’m <b>Rohan</b> Alexander.</p>"
```

rvest is part of the tidyverse so it does not have to be installed, but it is not part of the core, so it does need to be loaded. After that, use read_html() to read in the data.

```
rohans_data <- read_html(website_extract)

rohans_data
```

```
{html_document}
<html>
[1] <body><p>Hi, I'm <b>Rohan</b> Alexander.</p></body>
```

The language used by rvest to look for tags is "node", so we focus on bold nodes. By default html_elements() returns the tags as well. We extract the text with html_text().

```
rohans_data |>
  html_elements("b")
```

```
{xml_nodeset (1)}
[1] <b>Rohan</b>
```

```
rohans_data |>
  html_elements("b") |>
  html_text()
```

```
[1] "Rohan"
```

Web scraping is an exciting source of data, and we will now go through some examples. But in contrast to these examples, information is not usually all on one page. Web scraping quickly becomes a difficult art form that requires a lot of practice. For instance, we distinguish between an index scrape and a contents scrape. The former is scraping to build the list of URLs that have the content you want, while the latter is to get the content from those URLs. An example is provided by Luscombe, Duncan, and Walby (2022). If you end up doing a lot of web scraping, then polite (Perepolkin 2022) may be helpful to better optimize your workflow. And using GitHub Actions to allow for larger and slower scrapes over time.

7.3.3 Book information

In this case study we will scrape a list of books available here[8]. We will then clean the data and look at the distribution of the first letters of author surnames. It is slightly more complicated than the example above, but the underlying workflow is the same: download the website, look for the nodes of interest, extract the information, and clean it.

We use rvest to download a website, and to then navigate the HTML to find the aspects that we are interested in. And we use the tidyverse to clean the dataset. We first need to go to the website and then save a local copy.

---

[8]https://rohansbooks.com

```
books_data <- read_html("https://rohansbooks.com")

write_html(books_data, "raw_data.html")
```

We need to navigate the HTML to get the aspects that we want. And then try to get the data into a tibble as quickly as possible because this will allow us to more easily use `dplyr` verbs and other functions from the `tidyverse`.

See "R essentials"[9] if this is unfamiliar to you.

```
books_data <- read_html("raw_data.html")
```

```
books_data
```

```
{html_document}
<html>
[1] <head>\n<meta http-equiv="Content-Type" content="text/html; charset=UTF-8 ...
[2] <body>\n    <h1>Books</h1>\n\n    <p>\n      This is a list of books that ...
```

To get the data into a tibble we first need to use HTML tags to identify the data that we are interested in. If we look at the website then we know we need to focus on list items (Figure 7.6a). And we can look at the source, focusing particularly on looking for a list (Figure 7.6b).

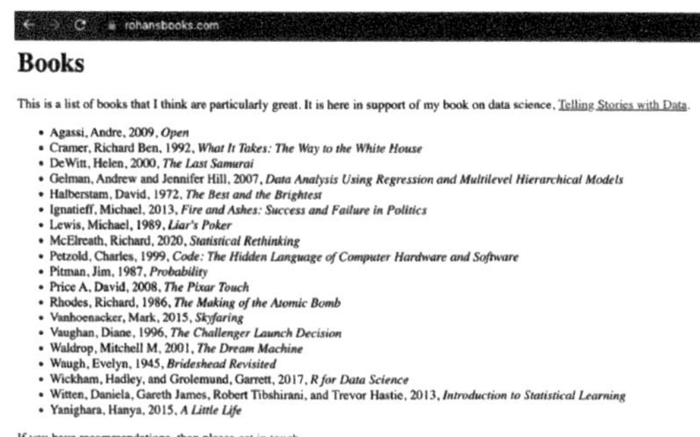

(**a**) Books website as displayed

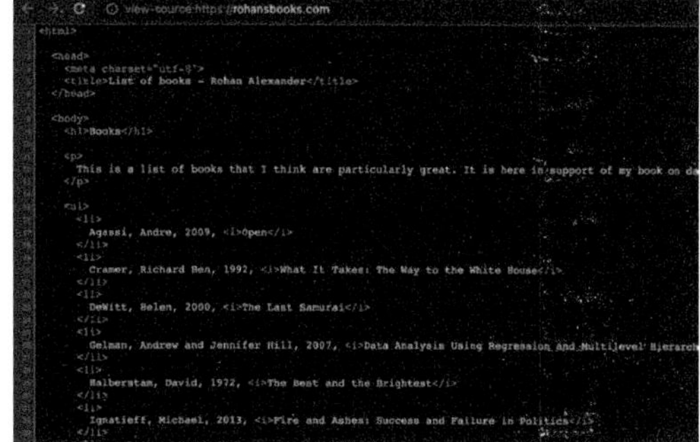

(**b**) HTML for the top of the books website and the list of books

Figure 7.6: Screen captures from the books website as at 16 June 2022

The tag for a list item is "li", so we can use that to focus on the list.

```
text_data <-
  books_data |>
  html_elements("li") |>
  html_text()

all_books <-
  tibble(books = text_data)
```

[9] https://tellingstorieswithdata.com/20-r_essentials.html

```
head(all_books)
```

```
# A tibble: 6 x 1
  books
  <chr>
1 "\n          Agassi, Andre, 2009, Open\n          "
2 "\n          Cramer, Richard Ben, 1992, What It Takes: The Way to the White Hou~
3 "\n          DeWitt, Helen, 2000, The Last Samurai\n          "
4 "\n          Gelman, Andrew and Jennifer Hill, 2007, Data Analysis Using Regres~
5 "\n          Halberstam, David, 1972, The Best and the Brightest\n          "
6 "\n          Ignatieff, Michael, 2013, Fire and Ashes: Success and Failure in P~
```

We now need to clean the data. First we want to separate the title and the author using `separate()` and then clean up the author and title columns. We can take advantage of the fact that the year is present and separate based on that.

```
all_books <-
  all_books |>
  mutate(books = str_squish(books)) |>
  separate(books, into = c("author", "title"), sep = "\\, [[:digit:]]{4}\\, ")

head(all_books)
```

```
# A tibble: 6 x 2
  author                           title
  <chr>                            <chr>
1 Agassi, Andre                    Open
2 Cramer, Richard Ben              What It Takes: The Way to the White House
3 DeWitt, Helen                    The Last Samurai
4 Gelman, Andrew and Jennifer Hill Data Analysis Using Regression and Multileve~
5 Halberstam, David                The Best and the Brightest
6 Ignatieff, Michael               Fire and Ashes: Success and Failure in Polit~
```

Finally, we could make, say, a table of the distribution of the first letter of the names (Table 7.1).

```
all_books |>
  mutate(
    first_letter = str_sub(author, 1, 1)
  ) |>
  count(.by = first_letter) |>
  kable(
    col.names = c("First letter", "Number of times")
  )
```

Table 7.1: Distribution of first letter of author names in a collection of books

First letter	Number of times
A	1
C	1
D	1
G	1
H	1
I	1
L	1
M	1
P	3
R	1
V	2
W	4
Y	1

7.3.4 Prime Ministers of the United Kingdom

In this case study we are interested in how long prime ministers of the United Kingdom lived, based on the year they were born. We will scrape data from Wikipedia using `rvest`, clean it, and then make a graph. From time to time a website will change. This makes many scrapes largely bespoke, even if we can borrow some code from earlier projects. It is normal to feel frustrated at times. It helps to begin with an end in mind.

To that end, we can start by generating some simulated data. Ideally, we want a table that has a row for each prime minister, a column for their name, and a column each for the birth and death years. If they are still alive, then that death year can be empty. We know that birth and death years should be somewhere between 1700 and 1990, and that death year should be larger than birth year. Finally, we also know that the years should be integers, and the names should be characters. We want something that looks roughly like this:

```
set.seed(853)

simulated_dataset <-
  tibble(
    prime_minister = babynames |>
      filter(prop > 0.01) |>
      distinct(name) |>
      unlist() |>
      sample(size = 10, replace = FALSE),
    birth_year = sample(1700:1990, size = 10, replace = TRUE),
    years_lived = sample(50:100, size = 10, replace = TRUE),
    death_year = birth_year + years_lived
  ) |>
  select(prime_minister, birth_year, death_year, years_lived) |>
  arrange(birth_year)

simulated_dataset
```

```
# A tibble: 10 x 4
   prime_minister birth_year death_year years_lived
```

```
   <chr>                <int>     <int>       <int>
 1 Kevin                 1813      1908          95
 2 Karen                 1832      1896          64
 3 Robert                1839      1899          60
 4 Bertha                1846      1915          69
 5 Jennifer              1867      1943          76
 6 Arthur                1892      1984          92
 7 Donna                 1907      2006          99
 8 Emma                  1957      2031          74
 9 Ryan                  1959      2053          94
10 Tyler                 1990      2062          72
```

One of the advantages of generating a simulated dataset is that if we are working in groups then one person can start making the graph, using the simulated dataset, while the other person gathers the data. In terms of a graph, we are aiming for something like Figure 7.7.

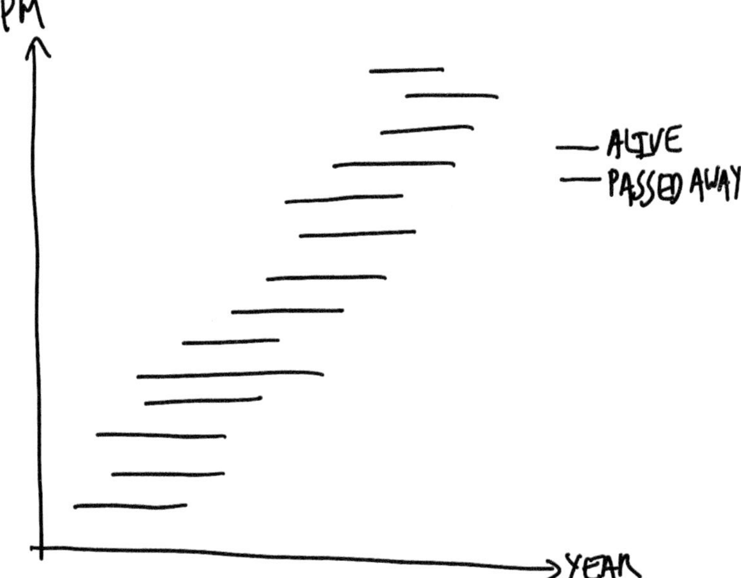

Figure 7.7: Sketch of planned graph showing how long United Kingdom prime ministers lived

We are starting with a question that is of interest, which is how long each prime minister of the United Kingdom lived. As such, we need to identify a source of data. While there are plenty of data sources that have the births and deaths of each prime minister, we want one that we can trust, and as we are going to be scraping, we want one that has some structure to it. The Wikipedia page about prime ministers of the United Kingdom[10] fits both these criteria. As it is a popular page the information is likely to be correct, and the data are available in a table.

We load `rvest` and then download the page using `read_html()`. Saving it locally provides us with a copy that we need for reproducibility in case the website changes, and means that we do not have to keep visiting the website. But it is not ours, and so this is typically not something that should be publicly redistributed.

[10] https://en.wikipedia.org/wiki/List_of_prime_ministers_of_the_United_Kingdom

```
raw_data <-
  read_html(
    "https://en.wikipedia.org/wiki/List_of_prime_ministers_of_the_United_Kingdom"
  )
write_html(raw_data, "pms.html")
```

As with the earlier case study, we are looking for patterns in the HTML that we can use to help us get closer to the data that we want. This is an iterative process and requires a lot of trial and error. Even simple examples will take time.

One tool that may help is the SelectorGadget[11]. This allows us to pick and choose the elements that we want, and then gives us the input for `html_element()` (Figure 7.8). By default, SelectorGadget uses CSS selectors. These are not the only way to specify the location of the information you want, and using an alternative, such as XPath, can be a useful option to consider.

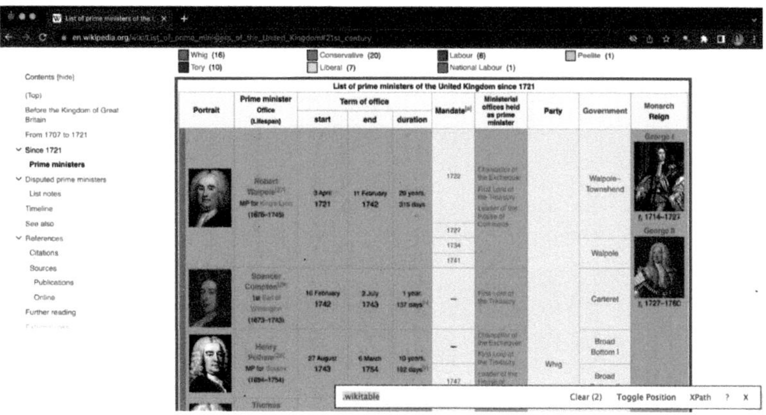

Figure 7.8: Using the Selector Gadget to identify the tag, as at 12 February 2023

```
raw_data <- read_html("pms.html")
```

```
parse_data_selector_gadget <-
  raw_data |>
  html_element(".wikitable") |>
  html_table()

head(parse_data_selector_gadget)
```

```
# A tibble: 6 x 11
  Portrait Portrait   Prime ministerOffice(L~1 `Term of office` `Term of office`
  <chr>    <chr>      <chr>                    <chr>            <chr>
1 Portrait "Portrait" Prime ministerOffice(Li~ start            end
2          ""         Robert Walpole[27]MP fo~ 3 April1721      11 February1742
3          ""         Robert Walpole[27]MP fo~ 3 April1721      11 February1742
4          ""         Robert Walpole[27]MP fo~ 3 April1721      11 February1742
```

[11] https://rvest.tidyverse.org/articles/articles/selectorgadget.html

```
5          ""          Robert Walpole[27]MP fo~ 3 April1721      11 February1742
6          ""          Spencer Compton[28]1st ~ 16 February1742  2 July1743
# i abbreviated name: 1: `Prime ministerOffice(Lifespan)`
# i 6 more variables: `Term of office` <chr>, `Mandate[a]` <chr>,
#   `Ministerial offices held as prime minister` <chr>, Party <chr>,
#   Government <chr>, MonarchReign <chr>
```

In this case there are many columns that we do not need, and some duplicated rows.

```
parsed_data <-
  parse_data_selector_gadget |>
  clean_names() |>
  rename(raw_text = prime_minister_office_lifespan) |>
  select(raw_text) |>
  filter(raw_text != "Prime ministerOffice(Lifespan)") |>
  distinct()

head(parsed_data)
```

```
# A tibble: 6 x 1
  raw_text
  <chr>
1 Robert Walpole[27]MP for King's Lynn(1676-1745)
2 Spencer Compton[28]1st Earl of Wilmington(1673-1743)
3 Henry Pelham[29]MP for Sussex(1694-1754)
4 Thomas Pelham-Holles[30]1st Duke of Newcastle(1693-1768)
5 William Cavendish[31]4th Duke of Devonshire(1720-1764)
6 Thomas Pelham-Holles[32]1st Duke of Newcastle(1693-1768)
```

Now that we have the parsed data, we need to clean it to match what we wanted. We want a names column, as well as columns for birth year and death year. We use `separate()` to take advantage of the fact that it looks like the names and dates are distinguished by brackets. The argument in `str_extract()` is a regular expression. It looks for four digits in a row, followed by a dash, followed by four more digits in a row. We use a slightly different regular expression for those prime ministers who are still alive.

```
initial_clean <-
  parsed_data |>
  separate(
    raw_text, into = c("name", "not_name"), sep = "\\[", extra = "merge",
  ) |>
  mutate(date = str_extract(not_name, "[[:digit:]]{4}-[[:digit:]]{4}"),
         born = str_extract(not_name, "born[[:space:]][[:digit:]]{4}")
         ) |>
  select(name, date, born)

head(initial_clean)
```

```
# A tibble: 6 x 3
  name                    date       born
  <chr>                   <chr>      <chr>
```

```
1 Robert Walpole        1676-1745 <NA>
2 Spencer Compton       1673-1743 <NA>
3 Henry Pelham          1694-1754 <NA>
4 Thomas Pelham-Holles 1693-1768 <NA>
5 William Cavendish     1720-1764 <NA>
6 Thomas Pelham-Holles 1693-1768 <NA>
```

Finally, we need to clean up the columns.

```
cleaned_data <-
  initial_clean |>
  separate(date, into = c("birth", "died"),
           sep = "-") |>    # PMs who have died have their birth and death years
  # separated by a hyphen, but we need to be careful with the hyphen as it seems
  # to be a slightly odd type of hyphen and we need to copy/paste it.
  mutate(
    born = str_remove_all(born, "born[[:space:]]"),
    birth = if_else(!is.na(born), born, birth)
  ) |> # Alive PMs have slightly different format
  select(-born) |>
  rename(born = birth) |>
  mutate(across(c(born, died), as.integer)) |>
  mutate(Age_at_Death = died - born) |>
  distinct() # Some of the PMs had two goes at it.

head(cleaned_data)
```

```
# A tibble: 6 x 4
  name                  born  died Age_at_Death
  <chr>                <int> <int>        <int>
1 Robert Walpole        1676  1745           69
2 Spencer Compton       1673  1743           70
3 Henry Pelham          1694  1754           60
4 Thomas Pelham-Holles  1693  1768           75
5 William Cavendish     1720  1764           44
6 John Stuart           1713  1792           79
```

Our dataset looks similar to the one that we said we wanted at the start (Table 7.2).

```
cleaned_data |>
  head() |>
  kable(
    col.names = c("Prime Minister", "Birth year", "Death year", "Age at death")
    )
```

Table 7.2: UK Prime Ministers, by how old they were when they died

Prime Minister	Birth year	Death year	Age at death
Robert Walpole	1676	1745	69
Spencer Compton	1673	1743	70

Prime Minister	Birth year	Death year	Age at death
Henry Pelham	1694	1754	60
Thomas Pelham-Holles	1693	1768	75
William Cavendish	1720	1764	44
John Stuart	1713	1792	79

At this point we would like to make a graph that illustrates how long each prime minister lived (Figure 7.9). If they are still alive then we would like them to run to the end, but we would like to color them differently.

```
cleaned_data |>
  mutate(
    still_alive = if_else(is.na(died), "Yes", "No"),
    died = if_else(is.na(died), as.integer(2023), died)
  ) |>
  mutate(name = as_factor(name)) |>
  ggplot(
    aes(x = born, xend = died, y = name, yend = name, color = still_alive)
    ) +
  geom_segment() +
  labs(
    x = "Year of birth", y = "Prime minister", color = "PM is currently alive"
    ) +
  theme_minimal() +
  scale_color_brewer(palette = "Set1") +
  theme(legend.position = "bottom")
```

7.3.5 Iteration

Considering text as data is exciting and opens a lot of different research questions. We will draw on it in Chapter 16. Many guides assume that we already have a nicely formatted text dataset, but that is rarely actually the case. In this case study we will download files from a few different pages. While we have already seen two examples of web scraping, those were focused on just one page, whereas we often need many. Here we will focus on this iteration. We will use `download.file()` to do the download, and use `purrr` to apply this function across multiple sites. You do not need to install or load that package because it is part of the core `tidyverse` so it is loaded when you load the `tidyverse`.

The Reserve Bank of Australia (RBA) is Australia's central bank. It has responsibility for setting the cash rate, which is the interest rate used for loans between banks. This interest rate is an especially important one and has a large impact on the other interest rates in the economy. Four times a year—February, May, August, and November—the RBA publishes a statement on monetary policy, and these are available as PDFs. In this example we will download two statements published in 2023.

First we set up a tibble that has the information that we need. We will take advantage of commonalities in the structure of the URLs. We need to specify both a URL and a local file name for each state.

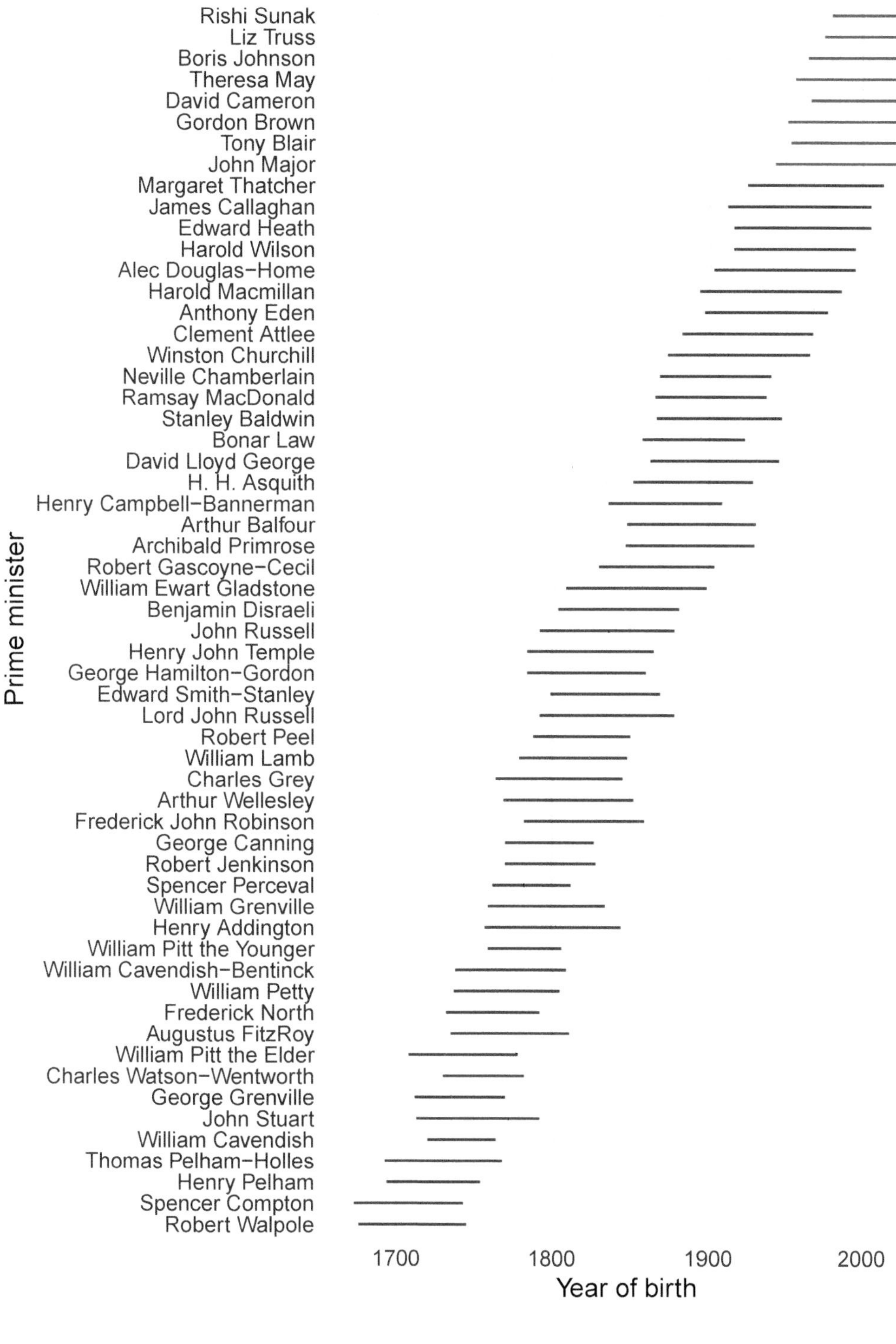

Figure 7.9: How long each prime minister of the United Kingdom lived

```
first_bit <- "https://www.rba.gov.au/publications/smp/2023/"
last_bit <- "/pdf/overview.pdf"

statements_of_interest <-
  tibble(
    address =
      c(
        paste0(first_bit, "feb", last_bit),
        paste0(first_bit, "may", last_bit)
      ),
    local_save_name = c("2023-02.pdf", "2023-05.pdf")
    )
```

We want to apply the function `download.files()` to these two statements. To do this we write a function that will download the file, let us know that it was downloaded, wait a polite amount of time, and then go get the next file.

```
visit_download_and_wait <-
  function(address_to_visit,
           where_to_save_it_locally) {
    download.file(url = address_to_visit,
                  destfile = where_to_save_it_locally)

    print(paste("Done with", address_to_visit, "at", Sys.time()))

    Sys.sleep(sample(5:10, 1))
  }
```

We now apply that function to our tibble of URLs and save names using the function `walk2()`.

```
walk2(
  statements_of_interest$address,
  statements_of_interest$local_save_name,
  ~ visit_download_and_wait(.x, .y)
)
```

The result is that we have downloaded these PDFs and saved them to our computer. An alternative to writing these functions ourselves would be to use `heapsofpapers` (R. Alexander and Mahfouz 2021). This includes various helpful options for downloading lists of files, especially PDF, CSV, and txt files. For instance, Collins and Alexander (2022) use this to obtain thousands of PDFs and estimate the extent to which COVID-19 research was reproducible. In the next section we will build on this to discuss getting information from PDFs.

7.4 PDFs

PDF files were developed in the 1990s by the technology company Adobe. They are useful for documents because they are meant to display in a consistent way independent of the environment that created them or the environment in which they are being viewed. A PDF viewed on an iPhone should look the same as on an Android phone, as on a Linux desktop. One feature of PDFs is that they can include a variety of objects, for instance, text, photos, figures, etc. However, this variety can limit the capacity of PDFs to be used directly as data. The data first needs to be extracted from the PDF.

It is often possible to copy and paste the data from the PDF. This is more likely when the PDF only contains text or regular tables. In particular, if the PDF has been created by an application such as Microsoft Word, or another document- or form-creation system, then often the text data can be extracted in this way because they are actually stored as text within the PDF. We begin with that case. But it is not as easy if the text has been stored as an image which is then part of the PDF. This may be the case for PDFs produced through scans or photos of physical documents, and some older document preparation software. We go through that case later.

In contrast to an API, a PDF is usually produced for human rather than computer consumption. The nice thing about PDFs is that they are static and constant. And it is great that data are available. But the trade-off is that:

- It is not overly useful to do larger-scale data.
- We do not know how the PDF was put together so we do not know whether we can trust it.
- We cannot manipulate the data to get results that we are interested in.

There are two important aspects to keep in mind when extracting data from a PDF:

1. Begin with an end in mind. Plan and sketch what we want from a final dataset/graph/paper to limit time wastage.
2. Start simple, then iterate. The quickest way to make something that needs to be complicated is often to first build a simple version and then add to it. Start with just trying to get one page of the PDF working or even just one line. Then iterate from there.

We will go through several examples and then go through a case study where we will gather data on United States Total Fertility Rate, by state.

7.4.1 *Jane Eyre*

Figure 7.10 is a PDF that consists of just the first sentence from Charlotte Brontë's novel *Jane Eyre* taken from Project Gutenberg (Brontë 1847). You can get it here[12]. If we assume that it was saved as "first_example.pdf", then after installing and loading `pdftools` to get the text from this one-page PDF into R.

[12]https://github.com/RohanAlexander/telling_stories/blob/aa6e2d76c80eba7bd31ca68161f0065344449ed8/inputs/pdfs/first_example.pdf

There was no possibility of taking a walk that day.

Figure 7.10: First sentence of Jane Eyre

```
first_example <- pdf_text("first_example.pdf")

first_example

class(first_example)
```

```
[1] "There was no possibility of taking a walk that day.\n"
[1] "character"
```

We can see that the PDF has been correctly read in, as a character vector.

We will now try a slightly more complicated example that consists of the first few paragraphs of *Jane Eyre* (Figure 7.11). Now we have the chapter heading as well.

We use the same function as before.

CHAPTER I

There was no possibility of taking a walk that day. We had been wandering, indeed, in the leafless shrubbery an hour in the morning; but since dinner (Mrs. Reed, when there was no company, dined early) the cold winter wind had brought with it clouds so sombre, and a rain so penetrating, that further out-door exercise was now out of the question.

I was glad of it: I never liked long walks, especially on chilly afternoons: dreadful to me was the coming home in the raw twilight, with nipped fingers and toes, and a heart saddened by the chidings of Bessie, the nurse, and humbled by the consciousness of my physical inferiority to Eliza, John, and Georgiana Reed.

The said Eliza, John, and Georgiana were now clustered round their mama in the drawing-room: she lay reclined on a sofa by the fireside, and with her darlings about her (for the time neither quarrelling nor crying) looked perfectly happy. Me, she had dispensed from joining the group; saying, "She regretted to be under the necessity of keeping me at a distance; but that until she heard from Bessie, and could discover by her own observation, that I was endeavouring in good earnest to acquire a more sociable and childlike disposition, a more attractive and sprightly manner—something lighter, franker, more natural, as it were—she really must exclude me from privileges intended only for contented, happy, little children."

"What does Bessie say I have done?" I asked.

"Jane, I don't like cavillers or questioners; besides, there is something truly forbidding in a child taking up her elders in that manner. Be seated somewhere; and until you can speak pleasantly, remain silent."

A breakfast-room adjoined the drawing-room, I slipped in there. It contained a bookcase: I soon possessed myself of a volume, taking care that it should be one stored with pictures. I mounted into the window-seat: gathering up my feet, I sat cross-legged, like a Turk; and, having drawn the red moreen curtain nearly close, I was shrined in double retirement.

Folds of scarlet drapery shut in my view to the right hand; to the left were the clear panes of glass, protecting, but not separating me from the drear November day. At intervals, while turning over the leaves of my book, I studied the aspect of that winter afternoon. Afar, it offered a pale blank of mist and cloud; near a scene of wet lawn and storm-beat shrub, with ceaseless rain sweeping away wildly before a long and lamentable blast.

Figure 7.11: First few paragraphs of Jane Eyre

```
second_example <- pdf_text("second_example.pdf")
class(second_example)
second_example
```

```
[1] "character"
```

```
[1] "CHAPTER I\nThere was no possibility of taking a walk that day. We ha..."
```

Again, we have a character vector. The end of each line is signaled by "\n", but other than that it looks pretty good. Finally, we consider the first two pages.

```
third_example <- pdf_text("third_example.pdf")
class(third_example)
third_example
```

```
[1] "character"
```

```
[1] "CHAPTER I\nThere was no possibility of taking a walk that day. We ha..."
[2] "Of farthest Thule; and the Atlantic surge\nPours in among the stormy..."
```

Notice that the first page is the first element of the character vector, and the second page is the second element. As we are most familiar with rectangular data, we will try to get it into that format as quickly as possible. And then we can use functions from the `tidyverse` to deal with it.

First we want to convert the character vector into a tibble. At this point we may like to add page numbers as well.

```
jane_eyre <- tibble(
  raw_text = third_example,
  page_number = c(1:2)
)
```

We then want to separate the lines so that each line is an observation. We can do that by looking for "\n" remembering that we need to escape the backslash as it is a special character.

```
jane_eyre <-
  separate_rows(jane_eyre, raw_text, sep = "\\n", convert = FALSE)

jane_eyre
```

```
# A tibble: 93 x 2
  raw_text                                                          page_number
  <chr>                                                                   <int>
1 "CHAPTER I"                                                                 1
2 "There was no possibility of taking a walk that day. We had been~           1
3 "leafless shrubbery an hour in the morning; but since dinner (Mr~           1
4 "company, dined early) the cold winter wind had brought with it ~           1
5 "penetrating, that further out-door exercise was now out of the ~           1
6 ""                                                                            1
7 "I was glad of it: I never liked long walks, especially on chill~           1
```

```
 8 "coming home in the raw twilight, with nipped fingers and toes, ~        1
 9 "chidings of Bessie, the nurse, and humbled by the consciousness~        1
10 "Eliza, John, and Georgiana Reed."                                       1
# i 83 more rows
```

7.4.2 Total Fertility Rate in the United States

The United States Department of Health and Human Services Vital Statistics Report provides information about the Total Fertility Rate (TFR) for each state. The average number of births per woman if women experience the current age-specific fertility rates throughout their reproductive years. The data are available in PDFs. We can use the approaches above to get the data into a dataset.

The table that we are interested in is on page 40 of a PDF that is available here[13] or here[14]. The column of interest is labelled: "Total fertility rate" (Figure 7.12).

40 National Vital Statistics Report, Vol. 50, No. 5, Revised May 15, 2002

Table 10. Number of births, birth rates, fertility rates, total fertility rates, and birth rates for teenagers 15-19 years by age of mother: United States, each State and territory, 2000

[By place of residence. Birth rates are live births per 1,000 estimated population in each area; fertility rates are live births per 1,000 women aged 15-44 years estimated in each area; total fertility rates are sums of birth rates for 5-year age groups multiplied by 5; birth rates by age are live births per 1,000 women in specified age group estimated in each area]

State	Number of births	Birth rate	Fertility rate	Total fertility rate	Teenage birth rate		
					Total	15-19 years: 15-17 years	15-19 years: 18-19 years
United States [1]	4,058,814	14.7	67.5	2,130.0	48.5	27.4	79.2
Alabama	63,299	14.4	65.0	2,021.0	62.9	37.9	97.3
Alaska	9,974	16.0	74.6	2,437.0	42.4	23.6	69.4
Arizona	85,273	17.5	84.4	2,652.5	69.1	41.1	111.3
Arkansas	37,783	14.7	69.1	2,140.0	68.5	36.7	114.1
California	531,959	15.8	70.7	2,186.0	48.5	28.6	75.6
Colorado	65,438	15.8	73.1	2,356.5	49.2	28.6	79.8
Connecticut	43,026	13.0	61.2	1,931.5	31.9	16.9	56.3
Delaware	11,051	14.5	63.5	2,014.0	51.6	30.5	80.2
District of Columbia	7,666	14.8	63.0	1,975.5	80.7	60.7	101.8
Florida	204,125	13.3	66.9	2,157.5	52.6	29.7	88.0
Georgia	132,644	16.7	71.4	2,239.5	64.2	36.8	104.3
Hawaii	17,551	14.9	72.3	2,337.0	45.1	24.7	70.5
Idaho	20,366	16.0	74.8	2,314.0	43.1	21.3	72.8
Illinois	185,036	15.2	69.5	2,190.5	49.5	28.5	81.1
Indiana	87,699	14.7	66.8	2,109.0	50.3	26.2	85.9
Iowa	38,266	13.3	64.0	2,052.5	34.7	17.4	60.3
Kansas	39,666	14.9	69.2	2,205.0	45.3	22.4	78.5
Kentucky	56,029	14.1	63.6	1,992.5	55.3	29.2	92.2
Louisiana	67,898	15.5	69.1	2,128.5	62.1	36.3	97.1
Maine	13,603	10.8	49.5	1,611.5	28.7	13.4	52.8
Maryland	74,316	14.2	61.9	1,974.5	41.6	23.8	68.8
Massachusetts	81,614	13.2	59.2	1,799.0	27.1	15.0	44.9
Michigan	136,171	13.7	62.0	1,969.5	39.2	21.3	66.3
Minnesota	67,604	14.0	63.8	2,062.0	29.6	15.6	51.0
Mississippi	44,075	15.8	70.3	2,124.0	72.0	45.0	109.9
Missouri	76,463	13.9	64.0	2,047.5	48.8	26.5	82.2
Montana	10,957	12.3	61.3	2,003.0	35.8	19.1	60.8
Nebraska	24,646	14.8	68.9	2,209.0	37.2	19.3	62.7
Nevada	30,829	16.4	79.8	2,560.0	62.2	34.2	106.7
New Hampshire	14,609	12.0	52.2	1,664.0	23.4	9.8	45.4
New Jersey	115,632	14.1	65.8	2,086.0	31.7	17.0	54.9
New Mexico	27,223	15.6	72.7	2,313.0	66.2	40.2	105.1
New York	258,737	14.2	65.0	2,022.0	35.6	20.1	58.1
North Carolina	120,311	15.5	71.6	2,269.5	59.9	32.8	101.4
North Dakota	7,676	12.2	58.7	1,875.5	28.2	12.5	51.4
Ohio	155,472	13.8	63.0	1,995.5	45.6	24.1	77.2
Oklahoma	49,782	14.7	69.9	2,184.0	60.1	32.9	99.8
Oregon	45,804	13.7	65.8	2,086.0	43.2	23.5	72.8
Pennsylvania	146,281	12.2	58.2	1,868.0	35.2	19.6	58.8
Rhode Island	12,505	12.6	58.1	1,822.0	38.4	21.3	64.0
South Carolina	56,114	14.3	63.3	1,971.5	60.6	36.7	92.9
South Dakota	10,345	14.0	66.7	2,148.0	37.2	19.4	62.2
Tennessee	79,611	14.4	65.2	2,063.5	61.5	34.2	101.6
Texas	363,414	17.8	80.0	2,500.5	69.2	42.7	107.1
Utah	47,353	21.9	94.5	2,761.5	40.0	22.0	62.7
Vermont	6,500	10.9	48.8	1,565.5	24.1	10.6	44.5
Virginia	98,938	14.2	61.2	1,904.0	40.8	21.7	66.9
Washington	81,036	13.9	63.2	2,011.5	38.2	20.3	64.5
West Virginia	20,865	11.6	55.9	1,723.5	46.4	22.8	79.8
Wisconsin	69,326	13.1	60.4	1,940.0	34.5	18.3	58.8
Wyoming	6,253	13.0	62.7	1,976.5	40.8	19.0	73.4

Figure 7.12: Example Vital Statistics Report, from 2000

[13] https://www.cdc.gov/nchs/data/nvsr/nvsr50/nvsr50_05.pdf

[14] https://github.com/RohanAlexander/telling_stories/blob/main/inputs/pdfs/dhs/year_2000.pdf

The first step when getting data out of a PDF is to sketch out what we eventually want. A PDF typically contains a lot of information, and so we should be clear about what is needed. This helps keep you focused, and prevents scope creep, but it is also helpful when thinking about data checks. We literally write down on paper what we have in mind. In this case, what is needed is a table with a column for state, year, and total fertility rate (TFR) (Figure 7.13).

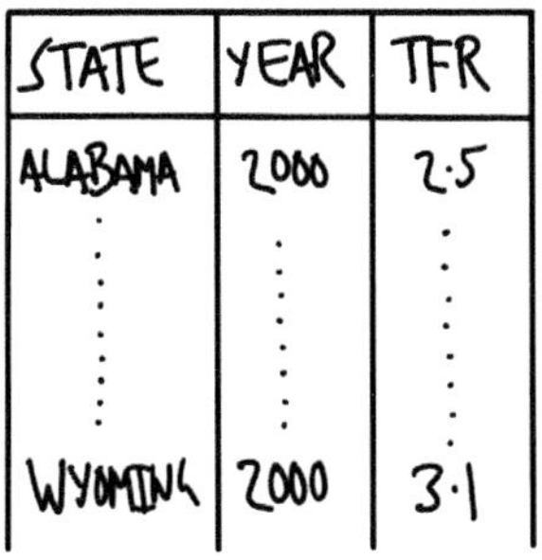

STATE	YEAR	TFR
ALABAMA	2000	2.5
⋮	⋮	⋮
WYOMING	2000	3.1

Figure 7.13: Planned dataset of TFR for each US state

We are interested in a particular column in a particular table for this PDF. Unfortunately, there is nothing magical about what is coming. This first step requires finding the PDF online, working out the link for each, and searching for the page and column name that is of interest. We have built a CSV with the details that we need and can read that in.

```
summary_tfr_dataset <- read_csv(
  paste0("https://raw.githubusercontent.com/RohanAlexander/",
         "telling_stories/main/inputs/tfr_tables_info.csv")
  )
```

We first download and save the PDF using `download.file()`.

```
download.file(
  url = summary_tfr_dataset$url[1],
  destfile = "year_2000.pdf"
)
```

We then read the PDF in as a character vector using `pdf_text()` from `pdftools`. And then convert it to a tibble, so that we can use familiar verbs on it.

```
dhs_2000 <- pdf_text("year_2000.pdf")
```

```
dhs_2000_tibble <- tibble(raw_data = dhs_2000)

head(dhs_2000_tibble)
```

```
# A tibble: 6 x 1
```

```
  raw_data
  <chr>
1 "Volume 50, Number 5                                                          ~
2 "2   National Vital Statistics Report, Vol. 50, No. 5, February 12, 2002\n\n\~
3 "                                                                             ~
4 "4   National Vital Statistics Report, Vol. 50, No. 5, February 12, 2002\n\n\~
5 "                                                                             ~
6 "6   National Vital Statistics Report, Vol. 50, No. 5, February 12, 2002\n\n ~
```

Grab the page that is of interest (remembering that each page is an element of the character vector, hence a row in the tibble).

```
dhs_2000_relevant_page <-
  dhs_2000_tibble |>
  slice(summary_tfr_dataset$page[1])

head(dhs_2000_relevant_page)
```

```
# A tibble: 1 x 1
  raw_data
  <chr>
1 "40 National Vital Statistics Report, Vol. 50, No. 5, Revised May 15, 20022\n~
```

We want to separate the rows and use `separate_rows()` from `tidyr`, which is part of the core tidyverse.

```
dhs_2000_separate_rows <-
  dhs_2000_relevant_page |>
  separate_rows(raw_data, sep = "\\n", convert = FALSE)

head(dhs_2000_separate_rows)
```

```
# A tibble: 6 x 1
  raw_data
  <chr>
1 "40 National Vital Statistics Report, Vol. 50, No. 5, Revised May 15, 20022"
2 ""
3 "Table 10. Number of births, birth rates, fertility rates, total fertility ra~
4 "United States, each State and territory, 2000"
5 "[By place of residence. Birth rates are live births per 1,000 estimated popu~
6 "estimated in each area; total fertility rates are sums of birth rates for 5-~
```

We are searching for patterns that we can use. Let us look at the first ten lines of content (ignoring aspects such as headings and page numbers at the top of the page).

```
dhs_2000_separate_rows[13:22, ] |>
  mutate(raw_data = str_remove(raw_data, "\\.{40}"))
```

```
# A tibble: 10 x 1
   raw_data
   <chr>
```

```
 1 "                                    State                                      ~
 2 "                                                                               ~
 3 "                                                                               ~
 4 ""
 5 ""
 6 "United States 1 ..............          4,058,814   14.7       67.5       2,1~
 7 ""
 8 "Alabama .......................            63,299   14.4       65.0       2,0~
 9 "Alaska ...........................          9,974   16.0       74.6       2,4~
10 "Arizona ........................           85,273   17.5       84.4       2,6~
```

And now at just one line.

```
dhs_2000_separate_rows[20, ] |>
  mutate(raw_data = str_remove(raw_data, "\\.{40}"))
```

```
# A tibble: 1 x 1
  raw_data
  <chr>
1 Alabama .......................           63,299    14.4       65.0       2,021~
```

It does not get much better than this:

1. We have dots separating the states from the data.
2. We have a space between each of the columns.

We can now separate this into columns. First, we want to match on when there are at least two dots (remembering that the dot is a special character and so needs to be escaped).

```
dhs_2000_separate_columns <-
  dhs_2000_separate_rows |>
  separate(
    col = raw_data,
    into = c("state", "data"),
    sep = "\\.{2,}",
    remove = FALSE,
    fill = "right"
  )

dhs_2000_separate_columns[18:28, ] |>
  select(state, data)
```

```
# A tibble: 11 x 2
   state                    data
   <chr>                    <chr>
 1 "United States 1 "       "          4,058,814   14.7       67.5        2,130.0  ~
 2 ""                        <NA>
 3 "Alabama "               "            63,299    14.4      65.0        2,021.0  ~
 4 "Alaska "                "          9,974     16.0      74.6       2,437.0     ~
 5 "Arizona "               "          85,273     17.5      84.4       2,652.5    ~
 6 "Arkansas "              "           37,783     14.7      69.1       2,140.0   ~
```

```
 7 "California "            "         531,959    15.8      70.7      2,186.0    ~
 8 "Colorado "              "           65,438    15.8      73.1      2,356.5    ~
 9 "Connecticut "           "             43,026    13.0      61.2      1,931.5    ~
10 "Delaware "              "             11,051    14.5      63.5      2,014.0    ~
11 "District of Columbia " "                   7,666    14.8      63.0      1,975.~
```

We then separate the data based on spaces. There is an inconsistent number of spaces, so we first squish any example of more than one space into just one with `str_squish()` from `stringr`.

```
dhs_2000_separate_data <-
  dhs_2000_separate_columns |>
  mutate(data = str_squish(data)) |>
  separate(
    col = data,
    into = c(
      "number_of_births",
      "birth_rate",
      "fertility_rate",
      "TFR",
      "teen_births_all",
      "teen_births_15_17",
      "teen_births_18_19"
    ),
    sep = "\\s",
    remove = FALSE
  )

dhs_2000_separate_data[18:28, ] |>
  select(-raw_data, -data)
```

```
# A tibble: 11 x 8
   state         number_of_births birth_rate fertility_rate TFR   teen_births_all
   <chr>         <chr>            <chr>      <chr>          <chr> <chr>
 1 "United Sta~ 4,058,814        14.7       67.5           2,13~ 48.5
 2 ""            <NA>             <NA>       <NA>           <NA>  <NA>
 3 "Alabama "    63,299           14.4       65.0           2,02~ 62.9
 4 "Alaska "     9,974            16.0       74.6           2,43~ 42.4
 5 "Arizona "    85,273           17.5       84.4           2,65~ 69.1
 6 "Arkansas "   37,783           14.7       69.1           2,14~ 68.5
 7 "California~ 531,959          15.8       70.7           2,18~ 48.5
 8 "Colorado "   65,438           15.8       73.1           2,35~ 49.2
 9 "Connecticu~ 43,026           13.0       61.2           1,93~ 31.9
10 "Delaware "   11,051           14.5       63.5           2,01~ 51.6
11 "District o~ 7,666            14.8       63.0           1,97~ 80.7
# i 2 more variables: teen_births_15_17 <chr>, teen_births_18_19 <chr>
```

This is all looking fairly great. The only thing left is to clean up.

```
dhs_2000_cleaned <-
  dhs_2000_separate_data |>
  select(state, TFR) |>
  slice(18:74) |>
  drop_na() |>
  mutate(
    TFR = str_remove_all(TFR, ","),
    TFR = as.numeric(TFR),
    state = str_trim(state),
    state = if_else(state == "United States 1", "Total", state)
  )
```

And run some checks, for instance that we have all the states.

```
all(state.name %in% dhs_2000_cleaned$state)
```

```
[1] TRUE
```

And we are done (Table 7.3). We can see that there is quite a wide distribution of TFR by US state (Figure 7.14). Utah has the highest and Vermont the lowest.

```
dhs_2000_cleaned |>
  slice(1:10) |>
  kable(
    col.names = c("State", "TFR"),
    digits = 0,
    format.args = list(big.mark = ",")
  )
```

Table 7.3: First ten rows of a dataset of TFR by United States state, 2000-2019

State	TFR
Total	2,130
Alabama	2,021
Alaska	2,437
Arizona	2,652
Arkansas	2,140
California	2,186
Colorado	2,356
Connecticut	1,932
Delaware	2,014
District of Columbia	1,976

```
dhs_2000_cleaned |>
  filter(state != "Total") |>
  ggplot(aes(x = TFR, y = fct_reorder(state, TFR))) +
  geom_point() +
  theme_classic() +
```

```
labs(y = "State", x = "Total Fertility Rate")
```

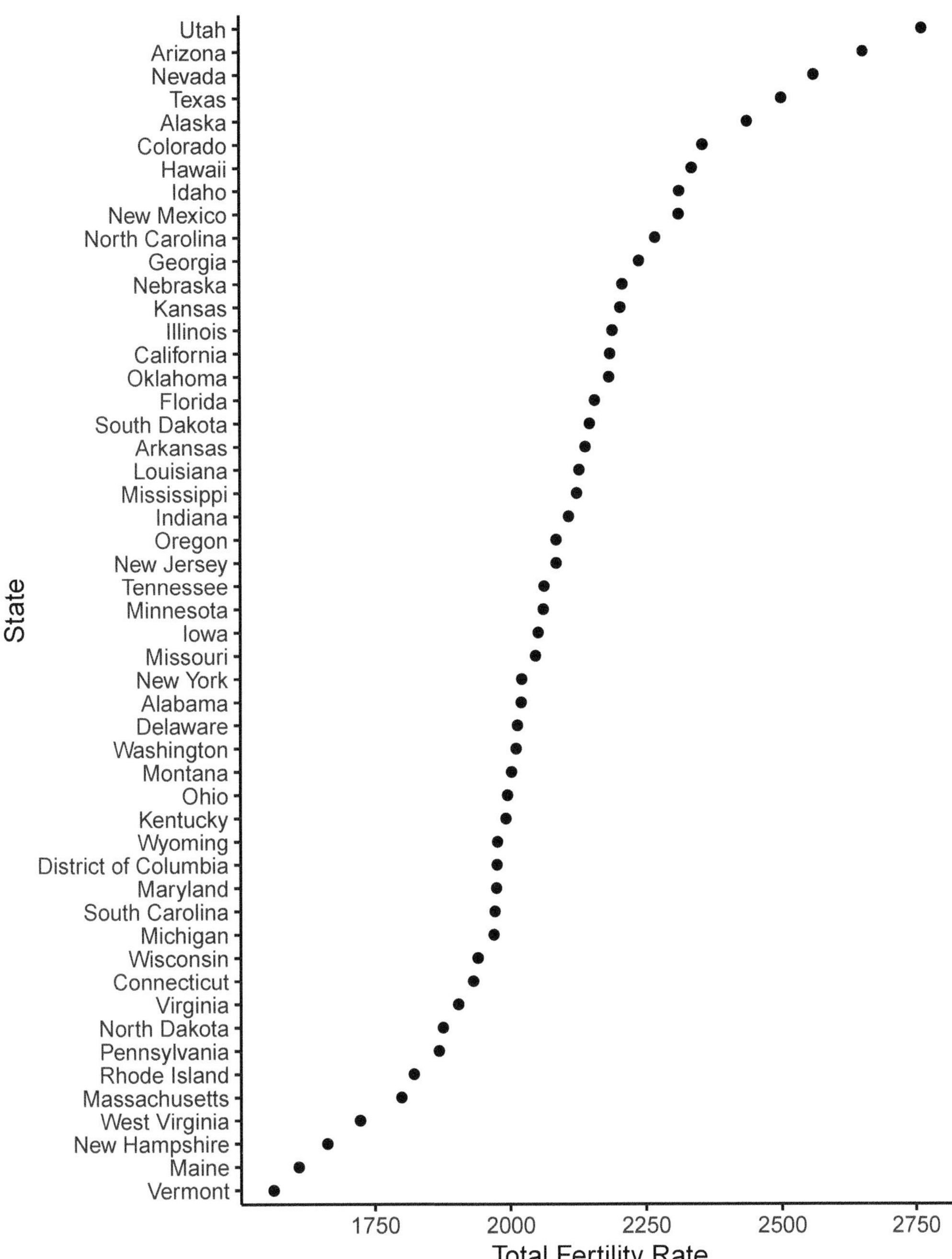

Figure 7.14: Distribution of TFR by US state in 2000

Healy (2022) provides another example of using this approach in a different context.

7.4.3 Optical Character Recognition

All of the above is predicated on having a PDF that is already "digitized". But what if it is made of images, such as the result of a scan. Such PDFs often contain unstructured data, meaning that the data are not tagged nor organized in a regular way. Optical Character Recognition (OCR) is a process that transforms an image of text into actual text. Although there may not be much difference to a human reading a PDF before and after OCR, the PDF becomes machine-readable which allows us to use scripts (Cheriet et al. 2007). OCR has been used to parse images of characters since the 1950s, initially using manual approaches. While manual approaches remain the gold standard, for reasons of cost effectiveness, this has been largely replaced with statistical models.

In this example we use `tesseract` to OCR a document. This is a R wrapper around the Tesseract open-source OCR engine. Tesseract was initially developed at HP in the 1980s, and is now mostly developed by Google. After we install and load `tesseract` we can use `ocr()`.

Let us see an example with a scan from the first page of *Jane Eyre* (Figure 7.15).

```
text <- ocr(
  here("jane_scan.png"),
  engine = tesseract("eng")
)
cat(text)
```

```
1 THERE was no possibility of taking a walk that day. We had
been wandering, indeed, in the leafless shrubbery an hour in
the morning; but since dinner (Mrs Reed, when there was no com-
pany, dined early) the cold winter wind had brought with it clouds
so sombre, and a rain so penetrating, that further out-door exercise

was now out of the question.

I was glad of it: I never liked long walks, especially on chilly
afternoons: dreadful to me was the coming home in the raw twi-
light, with nipped fingers and toes, and a heart saddened by the
chidings of Bessie, the nurse, and humbled by the consciousness of
my physical inferiority to Eliza, John, and Georgiana Reed.

The said Eliza, John, and Georgiana were now clustered round
their mama in the drawing-room: she lay reclined on a sofa by the
fireside, and with her darlings about her (for the time neither quar-
relling nor crying) looked perfectly happy. Me, she had dispensed
from joining the group; saying, 'She regretted to be under the
necessity of keeping me at a distance; but that until she heard from
Bessie, and could discover by her own observation that I was
endeavouring in good earnest to acquire a more sociable and
child-like disposition, a more attractive and sprightly manner—
something lighter, franker, more natural as it were—she really
must exclude me from privileges intended only for contented,
happy, littie children.'
```

I THERE was no possibility of taking a walk that day. We had been wandering, indeed, in the leafless shrubbery an hour in the morning; but since dinner (Mrs Reed, when there was no company, dined early) the cold winter wind had brought with it clouds so sombre, and a rain so penetrating, that further out-door exercise was now out of the question.

I was glad of it: I never liked long walks, especially on chilly afternoons: dreadful to me was the coming home in the raw twilight, with nipped fingers and toes, and a heart saddened by the chidings of Bessie, the nurse, and humbled by the consciousness of my physical inferiority to Eliza, John, and Georgiana Reed.

The said Eliza, John, and Georgiana were now clustered round their mama in the drawing-room: she lay reclined on a sofa by the fireside, and with her darlings about her (for the time neither quarrelling nor crying) looked perfectly happy. Me, she had dispensed from joining the group; saying, 'She regretted to be under the necessity of keeping me at a distance; but that until she heard from Bessie, and could discover by her own observation that I was endeavouring in good earnest to acquire a more sociable and child-like disposition, a more attractive and sprightly manner—something lighter, franker, more natural as it were—she really must exclude me from privileges intended only for contented, happy, little children.'

'What does Bessie say I have done?' I asked.

'Jane, I don't like cavillers or questioners: besides, there is something truly forbidding in a child taking up her elders in that manner. Be seated somewhere; and until you can speak pleasantly, remain silent.'

15

Figure 7.15: Scan of first page of Jane Eyre

```
'What does Bessie say I have done?' I asked.

'Jane, I don't like cavillers or questioners: besides, there is
something truly forbidding in a child taking up her elders in that
manner. Be seated somewhere; and until you can speak pleasantly,
remain silent.'

. a TV

i; STA AEE LT JEUNE TIS Sis
a) | | | a) ee
i Ni 4 | | | ae ST | | a eg

ce A FEM yi | eS ee
Pe TT (SB ag ie pe
is \ ie mu) i i es SS
veal | Dy eT |
pa || i er itl |

aes : Oty ZR UIE OR HMR Sa ote ariel
SEEN ed — =
15
```

In general the result is not too bad. OCR is a useful tool but is not perfect and the resulting data may require extra attention in terms of cleaning. For instance, in the OCR results of Figure 7.15 we see irregularities that would need to be fixed. Various options, such as focusing on the particular data of interest and increasing the contrast can help. Other popular OCR engines include Amazon Textract, Google Vision API, and ABBYY.

7.5 Exercises

Scales

1. *(Plan)* Consider the following scenario: *A group of five undergraduates—Matt, Ash, Jacki, Rol, and Mike—each read some number of pages from a book each day for 100 days. Two of the undergraduates are a couple and so their number of pages is positively correlated, however all the others are independent.* Please sketch what that dataset could look like and then sketch a graph that you could build to show all observations.
2. *(Simulate)* Please further consider the scenario described and simulate the situation. Please include five tests based on the simulated data. Submit a link to a GitHub Gist that contains your code.
3. *(Acquire)* Please describe a possible source of such a dataset.
4. *(Explore)* Please use `ggplot2` to build the graph that you sketched using the data that you simulated. Submit a link to a GitHub Gist that contains your code.
5. *(Communicate)* Please write two paragraphs about what you did.

Questions

1. Separately for both an API of interest to you, and an API that has an R package written around it, please list its name, a link, and a brief description of the data that are available.
2. Please consider the following code, which uses `gh` to access the GitHub API (you will need to have set up GitHub on your computer, as covered in Chapter 3). When was the repo for `heapsofpapers` created (pick one)?
   a. 2021-02-23
   b. 2021-03-06
   c. 2021-05-25
   d. 2021-04-27

```
# Based on Tyler Bradley and Monica Alexander
repos <- gh("/users/RohanAlexander/repos", per_page = 100)
repo_info <- tibble(
  name = map_chr(repos, "name"),
  created = map_chr(repos, "created_at"),
  full_name = map_chr(repos, "full_name"),
)
```

3. Please consider the UN's Data API[15] and the introductory note on how to use it by Schmertmann (2022). Argentina's location code is 32. Modify the following code to determine what Argentina's single-year fertility rate was for 20-year-olds in 1995 (pick one)?
   a. 147.679
   b. 172.988
   c. 204.124
   d. 128.665

```
my_indicator <- 68
my_location <- 50
my_startyr <- 1996
my_endyr <- 1999

url <- paste0(
  "https://population.un.org/dataportalapi/api/v1",
  "/data/indicators/", my_indicator, "/locations/",
  my_location, "/start/", my_startyr, "/end/",
  my_endyr, "/?format=csv"
)

un_data <- read_delim(file = url, delim = "|", skip = 1)

un_data |>
  filter(AgeLabel == 25 & TimeLabel == 1996) |>
  select(Value)
```

[15]https://population.un.org/dataportal/about/dataapi

4. What is the main argument to `GET()` from `httr` (pick one)?
   a. "url"
   b. "website"
   c. "domain"
   d. "location"
5. What are three reasons why we should be respectful when getting scraping data from websites (write at least two paragraphs)?
6. What features of a website do we typically take advantage of when we parse the code (pick one)?
   a. HTML/CSS mark-up.
   b. Cookies.
   c. Facebook beacons.
   d. Code comments.
7. What are three advantages and three disadvantages of scraping compared with using an API?
8. What are three delimiters that could be useful when trying to bring order to a PDF that you read in as a character vector (the use of dot points is fine)?
9. Which of the following, used as part of a regular expression, would match a full stop (hint: see the "strings" cheat sheet) (pick one)?
   a. "."
   b. "."
   c. "\."
   d. "\."
10. What are three checks that we might like to use for demographic data, such as the number of births in a country in a particular year?
11. Which of these are functions from the `purrr` package (select all that apply)?
    a. `map()`
    b. `walk()`
    c. `run()`
    d. `safely()`
12. What are some principles to follow when scraping (select all that apply)?
    a. Avoid it if possible
    b. Follow the site's guidance
    c. Slow down
    d. Use a scalpel not an axe.
13. What is the HTML tag for an item in a list (pick one)?
    a. `li`
    b. `body`
    c. `b`
    d. `em`
14. Which function should we use if we have the following text data: "rohan_alexander" in a column called "names" and want to split it into first name and surname based on the underscore (pick one)?
    a. `separate()`
    b. `slice()`
    c. `spacing()`
    d. `text_to_columns()`

Tutorial

Please redo the web scraping example, but for one of: Australia[16], Canada[17], India[18], or New Zealand[19].

Plan, gather, and clean the data, and then use it to create a similar table to the one created above. Write a few paragraphs about your findings. Then write a few paragraphs about the data source, what you gathered, and how you went about it. What took longer than you expected? When did it become fun? What would you do differently next time you do this? Your submission should be at least two pages, but likely more.

Use Quarto, and include an appropriate title, author, date, link to a GitHub repo, and citations. Submit a PDF.

[16]https://en.wikipedia.org/wiki/List_of_prime_ministers_of_Australia
[17]https://en.wikipedia.org/wiki/List_of_prime_ministers_of_Canada
[18]https://en.wikipedia.org/wiki/List_of_prime_ministers_of_India
[19]https://en.wikipedia.org/wiki/List_of_prime_ministers_of_New_Zealand

8

Hunt data

Prerequisites

- Read *Impact evaluation in practice*, (Gertler et al. 2016)
  - Focus on Chapters 3 and 4 which provide a broad discussion of causal inference and randomization.
- Read *The Psychology of Survey Response*, (Tourangeau, Rips, and Rasinski 2000)
  - Focus on Chapter 2 "Respondents' Understanding of Survey Questions", which discusses the wording of survey questions.
- Read *How to Run Surveys*, (Stantcheva 2023)
  - This paper provides an overview of practice concerns when putting surveys together.
- Read *Q&A: How Pew Research Center surveyed nearly 30,000 people in India*, (Letterman 2021)
  - Discusses many practical issues that occurred during a large survey about religious beliefs.
- Read *Statistics and causal inference*, (Holland 1986)
  - Focus on Parts 1-3 which discuss how we can use statistical models, especially Rubin's model, to understand the effect of causes.
- Read *Big tech is testing you*, (Fry 2020)
  - This article discusses the use of A/B testing in tech firms.
- Watch *Causal Inference Challenges in Industry: A perspective from experiences at LinkedIn*, (Xu 2020)
  - Focus on the first half of this video, which provides an overview of A/B testing.

Key concepts and skills

- Randomization is used to establish treatment and control groups. The idea is that, but for the treatment, these groups would be the same. This then allows us to measure an average effect of the treatment. But there are many threats to the validity of that estimate.
- Once we have estimates, we want to know the extent to which they apply. If they apply to only the context of the experiment, then they have internal validity. If they generalize outside of that context, then they have external validity.
- Appreciating why informed consent and establishing the need for an experiment are important.
- A/B testing and some of its nuances.
- Designing and implementing surveys.

Software and packages

- Base R (R Core Team 2023)
- `haven` (Wickham, Miller, and Smith 2023)
- `knitr` (Xie 2023)
- `labelled` (Larmarange 2023)
- `tidyverse` (Wickham et al. 2019)

```
library(haven)
library(knitr)
library(labelled)
library(tidyverse)
```

8.1 Introduction

This chapter is about obtaining data with experiments. This is a situation in which we can explicitly control and vary what we are interested in. The advantage of this is that identifying and estimating an effect should be clear. There is a treatment group that is subject to what we are interested in, and a control group that is not. These are randomly split before treatment. And so, if they end up different, then it must be because of the treatment. Unfortunately, life is rarely so smooth. Arguing about how similar the treatment and control groups were tends to carry on indefinitely. And before we can estimate an effect, we need to be able to measure whatever it is that we are interested in, which is often surprisingly difficult.

By way of motivation, consider the situation of someone who moved to San Francisco in 2014—as soon as they moved the Giants won the World Series and the Golden State Warriors began a historic streak of World Championships. They then moved to Chicago, and immediately the Cubs won the World Series for the first time in 100 years. They then moved to Massachusetts, and the Patriots won the Super Bowl again, and again, and again. And finally, they moved to Toronto, where the Raptors immediately won the World Championship. Should a city pay them to move, or could municipal funds be better spent elsewhere?

One way to get at the answer would be to run an experiment. Make a list of the North American cities with major sports teams. Then roll some dice, send them to live there for a year, and measure the outcomes of the sports teams. With enough lifetimes, we could work it out. This would take a long time because we cannot both live in a city and not live in a city. This is the fundamental problem of causal inference: a person cannot be both treated and untreated. Experiments and randomized controlled trials are circumstances in which we try to randomly allocate some treatment, to have a belief that everything else was the same (or at least ignorable). We use the Neyman-Rubin potential outcomes framework to formalize the situation (Holland 1986).

A treatment, t, will often be a binary variable, that is either 0 or 1. It is 0 if the person, i, is not treated, which is to say they are in the control group, and 1 if they are treated. We will typically have some outcome, Y_i, of interest for that person which could be binary, categorical, multinomial, ordinal, continuous, or possibly even some other type of variable. For instance, it could be vote choice, in which case we could measure whether the person is: "Conservative" or "Not Conservative"; which party they support, say: "Conservative", "Liberal", "Democratic", "Green"; or maybe a probability of supporting some particular leader.

The effect of a treatment is then causal if $(Y_i|t = 0) \neq (Y_i|t = 1)$. That is to say, the outcome for person i, given they were not treated, is different to their outcome given they were treated. If we could both treat and control the one individual at the one time, then we would know that it was only the treatment that had caused any change in outcome. There could be no other factor to explain it. But the fundamental problem of causal inference remains: we cannot both treat and control the one individual at the one time. So, when we want to know the effect of the treatment, we need to compare it with a counterfactual. The counterfactual, introduced in Chapter 4, is what would have happened if the treated individual were not treated. As it turns out, this means one way to think of causal inference is as a missing data problem, where we are missing the counterfactual.

We cannot compare treatment and control in one individual. So we instead compare the average of two groups—those treated and those not. We are looking to estimate the counterfactual at a group level because of the impossibility of doing it at an individual level. Making this trade-off allows us to move forward but comes at the cost of certainty. We must instead rely on randomization, probabilities, and expectations.

We usually consider a default of there being no effect and we look for evidence that would cause us to change our mind. As we are interested in what is happening in groups, we turn to expectations and notions of probability to express ourselves. Hence, we will make claims that apply on average. Maybe wearing fun socks really does make you have a lucky day, but on average, across the group, it is probably not the case. It is worth pointing out that we do not just have to be interested in the average effect. We may consider the median, or variance, or whatever. Nonetheless, if we were interested in the average effect, then one way to proceed would be to:

1. divide the dataset in two—treated and not treated—and have a binary effect variable—lucky day or not;
2. sum the variable, then divide it by the length of the variable; and
3. compare this value between the two groups.

This is an estimator, introduced in Chapter 4, which is a way of putting together a guess of something of interest. The estimand is the thing of interest, in this case the average effect, and the estimate is whatever our guess turns out to be. We can simulate data to illustrate the situation.

```
set.seed(853)

treat_control <-
  tibble(
    group = sample(x = c("Treatment", "Control"), size = 100, replace = TRUE),
    binary_effect = sample(x = c(0, 1), size = 100, replace = TRUE)
    )

treat_control
```

```
# A tibble: 100 x 2
   group     binary_effect
   <chr>             <dbl>
 1 Treatment             0
 2 Control               1
 3 Control               1
 4 Treatment             1
 5 Treatment             1
 6 Treatment             0
```

```
 7 Treatment                1
 8 Treatment                1
 9 Control                  0
10 Control                  0
# i 90 more rows
```

```
treat_control |>
  summarise(
    treat_result = sum(binary_effect) / length(binary_effect),
    .by = group
  )
```

```
# A tibble: 2 x 2
  group     treat_result
  <chr>            <dbl>
1 Treatment        0.552
2 Control          0.333
```

In this case, we draw either 0 or 1, 100 times, for each the treatment and control group, and then the estimate of the average effect of being treated is 0.22.

More broadly, to tell causal stories we need to bring together theory and a detailed knowledge of what we are interested in (Cunningham 2021, 4). In Chapter 7 we discussed gathering data that we observed about the world. In this chapter we are going to be more active about turning the world into the data that we need. As the researcher, we will decide what to measure and how, and we will need to define what we are interested in. We will be active participants in the data-generating process. That is, if we want to use this data, then as researchers we must go out and hunt it.

In this chapter we cover experiments, especially constructing treatment and control groups, and appropriately considering their results. We go through implementing a survey. We discuss some aspects of ethical behavior in experiments through reference to the Tuskegee Syphilis Study and the Extracorporeal Membrane Oxygenation (ECMO) experiment and go through various case studies. Finally, we then turn to A/B testing, which is extensively used in industry, and consider a case study based on Upworthy data.

Ronald Fisher, the twentieth century statistician, and Francis Galton, the nineteenth century statistician, are the intellectual grandfathers of much of the work that we cover in this chapter. In some cases it is directly their work, in other cases it is work that built on their contributions. Both men believed in eugenics, amongst other things that are generally reprehensible. In the same way that art history acknowledges, say, Caravaggio as a murderer, while also considering his work and influence, so too must statistics and data science more generally concern themselves with this past, at the same time as we try to build a better future.

8.2 Field experiments and randomized controlled trials

8.2.1 Randomization

Correlation can be enough in some settings (Hill 1965), but to be able to make forecasts when things change, and circumstances are slightly different, we should try to understand causation. Economics went through a credibility revolution in the 2000s (Angrist and Pischke 2010). Economists realized previous work was not as reliable as it could be. There was increased concern with research design and use of experiments. This also happened in other social sciences, such as political science at a similar time (Druckman and Green 2021).

The key is the counterfactual: what would have happened in the absence of the treatment. Ideally, we could keep everything else constant, randomly divide the world into two groups, and treat one and not the other. Then we could be confident that any difference between the two groups was due to that treatment. The reason for this is that if we have some population and we randomly select two groups from it, then those two groups (provided they are both big enough) should have the same characteristics as the population. Randomized controlled trials (RCTs) and A/B testing attempt to get us as close to this "gold standard" as we can hope.

When we, and others such as Athey and Imbens (2017b), use such positive language to refer to these approaches, we do not mean to imply that they are perfect. Just that they can be better than most of the other options. For instance, in Chapter 14 we will consider causality from observational data, and while this is sometimes all that we can do, the circumstances in which it is possible to evaluate both makes it clear that approaches based on observational data are usually second-best (Gordon et al. 2019; Gordon, Moakler, and Zettelmeyer 2022). RCTs and A/B testing also bring other benefits, such as the chance to design a study that focuses on a particular question and tries to uncover the mechanism by which the effect occurs (Alsan and Finkelstein 2021). But they are not perfect, and the embrace of RCTs has not been unanimous (Deaton 2010).

One bedrock of experimental practice is that it be blinded, that is, a participant does not know whether they are in the treatment or control group. A failure to blind, especially with subjective outcomes, is grounds for the dismissal of an entire experiment in some disciplines (Edwards 2017). Ideally experiments should be double-blind, that is, even the researcher does not know. Stolberg (2006) discusses an early example of a randomized double-blind trial in 1835 to evaluate the effect of homeopathic drugs where neither the participants nor the organizers knew who was in which group. This is rarely the case for RCTs and A/B testing. Again, this is not to say they are not useful—after all in 1847 Semmelweis identified the benefit of having an intern wash their hands before delivering babies without a blinded study (Morange 2016, 121). Another major concern is with the extent to which the result found in the RCT generalizes to outside of that setting. There are typically few RCTs conducted over a long time, although it is possible this is changing and Bouguen et al. (2019) provide some RCTs that could be followed up on to assess long-term effects. Finally, the focus on causality has not been without cost in social sciences. Some argue that a causality-focused approach centers attention on the types of questions that it can answer at the expense of other types of questions.

8.2.2 Simulated example: cats or dogs

We hope to be able to establish treatment and control groups that are the same, but for the treatment. This means creating the control group is critical because when we do that, we establish the counterfactual. We might be worried about, say, underlying trends, which is one issue with a before-and-after comparison, or selection bias, which could occur when we allow self-selection into the treatment group. Either of these issues could result in biased estimates. We use randomization to go some way to addressing these.

To get started, we simulate a population, and then randomly sample from it. We will set it up so that half the population likes blue, and the other half likes white. And further, if someone likes blue then they almost surely prefer dogs, but if they like white then they almost surely prefer cats. Simulation is a critical part of the workflow advocated in this book. This is because we know what the outcomes should be from the analysis of simulated data. Whereas if we go straight to analyzing real data, then we do not know if unexpected outcomes are due to our own analysis errors, or actual results. Another good reason it is useful to take this approach of simulation is that when you are working in teams the analysis can get started before the data collection and cleaning is completed. The simulation will also help the collection and cleaning team think about tests they should run on their data.

```
set.seed(853)

num_people <- 5000

population <- tibble(
  person = 1:num_people,
  favorite_color = sample(c("Blue", "White"), size = num_people, replace = TRUE),
  prefers_dogs = if_else(favorite_color == "Blue",
                         rbinom(num_people, 1, 0.9),
                         rbinom(num_people, 1, 0.1))
  )

population |>
  count(favorite_color, prefers_dogs)
```

```
# A tibble: 4 x 3
  favorite_color prefers_dogs     n
  <chr>                 <int> <int>
1 Blue                      0   256
2 Blue                      1  2291
3 White                     0  2239
4 White                     1   214
```

Building on the terminology and concepts introduced in Chapter 6, we now construct a sampling frame that contains about 80 per cent of the target population.

```
set.seed(853)

frame <-
  population |>
  mutate(in_frame = rbinom(n = num_people, 1, prob = 0.8)) |>
```

```
    filter(in_frame == 1)

  frame |>
    count(favorite_color, prefers_dogs)
```

```
# A tibble: 4 x 3
  favorite_color prefers_dogs     n
  <chr>                 <int> <int>
1 Blue                      0   201
2 Blue                      1  1822
3 White                     0  1803
4 White                     1   177
```

For now, we will set aside dog or cat preferences and focus on creating treatment and control groups with favorite color only.

```
set.seed(853)

sample <-
  frame |>
  select(-prefers_dogs) |>
  mutate(
    group =
      sample(x = c("Treatment", "Control"), size = nrow(frame), replace = TRUE
  ))
```

When we look at the mean for the two groups, we can see that the proportions that prefer blue or white are very similar to what we specified (Table 8.1).

```
sample |>
  count(group, favorite_color) |>
  mutate(prop = n / sum(n),
         .by = group) |>
  kable(
    col.names = c("Group", "Prefers", "Number", "Proportion"),
    digits = 2,
    format.args = list(big.mark = ",")
  )
```

Table 8.1: Proportion of the groups that prefer blue or white

Group	Prefers	Number	Proportion
Control	Blue	987	0.50
Control	White	997	0.50
Treatment	Blue	1,036	0.51
Treatment	White	983	0.49

We randomized with favorite color only. But we should also find that we took dog or cat preferences along at the same time and will have a "representative" share of people who prefer dogs to cats. We can look at our dataset (Table 8.2).

```
sample |>
  left_join(
    frame |> select(person, prefers_dogs),
    by = "person"
  ) |>
  count(group, prefers_dogs) |>
  mutate(prop = n / sum(n),
         .by = group) |>
  kable(
    col.names = c(
      "Group",
      "Prefers dogs to cats",
      "Number",
      "Proportion"
    ),
    digits = 2,
    format.args = list(big.mark = ",")
  )
```

Table 8.2: Proportion of the treatment and control group that prefer dogs or cats

Group	Prefers dogs to cats	Number	Proportion
Control	0	1,002	0.51
Control	1	982	0.49
Treatment	0	1,002	0.50
Treatment	1	1,017	0.50

It is exciting to have a representative share on "unobservables". (In this case, we do "observe" them—to illustrate the point—but we did not select on them). We get this because the variables were correlated. But it will break down in several ways that we will discuss. It also assumes large enough groups. For instance, if we considered specific dog breeds, instead of dogs as an entity, we may not find ourselves in this situation. To check that the two groups are the same, we look to see if we can identify a difference between the two groups based on observables, theory, experience, and expert opinion. In this case we looked at the mean, but we could look at other aspects as well.

This would traditionally bring us to Analysis of Variance (ANOVA). ANOVA was introduced around 100 years ago by Fisher while he was working on statistical problems in agriculture. (Stolley (1991) provides additional background on Fisher.) This is less unexpected than it may seem because historically agricultural research was closely tied to statistical innovation. Often statistical methods were designed to answer agricultural questions such as "does fertilizer work?" and were only later adapted to clinical trials (Yoshioka 1998). It was relatively easily to divide a field into "treated" and "non-treated", and the magnitude of any effect was likely to be large. While appropriate for that context, often these same statistical approaches are still taught today in introductory material, even when they are being applied in different circumstances to those they were designed for. It almost always pays to take a step back and think about what is being done and whether it is appropriate to the circumstances. We mention ANOVA here because of its importance historically. There is nothing wrong with it in the right setting. But the number of modern use-cases where it is the best option tends to be small. It might be better to build the model that underpins ANOVA ourselves, which we cover in Chapter 12.

8.2.3 Treatment and control

If the treatment and control groups are the same in all ways and remain that way, but for the treatment, then we have internal validity, which is to say that our control will work as a counterfactual and our results can speak to a difference between the groups in that study. Internal validity means that our estimates of the effect of the treatment speak to the treatment and not some other aspect. It means that we can use our results to make claims about what happened in the experiment.

If the group to which we applied our randomization were representative of the broader population, and the experimental set-up was like outside conditions, then we further could have external validity. That would mean that the difference that we find does not just apply in our own experiment, but also in the broader population. External validity means that we can use our experiment to make claims about what would happen outside the experiment. It is randomization that has allowed that to happen. In practice we would not just rely on one experiment but would instead consider that a contribution to a broader evidence-collection effort (Duflo 2020, 1955).

> **i Shoulders of giants**
>
> Dr Esther Duflo is Abdul Latif Jameel Professor of Poverty Alleviation and Development Economics at MIT. After earning a PhD in Economics from MIT in 1999, she remained at MIT as an assistant professor, being promoted to full professor in 2003. One area of her research is economic development where she uses randomized controlled trials to understand how to address poverty. One of her most important books is *Poor Economics* (Banerjee and Duflo 2011). One of her most important papers is Banerjee et al. (2015) which uses randomization to examine the effect of microfinance. She was awarded the Sveriges Riksbank Prize in Economic Sciences in Memory of Alfred Nobel in 2019.

But this means we need randomization twice. Firstly, into the group that was subject to the experiment, and then secondly, between treatment and control. How do we think about this randomization, and to what extent does it matter?

We are interested in the effect of being treated. It may be that we charge different prices, which would be a continuous treatment variable, or that we compare different colors on a website, which would be a discrete treatment variable. Either way, we need to make sure that the groups are otherwise the same. How can we be convinced of this? One way is to ignore the treatment variable and to examine all other variables, looking for whether we can detect a difference between the groups based on any other variables. For instance, if we are conducting an experiment on a website, then are the groups roughly similar in terms of, say:

- Microsoft and Apple users?
- Safari, Chrome, and Firefox users?

- Mobile and desktop users?
- Users from certain locations?

Further, are the groups representative of the broader population? These are all threats to the validity of our claims. For instance, the Nationscape survey which we consider later in this chapter was concerned about the number of Firefox users who completed the survey. In the end they exclude a subset of those respondents (Vavreck and Tausanovitch 2021, 5).

When done properly, that is if the treatment is truly independent, then we can estimate the average treatment effect (ATE). In a binary treatment variable setting this is:

$$\text{ATE} = \mathbb{E}[Y|t = 1] - \mathbb{E}[Y|t = 0].$$

That is, the difference between the treated group, $t = 1$, and the control group, $t = 0$, when measured by the expected value of the outcome, Y. The ATE becomes the difference between two conditional expectations.

To illustrate this concept, we simulate some data that shows an average difference of one between the treatment and control groups.

```
set.seed(853)

ate_example <-
  tibble(person = 1:1000,
         treated = sample(c("Yes", "No"), size = 1000, replace = TRUE)) |>
  mutate(outcome = case_when(
    treated == "No" ~ rnorm(n(), mean = 5, sd = 1),
    treated == "Yes" ~ rnorm(n(), mean = 6, sd = 1),
  ))
```

We can see the difference, which we simulated to be one, between the two groups in Figure 8.1. And we can compute the average between the groups and then the difference to see also that we roughly get back the result that we put in (Table 8.3).

```
ate_example |>
  ggplot(aes(x = outcome, fill = treated)) +
  geom_histogram(position = "dodge2", binwidth = 0.2) +
  theme_minimal() +
  labs(x = "Outcome",
       y = "Number of people",
       fill = "Person was treated") +
  scale_fill_brewer(palette = "Set1") +
  theme(legend.position = "bottom")
```

```
ate_example |>
  summarise(mean = mean(outcome),
            .by = treated) |>
  kable(
    col.names = c(
      "Was treated?",
      "Average effect"
```

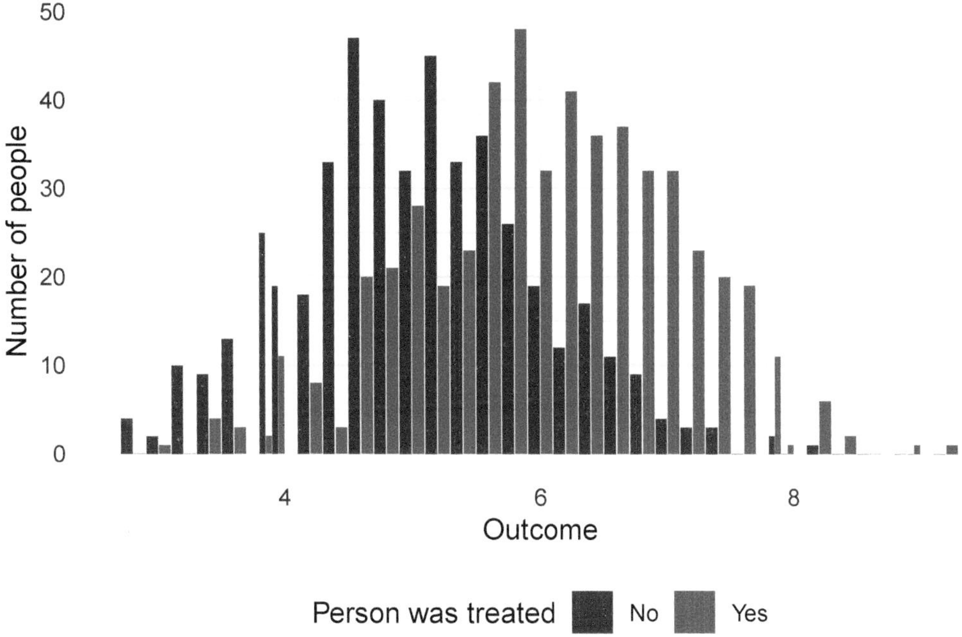

Figure 8.1: Simulated data showing a difference between the treatment and control group

```
    ),
    digits = 2
  )
```

Table 8.3: Average difference between the treatment and control groups for data simulated to have an average difference of one

Was treated?	Average effect
Yes	6.06
No	5.03

Unfortunately, there is often a difference between simulated data and reality. For instance, an experiment cannot run for too long otherwise people may be treated many times or become inured to the treatment; but it cannot be too short otherwise we cannot measure longer-term outcomes. We cannot have a "representative" sample across every facet of a population, but if not, then the treatment and control may be different. Practical difficulties may make it difficult to follow up with certain groups and so we end up with a biased collection. Some questions to explore when working with real experimental data include:

- How are the participants being selected into the frame for consideration?
- How are they being selected for treatment? We would hope this is being done randomly, but this term is applied to a variety of situations. Additionally, early "success" can lead to pressure to treat everyone, especially in medical settings.
- How is treatment being assessed?
- To what extent is random allocation ethical and fair? Some argue that shortages mean it is reasonable to randomly allocate, but that may depend on how linear the benefits are. It may also be difficult to establish definitions, and the power imbalance between those making these decisions and those being treated should be considered.

Bias and other issues are not the end of the world. But we need to think about them carefully. Selection bias, introduced in Chapter 4, can be adjusted for, but only if it is recognized. For instance, how would the results of a survey about the difficulty of a university course differ if only students who completed the course were surveyed, and not those who dropped out? We should always work to try to make our dataset as representative as possible when we are creating it, but it may be possible to use a model to adjust for some of the bias after the fact. For instance, if there were a variable that was correlated with, say, attrition, then it could be added to the model either by itself, or as an interaction. Similarly, if there was correlation between the individuals. For instance, if there was some "hidden variable" that we did not know about that meant some individuals were correlated, then we could use wider standard errors. This needs to be done carefully and we discuss this further in Chapter 14. That said, if such issues can be anticipated, then it may be better to change the experiment. For instance, perhaps it would be possible to stratify by that variable.

8.2.4 Fisher's tea party

The British are funny when it comes to tea. There is substantial, persistent, debate in Britain about how to make the perfect "cuppa" with everyone from George Orwell to John Lennon weighing in. Some say to add the milk first. Others, to add it last. YouGov, a polling company, found that most respondents put milk in last (M. Smith 2018). But one might wonder whether the order matters at all.

Fisher introduced an experiment designed to see if a person can distinguish between a cup of tea where the milk was added first, or last. We begin by preparing eight cups of tea: four with milk added first and the other four with milk added last. We then randomize the order of all eight cups. We tell the taster, whom we will call "Ian", about the experimental set-up: there are eight cups of tea, four of each type, he will be given cups of tea in a random order, and his task is to group them into two groups.

One of the nice aspects of this experiment is that we can do it ourselves. There are a few things to be careful of in practice. These include:

1) that the quantities of milk and tea are consistent,
2) the groups are marked in some way that the taster cannot see, and
3) the order is randomized.

Another nice aspect of this experiment is that we can calculate the chance that Ian is able to randomly get the groupings correct. To decide if his groupings were likely to have occurred at random, we need to calculate the probability this could happen. First, we count the number of successes out of the four that were chosen. There are: $\binom{8}{4} = \frac{8!}{4!(8-4)!} = 70$ possible outcomes (Fisher [1935] 1949, 14). This notation means there are eight items in the set, and we are choosing four of them, and is used when the order of choice does not matter.

We are asking Ian to group the cups, not to identify which is which, and so there are two ways for him to be perfectly correct. He could either correctly identify all the ones that were milk-first (one outcome out of 70) or correctly identify all the ones that were tea-first (one outcome out of 70). This means the probability of this event is: $\frac{2}{70}$, or about three per cent.

As Fisher ([1935] 1949, 15) makes clear, this now becomes a judgement call. We need to consider the weight of evidence that we require before we accept the groupings did not occur by chance and that Ian was aware of what he was doing. We need to decide what evidence it takes for us to be convinced. If there is no possible evidence that would dissuade us from the view that we held coming into the experiment, say, that there is no difference between milk-first and tea-first, then what is the point of doing an experiment? We expect that if Ian got it completely right, then the reasonable person would accept that he was able to tell the difference.

What if he is almost perfect? By chance, there are 16 ways for a person to be "off-by-one". Either Ian thinks there was one cup that was milk-first when it was tea-first—there are, $\binom{4}{1} = 4$, four ways this could happen—or he thinks there was one cup that was tea-first when it was milk-first—again, there are, $\binom{4}{1} = 4$, four ways this could happen. These outcomes are independent, so the probability is $\frac{4\times4}{70}$, or about 23 per cent. Given there is an almost 23 per cent chance of being off-by-one just by randomly grouping the teacups, this outcome probably would not convince us that Ian could tell the difference between tea-first and milk-first.

What we are looking for, in order to claim something is experimentally demonstrable is that we have come to know the features of an experiment where such a result is reliably found (Fisher [1935] 1949, 16). We need a weight of evidence rather than just one experiment. We are looking to thoroughly interrogate our data and our experiments, and to think precisely about the analysis methods we are using. Rather than searching for meaning in constellations of stars, we want to make it as easy as possible for others to reproduce our work. It is in that way that our conclusions stand a better chance of holding up in the long term.

8.2.5 Ethical foundations

The weight of evidence in medical settings can be measured in lost lives. One reason ethical practice in medical experiments developed is to prevent the unnecessary loss of life. We now detail two cases where human life may have been unnecessarily lost that helped establish foundations of ethical practice. We consider the need to obtain informed consent by discussing the Tuskegee Syphilis Study. And the need to ensure that an experiment is necessary by discussing the ECMO experiments.

8.2.5.1 Tuskegee Syphilis Study

Following Brandt (1978) and Alsan and Wanamaker (2018), the Tuskegee Syphilis Study is an infamous medical trial that began in 1932. As part of this experiment, 400 Black Americans with syphilis were not given appropriate treatment, nor even told they had syphilis, well after a standard treatment for syphilis was established and widely available. A control group, without syphilis, were also given non-effective drugs. These financially poor Black Americans in the United States South were offered minimal compensation and not told they were part of an experiment. Further, extensive work was undertaken to ensure the men would not receive treatment from anywhere, including writing to local doctors and the local health department. Even after some of the men were drafted and told to immediately get treatment, the draft board complied with a request to have the men excluded from treatment. By the time the study was stopped in 1972, more than half of the men were deceased and many of deaths were from syphilis-related causes.

The effect of the Tuskegee Syphilis Study was felt not just by the men in the study, but more broadly. Alsan and Wanamaker (2018) found that it is associated with a decrease in life expectancy at age 45 of up to 1.5 years for Black men located around central Alabama because of medical mistrust and decreased interactions with physicians. In response the United States established requirements for Institutional Review Boards and President Clinton made a formal apology in 1997. Brandt (1978, 27) says:

> In retrospect the Tuskegee Study revealed more about the pathology of racism than the pathology of syphilis; more about the nature of scientific inquiry than the nature of the disease process... [T]he notion that science is a value-free discipline must be rejected. The need for greater vigilance in assessing the specific ways in which social values and attitudes affect professional behavior is clearly indicated.

Heller (2022) provides further background on the Tuskegee Syphilis Study.

> **i Shoulders of giants**
>
> Dr Marcella Alsan is a Professor of Public Policy at Harvard University. She has an MD from Loyola University and earned a PhD in Economics from Harvard University in 2012. She was appointed as an assistant professor at Stanford, being promoted to full professor in 2019 when she returned to Harvard. One area of her research is health inequality, and one particularly important paper is Alsan and Wanamaker (2018), which we discussed above. She was awarded a MacArthur Foundation Fellowship in 2021.

8.2.5.2 Extracorporeal membrane oxygenation (ECMO)

Turning to the evaluation of extracorporeal membrane oxygenation (ECMO), Ware (1989) describes how they viewed ECMO as a possible treatment for persistent pulmonary hypertension in newborn children. They enrolled 19 patients and used conventional medical therapy on ten of them, and ECMO on nine of them. It was found that six of the ten in the control group survived while all in the treatment group survived. Ware (1989) used randomized consent whereby only the parents of infants randomly selected to be treated with ECMO were asked to consent.

We are concerned with "equipoise", by which we refer to a situation in which there is genuine uncertainty about whether the treatment is more effective than conventional procedures. In medical settings even if there is initial equipoise it could be undermined if the treatment is found to be effective early in the study. Ware (1989) describes how after the results of these first 19 patients, randomization stopped and only ECMO was used. The recruiters and those treating the patients were initially not told that randomization had stopped. It was decided that this complete allocation to ECMO would continue "until either the 28th survivor or the 4th death was observed". After 19 of 20 additional patients survived the trial was terminated. The experiment was effectively divided into two phases: in the first there was randomized use of ECMO, and in the second only ECMO was used.

One approach in these settings is a "randomized play-the-winner" rule following Wei and Durham (1978). Treatment is still randomized, but the probability shifts with each successful treatment to make treatment more likely, and there is some stopping rule. Berry (1989) argues that far from the need for a more sophisticated stopping rule, there was no need for this study of ECMO because equipoise never existed. Berry (1989) re-visits the literature mentioned by Ware (1989) and finds extensive evidence that ECMO was already known to be effective. Berry (1989) points out that there is almost never complete consensus and so one could almost always argue, inappropriately, for the existence of equipoise even in the face of a substantial weight of evidence. Berry (1989) further criticizes Ware (1989) for the use of randomized consent because of the potential that there may have been different outcomes for the infants subject to conventional medical therapy had their parents known there were other options.

The Tuskegee Syphilis Study and ECMO experiments may seem quite far from our present circumstances. While it may be illegal to do this exact research these days, it does not mean that unethical research does not still happen. For instance, we see it in machine learning applications in health and other areas; while we are not meant to explicitly discriminate and we are meant to get consent, it does not mean that we cannot implicitly discriminate without any type of consumer buy-in. For instance, Obermeyer et al. (2019) describes how many health care systems in the United States use algorithms to score the severity of how sick a patient is. They show that for the same score, Black patients are sicker, and that if Black patients were scored in the same way as White patients, then they would receive considerably more care. They find that the discrimination occurs because the algorithm is based on health care costs, rather than sickness. But because access to healthcare is unequally distributed between Black and White patients, the algorithm, however inadvertently, perpetuates racial bias.

8.3 Surveys

Having decided what to measure, one common way to get values is to use a survey. This is especially challenging, and there is an entire field—survey research—focused on it. Edelman, Vittert, and Meng (2021) make it clear that there are no new problems here, and the challenges that we face today are closely related to those that were faced in the past. There are many ways to implement surveys, and this decision matters. For some time, the only option was face-to-face surveys, where an enumerator conducted the survey in-person with the respondent. Eventually surveys began to be conducted over the telephone, again by an enumerator. One issue in both these settings was a considerable interviewer effect (Elliott et al. 2022). The internet brought a third era of survey research, characterized by low participation rates (Groves 2011). Surveys are a popular and invaluable way to get data. Face-to-face and telephone surveys are still used and have an important role to play, but many surveys are now internet-based.

There are many dedicated survey platforms, such as Survey Monkey and Qualtrics, that are largely internet-based. One especially common approach, because it is free, is to use Google Forms. In general, the focus of those platforms is enabling the user to construct and send a survey form. They typically expect the user already has contact details for some sampling frame.

Other platforms, such as Amazon Mechanical Turk, mentioned in Chapter 3, and Prolific, focus on providing respondents. When using platforms like those we should try to understand who those respondents are and how they might differ from the population of interest (Levay, Freese, and Druckman 2016; Enns and Rothschild 2022).

The survey form needs to be considered within the context of the broader research and with special concern for the respondent. Try to conduct a test of the survey before releasing it. Light, Singer, and Willett (1990, 213), in the context of studies to evaluate higher education, say that there is no occasion in which a pilot study will not bring improvements, and that they are almost always worth it. In the case of surveys, we go further. If you do not have the time, or budget, to test a survey then it might be better to re-consider whether the survey should be done.

Try to test the wording of a survey (Tourangeau, Rips, and Rasinski 2000, 23). When designing the survey, we need to have survey questions that are conversational and flow from one to the next, grouped within topics (Elson 2018). But we should also consider the cognitive load that we place on the respondent, and vary the difficulty of the questions.

When designing a survey, the critical task is to keep the respondent front-of-mind (Dillman, Smyth, and Christian [1978] 2014, 94). Drawing on Swain (1985), all questions need to be relevant and able to be answered by the respondent. The wording of the questions should be based on what the respondent would be comfortable with. The decision between different question types turns on minimizing both error and the burden that we impose on the respondent. In general, if there are a small number of clear options then multiple-choice questions are appropriate. In that case, the responses should usually be mutually exclusive and collectively exhaustive. If they are not mutually exclusive, then this needs to be signaled in the text of the question. It is also important that units are specified, and that standard concepts are used, to the extent possible.

Open text boxes may be appropriate if there are many potential answers. This will increase both the time the respondent spends completing the survey and the time it will take to analyze the answers. Only ask one question at a time and try to ask questions in a neutral way that does not lead to one particular response. Testing the survey helps avoid ambiguous or double-barreled questions, which could confuse respondents. The subject matter of the survey will also affect the appropriate choice of question type. For instance, potentially "threatening" topics may be better considered with open-ended questions (E. Blair et al. 1977).

All surveys need to have an introduction that specifies a title for the survey, who is conducting it, their contact details, and the purpose. It should also include a statement about the confidentiality protections that are in place, and any ethics review board clearances that were obtained.

When doing surveys, it is critical to ask the right person. For instance, Lichand and Wolf (2022) consider child labor. The extent of child labor is typically based on surveys of parents. When children were surveyed a considerable under-reporting by parents was found.

One aspect of particular concern is questions about sexual orientation and gender identity. While this is an evolving area, The White House (2023) provides recommendations for best practice, such as considering how the data will be used, and ensuring sufficient sample size. With regard to asking about sexual orientation they recommend the following question:

- "Which of the following best represents how you think of yourself?"
    a) "Gay or lesbian"
    b) "Straight, that is not gay or lesbian"
    c) "Bisexual"
    d) "I use a different term [free-text]"
    e) "I don't know"

And with regard to gender, they recommend a multi-question approach:

- "What sex were you assigned at birth, on your original birth certificate?"
    a) "Female"
    b) "Male"
- "How do you currently describe yourself (mark all that apply)?"
    a) "Female"
    b) "Male"
    c) "Transgender"
    d) "I use a different term [free-text]"

Again, this is an evolving area and best practice is likely to change.

Finally, returning to the reason for doing surveys in the first place, while doing all this, it is important to also keep what we are interested in measuring in mind. Check that the survey questions relate to the estimand.

8.3.1 Democracy Fund Voter Study Group

As an example of survey data, we will consider the Democracy Fund Voter Study Group Nationscape dataset (Tausanovitch and Vavreck 2021). This is a large series of surveys conducted between July 2019 and January 2021. It is weighted on a number of variables including: gender, major census regions, race, Hispanic ethnicity, household income, education, and age. Holliday et al. (2021) describe it as a convenience sample, which was introduced in Chapter 6, based on demographics. In this case, Holliday et al. (2021) detail how the sample was provided by Lucid, who operate an online platform for survey respondents, based on certain demographic quotas. Holliday et al. (2021) found that results are similar to government and commercial surveys.

To get the dataset, go to the Democracy Fund Voter Study Group website[1], then look for "Nationscape" and request access to the data. This could take a day or two. After getting access, focus on the ".dta" files. Nationscape conducted many surveys in the lead-up to the 2020 United States election, so there are many files. The filename is the reference date, where "ns20200625" refers to 25 June 2020. That is the file that we use here, but many of them are similar. We download and save it as "ns20200625.dta".

As introduced in the "R essentials" Online Appendix[2], we can import ".dta" files after installing `haven` and `labelled`. The code that we use to import and prepare the survey dataset is based on that of Mitrovski, Yang, and Wankiewicz (2020).

```
raw_nationscape_data <-
  read_dta("ns20200625.dta")


# The Stata format separates labels so reunite those
raw_nationscape_data <-
  to_factor(raw_nationscape_data)

# Just keep relevant variables
nationscape_data <-
```

[1] https://www.voterstudygroup.org
[2] https://tellingstorieswithdata.com/20-r_essentials.html

```
    raw_nationscape_data |>
    select(vote_2020, gender, education, state, age)

  nationscape_data
```

```
# A tibble: 6,479 x 5
   vote_2020                 gender education                           state   age
 * <fct>                     <fct>  <fct>                               <chr> <dbl>
 1 Donald Trump              Female Associate Degree                    WI       49
 2 I am not sure/don't know  Female College Degree (such as B.A., B.~ VA       39
 3 Donald Trump              Female College Degree (such as B.A., B.~ VA       46
 4 Donald Trump              Female High school graduate                TX       75
 5 Donald Trump              Female High school graduate                WA       52
 6 I would not vote          Female Other post high school vocationa~ OH       44
 7 Joe Biden                 Female Completed some college, but no d~ MA       21
 8 Joe Biden                 Female Completed some college, but no d~ TX       38
 9 Donald Trump              Female Completed some college, but no d~ CA       69
10 Donald Trump              Female College Degree (such as B.A., B.~ NC       59
# i 6,469 more rows
```

At this point we want to clean up a few issues. For instance, for simplicity, remove anyone not voting for Trump or Biden.

```
nationscape_data <-
  nationscape_data |>
  filter(vote_2020 %in% c("Joe Biden", "Donald Trump")) |>
  mutate(vote_biden = if_else(vote_2020 == "Joe Biden", 1, 0)) |>
  select(-vote_2020)
```

We then want to create some variables of interest.

```
nationscape_data <-
  nationscape_data |>
  mutate(
    age_group = case_when(
      age <= 29 ~ "18-29",
      age <= 44 ~ "30-44",
      age <= 59 ~ "45-59",
      age >= 60 ~ "60+",
      TRUE ~ "Trouble"
    ),
    gender = case_when(
      gender == "Female" ~ "female",
      gender == "Male" ~ "male",
      TRUE ~ "Trouble"
    ),
    education_level = case_when(
      education %in% c(
        "3rd Grade or less",
```

```
        "Middle School - Grades 4 - 8",
        "Completed some high school",
        "High school graduate"
      ) ~ "High school or less",
      education %in% c(
        "Other post high school vocational training",
        "Completed some college, but no degree"
      ) ~ "Some post sec",
      education %in% c(
        "Associate Degree",
        "College Degree (such as B.A., B.S.)",
        "Completed some graduate, but no degree"
      ) ~ "Post sec +",
      education %in% c("Masters degree",
                       "Doctorate degree") ~ "Grad degree",
      TRUE ~ "Trouble"
    )
  ) |>
  select(-education,-age)
```

We will draw on this dataset in Chapter 15, so we will save it.

```
write_csv(x = nationscape_data,
          file = "nationscape_data.csv")
```

We can also have a look at some of the variables (Figure 8.2).

```
nationscape_data |>
  mutate(supports = if_else(vote_biden == 1, "Biden", "Trump")) |>
  mutate(supports = factor(supports, levels = c("Trump", "Biden"))) |>
  ggplot(mapping = aes(x = age_group, fill = supports)) +
  geom_bar(position = "dodge2") +
  theme_minimal() +
  labs(
    x = "Age-group of respondent",
    y = "Number of respondents",
    fill = "Voted for"
  ) +
  facet_wrap(vars(gender)) +
  guides(x = guide_axis(angle = 90)) +
  theme(legend.position = "bottom") +
  scale_fill_brewer(palette = "Set1")
```

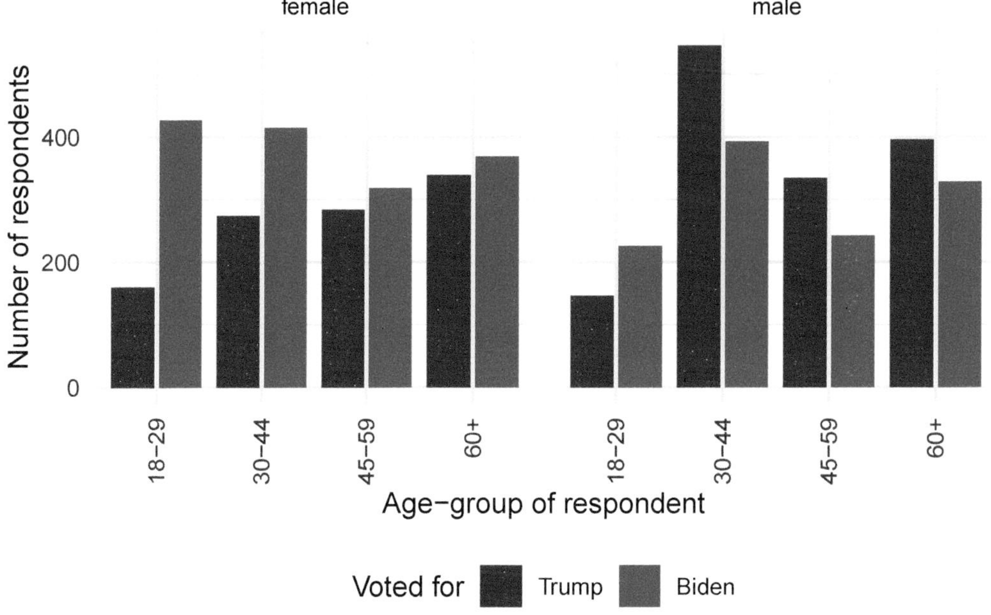

Figure 8.2: Examining some of the variables from the Nationscape survey dataset

8.4 RCT examples

8.4.1 The Oregon Health Insurance Experiment

In the United States, unlike many developed countries, basic health insurance is not necessarily available to all residents, even those on low incomes. The Oregon Health Insurance Experiment involved low-income adults in Oregon, a state in the northwest of the United States, from 2008 to 2010 (Finkelstein et al. 2012).

> **Shoulders of giants**
>
> Dr Amy Finkelstein is John & Jennie S. Macdonald Professor of Economics at MIT. After earning a PhD in Economics from MIT in 2001, she was a Junior Fellow at the Harvard Society of Fellows, before returning to MIT as an assistant professor in 2005, being promoted to full professor in 2008. One area of her research is health economics where she uses randomized controlled trials to understand insurance. She was one of the lead researchers on Finkelstein et al. (2012) which examined the Oregon Health Insurance Experiment. She was awarded the John Bates Clark Medal in 2012 and a MacArthur Foundation Fellowship in 2018.

Oregon funded 10,000 places in the state-run Medicaid program, which provides health insurance for people with low incomes. A lottery was used to allocate these places, and this was judged fair because it was expected, correctly as it turned out, that demand for places would exceed the supply. In the end, 89,824 individuals signed up.

The draws were conducted over a six-month period and 35,169 individuals were selected (the household of those who won the draw were given the opportunity) but only 30 per cent of them turned out to be eligible and completed the paperwork. The insurance lasted indefinitely. This random allocation of insurance allowed the researchers to understand the effect of health insurance.

The reason that this random allocation is important is that it is not usually possible to compare those with and without insurance because the type of people that sign up to get health insurance differ to those who do not. That decision is "confounded" with other variables and results in selection bias.

As the opportunity to apply for health insurance was randomly allocated, the researchers were able to evaluate the health and earnings of those who received health insurance and compare them to those who did not. To do this they used administrative data, such as hospital discharge data, matched credit reports, and, uncommonly, mortality records. The extent of this data is limited and so they also conducted a survey.

The specifics of this are not important, and we will have more to say in Chapter 12, but they estimate the model:

$$y_{ihj} = \beta_0 + \beta_1 \text{Lottery} + X_{ih}\beta_2 + V_{ih}\beta_3 + \epsilon_{ihj} \tag{8.1}$$

Equation 8.1 explains various j outcomes (such as health) for an individual i in household h as a function of an indicator variable as to whether household h was selected by the lottery. It is the β_1 coefficient that is of particular interest. That is the estimate of the mean difference between the treatment and control groups. X_{ih} is a set of variables that are correlated with the probability of being treated. These adjust for that impact to a certain extent. An example of that is the number of individuals in a household. And finally, V_{ih} is a set of variables that are not correlated with the lottery, such as demographics and previous hospital discharges.

Like earlier studies such as Brook et al. (1984), Finkelstein et al. (2012) found that the treatment group used more health care including both primary and preventive care as well as hospitalizations but had lower out-of-pocket medical expenditures. More generally, the treatment group reported better physical and mental health.

8.4.2 Civic Honesty Around The Globe

Trust is not something that we think regularly about, but it is fundamental to most interactions, both economic and personal. For instance, many people get paid after they do some work—they are trusting their employer will make good, and vice versa. If you get paid in advance, then they are trusting you. In a strictly naive, one-shot, world without transaction costs, this does not make sense. If you get paid in advance, the incentive is for you to take the money and run in the last pay period before you quit, and through backward induction everything falls apart. We do not live in such a world. For one thing there are transaction costs, for another, generally, we have repeated interactions, and finally, the world usually ends up being fairly small.

Understanding the extent of honesty in different countries may help us to explain economic development and other aspects of interest such as tax compliance, but it is hard to measure. We cannot ask people how honest they are—the liars would lie, resulting in a lemons problem (Akerlof 1970). This is a situation of adverse selection, where the liars know they are liars, but others do not. To get around this A. Cohn et al. (2019a) conduct an experiment in

355 cities across 40 countries where they "turned in" a wallet that was either empty or contained the local equivalent of US$13.45. They were interested in whether the "recipient" attempted to return the wallet. They found that generally wallets with money were more likely to be returned (A. Cohn et al. 2019a, 1).

In total A. Cohn et al. (2019a) "turn in" 17,303 wallets to various institutions including banks, museums, hotels, and police stations. The importance of such institutions to an economy is well accepted (Acemoglu, Johnson, and Robinson 2001) and they are common across most countries. Importantly, for the experiment, they usually have a reception area where the wallet could be turned in (A. Cohn et al. 2019a, 1).

In the experiment a research assistant turned in the wallet to an employee at the reception area, using a set form of words. The research assistant had to note various features of the setting, such as the gender, age-group, and busyness of the "recipient". The wallets were transparent and contained a key, a grocery list, and a business card with a name and email address. The outcome of interest was whether an email was sent to the unique email address on the business card in the wallet. The grocery list was included to signal that the owner of the wallet was a local. The key was included as something that was only useful to the owner of the wallet, and never the recipient, in contrast to the cash, to adjust for altruism. The language and currency were adapted to local conditions.

The primary treatment in the experiment is whether the wallet contained money or not. The key outcome was whether the wallet was attempted to be returned or not. It was found that the median response time was 26 minutes, and that if an email was sent then it usually happened within a day (A. Cohn et al. 2019b, 10).

Using the data for the paper that is made available (A. Cohn 2019) we can see that considerable differences were found between countries (Figure 8.3). In almost all countries wallets with money were more likely to be returned than wallets without. The experiments were conducted across 40 countries, which were chosen based on them having enough cities with populations of at least 100,000, as well as the ability for the research assistants to safely visit and withdraw cash. Within those countries, the cities were chosen starting with the largest ones and there were usually 400 observations in each country (A. Cohn et al. 2019b, 5). A. Cohn et al. (2019a) further conducted the experiment with the equivalent of US$94.15 in three countries—Poland, the UK, and the US—and found that reporting rates further increased.

In addition to the experiments, A. Cohn et al. (2019a) conducted surveys that allowed them to understand some reasons for their findings. During the survey, participants were given one of the scenarios and then asked to answer questions. The use of surveys also allowed them to be specific about the respondents. The survey involved 2,525 respondents (829 in the UK, 809 in Poland, and 887 in the US) (A. Cohn et al. 2019b, 36). Participants were chosen using attention checks and demographic quotas based on age, gender, and residence, and they received US$4.00 for their participation (A. Cohn et al. 2019b, 36). The survey did not find that larger rewards were expected for turning in a wallet with more money. But it did find that failure to turn in a wallet with more money caused the respondent to feel more like they had stolen money.

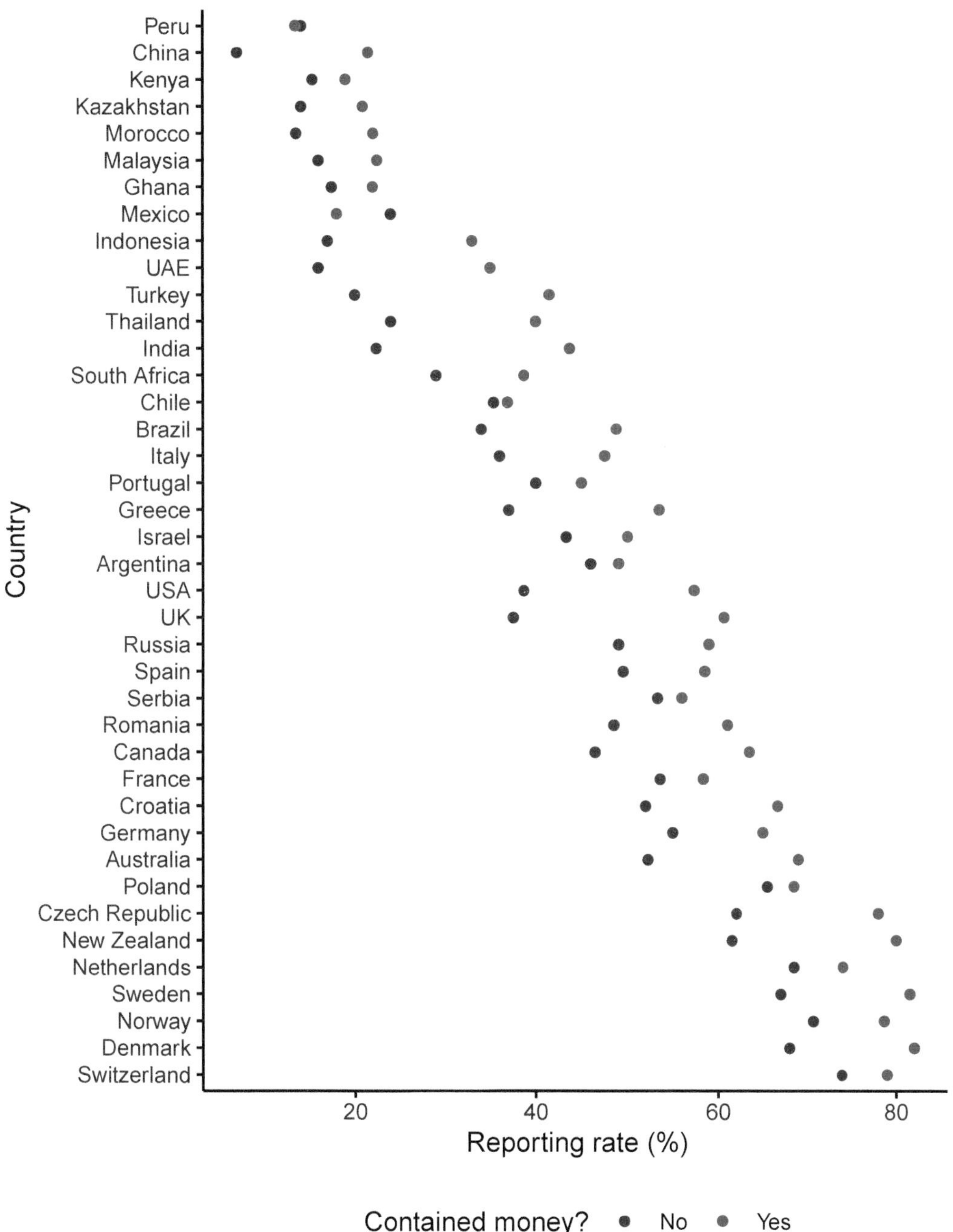

Figure 8.3: Comparison of the proportion of wallets handed in, by country, depending on whether they contained money

8.5 A/B testing

The past two decades have probably seen the most experiments ever run, likely by several orders of magnitude. This is because of the extensive use of A/B testing at tech firms (Kohavi et al. 2012). For a long time decisions such as what font to use were based on the Highest Paid Person's Opinion (HIPPO) (Christian 2012). These days, many large tech companies have extensive infrastructure for experiments. They term them A/B tests because of the comparison of two groups: one that gets treatment A and the other that either gets treatment B or does not see any change (Salganik 2018, 185). We could additionally consider more than two options at which point we typically use the terminology of "arms" of the experiment.

The proliferation of experiments in the private sector has brought with it a host of ethical concerns. Some private companies do not have ethical review boards, and there are different ethical concerns in the private sector compared with academia. For instance, many A/B tests are designed, explicitly, to make a consumer more likely to spend money. While society may not generally have a concern with that in the case of an online grocery retailer, society may have a problem in the case of an online gambling website. More extensive legislation and the development of private-sector ethical best practice are both likely as the extent of experimentation in the private sector becomes better known.

Every time you are online you are probably subject to tens, hundreds, or potentially thousands, of different A/B tests. While, at their heart, they are just experiments that use sensors to measure data that need to be analyzed, they have many special features that are interesting in their own light. For instance, Kohavi, Tang, and Xu (2020, 3) discuss the example of Microsoft's search engine Bing. They used A/B testing to examine how to display advertisements. Based on these tests they ended up lengthening the title on the advertisement. They found this caused revenue to increase by 12 per cent, or around $100 million annually, without any significant measured trade-off.

In this book we use the term A/B test to refer to the situation in which we primarily implement an experiment through a technology stack about something that is primarily of the internet, such as a change to a website or similar and measured with sensors rather than a survey. While at their heart they are just experiments, A/B tests have a range of specific concerns. Bosch and Revilla (2022) detail some of these from a statistical perspective. There is something different about doing tens of thousands of small experiments all the time, compared with the typical RCT set-up of conducting one experiment over the course of months.

RCTs are often, though not exclusively, done in academia or by government agencies, but much of A/B testing occurs in industry. This means that if you are in industry and want to introduce A/B testing to your firm there can be aspects such as culture and relationship building that become important. It can be difficult to convince a manager to run an experiment. Indeed, sometimes it can be easier to experiment by not delivering, or delaying, a change that has been decided to create a control group rather than a treatment group (Salganik 2018, 188). Sometimes the most difficult aspect of A/B testing is not the analysis, it is the politics. This is not unique to A/B testing and, for instance, looking at the history of biology, we see that even aspects such as germ theory were not resolved by experiment, but instead by ideology and social standing (Morange 2016, 124).

Following Kohavi, Tang, and Xu (2020, 153), when conducting A/B testing, as with all experiments, we need to be concerned with delivery. In the case of an experiment, it is usually clear how it is being delivered. For instance, we may have the person come to a doctor's clinic and then inject them with either a drug or a placebo. But in the case of A/B testing, it is less obvious. For instance, should we make a change to a website, or to an app? This decision affects our ability to both conduct the experiment and to gather data from it. (Urban, Sreenivasan, and Kannan (2016) provide an overview of A/B testing at Netflix, assuming an app is installed on a PlayStation 4.)

It is relatively easy and normal to update a website all the time. This means that small changes can be easily implemented if the A/B test is delivered that way. But in the case of an app, conducting an A/B test becomes a bigger deal. For instance, the release may need to go through an app store, and so would need to be part of a regular release cycle. There is also a selection concern: some users will not update the app and it is possible they are different to those that do regularly update the app.

The delivery decision also affects our ability to gather data from the A/B test. A website change is less of a big deal because we get data from a website whenever a user interacts with it. But in the case of an app, the user may use the app offline or with limited data upload which can add complications.

We need to plan! For instance, results are unlikely to be available the day after a change to an app, but they could be available the day after a change to a website. Further, we may need to consider our results in the context of different devices and platforms, potentially using, say, regression which will be covered in Chapter 12.

The second aspect of concern, as introduced in Chapter 6, is instrumentation. When we conduct a traditional experiment we might, for instance, ask respondents to fill out a survey. But this is usually not done with A/B testing. Instead we usually use various sensors (Kohavi, Tang, and Xu 2020, 162). One approach is to use cookies but different types of users will clear these at different rates. Another approach is to force the user to download a tiny image from a server, so that we know when they have completed some action. For instance, this is commonly used to track whether a user has opened an email. But again different types of users will block these at different rates.

The third aspect of concern is what are we randomizing over (Kohavi, Tang, and Xu 2020, 166)? In the case of traditional experiments, this is often a person, or sometimes various groups of people. But in the case of A/B testing it can be less clear. For instance, are we randomizing over the page, the session, or the user?

To think about this, let us consider color. For instance, say we are interested in whether we should change our logo from red to blue on the homepage. If we are randomizing at the page level, then if the user goes to some other page of our website, and then back to the homepage, the logo could change colors. If we are randomizing at the session level, then it could be blue while they use the website this time, if they close it and come back, then it could be red. Finally, if we are randomizing at a user level then possibly it would always be red for one user, but always blue for another.

The extent to which this matters depends on a trade-off between consistency and importance. For instance, if we are A/B testing product prices then consistency is likely an important feature. But if we are A/B testing background colors then consistency might not be as important. On the other hand, if we are A/B testing the position of a log-in button then it might be important that we not move that around too much for the one user, but between users it might matter less.

In A/B testing, as in traditional experiments, we are concerned that our treatment and control groups are the same, but for the treatment. In the case of traditional experiments, we satisfy ourselves of this by conducting analysis based on the data that we have after the experiment is conducted. That is usually all we can do because it would be weird to treat or control both groups. But in the case of A/B testing, the pace of experimentation allows us to randomly create the treatment and control groups, and then check, before we subject the treatment group to the treatment, that the groups are the same. For instance, if we were to show each group the same website, then we would expect the same outcomes across the two groups. If we found different outcomes then we would know that we may have a randomization issue (Taddy 2019, 129). This is termed an A/A test and was mentioned in Chapter 4.

We usually run A/B tests not because we desperately care about the specific outcome, but because that feeds into some other measure that we care about. For instance, do we care whether the website is quite-dark-blue or slightly-dark-blue? Probably not. We probably actually care a lot about the company share price. But what if the A/B test outcome of what is the best blue comes at a cost to the share price?

To illustrate this, pretend that we work at a food delivery app, and we are concerned with driver retention. Say we do some A/B tests and find that drivers are always more likely to be retained when they can deliver food to the customer faster. Our hypothetical finding is that faster is better, for driver retention, always. But one way to achieve faster deliveries is for the driver to not put the food into a hot box that would maintain the food's temperature. Something like that might save 30 seconds, which is significant on a ten-minute delivery. Unfortunately, although we would decide to encourage that based on A/B tests designed to optimize driver-retention, such a decision would likely make the customer experience worse. If customers receive cold food that is meant to be hot, then they may stop using the app, which would be bad for the business. Weijun Chen et al. (2022) describe how they found a similar situation at Facebook in terms of notifications—although reducing the number of notifications reduced user engagement in the short-term, over the long-term it increased both user satisfaction and app usage.

This trade-off could become known during the hypothetical driver experiment if we were to look at customer complaints. It is possible that on a small team the A/B test analyst would be exposed to those tickets, but on a larger team they may not be. Ensuring that A/B tests are not resulting in false optimization is especially important. This is not something that we typically have to worry about in normal experiments. As another example of this Aprameya (2020) describes testing a feature of Duolingo, a language-learning application, which served an ad for Duolingo Plus when a regular Duolingo user was offline. The feature was found to be positive for Duolingo's revenue, but negative for customer learning habits. Presumably enough customer negativity would eventually have resulted in the feature having a negative effect on revenue. Related to this, we want to think carefully about the nature of the result that we expect. For instance, in the shades of blues example, we are unlikely to find substantial surprises, and so it might be sufficient to try a small range of blues. But what if we considered a wider variety of colors?

> **Shoulders of giants**
>
> Dr Susan Athey is the Economics of Technology Professor at Stanford University. After earning a PhD in Economics from Stanford in 1995, she joined MIT as an assistant professor, returning to Stanford in 2001, where she was promoted to full professor in 2004. One area of her research is applied economics, and one particularly important paper is Abadie et al. (2017), which considers when standard errors need to be clustered. Another is Athey and Imbens (2017a), which considers how to analyze randomized experiments. In addition to her academic appointments, she has worked at Microsoft and other technology firms and been extensively involved in running experiments in this context. She was awarded the John Bates Clark Medal in 2007.

8.5.1 Upworthy

The trouble with much of A/B testing is that it is done by private firms and so we typically do not have access to their datasets. But Matias et al. (2021) provide access to a dataset of A/B tests from Upworthy, a media website that used A/B testing to optimize their content. Fitts (2014) provides more background information about Upworthy. And the datasets of A/B tests are available here[3].

We can look at what the dataset looks like and get a sense for it by looking at the names and an extract.

```
upworthy <- read_csv("https://osf.io/vy8mj/download")
```

```
upworthy |>
  names()
```

```
 [1] "...1"                 "created_at"           "updated_at"
 [4] "clickability_test_id" "excerpt"              "headline"
 [7] "lede"                 "slug"                 "eyecatcher_id"
[10] "impressions"          "clicks"               "significance"
[13] "first_place"          "winner"               "share_text"
[16] "square"               "test_week"
```

It is also useful to look at the documentation for the dataset. This describes the structure of the dataset, which is that there are packages within tests. A package is a collection of headlines and images that were shown randomly to different visitors to the website, as part of a test. A test can include many packages. Each row in the dataset is a package and the test that it is part of is specified by the "clickability_test_id" column.

There are many variables. We will focus on:

- "created_at";
- "clickability_test_id", so that we can create comparison groups;
- "headline";
- "impressions", which is the number of people that saw the package; and
- "clicks" which is the number of clicks on that package.

[3] https://osf.io/jd64p/

Within each batch of tests, we are interested in the effect of the varied headlines on impressions and clicks.

```
upworthy_restricted <-
  upworthy |>
  select(
    created_at, clickability_test_id, headline, impressions, clicks
    )
```

We will focus on the text contained in headlines, and look at whether headlines that asked a question got more clicks than those that did not. We want to remove the effect of different images and so will focus on those tests that have the same image. To identify whether a headline asks a question, we search for a question mark. Although there are more complicated constructions that we could use, this is enough to get started.

```
upworthy_restricted <-
  upworthy_restricted |>
  mutate(
    asks_question =
      str_detect(string = headline, pattern = "\\?")
    )

upworthy_restricted |>
  count(asks_question)
```

```
# A tibble: 2 x 2
  asks_question     n
  <lgl>         <int>
1 FALSE         19130
2 TRUE           3536
```

For every test, and for every picture, we want to know whether asking a question affected the number of clicks.

```
question_or_not <-
  upworthy_restricted |>
  summarise(
    ave_clicks = mean(clicks),
    .by = c(clickability_test_id, asks_question)
  )

question_or_not |>
  pivot_wider(names_from = asks_question,
              values_from = ave_clicks,
              names_prefix = "ave_clicks_") |>
  drop_na(ave_clicks_FALSE, ave_clicks_TRUE) |>
  mutate(difference_in_clicks = ave_clicks_TRUE - ave_clicks_FALSE) |>
  summarise(average_differce = mean(difference_in_clicks))
```

```
# A tibble: 1 x 1
  average_differce
```

```
            <dbl>
1           -4.89
```

We could also consider a cross-tab (Table 8.4).

```
question_or_not |>
  summarise(mean = mean(ave_clicks),
            .by = asks_question) |>
  kable(
    col.names = c("Asks a question?", "Mean clicks"),
    digits = 0
  )
```

Table 8.4: Difference between the average number of clicks

Asks a question?	Mean clicks
FALSE	57
TRUE	44

We find that in general, having a question in the headline may slightly decrease the number of clicks on a headline, although if there is an effect it does not appear to be very large (Figure 8.4).

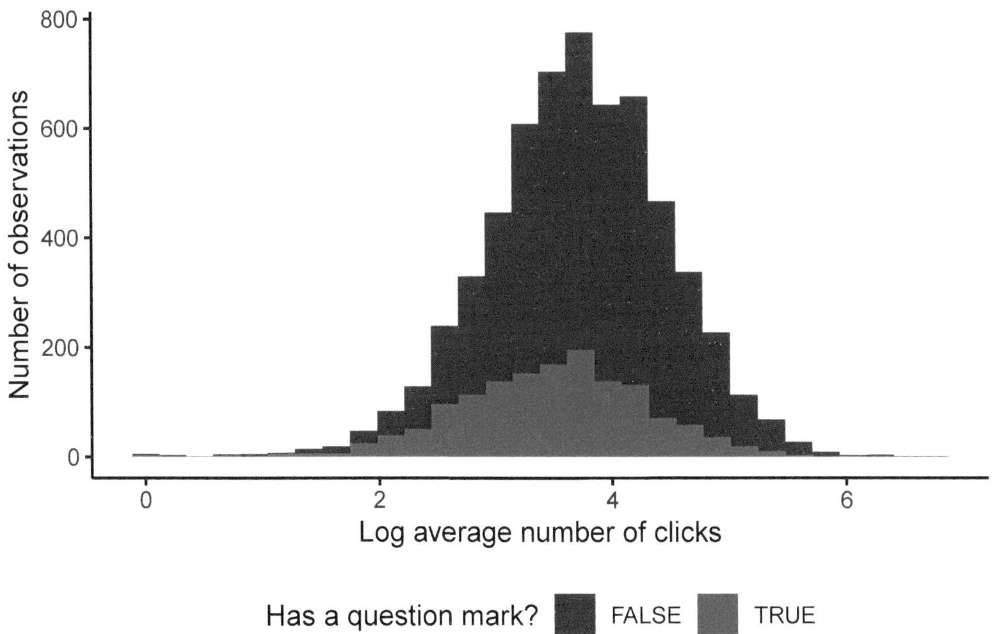

Figure 8.4: Comparison of the average number of clicks when a headline contains a question mark or not

8.6 Exercises

Scales

1. *(Plan)* Consider the following scenario: *A political candidate is interested in how two polling values change over the course of an election campaign: approval rating and vote-share. The two are measured as percentages, and are somewhat correlated. There tends to be large changes when there is a debate between candidates.* Please sketch what that dataset could look like and then sketch a graph that you could build to show all observations.
2. *(Simulate)* Please further consider the scenario described and simulate the situation. Please include five tests based on the simulated data. Submit a link to a GitHub Gist that contains your code.
3. *(Acquire)* Please identify and document a possible source of such a dataset.
4. *(Explore)* Please use `ggplot2` to build the graph that you sketched using the simulated data. Submit a link to a GitHub Gist that contains your code.
5. *(Communicate)* Please write two paragraphs about what you did.

Questions

1. In your own words, what is the fundamental problem of causal inference (write at least three paragraphs and include both examples and references)?
2. In your own words, what is the role of randomization in constructing a counterfactual (write at least three paragraphs and include both examples and references)?
3. What is external validity (pick one)?
   a. Findings from an experiment hold in that setting.
   b. Findings from an experiment hold outside that setting.
   c. Findings from an experiment that has been repeated many times.
   d. Findings from an experiment for which code and data are available.
4. What is internal validity (pick one)?
   a. Findings from an experiment hold in that setting.
   b. Findings from an experiment hold outside that setting.
   c. Findings from an experiment that has been repeated many times.
   d. Findings from an experiment for which code and data are available.
5. Please write some code for the following dataset that would randomly assign people into one of two groups.

```
netflix_data <-
  tibble(
    person = c("Ian", "Ian", "Roger", "Roger",
      "Roger", "Patricia", "Patricia", "Helen"
    ),
    tv_show = c(
      "Broadchurch", "Duty-Shame", "Broadchurch", "Duty-Shame",
      "Shetland", "Broadchurch", "Shetland", "Duty-Shame"
    ),
    hours = c(6.8, 8.0, 0.8, 9.2, 3.2, 4.0, 0.2, 10.2)
  )
```

6. How could you check that your randomization had been done appropriately (write at least three paragraphs and include both examples and references)?
7. Pretend that you work as a junior analyst for a large consulting firm. Further, pretend that your consulting firm has taken a contract to put together a facial recognition model for a government border security department. Write at least three paragraphs, with examples and references, discussing your thoughts, with regard to ethics, on this matter.
8. Ware (1989, 299) mentions "randomized-consent" and continues that it was "attractive in this setting because a standard approach to informed consent would require that parents of infants near death be approached to give informed consent for an invasive surgical procedure that would then, in some instances, not be administered. Those familiar with the agonizing experience of having a child in a neonatal intensive care unit can appreciate that the process of obtaining informed consent would be both frightening and stressful to parents." To what extent do you agree with this position, especially given, as Ware (1989, 305), mentions "the need to withhold information about the study from parents of infants receiving Conventional Medical Therapy (CMT)"?
9. Ware (1989, 300) mentions "equipoise". In your own words, could you please define and discuss it (write at least three paragraphs and include both examples and references)?
10. Please redo the Upworthy analysis, but for "!" instead of "?". What is the difference in clicks?
    a. -8.3
    b. -7.2
    c. -4.5
    d. -5.6

Tutorial

Please consider the Special Virtual Issue on Nonresponse Rates and Nonresponse Adjustments[4] of the *Journal of Survey Statistics and Methodology*. Focus on one aspect of the editorial, and with reference to relevant literature, please discuss it in at least two pages. Use Quarto, and include an appropriate title, author, date, link to a GitHub repo, and citations. Submit a PDF.

Paper

At about this point the *Howrah* Paper in the "Papers" Online Appendix[5] would be appropriate.

[4]https://academic.oup.com/jssam/pages/special-virtual-issue-on-nonresponse-rates-and-nonresponse-adjustments

[5]https://tellingstorieswithdata.com/23-assessment.html

Part IV

Preparation

9

Clean and prepare

Prerequisites

- Read *Data Feminism*, (D'Ignazio and Klein 2020)
  - Focus on Chapter 5 "Unicorns, Janitors, Ninjas, Wizards, and Rock Stars", which discusses the importance of considering different sources of data about the same process.
- Read *R for Data Science*, (Wickham, Çetinkaya-Rundel, and Grolemund [2016] 2023)
  - Focus on Chapter 6 "Data tidying", which provides an overview of tidy data and some strategies to obtain it.
- Read *An introduction to data cleaning with R*, (De Jonge and van der Loo 2013)
  - Focus on Chapter 2 "From raw data to technically correct data", which provides detailed information about reading data into R and various classes.
- Read *What The Washington Post Elections Engineering team had to learn about election data* (Liu, Bronner, and Bowers 2022)
  - Details several practical issues about real-world datasets.
- Read *Column Names as Contracts*, (Riederer 2020)
  - Introduces the benefits of having a limited vocabulary for naming variables.
- Read *Combining Statistical, Physical, and Historical Evidence to Improve Historical Sea-Surface Temperature Records*, (Chan 2021)
  - Details the difficulty of creating a dataset of temperatures from observations taken by different ships at different times.

Key concepts and skills

- Cleaning and preparing a dataset is difficult work that involves making many decisions. Planning an endpoint and simulating the dataset that we would like to end up with are key elements of cleaning and preparing data.
- It can help to work in an iterative way, beginning with a small sample of the dataset. Write code to fix some aspect, and then iterate and generalize to additional tranches.
- During that process we should also develop a series of tests and checks that the dataset should pass. This should focus on key features that we would expect of the dataset.
- We should be especially concerned about the class of variables, having clear names, and that the unique values of each variable are as expected given all this.

Software and packages

- Base R (R Core Team 2023)
- `janitor` (Firke 2023)
- `knitr` (Xie 2023)
- `lubridate` (Grolemund and Wickham 2011)
- `modelsummary` (Arel-Bundock 2022)
- `opendatatoronto` (Gelfand 2022b)
- `pdftools` (Ooms 2022b)

- `pointblank` (Iannone and Vargas 2022)
- `readxl` (Wickham and Bryan 2023)
- `scales` (Wickham and Seidel 2022)
- `stringi` (Gagolewski 2022)
- `testthat` (Wickham 2011)
- `tidyverse` (Wickham et al. 2019)
- `validate` (van der Loo and De Jonge 2021)

```
library(janitor)
library(knitr)
library(lubridate)
library(modelsummary)
library(opendatatoronto)
library(pdftools)
library(pointblank)
library(readxl)
library(scales)
library(stringi)
library(testthat)
library(tidyverse)
library(validate)
```

9.1 Introduction

> "Well, Lyndon, you may be right and they may be every bit as intelligent as you say," said Rayburn, "but I'd feel a whole lot better about them if just one of them had run for sheriff once."
>
> Sam Rayburn reacting to Lyndon Johnson's enthusiasm about John Kennedy's incoming cabinet, as quoted in *The Best and the Brightest* (Halberstam 1972, 41).

In this chapter we put in place more formal approaches for data cleaning and preparation. These are centered around:

1. validity;
2. internal consistency; and
3. external consistency.

Your model does not care whether you validated your data, but you should. Validity means that the values in the dataset are not obviously wrong. For instance, with few exceptions, currencies should not have letters in them, names should not have numbers, and velocities should not be faster than the speed of light. Internal consistency means the dataset does not contradict itself. For instance, that might mean that constituent columns add to the total column. External consistency means that the dataset does not, in general, contradict outside sources, and is deliberate when it does. For instance, if our dataset purports to be about the population of cities, then we would expect that they are the same as, to a rough approximation, say, those available from relevant censuses on Wikipedia.

SpaceX, the United States rocket company, uses cycles of ten or 50 Hertz (equivalent to 0.1 and 0.02 seconds, respectively) to control their rockets. Each cycle, the inputs from sensors, such as temperature and pressure, are read, processed, and used to make a decision, such as whether to adjust some setting (Martin and Popper 2021). We recommend a similar iterative approach of small adjustments during data cleaning and preparation. Rather than trying to make everything perfect from the start, just get started, and iterate through a process of small, continuous improvements.

To a large extent, the role of data cleaning and preparation is so great that the only people that understand a dataset are those that have cleaned it. Yet, the paradox of data cleaning is that often those that do the cleaning and preparation are those that have the least trust in the resulting dataset. At some point in every data science workflow, those doing the modeling should do some data cleaning. Even though few want to do it (Sambasivan et al. 2021), it can be as influential as modeling. To clean and prepare data is to make many decisions, some of which may have important effects on our results. For instance, Northcutt, Athalye, and Mueller (2021) find the test sets of some popular datasets in computer science contain, on average, labels that are wrong in around three per cent of cases. Banes et al. (2022) re-visit the Sumatran orang-utan *(Pongo abelii)* reference genome and find that nine of the ten samples had some issue. And Du, Huddart, and Jiang (2022) find a substantial difference between the as-filed and standardized versions of a company's accounting data, especially for complex financial situations. Like Sam Rayburn wishing that Kennedy's cabinet despite their intelligence, had experience in the nitty-gritty, a data scientist needs to immerse themselves in the messy reality of their dataset.

The reproducibility crisis, which was identified early in psychology (Open Science Collaboration 2015) but since extended to many other disciplines in the physical and social sciences, brought to light issues such as p-value "hacking", researcher degrees of freedom, file-drawer issues, and even data and results fabrication (Gelman and Loken 2013). Steps are now being put in place to address these. But there has been relatively little focus on the data gathering, cleaning, and preparation aspects of applied statistics, despite evidence that decisions made during these steps greatly affect statistical results (Huntington-Klein et al. 2021). In this chapter we focus on these issues.

While the statistical practices that underpin data science are themselves correct and robust when applied to simulated datasets, data science is not typically conducted with data that follow the assumptions underlying the models that are commonly fit. For instance, data scientists are interested in "messy, unfiltered, and possibly unclean data—tainted by heteroskedasticity, complex dependence and missingness patterns—that until recently were avoided in polite conversations between more traditional statisticians" (Craiu 2019). Big data does not resolve this issue and may even exacerbate it. For instance, population inference based on larger amounts of poor-quality data, without adjusting for data issues, will just lead to more confidently wrong conclusions (Meng 2018). The problems that are found in much of applied statistics research are not necessarily associated with researcher quality, or their biases (Silberzahn et al. 2018). Instead, they are a result of the context within which data science is conducted. This chapter provides an approach and tools to explicitly think about this work.

Gelman and Vehtari (2021), writing about the most important statistical ideas of the past 50 years, say that each of them enabled new ways of thinking about data analysis. These ideas brought into the tent of statistics, approaches that "had been considered more a matter of taste or philosophy". The focus on data cleaning and preparation in this chapter is analogous, insofar as it represents a codification, or bringing inside the tent, of aspects that are typically, incorrectly, considered those of taste rather than core statistical concerns.

The workflow for data cleaning and preparation that we advocate is:

1. Save the original, unedited data.
2. Begin with an end in mind by sketching and simulating.
3. Write tests and documentation.
4. Execute the plan on a small sample.
5. Iterate the plan.
6. Generalize the execution.
7. Update tests and documentation.

We will need a variety of skills to be effective, but this is the very stuff of data science. The approach needed is some combination of dogged and sensible. Perfect is very much the enemy of good enough when it comes to data cleaning. And to be specific, it is better to have 90 per cent of the data cleaned and prepared, and to start exploring that, before deciding whether it is worth the effort to clean and prepare the remaining 10 per cent. Because that remainder will likely take an awful lot of time and effort.

All data regardless of whether they were obtained from farming, gathering, or hunting, will have issues. We need approaches that can deal with a variety of concerns, and more importantly, understand how they might affect our modeling (Van den Broeck et al. 2005). To clean data is to analyze data. This is because the process forces us to make choices about what we value in our results (Au 2020).

9.2 Workflow

9.2.1 Save the original, unedited data

The first step is to save the original, unedited data into a separate, local folder. The original, unedited data establishes the foundation for reproducibility (Wilson et al. 2017). If we obtained our data from a third-party, such as a government website, then we have no control over whether they will continue to host that data, update it, or change the address at which it is available. Saving a local copy also reduces the burden that we impose on their servers.

Having locally saved the original, unedited data we must maintain a copy of it in that state, and not modify it. As we begin to clean and prepare it, we instead make these changes to a copy of the dataset. Maintaining the original, unedited dataset, and using scripts to create the dataset that we are interested in analyzing, ensures that our entire workflow is reproducible. It may be that the changes that we decide to make today, are not ones that we would make tomorrow, having learnt more about the dataset. We need to ensure that we have that data in the original, unedited state in case we need to return to it (Borer et al. 2009).

We may not always be allowed to share that original, unedited data, but we can almost always create something similar. For instance, if we are using a restricted-use computer, then it may be that the best we can do is create a simulated version of the original, unedited data that conveys the main features, and include detailed access instructions in a README file.

9.2.2 Plan

Planning the endpoint forces us to begin with an end in mind and is important for a variety of reasons. As with scraping data, introduced in Chapter 7, it helps us to be proactive about scope-creep. But with data cleaning it additionally forces us to really think about what we want the final dataset to look like.

The first step is to sketch the dataset that we are interested in. The key features of the sketch will be aspects such as the names of the columns, their class, and the possible range of values. For instance, we might be interested in the populations of US states. Our sketch might look like Figure 9.1.

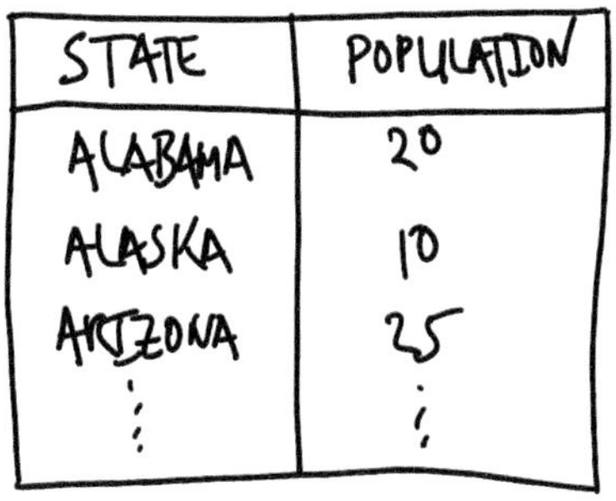

STATE	POPULATION
ALABAMA	20
ALASKA	10
ARIZONA	25
⋮	⋮

Figure 9.1: Planned dataset of US states and their populations

In this case, the sketch forces us to decide that we want full names rather than abbreviations for the state names, and the population to be measured in millions. The process of sketching this endpoint has forced us to make decisions early on and be clear about our desired endpoint.

We then implement that using code to simulate data. Again, this process forces us to think about what reasonable values look like in our dataset because we must decide which functions to use. We need to think carefully about the unique values of each variable. For instance, if the variable is meant to be "gender" then unique values such as "male", "female", "other", and "unknown" may be expected, but a number such as "1,000" would likely be wrong. It also forces us to be explicit about names because we must assign the output of those functions to a variable. For instance, we could simulate some population data for the US states.

```
set.seed(853)

simulated_population <-
  tibble(
    state = state.name,
    population = runif(n = 50, min = 0, max = 50) |>
      round(digits = 2)
```

```
)

simulated_population
```

```
# A tibble: 50 x 2
   state       population
   <chr>            <dbl>
 1 Alabama          18.0
 2 Alaska            6.01
 3 Arizona          24.2
 4 Arkansas         15.8
 5 California        1.87
 6 Colorado         20.2
 7 Connecticut       6.54
 8 Delaware         12.1
 9 Florida           7.9
10 Georgia           9.44
# i 40 more rows
```

Our purpose, during data cleaning and preparation, is to then bring our original, unedited data close to that plan. Ideally, we would plan so that the desired endpoint of our dataset is "tidy data". This is introduced in the "R essentials" Online Appendix[1], but briefly, it means that (Wickham, Çetinkaya-Rundel, and Grolemund [2016] 2023; Wickham 2014, 4):

1. each variable is in its own column;
2. each observation is in its own row; and
3. each value is in its own cell.

Begin thinking about validity and internal consistency at this stage. What are some of the features that these data should have? Note these as you go through the process of simulating the dataset because we will draw on them to write tests.

9.2.3 Start small

Having thoroughly planned we can turn to the original, unedited data that we are dealing with. Usually we want to manipulate the original, unedited data into a rectangular dataset as quickly as possible. This allows us to use familiar functions from the `tidyverse`. For instance, let us assume that we are starting with a `.txt` file.

The first step is to look for regularities in the dataset. We want to end up with tabular data, which means that we need some type of delimiter to distinguish different columns. Ideally this might be features such as a comma, a semicolon, a tab, a double space, or a line break. In the following case we could take advantage of the comma.

```
Alabama, 5
Alaska, 0.7
Arizona, 7
Arkansas, 3
California, 40
```

[1]https://tellingstorieswithdata.com/20-r_essentials.html

In more challenging cases there may be some regular feature of the dataset that we can take advantage of. Sometimes various text is repeated, as in the following case.

```
State is Alabama and population is 5 million.
State is Alaska and population is 0.7 million.
State is Arizona and population is 7 million.
State is Arkansas and population is 3 million.
State is California and population is 40 million.
```

In this case, although we do not have a traditional delimiter, we can use the regularity of "State is", "and population is", and "million" to get what we need. A more difficult case is when we do not have line breaks. This final case is illustrative of that.

```
Alabama 5 Alaska 0.7 Arizona 7 Arkansas 3 California 40
```

One way to approach this is to take advantage of the different classes and values that we are looking for. For instance, we know that we are after US states, so there are only 50 possible options (setting D.C. to one side for the time being), and we could use the these as a delimiter. We could also use the fact that population is a number, and so separate based on a space followed by a number.

We will now convert this final case into tidy data.

```
unedited_data <-
  c("Alabama 5 Alaska 0.7 Arizona 7 Arkansas 3 California 40")

tidy_data <-
  tibble(raw = unedited_data) |>
  separate(
    col = raw,
    into = letters[1:5],
    sep = "(?<=[[:digit:]]) " # A bracket preceded by numbers
  ) |>
  pivot_longer(
    cols = letters[1:5],
    names_to = "drop_me",
    values_to = "separate_me"
  ) |>
  separate(
    col = separate_me,
    into = c("state", "population"),
    sep = " (?=[[:digit:]])" # A space followed by a number
  ) |>
  select(-drop_me)

tidy_data
```

```
# A tibble: 5 x 2
  state      population
  <chr>      <chr>
1 Alabama    5
2 Alaska     0.7
3 Arizona    7
```

```
4 Arkansas    3
5 California 40
```

9.2.4 Write tests and documentation

Having established a rectangular dataset, albeit a messy one, we should begin to look at the classes that we have. We do not necessarily want to fix the classes at this point, because that can result in lost data. But we look at the class to see what it is, compare it to our simulated dataset, and note the columns where it is different to see what changes need to be made. Background on `class()` is available in the "R essentials" Online Appendix[2].

Before changing the class and before going on to more bespoke issues, we should deal with some common issues including:

- Commas and other punctuation, such as denomination signs ($, €, £, etc.), in variables that should be numeric.
- Inconsistent formatting of dates, such as "December" and "Dec" and "12" all in the one variable.
- Unexpected character encoding, especially in Unicode, which may not display consistently.[3]

Typically, we want to fix anything immediately obvious. For instance, we should remove commas that have been used to group digits in currencies. However, the situation will often feel overwhelming. What we need to do is to look at the unique values in each variable, and then triage what we will fix. We make the triage decision based on what is likely to have the largest impact. That usually means creating counts of the observations, sorting them in descending order, and then dealing with them in this order.

When the tests of membership are passed—which we initially establish based on simulation and experience—then we can change the class, and run all the tests again. We have adapted this idea from the software development approach of unit testing. Tests are crucial because they enable us to understand whether software (or in this case data) is fit for our purpose (Irving et al. 2021). Tests, especially in data science, are not static things that we just write once and then forget. Instead they should update and evolve as needed.

---

[2]https://tellingstorieswithdata.com/20-r_essentials.html

[3]By way of background, character encoding is needed for computers, which are based on strings of 0s and 1s, to be able to consider symbols such as alphabets. One source of particularly annoying data cleaning issues is different character encoding. This is especially common when dealing with foreign languages and odd characters. In general, we use an encoding called UTF-8. The encoding of a character vector can be found using `Encoding()`.

i Oh, you think we have good data on that!

The simplification of reality can be especially seen in sports records, which necessarily must choose what to record. Sports records are fit for some purposes and not for others. For instance, chess is played on an 8 x 8 board of alternating black and white squares. The squares are detonated by a unique combination of both a letter (A-G) and a number (1-8). Most pieces have a unique abbreviation, for instance knights are N and bishops are B. Each game is independently recorded using this "algebraic notation" by each player. These records allow us to recreate the moves of the game. The 2021 Chess World Championship was contested by Magnus Carlsen and Ian Nepomniachtchi. There were a variety of reasons this game was particularly noteworthy—including it being the longest world championship game—but one is the uncharacteristic mistakes that both Carlsen and Nepomniachtchi made. For instance, at Move 33 Carlsen did not exploit an opportunity; and at Move 36 a different move would have provided Nepomniachtchi with a promising endgame (Doggers 2021). One reason for these mistakes may have been that both players at that point in the game had very little time remaining—they had to decide on their moves very quickly. But there is no sense of that in the representation provided by the game sheet because it does not record time remaining. The record is fit for purpose as a "correct" representation of what happened in the game; but not necessarily why it happened.

Let us run through an example with a collection of strings, some of which are slightly wrong. This type of output is typical of OCR, introduced in Chapter 7, which often gets most of the way there, but not quite.

```
messy_string <- paste(
  c("Patricia, Ptricia, PatricIa, Patric1a, PatricIa"),
  c("PatrIcia, Patricia, Patricia, Patricia , 8atricia"),
  sep = ", "
)
```

As before, we first get this into a rectangular dataset.

```
messy_dataset <-
  tibble(names = messy_string) |>
  separate_rows(names, sep = ", ")

messy_dataset
```

```
# A tibble: 10 x 1
   names
   <chr>
 1 "Patricia"
 2 "Ptricia"
 3 "PatricIa"
 4 "Patric1a"
 5 "PatricIa"
 6 "PatrIcia"
 7 "Patricia"
```

```
 8 "Patricia"
 9 "Patricia "
10 "8atricia"
```

We now need to decide which of these errors we are going to fix. To help us decide which are most important, we create a count.

```
messy_dataset |>
  count(names, sort = TRUE)
```

```
# A tibble: 7 x 2
  names          n
  <chr>      <int>
1 "Patricia"     3
2 "PatricIa"     2
3 "8atricia"     1
4 "PatrIcia"     1
5 "Patric1a"     1
6 "Patricia "    1
7 "Ptricia"      1
```

The most common unique observation is the correct one. The next one—"PatricIa"—looks like the "i" has been incorrectly capitalized. This is true for "PatrIcia" as well. We can fix the capitalization issues with `str_to_title()`, which converts the first letter of each word in a string to uppercase and the rest to lowercase, and then redo the count.

Background on strings is available in the "R essentials" Online Appendix[4].

```
messy_dataset_fix_I_8 <-
  messy_dataset |>
  mutate(
    names = str_to_title(names)
  )

messy_dataset_fix_I_8 |>
  count(names, sort = TRUE)
```

```
# A tibble: 5 x 2
  names          n
  <chr>      <int>
1 "Patricia"     6
2 "8atricia"     1
3 "Patric1a"     1
4 "Patricia "    1
5 "Ptricia"      1
```

Already this is much better with 60 per cent of the values are correct, compared with the earlier 30 per cent. There are two more clear errors—"8tricia" and "Ptricia"—with the first distinguished by an "8" instead of a "P", and the second missing an "a". We can fix these issues with `str_replace_all()`.

[4] https://tellingstorieswithdata.com/20-r_essentials.html

```r
messy_dataset_fix_a_n <-
  messy_dataset_fix_I_8 |>
  mutate(
    names = str_replace_all(names, "8atricia", "Patricia"),
    names = str_replace_all(names, "Ptricia", "Patricia")
  )

messy_dataset_fix_a_n |>
  count(names, sort = TRUE)
```

```
# A tibble: 3 x 2
  names          n
  <chr>      <int>
1 "Patricia"     8
2 "Patric1a"     1
3 "Patricia "    1
```

We have achieved an 80 per cent outcome with not too much effort. The final two issues are more subtle. The first has occurred because the "i" has been incorrectly coded as a "1". In some fonts this will show up, but in others it will be more difficult to see. This is a common issue, especially with OCR, and something to be aware of. The second occurs because of a trailing space. Trailing and leading spaces are another common issue and we can address them with `str_trim()`. After we fix these two remaining issues we have all entries corrected.

```r
cleaned_data <-
  messy_dataset_fix_a_n |>
  mutate(
    names = str_replace_all(names, "Patric1a", "Patricia"),
    names = str_trim(names, side = c("right"))
  )

cleaned_data |>
  count(names, sort = TRUE)
```

```
# A tibble: 1 x 2
  names        n
  <chr>    <int>
1 Patricia    10
```

We have been doing the tests in our head in this example. We know that we are hoping for "Patricia". But we can start to document this test as well. One way is to look to see if values other than "Patricia" exist in the dataset.

```r
check_me <-
  cleaned_data |>
  filter(names != "Patricia")

if (nrow(check_me) > 0) {
  print("Still have values that are not Patricia!")
}
```

We can make things a little more imposing by stopping our code execution if the condition is not met with `stopifnot()`. To use this function we define a condition that we would like met. We could implement this type of check throughout our code. For instance if we expected there to be a certain number of observations in the dataset, or for a certain variable to have various properties, such as being an integer or a factor.

```
stopifnot(nrow(check_me) == 0)
```

We can use `stopifnot()` to ensure that our script is working as expected as it runs.

Another way to write tests for our dataset is to use `testthat`. Although developed for testing packages, we can use the functionality to test our datasets. For instance, we can use `expect_length()` to check the length of a dataset and `expect_equal()` to check the content.

```
# Is the dataset of length one?
expect_length(check_me, 1)
# Are the observations characters?
expect_equal(class(cleaned_data$names), "character")
# Is every unique observation "Patricia"?
expect_equal(unique(cleaned_data$names), "Patricia")
```

If the tests pass then nothing happens, but if the tests fail then the script will stop.

What do we test? It is a difficult problem, and we detail a range of more-specific tests in the next section. But broadly we test what we have, against what we expect. The engineers working on the software for the Apollo program in the 1960s initially considered writing tests to be "busy work" (Mindell 2008, 170). But they eventually came to realize that NASA would not have faith that software could be used to send men to the moon unless it was accompanied by a comprehensive suite of tests. And it is the same for data science.

Start with tests for validity. These will typically check the class of the variables, their unique values, and the number of observations. For instance, if we were using a recent dataset then columns that are years could be tested to ensure that all elements have four digits and start with a "2". P. Baumgartner (2021) describes this as tests on the schema.

After that, turn to checks of internal consistency. For instance, if there are variables of different numeric responses, then check that the sum of those equals a total variable, or if it does not then this difference is explainable. Finally, turn to tests for external consistency. Here we want to use outside information to inform our tests. For instance, if we had a variable of the neonatal mortality rate (NMR) for Germany (this concept was introduced in Chapter 2), then we could look at the estimates from the World Health Organization (WHO), and ensure our NMR variable aligns. Experienced analysts do this all in their head. The issue is that it does not scale, can be inconsistent, and overloads on reputation. We return to this issue in Chapter 12 in the context of modeling.

We write tests throughout our code, rather than right at the end. In particular, using `stopifnot()` statements on intermediate steps ensures that the dataset is being cleaned in a way that we expect. For instance, when merging two datasets we could check:

1) The variable names in the datasets are unique, apart from the column/s to be used as the key/s.
2) The number of observations of each type is being carried through appropriately.
3) The dimensions of the dataset are not being unexpectedly changed.

9.2.5 Iterate, generalize, and update

We could now iterate the plan. In this most recent case, we started with ten entries. There is no reason that we could not increase this to 100 or even 1,000. We may need to generalize the cleaning procedures and tests. But eventually we would start to bring the dataset into some sort of order.

9.3 Checking and testing

Robert Caro, the biographer of Lyndon Johnson introduced in Chapter 4, spent years tracking down everyone connected to the 36th President of the United States. Caro and his wife Ina went so far as to live in Texas Hill Country for three years so that they could better understand where Johnson was from. When Caro heard that Johnson, as a senator, would run to the Senate from where he stayed in D.C., he ran that route multiple times himself to try to understand why Johnson was running. Caro eventually understood it only when he ran the route as the sun was rising, just as Johnson had done; it turns out that the sun hits the Senate Rotunda in a particularly inspiring way (Caro 2019, 156). This background work enabled him to uncover aspects that no one else knew. For instance, Johnson almost surely stole his first election win (Caro 2019, 116). We need to understand our data to this same extent. We want to metaphorically turn every page.

The idea of negative space is well established in design. It refers to that which surrounds the subject. Sometimes negative space is used as an effect. For instance the logo of FedEx, an American logistics company, has negative space between the E and X that creates an arrow. In a similar way, we want to be cognizant of the data that we have, and the data that we do not have (Hodgetts 2022). We are worried that the data that we do not have somehow has meaning, potentially even to the extent of changing our conclusions. When we are cleaning data, we are looking for anomalies. We are interested in values that are in the dataset that should not be, but also the opposite situation—values that should be in the dataset but are not. There are three tools that we use to identify these situations: graphs, counts, and tests.

We also use these tools to ensure that we are not changing correct observations to incorrect. Especially when our cleaning and preparation requires many steps, it may be that fixes at one stage are undone later. We use graphs, counts, and especially tests, to prevent this. The importance of these grows exponentially with the size of the dataset. Small and medium datasets are more amenable to manual inspection and other aspects that rely on the analyst, while larger datasets especially require more efficient strategies (Hand 2018).

9.3.1 Graphs

Graphs are an invaluable tool when cleaning data, because they show each observation in the dataset, potentially in relation to the other observations. They are useful for identifying when a value does not belong. For instance, if a value is expected to be numerical, but is still a character then it will not plot, and a warning will be displayed. Graphs will be especially useful for numerical data, but are still useful for text and categorical data. Let us pretend that we have a situation where we are interested in a person's age, for some youth survey. We have the following data:

```
youth_survey_data <-
  tibble(ages = c(
    15.9, 14.9, 16.6, 15.8, 16.7, 17.9, 12.6, 11.5, 16.2, 19.5, 150
  ))


youth_survey_data |>
  ggplot(aes(x = ages)) +
  geom_histogram(binwidth = 1) +
  theme_minimal() +
  labs(
    x = "Age of respondent",
    y = "Number of respondents"
  )

youth_survey_data_fixed |>
  ggplot(aes(x = ages)) +
  geom_histogram(binwidth = 1) +
  theme_minimal() +
  labs(
    x = "Age of respondent",
    y = "Number of respondents"
  )
```

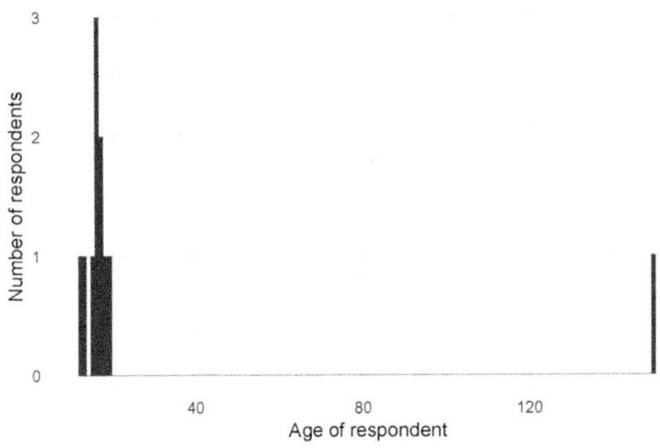

(a) Before cleaning

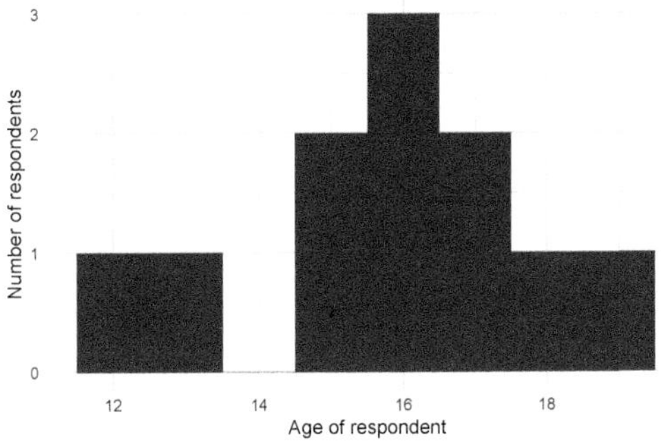

(b) After cleaning

Figure 9.2: The ages in the simulated youth survey dataset identify a data issue

Figure 9.2a shows an unexpected value of 150. The most likely explanation is that the data were incorrectly entered, missing the decimal place, and should be 15.0. We could fix that, document it, and then redo the graph, which would show that everything seemed more valid (Figure 9.2b).

9.3.2 Counts

We want to focus on getting most of the data right, so we are interested in the counts of unique values. Hopefully most of the data are concentrated in the most common counts. But it can also be useful to invert it and see what is especially uncommon. The extent to which we want to deal with these depends on what we need. Ultimately, each time we fix one we are getting very few additional observations, potentially even just one. Counts are especially useful with text or categorical data but can be helpful with numerical data as well.

Let us see an example of text data, each of which is meant to be "Australia".

```
australian_names_data <-
  tibble(
    country = c(
      "Australie", "Austrelia", "Australie", "Australie", "Aeustralia",
      "Austraia", "Australia", "Australia", "Australia", "Australia"
    )
  )

australian_names_data |>
  count(country, sort = TRUE)
```

```
# A tibble: 5 x 2
  country        n
  <chr>      <int>
1 Australia      4
2 Australie      3
3 Aeustralia     1
4 Austraia       1
5 Austrelia      1
```

The use of this count identifies where we should spend our time: changing "Australie" to "Australia" would almost double the amount of usable data.

Turning, briefly to numeric data, Preece (1981) recommends plotting counts of the final digit of each observation in a variable. For instance, if the observations of the variable were "41.2", "80.3", "20.7", "1.2", "46.5", "96.2", "32.7", "44.3", "5.1", and "49.0". Then we note that 0, 1 and 5 all occur once, 3 and 7 occur twice, and 2 occurs three times. We might expect that there should be a uniform distribution of these final digits. But that is surprisingly often not the case, and the ways in which it differs can be informative. For instance, it may be that data were rounded, or recorded by different collectors.

For instance, later in this chapter we will gather, clean, and prepare some data from the 2019 Kenyan census. We pre-emptively use that dataset here and look at the count of the final digits of the ages. That is, say, from age 35 we take "5", from age 74, we take "4". Table 9.1 shows the expected age-heaping that occurs because some respondents reply to questions about age with a value to the closest 5 or 10. If we had an age variable without that pattern then we might expect it had been constructed from a different type of question.

9.3.3 Tests

As we said in Chapter 3, if you write code, then you are a programmer, but there is a difference between someone coding for fun, and, say, writing the code that runs the James Webb Telescope. Following Weinberg (1971, 122), we can distinguish between amateurs and professionals based the existence of subsequent users. When you first start out coding, you typically write code that only you will use. For instance, you may write some code for a class paper. After you get a grade, then in most cases, the code will not be run again. In contrast, a professional writes code for, and often with, other people.

Table 9.1: Excess of 0 and 5 digits in counts of the final digits of single-year ages in Nairobi from the 2019 Kenyan census

Final digit of age	Number of times
0	347,233
1	278,930
2	308,933
3	285,745
4	270,355
5	303,817
6	246,582
7	242,688
8	207,739
9	216,355

Much academic research these days relies on code. If that research is to contribute to lasting knowledge, then the code that underpins it is being written for others and must work for others well after the researcher has moved to other projects. A professional places appropriate care on tasks that ensure code can be considered by others. A large part of that is tests.

Jet Propulsion Laboratory (2009, 14) claim that analysis after the fact "often find at least one defect per one hundred lines of code written". There is no reason to believe that code without tests is free of defects, just that they are not known. As such, we should strive to include tests in our code when possible. There is some infrastructure for testing data science code. For instance, in Python there is the Test-Driven Data Analysis library of Radcliffe (2023), but more is needed.

Some things are so important that we require that the cleaned dataset have them. These are conditions that we should check. They would typically come from experience, expert knowledge, or the planning and simulation stages. For instance, there should be no negative numbers in an age variable, and few ages above 110. For these we could specifically require that the condition is met. Another example is when doing cross-country analysis, a list of country names that we know should be in our dataset would be useful. Our test would then be that there were:

1) values not in that list that were in our dataset, or vice versa; and
2) countries that we expected to be in our dataset that were not.

To have a concrete example, let us consider if we were doing some analysis about the five largest counties in Kenya. From looking it up, we find these are: "Nairobi", "Kiambu", "Nakuru", "Kakamega", and "Bungoma". We can create that variable.

```
correct_kenya_counties <-
  c(
    "Nairobi", "Kiambu", "Nakuru", "Kakamega", "Bungoma"
  )
```

Then pretend we have the following dataset, which contains errors.

```
top_five_kenya <-
  tibble(county = c(
    "Nairobi",  "Nairob1", "Nakuru", "Kakamega", "Nakuru",
    "Kiambu", "Kiambru", "Kabamega", "Bun8oma", "Bungoma"
  ))

top_five_kenya |>
  count(county, sort = TRUE)
```

```
# A tibble: 9 x 2
  county       n
  <chr>    <int>
1 Nakuru       2
2 Bun8oma      1
3 Bungoma      1
4 Kabamega     1
5 Kakamega     1
6 Kiambru      1
7 Kiambu       1
8 Nairob1      1
9 Nairobi      1
```

Based on the count we know that we must fix some of them. There are two with numbers in the names.

```
top_five_kenya_fixed_1_8 <-
  top_five_kenya |>
  mutate(
    county = str_replace_all(county, "Nairob1", "Nairobi"),
    county = str_replace_all(county, "Bun8oma", "Bungoma")
  )

top_five_kenya_fixed_1_8 |>
  count(county, sort = TRUE)
```

```
# A tibble: 7 x 2
  county       n
  <chr>    <int>
1 Bungoma      2
2 Nairobi      2
3 Nakuru       2
4 Kabamega     1
5 Kakamega     1
6 Kiambru      1
7 Kiambu       1
```

At this point we can compare this with our known correct variable. We check both ways, i.e. is there anything in the correct variable not in our dataset, and is there anything in the dataset not in our correct variable. We use our check conditions to decide whether we are finished.

```r
if (all(top_five_kenya_fixed_1_8$county |>
  unique() %in% correct_kenya_counties)) {
  "The cleaned counties match the expected countries"
} else {
  "Not all of the counties have been cleaned completely"
}
```

```
[1] "Not all of the counties have been cleaned completely"
```

```r
if (all(correct_kenya_counties %in% top_five_kenya_fixed_1_8$county |>
  unique())) {
  "The expected countries are in the cleaned counties"
} else {
  "Not all the expected countries are in the cleaned counties"
}
```

```
[1] "The expected countries are in the cleaned counties"
```

It is clear that we still have cleaning to do because not all the counties match what we were expecting.

9.3.3.1 Aspects to test

We will talk about explicit tests for class and dates, given their outsized importance, and how common it is for them to go wrong. But other aspects to explicitly consider testing include:

- Variables of monetary values should be tested for reasonable bounds given the situation. In some cases negative values will not be possible. Sometimes an upper bound can be identified. Monetary variables should be numeric. They should not have commas or other separators. They should not contain symbols such as currency signs or semicolons.
- Variables of population values should likely not be negative. Populations of cities should likely be somewhere between 100,000 and 50,000,000. They again should be numeric, and contain only numbers, no symbols.
- Names should be character variables. They likely do not contain numbers. They may contain some limited set of symbols, and this would be context specific.
- The number of observations is surprisingly easy to inadvertently change. While it is fine for this to happen deliberately, when it happens accidentally it can create substantial problems. The number of observations should be tested at the start of any data cleaning process against the data simulation and this expectation updated as necessary. It should be tested throughout the data cleaning process, but especially before and after any joins.

More generally, work with experts and draw on prior knowledge to work out some reasonable features for the variables of interest and then implement these. For instance, consider how D. Baker (2023) was able to quickly identify an error in a claim about user numbers by roughly comparing it with how many institutions in the US receive federal financial aid.

We can use `validate` to set up a series of tests. For instance, here we will simulate some data with clear issues.

```
set.seed(853)

dataset_with_issues <-
  tibble(
    age = c(
      runif(n = 9, min = 0, max = 100) |> round(),
      1000
    ),
    gender = c(
      sample(
        x = c("female", "male", "other", "prefer not to disclose"),
        size = 9,
        replace = TRUE,
        prob = c(0.4, 0.4, 0.1, 0.1)
      ),
      "tasmania"
    ),
    income = rexp(n = 10, rate = 0.10) |> round() |> as.character()
  )

dataset_with_issues
```

```
# A tibble: 10 x 3
     age gender                 income
   <dbl> <chr>                  <chr>
 1    36 female                 20
 2    12 prefer not to disclose 16
 3    48 male                   0
 4    32 female                 2
 5     4 female                 1
 6    40 female                 13
 7    13 female                 13
 8    24 female                 7
 9    16 male                   3
10  1000 tasmania               2
```

In this case, there is an impossible age, one observation in the gender variable that should not be there, and finally, income is a character variable instead of a numeric. We use `validator()` to establish rules we expect the data to satisfy and `confront()` to determine whether it does.

```
rules <- validator(
  is.numeric(age),
  is.character(gender),
  is.numeric(income),
  age < 120,
  gender %in% c("female", "male", "other", "prefer not to disclose")
)

out <-
```

```
    confront(dataset_with_issues, rules)

  summary(out)
```

```
  name items passes fails nNA error warning
1   V1     1      1     0   0 FALSE   FALSE
2   V2     1      1     0   0 FALSE   FALSE
3   V3     1      0     1   0 FALSE   FALSE
4   V4    10      9     1   0 FALSE   FALSE
5   V5    10      9     1   0 FALSE   FALSE
                                                   expression
1                                             is.numeric(age)
2                                        is.character(gender)
3                                          is.numeric(income)
4                                                   age < 120
5 gender %vin% c("female", "male", "other", "prefer not to disclose")
```

In this case, we can see that there are issues with the final three rules that we established. More generally, van der Loo (2022) provides many example tests that can be used.

As mentioned in Chapter 6, gender is something that we need to be especially careful about. We will typically have a small number of responses that are neither "male" or "female". The correct way to deal with the situation depends on context. But if responses other than "male" or "female" are going to be removed from the dataset and ignored, because there are too few of them, showing respect for the respondent might mean including a brief discussion of how they were similar or different to the rest of the dataset. Plots and a more extensive discussion could then be included in an appendix.

9.3.3.2 Class

It is sometimes said that Americans are obsessed with money, while the English are obsessed with class. In the case of data cleaning and preparation we need to be English. Class is critical and worthy of special attention. We introduce class in the "R essentials" Online Appendix[5] and here we focus on "numeric", "character", and "factor". Explicit checks of the class of variables are essential. Accidentally assigning the wrong class to a variable can have a large effect on subsequent analysis. It is important to:

- check whether some value should be a number or a factor; and
- check that values are numbers not characters.

To understand why it is important to be clear about whether a value is a number or a factor, consider the following situation:

```
simulated_class_data <-
  tibble(
    response = c(1, 1, 0, 1, 0, 1, 1, 0, 0),
    group = c(1, 2, 1, 1, 2, 3, 1, 2, 3)
  ) |>
  mutate(
    group_as_integer = as.integer(group),
```

[5] https://tellingstorieswithdata.com/20-r_essentials.html

Table 9.2: Examining the effect of class on regression results

	Group as integer	Group as factor
(Intercept)	1.417	1.099
	(1.755)	(1.155)
group_as_integer	−0.666	
	(0.894)	
group_as_factor2		−1.792
		(1.683)
group_as_factor3		−1.099
		(1.826)
Num.Obs.	9	9
AIC	15.8	17.1
BIC	16.2	17.7
Log.Lik.	−5.891	−5.545
F	0.554	0.579
RMSE	0.48	0.46

```
    group_as_factor = as.factor(group),
  )
```

We use logistic regression, which we cover in more detail in Chapter 12, and first include "group" as an integer, then we include it as a factor. Table 9.2 shows how different the results are and highlights the importance of getting the class of variables used in regression right. In the former, where group is an integer, we impose a consistent relationship between the different levels of the observations, whereas in the latter, where it is a factor, we enable more freedom.

```
models <- list(
  "Group as integer" = glm(
    response ~ group_as_integer,
    data = simulated_class_data,
    family = "binomial"
  ),
  "Group as factor" = glm(
    response ~ group_as_factor,
    data = simulated_class_data,
    family = "binomial"
  )
)
modelsummary(models)
```

Class is so important, subtle, and can have such a pernicious effect on analysis, that analysis with a suite of tests that check class is easier to believe. Establishing this suite is especially valuable just before modeling, but it is worthwhile setting this up as part of data cleaning and preparation. One reason that Jane Street, the US proprietary trading firm, uses a particular programming language, OCaml, is that its type system makes it more reliable with regard to class (Somers 2015). When code matters, class is of vital concern.

There are many open questions around the effect and implications of type in computer science more generally but there has been some work. For instance, Z. Gao, Bird, and Barr (2017) find that the use of a static type system would have caught around 15 per cent of errors in production JavaScript systems. Languages have been developed, such as Typescript, where the primary difference, in this case from JavaScript, is that they are strongly typed. Turcotte et al. (2020) examine some of the considerations for adding a type system in R. They develop a prototype that goes some way to addressing the technical issues, but acknowledge that large-scale implementation would be challenging for many reasons including the need for users to change.

To this point in this book when we have used `read_csv()`, and other functions for importing data, we have allowed the function to guess the class of the variables. Moving forward we will be more deliberate and instead specify it ourselves using "col_types". For instance, instead of:

```
raw_igme_data <-
  read_csv(
    file =
      paste0("https://childmortality.org/wp-content",
             "/uploads/2021/09/UNIGME-2021.csv"),
    show_col_types = FALSE
  )
```

We recommend using:

```
raw_igme_data <-
  read_csv(
    file =
      paste0("https://childmortality.org/wp-content",
             "/uploads/2021/09/UNIGME-2021.csv"),
    col_select = c(`Geographic area`, TIME_PERIOD, OBS_VALUE),
    col_types = cols(
      `Geographic area` = col_character(),
      TIME_PERIOD = col_character(),
      OBS_VALUE = col_double(),
    )
  )
```

This is typically an iterative process of initially reading in the dataset, getting a quick sense of it, and then reading it in properly with only the necessary columns and classes specified. While this will require a little extra work of us, it is important that we are clear about class.

9.3.3.3 Dates

A shibboleth for whether someone has worked with dates is their reaction when you tell them you are going to be working with dates. If they share a horror story, then they have likely worked with dates before!

Extensive checking of dates is important. Ideally, we would like dates to be in the following format: YYYY-MM-DD. There are differences of opinion as to what is an appropriate date format in the broader world. Reasonable people can differ on whether 1 July 2022 or July

1, 2022 is better, but YYYY-MM-DD is the international standard and we should use that in our date variables where possible.

A few tests that could be useful include:

- If a column is days of the week, then test that the only components are Monday, Tuesday, ..., Sunday. Further, test that all seven days are present. Similarly, for month.
- Test that the number of days is appropriate for each month, for instance, check that September has 30 days, etc.
- Check whether the dates are in order in the dataset. This need not necessarily be the case, but often when it is not, there are issues worth exploring.
- Check that the years are complete and appropriate to the analysis period.

In Chapter 2 we introduced a dataset of shelter usage in Toronto in 2021 using `opendatatoronto`. Here we examine that same dataset, but for 2017, to illustrate some issues with dates. We first need to download the data.[6]

```
toronto_shelters_2017 <-
  search_packages("Daily Shelter Occupancy") |>
  list_package_resources() |>
  filter(name == "Daily shelter occupancy 2017.csv") |>
  group_split(name) |>
  map_dfr(get_resource, .id = "file")

write_csv(
  x = toronto_shelters_2017,
  file = "toronto_shelters_2017.csv"
)
```

We need to make the names easier to type and only keep relevant columns.

```
toronto_shelters_2017 <-
  toronto_shelters_2017 |>
  clean_names() |>
  select(occupancy_date, sector, occupancy, capacity)
```

The main issue with this dataset will be the dates. We will find that the dates appear to be mostly year-month-day, but certain observations may be year-day-month. We use `ymd()` from `lubridate` to parse the date in that order.

```
toronto_shelters_2017 <-
  toronto_shelters_2017 |>
  mutate(
    # remove times
    occupancy_date =
      str_remove(
        occupancy_date,
        "T[:digit:]{2}:[:digit:]{2}:[:digit:]{2}"
```

[6]If this does not work, then the City of Toronto government may have moved the datasets. Instead use: `earlier_toronto_shelters <- read_csv("https://www.tellingstorieswithdata.com/inputs/data/earlier_toronto_shelters.csv")`.

```
      )) |>
    mutate(generated_date = ymd(occupancy_date, quiet = TRUE))

  toronto_shelters_2017
```

```
# A tibble: 38,700 x 5
   occupancy_date sector   occupancy capacity generated_date
   <chr>          <chr>        <dbl>    <dbl> <date>
 1 2017-01-01     Co-ed           16       16 2017-01-01
 2 2017-01-01     Men             13       17 2017-01-01
 3 2017-01-01     Men             63       63 2017-01-01
 4 2017-01-01     Families        66       70 2017-01-01
 5 2017-01-01     Men             58       60 2017-01-01
 6 2017-01-01     Families       168      160 2017-01-01
 7 2017-01-01     Families       119      150 2017-01-01
 8 2017-01-01     Men             23       28 2017-01-01
 9 2017-01-01     Families         8        0 2017-01-01
10 2017-01-01     Co-ed           14       40 2017-01-01
# i 38,690 more rows
```

The plot of the distribution of what purports to be the day component makes it clear that there are concerns (Figure 9.3a). In particular we are concerned that the distribution of the days is not roughly uniform.

```
toronto_shelters_2017 |>
  separate(
    generated_date,
    into = c("one", "two", "three"),
    sep = "-",
    remove = FALSE
  ) |>
  count(three) |>
  ggplot(aes(x = three, y = n)) +
  geom_point() +
  theme_minimal() +
  labs(x = "Third component of occupancy date",
       y = "Number")

toronto_shelters_2017 |>
  mutate(row_number = c(seq_len(nrow(toronto_shelters_2017)))) |>
  ggplot(aes(x = row_number, y = generated_date), alpha = 0.1) +
  geom_point(alpha = 0.3) +
  theme_minimal() +
  labs(
    x = "Row number",
    y = "Date"
  )
```

As mentioned, one graph that is especially useful when cleaning a dataset is the order the observations appear in the dataset. For instance, we would generally expect that there would

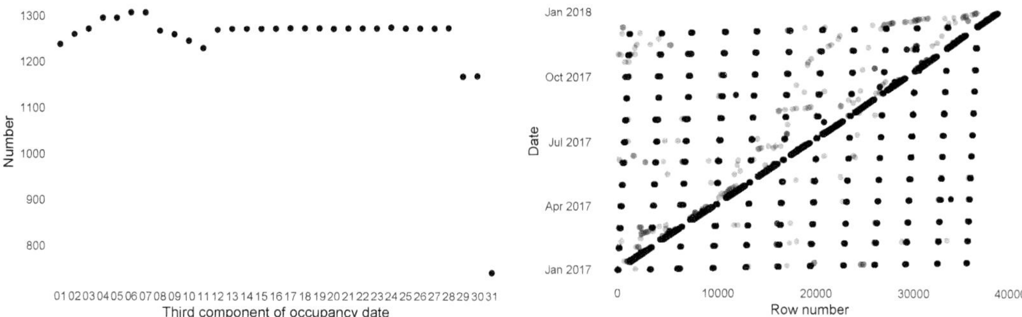

(a) Counts, by third component of occupancy date

(b) Comparison of row number with date

Figure 9.3: Examining the date in more detail

be a rough ordering in terms of date. To examine whether this is the case, we can graph the date variable in the order it appears in the dataset (Figure 9.3b).

While this is just a quick graph it illustrates the point—there are a lot in order, but not all. If they were in order, then we would expect them to be along the diagonal. It is odd that the data are not in order, especially as there appears to be something systematic initially. We can summarize the data to get a count of occupancy by day.

```
# Idea from Lisa Lendway
toronto_shelters_by_day <-
  toronto_shelters_2017 |>
  drop_na(occupancy, capacity) |>
  summarise(
    occupancy = sum(occupancy),
    capacity = sum(capacity),
    usage = occupancy / capacity,
    .by = generated_date
  )
```

We are interested in the availability of shelter spots in Toronto for each day (Figure 9.4).

```
toronto_shelters_by_day |>
  ggplot(aes(x = day(generated_date), y = occupancy)) +
  geom_point(alpha = 0.3) +
  scale_y_continuous(limits = c(0, NA)) +
  labs(
    color = "Type",
    x = "Day",
    y = "Occupancy (number)"
  ) +
  facet_wrap(
    vars(month(generated_date, label = TRUE)),
    scales = "free_x"
  ) +
```

```
  theme_minimal() +
  scale_color_brewer(palette = "Set1")
```

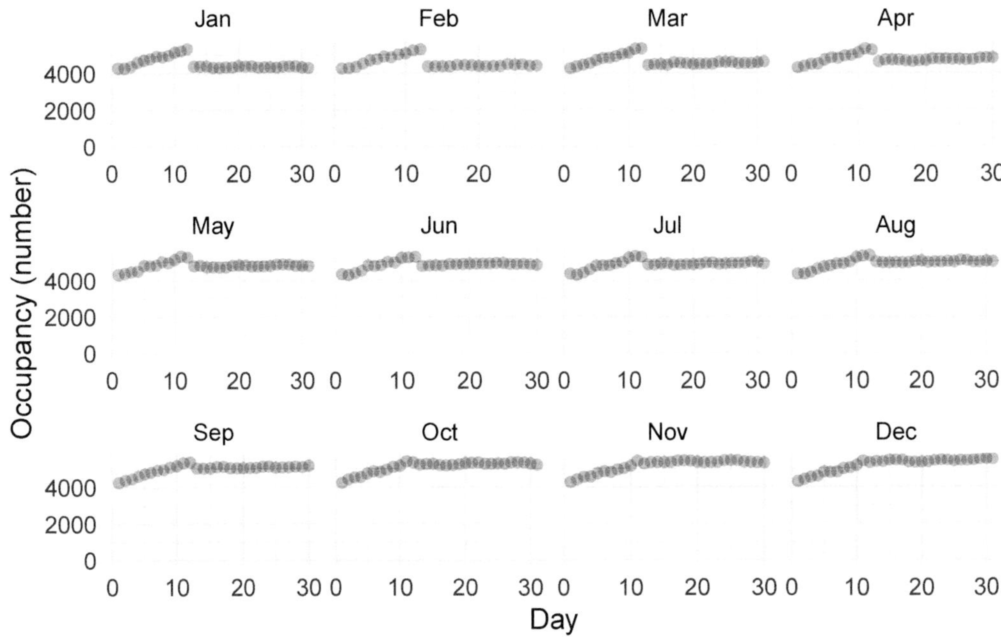

Figure 9.4: Occupancy per day in Toronto shelters

It is clear there seems to be an issue with the first 12 days of the month. We noted that when we look at the data it is a bit odd that it is not in order. From Figure 9.3b it looks like there are some systematic issue that affects many observations. In general, it seems that it might be the case that in the date variable the first 12 days are the wrong way around, i.e. we think it is year-month-day, but it is actually year-day-month. But there are exceptions. As a first pass, we can flip those first 12 days of each month and see if that helps. It will be fairly blunt, but hopefully gets us somewhere.

```
# Code by Monica Alexander
padded_1_to_12 <- sprintf("%02d", 1:12)

list_of_dates_to_flip <-
  paste(2017, padded_1_to_12,
        rep(padded_1_to_12, each = 12), sep = "-")

toronto_shelters_2017_flip <-
  toronto_shelters_2017 |>
  mutate(
    year = year(generated_date),
    month = month(generated_date),
    day = day(generated_date),
    generated_date = as.character(generated_date),
    changed_date = if_else(
```

```
      generated_date %in% list_of_dates_to_flip,
      paste(year, day, month, sep = "-"),
      paste(year, month, day, sep = "-"),
    ),
    changed_date = ymd(changed_date)
  ) |>
  select(-year, -month, -day)
```

Now let us take a look (Figure 9.5).

```
toronto_shelters_2017_flip |>
  mutate(counter = seq_len(nrow(toronto_shelters_2017_flip))) |>
  ggplot(aes(x = counter, y = changed_date)) +
  geom_point(alpha = 0.3) +
  labs(x = "Row in the dataset",
       y = "Date of that row") +
  theme_minimal()

toronto_shelters_2017_flip |>
  drop_na(occupancy, capacity) |>
  summarise(occupancy = sum(occupancy),
            .by = changed_date) |>
  ggplot(aes(x = day(changed_date), y = occupancy)) +
  geom_point(alpha = 0.3) +
  scale_y_continuous(limits = c(0, NA)) +
  labs(color = "Type",
       x = "Changed day",
       y = "Occupancy (number)") +
  facet_wrap(vars(month(changed_date, label = TRUE)),
             scales = "free_x") +
  theme_minimal()
```

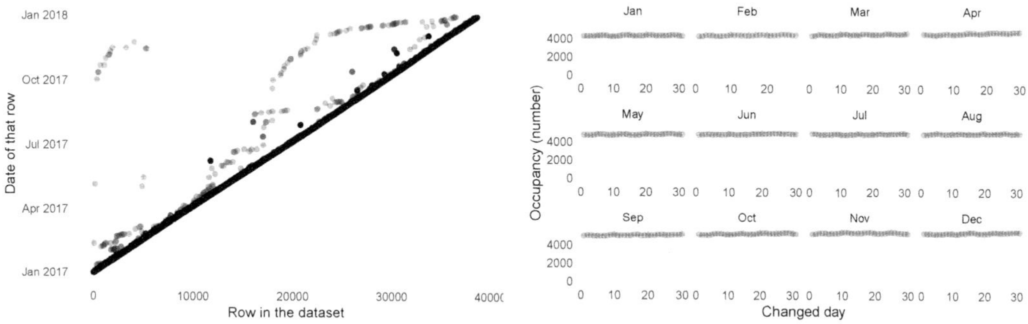

(a) Date of each row in order after adjustment

(b) Toronto shelters daily occupancy after adjustment

Figure 9.5: Adjusted dates, occupancy in Toronto shelters

It has not fixed all the issues. For instance, notice there are now no entries below the diagonal (Figure 9.5a). But we can see that has almost entirely taken care of the systematic differences (Figure 9.5b). This is where we will leave this example.

9.4 Simulated example: running times

To provide a specific example, which we will return to in Chapter 12, consider the time it takes someone to run five kilometers (which is a little over three miles), compared with the time it takes them to run a marathon (Figure 12.2a).

Here we consider "simulate" and "acquire", focused on testing. In the simulation we specify a relationship of 8.4, as that is roughly the ratio between a five-kilometer run and the 42.2 kilometer distance of a marathon (a little over 26 miles).

```
set.seed(853)

num_observations <- 200
expected_relationship <- 8.4
fast_time <- 15
good_time <- 30

sim_run_data <-
  tibble(
    five_km_time =
      runif(n = num_observations, min = fast_time, max = good_time),
    noise = rnorm(n = num_observations, mean = 0, sd = 20),
    marathon_time = five_km_time * expected_relationship + noise
  ) |>
  mutate(
    five_km_time = round(x = five_km_time, digits = 1),
    marathon_time = round(x = marathon_time, digits = 1)
  ) |>
  select(-noise)

sim_run_data
```

```
# A tibble: 200 x 2
   five_km_time marathon_time
          <dbl>         <dbl>
 1         20.4          164.
 2         16.8          158
 3         22.3          196.
 4         19.7          160.
 5         15.6          121.
 6         21.1          178.
 7         17            157.
 8         18.6          169.
 9         17.4          150.
10         17.8          126.
# i 190 more rows
```

We can use our simulation to put in place various tests that we would want the actual data to satisfy. For instance, we want the class of the five kilometer and marathon run times to be numeric. And we want 200 observations.

```
stopifnot(
  class(sim_run_data$marathon_time) == "numeric",
  class(sim_run_data$five_km_time) == "numeric",
  nrow(sim_run_data) == 200
)
```

We know that any value that is less than 15 minutes or more than 30 minutes for the five-kilometer run time is likely something that needs to be followed up on.

```
stopifnot(
  min(sim_run_data$five_km_time) >= 15,
  max(sim_run_data$five_km_time) <= 30
)
```

Based on this maximum and the simulated relationship of 8.4, we would be surprised if we found any marathon times that were substantially over $30 \times 8.4 = 252$ minutes, after we allow for a little bit of drift, say 300 minutes. (To be clear, there is nothing wrong with taking longer than this to run a marathon, but it is just unlikely based on our simulation parameters). And we would be surprised if the world record marathon time, 121 minutes as at the start of 2023, were improved by anything more than a minute or two, say, anything faster than 118 minutes. (It will turn out that our simulated data do not satisfy this and result in a implausibly fast 88 minute marathon time, which suggests a need to improve the simulation.)

```
stopifnot(
  min(sim_run_data$marathon_time) >= 118,
  max(sim_run_data$marathon_time) <= 300
)
```

We can then take these tests to real data. Actual survey data on the relationship between five kilometer and marathon run times are available from Vickers and Vertosick (2016). After downloading the data, which Vickers and Vertosick (2016) make available as an "Additional file", we can focus on the variables of interest and only individuals with both a five-kilometer time and a marathon time.

```
vickers_data <-
  read_excel("13102_2016_52_MOESM2_ESM.xlsx") |>
  select(k5_ti, mf_ti) |>
  drop_na()

vickers_data
```

```
# A tibble: 430 x 2
   k5_ti mf_ti
   <dbl> <dbl>
 1  1075 10295
```

```
 2  1292 12292
 3  1222 13452
 4   893  9515
 5  1050 10875
 6  1603 16580
 7  1457 15440
 8  1256 13113
 9  1572 17190
10  2575 22139
# i 420 more rows
```

The first thing that we notice is that our data are in seconds, whereas we were expecting them to be in minutes. This is fine. Our simulation and tests can update, or we can adjust our data. Our simulation and tests retain their value even when the data turn out to be slightly different, which they inevitably will.

In this case, we will divide by sixty, and round, to shift our data into minutes.

```
vickers_data <-
  vickers_data |>
  mutate(five_km_time = round(k5_ti / 60, 1),
         marathon_time = round(mf_ti / 60, 1)
         ) |>
  select(five_km_time, marathon_time)

vickers_data
```

```
# A tibble: 430 x 2
   five_km_time marathon_time
          <dbl>         <dbl>
 1         17.9          172.
 2         21.5          205.
 3         20.4          224.
 4         14.9          159.
 5         17.5          181.
 6         26.7          276.
 7         24.3          257.
 8         20.9          219.
 9         26.2          286.
10         42.9          369
# i 420 more rows
```

```
stopifnot(
  class(vickers_data$marathon_time) == "numeric",
  class(vickers_data$five_km_time) == "numeric",
  min(vickers_data$five_km_time) >= 15,
  max(vickers_data$five_km_time) <= 30,
  min(vickers_data$marathon_time) >= 118,
  max(vickers_data$marathon_time) <= 300
)
```

In this case, our tests, which were written for the simulated data, identify that we have five kilometer run times that are faster that 15 minutes and longer than 30 minutes. They also identify marathon times that are longer than 300 minutes. If we were actually using this data for analysis, then our next step would be to plot the data, taking care to examine each of these points that our tests identified, and then either adjust the tests or the dataset.

9.5 Names

> An improved scanning software we developed identified gene name errors in 30.9% (3,436/11,117) of articles with supplementary Excel gene lists; a figure significantly higher than previously estimated. This is due to gene names being converted not just to dates and floating-point numbers, but also to internal date format (five-digit numbers).
>
> Abeysooriya et al. (2021)

Names matter. The land on which much of this book was written is today named Canada, but for a long time was known as Turtle Island. Similarly, there is a big rock in the center of Australia. For a long time, it was called Uluru, then it was known as Ayers Rock. Today it has a dual name that combines both. And in parts of the US South, including signage surrounding the South Carolina State House, the US Civil War is referred to as the War of Northern Aggression. In these examples, the name that is used conveys information, not only about the user, but about the circumstances. Even the British Royal Family recognizes the power of names. In 1917 they changed from the House of Saxe-Coburg and Gotha to the House of Windsor. It was felt that the former was too Germanic given World War I. Names matter in everyday life. And they matter in our code, too.

When coding, names are critical and worthy of special attention because (Hermans 2021):

1) they help document our code as they are contained in the code;
2) they make up a large proportion of any script;
3) they are referred to a lot by others; and
4) they help the reader understand what is happening in the code.

In addition to respecting the nature of the data, names need to satisfy two additional considerations:

1) they need to be machine readable, and
2) they need to be human readable.

9.5.1 Machine-readable

Ensuring machine-readable names can be an easier standard to meet. It usually means avoiding spaces and special characters. A space can be replaced with an underscore. For instance, we prefer "my_data" to "my data". Avoiding spaces enables tab-completion which makes us more efficient. It also helps with reproducibility because spaces are considered differently by different operating systems.

Usually, special characters should be removed because they can be inconsistent between different computers and languages. This is especially the case with slash, backslash, asterisk, and both single, and double quotation marks. Try to avoid using those in names.

Names should also be unique within a dataset, and unique within a collection of datasets unless that particular variable is being deliberately used as a key to join different datasets. This usually means that the domain is critical for effective names, and when working as part of a team this all gets much more difficult (Hermans 2017). Names need to not only be unique, but notably different when there is a potential for confusion. For instance, for many years, the language PHP had both `mysql_escape_string` and `mysql_real_escape_string` (Somers 2015). It is easy to see how programmers may have accidentally written one when they meant the other.

An especially useful function to use to get closer to machine-readable names is `clean_names()` from `janitor`. This deals with those issues mentioned above as well as a few others.

```
some_bad_names <-
  tibble(
    "Second Name has spaces" = c(1),
    "weird#symbol" = c(1),
    "InCoNsIsTaNtCaPs" = c(1)
  )

bad_names_made_better <-
  some_bad_names |>
  clean_names()

some_bad_names
```

```
# A tibble: 1 x 3
  `Second Name has spaces` `weird#symbol` InCoNsIsTaNtCaPs
                     <dbl>          <dbl>            <dbl>
1                        1              1                1
```

```
bad_names_made_better
```

```
# A tibble: 1 x 3
  second_name_has_spaces weird_number_symbol in_co_ns_is_ta_nt_ca_ps
                   <dbl>               <dbl>                   <dbl>
1                      1                   1                       1
```

9.5.2 Human-readable

> Programs must be written for people to read, and only incidentally for machines to execute
>
> Abelson and Sussman (1996)

In the same way that we emphasized in Chapter 4 that we write papers for the reader, here we emphasize that we write code for the reader. Human-readable names require an additional layer, and extensive consideration. Following Lockheed Martin (2005, 25), we should avoid names that only differ by the use of the letter "O", instead of the number "0" or the letter "D". Similarly, "S" with "5".

We should consider other cultures and how they may interpret some of the names that we use. We also need to consider different experience levels that subsequent users of the dataset may have. This is both in terms of experience with data science, but also experience with similar datasets. For instance, a variable called "flag" is often used to signal that a variable contains data that needs to be followed up with or treated carefully in some way. An experienced analyst will know this, but a beginner will not. Try to use meaningful names wherever possible (S. Lin, Ali, and Wilson 2021). It has been found that shorter names may take longer to comprehend (Hofmeister, Siegmund, and Holt 2017), and so it is often useful to avoid uncommon abbreviations where possible.

Bryan (2015) recommends that file names, in particular, should consider the default ordering that a file manager will impose. This might mean adding prefixes such as "00-", "01-", etc to filenames (which might involve left-padding with zeros depending on the number of files). Critically it means using ISO 8601 for dates. That was introduced earlier and means that 2 December 2022 would be written "2022-12-02". The reason for using such file names is to provide information to other people about the order of the files.

One interesting feature of R is that in certain cases partial matching on names is possible. For instance:

```
partial_matching_example <-
  data.frame(
    my_first_name = c(1, 2),
    another_name = c("wow", "great")
  )

partial_matching_example$my_first_name
```

```
[1] 1 2
```

```
partial_matching_example$my
```

```
[1] 1 2
```

This behavior is not possible within the `tidyverse` (for instance, if `data.frame` were replaced with `tibble` in the above code). Partial matching should rarely be used. It makes it more difficult to understand code after a break, and for others to come to it fresh.

Variable names should have a consistent structure. For instance, imposing the naming pattern `verb_noun`, as in `read_csv()`, then having one function that was `noun_verb`, perhaps `csv_read()`, would be inconsistent. That inconsistency imposes a significant cost because it makes it more difficult to remember the name of the function.

R, Python, and many of the other languages that are commonly used for data science are dynamically typed, as opposed to static typed. This means that class can be defined independently of declaring a variable. One interesting area of data science research is going partially toward static typed and understanding what that might mean. For instance, Python enabled[7] type hints in 2014 (Boykis 2019). While not required, this goes someway to being more explicit about types.

Riederer (2020) advises using variable names as contracts. We do this by establishing a controlled vocabulary for them. In this way, we would define a set of words that we can use in names. In the controlled vocabulary of Riederer (2020) a variable could start with an abbreviation for its class, then something specific to what it pertains to, and then various details.

For instance, we could consider column names of "age" and "sex". Following Riederer (2020) we may change these to be more informative of the class and other information. This issue is not settled, and there is not yet best practice. For instance, there are arguments against this in terms of readability.

```
some_names <-
  tibble(
    age = as.integer(c(1, 3, 35, 36)),
    sex = factor(c("male", "male", "female", "male"))
  )

riederer_names <-
  some_names |>
  rename(
    integer_age_respondent = age,
    factor_sex_respondent = sex
  )

some_names
```

```
# A tibble: 4 x 2
    age sex
  <int> <fct>
1     1 male
2     3 male
3    35 female
4    36 male
```

[7] https://peps.python.org/pep-0484/

```
riederer_names
```

```
# A tibble: 4 x 2
  integer_age_respondent factor_sex_respondent
                   <int> <fct>
1                      1 male
2                      3 male
3                     35 female
4                     36 male
```

Even just trying to be a little more explicit and consistent about names throughout a project typically brings substantial benefits when we come to revisit the project later. Would a rose by any other name smell as sweet? Of course. But we call it a rose—or even better *Rosa rubiginosa*—because that helps others know what we are talking about, compared with, say, "red_thing", "five_petaled_smell_nice", "flower", or "r_1". It is clearer, and helps others efficiently understand.

9.6 1996 Tanzanian DHS

We will now go through the first of two examples. The Demographic and Health Surveys (DHS) play an important role in gathering data in areas where we may not have other datasets. Here we will clean and prepare a DHS table about household populations in Tanzania in 1996. As a reminder, the workflow that we advocate in this book is:

Plan → Simulate → Acquire → Explore → Share

We are interested in the distribution of age-groups, gender, and urban/rural. A quick sketch might look like Figure 9.6.

AGE GROUP	URBAN MALE	URBAN FEMALE	...	...	TOTAL FEMALE	TOTAL TOTAL
0-4	10	12	...	...	11	10
5-9	8	10	...	...	9	9
⋮	⋮	⋮	⋮	⋮	⋮	⋮
TOTAL	5,000	5,500	...	...	10,500	20,000

Figure 9.6: Quick sketch of a dataset that we might be interested in

We can then simulate a dataset.

```
set.seed(853)

age_group <- tibble(starter = 0:19) |>
  mutate(lower = starter * 5, upper = starter * 5 + 4) |>
  unite(string_sequence, lower, upper, sep = "-") |>
  pull(string_sequence)

mean_value <- 10

simulated_tanzania_dataset <-
  tibble(
    age_group = age_group,
    urban_male = round(rnorm(length(age_group), mean_value)),
    urban_female = round(rnorm(length(age_group), mean_value)),
    rural_male = round(rnorm(length(age_group), mean_value)),
    rural_female = round(rnorm(length(age_group), mean_value)),
    total_male = round(rnorm(length(age_group), mean_value)),
    total_female = round(rnorm(length(age_group), mean_value))
  ) |>
  mutate(
    urban_total = urban_male + urban_female,
    rural_total = rural_male + rural_female,
    total_total = total_male + total_female
  )

simulated_tanzania_dataset
```

```
# A tibble: 20 x 10
   age_group urban_male urban_female rural_male rural_female total_male
   <chr>          <dbl>        <dbl>      <dbl>        <dbl>      <dbl>
 1 0-4               10           10          9            9         11
 2 5-9               10            9          9           10          9
 3 10-14              8           11         11           11         10
 4 15-19              9           11         10            9         10
 5 20-24              9            8         11           10          9
 6 25-29             12            9         10           10         10
 7 30-34              9            8         10           10          8
 8 35-39             10           11          8           10         10
 9 40-44              9            9          9           10         11
10 45-49              9           10         11           10         11
11 50-54             12           10          9           13         10
12 55-59              9           11         10            9          9
13 60-64             10            9         11           11         10
14 65-69             10           10         10           10         11
15 70-74             10           10         12            9          8
16 75-79             10            8         10            9         10
17 80-84             10            9          9           10          9
18 85-89             10            9         10           11         11
19 90-94             11           11         11           10         11
20 95-99             10           10         10           11         11
```

```
# i 4 more variables: total_female <dbl>, urban_total <dbl>, rural_total <dbl>,
#   total_total <dbl>
```

Based on this simulation we are interested to test:

a) Whether there are only numbers.
b) Whether the sum of urban and rural match the total column.
c) Whether the sum of the age-groups match the total.

We begin by downloading the data.[8]

```
download.file(
  url = "https://dhsprogram.com/pubs/pdf/FR83/FR83.pdf",
  destfile = "1996_Tanzania_DHS.pdf",
  mode = "wb"
)
```

When we have a PDF and want to read the content into R, then `pdf_text()` from `pdftools` is useful, as introduced in Chapter 7. It works well for many recently produced PDFs because the content is text which it can extract. But if the PDF is an image, then `pdf_text()` will not work. Instead, the PDF will first need to go through OCR, which was also introduced in Chapter 7.

```
tanzania_dhs <-
  pdf_text(
    pdf = "1996_Tanzania_DHS.pdf"
  )
```

In this case we are interested in Table 2.1, which is on the 33rd page of the PDF (Figure 9.7).

We use `stri_split_lines()` from `stringi` to focus on that particular page.

```
# From Bob Rudis: https://stackoverflow.com/a/47793617
tanzania_dhs_page_33 <- stri_split_lines(tanzania_dhs[[33]])[[1]]
```

We first want to remove all the written content and focus on the table. We then want to convert that into a tibble so that we can use our familiar `tidyverse` approaches.

```
tanzania_dhs_page_33_only_data <- tanzania_dhs_page_33[31:55]

tanzania_dhs_raw <- tibble(all = tanzania_dhs_page_33_only_data)

tanzania_dhs_raw
```

```
# A tibble: 25 x 1
   all
   <chr>
 1 "                                    Urban                                    Rural ~
 2 ""
```

[8]Or use: https://www.tellingstorieswithdata.com/inputs/pdfs/1996_Tanzania_DHS.pdf.

CHAPTER 2

CHARACTERISTICS OF HOUSEHOLDS AND RESPONDENTS

This chapter presents information on selected socioeconomic characteristics of the household population and the individual survey respondents, such as age, sex, marital status, urban-rural residence, and regional distribution. The chapter also considers the conditions surrounding the households in which the survey population live, including sources of drinking water, availability of electricity, sanitation facilities, building materials, and persons per sleeping room.

The 1996 TDHS collected information on individual socioeconomic characteristics of all usual residents and visitors who had spent the previous night preceding the survey interview. This was done by using a questionnaire which was completed for each household. A household was defined as a person or group of persons who live together and share a common source of food.

2.1 Population by Age and Sex

Table 2.1 shows the distribution of the household population by five-year age groups, according to sex and urban-rural residence. As was observed in the censuses and the 1991-92 TDHS, the distribution conforms to the pattern typical of high-fertility populations, that is, a much higher proportion of the population is in the younger age groups than in the older age groups as clearly seen in the population pyramid (Figure 2.1). The slight irregular bulge of women at age 50-54 indicates that some women from ages 45-49 were shifted to the 50-54 age group, perhaps to reduce the workload of the interviewer. There is also an unusually large

Table 2.1 Household population by age, residence, and sex

Percent distribution of the de facto household population by five-year age group, according to urban-rural residence and sex, Tanzania 1996

	Urban			Rural			Total		
Age group	Male	Female	Total	Male	Female	Total	Male	Female	Total
0-4	16.4	13.8	15.1	18.1	17.1	17.6	17.8	16.4	17.1
5-9	13.5	13.0	13.2	17.5	16.0	16.7	16.7	15.4	16.0
10-14	12.6	13.1	12.8	15.3	13.5	14.4	14.8	13.4	14.1
15-19	10.8	11.3	11.1	9.8	8.8	9.3	10.0	9.3	9.6
20-24	9.4	12.2	10.8	5.9	8.2	7.1	6.6	9.0	7.8
25-29	8.4	9.8	9.1	5.6	7.1	6.4	6.2	7.6	6.9
30-34	6.6	6.3	6.4	5.2	5.6	5.4	5.5	5.8	5.6
35-39	5.8	5.9	5.8	4.0	4.5	4.3	4.4	4.8	4.6
40-44	4.4	3.5	3.9	3.3	3.5	3.4	3.5	3.5	3.5
45-49	3.2	2.3	2.7	3.2	3.3	3.2	3.2	3.1	3.1
50-54	2.0	2.4	2.2	2.2	3.4	2.9	2.2	3.2	2.7
55-59	1.8	1.8	1.8	2.1	2.9	2.5	2.0	2.7	2.4
60-64	2.1	1.7	1.9	2.4	2.0	2.2	2.3	2.0	2.1
65-69	1.3	1.3	1.3	2.2	1.6	1.9	2.0	1.5	1.8
70-74	0.9	0.7	0.8	1.3	1.2	1.2	1.2	1.1	1.1
75-79	0.3	0.4	0.4	0.8	0.6	0.7	0.7	0.6	0.6
80 +	0.3	0.5	0.4	0.9	0.7	0.8	0.8	0.7	0.7
Total	100.0	100.0	100.0	100.0	100.0	100.0	100.0	100.0	100.0
Number	3,690	3,876	7,567	14,775	15,931	30,714	18,464	19,807	38,281

Note: Total includes 9 persons whose sex was not stated.

9

Figure 9.7: The page of interest in the 1996 Tanzanian DHS

```
 3 " Age group                  Male      Female      Total          Male   Female ~
 4 ""
 5 ""
 6 " 0-4                        16.4        13.8       15.1          18.1     17.1 ~
 7 " 5-9                        13.5        13.0       13.2          17.5     16,0 ~
 8 " 10-14                      12.6        13.1       12.8          15.3     13.5 ~
 9 " 15-19                      10.8        11.3       11.1           9.8      8.8 ~
10 " 20-~                        9.4        12.2       10,8           5.9      8.2 ~
# i 15 more rows
```

All the columns have been collapsed into one, so we need to separate them. We will do this based on the existence of a space, which means we first need to change "Age group" to "Age-group" because we do not want that separated.

```
# Separate columns
tanzania_dhs_separated <-
  tanzania_dhs_raw |>
  mutate(all = str_squish(all)) |>
  mutate(all = str_replace(all, "Age group", "Age-group")) |>
  separate(
    col = all,
    into = c(
      "age_group",
      "male_urban", "female_urban", "total_urban",
      "male_rural", "female_rural", "total_rural",
      "male_total", "female_total", "total_total"
    ),
    sep = " ",
    remove = TRUE,
    fill = "right",
    extra = "drop"
  )

tanzania_dhs_separated
```

```
# A tibble: 25 x 10
   age_group   male_urban female_urban total_urban male_rural female_rural
   <chr>       <chr>      <chr>        <chr>       <chr>      <chr>
 1 "Urban"     Rural      Total        <NA>        <NA>       <NA>
 2 ""          <NA>       <NA>         <NA>        <NA>       <NA>
 3 "Age-group" Male       Female       Total       Male       Female
 4 ""          <NA>       <NA>         <NA>        <NA>       <NA>
 5 ""          <NA>       <NA>         <NA>        <NA>       <NA>
 6 "0-4"       16.4       13.8         15.1        18.1       17.1
 7 "5-9"       13.5       13.0         13.2        17.5       16,0
 8 "10-14"     12.6       13.1         12.8        15.3       13.5
 9 "15-19"     10.8       11.3         11.1        9.8        8.8
10 "20-~"      9.4        12.2         10,8        5.9        8.2
# i 15 more rows
# i 4 more variables: total_rural <chr>, male_total <chr>, female_total <chr>,
#   total_total <chr>
```

Now we need to clean the rows and columns. One helpful "negative space" approach to work out what we need to remove, is to look at what is left if we temporarily remove everything that we know we want. Whatever is left is then a candidate for being removed. In this case we know that we want the columns to contain numbers, so we remove numeric digits from all columns to see what might stand in our way of converting from string to numeric.

```
tanzania_dhs_separated |>
  mutate(across(everything(), ~ str_remove_all(., "[:digit:]"))) |>
  distinct()
```

```
# A tibble: 15 x 10
   age_group   male_urban female_urban total_urban male_rural female_rural
   <chr>       <chr>      <chr>        <chr>       <chr>      <chr>
 1 "Urban"     Rural      Total        <NA>        <NA>       <NA>
 2 ""          <NA>       <NA>         <NA>        <NA>       <NA>
 3 "Age-group" Male       Female       Total       Male       Female
 4 "-"         .          .            .           .          .
 5 "-"         .          .            .           .          ,
 6 "-"         .          .            .           .          .
 7 "-~"        .          .            ,           .          .
 8 "-"         .          .            ,           ,          ,
 9 "-"         ,          .            .           .          .
10 "-"         .          .            .           .          .
11 "-"         ,          .            .           ;          .
12 "-"         .          .            .           ,          .
13 "+"         .          .            .           .          .
14 "Total"     .          .            .           .          .
15 "Number"    ,          ,            ,           .          ,
# i 4 more variables: total_rural <chr>, male_total <chr>, female_total <chr>,
#   total_total <chr>
```

In this case we can see that some commas and semicolons have been incorrectly considered decimal places. Also, some tildes and blank lines need to be removed. After that we can impose the correct class.

```
tanzania_dhs_cleaned <-
  tanzania_dhs_separated |>
  slice(6:22, 24, 25) |>
  mutate(across(everything(), ~ str_replace_all(., "[,;]", "."))) |>
  mutate(
    age_group = str_replace(age_group, "20-~", "20-24"),
    age_group = str_replace(age_group, "40-~", "40-44"),
    male_rural = str_replace(male_rural, "14.775", "14775")
  ) |>
  mutate(across(starts_with(c(
    "male", "female", "total"
  )),
  as.numeric))

tanzania_dhs_cleaned
```

```
# A tibble: 19 x 10
   age_group male_urban female_urban total_urban male_rural female_rural
   <chr>          <dbl>        <dbl>       <dbl>      <dbl>        <dbl>
 1 0-4             16.4         13.8        15.1       18.1         17.1
 2 5-9             13.5         13          13.2       17.5         16
 3 10-14           12.6         13.1        12.8       15.3         13.5
 4 15-19           10.8         11.3        11.1        9.8          8.8
 5 20-24            9.4         12.2        10.8        5.9          8.2
 6 25-29            8.4          9.8         9.1        5.6          7.1
 7 30-34            6.6          6.3         6.4        5.2          5.6
 8 35-39            5.8          5.9         5.8        4            4.5
 9 40-44            4.4          3.5         3.9        3.3          3.5
10 45-49            3.2          2.3         2.7        3.2          3.3
11 50-54            2            2.4         2.2        2.2          3.4
12 55-59            1.8          1.8         1.8        2.1          2.9
13 60-64            2.1          1.7         1.9        2.4          2
14 65-69            1.3          1.3         1.3        2.2          1.6
15 70-74            0.9          0.7         0.8        1.3          1.2
16 75-79            0.3          0.4         0.4        0.8          0.6
17 80+              0.3          0.5         0.4        0.9          0.7
18 Total          100          100         100        100          100
19 Number           3.69         3.88        7.57   14775           15.9
# i 4 more variables: total_rural <dbl>, male_total <dbl>, female_total <dbl>,
#   total_total <dbl>
```

Finally, we may wish to check that the sum of the constituent parts equals the total.

```
tanzania_dhs_cleaned |>
  filter(!age_group %in% c("Total", "Number")) |>
  summarise(sum = sum(total_total))
```

```
# A tibble: 1 x 1
    sum
  <dbl>
1  99.7
```

In this case we can see that it is a few tenths of a percentage point off.

9.7 2019 Kenyan census

As a final example, let us consider a more extensive situation and gather, clean, and prepare some data from the 2019 Kenyan census. We will focus on creating a dataset of single-year counts, by gender, for Nairobi.

The distribution of population by age, sex, and administrative unit from the 2019 Kenyan census can be downloaded here[9]. While this format as a PDF makes it easy to look up a

[9] https://www.knbs.or.ke/?wpdmpro=2019-kenya-population-and-housing-census-volume-iii-distribution-of-population-by-age-sex-and-administrative-units

particular result, it is not overly useful if we want to model the data. In order to be able to do that, we need to convert this PDF into a tidy dataset that can be analyzed.

9.7.1 Gather and clean

We first need to download and read in the PDF of the 2019 Kenyan census.[10]

```
census_url <-
  paste0(
    "https://www.knbs.or.ke/download/2019-kenya-population-and-",
    "housing-census-volume-iii-distribution-of-population-by-age-",
    "sex-and-administrative-units/?wpdmdl=5729&refresh=",
    "620561f1ce3ad1644519921"
  )

download.file(
  url = census_url,
  destfile = "2019_Kenya_census.pdf",
  mode = "wb"
)
```

We can use `pdf_text()` from `pdftools` again here.

```
kenya_census <-
  pdf_text(
    pdf = "2019_Kenya_census.pdf"
  )
```

In this example we will focus on the page of the PDF about Nairobi (Figure 9.8).

9.7.1.1 Make rectangular

The first challenge is to get the dataset into a format that we can more easily manipulate. We will extract the relevant parts of the page. In this case, data about Nairobi is on page 410.

```
# Focus on the page of interest
just_nairobi <- stri_split_lines(kenya_census[[410]])[[1]]

# Remove blank lines
just_nairobi <- just_nairobi[just_nairobi != ""]

# Remove titles, headings and other content at the top of the page
just_nairobi <- just_nairobi[5:length(just_nairobi)]

# Remove page numbers and other content at the bottom of the page
just_nairobi <- just_nairobi[1:62]
```

[10]If the Kenyan government link breaks then replace their URL with: https://www.tellingstorieswithdata.com/inputs/pdfs/2019_Kenya_census.pdf.

Table 2.3: Distribution of Population by Age, Sex*, County and Sub- County

NAIROBI

Age	Male	Female	Total	Age	Male	Female	Total
Total	**2,192,452**	**2,204,376**	**4,396,828**	51	12,961	9,112	22,073
0	57,265	56,523	113,788	52	13,381	9,179	22,560
1	56,019	54,601	110,620	53	9,905	7,611	17,516
2	52,518	51,848	104,366	54	11,271	7,798	19,069
3	51,115	51,027	102,142	50-54	66,217	47,732	113,949
4	47,182	46,889	94,071	55	10,869	7,263	18,132
0 - 4	264,099	260,888	524,987	56	10,179	7,370	17,549
5	45,203	44,711	89,914	57	8,966	6,677	15,643
6	43,635	44,226	87,861	58	7,164	5,147	12,311
7	43,507	43,655	87,162	59	7,561	5,405	12,966
8	40,916	41,615	82,531	55-59	44,739	31,862	76,601
9	41,969	43,275	85,244	60	7,694	6,148	13,842
5-9	215,230	217,482	432,712	61	5,197	3,948	9,145
10	40,791	40,892	81,683	62	4,853	3,447	8,300
11	35,581	37,513	73,094	63	4,051	3,103	7,154
12	37,907	39,622	77,529	64	3,106	2,437	5,543
13	36,701	39,479	76,180	60-64	24,901	19,083	43,984
14	34,028	36,036	70,064	65	3,992	3,256	7,248
10 -14	185,008	193,542	378,550	66	2,591	2,191	4,782
15	30,919	35,136	66,055	67	3,553	2,762	6,315
16	30,408	35,599	66,007	68	1,914	1,612	3,526
17	32,413	37,865	70,278	69	2,408	2,104	4,512
18	29,102	36,415	65,517	65-69	14,458	11,925	26,383
19	36,256	47,740	83,996	70	2,676	2,653	5,329
15-19	159,098	192,755	351,853	71	1,797	1,541	3,338
20	39,853	55,625	95,478	72	1,672	1,376	3,048
21	45,052	57,938	102,990	73	1,295	1,119	2,414
22	49,186	62,338	111,524	74	1,129	1,096	2,225
23	57,179	70,152	127,331	70-74	8,569	7,785	16,354
24	58,264	67,432	125,696	75	909	1,084	1,993
20-24	249,534	313,485	563,019	76	849	947	1,796
25	63,693	69,680	133,373	77	682	763	1,445
26	56,174	62,288	118,462	78	505	516	1,021
27	57,764	60,383	118,147	79	530	652	1,182
28	50,792	53,563	104,355	75-79	3,475	3,962	7,437
29	54,280	54,931	109,211	80	603	917	1,520
25-29	282,703	300,845	583,548	81	302	432	734
30	64,070	65,757	129,827	82	341	408	749
31	44,601	42,537	87,138	83	335	388	723
32	56,015	54,958	110,973	84	275	384	659
33	43,556	42,761	86,317	80-84	1,856	2,529	4,385
34	41,234	39,981	81,215	85	243	335	578
30-34	249,476	245,994	495,470	86	172	268	440
35	49,053	44,052	93,105	87	155	270	425
36	35,610	33,131	68,741	88	111	132	243
37	34,835	30,671	65,506	89	116	248	364
38	30,710	28,604	59,314	85-89	797	1,253	2,050
39	31,593	27,537	59,130	90	89	218	307
35-39	181,801	163,995	345,796	91	65	135	200
40	37,229	30,970	68,199	92	47	98	145
41	29,619	23,693	53,312	93	39	75	114
42	28,657	22,977	51,634	94	30	77	107
43	24,278	19,898	44,176	90-94	270	603	873
44	19,495	16,346	35,841	95	32	108	140
40-44	139,278	113,884	253,162	96	29	65	94
45	28,137	21,111	49,248	97	22	46	68
46	19,749	14,969	34,718	98	16	34	50
47	20,398	14,741	35,139	99	16	66	82
48	15,447	11,472	26,919	95-99	115	319	434
49	16,988	11,920	28,908	100+	35	171	206
45-49	100,719	74,213	174,932	Not Stated	74	69	143
50	18,699	14,032	32,731				

**Intersex population is excluded from the table since it is too small to be distributed by age*

Figure 9.8: Page from the 2019 Kenyan census about Nairobi

```
# Convert into a tibble
demography_data <- tibble(all = just_nairobi)
```

At this point the data are in a tibble. This allows us to use our familiar `dplyr` verbs. In particular we want to separate the columns.

```
demography_data <-
  demography_data |>
  mutate(all = str_squish(all)) |>
  mutate(all = str_replace(all, "10 -14", "10-14")) |>
  mutate(all = str_replace(all, "Not Stated", "NotStated")) |>
  # Deal with the two column set-up
  separate(
    col = all,
    into = c(
      "age", "male", "female", "total",
      "age_2", "male_2", "female_2", "total_2"
    ),
    sep = " ",
    remove = TRUE,
    fill = "right",
    extra = "drop"
  )
```

They are side by side at the moment. We need to instead append to the bottom.

```
demography_data_long <-
  rbind(
    demography_data |> select(age, male, female, total),
    demography_data |>
      select(age_2, male_2, female_2, total_2) |>
      rename(
        age = age_2,
        male = male_2,
        female = female_2,
        total = total_2
        )
    )


# There is one row of NAs, so remove it
demography_data_long <-
  demography_data_long |>
  remove_empty(which = c("rows"))

demography_data_long
```

```
# A tibble: 123 x 4
   age   male      female    total
   <chr> <chr>     <chr>     <chr>
```

```
 1 Total 2,192,452 2,204,376 4,396,828
 2 0     57,265    56,523    113,788
 3 1     56,019    54,601    110,620
 4 2     52,518    51,848    104,366
 5 3     51,115    51,027    102,142
 6 4     47,182    46,889    94,071
 7 0-4   264,099   260,888   524,987
 8 5     45,203    44,711    89,914
 9 6     43,635    44,226    87,861
10 7     43,507    43,655    87,162
# i 113 more rows
```

Having got it into a rectangular format, we now need to clean the dataset to make it useful.

9.7.1.2 Validity

To attain validity requires a number of steps. The first step is to make the numbers into actual numbers, rather than characters. Before we can convert the type, we need to remove anything that is not a number otherwise that cell will be converted into an NA. We first identify any values that are not numbers so that we can remove them, and `distinct()` is especially useful.

```
demography_data_long |>
  select(male, female, total) |>
  mutate(across(everything(), ~ str_remove_all(., "[:digit:]"))) |>
  distinct()
```

```
# A tibble: 5 x 3
  male  female total
  <chr> <chr>  <chr>
1 ",,"  ",,"   ",,"
2 ","   ","    ","
3 ""    ","    ","
4 ""    ""     ","
5 ""    ""     ""
```

We need to remove commas. While we could use `janitor` here, it is worthwhile to at least first look at what is going on because sometimes there is odd stuff that `janitor` (and other packages) will not deal with in a way that we want. Nonetheless, having identified everything that needs to be removed, we can do the actual removal and convert our character column of numbers to integers.

```
demography_data_long <-
  demography_data_long |>
  mutate(across(c(male, female, total), ~ str_remove_all(., ","))) |>
  mutate(across(c(male, female, total), ~ as.integer(.)))

demography_data_long
```

```
# A tibble: 123 x 4
   age      male  female   total
   <chr>   <int>   <int>   <int>
```

```
 1 Total 2192452 2204376 4396828
 2 0        57265   56523  113788
 3 1        56019   54601  110620
 4 2        52518   51848  104366
 5 3        51115   51027  102142
 6 4        47182   46889   94071
 7 0-4     264099  260888  524987
 8 5        45203   44711   89914
 9 6        43635   44226   87861
10 7        43507   43655   87162
# i 113 more rows
```

9.7.1.3 Internal consistency

The census has done some of the work of putting together age-groups for us, but we want to make it easy to just focus on the counts by single-year age. As such we will add a flag as to the type of age it is: an age-group, such as "ages 0 to 5", or a single age, such as "1".

```
demography_data_long <-
  demography_data_long |>
  mutate(
    age_type = if_else(str_detect(age, "-"),
                       "age-group",
                       "single-year"),
    age_type = if_else(str_detect(age, "Total"),
                       "age-group",
                       age_type)
  )
```

At the moment, age is a character variable. We have a decision to make here. We do not want it to be a character variable (because it will not graph properly), but we do not want it to be numeric, because there is `total` and `100+` in there. For now, we will just make it into a factor, and at least that will be able to be nicely graphed.

```
demography_data_long <-
  demography_data_long |>
  mutate(
    age = as_factor(age)
  )
```

9.7.2 Check and test

Having gathered and cleaned the data, we would like to run a few checks. Given the format of the data, we can check that "total" is the sum of "male" and "female", which are the only two gender categories available.

```
demography_data_long |>
  mutate(
    check_sum = male + female,
```

```
    totals_match = if_else(total == check_sum, 1, 0)
  ) |>
  filter(totals_match == 0)
```

```
# A tibble: 0 x 7
# i 7 variables: age <fct>, male <int>, female <int>, total <int>,
#   age_type <chr>, check_sum <int>, totals_match <dbl>
```

Finally, we want to check that the single-age counts sum to the age-groups.

```
demography_data_long |>
  mutate(age_groups = if_else(age_type == "age-group",
                              age,
                              NA_character_)) |>
  fill(age_groups, .direction = "up") |>
  mutate(
    group_sum = sum(total),
    group_sum = group_sum / 2,
    difference = total - group_sum,
    .by = c(age_groups)
  ) |>
  filter(age_type == "age-group" & age_groups != "Total") |>
  head()
```

```
# A tibble: 6 x 8
  age     male female  total age_type  age_groups group_sum difference
  <fct>  <int>  <int>  <int> <chr>     <chr>          <dbl>      <dbl>
1 0-4   264099 260888 524987 age-group 0-4           524987          0
2 5-9   215230 217482 432712 age-group 5-9           432712          0
3 10-14 185008 193542 378550 age-group 10-14         378550          0
4 15-19 159098 192755 351853 age-group 15-19         351853          0
5 20-24 249534 313485 563019 age-group 20-24         563019          0
6 25-29 282703 300845 583548 age-group 25-29         583548          0
```

9.7.3 Tidy-up

Now that we are reasonably confident that everything is looking good, we can convert it to tidy format. This will make it easier to work with.

```
demography_data_tidy <-
  demography_data_long |>
  rename_with(~paste0(., "_total"), male:total) |>
  pivot_longer(cols = contains("_total"),
               names_to = "type",
               values_to = "number") |>
  separate(
    col = type,
    into = c("gender", "part_of_area"),
    sep = "_"
```

```
  ) |>
  select(age, age_type, gender, number)
```

The original purpose of cleaning this dataset was to make a table that is used by M. Alexander and Alkema (2022). We will return to this dataset, but just to bring this all together, we may like to make a graph of single-year counts, by gender, for Nairobi (Figure 9.9).

```
demography_data_tidy |>
  filter(age_type == "single-year") |>
  select(age, gender, number) |>
  filter(gender != "total") |>
  ggplot(aes(x = age, y = number, fill = gender)) +
  geom_col(aes(x = age, y = number, fill = gender),
           position = "dodge") +
  scale_y_continuous(labels = comma) +
  scale_x_discrete(breaks = c(seq(from = 0, to = 99, by = 5), "100+")) +
  theme_classic() +
  scale_fill_brewer(palette = "Set1") +
  labs(
    y = "Number",
    x = "Age",
    fill = "Gender",
    caption = "Data source: 2019 Kenya Census"
  ) +
  theme(legend.position = "bottom") +
  coord_flip()
```

A variety of features are clear from Figure 9.9, including age-heaping, a slight difference in the ratio of male-female birth, and a substantial difference between ages 15 and 25.

Finally, we may wish to use more informative names. For instance, in the Kenyan data example earlier we have the following column names: "area", "age", "gender", and "number". If we were to use our column names as contracts, then these could be: "chr_area", "fctr_group_age", "chr_group_gender", and "int_group_count".

```
column_names_as_contracts <-
  demography_data_tidy |>
  filter(age_type == "single-year") |>
  select(age, gender, number) |>
  rename(
    "fctr_group_age" = "age",
    "chr_group_gender" = "gender",
    "int_group_count" = "number"
  )
```

We can then use `pointblank` to set up tests for us (Figure 9.10).

```
agent <-
  create_agent(tbl = column_names_as_contracts) |>
```

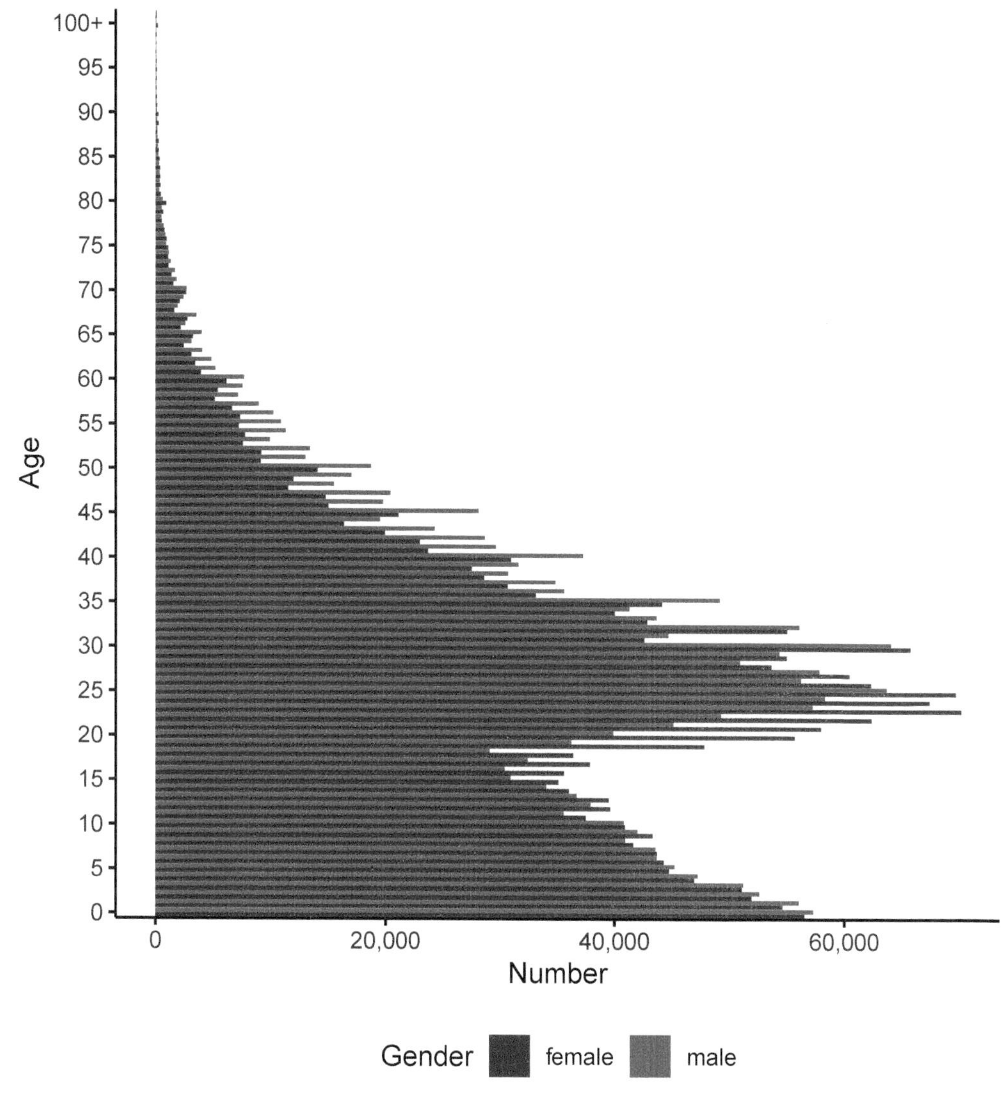

Figure 9.9: Distribution of age and gender in Nairobi in 2019, based on Kenyan census

```
  col_is_character(columns = vars(chr_area, chr_group_gender)) |>
  col_is_factor(columns = vars(fctr_group_age)) |>
  col_is_integer(columns = vars(int_group_count)) |>
  col_vals_in_set(
    columns = chr_group_gender,
    set = c("male", "female", "total")
  ) |>
  interrogate()

agent
```

Pointblank Validation

[2022-08-25|07:18:33]

TIBBLE column_names_as_contracts

	STEP	COLUMNS	VALUES	TBL	EVAL	UNITS	PASS	FAIL	W
1	c col_is_character()	chr_area	—	O→	✓	1	1 1	0 0	—
2	c col_is_character()	chr_group_gender	—	O→	✓	1	1 1	0 0	—
3	f col_is_factor()	fctr_group_age	—	O→	✓	1	1 1	0 0	—
4	i col_is_integer()	int_group_count	—	O→	✓	1	1 1	0 0	—
5	∈ col_vals_in_set()	chr_group_gender	male, female, to...	O→	✓	14K	14K 1	0 0	—

2022-08-25 07:18:33 EDT | < 1 s | 2022-08-25 07:18:33 EDT

Figure 9.10: Example of Pointblank Validation

9.8 Exercises

Scales

1. *(Plan)* Consider the following scenario: *You manage a shop with two employees and are interested in modeling their efficiency. The shop opens at 9am and closes at 5pm. The efficiency of the employees is mildly correlated and defined by the number of customers that they serve each hour. Be clear about whether you assume a negative or positive correlation.* Please sketch what that dataset could look like and then sketch a graph that you could build to show all observations.
2. *(Simulate)* Please further consider the scenario described and simulate the situation. Please include five tests based on the simulated data. Submit a link to a GitHub Gist that contains your code.
3. *(Acquire)* Please describe a possible source of such a dataset.
4. *(Explore)* Please use `ggplot2` to build the graph that you sketched using the simulated data from step 1. Submit a link to a GitHub Gist that contains your code.
5. *(Communicate)* Please write two paragraphs about what you did.

Questions

1. If we had a character variable "some_words" with one observation `"You know what"` within a dataset called `sayings`, then which of the following would split it into its constituent words (pick one)?
   a. `separate(data = sayings, col = some_words, into = c("one", "two", "three"), sep = " ")`
   b. `split(data = sayings, col = some_words, into = c("one", "two", "three"), sep = " ")`
   c. `divide(data = sayings, col = some_words, into = c("one", "two", "three"), sep = " ")`
   d. `part(data = sayings, col = some_words, into = c("one", "two", "three"), sep = " ")`
   e. `unattach(data = sayings, col = some_words, into = c("one", "two",`

```
"three"), sep = " ")
```

2. Is the following an example of tidy data? Why or why not?

```
tibble(
  name = c("Ian", "Patricia", "Ville", "Karen"),
  age_group = c("18-29", "30-44", "45-60", "60+"),
)
```

3. Which function would change "lemons" into "lemonade"?
   a. `str_replace(string = "lemons", pattern = "lemons", replacement = "lemonade")`
   b. `chr_replace(string = "lemons", pattern = "lemons", replacement = "lemonade")`
   c. `str_change(string = "lemons", pattern = "lemons", replacement = "lemonade")`
   d. `chr_change(string = "lemons", pattern = "lemons", replacement = "lemonade")`
4. When dealing with ages, what are some desirable classes for the variable (select all that apply)?
   a. integer
   b. matrix
   c. numeric
5. Please consider the following cities in Germany: "Berlin", "Hamburg", "Munich", "Cologne", "Frankfurt", and "Rostock". Use `testthat` to define three tests that could apply if we had a dataset with a variable "german_cities" that claimed to contain these, and only these, cities. Submit a link to a GitHub Gist.
6. Which is the most acceptable format for dates in data science?
   a. YYYY-DD-MM
   b. YYYY-MM-DD
   c. DD-MM-YYYY
   d. MM-MM-YYYY
7. Which of the following does not belong? `c(15.9, 14.9, 16.6, 15.8, 16.7, 17.9, I2.6, 11.5, 16.2, 19.5, 15.0)`
8. With regard to "AV Rule 48" from Lockheed Martin (2005, 25) which of the following are not allowed to differ identifiers (select all that apply)?
   a. Only a mixture of case
   b. The presence/absence of the underscore character
   c. The interchange of the letter "O" with the number "0" or the letter "D"
   d. The interchange of the letter "I" with the number "1" or the letter "l"
9. With regard to Preece (1981) please discuss two ways in which final digits can be informative. Write at least a paragraph about each and include examples.

Tutorial

With regard to Jordan (2019), D'Ignazio and Klein (2020, chap. 6), Au (2020), and other relevant work, to what extent do you think we should let the data speak for themselves? Please write at least two pages.

Use Quarto, and include an appropriate title, author, date, link to a GitHub repo, and citations to produce a draft. After this, please pair with another student and exchange your written work. Update it based on their feedback, and be sure to acknowledge them by name in your paper. Submit a PDF.

10

Store and share

Prerequisites

- Read *Promoting Open Science Through Research Data Management*, (Borghi and Van Gulick 2022)
  - Describes the state of data management, and some strategies for conducting research that is more reproducible.
- Read *Data Management in Large-Scale Education Research*, (Lewis 2023)
  - Focus on Chapter 2 "Research Data Management", which provides an overview of data management concerns, workflow, and terminology.
- Read *Transparent and reproducible social science research*, (Christensen, Freese, and Miguel 2019)
  - Focus on Chapter 10 "Data Sharing", which specifies ways to share data.
- Read *Datasheets for datasets*, (Gebru et al. 2021)
  - Introduces the idea of a datasheet.
- Read *Data and its (dis)contents: A survey of dataset development and use in machine learning research*, (Paullada et al. 2021)
  - Details the state of data in machine learning.

Key concepts and skills

- The FAIR principles provide the foundation from which we consider data sharing and storage. These specify that data should be findable, accessible, interoperable, and reusable.
- The most important step is the first one, and that is to get the data off our local computer, and to then make it accessible by others. After that, we build documentation, and datasheets, to make it easier for others to understand and use it. Finally, we ideally enable access without our involvement.
- At the same time as wanting to share our datasets as widely as possible, we should respect those whose information are contained in them. This means, for instance, protecting, to a reasonable extent, and informed by costs and benefits, personally identifying information through selective disclosure, hashing, data simulation, and differential privacy.
- Finally, as our data get larger, approaches that were viable when they were smaller start to break down. We need to consider efficiency, and explore other approaches, formats, and languages.

Software and packages

- Base R (R Core Team 2023)
- `arrow` (Richardson et al. 2023)
- `devtools` (Wickham, Hester, et al. 2022)
- `diffpriv` (Rubinstein and Alda 2017)
- `fs` (Hester, Wickham, and Csárdi 2021)
- `janitor` (Firke 2023)
- `knitr` (Xie 2023)

- `openssl` (Ooms 2022a)
- `tictoc` (Izrailev 2022)
- `tidyverse` (Wickham et al. 2019)

```
library(arrow)
library(devtools)
library(diffpriv)
library(fs)
library(janitor)
library(knitr)
library(openssl)
library(tictoc)
library(tidyverse)
```

10.1 Introduction

After we have put together a dataset we must store it appropriately and enable easy retrieval both for ourselves and others. There is no completely agreed on approach, but there are best standards, and this is an evolving area of research (Lewis 2023). Wicherts, Bakker, and Molenaar (2011) found that a reluctance to share data was associated with research papers that had weaker evidence and more potential errors. While it is possible to be especially concerned about this—and entire careers and disciplines are based on the storage and retrieval of data—to a certain extent, the baseline is not onerous. If we can get our dataset off our own computer, then we are much of the way there. Further confirming that someone else can retrieve and use it, ideally without our involvement, puts us much further than most. Just achieving that for our data, models, and code meets the "bronze" standard of Heil et al. (2021).

The FAIR principles are useful when we come to think more formally about data sharing and management. This requires that datasets are (M. Wilkinson et al. 2016):

1. Findable. There is one, unchanging, identifier for the dataset and the dataset has high-quality descriptions and explanations.
2. Accessible. Standardized approaches can be used to retrieve the data, and these are open and free, possibly with authentication, and their metadata persist even if the dataset is removed.
3. Interoperable. The dataset and its metadata use a broadly-applicable language and vocabulary.
4. Reusable. There are extensive descriptions of the dataset and the usage conditions are made clear along with provenance.

One reason for the rise of data science is that humans are at the heart of it. And often the data that we are interested in directly concern humans. This means that there can be tension between sharing a dataset to facilitate reproducibility and maintaining privacy. Medicine developed approaches to this over a long time. And out of that we have seen the Health Insurance Portability and Accountability Act (HIPAA) in the US, the broader General Data Protection Regulation (GDPR) in Europe introduced in 2016, and the California Consumer

Privacy Act (CCPA) introduced in 2018, among others.

Our concerns in data science tend to be about personally identifying information. We have a variety of ways to protect especially private information, such as emails and home addresses. For instance, we can hash those variables. Sometimes we may simulate data and distribute that instead of sharing the actual dataset. More recently, approaches based on differential privacy are being implemented, for instance for the US census. The fundamental problem of data privacy is that increased privacy reduces the usefulness of a dataset. The trade-off means the appropriate decision is nuanced and depends on costs and benefits, and we should be especially concerned about differentiated effects on population minorities.

Just because a dataset is FAIR, it is not necessarily an unbiased representation of the world. Further, it is not necessarily fair in the everyday way that word is used, i.e. impartial and honest (Lima et al. 2022). FAIR reflects whether a dataset is appropriately available, not whether it is appropriate.

Finally, in this chapter we consider efficiency. As datasets and code bases get larger it becomes more difficult to deal with them, especially if we want them to be shared. We come to concerns around efficiency, not for its own sake, but to enable us to tell stories that could not otherwise be told. This might mean moving beyond CSV files to formats with other properties, or even using databases, such as Postgres, although even as we do so acknowledging that the simplicity of a CSV, as it is text-based which lends itself to human inspection, can be a useful feature.

10.2 Plan

The storage and retrieval of information is especially connected with libraries, in the traditional sense of a collection of books. These have existed since antiquity and have well-established protocols for deciding what information to store and what to discard, as well as information retrieval. One of the defining aspects of libraries is deliberate curation and organization. The use of a cataloging system ensures that books on similar topics are located close to each other, and there are typically also deliberate plans for ensuring the collection is up to date. This enables information storage and retrieval that is appropriate and efficient.

Data science relies heavily on the internet when it comes to storage and retrieval. Vannevar Bush, the twentieth century engineer, defined a "memex" in 1945 as a device to store books, records, and communications in a way that supplements memory (Bush 1945). The key to it was the indexing, or linking together, of items. We see this concept echoed just four decades later in the proposal by Tim Berners-Lee for hypertext (Berners-Lee 1989). This led to the World Wide Web and defines the way that resources are identified. They are then transported over the internet, using Hypertext Transfer Protocol (HTTP).

At its most fundamental, the internet is about storing and retrieving data. It is based on making various files on a computer available to others. When we consider the storage and retrieval of our datasets we want to especially contemplate for how long they should be stored and for whom (Michener 2015). For instance, if we want some dataset to be available for a decade, and widely available, then it becomes important to store it in open and persistent formats (Hart et al. 2016). But if we are just using a dataset as part of an intermediate step, and we have the original, unedited data and the scripts to create it, then it might be fine to not worry too much about such considerations. The evolution of physical storage media has similar complicated issues. For instance, datasets and recordings made on media such as wax cylinders, magnetic tapes, and proprietary optical disks, now have a variable ease of use.

Storing the original, unedited data is important and there are many cases where unedited data have revealed or hinted at fraud (Simonsohn 2013). Shared data also enhances the credibility of our work, by enabling others to verify it, and can lead to the generation of new knowledge as others use it to answer different questions (Christensen, Freese, and Miguel 2019). Christensen et al. (2019) suggest that research that shares its data may be more highly cited, although Tierney and Ram (2021) caution that widespread data sharing may require a cultural change.

We should try to invite scrutiny and make it as easy as possible to receive criticism. We should try to do this even when it is the difficult choice and results in discomfort because that is the only way to contribute to the stock of lasting knowledge. For instance, Piller (2022) details potential fabrication in research about Alzheimer's disease. In that case, one of the issues that researchers face when trying to understand whether the results are legitimate is a lack of access to unpublished images.

Data provenance is especially important. This refers to documenting "where a piece of data came from and the process by which it arrived in the database" (Buneman, Khanna, and Wang-Chiew 2001, 316). Documenting and saving the original, unedited dataset, using scripts to manipulate it to create the dataset that is analyzed, and sharing all of this—as recommended in this book—goes some way to achieving this. In some fields it is common for just a handful of databases to be used by many different teams, for instance, in genetics, the UK BioBank, and in the life sciences a cloud-based platform called ORCESTRA (Mammoliti et al. 2021) has been established to help.

10.3 Share

10.3.1 GitHub

The easiest place for us to get started with storing a dataset is GitHub because that is already built into our workflow. For instance, if we push a dataset to a public repository, then our dataset becomes available. One benefit of this is that if we have set up our workspace appropriately, then we likely store our original, unedited data and the tidy data, as well as the scripts that are needed to transform one to the other. We are most of the way to the "bronze" standard of Heil et al. (2021) without changing anything.

As an example of how we have stored some data, we can access "raw_data.csv" from the "starter_folder"[1]. We navigate to the file in GitHub ("inputs" → "data" → "raw_data.csv"), and then click "Raw" (Figure 10.1).

We can then add that URL as an argument to `read_csv()`.

```
data_location <-
  paste0(
    "https://raw.githubusercontent.com/RohanAlexander/",
```

[1] https://github.com/RohanAlexander/starter_folder

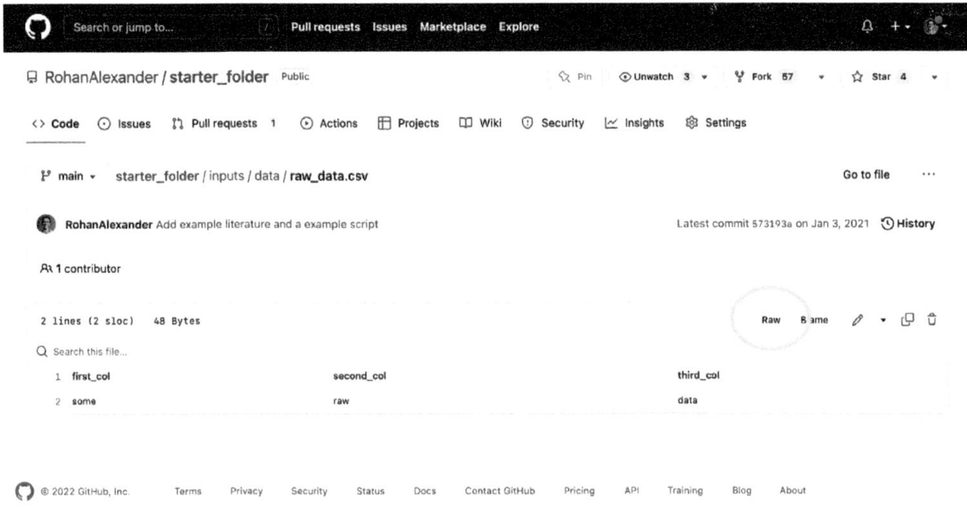

Figure 10.1: Getting the necessary link to be able to read a CSV from a GitHub repository

```
    "starter_folder/main/inputs/data/raw_data.csv"
  )

starter_data <-
  read_csv(file = data_location,
           col_types = cols(
             first_col = col_character(),
             second_col = col_character(),
             third_col = col_character()
             )
           )

starter_data
```

```
# A tibble: 1 x 3
  first_col second_col third_col
  <chr>     <chr>      <chr>
1 some      raw        data
```

While we can store and retrieve a dataset easily in this way, it lacks explanation, a formal dictionary, and aspects such as a license that would bring it closer to aligning with the FAIR principles. Another practical concern is that the maximum file size on GitHub is 100MB, although Git Large File Storage (LFS) can be used if needed. And a final concern, for some, is that GitHub is owned by Microsoft, a for-profit US technology firm.

10.3.2 R packages for data

To this point we have largely used R packages for their code, although we have seen a few that were focused on sharing data, for instance, `troopdata` and `babynames`. We can build a R package for our dataset and then add it to GitHub and potentially CRAN. This will make it easier to store and retrieve because we can obtain the dataset by loading the package. In contrast to a CSV-based approach, it also means a dataset brings its documentation along with it.

This will be the first R package that we build, and so we will skip over a number of steps. The key is to just try to get something working. In "Production" Online Appendix[2], we return to R packages and use them to deploy models. This gives us another chance to further develop experience with them.

To get started, create a new package: "File" → "New project" → "New Directory" → "R Package". Give the package a name, such as "favcolordata" and select "Open in new session". Create a new folder called "data". We will simulate a dataset of people and their favorite colors to include in our R package.

```
set.seed(853)

color_data <-
  tibble(
    name =
      c(
        "Edward", "Helen", "Hugo", "Ian", "Monica",
        "Myles", "Patricia", "Roger", "Rohan", "Ruth"
      ),
    fav_color =
      sample(
        x = colors(),
        size = 10,
        replace = TRUE
      )
  )
```

To this point we have largely been using CSV files for our datasets. To include our data in this R package, we save our dataset in a different format, ".rda", using `save()`.

```
save(color_data, file = "data/color_data.rda")
```

Then we create a R file "data.R" in the "R" folder. This file will only contain documentation using `roxygen2` comments. These start with `#'`, and we follow the documentation for `troopdata` closely.

```
#' Favorite color of various people data
#'
#' @description \code{favcolordata} returns a dataframe
#' of the favorite color of various people.
#'
#' @return Returns a dataframe of the favorite color
#' of various people.
#'
#' @docType data
#'
```

[2]https://tellingstorieswithdata.com/28-deploy.html

```
#' @usage data(color_data)
#'
#' @format A dataframe of individual-level observations
#' with the following variables:
#'
#' \describe{
#' \item{\code{name}}{A character vector of individual names.}
#' \item{\code{fav_color}}{A character vector of colors.}
#' }
#'
#' @keywords datasets
#'
#' @source \url{tellingstorieswithdata.com/10-store_and_share.html}
#'
"color_data"
```

Finally, add a README that provides a summary of all of this for someone coming to the project for the first time. Examples of packages with excellent READMEs include `ggplot2`[3], `pointblank`[4], `modelsummary`[5], and `janitor`[6].

We can now go to the "Build" tab and click "Install and Restart". After this, the package "favcolordata", will be loaded and the data can be accessed locally using "color_data". If we were to push this package to GitHub, then anyone would be able to install the package using `devtools` and use our dataset. Indeed, the following should work.

```
install_github("RohanAlexander/favcolordata")

library(favcolordata)

color_data
```

This has addressed many of the issues that we faced earlier. For instance, we have included a README and a data dictionary, of sorts, in terms of the descriptions that we added. But if we were to try to put this package onto CRAN, then we might face some issues. For instance, the maximum size of a package is 5MB and we would quickly come up against that. We have also largely forced users to use R. While there are benefits of that, we may like to be more language agnostic (Tierney and Ram 2020), especially if we are concerned about the FAIR principles.

Wickham (2022a, chap. 8) provides more information about including data in R packages.

10.3.3 Depositing data

While it is possible that a dataset will be cited if it is available through GitHub or a R package, this becomes more likely if the dataset is deposited somewhere. There are several reasons for this, but one is that it seems a bit more formal. Another is that it is associated

[3]https://github.com/tidyverse/ggplot2#readme
[4]https://github.com/rich-iannone/pointblank#readme
[5]https://github.com/vincentarelbundock/modelsummary#readme
[6]https://github.com/sfirke/janitor#readme

with a DOI. Zenodo[7] and the Open Science Framework[8] (OSF) are two depositories that are commonly used. For instance, Carleton (2021) uses Zenodo to share the dataset and analysis supporting Carleton, Campbell, and Collard (2021), Geuenich et al. (2021b) use Zenodo to share the dataset that underpins Geuenich et al. (2021a), and Katz and Alexander (2023b) use Zenodo to share the dataset that underpins Katz and Alexander (2023a). Similarly, Arel-Bundock et al. (2022) use OSF to share code and data.

Another option is to use a dataverse, such as the Harvard Dataverse[9] or the Australian Data Archive[10]. This is a common requirement for journal publications. One nice aspect of this is that we can use `dataverse` to retrieve the dataset as part of a reproducible workflow. We have an example of this in Chapter 13.

In general, these options are free and provide a DOI that can be useful for citation purposes. The use of data deposits such as these is a way to offload responsibility for the continued hosting of the dataset (which in this case is a good thing) and prevent the dataset from being lost. It also establishes a single point of truth, which should act to reduce errors (Byrd et al. 2020). Finally, it makes access to the dataset independent of the original researchers, and results in persistent metadata. That all being said, the viability of these options rests on their underlying institutions. For instance, Zenodo is operated by CERN and many dataverses are operated by universities. These institutions are subject to, as we all are, social and political forces.

10.4 Data documentation

Dataset documentation has long consisted of a data dictionary. This may be as straightforward a list of the variables, a few sentences of description, and ideally a source. The data dictionary of the ACS[11], which was introduced in Chapter 6, is particularly comprehensive. And OSF provides instructions[12] for how to make a data dictionary. Given the workflow advocated in this book, it might be worthwhile to actually begin putting together a data dictionary as part of the simulation step i.e. before even collecting the data. While it would need to be updated, it would be another opportunity to think deeply about the data situation.

Datasheets (Gebru et al. 2021) are an increasingly common addition to documentation. If we think of a data dictionary as a list of ingredients for a dataset, then we could think of a datasheet as basically a nutrition label for datasets. The process of creating them enables us to think more carefully about what we will feed our model. More importantly, they enable others to better understand what we fed our model. One important task is going back and putting together datasheets for datasets that are widely used. For instance, researchers went back and wrote a datasheet for "BookCorpus", which is one of the most popular datasets in computer science, and they found that around 30 per cent of the data were duplicated (Bandy and Vincent 2021).

[7]https://zenodo.org
[8]https://osf.io
[9]https://dataverse.harvard.edu
[10]https://ada.edu.au
[11]https://www2.census.gov/programs-surveys/acs/tech_docs/pums/data_dict/PUMS_Data_Dictionary_2016-2020.pdf
[12]https://help.osf.io/article/217-how-to-make-a-data-dictionary

Shoulders of giants

Timnit Gebru is the founder of the Distributed Artificial Intelligence Research Institute (DAIR). After earning a PhD in Computer Science from Stanford University, Gebru joined Microsoft and then Google. In addition to Bandy and Vincent (2021), which introduced datasheets, one notable paper is Bender et al. (2021), which discussed the dangers of language models being too large. She has made many other substantial contributions to fairness and accountability, especially Buolamwini and Gebru (2018), which demonstrated racial bias in facial analysis algorithms.

Instead of telling us how unhealthy various foods are, a datasheet tells us things like:

- Who put the dataset together?
- Who paid for the dataset to be created?
- How complete is the dataset? (Which is, of course, unanswerable, but detailing the ways in which it is known to be incomplete is valuable.)
- Which variables are present, and, equally, not present, for particular observations?

Sometimes, a lot of work is done to create a datasheet. In that case, we may like to publish and share it on its own, for instance, Biderman, Bicheno, and Gao (2022) and Bandy and Vincent (2021). But typically a datasheet might live in an appendix to the paper, for instance S. Zhang et al. (2022), or be included in a file adjacent to the dataset.

As an example, a datasheet for the dataset that underpins R. Alexander and Hodgetts (2021) is included in the "Datasheet" Online Appendix[13]. The text of the questions directly comes from Gebru et al. (2021). When creating a datasheet for a dataset, especially a dataset that we did not put together ourselves, it is possible and understandable that the answer to some questions will simply be "Unknown", but we should do what we can to minimize that.

The datasheet template created by Gebru et al. (2021) is not the final word. It is possible to improve on it, and add additional detail sometimes. For instance, Miceli, Posada, and Yang (2022) argue for the addition of questions to do with power relations.

10.5 Personally identifying information

By way of background, Christensen, Freese, and Miguel (2019, 180) define a variable as "confidential" if the researchers know who is associated with each observation, but the public version of the dataset removes this association. A variable is "anonymous" if even the researchers do not know.

Personally identifying information (PII) is that which enables us to link an observation in our dataset with an actual person. This is a significant concern in fields focused on data about people. Email addresses are often PII, as are names and addresses. While some variables may not be PII for many respondents, it could be PII for some. For instance, consider a survey that is representative of the population age distribution. There is not likely to be many respondents aged over 100, and so the variable age may then become PII. The same scenario applies to income, wealth, and many other variables. One response to

[13]https://tellingstorieswithdata.com/25-datasheet.html

this is for data to be censored, which was discussed in Chapter 6. For instance, we may record age between zero and 90, and then group everyone over that into "90+". Another is to construct age-groups: "18-29", "30-44", ... Notice that with both these solutions we have had to trade-off privacy and usefulness. More concerningly, a variable may be PII, not by itself, but when combined with another variable.

Our primary concern should be with ensuring that the privacy of our dataset is appropriate, given the expectations of the reasonable person. This requires weighing costs and benefits. In national security settings there has been considerable concern about the over-classification of documents (H. Lin 2014). The reduced circulation of information because of this may result in unrealized benefits. To avoid this in data science, the test of the need to protect a dataset needs to be made by the reasonable person weighing up costs and benefits. It is easy, but incorrect, to argue that data should not be released unless it is perfectly anonymized. The fundamental problem of data privacy implies that such data would have limited utility. That approach, possibly motivated by the precautionary principle, would be too conservative and could cause considerable loss in terms of unrealized benefits.

Randomized response (Greenberg et al. 1969) is a clever way to enable anonymity without much overhead. Each respondent flips a coin before they answer a question but does not show the researcher the outcome of the coin flip. The respondent is instructed to respond truthfully to the question if the coin lands on heads, but to always give some particular (but still plausible) response if tails. The results of the other options can then be re-weighted to enable an estimate, without a researcher ever knowing the truth about any particular respondent. This is especially used in association with snowball sampling, discussed in Chapter 6. One issue with randomized response is that the resulting dataset can be only used to answer specific questions. This requires careful planning, and the dataset will be of less general value.

Zook et al. (2017) recommend considering whether data even need to be gathered in the first place. For instance, if a phone number is not absolutely required then it might be better to not ask for it, rather than need to worry about protecting it before data dissemination. GDPR and HIPAA are two legal structures that govern data in Europe, and the United States, respectively. Due to the influence of these regions, they have a significant effect outside those regions also. GDPR concerns data generally, while HIPAA is focused on healthcare. GDPR applies to all personal data, which is defined as:

> ...any information relating to an identified or identifiable natural person ("data subject"); an identifiable natural person is one who can be identified, directly or indirectly, in particular by reference to an identifier such as a name, an identification number, location data, an online identifier or to one or more factors specific to the physical, physiological, genetic, mental, economic, cultural or social identity of that natural person;
>
> Council of European Union (2016), Article 4, "Definitions"

HIPAA refers to the privacy of medical records in the US and codifies the idea that the patient should have access to their medical records, and that only the patient should be able to authorize access to their medical records (Annas 2003). HIPAA only applies to certain entities. This means it sets a standard, but coverage is inconsistent. For instance, a person's social media posts about their health would generally not be subject to it, nor would knowledge of a person's location and how active they are, even though based on that information we may be able to get some idea of their health (G. Cohen and Mello 2018). Such data are hugely valuable (Ross 2022).

There are a variety of ways of protecting PII, while still sharing some data, that we will now go through. We focus here initially on what we can do when the dataset is considered by itself, which is the main concern. But sometimes the combination of several variables, none of which are PII in and of themselves, can be PII. For instance, age is unlikely PII by itself, but age combined with city, education, and a few other variables could be. One concern is that re-identification could occur by combining datasets and this is a potential role for differential privacy.

10.5.1 Hashing

A cryptographic hash is a one-way transformation, such that the same input always provides the same output, but given the output, it is not reasonably possible to obtain the input. For instance, a function that doubled its input always gives the same output, for the same input, but is also easy to reverse, so would not work well as a hash. In contrast, the modulo, which for a non-negative number is the remainder after division and can be implemented in R using `%%`, would be difficult to reverse.

Knuth (1998, 514) relates an interesting etymology for "hash". He first defines "to hash" as relating to chop up or make a mess, and then explaining that hashing relates to scrambling the input and using this partial information to define the output. A collision is when different inputs map to the same output, and one feature of a good hashing algorithm is that collisions are reduced. As mentioned, one simple approach is to rely on the modulo operator. For instance, if we were interested in ten different groupings for the integers 1 through to 10, then modulo would enable this. A better approach would be for the number of groupings to be a larger number, because this would reduce the number of values with the same hash outcome.

For instance, consider some information that we would like to keep private, such as names and ages of respondents.

```
some_private_information <-
  tibble(
    names = c("Rohan", "Monica"),
    ages = c(36, 35)
  )

some_private_information
```

```
# A tibble: 2 x 2
  names   ages
  <chr>  <dbl>
1 Rohan     36
2 Monica    35
```

One option for the names would be to use a function that just took the first letter of each name. And one option for the ages would be to convert them to Roman numerals.

```
some_private_information |>
  mutate(
    names = substring(names, 1, 1),
    ages = as.roman(ages)
  )
```

```
# A tibble: 2 x 2
  names ages
  <chr> <roman>
1 R     XXXVI
2 M     XXXV
```

While the approach for the first variable, names, is good because the names cannot be backed out, the issue is that as the dataset grows there are likely to be lots of "collisions"—situations where different inputs, say "Rohan" and "Robert", both get the same output, in this case "R". It is the opposite situation for the approach for the second variable, ages. In this case, there will never be any collisions—"36" will be the only input that ever maps to "XXXVI". However, it is easy to back out the actual data, for anyone who knows roman numerals.

Rather than write our own hash functions, we can use cryptographic hash functions such as `md5()` from `openssl`.

```
some_private_information |>
  mutate(
    md5_names = md5(names),
    md5_ages = md5(ages |> as.character())
  )
```

```
# A tibble: 2 x 4
  names    ages md5_names              md5_ages
  <chr>   <dbl> <hash>                 <hash>
1 Rohan      36 02df8936eee3d4d25... 19ca14e7ea6328a42...
2 Monica     35 09084cc0cda34fd80... 1c383cd30b7c298ab...
```

We could share either of these transformed variables and be comfortable that it would be difficult for someone to use only that information to recover the names of our respondents. That is not to say that it is impossible. Knowledge of the key, which is the term given to the string used to encrypt the data, would allow someone to reverse this. If we made a mistake, such as accidentally pushing the original dataset to GitHub then they could be recovered. And it is likely that governments and some private companies can reverse the cryptographic hashes used here.

One issue that remains is that anyone can take advantage of the key feature of hashes to back out the input. In particular, the same input always gets the same output. So they could test various options for inputs. For instance, they could themselves try to hash "Rohan", and then noticing that the hash is the same as the one that we published in our dataset, know that data relates to that individual. We could try to keep our hashing approach secret, but that is difficult as there are only a few that are widely used. One approach is to add a salt that we keep secret. This slightly changes the input. For instance, we could add the salt "_is_a_person" to all our names and then hash that, although a large random number might be a better option. Provided the salt is not shared, then it would be difficult for most people to reverse our approach in that way.

```
some_private_information |>
  mutate(names = paste0(names, "_is_a_person")) |>
  mutate(
    md5_of_salt = md5(names)
  )
```

```
# A tibble: 2 x 3
  names                ages md5_of_salt
  <chr>               <dbl> <hash>
1 Rohan_is_a_person      36 3ab064d7f746fde604122d072fd4fa97
2 Monica_is_a_person     35 50bb9dfffa926c855b830845ac61b659
```

10.5.2 Simulation

One common approach to deal with the issue of being unable to share the actual data that underpins an analysis, is to use data simulation. We have used data simulation throughout this book toward the start of the workflow to help us to think more deeply about our dataset. We can use data simulation again at the end, to ensure that others cannot access the actual dataset.

The approach is to understand the critical features of the dataset and the appropriate distribution. For instance, if our data were the ages of some population, then we may want to use the Poisson distribution and experiment with different parameters for the rate. Having simulated a dataset, we conduct our analysis using this simulated dataset and ensure that the results are broadly similar to when we use the real data. We can then release the simulated dataset along with our code.

For more nuanced situations, Koenecke and Varian (2020) recommend using the synthetic data vault (Patki, Wedge, and Veeramachaneni 2016) and then the use of Generative Adversarial Networks, such as implemented by Athey et al. (2021).

10.5.3 Differential privacy

Differential privacy is a mathematical definition of privacy (Dwork and Roth 2013, 6). It is not just one algorithm, it is a definition that many algorithms satisfy. Further, there are many definitions of privacy, of which differential privacy is just one. The main issue it solves is that there are many datasets available. This means there is always the possibility that some combination of them could be used to identify respondents even if PII were removed from each of these individual datasets. For instance, experience with the Netflix prize found that augmenting the available dataset with data from IMBD resulted in better predictions, which points to why this would so commonly happen. Rather than needing to anticipate how various datasets could be combined to re-identify individuals and adjust variables to remove this possibility, a dataset that is created using a differentially private approach provides assurances that privacy will be maintained.

> **Shoulders of giants**
>
> Cynthia Dwork is the Gordon McKay Professor of Computer Science at Harvard University. After earning a PhD in Computer Science from Cornell University, she was a Post-Doctoral Research Fellow at MIT and then worked at IBM, Compaq, and Microsoft Research where she is a Distinguished Scientist. She joined Harvard in 2017. One of her major contributions is differential privacy (Dwork et al. 2006), which has become widely used.

To motivate the definition, consider a dataset of responses and PII that only has one person in it. The release of that dataset, as is, would perfectly identify them. At the other end of the scale, consider a dataset that does not contain a particular person. The release of that dataset could, in general, never be linked to them because they are not in it.[14] Differential privacy, then, is about the inclusion or exclusion of particular individuals in a dataset. An algorithm is differentially private if the inclusion or exclusion of any particular person in a dataset has at most some given factor of an effect on the probability of some output (Oberski and Kreuter 2020). The fundamental problem of data privacy is that we cannot have completely anonymized data that remains useful (Dwork and Roth 2013, 6). Instead, we must trade-off utility and privacy.

A dataset is differentially private to different levels of privacy, based on how much it changes when one person's results are included or excluded. This is the key parameter, because at the same time as deciding how much of an individual's information we are prepared to give up, we are deciding how much random noise to add, which will impact our output. The choice of this level is a nuanced one and should involve consideration of the costs of undesired disclosures, compared with the benefits of additional research. For public data that will be released under differential privacy, the reasons for the decision should be public because of the costs that are being imposed. Indeed, Jun Tang et al. (2017) argue that even in the case of private companies that use differential privacy, such as Apple, users should have a choice about the level of privacy loss.

Consider a situation in which a professor wants to release the average mark for a particular assignment. The professor wants to ensure that despite that information, no student can work out the grade that another student got. For instance, consider a small class with the following marks.

```
set.seed(853)

grades <-
  tibble(ps_1 = sample(x = (1:100), size = 10, replace = TRUE))

mean(grades$ps_1)
```

```
[1] 50.5
```

The professor could announce the exact mean, for instance, "The mean for the first problem set was 50.5". Theoretically, all-but-one student could let the others know their mark. It

[14] An interesting counterpoint is the recent use, by law enforcement, of DNA databases to find suspects. The suspect themselves might not be in the database, but the nature of DNA means that some related individuals can nonetheless still be identified.

would then be possible for that group to determine the mark of the student who did not agree to make their mark public.

A non-statistical approach would be for the professor to add the word "roughly". For instance, the professor could say "The mean for the first problem set was roughly 50.5". The students could attempt the same strategy, but they would never know with certainty. The professor could implement a more statistical approach to this by adding noise to the mean.

```
mean(grades$ps_1) + runif(n = 1, min = -2, max = 2)
```

```
[1] 48.91519
```

The professor could then announce this modified mean. This would make the students' plan more difficult. One thing to notice about that approach is that it would not work with persistent questioning. For instance, eventually the students would be able to back out the distribution of the noise that the professor added. One implication is that the professor would need to limit the number of queries they answered about the mean of the problem set.

A differentially private approach is a sophisticated version of this. We can implement it using `diffpriv`. This results in a mean that we could announce (Table 10.1).

```
# Code based on the diffpriv example
target <- function(X) mean(X)

mech <- DPMechLaplace(target = target)

distr <- function(n) rnorm(n)

mech <- sensitivitySampler(mech, oracle = distr, n = 5, gamma = 0.1)

r <- releaseResponse(mech,
                     privacyParams = DPParamsEps(epsilon = 1),
                     X = grades$ps_1)
```

Table 10.1: Comparing the actual mean with a differentially private mean

Actual mean	Announceable mean
50.5	52.46028

The implementation of differential privacy is a costs and benefits issue (Hotz et al. 2022; Kenny et al. 2022). Stronger privacy protection fundamentally must mean less information (Bowen 2022, 39), and this differently affects various aspects of society. For instance, Suriyakumar et al. (2021) found that, in the context of health care, differentially private learning can result in models that are disproportionately affected by large demographic groups. A variant of differential privacy has recently been implemented by the US census. It may have a significant effect on redistricting (Kenny et al. 2021) and result in some publicly available data that are unusable in the social sciences (Ruggles et al. 2019).

10.6 Data efficiency

For the most part, done is better than perfect, and unnecessary optimization is a waste of resources. However, at a certain point, we need to adapt new ways of dealing with data, especially as our datasets start to get larger. Here we discuss iterating through multiple files, and then turn to the use of Apache Arrow and parquet. Another natural step would be the use of SQL, which is covered in the "SQL" Online Appendix[15].

10.6.1 Iteration

There are several ways to become more efficient with our data, especially as it becomes larger. The first, and most obvious, is to break larger datasets into smaller pieces. For instance, if we have a dataset for a year, then we could break it into months, or even days. To enable this, we need a way of quickly reading in many different files.

The need to read in multiple files and combine them into the one tibble is a surprisingly common task. For instance, it may be that the data for a year, are saved into individual CSV files for each month. We can use `purrr` and `fs` to do this. To illustrate this situation we will simulate data from the exponential distribution using `rexp()`. Such data may reflect, say, comments on a social media platform, where the vast majority of comments are made by a tiny minority of users. We will use `dir_create()` from `fs` to create a folder, simulate monthly data, and save it. We will then illustrate reading it in.

```
dir_create(path = "user_data")

set.seed(853)

simulate_and_save_data <- function(month) {
  num_obs <- 1000
  file_name <- paste0("user_data/", month, ".csv")
  user_comments <-
    tibble(
      user = c(1:num_obs),
      month = rep(x = month, times = num_obs),
      comments = rexp(n = num_obs, rate = 0.3) |> round()
    )
  write_csv(
    x = user_comments,
    file = file_name
  )
}

walk(month.name |> tolower(), simulate_and_save_data)
```

Having created our dataset with each month saved to a different CSV, we can now read it in. There are a variety of ways to do this. The first step is that we need to get a list of all the CSV files in the directory. We use the "glob" argument here to specify that we are

[15] https://tellingstorieswithdata.com/26-sql.html

interested only in the ".csv" files, and that could change to whatever files it is that we are interested in.

```
files_of_interest <-
  dir_ls(path = "user_data/", glob = "*.csv")

files_of_interest
```

```
[1] "april.csv"     "august.csv"    "december.csv"  "february.csv"
[5] "january.csv"   "july.csv"      "june.csv"      "march.csv"
[9] "may.csv"       "november.csv"  "october.csv"   "september.csv"
```

We can pass this list to `read_csv()` and it will read them in and combine them.

```
year_of_data <-
  read_csv(
    files_of_interest,
    col_types = cols(
      user = col_double(),
      month = col_character(),
      comments = col_double(),
    )
  )

year_of_data
```

```
# A tibble: 12,000 x 3
    user month comments
   <dbl> <chr>    <dbl>
 1     1 april        0
 2     2 april        2
 3     3 april        2
 4     4 april        5
 5     5 april        1
 6     6 april        3
 7     7 april        2
 8     8 april        1
 9     9 april        4
10    10 april        3
# i 11,990 more rows
```

It prints out the first ten days of April, because alphabetically April is the first month of the year and so that was the first CSV that was read.

This works well when we have CSV files, but we might not always have CSV files and so will need another way, and can use `map_dfr()` to do this. One nice aspect of this approach is that we can include the name of the file alongside the observation using ".id". Here we specify that we would like that column to be called "file", but it could be anything.

```
year_of_data_using_purrr <-
  files_of_interest |>
```

```
    map_dfr(read_csv, .id = "file")
```

```
# A tibble: 12,000 x 4
   file       user month comments
   <chr>     <dbl> <chr>    <dbl>
 1 april.csv     1 april        0
 2 april.csv     2 april        2
 3 april.csv     3 april        2
 4 april.csv     4 april        5
 5 april.csv     5 april        1
 6 april.csv     6 april        3
 7 april.csv     7 april        2
 8 april.csv     8 april        1
 9 april.csv     9 april        4
10 april.csv    10 april        3
# i 11,990 more rows
```

10.6.2 Apache Arrow

CSVs are commonly used without much thought in data science. And while CSVs are good because they have little overhead and can be manually inspected, this also means they are quite minimal. This can lead to issues, for instance class is not preserved, and file sizes can become large leading to storage and performance issues. There are various alternatives, including Apache Arrow, which stores data in columns rather than rows like CSV. We focus on the ".parquet" format from Apache Arrow. Like a CSV, parquet is an open standard. The R package, `arrow`, enables us to use this format. The use of parquet has the advantage of requiring little change from us while delivering significant benefits.

> **Shoulders of giants**
>
> Wes McKinney holds an undergraduate degree in theoretical mathematics from MIT. Starting in 2008, while working at AQR Capital Management, he developed the Python package, pandas, which has become a cornerstone of data science. He later wrote *Python for Data Analysis* (McKinney [2011] 2022). In 2016, with Hadley Wickham, he designed Feather, which was released in 2016. He now works as CTO of Voltron Data, which focuses on the Apache Arrow project.

In particular, we focus on the benefit of using parquet for data storage, such as when we want to save a copy of an analysis dataset that we cleaned and prepared. Among other aspects, parquet brings two specific benefits, compared with CSV:

- the file sizes are typically smaller; and
- class is preserved because parquet attaches a schema, which makes dealing with, say, dates and factors considerably easier.

Having loaded `arrow`, we can use parquet files in a similar way to CSV files. Anywhere in our code that we used `write_csv()` and `read_csv()` we could alternatively, or additionally, use `write_parquet()` and `read_parquet()`, respectively. The decision to use parquet needs to consider both costs and benefits, and it is an active area of development.

```
num_draws <- 1000000

# Homage: https://www.rand.org/pubs/monograph_reports/MR1418.html
a_million_random_digits <-
  tibble(
    numbers = runif(n = num_draws),
    letters = sample(x = letters, size = num_draws, replace = TRUE),
    states = sample(x = state.name, size = num_draws, replace = TRUE),
  )

write_csv(x = a_million_random_digits,
          file = "a_million_random_digits.csv")

write_parquet(x = a_million_random_digits,
              sink = "a_million_random_digits.parquet")

file_size("a_million_random_digits.csv")
```

```
29.3M
```

```
file_size("a_million_random_digits.parquet")
```

```
8.17M
```

We can write a parquet file with `write_parquet()` and we can read a parquet with `read_parquet()`. We get significant reductions in file size when we compare the size of the same datasets saved in each format, especially as they get larger (Table 10.2). The speed benefits of using parquet are most notable for larger datasets. It turns them from being impractical to being usable.

Table 10.2: Comparing the file sizes, and read and write times, of CSV and parquet as the file size increases

Number	CSV size	CSV write time (sec)	CSV read time (sec)	Parquet size	Parquet write time (sec)	Parquet read time (sec)
1e+02	3.03K	0.005	0.262	2.65K	0.007	0.004
1e+03	30K	0.019	0.272	11.1K	0.011	0.004
1e+04	300.21K	0.023	0.305	99.58K	0.010	0.005
1e+05	2.93M	0.029	0.281	1016.49K	0.043	0.008
1e+06	29.29M	0.151	0.580	8.17M	0.224	0.046
1e+07	292.89M	0.998	2.953	79.11M	1.763	0.416
1e+08	2.86G	7.648	32.892	788.82M	16.124	4.847

Crane (2022) provides further information about specific tasks, Navarro (2022) provides helpful examples of implementation, and Navarro, Keane, and Hazlitt (2022) provides an extensive set of materials. There is no settled consensus on whether parquet files should be used exclusively for dataset. But it is indisputable that the persistence of class alone provides a compelling reason for including them in addition to a CSV.

We will use parquet more in the remainder of this book.

10.7 Exercises

Scales

1. *(Plan)* Consider the following scenario: *You work for a large news media company and focus on subscriber management. Over the course of a year most subscribers will never post a comment beneath a news article, but a few post an awful lot.* Please sketch what that dataset could look like and then sketch a graph that you could build to show all observations.
2. *(Simulate)* Please further consider the scenario described and simulate the situation. Carefully pick an appropriate distribution. Please include five tests based on the simulated data. Submit a link to a GitHub Gist that contains your code.
3. *(Acquire)* Please describe one possible source of such a dataset.
4. *(Explore)* Please use `ggplot2` to build the graph that you sketched. Submit a link to a GitHub Gist that contains your code.
5. *(Communicate)* Please write two paragraphs about what you did.

Questions

1. Following M. Wilkinson et al. (2016), please discuss the FAIR principles in the context of a dataset that you are familiar with (begin with a one-paragraph summary of the dataset, then write one paragraph per principle).
2. Please create a R package for a simulated dataset, push it to GitHub, and submit code to install the package (e.g. `devtools::install_github("RohanAlexander/favcolordata")`).
3. According to Gebru et al. (2021), a datasheet should document a dataset's (please select all that apply):
   a. composition.
   b. recommended uses.
   c. motivation.
   d. collection process.
4. Discuss, with the help of examples and references, whether a person's name is PII (please write at least three paragraphs)?
5. Using `md5()` what is the hash of "Monica" (pick one)?
   a. 243f63354f4c1cc25d50f6269b844369
   b. 09084cc0cda34fd80bfa3cc0ae8fe3dc
   c. 09084cc0cda34fd80bfa3cc0ae8fe3dc
   d. 1b3840b0b70d91c17e70014c8537dbba
6. Please save the `penguins` data from from `palmerpenguins` as a CSV file and as a Parquet file. How big are they?
   a. 12.5K; 6.03K
   b. 14.9K; 6.03K
   c. 14.9K; 5.02K
   d. 12.5K; 5.02K

Tutorial

Please identify a dataset you consider interesting and important, that does not have a datasheet (Gebru et al. 2021). As a reminder, datasheets accompany datasets and document "motivation, composition, collection process, recommended uses," among other aspects. Please put together a datasheet for this dataset. You are welcome to use the template in the starter folder[16].

Use Quarto, and include an appropriate title, author, date, link to a GitHub repo, and citations to produce a draft. Following this, please pair with another student and exchange your written work. Update it based on their feedback, and be sure to acknowledge them by name in your paper. Submit a PDF.

Paper

At about this point the *Dysart* Paper in the "Papers" Online Appendix[17] would be appropriate.

[16]https://github.com/RohanAlexander/starter_folder
[17]https://tellingstorieswithdata.com/23-assessment.html

Part V

Modeling

11

Exploratory data analysis

Prerequisites

- Read *The Future of Data Analysis*, (Tukey 1962)
  - John Tukey, the twentieth century statistician, made many contributions to statistics. From this paper focus on Part 1 "General Considerations", which was ahead of its time about the ways in which we ought to learn something from data.
- Read *Best Practices in Data Cleaning*, (Osborne 2012)
  - Focus on Chapter 6 "Dealing with Missing or Incomplete Data" which is a chapter-length treatment of this issue.
- Read *R for Data Science*, (Wickham, Çetinkaya-Rundel, and Grolemund [2016] 2023)
  - Focus on Chapter 12 "Exploratory data analysis", which provides a written self-contained EDA worked example.
- Watch *Whole game*, (Wickham 2018)
  - A video providing a self-contained EDA worked example. One nice aspect is that you get to see an expert make mistakes and then fix them.

Key concepts and skills

- Exploratory data analysis is the process of coming to terms with a new dataset by looking at the data, constructing graphs, tables, and models. We want to understand three aspects:

  1) each individual variable by itself;
  2) each individual in the context of other, relevant, variables; and
  3) the data that are not there.

- During EDA we want to come to understand the issues and features of the dataset and how this may affect analysis decisions. We are especially concerned about missing values and outliers.

Software and packages

- Base R (R Core Team 2023)
- `arrow` (Richardson et al. 2023)
- `janitor` (Firke 2023)
- `knitr` (Xie 2023)
- `lubridate` (Grolemund and Wickham 2011)
- `mice` (van Buuren and Groothuis-Oudshoorn 2011)
- `modelsummary` (Arel-Bundock 2022)
- `naniar` (Tierney et al. 2021)
- `opendatatoronto` (Gelfand 2022b)
- `tidyverse` (Wickham et al. 2019)

```
library(arrow)
library(janitor)
library(knitr)
```

```
library(lubridate)
library(mice)
library(modelsummary)
library(naniar)
library(opendatatoronto)
library(tidyverse)
```

11.1 Introduction

> The future of data analysis can involve great progress, the overcoming of real difficulties, and the provision of a great service to all fields of science and technology. Will it? That remains to us, to our willingness to take up the rocky road of real problems in preference to the smooth road of unreal assumptions, arbitrary criteria, and abstract results without real attachments. Who is for the challenge?
>
> Tukey (1962, 64).

Exploratory data analysis is never finished. It is the active process of exploring and becoming familiar with our data. Like a farmer with their hands in the earth, we need to know every contour and aspect of our data. We need to know how it changes, what it shows, hides, and what are its limits. Exploratory data analysis (EDA) is the unstructured process of doing this.

EDA is a means to an end. While it will inform the entire paper, especially the data section, it is not typically something that ends up in the final paper. The way to proceed is to make a separate Quarto document. Add code and brief notes on-the-go. Do not delete previous code, just add to it. By the end of it we will have created a useful notebook that captures your exploration of the dataset. This is a document that will guide the subsequent analysis and modeling.

EDA draws on a variety of skills and there are a lot of options when conducting EDA (Staniak and Biecek 2019). Every tool should be considered. Look at the data and scroll through it. Make tables, plots, summary statistics, even some models. The key is to iterate, move quickly rather than perfectly, and come to a thorough understanding of the data. Interestingly, coming to thoroughly understand the data that we have often helps us understand what we do not have.

We are interested in the following process:

- Understand the distribution and properties of individual variables.
- Understand relationships between variables.
- Understand what is not there.

There is no one correct process or set of steps that are required to undertake and complete EDA. Instead, the relevant steps and tools depend on the data and question of interest. As such, in this chapter we will illustrate approaches to EDA through various examples of EDA including US state populations, subway delays in Toronto, and Airbnb listings in London. We also build on Chapter 6 and return to missing data.

11.2 1975 United States population and income data

As a first example we consider US state populations as of 1975. This dataset is built into R with `state.x77`. Here is what the dataset looks like:

```
us_populations <-
  state.x77 |>
  as_tibble() |>
  clean_names() |>
  mutate(state = rownames(state.x77)) |>
  select(state, population, income)

us_populations
```

```
# A tibble: 50 x 3
   state       population income
   <chr>            <dbl>  <dbl>
 1 Alabama           3615   3624
 2 Alaska             365   6315
 3 Arizona           2212   4530
 4 Arkansas          2110   3378
 5 California       21198   5114
 6 Colorado          2541   4884
 7 Connecticut       3100   5348
 8 Delaware           579   4809
 9 Florida           8277   4815
10 Georgia           4931   4091
# i 40 more rows
```

We want to get a quick sense of the data. The first step is to have a look at the top and bottom of it with `head()` and `tail()`, then a random selection, and finally to focus on the variables and their class with `glimpse()`. The random selection is an important aspect, and when you use `head()` you should also quickly consider a random selection.

```
us_populations |>
  head()
```

```
# A tibble: 6 x 3
  state      population income
  <chr>           <dbl>  <dbl>
1 Alabama          3615   3624
2 Alaska            365   6315
```

```
3 Arizona          2212   4530
4 Arkansas         2110   3378
5 California      21198   5114
6 Colorado         2541   4884
```

```
us_populations |>
  tail()
```

```
# A tibble: 6 x 3
  state         population income
  <chr>              <dbl>  <dbl>
1 Vermont              472   3907
2 Virginia            4981   4701
3 Washington          3559   4864
4 West Virginia       1799   3617
5 Wisconsin           4589   4468
6 Wyoming              376   4566
```

```
us_populations |>
  slice_sample(n = 6)
```

```
# A tibble: 6 x 3
  state        population income
  <chr>             <dbl>  <dbl>
1 Pennsylvania      11860   4449
2 Oklahoma           2715   3983
3 Alaska              365   6315
4 North Dakota        637   5087
5 Maryland           4122   5299
6 Vermont             472   3907
```

```
us_populations |>
  glimpse()
```

```
Rows: 50
Columns: 3
$ state      <chr> "Alabama", "Alaska", "Arizona", "Arkansas", "California", "~
$ population <dbl> 3615, 365, 2212, 2110, 21198, 2541, 3100, 579, 8277, 4931, ~
$ income     <dbl> 3624, 6315, 4530, 3378, 5114, 4884, 5348, 4809, 4815, 4091,~
```

We are then interested in understanding key summary statistics, such as the minimum, median, and maximum values for numeric variables with `summary()` from base R and the number of observations.

```
us_populations |>
  summary()
```

```
    state             population        income
 Length:50          Min.   :  365   Min.   :3098
 Class :character   1st Qu.: 1080   1st Qu.:3993
```

Table 11.1: Comparing the mean population when different states are randomly removed

Seed	Mean	Ignored states
1	4,469	Arkansas, Rhode Island, Alabama, North Dakota, Minnesota
2	4,027	Massachusetts, Iowa, Colorado, West Virginia, New York
3	4,086	California, Idaho, Rhode Island, Oklahoma, South Carolina
4	4,391	Hawaii, Arizona, Connecticut, Utah, New Jersey
5	4,340	Alaska, Texas, Iowa, Hawaii, South Dakota

```
Mode  :character   Median : 2838   Median :4519
                   Mean   : 4246   Mean   :4436
                   3rd Qu.: 4968   3rd Qu.:4814
                   Max.   :21198   Max.   :6315
```

Finally, it is especially important to understand the behavior of these key summary statistics at the limits. In particular, one approach is to randomly remove some observations and compare what happens to them. For instance, we can randomly create five datasets that differ on the basis of which observations were removed. We can then compare the summary statistics. If any of them are especially different, then we would want to look at the observations that were removed as they may contain observations with high influence.

```
sample_means <- tibble(seed = c(), mean = c(), states_ignored = c())

for (i in c(1:5)) {
  set.seed(i)
  dont_get <- c(sample(x = state.name, size = 5))
  sample_means <-
    sample_means |>
    rbind(tibble(
      seed = i,
      mean =
        us_populations |>
          filter(!state %in% dont_get) |>
          summarise(mean = mean(population)) |>
          pull(),
      states_ignored = str_c(dont_get, collapse = ", ")
    ))
}

sample_means |>
  kable(
    col.names = c("Seed", "Mean", "Ignored states"),
    digits = 0,
    format.args = list(big.mark = ","),
    booktabs = TRUE
  )
```

In the case of the populations of US states, we know that larger states, such as California and New York, will have an out sized effect on our estimate of the mean. Table 11.1 supports that, as we can see that when we use seeds 2 and 3, there is a lower mean.

11.3 Missing data

We have discussed missing data a lot throughout this book, especially in Chapter 6. Here we return to it because understanding missing data tends to be a substantial focus of EDA. When we find missing data—and there are always missing data of some sort or another—we want to establish what type of missingness we are dealing with. Focusing on known-missing observations, that is where there are observations that we can see are missing in the dataset, based on Gelman, Hill, and Vehtari (2020, 323) we consider three main categories of missing data:

1) Missing Completely At Random;
2) Missing at Random; and
3) Missing Not At Random.

When data are Missing Completely At Random (MCAR), observations are missing from the dataset independent of any other variables—whether in the dataset or not. As discussed in Chapter 6, when data are MCAR there are fewer concerns about summary statistics and inference, but data are rarely MCAR. Even if they were it would be difficult to be convinced of this. Nonetheless we can simulate an example. For instance we can remove the population data for three randomly selected states.

```
set.seed(853)

remove_random_states <-
  sample(x = state.name, size = 3, replace = FALSE)

us_states_MCAR <-
  us_populations |>
  mutate(
    population =
      if_else(state %in% remove_random_states, NA_real_, population)
  )

summary(us_states_MCAR)
```

```
    state             population        income
 Length:50          Min.   :  365   Min.   :3098
 Class :character   1st Qu.: 1174   1st Qu.:3993
 Mode  :character   Median : 2861   Median :4519
                    Mean   : 4308   Mean   :4436
                    3rd Qu.: 4956   3rd Qu.:4814
                    Max.   :21198   Max.   :6315
                    NA's   :3
```

When observations are Missing at Random (MAR) they are missing from the dataset in a way that is related to other variables in the dataset. For instance, it may be that we are interested in understanding the effect of income and gender on political participation, and so we gather information on these three variables. But perhaps for some reason males are less likely to respond to a question about income.

In the case of the US states dataset, we can simulate a MAR dataset by making the three US states with the highest population not have an observation for income.

```
highest_income_states <-
  us_populations |>
  slice_max(income, n = 3) |>
  pull(state)

us_states_MAR <-
  us_populations |>
  mutate(population =
           if_else(state %in% highest_income_states, NA_real_, population)
         )

summary(us_states_MAR)
```

```
    state             population          income
 Length:50          Min.   :  376   Min.   :3098
 Class :character   1st Qu.: 1101   1st Qu.:3993
 Mode  :character   Median : 2816   Median :4519
                    Mean   : 4356   Mean   :4436
                    3rd Qu.: 5147   3rd Qu.:4814
                    Max.   :21198   Max.   :6315
                    NA's   :3
```

Finally when observations are Missing Not At Random (MNAR) they are missing from the the dataset in a way that is related to either unobserved variables, or the missing variable itself. For instance, it may be that respondents with a higher income, or that respondents with higher education (a variable that we did not collect), are less likely to fill in their income.

In the case of the US states dataset, we can simulate a MNAR dataset by making the three US states with the highest population not have an observation for population.

```
highest_population_states <-
  us_populations |>
  slice_max(population, n = 3) |>
  pull(state)

us_states_MNAR <-
  us_populations |>
  mutate(population =
           if_else(state %in% highest_population_states,
                   NA_real_,
                   population))
```

```
us_states_MNAR
```

```
# A tibble: 50 x 3
   state       population income
   <chr>            <dbl>  <dbl>
 1 Alabama           3615   3624
 2 Alaska             365   6315
 3 Arizona           2212   4530
 4 Arkansas          2110   3378
 5 California          NA   5114
 6 Colorado          2541   4884
 7 Connecticut       3100   5348
 8 Delaware           579   4809
 9 Florida           8277   4815
10 Georgia           4931   4091
# i 40 more rows
```

The best approach will be bespoke to the circumstances, but in general we want to use simulation to better understand the implications of our choices. From a data side we can choose to remove observations that are missing or input a value. (There are also options on the model side, but those are beyond the scope of this book.) These approaches have their place, but need to be used with humility and well communicated. The use of simulation is critical.

We can return to our US states dataset, generate some missing data, and consider a few common approaches for dealing with missing data, and compare the implied values for each state, and the overall US mean population. We consider the following options:

1) Drop observations with missing data.
2) Impute the mean of observations without missing data.
3) Use multiple imputation.

To drop the observations with missing data, we can use `mean()`. By default it will exclude observations with missing values in its calculation. To impute the mean, we construct a second dataset with the observations with missing data removed. We then compute the mean of the population column, and impute that into the missing values in the original dataset. Multiple imputation involves creating many potential datasets, conducting inference, and then bringing them together potentially though averaging (Gelman and Hill 2007, 542). We can implement multiple imputation with `mice()` from `mice`.

```
multiple_imputation <-
  mice(
    us_states_MCAR,
    print = FALSE
  )

mice_estimates <-
  complete(multiple_imputation) |>
  as_tibble()
```

Table 11.2: Comparing the imputed values of population for three US states and the overall mean population

Observation	Drop missing	Input mean	Multiple imputation	Actual
Florida	NA	4,308	11,197	8,277
Montana	NA	4,308	4,589	746
New Hampshire	NA	4,308	813	812
Overall	4,308	4,308	4,382	4,246

Table 11.2 makes it clear that none of these approaches should be naively imposed. For instance, Florida's population should be 8,277. Imputing the mean across all the states would result in an estimate of 4,308, and multiple imputation results in an estimate of 5,814, both of which are too low. If imputation is the answer, it may be better to look for a different question. It is worth pointing out that it was developed for specific circumstances of limiting public disclosure of private information (Horton and Lipsitz 2001).

Nothing can make up for missing data (Manski 2022). The conditions under which it makes sense to impute the mean or the prediction based on multiple imputation are not common, and even more rare is our ability to verify them. What to do depends on the circumstances and purpose of the analysis. Simulating the removal of observations that we have and then implementing various options can help us better understand the trade-offs we face. Whatever choice is made—and there is rarely a clear-cut solution—try to document and communicate what was done, and explore the effect of different choices on subsequent estimates. We recommend proceeding by simulating different scenarios that remove some of the data that we have, and evaluating how the approaches differ.

Finally, more prosaically, but just as importantly, sometimes missing data is encoded in the variable with particular values. For instance, while R has the option of "NA", sometimes numerical data is entered as "-99" or alternatively as a very large integer such as "9999999", if it is missing. In the case of the Nationscape survey dataset introduced in Chapter 8, there are three types of known missing data:

- "888": "Asked in this wave, but not asked of this respondent"
- "999": "Not sure, don't know"
- ".": Respondent skipped

It is always worth looking explicitly for values that seem like they do not belong and investigating them. Graphs and tables are especially useful for this purpose.

11.4 TTC subway delays

As a second, and more involved, example of EDA we use `opendatatoronto`, introduced in Chapter 2, and the `tidyverse` to obtain and explore data about the Toronto subway system. We want to get a sense of the delays that have occurred.

To begin, we download the data on Toronto Transit Commission (TTC) subway delays in 2021. The data are available as an Excel file with a separate sheet for each month. We are interested in 2021 so we filter to just that year then download it using `get_resource()` from `opendatatoronto` and bring the months together with `bind_rows()`.

```
all_2021_ttc_data <-
  list_package_resources("996cfe8d-fb35-40ce-b569-698d51fc683b") |>
  filter(name == "ttc-subway-delay-data-2021") |>
  get_resource() |>
  bind_rows() |>
  clean_names()

write_csv(all_2021_ttc_data, "all_2021_ttc_data.csv")

all_2021_ttc_data
```

```
# A tibble: 16,370 x 10
   date                time   day    station code  min_delay min_gap bound line
   <dttm>              <time> <chr>  <chr>   <chr>     <dbl>   <dbl> <chr> <chr>
 1 2021-01-01 00:00:00 00:33  Friday BLOOR ~ MUPAA         0       0 N     YU
 2 2021-01-01 00:00:00 00:39  Friday SHERBO~ EUCO          5       9 E     BD
 3 2021-01-01 00:00:00 01:07  Friday KENNED~ EUCD          5       9 E     BD
 4 2021-01-01 00:00:00 01:41  Friday ST CLA~ MUIS          0       0 <NA>  YU
 5 2021-01-01 00:00:00 02:04  Friday SHEPPA~ MUIS          0       0 <NA>  YU
 6 2021-01-01 00:00:00 02:35  Friday KENNED~ MUIS          0       0 <NA>  BD
 7 2021-01-01 00:00:00 02:39  Friday VAUGHA~ MUIS          0       0 <NA>  YU
 8 2021-01-01 00:00:00 06:00  Friday TORONT~ MUO           0       0 <NA>  YU
 9 2021-01-01 00:00:00 06:00  Friday TORONT~ MUO           0       0 <NA>  SHP
10 2021-01-01 00:00:00 06:00  Friday TORONT~ MRO           0       0 <NA>  SRT
# i 16,360 more rows
# i 1 more variable: vehicle <dbl>
```

The dataset has a variety of columns, and we can find out more about each of them by downloading the codebook. The reason for each delay is coded, and so we can also download the explanations. One variable of interest appears is "min_delay", which gives the extent of the delay in minutes.

```
# Data codebook
delay_codebook <-
  list_package_resources(
    "996cfe8d-fb35-40ce-b569-698d51fc683b"
  ) |>
  filter(name == "ttc-subway-delay-data-readme") |>
  get_resource() |>
  clean_names()

write_csv(delay_codebook, "delay_codebook.csv")

# Explanation for delay codes
delay_codes <-
  list_package_resources(
    "996cfe8d-fb35-40ce-b569-698d51fc683b"
  ) |>
  filter(name == "ttc-subway-delay-codes") |>
  get_resource() |>
```

```
  clean_names()

write_csv(delay_codes, "delay_codes.csv")
```

There is no one way to explore a dataset while conducting EDA, but we are usually especially interested in:

- What should the variables look like? For instance, what is their class, what are the values, and what does the distribution of these look like?
- What aspects are surprising, both in terms of data that are there that we do not expect, such as outliers, but also in terms of data that we may expect but do not have, such as missing data.
- Developing a goal for our analysis. For instance, in this case, it might be understanding the factors such as stations and the time of day that are associated with delays. While we would not answer these questions formally here, we might explore what an answer could look like.

It is important to document all aspects as we go through and note anything surprising. We are looking to create a record of the steps and assumptions that we made as we were going because these will be important when we come to modeling. In the natural sciences, a research notebook of this type can even be a legal document (Ryan 2015).

11.4.1 Distribution and properties of individual variables

We should check that the variables are what they say they are. If they are not, then we need to work out what to do. For instance, should we change them, or possibly even remove them? It is also important to ensure that the class of the variables is as we expect. For instance, variables that should be a factor are a factor and those that should be a character are a character. And that we do not accidentally have, say, factors as numbers, or vice versa. One way to do this is to use `unique()`, and another is to use `table()`. There is no universal answer to which variables should be of certain classes, because the answer depends on the context.

```
unique(all_2021_ttc_data$day)
```

```
[1] "Friday"    "Saturday"  "Sunday"    "Monday"    "Tuesday"   "Wednesday"
[7] "Thursday"
```

```
unique(all_2021_ttc_data$line)
```

```
 [1] "YU"                        "BD"                        "SHP"
 [4] "SRT"                       "YU/BD"                     NA
 [7] "YONGE/UNIVERSITY/BLOOR" "YU / BD"                   "YUS"
[10] "999"                       "SHEP"                      "36 FINCH WEST"
[13] "YUS & BD"                  "YU & BD LINES"             "35 JANE"
[16] "52"                        "41 KEELE"                  "YUS/BD"
```

```
table(all_2021_ttc_data$day)
```

```
   Friday    Monday  Saturday    Sunday  Thursday   Tuesday Wednesday
```

```
      2600       2434       2073       1942       2425       2481       2415
```

```
table(all_2021_ttc_data$line)
```

```
             35 JANE          36 FINCH WEST              41 KEELE
                   1                      1                     1
                  52                    999                    BD
                   1                      1                  5734
                SHEP                    SHP                   SRT
                   1                    657                   656
YONGE/UNIVERSITY/BLOOR                   YU               YU / BD
                   1                   8880                    17
         YU & BD LINES                YU/BD                   YUS
                   1                    346                    18
           YUS & BD                  YUS/BD
                   1                      1
```

We have likely issues in terms of the subway lines. Some of them have a clear fix, but not all. One option would be to drop them, but we would need to think about whether these errors might be correlated with something that is of interest. If they were then we may be dropping important information. There is usually no one right answer, because it will usually depend on what we are using the data for. We would note the issue, as we continued with EDA and then decide later about what to do. For now, we will remove all the lines that are not the ones that we know to be correct based on the codebook.

```
delay_codebook |>
  filter(field_name == "Line")
```

```
# A tibble: 1 x 3
  field_name description                                 example
  <chr>      <chr>                                       <chr>
1 Line       TTC subway line i.e. YU, BD, SHP, and SRT YU
```

```
all_2021_ttc_data_filtered_lines <-
  all_2021_ttc_data |>
  filter(line %in% c("YU", "BD", "SHP", "SRT"))
```

Entire careers are spent understanding missing data, and the presence, or lack, of missing values can haunt an analysis. To get started we could look at known-unknowns, which are the NAs for each variable. For instance, we could create counts by variable.

In this case we have many missing values in "bound" and two in "line". For these known-unknowns, as discussed in Chapter 6, we are interested in whether they are missing at random. We want to, ideally, show that data happened to just drop out. But this is unlikely, and so we are usually trying to look at what is systematic about how the data are missing.

Sometimes data happen to be duplicated. If we did not notice this, then our analysis would be wrong in ways that we would not be able to consistently expect. There are a variety of ways to look for duplicated rows, but `get_dupes()` from `janitor` is especially useful.

```
get_dupes(all_2021_ttc_data_filtered_lines)
```

```
# A tibble: 36 x 11
   date                time   day    station code  min_delay min_gap bound line
   <dttm>              <time> <chr>  <chr>   <chr>     <dbl>   <dbl> <chr> <chr>
 1 2021-09-13 00:00:00 06:00  Monday TORONT~ MRO           0       0 <NA>  SRT
 2 2021-09-13 00:00:00 06:00  Monday TORONT~ MRO           0       0 <NA>  SRT
 3 2021-09-13 00:00:00 06:00  Monday TORONT~ MRO           0       0 <NA>  SRT
 4 2021-09-13 00:00:00 06:00  Monday TORONT~ MUO           0       0 <NA>  SHP
 5 2021-09-13 00:00:00 06:00  Monday TORONT~ MUO           0       0 <NA>  SHP
 6 2021-09-13 00:00:00 06:00  Monday TORONT~ MUO           0       0 <NA>  SHP
 7 2021-03-31 00:00:00 05:45  Wedne~ DUNDAS~ MUNCA         0       0 <NA>  BD
 8 2021-03-31 00:00:00 05:45  Wedne~ DUNDAS~ MUNCA         0       0 <NA>  BD
 9 2021-06-08 00:00:00 14:40  Tuesd~ VAUGHA~ MUNOA         3       6 S     YU
10 2021-06-08 00:00:00 14:40  Tuesd~ VAUGHA~ MUNOA         3       6 S     YU
# i 26 more rows
# i 2 more variables: vehicle <dbl>, dupe_count <int>
```

This dataset has many duplicates. We are interested in whether there is something systematic going on. Remembering that during EDA we are trying to quickly come to terms with a dataset, one way forward is to flag this as an issue to come back to and explore later, and to just remove duplicates for now using `distinct()`.

```
all_2021_ttc_data_no_dupes <-
  all_2021_ttc_data_filtered_lines |>
  distinct()
```

The station names have many errors.

```
all_2021_ttc_data_no_dupes |>
  count(station) |>
  filter(str_detect(station, "WEST"))
```

```
# A tibble: 17 x 2
   station                    n
   <chr>                  <int>
 1 DUNDAS WEST STATION      198
 2 EGLINTON WEST STATION    142
 3 FINCH WEST STATION       126
 4 FINCH WEST TO LAWRENCE     3
 5 FINCH WEST TO WILSON       1
 6 LAWRENCE WEST CENTRE       1
 7 LAWRENCE WEST STATION    127
 8 LAWRENCE WEST TO EGLIN     1
 9 SHEPPARD WEST - WILSON     1
10 SHEPPARD WEST STATION    210
11 SHEPPARD WEST TO LAWRE     3
12 SHEPPARD WEST TO ST CL     2
13 SHEPPARD WEST TO WILSO     7
14 ST CLAIR WEST STATION    205
15 ST CLAIR WEST TO ST AN     1
16 ST. CLAIR WEST TO KING     1
17 ST.CLAIR WEST TO ST.A      1
```

We could try to quickly bring a little order to the chaos by just taking just the first word or first few words, accounting for names like "ST. CLAIR" and "ST. PATRICK" by checking if the name starts with "ST", as well as distinguishing between stations like "DUNDAS" and "DUNDAS WEST" by checking if the name contains "WEST". Again, we are just trying to get a sense of the data, not necessarily make binding decisions here. We use `word()` from `stringr` to extract specific words from the station names.

```
all_2021_ttc_data_no_dupes <-
  all_2021_ttc_data_no_dupes |>
  mutate(
    station_clean =
      case_when(
        str_starts(station, "ST") &
          str_detect(station, "WEST") ~ word(station, 1, 3),
        str_starts(station, "ST") ~ word(station, 1, 2),
        str_detect(station, "WEST") ~ word(station, 1, 2),
        TRUE ~ word(station, 1)
      )
  )

all_2021_ttc_data_no_dupes
```

```
# A tibble: 15,908 x 11
   date                time   day    station code  min_delay min_gap bound line
   <dttm>              <time> <chr>  <chr>   <chr>     <dbl>   <dbl> <chr> <chr>
 1 2021-01-01 00:00:00 00:33  Friday BLOOR ~ MUPAA         0       0 N     YU
 2 2021-01-01 00:00:00 00:39  Friday SHERBO~ EUCO          5       9 E     BD
 3 2021-01-01 00:00:00 01:07  Friday KENNED~ EUCD          5       9 E     BD
 4 2021-01-01 00:00:00 01:41  Friday ST CLA~ MUIS          0       0 <NA>  YU
 5 2021-01-01 00:00:00 02:04  Friday SHEPPA~ MUIS          0       0 <NA>  YU
 6 2021-01-01 00:00:00 02:35  Friday KENNED~ MUIS          0       0 <NA>  BD
 7 2021-01-01 00:00:00 02:39  Friday VAUGHA~ MUIS          0       0 <NA>  YU
 8 2021-01-01 00:00:00 06:00  Friday TORONT~ MUO           0       0 <NA>  YU
 9 2021-01-01 00:00:00 06:00  Friday TORONT~ MUO           0       0 <NA>  SHP
10 2021-01-01 00:00:00 06:00  Friday TORONT~ MRO           0       0 <NA>  SRT
# i 15,898 more rows
# i 2 more variables: vehicle <dbl>, station_clean <chr>
```

We need to see the data in its original state to understand it, and we often use bar charts, scatterplots, line plots, and histograms for this. During EDA we are not so concerned with whether the graph looks nice, but are instead trying to acquire a sense of the data as quickly as possible. We can start by looking at the distribution of "min_delay", which is one outcome of interest.

```
all_2021_ttc_data_no_dupes |>
  ggplot(aes(x = min_delay)) +
  geom_histogram(bins = 30)

all_2021_ttc_data_no_dupes |>
  ggplot(aes(x = min_delay)) +
```

```
  geom_histogram(bins = 30) +
  scale_x_log10()
```

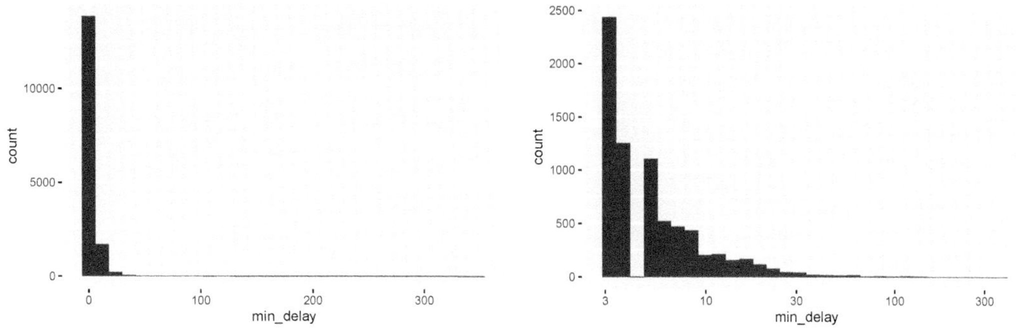

(a) Distribution of delay

(b) With a log scale

Figure 11.1: Distribution of delay, in minutes

The largely empty graph in Figure 11.1a suggests the presence of outliers. There are a variety of ways to try to understand what could be going on, but one quick way to proceed is to use logarithms, remembering that we would expect values of zero to drop away (Figure 11.1b).

This initial exploration suggests there are a small number of large delays that we might like to explore further. We will join this dataset with "delay_codes" to understand what is going on.

```
fix_organization_of_codes <-
  rbind(
    delay_codes |>
      select(sub_rmenu_code, code_description_3) |>
      mutate(type = "sub") |>
      rename(
        code = sub_rmenu_code,
        code_desc = code_description_3
      ),
    delay_codes |>
      select(srt_rmenu_code, code_description_7) |>
      mutate(type = "srt") |>
      rename(
        code = srt_rmenu_code,
        code_desc = code_description_7
      )
  )

all_2021_ttc_data_no_dupes_with_explanation <-
  all_2021_ttc_data_no_dupes |>
  mutate(type = if_else(line == "SRT", "srt", "sub")) |>
  left_join(
    fix_organization_of_codes,
    by = c("type", "code")
```

```
  )

all_2021_ttc_data_no_dupes_with_explanation |>
  select(station_clean, code, min_delay, code_desc) |>
  arrange(-min_delay)
```

```
# A tibble: 15,908 x 4
   station_clean code  min_delay code_desc
   <chr>         <chr>     <dbl> <chr>
 1 MUSEUM        PUTTP       348 Traction Power Rail Related
 2 EGLINTON      PUSTC       343 Signals - Track Circuit Problems
 3 WOODBINE      MUO         312 Miscellaneous Other
 4 MCCOWAN       PRSL        275 Loop Related Failures
 5 SHEPPARD WEST PUTWZ       255 Work Zone Problems - Track
 6 ISLINGTON     MUPR1       207 Priority One - Train in Contact With Person
 7 SHEPPARD WEST MUPR1       191 Priority One - Train in Contact With Person
 8 ROYAL         SUAP        182 Assault / Patron Involved
 9 ROYAL         MUPR1       180 Priority One - Train in Contact With Person
10 SHEPPARD      MUPR1       171 Priority One - Train in Contact With Person
# i 15,898 more rows
```

From this we can see that the 348 minute delay was due to "Traction Power Rail Related", the 343 minute delay was due to "Signals - Track Circuit Problems", and so on.

Another thing that we are looking for is various groupings of the data, especially where sub-groups may end up with only a small number of observations in them. This is because our analysis could be especially influenced by them. One quick way to do this is to group the data by a variable that is of interest, for instance, "line", using color.

```
all_2021_ttc_data_no_dupes_with_explanation |>
  ggplot() +
  geom_histogram(
    aes(
      x = min_delay,
      y = ..density..,
      fill = line
    ),
    position = "dodge",
    bins = 10
  ) +
  scale_x_log10()

all_2021_ttc_data_no_dupes_with_explanation |>
  ggplot() +
  geom_histogram(
    aes(x = min_delay, fill = line),
    position = "dodge",
    bins = 10
  ) +
  scale_x_log10()
```

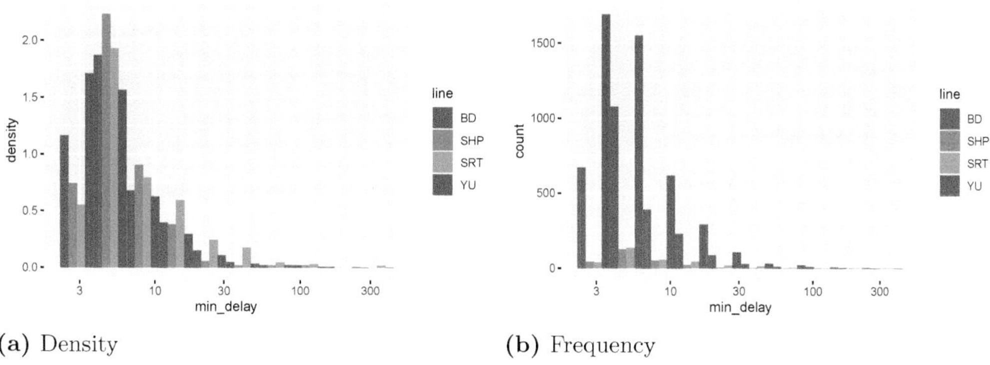

(a) Density

(b) Frequency

Figure 11.2: Distribution of delay, in minutes

Figure 11.2a uses density so that we can look at the distributions more comparably, but we should also be aware of differences in frequency (Figure 11.2b). In this case, we see that "SHP" and "SRT" have much smaller counts.

To group by another variable, we can add facets (Figure 11.3).

```
all_2021_ttc_data_no_dupes_with_explanation |>
  ggplot() +
  geom_histogram(
    aes(x = min_delay, fill = line),
    position = "dodge",
    bins = 10
  ) +
  scale_x_log10() +
  facet_wrap(vars(day)) +
  theme(legend.position = "bottom")
```

We can also plot the top five stations by mean delay, faceted by line (Figure 11.4). This raises something that we would need to follow up on, which is what is "ZONE" in "YU"?

```
all_2021_ttc_data_no_dupes_with_explanation |>
  summarise(mean_delay = mean(min_delay), n_obs = n(),
            .by = c(line, station_clean)) |>
  filter(n_obs > 1) |>
  arrange(line, -mean_delay) |>
  slice(1:5, .by = line) |>
  ggplot(aes(station_clean, mean_delay)) +
  geom_col() +
  coord_flip() +
  facet_wrap(vars(line), scales = "free_y")
```

As discussed in Chapter 9, dates are often difficult to work with because they are so prone to having issues. For this reason, it is especially important to consider them during EDA. Let us create a graph by week, to see if there is any seasonality over the course of a year. When

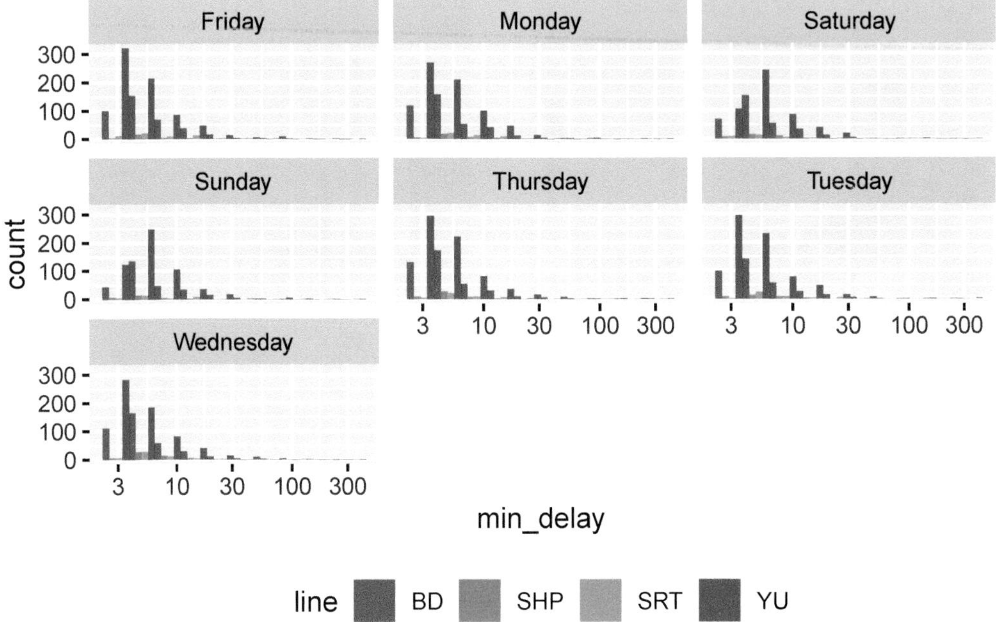

Figure 11.3: Frequency of the distribution of delay, in minutes, by day

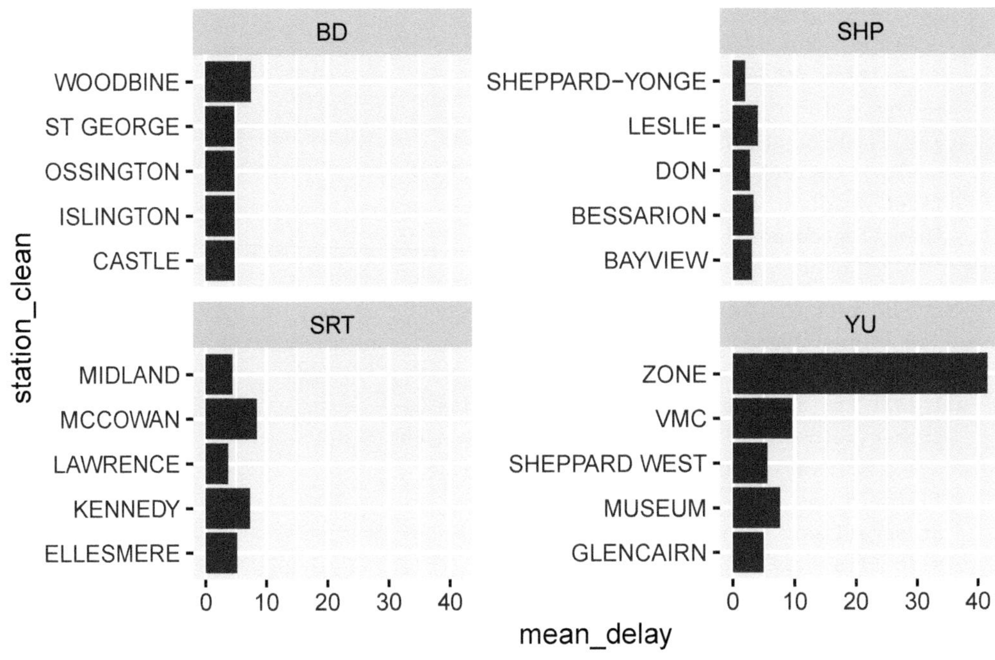

Figure 11.4: Top five stations, by mean delay and line

using dates, `lubridate` is especially useful. For instance, we can look at the average delay, of those that were delayed, by week, using `week()` to construct the weeks (Figure 11.5).

```
all_2021_ttc_data_no_dupes_with_explanation |>
  filter(min_delay > 0) |>
  mutate(week = week(date)) |>
  summarise(mean_delay = mean(min_delay),
            .by = c(week, line)) |>
  ggplot(aes(week, mean_delay, color = line)) +
  geom_point() +
  geom_smooth() +
  facet_wrap(vars(line), scales = "free_y")
```

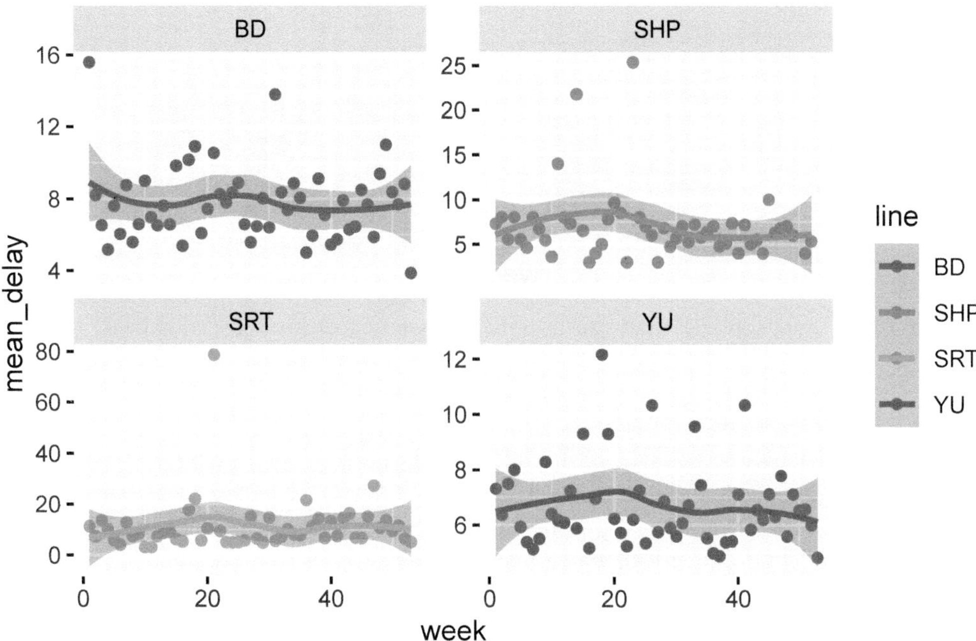

Figure 11.5: Average delay, in minutes, by week, for the Toronto subway

Now let us look at the proportion of delays that were greater than ten minutes (Figure 11.6).

```
all_2021_ttc_data_no_dupes_with_explanation |>
  mutate(week = week(date)) |>
  summarise(prop_delay = sum(min_delay > 10) / n(),
            .by = c(week, line)) |>
  ggplot(aes(week, prop_delay, color = line)) +
  geom_point() +
  geom_smooth() +
  facet_wrap(vars(line), scales = "free_y")
```

These figures, tables, and analysis may not have a place in a final paper. Instead, they allow us to become comfortable with the data. We note aspects about each that stand out, as well as the warnings and any implications or aspects to return to.

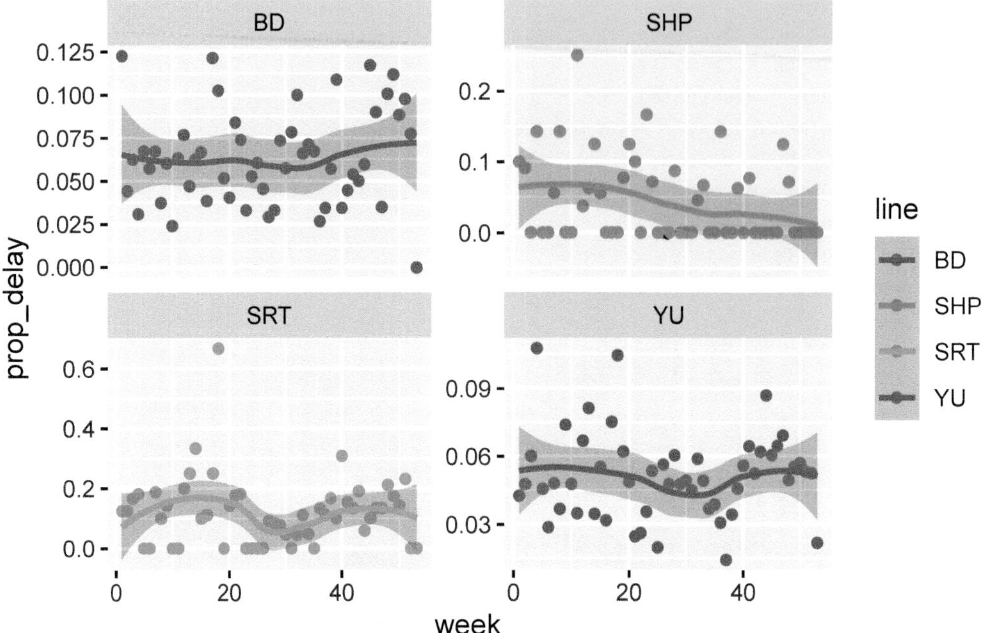

Figure 11.6: Delays longer than ten minutes, by week, for the Toronto subway

11.4.2 Relationships between variables

We are also interested in looking at the relationship between two variables. We will draw heavily on graphs for this. Appropriate types, for different circumstances, were discussed in Chapter 5. Scatter plots are especially useful for continuous variables, and are a good precursor to modeling. For instance, we may be interested in the relationship between the delay and the gap, which is the number of minutes between trains (Figure 11.7).

```
all_2021_ttc_data_no_dupes_with_explanation |>
  ggplot(aes(x = min_delay, y = min_gap, alpha = 0.1)) +
  geom_point() +
  scale_x_log10() +
  scale_y_log10()
```

The relationship between categorical variables takes more work, but we could also, for instance, look at the top five reasons for delay by station. We may be interested in whether they differ, and how any difference could be modelled (Figure 11.8).

```
all_2021_ttc_data_no_dupes_with_explanation |>
  summarise(mean_delay = mean(min_delay),
            .by = c(line, code_desc)) |>
  arrange(-mean_delay) |>
  slice(1:5) |>
  ggplot(aes(x = code_desc, y = mean_delay)) +
  geom_col() +
  facet_wrap(vars(line), scales = "free_y", nrow = 4) +
```

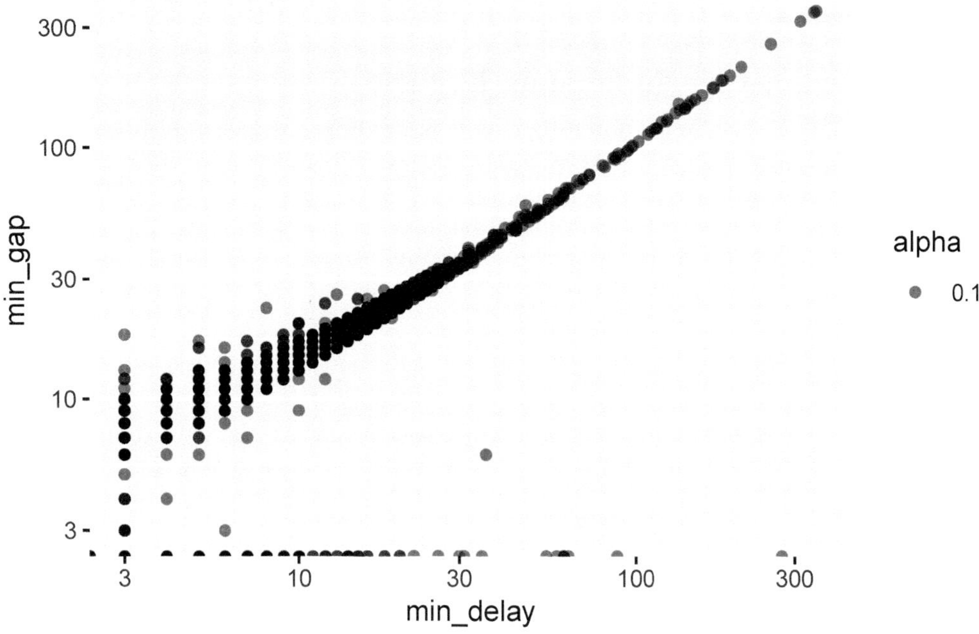

Figure 11.7: Relationship between delay and gap for the Toronto subway in 2021

```
coord_flip()
```

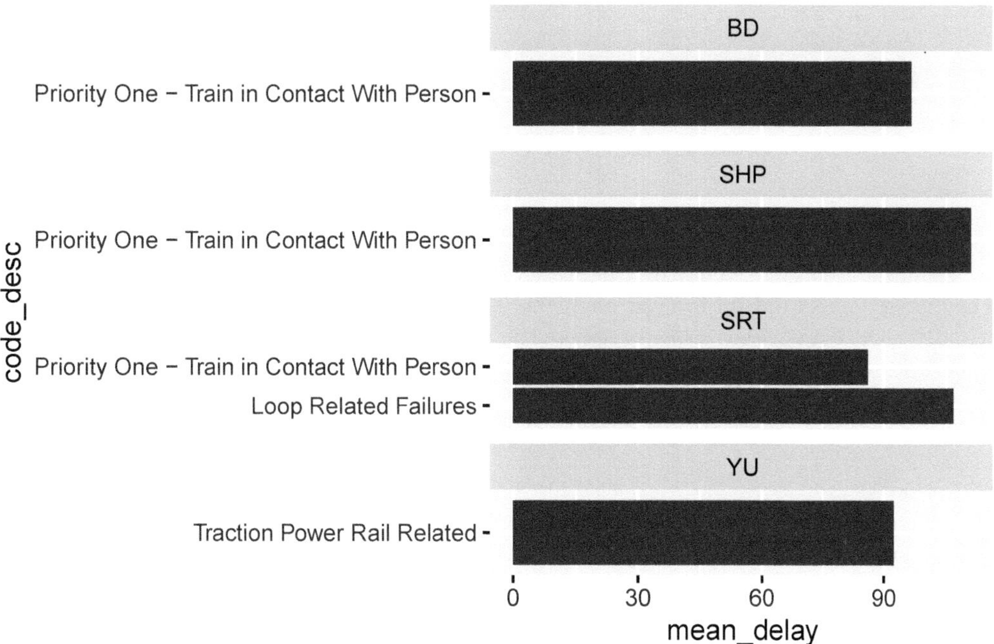

Figure 11.8: Relationship between categorical variables for the Toronto subway in 2021

11.5 Airbnb listings in London, England

In this case study we look at Airbnb listings in London, England, as at 14 March 2023. The dataset is from Inside Airbnb[1] (M. Cox 2021) and we will read it from their website, and then save a local copy. We can give `read_csv()` a link to where the dataset is and it will download it. This helps with reproducibility because the source is clear. But as that link could change at any time, longer-term reproducibility, as well as wanting to minimize the effect on the Inside Airbnb servers, suggests that we should also save a local copy of the data and then use that.

To get the dataset that we need, go to Inside Airbnb -> "Data" -> "Get the Data", then scroll down to London. We are interested in the "listings dataset", and we right click to get the URL that we need (Figure 11.9). Inside Airbnb update the data that they make available, and so the particular dataset that is available will change over time.

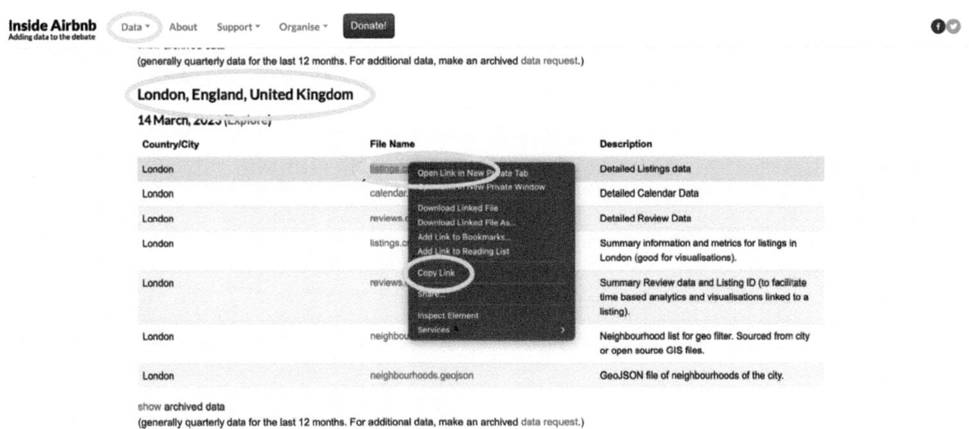

Figure 11.9: Obtaining the Airbnb data from Inside Airbnb

As the original dataset is not ours, we should not make that public without first getting written permission. For instance, we may want to add it to our inputs folder, but use a ".gitignore" entry, covered in Chapter 3, to ensure that we do not push it to GitHub. The "guess_max" option in `read_csv()` helps us avoid having to specify the column types. Usually `read_csv()` takes a best guess at the column types based on the first few rows. But sometimes those first ones are misleading and so "guess_max" forces it to look at a larger number of rows to try to work out what is going on. Paste the URL that we copied from Inside Airbnb into the URL part. And once it is downloaded, save a local copy.

```
url <-
  paste0(
    "http://data.insideairbnb.com/united-kingdom/england/",
    "london/2023-03-14/data/listings.csv.gz"
  )

airbnb_data <-
```

[1] http://insideairbnb.com

```
  read_csv(
    file = url,
    guess_max = 20000
  )

write_csv(airbnb_data, "airbnb_data.csv")

airbnb_data
```

We should refer to this local copy of our data when we run our scripts to explore the data, rather than asking the Inside Airbnb servers for the data each time. It might be worth even commenting out this call to their servers to ensure that we do not accidentally stress their service.

Again, add this filename—"airbnb_data.csv"—to the ".gitignore" file so that it is not pushed to GitHub. The size of the dataset will create complications that we would like to avoid.

While we need to archive this CSV because that is the original, unedited data, at more than 100MB it is a little unwieldy. For exploratory purposes we will create a parquet file with selected variables (we do this in an iterative way, using `names(airbnb_data)` to work out the variable names).

```
airbnb_data_selected <-
  airbnb_data |>
  select(
    host_id,
    host_response_time,
    host_is_superhost,
    host_total_listings_count,
    neighbourhood_cleansed,
    bathrooms,
    bedrooms,
    price,
    number_of_reviews,
    review_scores_rating,
    review_scores_accuracy,
    review_scores_value
  )

write_parquet(
  x = airbnb_data_selected,
  sink =
    "2023-03-14-london-airbnblistings-select_variables.parquet"
  )

rm(airbnb_data)
```

11.5.1 Distribution and properties of individual variables

First we might be interested in price. It is a character at the moment and so we need to convert it to a numeric. This is a common problem and we need to be a little careful that it does not all just convert to NAs. If we just force the price variable to be a numeric then it will go to NA because there are a lot of characters where it is unclear what the numeric equivalent is, such as "$". We need to remove those characters first.

```
airbnb_data_selected$price |>
  head()
```

```
[1] "$100.00" "$65.00"  "$132.00" "$100.00" "$120.00" "$43.00"
```

```
airbnb_data_selected$price |>
  str_split("") |>
  unlist() |>
  unique()
```

```
 [1] "$" "1" "0" "." "6" "5" "3" "2" "4" "9" "8" "7" ","
```

```
airbnb_data_selected |>
  select(price) |>
  filter(str_detect(price, ","))
```

```
# A tibble: 1,629 x 1
   price
   <chr>
 1 $3,070.00
 2 $1,570.00
 3 $1,480.00
 4 $1,000.00
 5 $1,100.00
 6 $1,433.00
 7 $1,800.00
 8 $1,000.00
 9 $1,000.00
10 $1,000.00
# i 1,619 more rows
```

```
airbnb_data_selected <-
  airbnb_data_selected |>
  mutate(
    price = str_remove_all(price, "[\\$,]"),
    price = as.integer(price)
  )
```

Now we can look at the distribution of prices (Figure 11.10a). There are outliers, so again we might like to consider it on the log scale (Figure 11.10b).

```
airbnb_data_selected |>
  ggplot(aes(x = price)) +
  geom_histogram(binwidth = 10) +
  theme_classic() +
  labs(
    x = "Price per night",
    y = "Number of properties"
  )

airbnb_data_selected |>
  filter(price > 1000) |>
  ggplot(aes(x = price)) +
  geom_histogram(binwidth = 10) +
  theme_classic() +
  labs(
    x = "Price per night",
    y = "Number of properties"
  ) +
  scale_y_log10()
```

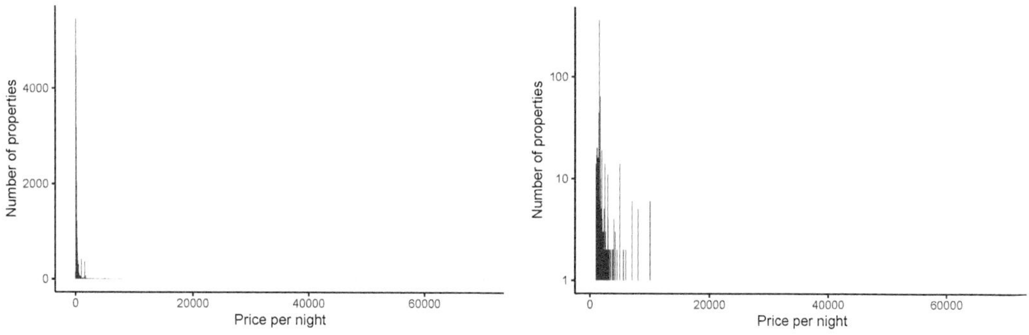

(a) Distribution of prices

(b) Using the log scale for prices more than $1,000

Figure 11.10: Distribution of prices of London Airbnb rentals in March 2023

If we focus on prices that are less than $1,000, then we see that most properties have a nightly price less than $250 (Figure 11.11a). In the same way that we saw some bunching in ages in Chapter 9, it looks like there is some bunching of prices here. It might be that this is happening around numbers ending in zero or nine. Let us just zoom in on prices between $90 and $210, out of interest, but change the bins to be smaller (Figure 11.11b).

```
airbnb_data_selected |>
  filter(price < 1000) |>
  ggplot(aes(x = price)) +
  geom_histogram(binwidth = 10) +
  theme_classic() +
  labs(
    x = "Price per night",
    y = "Number of properties"
```

```
  )

airbnb_data_selected |>
  filter(price > 90) |>
  filter(price < 210) |>
  ggplot(aes(x = price)) +
  geom_histogram(binwidth = 1) +
  theme_classic() +
  labs(
    x = "Price per night",
    y = "Number of properties"
  )
```

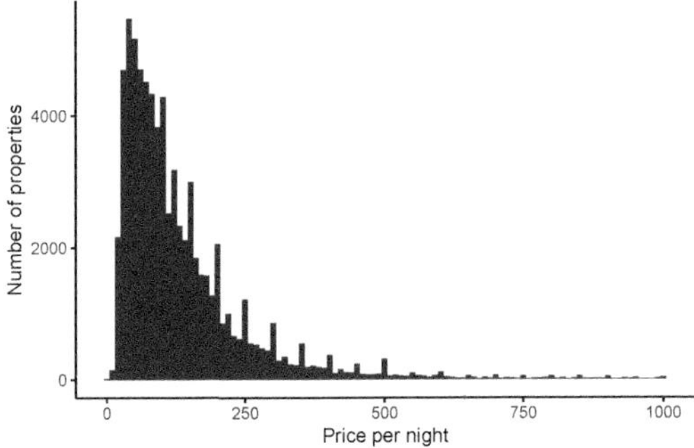

(a) Prices less than $1,000 suggest some bunching

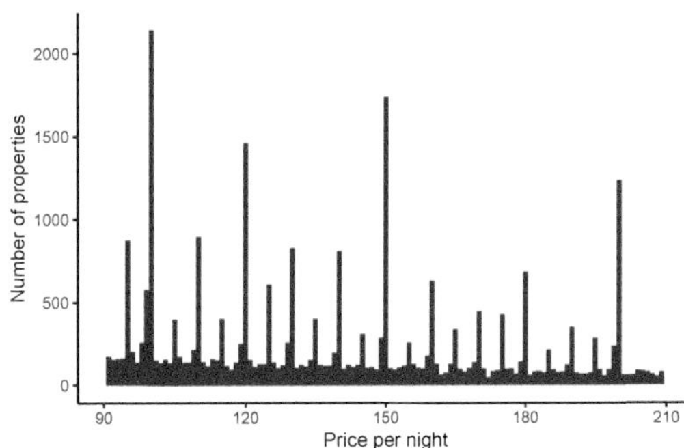

(b) Prices between $90 and $210 illustrate the bunching more clearly

Figure 11.11: Distribution of prices for Airbnb listings in London in March 2023

For now, we will just remove all prices that are more than $999.

```
airbnb_data_less_1000 <-
  airbnb_data_selected |>
  filter(price < 1000)
```

Superhosts are especially experienced Airbnb hosts, and we might be interested to learn more about them. For instance, a host either is or is not a superhost, and so we would not expect any NAs. But we can see that there are NAs. It might be that the host removed a listing or similar, but this is something that we would need to look further into.

```
airbnb_data_less_1000 |>
  filter(is.na(host_is_superhost))
```

```
# A tibble: 13 x 12
    host_id host_response_time host_is_superhost host_total_listings_count
      <dbl> <chr>              <lgl>                                 <dbl>
1 317054510 within an hour     NA                                        5
2 316090383 within an hour     NA                                        6
3 315016947 within an hour     NA                                        2
4 374424554 within an hour     NA                                        2
```

```
 5  97896300 N/A                NA                                       10
 6 316083765 within an hour     NA                                        7
 7 310628674 N/A                NA                                        5
 8 179762278 N/A                NA                                       10
 9 315037299 N/A                NA                                        1
10 316090018 within an hour     NA                                        6
11 375515965 within an hour     NA                                        2
12 341372520 N/A                NA                                        7
13 180634347 within an hour     NA                                        5
# i 8 more variables: neighbourhood_cleansed <chr>, bathrooms <lgl>,
#   bedrooms <dbl>, price <int>, number_of_reviews <dbl>,
#   review_scores_rating <dbl>, review_scores_accuracy <dbl>,
#   review_scores_value <dbl>
```

We will also want to create a binary variable from this. It is true/false at the moment, which is fine for the modeling, but there are a handful of situations where it will be easier if we have a 0/1. And for now we will just remove anyone with a NA for whether they are a superhost.

```
airbnb_data_no_superhost_nas <-
  airbnb_data_less_1000 |>
  filter(!is.na(host_is_superhost)) |>
  mutate(
    host_is_superhost_binary =
      as.numeric(host_is_superhost)
  )
```

On Airbnb, guests can give one to five star ratings across a variety of different aspects, including cleanliness, accuracy, value, and others. But when we look at the reviews in our dataset, it is clear that it is effectively a binary, and almost entirely the case that either the rating is five stars or not (Figure 11.12).

```
airbnb_data_no_superhost_nas |>
  ggplot(aes(x = review_scores_rating)) +
  geom_bar() +
  theme_classic() +
  labs(
    x = "Review scores rating",
    y = "Number of properties"
  )
```

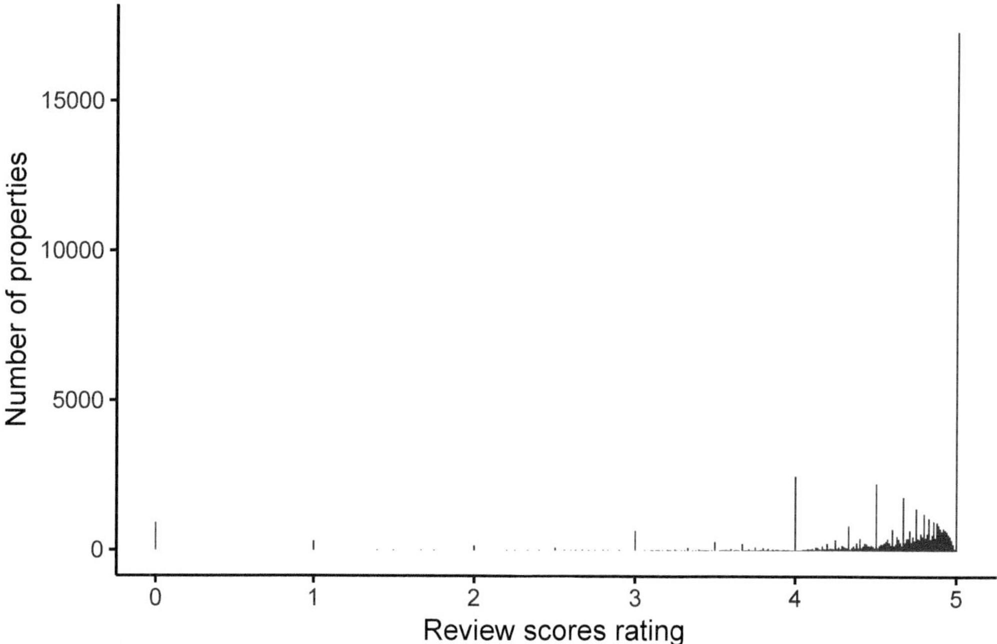

Figure 11.12: Distribution of review scores rating for London Airbnb rentals in March 2023

We would like to deal with the NAs in "review_scores_rating", but this is more complicated as there are a lot of them. It may be that this is just because they do not have any reviews.

```
airbnb_data_no_superhost_nas |>
  filter(is.na(review_scores_rating)) |>
  nrow()
```

```
[1] 17681
```

```
airbnb_data_no_superhost_nas |>
  filter(is.na(review_scores_rating)) |>
  select(number_of_reviews) |>
  table()
```

```
number_of_reviews
    0
17681
```

These properties do not have a review rating yet because they do not have enough reviews. It is a large proportion of the total, at almost a fifth of them so we might like to look at this in more detail using counts. We are interested to see whether there is something systematic happening with these properties. For instance, if the NAs were being driven by, say, some requirement of a minimum number of reviews, then we would expect they would all be missing.

One approach would be to just focus on those that are not missing and the main review score (Figure 11.13).

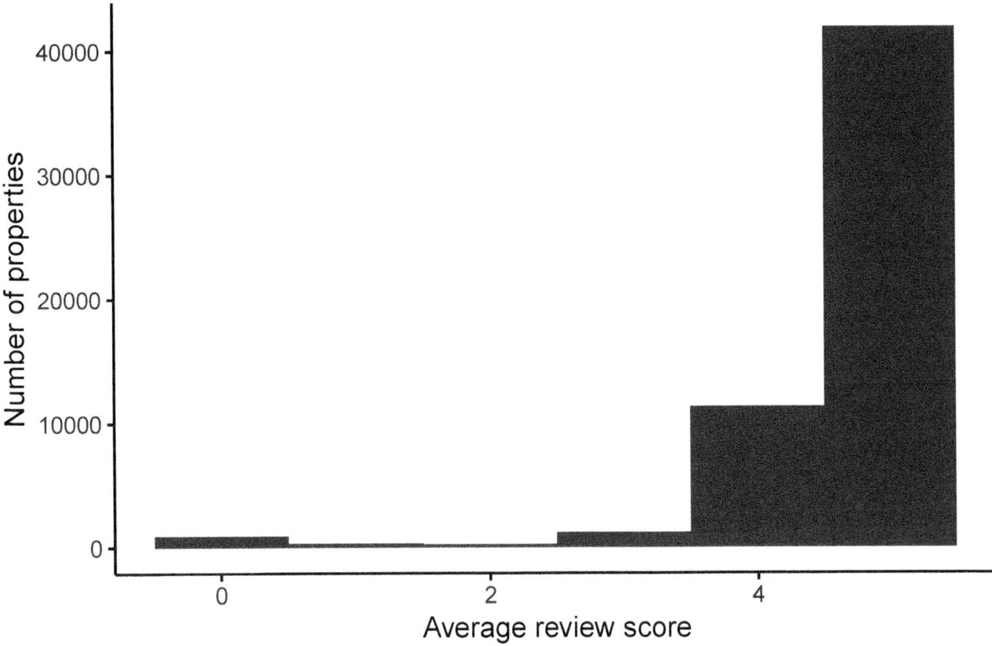

Figure 11.13: Distribution of review scores for London Airbnb rentals in March 2023

```
airbnb_data_no_superhost_nas |>
  filter(!is.na(review_scores_rating)) |>
  ggplot(aes(x = review_scores_rating)) +
  geom_histogram(binwidth = 1) +
  theme_classic() +
  labs(
    x = "Average review score",
    y = "Number of properties"
  )
```

For now, we will remove anyone with an NA in their main review score, even though this will remove roughly 20 per cent of observations. If we ended up using this dataset for actual analysis, then we would want to justify this decision in an appendix or similar.

```
airbnb_data_has_reviews <-
  airbnb_data_no_superhost_nas |>
  filter(!is.na(review_scores_rating))
```

Another important factor is how quickly a host responds to an inquiry. Airbnb allows hosts up to 24 hours to respond, but encourages responses within an hour.

```
airbnb_data_has_reviews |>
  count(host_response_time)
```

```
# A tibble: 5 x 2
  host_response_time     n
```

```
  <chr>                <int>
1 N/A                  19479
2 a few days or more     712
3 within a day          4512
4 within a few hours    6894
5 within an hour       24321
```

It is unclear how a host could have a response time of NA. It may be this is related to some other variable. Interestingly it seems like what looks like "NAs" in "host_response_time" variable are not coded as proper NAs, but are instead being treated as another category. We will recode them to be actual NAs and change the variable to be a factor.

```
airbnb_data_has_reviews <-
  airbnb_data_has_reviews |>
  mutate(
    host_response_time = if_else(
      host_response_time == "N/A",
      NA_character_,
      host_response_time
    ),
    host_response_time = factor(host_response_time)
  )
```

There is an issue with NAs as there are a lot of them. For instance, we might be interested to see if there is a relationship with the review score (Figure 11.14). There are a lot that have an overall review of 100.

```
airbnb_data_has_reviews |>
  filter(is.na(host_response_time)) |>
  ggplot(aes(x = review_scores_rating)) +
  geom_histogram(binwidth = 1) +
  theme_classic() +
  labs(
    x = "Average review score",
    y = "Number of properties"
  )
```

Usually missing values are dropped by `ggplot2`. We can use `geom_miss_point()` from `naniar` to include them in the graph (Figure 11.15).

```
airbnb_data_has_reviews |>
  ggplot(aes(
    x = host_response_time,
    y = review_scores_accuracy
  )) +
  geom_miss_point() +
  labs(
    x = "Host response time",
    y = "Review score accuracy",
    color = "Is missing?"
```

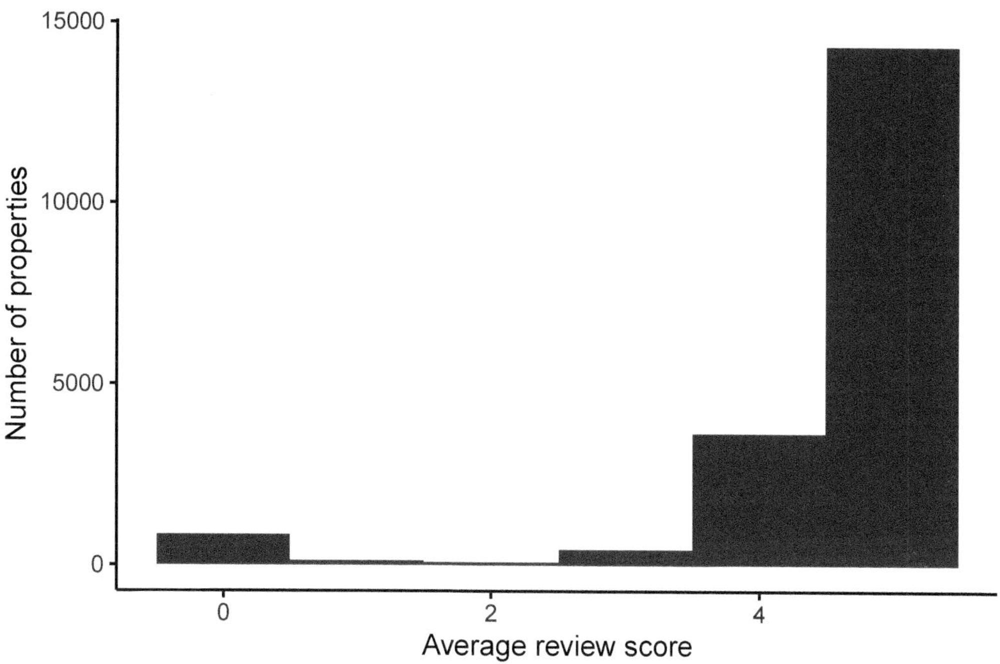

Figure 11.14: Distribution of review scores for properties with NA response time, for London Airbnb rentals in March 2023

```
) +
theme(axis.text.x = element_text(angle = 90, vjust = 0.5, hjust=1))
```

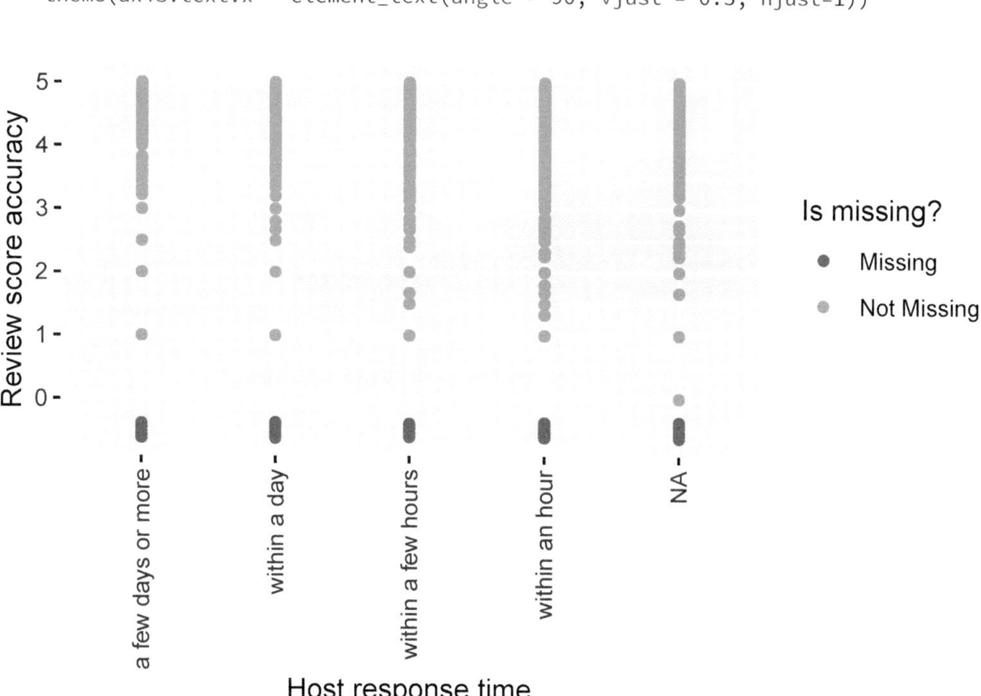

Figure 11.15: Missing values in London Airbnb data, by host response time

For now, we will remove anyone with a NA in their response time. This will again remove roughly another 20 per cent of the observations.

```
airbnb_data_selected <-
  airbnb_data_has_reviews |>
  filter(!is.na(host_response_time))
```

We might be interested in how many properties a host has on Airbnb (Figure 11.16).

```
airbnb_data_selected |>
  ggplot(aes(x = host_total_listings_count)) +
  geom_histogram() +
  scale_x_log10() +
  labs(
    x = "Total number of listings, by host",
    y = "Number of hosts"
  )
```

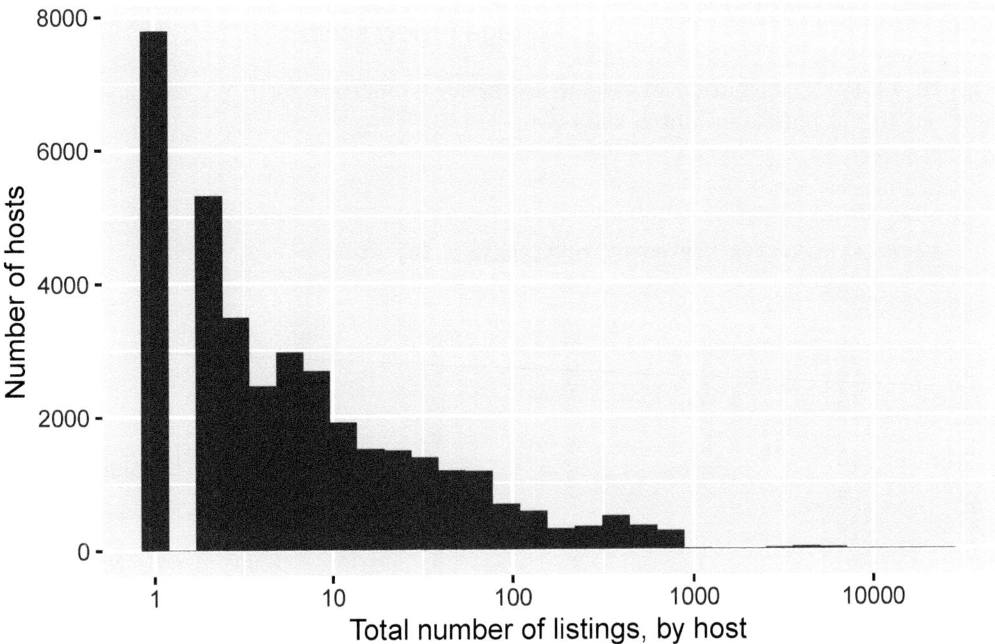

Figure 11.16: Distribution of the number of properties a host has on Airbnb, for London Airbnb rentals in March 2023

Based on Figure 11.16 we can see there are a large number who have somewhere in the 2-500 properties range, with the usual long tail. The number with that many listings is unexpected and worth following up on. And there are a bunch with NA that we will need to deal with.

```
airbnb_data_selected |>
  filter(host_total_listings_count >= 500) |>
  head()
```

```
# A tibble: 6 x 13
   host_id host_response_time host_is_superhost host_total_listings_count
     <dbl> <fct>              <lgl>                                 <dbl>
1 439074505 within an hour     FALSE                                  3627
2 156158778 within an hour     FALSE                                   558
3 156158778 within an hour     FALSE                                   558
4 156158778 within an hour     FALSE                                   558
5 156158778 within an hour     FALSE                                   558
6 156158778 within an hour     FALSE                                   558
# i 9 more variables: neighbourhood_cleansed <chr>, bathrooms <lgl>,
#   bedrooms <dbl>, price <int>, number_of_reviews <dbl>,
#   review_scores_rating <dbl>, review_scores_accuracy <dbl>,
#   review_scores_value <dbl>, host_is_superhost_binary <dbl>
```

There is nothing that immediately jumps out as odd about the people with more than ten listings, but at the same time it is still not clear. For now, we will move on and focus on only those with one property for simplicity.

```
airbnb_data_selected <-
  airbnb_data_selected |>
  add_count(host_id) |>
  filter(n == 1) |>
  select(-n)
```

11.5.2 Relationships between variables

We might like to make some graphs to see if there are any relationships between variables that become clear. Some aspects that come to mind are looking at prices and comparing with reviews, superhosts, number of properties, and neighborhood.

We can look at the relationship between price and reviews, and whether they are a superhost, for properties with more than one review (Figure 11.17).

```
airbnb_data_selected |>
  filter(number_of_reviews > 1) |>
  ggplot(aes(x = price, y = review_scores_rating,
             color = host_is_superhost)) +
  geom_point(size = 1, alpha = 0.1) +
  theme_classic() +
  labs(
    x = "Price per night",
    y = "Average review score",
    color = "Superhost"
  ) +
  scale_color_brewer(palette = "Set1")
```

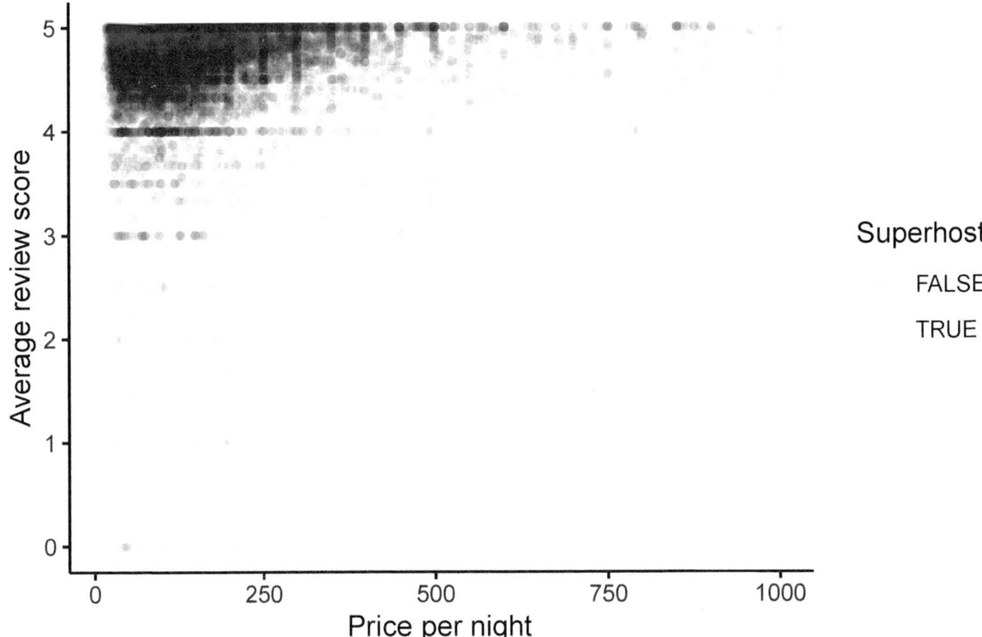

Figure 11.17: Relationship between price and review and whether a host is a superhost, for London Airbnb rentals in March 2023

One of the aspects that may make someone a superhost is how quickly they respond to inquiries. One could imagine that being a superhost involves quickly saying yes or no to inquiries. Let us look at the data. First, we want to look at the possible values of superhost by their response times.

```
airbnb_data_selected |>
  count(host_is_superhost) |>
  mutate(
    proportion = n / sum(n),
    proportion = round(proportion, digits = 2)
  )
```

```
# A tibble: 2 x 3
  host_is_superhost     n proportion
  <lgl>             <int>      <dbl>
1 FALSE             10480       0.74
2 TRUE               3672       0.26
```

Fortunately, it looks like when we removed the reviews rows we removed any NAs from whether they were a superhost, but if we go back and look into that we may need to check again. We could build a table that looks at a hosts response time by whether they are a superhost using `tabyl()` from `janitor`. It is clear that if a host does not respond within an hour then it is unlikely that they are a superhost.

```
airbnb_data_selected |>
  tabyl(host_response_time, host_is_superhost) |>
  adorn_percentages("col") |>
  adorn_pct_formatting(digits = 0) |>
  adorn_ns() |>
  adorn_title()
```

```
                       host_is_superhost
 host_response_time                FALSE            TRUE
 a few days or more          5%    (489)  0%         (8)
       within a day         22% (2,322) 11%        (399)
 within a few hours         23% (2,440) 25%        (928)
      within an hour        50% (5,229) 64%    (2,337)
```

Finally, we could look at neighborhood. The data provider has attempted to clean the neighborhood variable for us, so we will use that variable for now. Although if we ended up using this variable for our actual analysis we would want to examine how it was constructed.

```
airbnb_data_selected |>
  tabyl(neighbourhood_cleansed) |>
  adorn_pct_formatting() |>
  arrange(-n) |>
  filter(n > 100) |>
  adorn_totals("row") |>
  head()
```

```
 neighbourhood_cleansed    n percent
                Hackney 1172    8.3%
            Westminster  965    6.8%
          Tower Hamlets  956    6.8%
              Southwark  939    6.6%
                Lambeth  914    6.5%
             Wandsworth  824    5.8%
```

We will quickly run a model on our dataset. We will cover modeling in more detail in Chapter 12, but we can use models during EDA to help get a better sense of relationships that may exist between multiple variables in a dataset. For instance, we may like to see whether we can forecast whether someone is a superhost, and the factors that go into explaining that. As the outcome is binary, this is a good opportunity to use logistic regression. We expect that superhost status will be associated with faster responses and better reviews. Specifically, the model that we estimate is:

$$\text{Prob(Is superhost} = 1) = \text{logit}^{-1}\left(\beta_0 + \beta_1 \text{Response time} + \beta_2 \text{Reviews} + \epsilon\right)$$

We estimate the model using `glm`.

```
logistic_reg_superhost_response_review <-
  glm(
    host_is_superhost ~
      host_response_time +
```

Table 11.3: Explaining whether a host is a superhost based on their response time

	(1)
(Intercept)	−16.369
	(0.673)
host_response_timewithin a day	2.230
	(0.361)
host_response_timewithin a few hours	3.035
	(0.359)
host_response_timewithin an hour	3.279
	(0.358)
review_scores_rating	2.545
	(0.116)
Num.Obs.	14 152
AIC	14 948.4
BIC	14 986.2
Log.Lik.	−7469.197
F	197.407
RMSE	0.42

```
    review_scores_rating,
  data = airbnb_data_selected,
  family = binomial
)
```

After installing and loading `modelsummary` we can have a quick look at the results using `modelsummary()` (Table 11.3).

```
modelsummary(logistic_reg_superhost_response_review)
```

We see that each of the levels is positively associated with the probability of being a superhost. However, having a host that responds within an hour is associated with individuals that are superhosts in our dataset.

We will save this analysis dataset.

```
write_parquet(
  x = airbnb_data_selected,
  sink = "2023-05-05-london-airbnblistings-analysis_dataset.parquet"
  )
```

11.6 Concluding remarks

In this chapter we have considered exploratory data analysis (EDA), which is the active process of getting to know a dataset. We focused on missing data, the distributions of variables, and the relationships between variables. And we extensively used graphs and tables to do this.

The approaches to EDA will vary depending on context, and the issues and features that are encountered in the dataset. It will also depend on your skills, for instance it is common to consider regression models, and dimensionality reduction approaches.

11.7 Exercises

Scales

1. *(Plan)* Consider the following scenario: *We have some data on age from a social media company that has about 80 per cent of the US population on the platform.* Please sketch what that dataset could look like and then sketch a graph that you could build to show all observations.
2. *(Simulate)* Please further consider the scenario described and simulate the situation. Use parquet due to size. Please include ten tests based on the simulated data. Submit a link to a GitHub Gist that contains your code.
3. *(Acquire)* Please describe a possible source of such a dataset.
4. *(Explore)* Please use `ggplot2` to build the graph that you sketched. Submit a link to a GitHub Gist that contains your code.
5. *(Communicate)* Please write one page about what you did, and be careful to discuss some of the threats to the estimate that you make based on the sample.

Questions

1. Summarize Tukey (1962) in a few paragraphs and then relate it to data science.
2. In your own words what is exploratory data analysis (please write at least three paragraphs, and include citations and examples)?
3. Suppose you have a dataset called "my_data", which has two columns: "first_col" and "second_col". Please write some R code that would generate a graph (the type of graph does not matter). Submit a link to a GitHub Gist that contains your code.
4. Consider a dataset that has 500 observations and three variables, so there are 1,500 cells. If 100 of the rows are missing a cell for at least one of the columns, then would you: a) remove the whole row from your dataset, b) try to run your analysis on the data as is, or c) some other procedure? What if your dataset had 10,000 rows instead, but the same number of missing rows? Discuss, with examples and citations, in at least three paragraphs.
5. Please discuss three ways of identifying unusual values, writing at least one paragraph for each.
6. What is the difference between a categorical and continuous variable?
7. What is the difference between a factor and an integer variable?
8. How can we think about who is systematically excluded from a dataset?
9. Using `opendatatoronto`, download the data on mayoral campaign contributions for 2014. (Note: the 2014 file you will get from `get_resource()` contains many sheets, so just keep the sheet that relates to the mayor election).
    1. Clean up the data format (fixing the parsing issue and standardizing the column names using `janitor`).

   2. Summarize the variables in the dataset. Are there missing values, and if so, should we be worried about them? Is every variable in the format it should be? If not, create new variable(s) that are in the right format.
   3. Visually explore the distribution of values of the contributions. What contributions are notable outliers? Do they share similar characteristic(s)? It may be useful to plot the distribution of contributions without these outliers to get a better sense of most of the data.
   4. List the top five candidates in each of these categories: 1) total contributions; 2) mean contribution; and 3) number of contributions.
   5. Repeat that process, but without contributions from the candidates themselves.
   6. How many contributors gave money to more than one candidate?

10. List three geoms that produce graphs that have bars in `ggplot()`.
11. Consider a dataset with 10,000 observations and 27 variables. For each observation, there is at least one missing variable. Please discuss, in a paragraph or two, the steps that you would take to understand what is going on.
12. Known missing data are those that leave holes in your dataset. But what about data that were never collected? Please look at McClelland (2019) and Luscombe and McClelland (2020). Look into how they gathered their dataset and what it took to put this together. What is in the dataset and why? What is missing and why? How could this affect the results? How might similar biases enter into other datasets that you have used or read about?

Tutorial

Pick one of the following options. Use Quarto, and include an appropriate title, author, date, link to a GitHub repo, and citations. Submit a PDF.

Option 1:

Repeat the missing data exercise conducted for the US states and population, but for the "bill_length_mm" variable in the `penguins()` dataset available from `palmerpenguins`. Compare the imputed value with the actual value.

Write at least two pages about what you did and what you found.

Following this, please pair with another student and exchange your written work. Update it based on their feedback, and be sure to acknowledge them by name in your paper.

Option 2:

Carry out an Airbnb EDA but for Paris.

Option 3:

Please write at least two pages about the topic: "what is missing data and what should you do about it?"

Following this, please pair with another student and exchange your written work. Update it based on their feedback, and be sure to acknowledge them by name in your paper.

12

Linear models

Prerequisites

- Read *Regression and Other Stories*, (Gelman, Hill, and Vehtari 2020)
  - Focus on Chapters 6 "Background on regression modeling", 7 "Linear regression with a single predictor", and 10 "Linear regression with multiple predictors", which provide a detailed guide to linear models.
- Read *An Introduction to Statistical Learning with Applications in R*, (James et al. [2013] 2021)
  - Focus on Chapter 3 "Linear Regression", which provides a complementary treatment of linear models from a different perspective.
- Read *Why most published research findings are false*, (Ioannidis 2005)
  - Details aspects that can undermine the conclusions drawn from statistical models.

Key concepts and skills

- Linear models are a key component of statistical inference and enable us to quickly explore a wide range of data.
- Simple and multiple linear regression model a continuous outcome variable as a function of one, and multiple, predictor variables, respectively.
- Linear models tend to focus on either inference or prediction.

Software and packages

- Base R (R Core Team 2023)
- `beepr` (Bååth 2018)
- `broom` (D. Robinson, Hayes, and Couch 2022)
- `broom.mixed` (Bolker and Robinson 2022)
- `knitr` (Xie 2023)
- `modelsummary` (Arel-Bundock 2022)
- `purrr` (Wickham and Henry 2022)
- `rstanarm` (Goodrich et al. 2023)
- `testthat` (Wickham 2011)
- `tidyverse` (Wickham et al. 2019)

```
library(beepr)
library(broom)
library(broom.mixed)
library(knitr)
library(modelsummary)
library(purrr)
library(rstanarm)
library(testthat)
library(tidyverse)
```

12.1 Introduction

Linear models have been used in various forms for a long time. Stigler (1986, 16) describes how least squares, which is a method to fit simple linear regression, was associated with foundational problems in astronomy in the 1700s, such as determining the motion of the moon and reconciling the non-periodic motion of Jupiter and Saturn. The fundamental issue at the time with least squares was that of hesitancy by those coming from a statistical background to combine different observations. Astronomers were early to develop a comfort with doing this, possibly because they had typically gathered their observations themselves and knew that the conditions of the data gathering were similar, even though the value of the observation was different. For instance, Stigler (1986, 28) characterizes Leonhard Euler, the eighteenth century mathematician mentioned in Chapter 6, as considering that errors increase as they are aggregated, in comparison to Tobias Mayer, the eighteenth century astronomer, who was comfortable that errors would cancel each other. It took longer, again, for social scientists to become comfortable with linear models, possibly because they were hesitant to group together data they worried were not alike. In one sense astronomers had an advantage because they could compare their predictions with what happened whereas this was more difficult for social scientists (Stigler 1986, 163).

When we build models, we are not discovering "the truth". A model is not, and cannot be, a true representation of reality. We are using the model to help us explore and understand our data. There is no one best model, there are just useful models that help us learn something about the data that we have and hence, hopefully, something about the world from which the data were generated. When we use models, we are trying to understand the world, but there are constraints on the perspective we bring to this. We should not just throw data into a model and hope that it will sort it out. It will not.

> Regression is indeed an oracle, but a cruel one. It speaks in riddles and delights in punishing us for asking bad questions.
>
> McElreath ([2015] 2020, 162)

We use models to understand the world. We poke, push, and test them. We build them and rejoice in their beauty, and then seek to understand their limits and ultimately destroy them. It is this process that is important, it is this process that allows us to better understand the world; not the outcome, although they may be coincident. When we build models, we need to keep in mind both the world of the model and the broader world that we want to be able to speak about. The datasets that we have are often unrepresentative of real-world populations in certain ways. Models trained on such data are not worthless, but they are also not unimpeachable. To what extent does the model teach us about the data that we have? To what extent do the data that we have reflect the world about which we would like to draw conclusions? We need to keep such questions front of mind.

A lot of statistical methods commonly used today were developed for situations such as astronomy and agriculture. Ronald Fisher, introduced in Chapter 8, published Fisher ([1925]

1928) while he worked at an agricultural research institution. But many of the subsequent uses in the twentieth and twenty-first centuries concern applications that may have different properties. Statistical validity relies on assumptions, and so while what is taught is correct, our circumstances may not meet the starting criteria. Statistics is often taught as though it proceeds through some idealized process where a hypothesis appears, is tested against some data that similarly appears, and is either confirmed or not. But that is not what happens, in practice. We react to incentives. We dabble, guess, and test, and then follow our intuition, backfilling as we need. All of this is fine. But it is not a world in which a traditional null hypothesis, which we will get to later, holds completely. This means concepts such as p-values and power lose some of their meaning. While we need to understand these foundations, we also need to be sophisticated enough to know when we need to move away from them.

Statistical checks are widely used in modeling. And an extensive suite of them is available. But automated testing of code and data is also important. For instance, Knutson et al. (2022) built a model of excess deaths in a variety of countries, to estimate the overall death toll from the pandemic. After initially releasing the model, which had been extensively manually checked for statistical issues and reasonableness, some of the results were reexamined and it was found that the estimates for Germany and Sweden were oversensitive. The authors quickly addressed the issue, but the integration of automated testing of expected values for the coefficients, in addition to the usual manual statistical checks, would go some way to enabling us to have more faith in the models of others.

In this chapter we begin with simple linear regression, and then move to multiple linear regression, the difference being the number of explanatory variables that we allow. We go through two approaches for each of these: base R, in particular the `lm()` and `glm()` functions, which are useful when we want to quickly use the models in EDA; and `rstanarm` for when we are interested in inference. In general, a model is either optimized for inference or prediction. A focus on prediction is one of the hallmarks of machine learning. For historical reasons that has tended to be dominated by Python, although `tidymodels` (Kuhn and Wickham 2020) has been developed in R. Due to the need to also introduce Python, we devote the "Prediction" Online Appendix[1] to various approaches focused on prediction. Regardless of the approach we use, the important thing to remember that we are just doing something akin to fancy averaging, and our results always reflect the biases and idiosyncrasies of the dataset.

Finally a note on terminology and notation. For historical and context-specific reasons there are a variety of terms used to describe the same idea across the literature. We follow Gelman, Hill, and Vehtari (2020) and use the terms "outcome" and "predictor", we follow the frequentist notation of James et al. ([2013] 2021), and the Bayesian model specification of McElreath ([2015] 2020).

12.2 Simple linear regression

When we are interested in the relationship of some continuous outcome variable, say y, and some predictor variable, say x, we can use simple linear regression. This is based on the Normal, also called "Gaussian", distribution, but it is not these variables themselves that

[1] https://tellingstorieswithdata.com/27-prediction.html

are normally distributed. The Normal distribution is determined by two parameters, the mean, μ, and the standard deviation, σ (Pitman 1993, 94):

$$y = \frac{1}{\sqrt{2\pi\sigma}} e^{-\frac{1}{2}z^2},$$

where $z = (x - \mu)/\sigma$ is the difference between x and the mean, scaled by the standard deviation. Altman and Bland (1995) provide an overview of the Normal distribution.

As introduced in the "R essentials" Online Appendix[2], we use `rnorm()` to simulate data from the Normal distribution.

```
set.seed(853)

normal_example <-
  tibble(draws = rnorm(n = 20, mean = 0, sd = 1))

normal_example |> pull(draws)
```

```
 [1] -0.35980342 -0.04064753 -1.78216227 -1.12242282 -1.00278400  1.77670433
 [7] -1.38825825 -0.49749494 -0.55798959 -0.82438245  1.66877818 -0.68196486
[13]  0.06519751 -0.25985911  0.32900796 -0.43696568 -0.32288891  0.11455483
[19]  0.84239206  0.34248268
```

Here we specified 20 draws from a Normal distribution with a true mean, μ, of zero and a true standard deviation, σ, of one. When we deal with real data, we will not know the true value of these, and we want to use our data to estimate them. We can create an estimate of the mean, $\hat{\mu}$, and an estimate of the standard deviation, $\hat{\sigma}$, with the following estimators:

$$\hat{\mu} = \frac{1}{n} \times \sum_{i=1}^{n} x_i$$

$$\hat{\sigma} = \sqrt{\frac{1}{n-1} \times \sum_{i=1}^{n} (x_i - \hat{\mu})^2}$$

If $\hat{\sigma}$ is the estimate of the standard deviation, then the standard error (SE) of the estimate of the mean, $\hat{\mu}$, is:

$$\mbox{SE}(\hat{\mu}) = \frac{\hat{\sigma}}{\sqrt{n}}.$$

The standard error is a comment about the estimate of the mean compared with the actual mean, while the standard deviation is a comment about how widely distributed the data are.[3]

We can implement these in code using our simulated data to see how close our estimates are.

[2]https://tellingstorieswithdata.com/20-r_essentials.html

[3]Given the small sample size in the example of 20, we strictly should use the finite-sample adjustment, but as this is not the focus of this book we will move forward with the general approach.

Table 12.1: Estimates of the mean and standard deviation based on the simulated data

Estimated mean	Estimated standard deviation	Estimated standard error
-0.21	0.91	0.2

```
estimated_mean <-
  sum(normal_example$draws) / nrow(normal_example)

normal_example <-
  normal_example |>
  mutate(diff_square = (draws - estimated_mean) ^ 2)

estimated_standard_deviation <-
  sqrt(sum(normal_example$diff_square) / (nrow(normal_example) - 1))

estimated_standard_error <-
  estimated_standard_deviation / sqrt(nrow(normal_example))

kable(
  tibble(mean = estimated_mean,
         sd = estimated_standard_deviation,
         se = estimated_standard_error),
  col.names = c(
    "Estimated mean",
    "Estimated standard deviation",
    "Estimated standard error"
  ),
  digits = 2,
  align = c("l", "r", "r"),
  booktabs = TRUE,
  linesep = ""
  )
```

We should not be too worried that our estimates are slightly off (Table 12.1), relative to the "true" mean and SD of 0 and 1. We only considered 20 observations. It will typically take a larger number of draws before we get the expected shape, and our estimated parameters get close to the actual parameters, but it will almost surely happen (Figure 12.1). Wasserman (2005, 76) considers our certainty of this, which is due to the Law of Large Numbers, as a crowning accomplishment of probability, although Wood (2015, 15), perhaps more prosaically, describes it as "almost" a statement "of the obvious"!

```
set.seed(853)

normal_takes_shapes <-
  map_dfr(c(2, 5, 10, 50, 100, 500, 1000, 10000, 100000),
          ~ tibble(
            number_draws = rep(paste(.x, "draws"), .x),
            draws = rnorm(.x, mean = 0, sd = 1)
```

```
    ))

normal_takes_shapes |>
  mutate(number_draws = as_factor(number_draws)) |>
  ggplot(aes(x = draws)) +
  geom_density() +
  theme_minimal() +
  facet_wrap(vars(number_draws),
             scales = "free_y") +
  labs(x = "Draw",
       y = "Density")
```

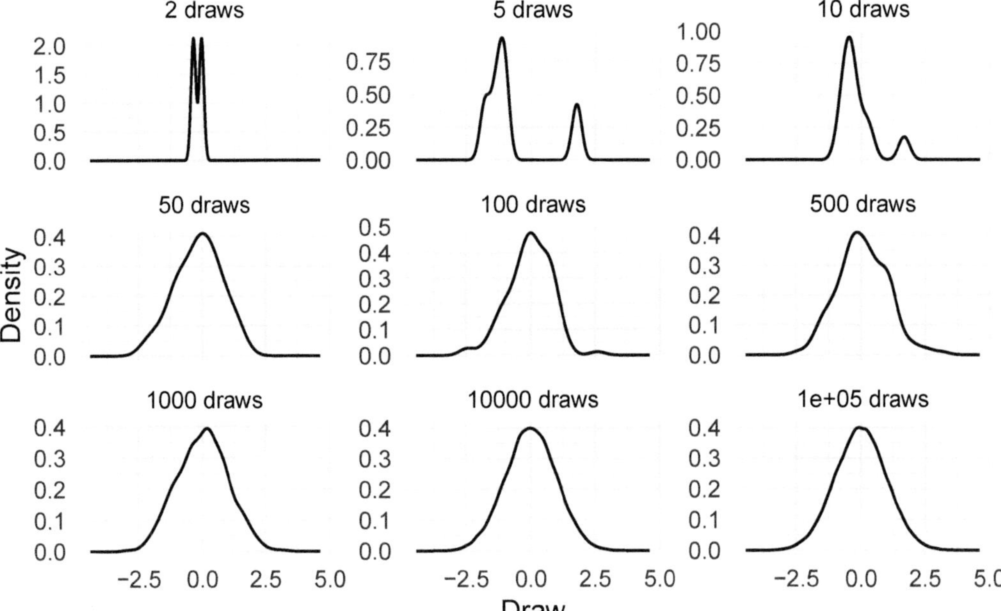

Figure 12.1: The Normal distribution takes its familiar shape as the number of draws increases

When we use simple linear regression, we assume that our relationship is characterized by the variables and the parameters. If we have two variables, Y and X, then we could characterize a linear relationship between these as:

$$Y = \beta_0 + \beta_1 X + \epsilon. \tag{12.1}$$

Here, there are two parameters, also referred to as coefficients: the intercept, β_0, and the slope, β_1. In Equation 12.1 we are saying that the expected value of Y is β_0 when X is 0, and that the expected value of Y will change by β_1 units for every one unit change in X. We may then take this relationship to the data that we have to estimate these parameters. The ϵ is noise and accounts for deviations away from this relationship. It is this noise that we generally assume to be normally distributed, and it is this that leads to $Y \sim N(\beta, \sigma^2)$.

12.2.1 Simulated example: running times

To make this example concrete, we revisit an example from Chapter 9 about the time it takes someone to run five kilometers, compared with the time it takes them to run a marathon (Figure 12.2a). We specified a relationship of 8.4, as that is roughly the ratio between a five-kilometer run and the 42.2-kilometer distance of a marathon. To help the reader, we include the simulation code again here. Notice that it is the noise that is normally distributed, not the variables. We do not require the variables themselves to be normally distributed in order to use linear regression.

```
set.seed(853)

num_observations <- 200
expected_relationship <- 8.4
fast_time <- 15
good_time <- 30

sim_run_data <-
  tibble(
    five_km_time =
      runif(n = num_observations, min = fast_time, max = good_time),
    noise = rnorm(n = num_observations, mean = 0, sd = 20),
    marathon_time = five_km_time * expected_relationship + noise
  ) |>
  mutate(
    five_km_time = round(x = five_km_time, digits = 1),
    marathon_time = round(x = marathon_time, digits = 1)
  ) |>
  select(-noise)
```

```
base_plot <-
  sim_run_data |>
  ggplot(aes(x = five_km_time, y = marathon_time)) +
  geom_point(alpha = 0.5) +
  labs(
    x = "Five-kilometer time (minutes)",
    y = "Marathon time (minutes)"
  ) +
  theme_classic()

# Panel (a)
base_plot

# Panel (b)
base_plot +
  geom_smooth(
    method = "lm",
    se = FALSE,
    color = "black",
    linetype = "dashed",
```

```
    formula = "y ~ x"
  )

# Panel (c)
base_plot +
  geom_smooth(
    method = "lm",
    se = TRUE,
    color = "black",
    linetype = "dashed",
    formula = "y ~ x"
  )
```

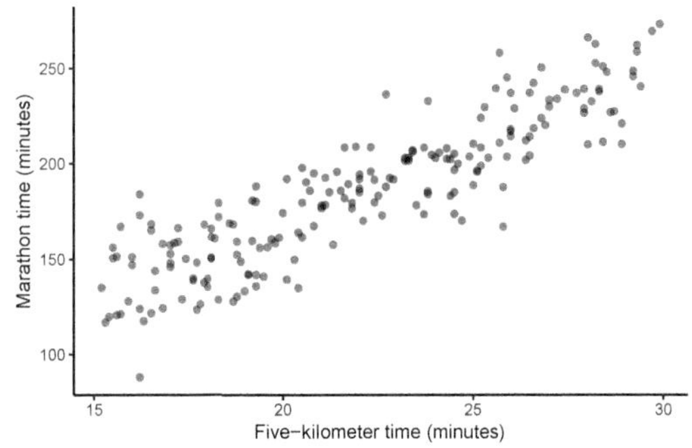

(a) Distribution of simulated data

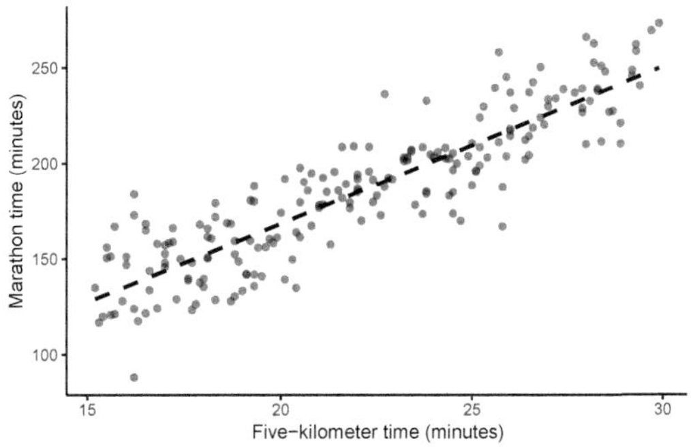

(b) With one linear best-fit line illustrating the implied relationship

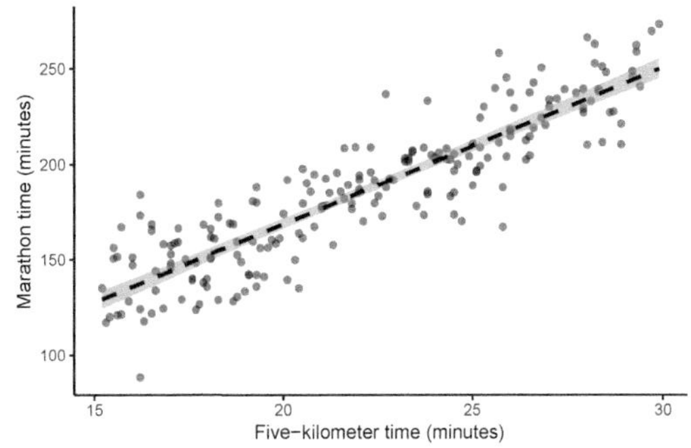

(c) Including standard errors

Figure 12.2: Simulated data of the relationship between the time to run five kilometers and a marathon

In this simulated example, we know the true values of β_0 and β_1, which are zero and 8.4, respectively. But our challenge is to see if we can use only the data, and simple linear regression, to recover them. That is, can we use x, which is the five-kilometer time, to produce estimates of y, which is the marathon time, and that we denote by $\hat{y}$ (by convention, hats are used to indicate that these are, or will be, estimated values) (James et al. [2013] 2021, 61):

$$\hat{y} = \hat{\beta}_0 + \hat{\beta}_1 x.$$

This involves estimating values for β_0 and β_1. But how should we estimate these coefficients? Even if we impose a linear relationship there are many options because many straight lines could be drawn. But some of those lines would fit the data better than others.

One way we could define a line as being "better" than another, is if it is as close as possible to each of the known x and y combinations. There are a lot of candidates for how we define as "close as possible", but one is to minimize the residual sum of squares. To do this we produce estimates for $\hat{y}$ based on some guesses of $\hat{\beta}_0$ and $\hat{\beta}_1$, given the x. We then work out how wrong, for every observation i, we were (James et al. [2013] 2021, 62):

$$e_i = y_i - \hat{y}_i.$$

To compute the residual sum of squares (RSS), we sum the errors across all the points (taking the square to account for negative differences) (James et al. [2013] 2021, 62):

$$\text{RSS} = e_1^2 + e_2^2 + \dots + e_n^2.$$

This results in one linear best-fit line (Figure 12.2b), but it is worth reflecting on all the assumptions and decisions that it took to get us to this point.

Underpinning our use of simple linear regression is a belief that there is some "true" relationship between X and Y. And that this is a linear function of X. We do not, and cannot, know the "true" relationship between X and Y. All we can do is use our sample to estimate it. But because our understanding depends on that sample, for every possible sample, we would get a slightly different relationship, as measured by the coefficients.

That ϵ is a measure of our error—what does the model not know in the small, contained world of the dataset? But it does not tell us whether the model is appropriate outside of the dataset (think, by way of analogy, to the concepts of internal and external validity for experiments introduced in Chapter 8). That requires our judgement and experience.

We can conduct simple linear regression with `lm()` from base R. We specify the outcome variable first, then `~`, followed by the predictor. The outcome variable is the variable of interest, while the predictor is the basis on which we consider that variable. Finally, we specify the dataset.

Before we run a regression, we may want to include a quick check of the class of the variables, and the number of observations, just to ensure that it corresponds with what we were expecting, although we may have done that earlier in the workflow. And after we run it, we may check that our estimate seems reasonable. For instance, (pretending that we had not ourselves imposed this in the simulation) based on our knowledge of the respective distances of a five-kilometer run and a marathon, we would expect β_1 to be somewhere between six and ten.

```
# Check the class and number of observations are as expected
stopifnot(
  class(sim_run_data$marathon_time) == "numeric",
  class(sim_run_data$five_km_time) == "numeric",
  nrow(sim_run_data) == 200
)

sim_run_data_first_model <-
  lm(
```

```
    marathon_time ~ five_km_time,
    data = sim_run_data
  )

stopifnot(between(
  sim_run_data_first_model$coefficients[2],
  6,
  10
))
```

To quickly see the result of the regression, we can use `summary()`.

```
summary(sim_run_data_first_model)
```

```
Call:
lm(formula = marathon_time ~ five_km_time, data = sim_run_data)

Residuals:
    Min      1Q  Median      3Q     Max 
-49.289 -11.948   0.153  11.396  46.511 

Coefficients:
             Estimate Std. Error t value Pr(>|t|)    
(Intercept)    4.4692     6.7517   0.662    0.509    
five_km_time   8.2049     0.3005  27.305   <2e-16 ***
---
Signif. codes:  0 '***' 0.001 '**' 0.01 '*' 0.05 '.' 0.1 ' ' 1

Residual standard error: 17.42 on 198 degrees of freedom
Multiple R-squared:  0.7902,	Adjusted R-squared:  0.7891 
F-statistic: 745.5 on 1 and 198 DF,  p-value: < 2.2e-16
```

But we can also use `modelsummary()` from `modelsummary` (Table 12.2). The advantage of that approach is that we get a nicely formatted table. We focus initially on those results in the "Five km only" column.

```
modelsummary(
  list(
    "Five km only" = sim_run_data_first_model,
    "Five km only, centered" = sim_run_data_centered_model
  ),
  fmt = 2
)
```

The top half of Table 12.2 provides our estimated coefficients and standard errors in brackets. And the second half provides some useful diagnostics, which we will not dwell too much in this book. The intercept in the "Five km only" column is the marathon time associated with a hypothetical five-kilometer time of zero minutes. Hopefully this example illustrates the need to always interpret the intercept coefficient carefully. And to disregard it at times. For instance, in this circumstance, we know that the intercept should be zero, and it is

Table 12.2: Explaining marathon times based on five-kilometer run times

	Five km only	Five km only, centered
(Intercept)	4.47	185.73
	(6.75)	(1.23)
five_km_time	8.20	
	(0.30)	
centered_time		8.20
		(0.30)
Num.Obs.	200	200
R2	0.790	0.790
R2 Adj.	0.789	0.789
AIC	1714.7	1714.7
BIC	1724.6	1724.6
Log.Lik.	−854.341	−854.341
F	745.549	745.549
RMSE	17.34	17.34

just being set to around four because that is the best fit given all the observations were for five-kilometer times between 15 and 30.

The intercept becomes more interpretable when we run the regression using centered five-kilometer time, which we do in the "Five km only, centered" column of Table 12.2. That is, for each of the five-kilometer times we subtract the mean five-kilometer time. In this case, the intercept is interpreted as the expected marathon time for someone who runs five kilometers in the average time. Notice that the slope estimate is unchanged it is only the intercept that has changed.

```
sim_run_data <-
  sim_run_data |>
  mutate(centered_time = five_km_time - mean(sim_run_data$five_km_time))

sim_run_data_centered_model <-
  lm(
    marathon_time ~ centered_time,
    data = sim_run_data
  )
```

Following Gelman, Hill, and Vehtari (2020, 84) we recommend considering the coefficients as comparisons, rather than effects. And to use language that makes it clear these are comparisons, on average, based on one dataset. For instance, we may consider that the coefficient on the five-kilometer run time shows how different individuals compare. When comparing the marathon times of individuals in our dataset whose five-kilometer run time differed by one minute, on average we find their marathon times differ by about eight minutes. This makes sense seeing as a marathon is roughly that many times longer than a five-kilometer run.

We can use `augment()` from `broom` to add the fitted values and residuals to our original dataset. This allows us to plot the residuals (Figure 12.3).

```
sim_run_data <-
  augment(
    sim_run_data_first_model,
    data = sim_run_data
  )


# Plot a)
ggplot(sim_run_data, aes(x = .resid)) +
  geom_histogram(binwidth = 1) +
  theme_classic() +
  labs(y = "Number of occurrences", x = "Residuals")

# Plot b)
ggplot(sim_run_data, aes(x = five_km_time, y = .resid)) +
  geom_point() +
  geom_hline(yintercept = 0, linetype = "dotted", color = "grey") +
  theme_classic() +
  labs(y = "Residuals", x = "Five-kilometer time (minutes)")

# Plot c)
ggplot(sim_run_data, aes(x = marathon_time, y = .resid)) +
  geom_point() +
  geom_hline(yintercept = 0, linetype = "dotted", color = "grey") +
  theme_classic() +
  labs(y = "Residuals", x = "Marathon time (minutes)")

# Plot d)
ggplot(sim_run_data, aes(x = marathon_time, y = .fitted)) +
  geom_point() +
  geom_abline(intercept = 0, slope = 1, linetype = "dashed") +
  theme_classic() +
  labs(y = "Estimated marathon time", x = "Actual marathon time")
```

We want to try to speak to the "true" relationship, so we need to try to capture how much we think our understanding depends on the sample that we have to analyze. And this is where the standard error comes in. It guides us, based on many assumptions, about how to think about the estimates of parameters based on the data that we have (Figure 12.2c). Part of this is captured by the fact that standard errors are a function of sample size n, and as the sample size increases, the standard errors decrease.

The most common way to summarize the range of uncertainty for a coefficient is to transform its standard error into a confidence interval. These intervals are often misunderstood to represent a statement of probability about a given realization of the coefficients (i.e. $\hat{\beta}$). In reality, confidence intervals are a statistic whose properties can only be understood "in expectation" (which is equivalent to repeating an experiment many times). A 95 per cent confidence interval is a range, such that there is "approximately a 95 per cent chance that the" range contains the population parameter, which is typically unknown (James et al. [2013] 2021, 66).

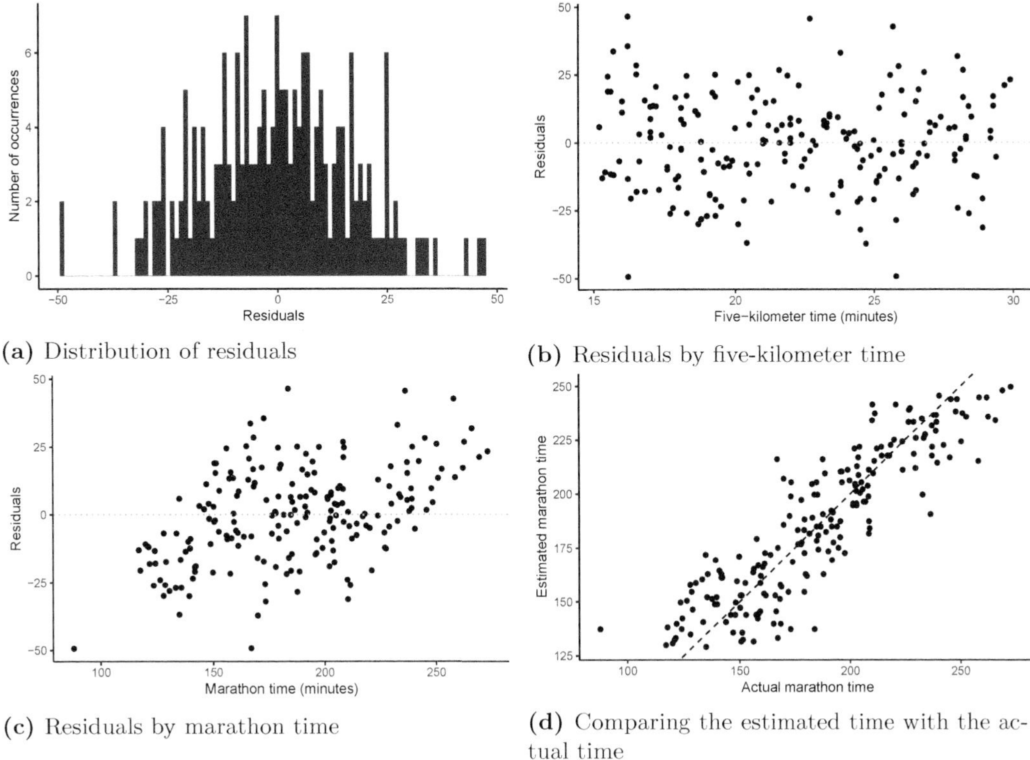

(a) Distribution of residuals

(b) Residuals by five-kilometer time

(c) Residuals by marathon time

(d) Comparing the estimated time with the actual time

Figure 12.3: Residuals from the simple linear regression with simulated data on the time someone takes to run five kilometers and a marathon

When the coefficient follows a Normal distribution, the lower and upper end of a 95 per cent confidence interval range will be about $\hat{\beta}_1 \pm 2 \times \mathrm{SE}\left(\hat{\beta}_1\right)$. For instance, in the case of the marathon time example, the lower end is $8.2 - 2 \times 0.3 = 7.6$ and the upper end is $8.2+2\times 0.3 = 8.8$, and the true value (which we only know in this case because we simulated it) is 8.4.

We can use this machinery to test claims. For instance, we could claim that there is no relationship between X and Y, i.e. $\beta_1 = 0$, as an alternative to a claim that there is some relationship between X and Y, i.e. $\beta_1 \neq 0$. This is the null hypothesis testing approach mentioned earlier. In Chapter 8 we needed to decide how much evidence it would take to convince us that our tea taster could distinguish whether milk or tea had been added first. In the same way, here we need to decide if the estimate of β_1, which we denote as $\hat{\beta}_1$, is far enough away from zero for us to be comfortable claiming that $\beta_1 \neq 0$. If we were very confident in our estimate of β_1 then it would not have to be far, but if we were not, then it would have to be substantial. For instance, if the confidence interval contains zero, then we lack evidence to suggest $\beta_1 \neq 0$. The standard error of $\hat{\beta}_1$ does an awful lot of work here in accounting for a variety of factors, only some of which it can actually account for, as does our choice as to what it would take to convince us.

We use this standard error and $\hat{\beta}_1$ to get the "test statistic" or t-statistic:

$$t = \frac{\hat{\beta}_1}{\mathrm{SE}(\hat{\beta}_1)}.$$

And we then compare our t-statistic to the t-distribution of Student (1908) to compute the probability of getting this absolute t-statistic or a larger one, if it was the case that $\beta_1 = 0$. This probability is the p-value. A smaller p-value means there is a smaller "probability of observing something at least as extreme as the observed test statistic" (Gelman, Hill, and Vehtari 2020, 57). Here we use the t-distribution of Student (1908) rather than the Normal distribution, because the t-distribution has slightly larger tails than a standard Normal distribution.

> Words! Mere words! How terrible they were! How clear, and vivid, and cruel! One could not escape from them. And yet what a subtle magic there was in them! They seemed to be able to give a plastic form to formless things, and to have a music of their own as sweet as that of viol or of lute. Mere words! Was there anything so real as words?
>
> *The Picture of Dorian Gray* (Wilde 1891).

We will not make much use of p-values in this book because they are a specific and subtle concept. They are difficult to understand and easy to abuse. Even though they are "little help" for "scientific inference" many disciplines are incorrectly fixated on them (Nelder 1999, 257). One issue is that they embody every assumption of the workflow, including everything that went into gathering and cleaning the data. While p-values have implications if all the assumptions were correct, when we consider the full data science workflow there are usually an awful lot of assumptions. And we do not get guidance from p-values about whether the assumptions are satisfied (Greenland et al. 2016, 339).

A p-value may reject a null hypothesis because the null hypothesis is false, but it may also be that some data were incorrectly gathered or prepared. We can only be sure that the p-value speaks to the hypothesis we are interested in testing if all the other assumptions are correct. There is nothing wrong about using p-values, but it is important to use them in sophisticated and thoughtful ways. D. Cox (2018) discusses what this requires.

One application where it is easy to see an inappropriate focus on p-values is in power analysis. Power, in a statistical sense, refers to probability of rejecting a null hypothesis that is false. As power relates to hypothesis testing, it also relates to sample size. There is often a worry that a study is "under-powered", meaning there was not a large enough sample, but rarely a worry that, say, the data were inappropriately cleaned, even though we cannot distinguish between these based only on a p-value. As Meng (2018) and Bradley et al. (2021) demonstrate, a focus on power can blind us from our responsibility to ensure our data are high quality.

Shoulders of giants

Dr Nancy Reid is University Professor in the Department of Statistical Sciences at the University of Toronto. After obtaining a PhD in Statistics from Stanford University in 1979, she took a position as a postdoctoral fellow at Imperial College London. She was appointed as an assistant professor at the University of British Columbia in 1980, and then moved to the University of Toronto in 1986, where she was promoted to full professor in 1988 and served as department chair between 1997 and 2002 (Staicu 2017). Her research focuses on obtaining accurate inference in small-sample regimes and developing inferential procedures for complex models featuring intractable likelihoods. D. Cox and Reid (1987) examine how re-parameterizing models can simplify inference, Varin, Reid, and Firth (2011) surveys methods for approximating intractable likelihoods, and Reid (2003) overviews inferential procedures in the small-sample regime. Dr Reid was awarded the 1992 COPSS Presidents' Award, the Royal Statistical Society Guy Medal in Silver in 2016 and in Gold in 2022, and the COPSS Distinguished Achievement Award and Lectureship in 2022.

12.3 Multiple linear regression

To this point we have just considered one explanatory variable. But we will usually have more than one. One approach would be to run separate regressions for each explanatory variable. But compared with separate linear regressions for each, adding more explanatory variables allows for associations between the outcome variable and the predictor variable of interest to be assessed while adjusting for other explanatory variables. The results can be quite different, especially when the explanatory variables are correlated with each other.

We may also like to consider explanatory variables that are not continuous. For instance: pregnant or not; day or night. When there are only two options then we can use a binary variable, which is considered either 0 or 1. If we have a column of character values that only has two values, such as: `c("Myles", "Ruth", "Ruth", "Myles", "Myles", "Ruth")`, then using this as an explanatory variable in the usual regression set-up would mean that it is treated as a binary variable. If there are more than two levels, then we can use a combination of binary variables, where some baseline outcome gets integrated into the intercept.

12.3.1 Simulated example: running times with rain and humidity

As an example, we add whether it was raining to our simulated relationship between marathon and five-kilometer run times. We then specify that if it was raining, the individual is ten minutes slower than they otherwise would have been.

```
slow_in_rain <- 10

sim_run_data <-
  sim_run_data |>
  mutate(was_raining = sample(
```

```
      c("Yes", "No"),
      size = num_observations,
      replace = TRUE,
      prob = c(0.2, 0.8)
    )) |>
    mutate(
      marathon_time = if_else(
        was_raining == "Yes",
        marathon_time + slow_in_rain,
        marathon_time
      )
    ) |>
    select(five_km_time, marathon_time, was_raining)
```

We can add additional explanatory variables to `lm()` with `+`. Again, we will include a variety of quick tests for class and the number of observations, and add another about missing values. We may not have any idea what the coefficient of rain should be, but if we did not expect it to make them faster, then we could also add a test of that with a wide interval of non-negative values.

```
stopifnot(
  class(sim_run_data$marathon_time) == "numeric",
  class(sim_run_data$five_km_time) == "numeric",
  class(sim_run_data$was_raining) == "character",
  all(complete.cases(sim_run_data)),
  nrow(sim_run_data) == 200
)

sim_run_data_rain_model <-
  lm(
    marathon_time ~ five_km_time + was_raining,
    data = sim_run_data
  )

stopifnot(
  between(sim_run_data_rain_model$coefficients[3], 0, 20)
  )

summary(sim_run_data_rain_model)
```

```
Call:
lm(formula = marathon_time ~ five_km_time + was_raining, data = sim_run_data)

Residuals:
    Min      1Q  Median      3Q     Max
-49.772 -11.236   0.484  11.352  46.028

Coefficients:
               Estimate Std. Error t value Pr(>|t|)
(Intercept)      5.0452     6.8025   0.742   0.4592
```

```
five_km_time      8.1992      0.3009  27.247   <2e-16 ***
was_rainingYes    7.6368      3.1449   2.428   0.0161 *
---
Signif. codes:  0 '***' 0.001 '**' 0.01 '*' 0.05 '.' 0.1 ' ' 1

Residual standard error: 17.44 on 197 degrees of freedom
Multiple R-squared:  0.791, Adjusted R-squared:  0.7888
F-statistic: 372.7 on 2 and 197 DF,  p-value: < 2.2e-16
```

The result, in the second column of Table 12.3, shows that when we compare individuals in our dataset who ran in the rain with those who did not, the ones in the rain tended to have a slower time. And this corresponds with what we expect if we look at a plot of the data (Figure 12.4a).

We have included two types of tests here. The ones run before `lm()` check inputs, and the ones run after `lm()` check outputs. We may notice that some of the input checks are the same as earlier. One way to avoid having to rewrite tests many times would be to install and load `testthat` to create a suite of tests of class in say an R file called "class_tests.R", which are then called using `test_file()`.

For instance, we could save the following as "test_class.R" in a dedicated tests folder.

```
test_that("Check class", {
  expect_type(sim_run_data$marathon_time, "double")
  expect_type(sim_run_data$five_km_time, "double")
  expect_type(sim_run_data$was_raining, "character")
})
```

We could save the following as "test_observations.R"

```
test_that("Check number of observations is correct", {
  expect_equal(nrow(sim_run_data), 200)
})

test_that("Check complete", {
  expect_true(all(complete.cases(sim_run_data)))
})
```

And finally, we could save the following as "test_coefficient_estimates.R".

```
test_that("Check coefficients", {
  expect_gt(sim_run_data_rain_model$coefficients[3], 0)
  expect_lt(sim_run_data_rain_model$coefficients[3], 20)
})
```

We could then change the regression code to call these test files rather than write them all out.

```
test_file("tests/test_observations.R")
test_file("tests/test_class.R")
```

```
sim_run_data_rain_model <-
  lm(
    marathon_time ~ five_km_time + was_raining,
    data = sim_run_data
  )

test_file("tests/test_coefficient_estimates.R")
```

It is important to be clear about what we are looking for in the checks of the coefficients. When we simulate data, we put in place reasonable guesses for what the data could look like, and it is similarly reasonable guesses that we test. A failing test is not necessarily a reason to go back and change things, but instead a reminder to look at what is going on in both, and potentially update the test if necessary.

In addition to wanting to include additional explanatory variables, we may think that they are related to each another. For instance, maybe rain really matters if it is also humid that day. We are interested in the humidity and temperature, but also how those two variables interact (Figure 12.4b). We can do this by using `*` instead of `+` when we specify the model. When we interact variables in this way, then we almost always need to include the individual variables as well and `lm()` will do this by default. The result is contained in the third column of Table 12.3.

```
slow_in_humidity <- 15

sim_run_data <- sim_run_data |>
  mutate(
    humidity = sample(c("High", "Low"), size = num_observations,
                      replace = TRUE, prob = c(0.2, 0.8)),
    marathon_time =
      marathon_time + if_else(humidity == "High", slow_in_humidity, 0),
    weather_conditions = case_when(
      was_raining == "No" & humidity == "Low" ~ "No rain, not humid",
      was_raining == "Yes" & humidity == "Low" ~ "Rain, not humid",
      was_raining == "No" & humidity == "High" ~ "No rain, humid",
      was_raining == "Yes" & humidity == "High" ~ "Rain, humid"
    )
  )


base <-
  sim_run_data |>
  ggplot(aes(x = five_km_time, y = marathon_time)) +
  labs(
    x = "Five-kilometer time (minutes)",
    y = "Marathon time (minutes)"
  ) +
  theme_classic() +
  scale_color_brewer(palette = "Set1") +
  theme(legend.position = "bottom")
```

```
base +
  geom_point(aes(color = was_raining)) +
  geom_smooth(
    aes(color = was_raining),
    method = "lm",
    alpha = 0.3,
    linetype = "dashed",
    formula = "y ~ x"
  ) +
  labs(color = "Was raining")

base +
  geom_point(aes(color = weather_conditions)) +
  geom_smooth(
    aes(color = weather_conditions),
    method = "lm",
    alpha = 0.3,
    linetype = "dashed",
    formula = "y ~ x"
  ) +
  labs(color = "Conditions")


sim_run_data_rain_and_humidity_model <-
  lm(
    marathon_time ~ five_km_time + was_raining * humidity,
    data = sim_run_data
  )

modelsummary(
  list(
    "Five km only" = sim_run_data_first_model,
    "Add rain" = sim_run_data_rain_model,
    "Add humidity" = sim_run_data_rain_and_humidity_model
  ),
  fmt = 2
)
```

There are a variety of threats to the validity of linear regression estimates, and aspects to think about, particularly when using an unfamiliar dataset. We need to address these when we use it, and usually graphs and associated text are sufficient to assuage most of them. Aspects of concern include:

1. Linearity of explanatory variables. We are concerned with whether the predictors enter in a linear way. We can usually be convinced there is enough linearity in our explanatory variables for our purposes by using graphs of the variables.
2. Homoscedasticity of errors. We are concerned that the errors are not becoming systematically larger or smaller throughout the sample. If that is happening, then we term it heteroscedasticity. Again, graphs of errors, such as Figure 12.3b, are used to convince us of this.

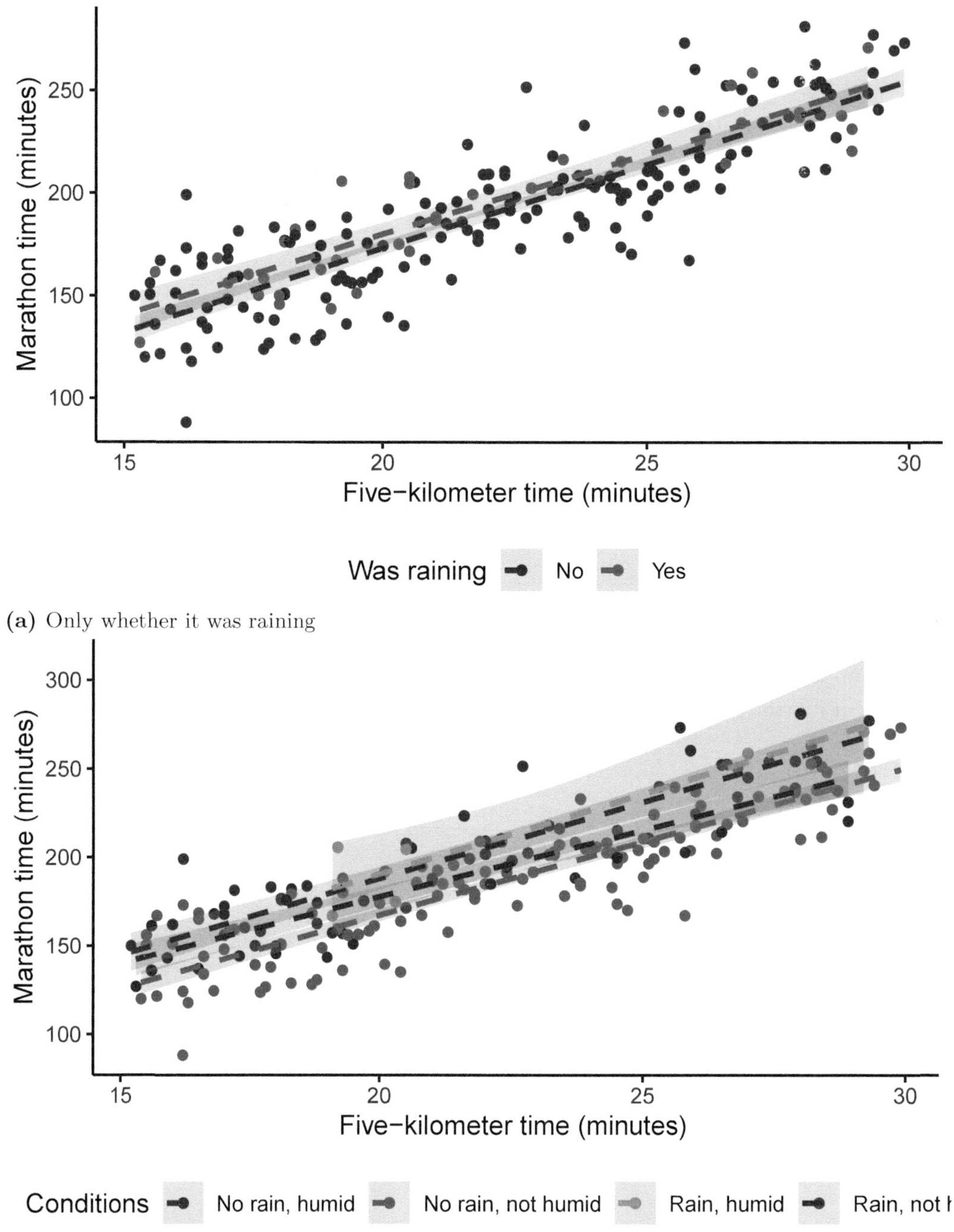

(a) Only whether it was raining

(b) Whether it was raining and the level of humidity

Figure 12.4: Simple linear regression with simulated data on the time someone takes to run five kilometers and a marathon, depending on the weather

Table 12.3: Explaining marathon times based on five-kilometer run times and weather features

	Five km only	Add rain	Add humidity
(Intercept)	4.47	5.05	23.54
	(6.75)	(6.80)	(7.00)
five_km_time	8.20	8.20	8.25
	(0.30)	(0.30)	(0.30)
was_rainingYes		7.64	3.94
		(3.14)	(7.60)
humidityLow			−21.14
			(3.15)
was_rainingYes × humidityLow			5.10
			(8.35)
Num.Obs.	200	200	200
R2	0.790	0.791	0.800
R2 Adj.	0.789	0.789	0.796
AIC	1714.7	1716.1	1716.2
BIC	1724.6	1729.3	1736.0
Log.Lik.	−854.341	−854.055	−852.113
F	745.549	372.701	195.296
RMSE	17.34	17.31	17.14

3. Independence of errors. We are concerned that the errors are not correlated with each other. For instance, if we are interested in weather-related measurement such as average daily temperature, then we may find a pattern because the temperature on one day is likely similar to the temperature on another. We can be convinced that we have satisfied this condition by looking at the residuals compared with observed values, such as Figure 12.3c, or estimates compared with actual outcomes, such as Figure 12.3d.
4. Outliers and other high-impact observations. Finally, we might be worried that our results are being driven by a handful of observations. For instance, thinking back to Chapter 5 and Anscombe's Quartet, we notice that linear regression estimates would be heavily influenced by the inclusion of one or two particular points. We can become comfortable with this by considering our analysis on various subsets. For instance, randomly removing some observation in the way we did to the US states in Chapter 11.

Those aspects are statistical concerns and relate to whether the model is working. The most important threat to validity and hence the aspect that must be addressed at some length, is whether this model is directly relevant to the research question of interest.

Shoulders of giants

Dr Daniela Witten is the Dorothy Gilford Endowed Chair of Mathematical Statistics and Professor of Statistics & Biostatistics at the University of Washington. After taking a PhD in Statistics from Stanford University in 2010, she joined the University of Washington as an assistant professor. She was promoted to full professor in 2018. One active area of her research is double-dipping which is focused on the effect of sample splitting (L. Gao, Bien, and Witten 2022). She is an author of the influential *Introduction to Statistical Learning* (James et al. [2013] 2021). Witten was appointed a Fellow of the American Statistical Association in 2020 and awarded the COPSS Presidents' Award in 2022.

12.4 Building models

Breiman (2001) describes two cultures of statistical modeling: one focused on inference and the other on prediction. In general, around the time Breiman (2001) was published, various disciplines tended to focus on either inference or prediction. For instance, Jordan (2004) describes how statistics and computer science had been separate for some time, but how the goals of each field were becoming more closely aligned. The rise of data science, and in particular machine learning has meant there is now a need to be comfortable with both (A. Neufeld and Witten 2021). The two cultures are being brought closer together, and there is an overlap and interaction between prediction and inference. But their separate evolution means there are still considerable cultural differences. As a small example of this, the term "machine learning" tends to be used in computer science, while the term "statistical learning" tends to be used in statistics, even though they usually refer to the same machinery.

In this book we will focus on inference using the probabilistic programming language Stan to fit models in a Bayesian framework, and interface with it using `rstanarm`. Inference and forecasting have different cultures, ecosystems, and priorities. You should try to develop a comfort in both. One way these different cultures manifest is in language choice. The primary language in this book is R, and for the sake of consistency we focus on that here. But there is an extensive culture, especially but not exclusively focused on prediction, that uses Python. We recommend focusing on only one language and approach initially, but after developing that initial familiarity it is important to become multilingual. We introduce prediction based on Python in the "Prediction" Online Appendix[4].

We will again not go into the details, but running a regression in a Bayesian setting is similar to the frequentist approach that underpins `lm()`. The main difference from a regression point of view, is that the parameters involved in the models (i.e. β_0, β_1, etc) are considered random variables, and so themselves have associated probability distributions. In contrast, the frequentist paradigm assumes that any randomness from these coefficients comes from a parametric assumption on the distribution of the error term, ϵ.

Before we run a regression in a Bayesian framework, we need to decide on a starting probability distribution for each of these parameters, which we call a "prior". While the presence of priors adds some additional complication, it has several advantages, and we will discuss the issue of priors in more detail below. This is another reason for the workflow advocated

[4]https://tellingstorieswithdata.com/27-prediction.html

in this book: the simulation stage leads directly to priors. We will again specify the model that we are interested in, but this time we include priors.

$$
\begin{aligned}
y_i|\mu_i, \sigma &\sim \text{Normal}(\mu_i, \sigma) \\
\mu_i &= \beta_0 + \beta_1 x_i \\
\beta_0 &\sim \text{Normal}(0, 2.5) \\
\beta_1 &\sim \text{Normal}(0, 2.5) \\
\sigma &\sim \text{Exponential}(1)
\end{aligned}
$$

We combine information from the data with the priors to obtain posterior distributions for our parameters. Inference is then carried out based on analyzing posterior distributions.

Another aspect that is different between Bayesian approaches and the way we have been doing modeling to this point, is that Bayesian models will usually take longer to run. Because of this, it can be useful to run the model in a separate R script and then save it with `saveRDS()`. With sensible Quarto chunk options for "eval" and "echo" (see Chapter 3), the model can then be read into the Quarto document with `readRDS()` rather than being run every time the paper is compiled. In this way, the model delay is only imposed once for a given model. It can also be useful to add `beep()` from `beepr` to the end of the model, to get an audio notification when the model is done.

```
sim_run_data_first_model_rstanarm <-
  stan_glm(
    formula = marathon_time ~ five_km_time + was_raining,
    data = sim_run_data,
    family = gaussian(),
    prior = normal(location = 0, scale = 2.5),
    prior_intercept = normal(location = 0, scale = 2.5),
    prior_aux = exponential(rate = 1),
    seed = 853
  )

beep()

saveRDS(
  sim_run_data_first_model_rstanarm,
  file = "sim_run_data_first_model_rstanarm.rds"
)
```

```
sim_run_data_first_model_rstanarm <-
  readRDS(file = "sim_run_data_first_model_rstanarm.rds")
```

We use `stan_glm()` with the "gaussian()" family to specify multiple linear regression and the model formula is written in the same way as base R and 'rstanarm". We have explicitly added the default priors, as we see this as good practice, although strictly this is not necessary.

The estimation results, which are in the first column of Table 12.4, are not quite what we expect. For instance, the rate of increase in marathon times is estimated to be around three minutes per minute of increase in five-kilometer time, which seems low given the ratio of a five-kilometer run to marathon distance.

The issue of picking priors is a challenging one and the subject of extensive research. For the purposes of this book, using the rstanarm defaults is fine. But even if they are just the default, priors should be explicitly specified in the model and included in the function. This is to make it clear to others what has been done. We could use default_prior_intercept() and default_prior_coef() to find the default priors in rstanarm and then explicitly include them in the model.

It is normal to find it difficult to know what prior to specify. Getting started by adapting someone else's rstanarm code is perfectly fine. If they have not specified their priors, then we can use the helper function prior_summary(), to find out which priors were used.

```
prior_summary(sim_run_data_first_model_rstanarm)
```

```
Priors for model 'sim_run_data_first_model_rstanarm'
------
Intercept (after predictors centered)
 ~ normal(location = 0, scale = 2.5)

Coefficients
 ~ normal(location = [0,0], scale = [2.5,2.5])

Auxiliary (sigma)
 ~ exponential(rate = 1)
------
See help('prior_summary.stanreg') for more details
```

We are interested in understanding what the priors imply before we involve any data. We do this by implementing prior predictive checks. This means simulating from the priors to look at what the model implies about the possible magnitude and direction of the relationships between the explanatory and outcome variables. This process is no different to all the other simulation that we have done to this point.

```
draws <- 1000

priors <-
  tibble(
    sigma = rep(rexp(n = draws, rate = 1), times = 16),
    beta_0 = rep(rnorm(n = draws, mean = 0, sd = 2.5), times = 16),
    beta_1 = rep(rnorm(n = draws, mean = 0, sd = 2.5), times = 16),
    five_km_time = rep(15:30, each = draws),
    mu = beta_0 + beta_1 * five_km_time
  ) |>
  rowwise() |>
  mutate(
    marathon_time = rnorm(n = 1, mean = mu, sd = sigma)
  )

priors |>
  ggplot(aes(x = marathon_time)) +
  geom_histogram(binwidth = 10) +
```

```
  theme_classic()

priors |>
  ggplot(aes(x = five_km_time, y = marathon_time)) +
  geom_point(alpha = 0.1) +
  theme_classic()
```

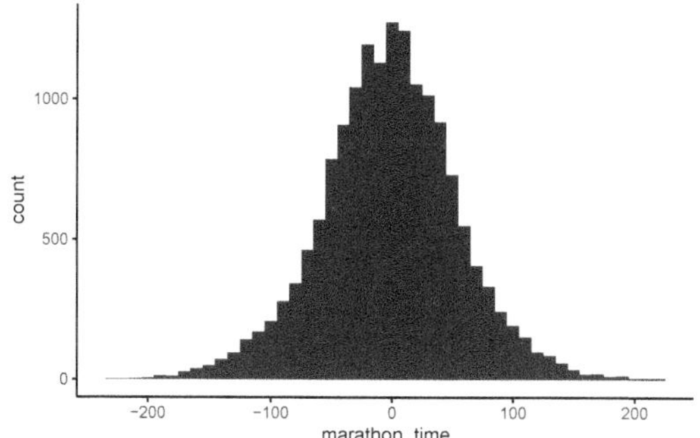

(a) Distribution of implied marathon times

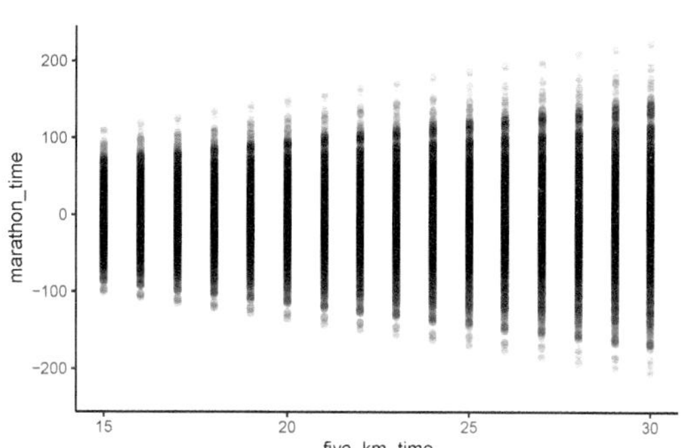

(b) Relationship between 5km and marathon times

Figure 12.5: Some implications from the priors that were used

Figure 12.5 suggests our model has been poorly constructed. Not only are there world record marathon times, but there are also negative marathon times! One issue is that our prior for β_1 does not take in all the information that we know. We know that a marathon is about eight times longer than a five-kilometer run and so we could center the prior for β_1 around that. Our re-specified model is:

$$
\begin{aligned}
y_i|\mu_i, \sigma &\sim \text{Normal}(\mu_i, \sigma) \\
\mu_i &= \beta_0 + \beta_1 x_i \\
\beta_0 &\sim \text{Normal}(0, 2.5) \\
\beta_1 &\sim \text{Normal}(8, 2.5) \\
\sigma &\sim \text{Exponential}(1)
\end{aligned}
$$

And we can see from prior prediction checks that it seems more reasonable (Figure 12.6).

```
draws <- 1000

updated_priors <-
  tibble(
    sigma = rep(rexp(n = draws, rate = 1), times = 16),
    beta_0 = rep(rnorm(n = draws, mean = 0, sd = 2.5), times = 16),
    beta_1 = rep(rnorm(n = draws, mean = 8, sd = 2.5), times = 16),
    five_km_time = rep(15:30, each = draws),
    mu = beta_0 + beta_1 * five_km_time
  ) |>
  rowwise() |>
  mutate(
    marathon_time = rnorm(n = 1, mean = mu, sd = sigma)
```

```
)
```

```
updated_priors |>
  ggplot(aes(x = marathon_time)) +
  geom_histogram(binwidth = 10) +
  theme_classic()

updated_priors |>
  ggplot(aes(x = five_km_time, y = marathon_time)) +
  geom_point(alpha = 0.1) +
  theme_classic()
```

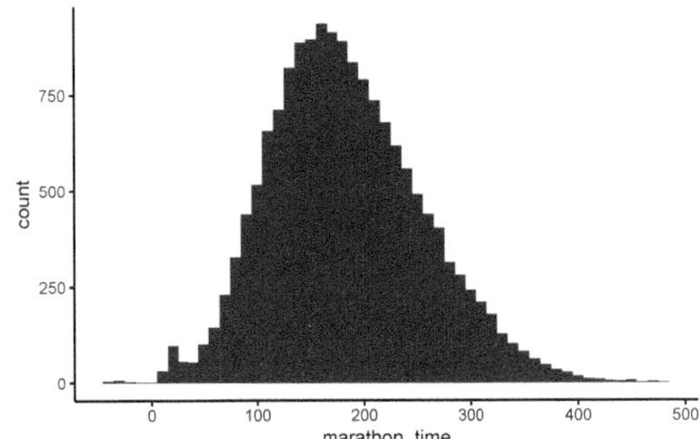

(a) Distribution of implied marathon times

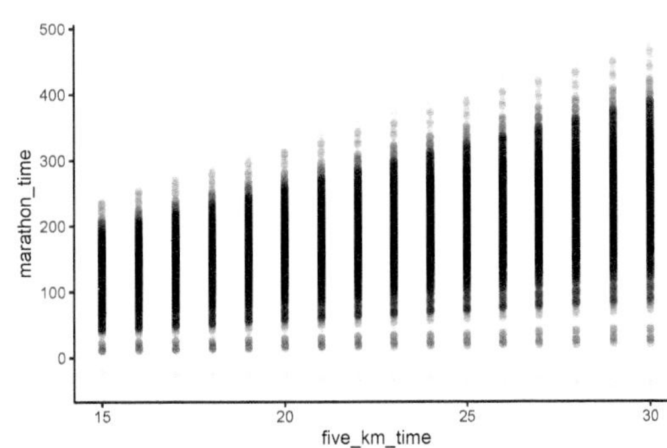

(b) Relationship between 5km and marathon times

Figure 12.6: Updated priors

If we were not sure what to do then `rstanarm` could help to improve the specified priors, by scaling them based on the data. Specify the prior that you think is reasonable, even if this is just the default, and include it in the function, but also include "autoscale = TRUE", and `rstanarm` will adjust the scale. When we re-run our model with these updated priors and allowing auto-scaling we get much better results, which are in the second column of Table 12.4. You can then add those to the written-out model instead.

```
sim_run_data_second_model_rstanarm <-
  stan_glm(
    formula = marathon_time ~ five_km_time + was_raining,
    data = sim_run_data,
    family = gaussian(),
    prior = normal(location = 8, scale = 2.5, autoscale = TRUE),
    prior_intercept = normal(0, 2.5, autoscale = TRUE),
    prior_aux = exponential(rate = 1, autoscale = TRUE),
    seed = 853
  )

saveRDS(
  sim_run_data_second_model_rstanarm,
  file = "sim_run_data_second_model_rstanarm.rds"
```

Table 12.4: Forecasting and explanatory models of marathon times based on five-kilometer run times

	Non-scaled priors	Auto-scaling priors
(Intercept)	−67.50	8.66
five_km_time	3.47	7.90
was_rainingYes	0.12	9.23
Num.Obs.	100	100
R2	0.015	0.797
R2 Adj.	−1.000	0.790
Log.Lik.	−678.336	−425.193
ELPD	−679.5	−429.0
ELPD s.e.	3.3	8.9
LOOIC	1359.0	858.0
LOOIC s.e.	6.6	17.8
WAIC	1359.0	857.9
RMSE	175.52	16.85

```
)
```

```
modelsummary(
  list(
    "Non-scaled priors" = sim_run_data_first_model_rstanarm,
    "Auto-scaling priors" = sim_run_data_second_model_rstanarm
  ),
  fmt = 2
)
```

As we used the "autoscale = TRUE" option, it can be helpful to look at how the priors were updated with `prior_summary()` from `rstanarm`.

```
prior_summary(sim_run_data_second_model_rstanarm)
```

```
Priors for model 'sim_run_data_second_model_rstanarm'
------
Intercept (after predictors centered)
  Specified prior:
    ~ normal(location = 0, scale = 2.5)
  Adjusted prior:
    ~ normal(location = 0, scale = 95)

Coefficients
  Specified prior:
    ~ normal(location = [8,8], scale = [2.5,2.5])
  Adjusted prior:
    ~ normal(location = [8,8], scale = [ 22.64,245.52])
```

```
Auxiliary (sigma)
  Specified prior:
    ~ exponential(rate = 1)
  Adjusted prior:
    ~ exponential(rate = 0.026)
------
See help('prior_summary.stanreg') for more details
```

Having built a Bayesian model, we may want to look at what it implies (Figure 12.7). One way to do this is to consider the posterior distribution.

One way to use the posterior distribution is to consider whether the model is doing a good job of fitting the data. The idea is that if the model is doing a good job of fitting the data, then the posterior should be able to be used to simulate data that are like the actual data (Gelman et al. 2020). We can implement a posterior predictive check with `pp_check()` from `rstanarm` (Figure 12.7a). This compares the actual outcome variable with simulations from the posterior distribution. And we can compare the posterior with the prior with `posterior_vs_prior()` to see how much the estimates change once data are taken into account (Figure 12.7b). Helpfully, `pp_check()` and `posterior_vs_prior()` return `ggplot2` objects so we can modify the look of them in the normal way we manipulate graphs. These checks and discussion would typically just be briefly mentioned in the main content of a paper, with the detail and graphs added to a dedicated appendix.

```
pp_check(sim_run_data_second_model_rstanarm) +
  theme_classic() +
  theme(legend.position = "bottom")

posterior_vs_prior(sim_run_data_second_model_rstanarm) +
  theme_minimal() +
  scale_color_brewer(palette = "Set1") +
  theme(legend.position = "bottom") +
  coord_flip()
```

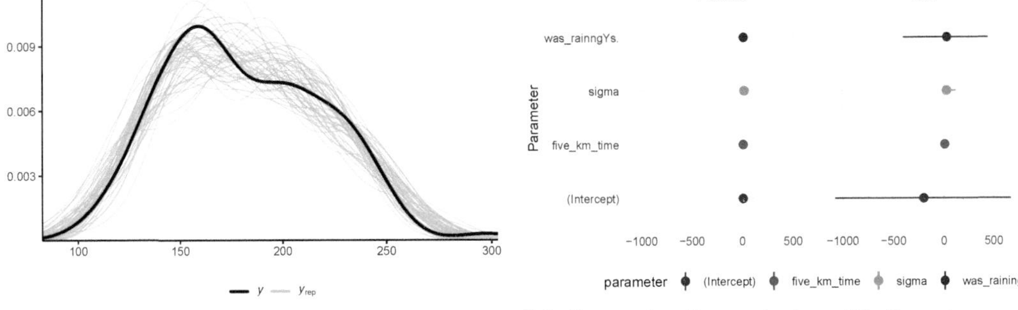

(a) Posterior prediction check

(b) Comparing the posterior with the prior

Figure 12.7: Examining how the model fits, and is affected by, the data

With a simple model like this, the differences between the prediction and inference approaches are minimal. But as model or data complexity increases these differences can become important.

We have already discussed confidence intervals and the Bayesian equivalent to a confidence interval is called a "credibility interval", and reflects two points where there is a certain probability mass between them, in this case 95 per cent. Bayesian estimation provides a distribution for each coefficient. This means there is an infinite number of points that we could use to generate this interval. The entire distribution should be shown graphically (Figure 12.8). This might be using a cross-referenced appendix.

```
plot(
  sim_run_data_second_model_rstanarm,
  "areas"
)
```

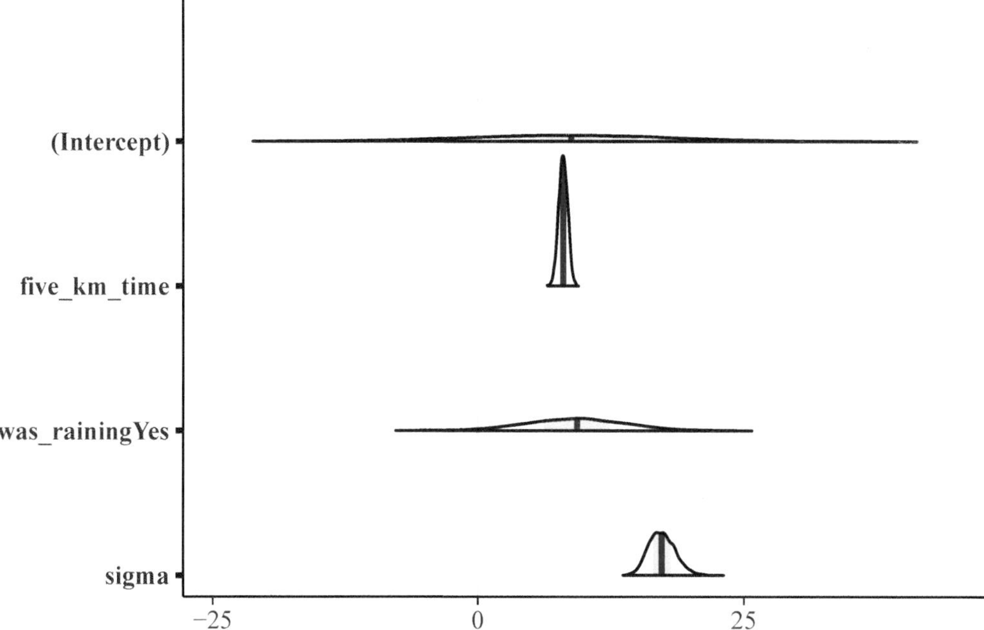

Figure 12.8: Credible intervals

The final aspect that we would like to check is a practical matter. `rstanarm` uses a sampling algorithm called Markov chain Monte Carlo (MCMC) to obtain samples from the posterior distributions of interest. We need to quickly check for the existence of signs that the algorithm ran into issues. We consider a trace plot, such as Figure 12.9a, and a Rhat plot, such as Figure 12.9b. These would typically go in a cross-referenced appendix.

```
plot(sim_run_data_second_model_rstanarm, "trace")
```

```
plot(sim_run_data_second_model_rstanarm, "rhat")
```

In the trace plot, we are looking for lines that appear to bounce around, but are horizontal, and have a nice overlap between the chains. The trace plot in Figure 12.9a does not suggest anything out of the ordinary. Similarly, with the Rhat plot, we are looking for everything to be close to 1, and ideally no more than 1.1. Again Figure 12.9b is an example that does

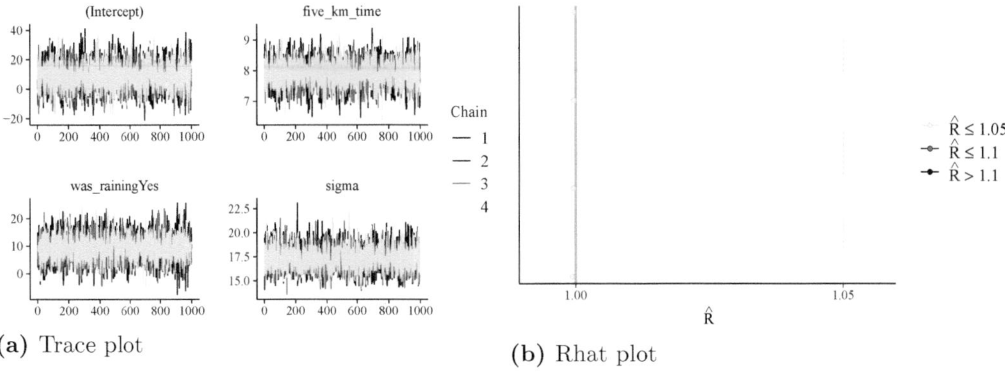

(a) Trace plot

(b) Rhat plot

Figure 12.9: Checking the convergence of the MCMC algorithm

not suggest any problems. If these diagnostics are not like this, then simplify the model by removing or modifying predictors, change the priors, and re-run it.

12.5 Concluding remarks

In this chapter we have considered linear models. We established a foundation for analysis, and described some essential approaches. We have also skimmed over a lot. This chapter and the next should be considered together. These provide you with enough to get started, but for doing more than that, going through the modeling books recommended in Chapter 17.

12.6 Exercises

Scales

1. *(Plan)* Consider the following scenario: *A person is interested in the heights of all the buildings in London. They walk around the city counting the number of floors for each building, and noting the year of construction.* Please sketch what that dataset could look like and then sketch a graph that you could build to show all observations.
2. *(Simulate)* Please further consider the scenario described and simulate the situation, along with three predictors that are associated the count of the number of levels. Please include at least ten tests based on the simulated data. Submit a link to a GitHub Gist that contains your code.
3. *(Acquire)* Please describe one possible source of such a dataset.
4. *(Explore)* Please use `ggplot2` to build the graph that you sketched. Then use `rstanarm` to build a model with number of floors as an outcome and the year of construction as a predictor. Submit a link to a GitHub Gist that contains your code.
5. *(Communicate)* Please write two paragraphs about what you did.

Questions

1. Please simulate the situation in which there are two predictors, "race" and "gender", and one outcome variable, "vote_preference", which is imperfectly related to them. Submit a link to a GitHub Gist that contains your code.
2. Please write a linear relationship between some outcome variable, Y, and some predictor, X. What is the intercept term? What is the slope term? What would adding a hat to these indicate?
3. Which of the following are examples of linear models (select all that apply)?
   a. `lm(y ~ x_1 + x_2 + x_3, data = my_data)`
   b. `lm(y ~ x_1 + x_2^2 + x_3, data = my_data)`
   c. `lm(y ~ x_1 * x_2 + x_3, data = my_data)`
   d. `lm(y ~ x_1 + x_1^2 + x_2 + x_3, data = my_data)`
4. What is the least squares criterion? Similarly, what is RSS and what are we trying to do when we run least squares regression?
5. What is bias (in a statistical context)?
6. Consider five variables: earth, fire, wind, water, and heart. Please simulate a scenario where heart depends on the other four, which are independent of each other. Then please write R code that would fit a linear regression model to explain heart as a function of the other variables. Submit a link to a GitHub Gist that contains your code.
7. According to Greenland et al. (2016), p-values test (pick one):
   a. All the assumptions about how the data were generated (the entire model), not just the targeted hypothesis it is supposed to test (such as a null hypothesis).
   b. Whether the hypothesis targeted for testing is true or not.
   c. A dichotomy whereby results can be declared "statistically significant".
8. According to Greenland et al. (2016), a p-value may be small because (select all that apply):
   a. The targeted hypothesis is false.
   b. The study protocols were violated.
   c. It was selected for presentation based on its small size.
9. Please explain what a p-value is, using only the term itself (i.e. "p-value") and words that are amongst the 1,000 most common in the English language according to the XKCD Simple Writer[5]. (Please write one or two paragraphs.)
10. What is power (in a statistical context)?
11. Look at the list of people awarded the COPSS Presidents' Award[6] or the Guy Medal in Gold[7] and write a short biography of them in the style of the "Shoulders of giants" entries in this book.
12. Discuss, with the help of examples and citations, the quote from McElreath ([2015] 2020, 162) included toward the start of this chapter. Write at least three paragraphs.

Tutorial

Allow that the true data generating process is a Normal distribution with mean of one, and standard deviation of 1. We obtain a sample of 1,000 observations using some instrument. Simulate the following situation:

[5] https://xkcd.com/simplewriter/
[6] https://en.wikipedia.org/wiki/COPSS_Presidents%27_Award
[7] https://en.wikipedia.org/wiki/Guy_Medal

1) Unknown to us, the instrument has a mistake in it, which means that it has a maximum memory of 900 observations, and begins over-writing at that point, so the final 100 observations are actually a repeat of the first 100.
2) We employ a research assistant to clean and prepare the dataset. During the process of doing this, unknown to us, they accidentally change half of the negative draws to be positive.
3) They additionally, accidentally, change the decimal place on any value between 1 and 1.1, so that, for instance 1 becomes 0.1, and 1.1 would become 0.11.
4) You finally get the cleaned dataset and are interested in understanding whether the mean of the true data generating process is greater than 0.

Write at least two pages about what you did and what you found. Also discuss what effect the issues had, and what steps you can put in place to ensure actual analysis has a chance to flag some of these issues.

Use Quarto, and include an appropriate title, author, date, link to a GitHub repo, and citations to produce a draft. Following this, please pair with another student and exchange your written work. Update it based on their feedback, and be sure to acknowledge them by name in your paper. Submit a PDF.

Paper

At about this point the *Murrumbidgee* Paper in the "Papers" Online Appendix[8] would be appropriate.

[8]https://tellingstorieswithdata.com/23-assessment.html

13

Generalized linear models

Prerequisites

- Read *Regression and Other Stories*, (Gelman, Hill, and Vehtari 2020)
  - Focus on Chapters 13 "Logistic regression" and 15 "Other generalized linear models", which provide a detailed guide to generalized linear models.
- Read *An Introduction to Statistical Learning with Applications in R*, (James et al. [2013] 2021)
  - Focus on Chapter 4 "Classification", which is a complementary treatment of generalized linear models from a different perspective.
- Read *We Gave Four Good Pollsters the Same Raw Data. They Had Four Different Results*, (N. Cohn 2016)
  - Details a situation in which different modeling choices, given the same dataset, result in different forecasts.

Key concepts and skills

- Linear regression can be generalized for alternative types of outcome variables.
- Logistic regression can be used when we have a binary outcome variable.
- Poisson regression can be used when we have an integer count outcome variable. A variant—negative binomial regression—is often also considered because the assumptions are less onerous.
- Multilevel modeling is an approach that can allow us to make better use of our data.

Software and packages

- Base R (R Core Team 2023)
- `boot` (Canty and Ripley 2021; Davison and Hinkley 1997)
- `broom.mixed` (Bolker and Robinson 2022)
- `collapse` (Krantz 2023)
- `dataverse` (Kuriwaki, Beasley, and Leeper 2023)
- `gutenbergr` (Johnston and Robinson 2022)
- `janitor` (Firke 2023)
- `knitr` (Xie 2023)
- `marginaleffects` (Arel-Bundock 2023)
- `modelsummary` (Arel-Bundock 2022)
- `rstanarm` (Goodrich et al. 2023)
- `tidybayes` (Kay 2022)
- `tidyverse` (Wickham et al. 2019)

```
library(boot)
library(broom.mixed)
library(collapse)
```

```
library(dataverse)
library(gutenbergr)
library(janitor)
library(knitr)
library(marginaleffects)
library(modelsummary)
library(rstanarm)
library(tidybayes)
library(tidyverse)
```

13.1 Introduction

Linear models, covered in Chapter 12, have evolved substantially over the past century. Francis Galton, mentioned in Chapter 8, and others of his generation used linear regression in earnest in the late 1800s and early 1900s. Binary outcomes quickly became of interest and needed special treatment, leading to the development and wide adaption of logistic regression and similar methods in the mid-1900s (Cramer 2003). The generalized linear model framework came into being, in a formal sense, in the 1970s with Nelder and Wedderburn (1972). Generalized linear models (GLMs) broaden the types of outcomes that are allowed. We still model outcomes as a linear function, but we are less constrained. The outcome can be anything in the exponential family, and popular choices include the logistic distribution and the Poisson distribution. For the sake of a completed story but turning to approaches that are beyond the scope of this book, a further generalization of GLMs is generalized additive models (GAMs) where we broaden the structure of the explanatory side. We still explain the outcome variable as an additive function of various bits and pieces, but those bits and pieces can be functions. This framework was proposed in the 1990s by Hastie and Tibshirani (1990).

In terms of generalized linear models, in this chapter we consider logistic, Poisson, and negative binomial regression. But we also explore a variant that is relevant to both linear models and generalized linear models: multilevel modeling. This is when we take advantage of some type of grouping that exists within our dataset.

13.2 Logistic regression

Linear regression is a useful way to better understand our data. But it assumes a continuous outcome variable that can take any number on the real line. We would like some way to use this same machinery when we cannot satisfy this condition. We turn to logistic and Poisson regression for binary and count outcome variables, respectively. They are still linear models, because the predictor variables enter in a linear fashion.

Logistic regression, and its close variants, are useful in a variety of settings, from elections (W. Wang et al. 2015) through to horse racing (Chellel 2018; Bolton and Chapman 1986). We use logistic regression when the outcome variable is a binary outcome, such as 0 or 1, or "yes" or "no". Although the presence of a binary outcome variable may sound limiting, there are a lot of circumstances in which the outcome either naturally falls into this situation or can be adjusted into it. For instance, win or lose, available or not available, support or not.

The foundation of this is the Bernoulli distribution. There is a certain probability, p, of outcome "1" and the remainder, $1-p$, for outcome "0". We can use `rbinom()` with one trial ("size $=1$") to simulate data from the Bernoulli distribution.

```
set.seed(853)

bernoulli_example <-
  tibble(draws = rbinom(n = 20, size = 1, prob = 0.1))

bernoulli_example |> pull(draws)
```

```
 [1] 0 0 0 0 0 0 0 0 0 1 0 0 0 0 0 0 0 0 0 0
```

One reason to use logistic regression is that we will be modeling a probability, hence it will be bounded between 0 and 1. With linear regression we may end up with values outside this. The foundation of logistic regression is the logit function:

$$\text{logit}(x) = \log\left(\frac{x}{1-x}\right).$$

This will transpose values between 0 and 1 onto the real line. For instance, `logit(0.1) = -2.2`, `logit(0.5) = 0`, and `logit(0.9) = 2.2` (Figure 13.1). We call this the "link function". It relates the distribution of interest in a generalized linear model to the machinery we use in linear models.

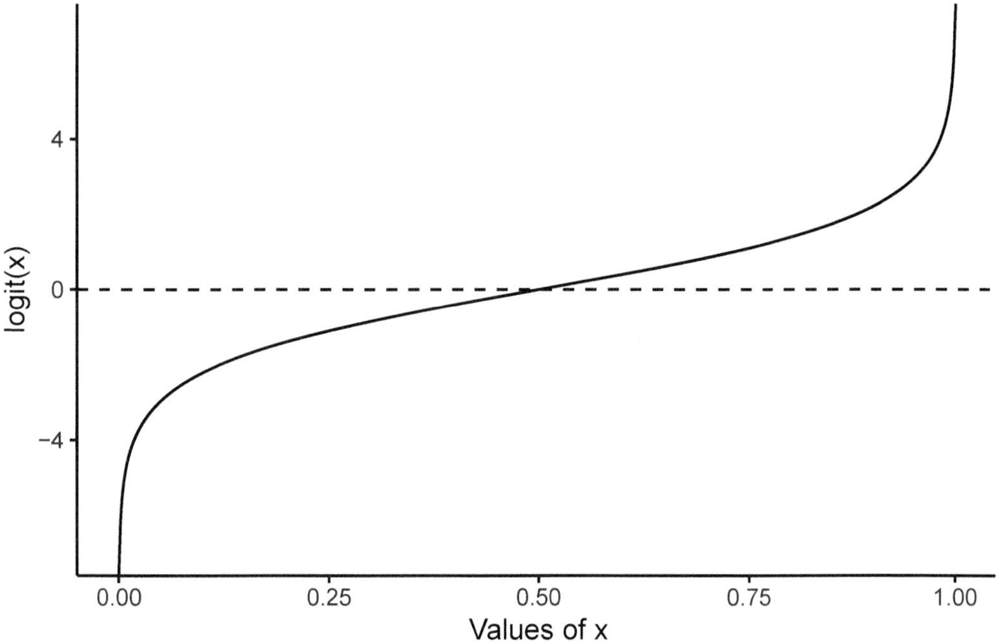

Figure 13.1: Example of the logit function for values between 0 and 1

13.2.1 Simulated example: day or night

To illustrate logistic regression, we will simulate data on whether it is a weekday or weekend, based on the number of cars on the road. We will assume that on weekdays the road is busier.

```
set.seed(853)

week_or_weekday <-
  tibble(
    num_cars = sample.int(n = 100, size = 1000, replace = TRUE),
    noise = rnorm(n = 1000, mean = 0, sd = 10),
    is_weekday = if_else(num_cars + noise > 50, 1, 0)
  ) |>
  select(-noise)

week_or_weekday
```

```
# A tibble: 1,000 x 2
   num_cars is_weekday
      <int>      <dbl>
 1        9          0
 2       64          1
 3       90          1
 4       93          1
 5       17          0
 6       29          0
 7       84          1
 8       83          1
 9        3          0
10       33          1
# i 990 more rows
```

We can use `glm()` from base R to do a quick estimation. In this case we will try to work out whether it is a weekday or weekend, based on the number of cars we can see. We are interested in estimating Equation 13.1:

$$\Pr(y_i = 1) = \text{logit}^{-1}(\beta_0 + \beta_1 x_i) \tag{13.1}$$

where y_i is whether it is a weekday and x_i is the number of cars on the road.

```
week_or_weekday_model <-
  glm(
    is_weekday ~ num_cars,
    data = week_or_weekday,
    family = "binomial"
  )

summary(week_or_weekday_model)
```

```
Call:
glm(formula = is_weekday ~ num_cars, family = "binomial", data = week_or_weekday)
```

```
Coefficients:
             Estimate Std. Error z value Pr(>|z|)
(Intercept) -9.48943    0.74492  -12.74   <2e-16 ***
num_cars     0.18980    0.01464   12.96   <2e-16 ***
---
Signif. codes:  0 '***' 0.001 '**' 0.01 '*' 0.05 '.' 0.1 ' ' 1

(Dispersion parameter for binomial family taken to be 1)

    Null deviance: 1386.26  on 999  degrees of freedom
Residual deviance:  337.91  on 998  degrees of freedom
AIC: 341.91

Number of Fisher Scoring iterations: 7
```

The estimated coefficient on the number of cars is 0.19. The interpretation of coefficients in logistic regression is more complicated than linear regression as they relate to changes in the log-odds of the binary outcome. For instance, the estimate of 0.19 is the average change in the log-odds of it being a weekday with observing one extra car on the road. The coefficient is positive which means an increase. As it is non-linear, if we want to specify a particular change, then this will be different for different baseline levels of the observation. That is, an increase of 0.19 log-odds has a larger impact when the baseline log-odds are 0, compared to 2.

We can translate our estimate into the probability of it being a weekday, for a given number of cars. We can add the implied probability that it is a weekday for each observation using `predictions()` from `marginaleffects`.

```
week_or_weekday_predictions <-
  predictions(week_or_weekday_model) |>
  as_tibble()

week_or_weekday_predictions
```

```
# A tibble: 1,000 x 7
   rowid estimate  p.value  conf.low conf.high is_weekday num_cars
   <int>    <dbl>    <dbl>     <dbl>     <dbl>      <dbl>    <int>
 1     1 0.000417 1.40e-36 0.000125   0.00139           0        9
 2     2 0.934    9.33e-27 0.898      0.959             1       64
 3     3 0.999    1.97e-36 0.998      1.00              1       90
 4     4 1.00     1.10e-36 0.999      1.00              1       93
 5     5 0.00190  1.22e-35 0.000711   0.00508           0       17
 6     6 0.0182   3.34e-32 0.00950    0.0348            0       29
 7     7 0.998    1.00e-35 0.996      0.999             1       84
 8     8 0.998    1.42e-35 0.995      0.999             1       83
 9     9 0.000134 5.22e-37 0.0000338  0.000529          0        3
10    10 0.0382   1.08e-29 0.0222     0.0649            1       33
# i 990 more rows
```

And we can then graph the probability that our model implies, for each observation, of it being a weekday (Figure 13.2). This is a nice opportunity to consider a few different ways of illustrating the fit. While it is common to use a scatterplot (Figure 13.2a), this is also an opportunity to use an ECDF (Figure 13.2b).

```
# Panel (a)
week_or_weekday_predictions |>
  mutate(is_weekday = factor(is_weekday)) |>
  ggplot(aes(x = num_cars, y = estimate, color = is_weekday)) +
  geom_jitter(width = 0.01, height = 0.01, alpha = 0.3) +
  labs(
    x = "Number of cars that were seen",
    y = "Estimated probability it is a weekday",
    color = "Was actually weekday"
  ) +
  theme_classic() +
  scale_color_brewer(palette = "Set1") +
  theme(legend.position = "bottom")

# Panel (b)
week_or_weekday_predictions |>
  mutate(is_weekday = factor(is_weekday)) |>
  ggplot(aes(x = num_cars, y = estimate, color = is_weekday)) +
  stat_ecdf(geom = "point", alpha = 0.75) +
  labs(
    x = "Number of cars that were seen",
    y = "Estimated probability it is a weekday",
    color = "Actually weekday"
  ) +
  theme_classic() +
  scale_color_brewer(palette = "Set1") +
  theme(legend.position = "bottom")
```

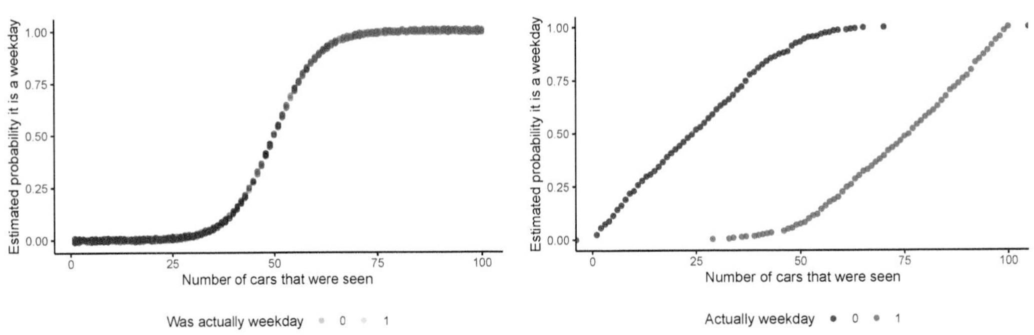

(a) Illustrating the fit with a scatterplot

(b) Illustrating the fit with an ECDF

Figure 13.2: Logistic regression probability results with simulated data of whether it is a weekday or weekend based on the number of cars that are around

The marginal effect at each observation is of interest because it provides a sense of how this probability is changing. It enables us to say that at the median (which in this case is if we were to see 50 cars) the probability of it being a weekday increases by almost five per cent if we were to see another car (Table 13.1).

Table 13.1: Marginal effect of another car on the probability that it is a weekday, at the median

Term	Estimate	Standard error
num_cars	0.047	0.004

```
slopes(week_or_weekday_model, newdata = "median") |>
  select(term, estimate, std.error) |>
  kable(
    col.names = c("Term", "Estimate", "Standard error"),
    digits = 3, booktabs = TRUE
  )
```

To more thoroughly examine the situation we might want to build a Bayesian model using `rstanarm`. As in Chapter 12 we will specify priors for our model, but these will just be the default priors that `rstanarm` uses:

$$
\begin{aligned}
y_i|\pi_i &\sim \text{Bern}(\pi_i) \\
\text{logit}(\pi_i) &= \beta_0 + \beta_1 x_i \\
\beta_0 &\sim \text{Normal}(0, 2.5) \\
\beta_1 &\sim \text{Normal}(0, 2.5)
\end{aligned}
$$

where y_i is whether it is a weekday (actually 0 or 1), x_i is the number of cars on the road, and π_i is the probability that observation i is a weekday.

```
week_or_weekday_rstanarm <-
  stan_glm(
    is_weekday ~ num_cars,
    data = week_or_weekday,
    family = binomial(link = "logit"),
    prior = normal(location = 0, scale = 2.5, autoscale = TRUE),
    prior_intercept = normal(location = 0, scale = 2.5, autoscale = TRUE),
    seed = 853
  )

saveRDS(
  week_or_weekday_rstanarm,
  file = "week_or_weekday_rstanarm.rds"
)
```

The results of our Bayesian model are similar to the quick model we built using base (Table 13.2).

```
modelsummary(
  list(
    "Day or night" = week_or_weekday_rstanarm
  )
)
```

Table 13.2: Explaining whether it is day or night, based on the number of cars on the road

	Day or night
(Intercept)	−9.464
number_of_cars	0.186
Num.Obs.	1000
R2	0.779
Log.Lik.	−177.899
ELPD	−179.8
ELPD s.e.	13.9
LOOIC	359.6
LOOIC s.e.	27.9
WAIC	359.6
RMSE	0.24

Table 13.2 makes it clear that each of the approaches is similar in this case. They agree on the direction of the effect of seeing an extra car on the probability of it being a weekday. Even the magnitude of the effect is estimated to be similar.

13.2.2 Political support in the United States

One area where logistic regression is often used is political polling. In many cases voting implies the need for one preference ranking, and so issues are reduced, whether appropriately or not, to "support" or "not support".

As a reminder, the workflow we advocate in this book is:

$$\text{Plan} \rightarrow \text{Simulate} \rightarrow \text{Acquire} \rightarrow \text{Explore} \rightarrow \text{Share}$$

While the focus here is the exploration of data using models, we still need to do the other aspects. We begin by planning. In this case, we are interested in US political support. In particular we are interested in whether we can forecast who a respondent is likely to vote for, based only on knowing their highest level of education and gender. That means we are interested in a dataset with variables for who an individual voted for, and some of their characteristics, such as gender and education. A quick sketch of such a dataset is Figure 13.3a. We would like our model to average over these points. A quick sketch is Figure 13.3b.

We will simulate a dataset where the chance that a person supports Biden depends on their gender and education.

```
set.seed(853)

num_obs <- 1000

us_political_preferences <- tibble(
  education = sample(0:4, size = num_obs, replace = TRUE),
  gender = sample(0:1, size = num_obs, replace = TRUE),
  support_prob = ((education + gender) / 5),
```

PERSON	VOTED	GENDER	EDUCATION
1	TRUMP	FEMALE	HS
2	BIDEN	MALE	COLLEGE
3	TRUMP	FEMALE	POST-GRAD
⋮	⋮	⋮	⋮

(a) Quick sketch of a dataset that could be used to examine US political support

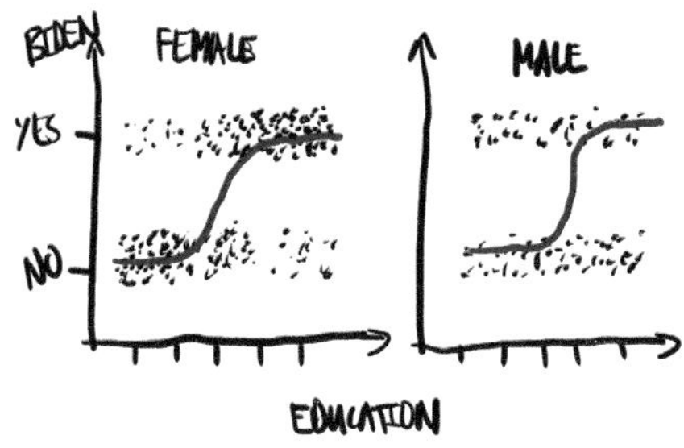

(b) Quick sketch of what we expect from the analysis before finalizing either the data or the analysis

Figure 13.3: Sketches of the expected dataset and analysis focus and clarify our thinking even if they will be updated later

```
) |>
  mutate(
    supports_biden = if_else(runif(n = num_obs) < support_prob, "yes", "no"),
    education = case_when(
      education == 0 ~ "< High school",
      education == 1 ~ "High school",
      education == 2 ~ "Some college",
      education == 3 ~ "College",
      education == 4 ~ "Post-grad"
    ),
    gender = if_else(gender == 0, "Male", "Female")
  ) |>
  select(-support_prob, supports_biden, gender, education)
```

For the actual data we can use the 2020 Cooperative Election Study (CES) (Schaffner, Ansolabehere, and Luks 2021). This is a long-standing annual survey of US political opinion. In 2020, there were 61,000 respondents who completed the post-election survey. The sampling methodology, detailed in Ansolabehere, Schaffner, and Luks (2021, 13), relies on matching and is an accepted approach that balances sampling concerns and cost.

We can access the CES using `get_dataframe_by_name()` after installing and loading `dataverse`. This approach was introduced in Chapter 7 and Chapter 10. We save the data that are of interest to us, and then refer to that saved dataset.

```
ces2020 <-
  get_dataframe_by_name(
    filename = "CES20_Common_OUTPUT_vv.csv",
    dataset = "10.7910/DVN/E9N6PH",
    server = "dataverse.harvard.edu",
    .f = read_csv
  ) |>
  select(votereg, CC20_410, gender, educ)
```

```
write_csv(ces2020, "ces2020.csv")
```

```
ces2020 <-
  read_csv(
    "ces2020.csv",
    col_types =
      cols(
        "votereg" = col_integer(),
        "CC20_410" = col_integer(),
        "gender" = col_integer(),
        "educ" = col_integer()
      )
  )

ces2020
```

```
# A tibble: 61,000 x 4
   votereg CC20_410 gender  educ
     <int>    <int>  <int> <int>
 1       1        2      1     4
 2       2       NA      2     6
 3       1        1      2     5
 4       1        1      2     5
 5       1        4      1     5
 6       1        2      1     3
 7       2       NA      1     3
 8       1        2      2     3
 9       1        2      2     2
10       1        1      2     5
# i 60,990 more rows
```

When we look at the actual data, there are concerns that we did not anticipate in our sketches. We use the codebook to investigate this more thoroughly. We only want respondents who are registered to vote, and we are only interested in those that voted for either Biden or Trump. We see that when the variable "CC20_410" is 1, then this means the respondent supported Biden, and when it is 2 that means Trump. We can filter to only those respondents and then add more informative labels. Genders of "female" and "male" is what is available from the CES, and when the variable "gender" is 1, then this means "male", and when it is 2 this means "females". Finally, the codebook tells us that "educ" is a variable from 1 to 6, in increasing levels of education.

```
ces2020 <-
  ces2020 |>
  filter(votereg == 1,
         CC20_410 %in% c(1, 2)) |>
  mutate(
    voted_for = if_else(CC20_410 == 1, "Biden", "Trump"),
    voted_for = as_factor(voted_for),
    gender = if_else(gender == 1, "Male", "Female"),
```

```
      education = case_when(
        educ == 1 ~ "No HS",
        educ == 2 ~ "High school graduate",
        educ == 3 ~ "Some college",
        educ == 4 ~ "2-year",
        educ == 5 ~ "4-year",
        educ == 6 ~ "Post-grad"
      ),
      education = factor(
        education,
        levels = c(
          "No HS",
          "High school graduate",
          "Some college",
          "2-year",
          "4-year",
          "Post-grad"
        )
      )
    ) |>
    select(voted_for, gender, education)
```

In the end we are left with 43,554 respondents (Figure 13.4).

```
ces2020 |>
  ggplot(aes(x = education, fill = voted_for)) +
  stat_count(position = "dodge") +
  facet_wrap(facets = vars(gender)) +
  theme_minimal() +
  labs(
    x = "Highest education",
    y = "Number of respondents",
    fill = "Voted for"
  ) +
  coord_flip() +
  scale_fill_brewer(palette = "Set1") +
  theme(legend.position = "bottom")
```

The model that we are interested in is:

$$
\begin{aligned}
y_i|\pi_i &\sim \text{Bern}(\pi_i) \\
\text{logit}(\pi_i) &= \beta_0 + \beta_1 \times \text{gender}_i + \beta_2 \times \text{education}_i \\
\beta_0 &\sim \text{Normal}(0, 2.5) \\
\beta_1 &\sim \text{Normal}(0, 2.5) \\
\beta_2 &\sim \text{Normal}(0, 2.5)
\end{aligned}
$$

where y_i is the political preference of the respondent and equal to 1 if Biden and 0 if Trump, gender_i is the gender of the respondent, and education_i is the education of the respondent. We could estimate the parameters using `stan_glm()`. Note that the model is a generally

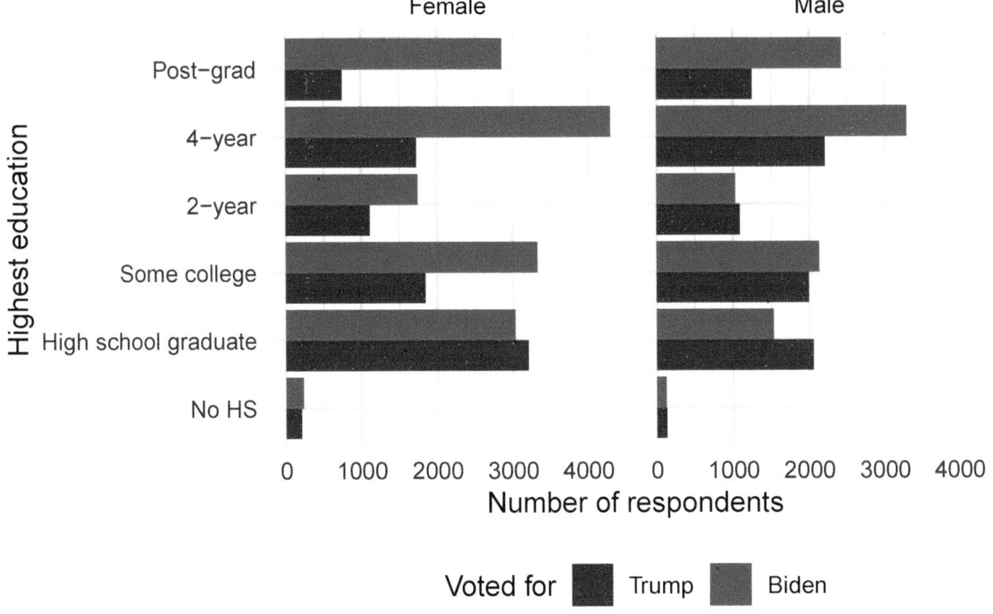

Figure 13.4: The distribution of presidential preferences, by gender, and highest education

accepted short-hand. In practice `rstanarm` converts categorical variables into a series of indicator variables and there are multiple coefficients estimated. In the interest of run-time we will randomly sample 1,000 observations and fit the model on that, rather than the full dataset.

```
set.seed(853)

ces2020_reduced <-
  ces2020 |>
  slice_sample(n = 1000)

political_preferences <-
  stan_glm(
    voted_for ~ gender + education,
    data = ces2020_reduced,
    family = binomial(link = "logit"),
    prior = normal(location = 0, scale = 2.5, autoscale = TRUE),
    prior_intercept =
      normal(location = 0, scale = 2.5, autoscale = TRUE),
    seed = 853
  )

saveRDS(
  political_preferences,
  file = "political_preferences.rds"
)
```

Table 13.3: Whether a respondent is likely to vote for Biden based on their gender and education

	Support Biden
(Intercept)	−0.745
	(0.517)
genderMale	−0.477
	(0.136)
educationHigh school graduate	0.617
	(0.534)
educationSome college	1.494
	(0.541)
education2-year	0.954
	(0.538)
education4-year	1.801
	(0.532)
educationPost-grad	1.652
	(0.541)
Num.Obs.	1000
R2	0.064
Log.Lik.	−646.335
ELPD	−653.5
ELPD s.e.	9.4
LOOIC	1307.0
LOOIC s.e.	18.8
WAIC	1307.0
RMSE	0.48

```
political_preferences <-
  readRDS(file = "political_preferences.rds")
```

The results of our model are interesting. They suggest males were less likely to vote for Biden, and that there is a considerable effect of education (Table 13.3).

```
modelsummary(
  list(
    "Support Biden" = political_preferences
  ),
  statistic = "mad"
  )
```

It can be useful to plot the credibility intervals of these predictors (Figure 13.5). In particular this might be something that is especially useful in an appendix.

```
modelplot(political_preferences, conf_level = 0.9) +
  labs(x = "90 per cent credibility interval")
```

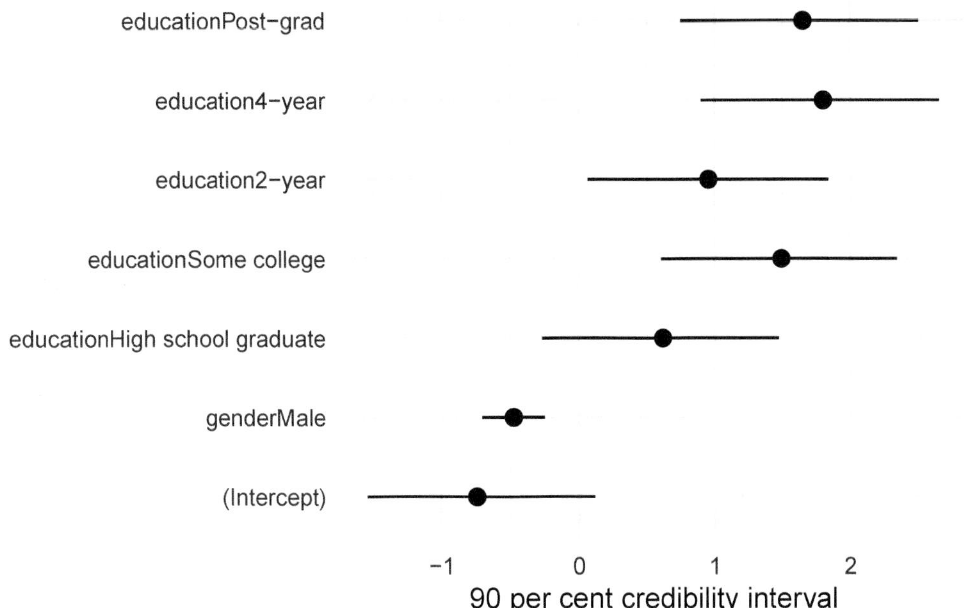

Figure 13.5: Credible intervals for predictors of support for Biden

13.3 Poisson regression

When we have count data we should initially think to take advantage of the Poisson distribution. One application of Poisson regression is modeling the outcomes of sports. For instance Burch (2023) builds a Poisson model of hockey outcomes, following Baio and Blangiardo (2010) who build a Poisson model of football outcomes.

The Poisson distribution is governed by one parameter, λ. This distributes probabilities over non-negative integers and hence governs the shape of the distribution. As such, the Poisson distribution has the interesting feature that the mean is also the variance. As the mean increases, so does the variance. The Poisson probability mass function is (Pitman 1993, 121):

$$P_\lambda(k) = e^{-\lambda}\lambda^k/k!, \text{ for } k = 0, 1, 2, ...$$

We can simulate $n = 20$ draws from the Poisson distribution with `rpois()`, where λ is equal to three.

```
rpois(n = 20, lambda = 3)
```

```
[1] 5 6 7 1 1 2 5 3 2 4 1 2 2 3 1 5 9 1 5 2
```

We can also look at what happens to the distribution as we change the value of λ (Figure 13.6).

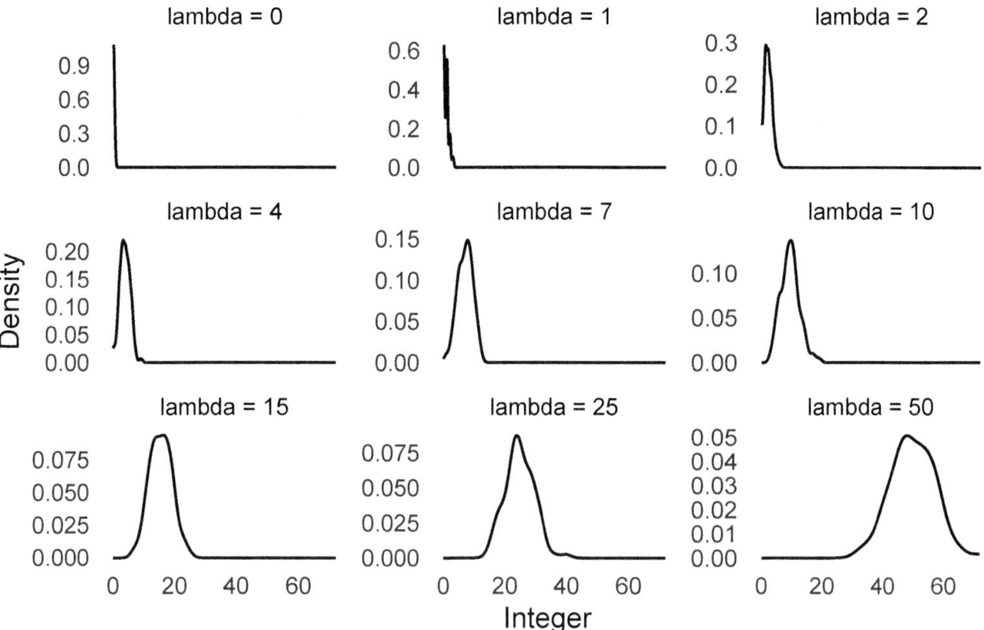

Figure 13.6: The Poisson distribution is governed by the value of the mean, which is the same as its variance

13.3.1 Simulated example: number of As by department

To illustrate the situation, we could simulate data about the number of As that are awarded in each university course. In this simulated example, we consider three departments, each of which has many courses. Each course will award a different number of As.

```
set.seed(853)

class_size <- 26

count_of_A <-
  tibble(
    # From Chris DuBois: https://stackoverflow.com/a/1439843
    department =
      c(rep.int("1", 26), rep.int("2", 26), rep.int("3", 26)),
    course = c(
      paste0("DEP_1_", letters),
      paste0("DEP_2_", letters),
      paste0("DEP_3_", letters)
    ),
    number_of_As = c(
      rpois(n = class_size, lambda = 5),
      rpois(n = class_size, lambda = 10),
      rpois(n = class_size, lambda = 20)
    )
  )
```

```
count_of_A |>
  ggplot(aes(x = number_of_As)) +
  geom_histogram(aes(fill = department), position = "dodge") +
  labs(
    x = "Number of As awarded",
    y = "Number of classes",
    fill = "Department"
  ) +
  theme_classic() +
  scale_fill_brewer(palette = "Set1") +
  theme(legend.position = "bottom")
```

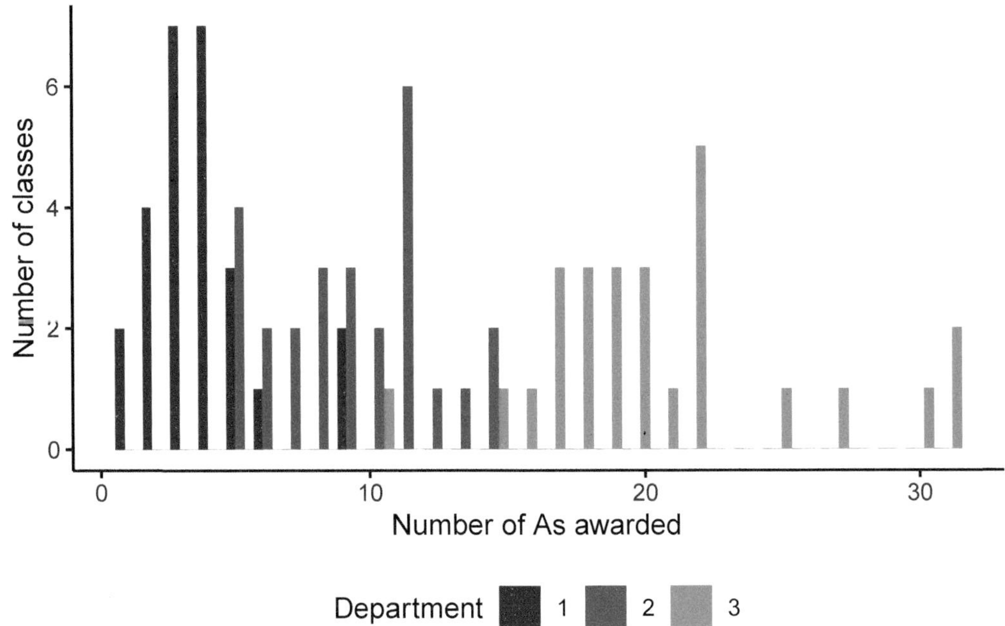

Figure 13.7: Simulated number of As in various classes across three departments

Our simulated dataset has the number of As awarded by courses, which are structured within departments (Figure 13.7). In Chapter 15, we will take advantage of this departmental structure, but for now we just ignore it and focus on differences between departments.

The model that we are interested in estimating is:

$$
\begin{aligned}
y_i|\lambda_i &\sim \text{Poisson}(\lambda_i)\\
\log(\lambda_i) &= \beta_0 + \beta_1 \times \text{department}_i
\end{aligned}
$$

where y_i is the number of A grades awarded, and we are interested in how this differs by department.

We can use `glm()` from base R to get a quick sense of the data. This function is quite general, and we specify Poisson regression by setting the "family" parameter. The estimates are contained in the first column of Table 13.4.

```
grades_base <-
  glm(
    number_of_As ~ department,
    data = count_of_A,
    family = "poisson"
  )

summary(grades_base)
```

```
Call:
glm(formula = number_of_As ~ department, family = "poisson",
    data = count_of_A)

Coefficients:
            Estimate Std. Error z value Pr(>|z|)
(Intercept)   1.3269     0.1010  13.135  < 2e-16 ***
department2   0.8831     0.1201   7.353 1.94e-13 ***
department3   1.7029     0.1098  15.505  < 2e-16 ***
---
Signif. codes:  0 '***' 0.001 '**' 0.01 '*' 0.05 '.' 0.1 ' ' 1

(Dispersion parameter for poisson family taken to be 1)

    Null deviance: 426.201  on 77  degrees of freedom
Residual deviance:  75.574  on 75  degrees of freedom
AIC: 392.55

Number of Fisher Scoring iterations: 4
```

As with logistic regression, the interpretation of the coefficients from Poisson regression can be difficult. The interpretation of the coefficient on "department2" is that it is the log of the expected difference between departments. We expect $e^{0.883} \approx 2.4$ and $e^{1.703} \approx 5.5$ as many A grades in departments 2 and 3, respectively, compared with department 1 (Table 13.4).

We could build a Bayesian model and estimate it with `rstanarm` (Table 13.4).

$$
\begin{aligned}
y_i|\lambda_i &\sim \text{Poisson}(\lambda_i)\\
\log(\lambda_i) &= \beta_0 + \beta_1 \times \text{department}_i\\
\beta_0 &\sim \text{Normal}(0, 2.5)\\
\beta_1 &\sim \text{Normal}(0, 2.5)
\end{aligned}
$$

where y_i is the number of As awarded.

```
grades_rstanarm <-
  stan_glm(
    number_of_As ~ department,
    data = count_of_A,
    family = poisson(link = "log"),
    prior = normal(location = 0, scale = 2.5, autoscale = TRUE),
    prior_intercept = normal(location = 0, scale = 2.5, autoscale = TRUE),
```

Table 13.4: Examining the number of A grades given in different departments

	Number of As
(Intercept)	1.321
department2	0.884
department3	1.706
Num.Obs.	78
Log.Lik.	−193.355
ELPD	−196.2
ELPD s.e.	7.7
LOOIC	392.4
LOOIC s.e.	15.4
WAIC	392.4
RMSE	3.41

```
    seed = 853
  )

saveRDS(
  grades_rstanarm,
  file = "grades_rstanarm.rds"
)
```

The results are in Table 13.4.

```
modelsummary(
  list(
    "Number of As" = grades_rstanarm
  )
)
```

As with logistic regression, we can use `slopes()` from `marginaleffects` to help with interpreting these results. It may be useful to consider how we expect the number of A grades to change as we go from one department to another. Table 13.5 suggests that in our dataset, classes in Department 2 tend to have around five additional A grades, compared with Department 1, and that classes in Department 3 tend to have around 17 more A grades, compared with Department 1.

```
slopes(grades_rstanarm) |>
  summary() |>
  select(-term) |>
  kable(
    col.names = c("Compare department", "Estimate", "2.5%", "97.5%"),
    digits = 2, booktabs = TRUE, linesep = ""
  )
```

Table 13.5: The estimated difference in the number of A grades awarded at each department

Compare department	Estimate	2.5%	97.5%
mean(2) - mean(1)	5.32	4.01	6.70
mean(3) - mean(1)	16.92	15.10	18.84

13.3.2 Letters used in *Jane Eyre*

In an earlier age, Edgeworth (1885) made counts of the dactyls in Virgil's *Aeneid* (Stigler (1978, 301) provides helpful background and the dataset is available using `Dactyl` from `HistData` (Friendly 2021)). Inspired by this we could use `gutenbergr` to get the text of *Jane Eyre* by Charlotte Brontë. (Recall that in Chapter 7 we converted PDFs of *Jane Eyre* into a dataset.) We could then consider the first ten lines of each chapter, count the number of words, and count the number of times either "E" or "e" appears. We are interested to see whether the number of e/Es increases as more words are used. If not, it could suggest that the distribution of e/Es is not consistent, which could be of interest to linguists.

Following the workflow advocated in this book, we first sketch our dataset and model. A quick sketch of what the dataset could look like is Figure 13.8a, and a quick sketch of our model is Figure 13.8b.

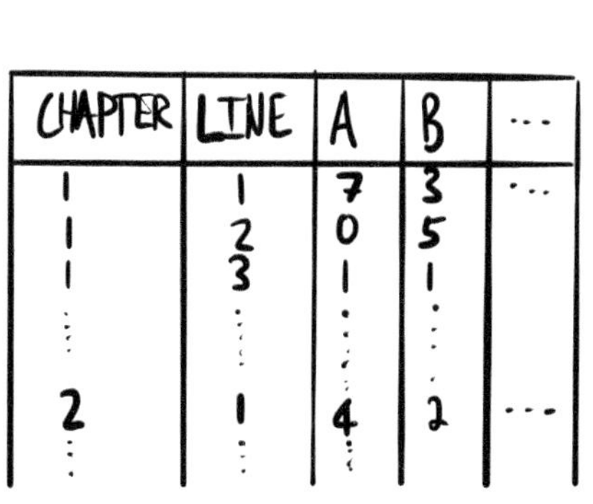

(a) Planned counts, by line and chapter, in *Jane Eyre*

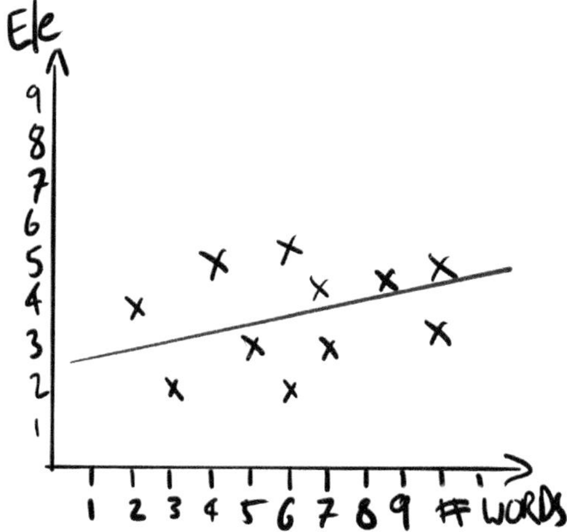

(b) Expected relationship between count of e/Es and number of words in the line

Figure 13.8: Sketches of the expected dataset and analysis force us to consider what we are interested in

We simulate a dataset of how the number of e/Es could be distributed following the Poisson distribution (Figure 13.9).

```
count_of_e_simulation <-
  tibble(
    chapter = c(rep(1, 10), rep(2, 10), rep(3, 10)),
```

```
    line = rep(1:10, 3),
    number_words_in_line = runif(min = 0, max = 15, n = 30) |> round(0),
    number_e = rpois(n = 30, lambda = 10)
  )

count_of_e_simulation |>
  ggplot(aes(y = number_e, x = number_words_in_line)) +
  geom_point() +
  labs(
    x = "Number of words in line",
    y = "Number of e/Es in the first ten lines"
  ) +
  theme_classic() +
  scale_fill_brewer(palette = "Set1")
```

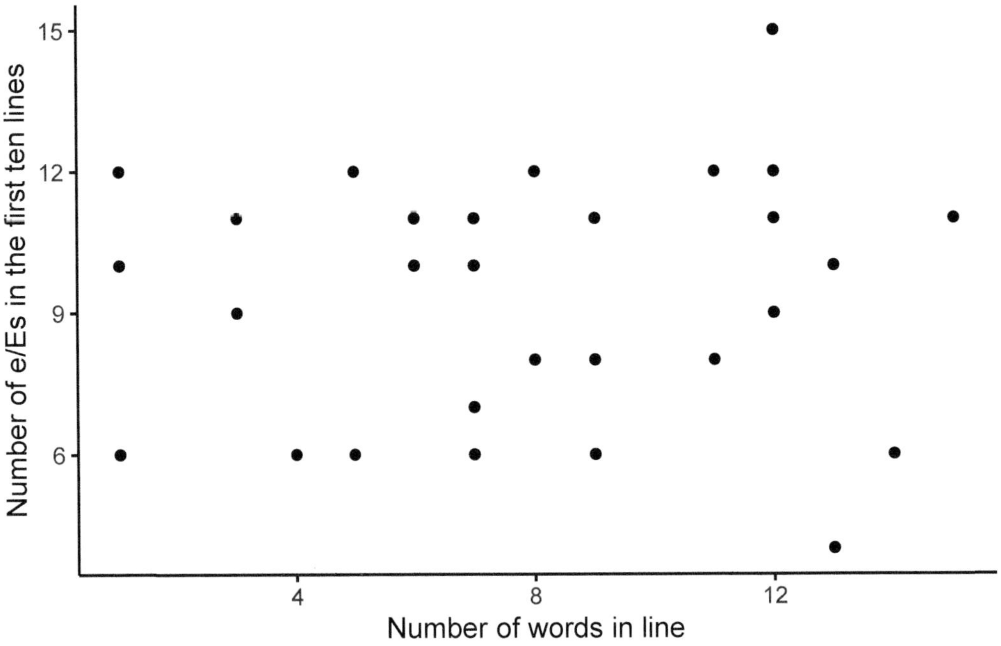

Figure 13.9: Simulated counts of e/Es

We can now gather and prepare our data. We download the text of the book from Project Gutenberg using `gutenberg_download()` from `gutenbergr`.

```
gutenberg_id_of_janeeyre <- 1260

jane_eyre <-
  gutenberg_download(
    gutenberg_id = gutenberg_id_of_janeeyre,
    mirror = "https://gutenberg.pglaf.org/"
  )
```

```
jane_eyre

write_csv(jane_eyre, "jane_eyre.csv")
```

We will download it and then use our local copy to avoid overly imposing on the Project Gutenberg servers.

```
jane_eyre <- read_csv(
  "jane_eyre.csv",
  col_types = cols(
    gutenberg_id = col_integer(),
    text = col_character()
  )
)

jane_eyre
```

```
# A tibble: 21,001 x 2
   gutenberg_id text
          <int> <chr>
 1         1260 JANE EYRE
 2         1260 AN AUTOBIOGRAPHY
 3         1260 <NA>
 4         1260 by Charlotte Brontë
 5         1260 <NA>
 6         1260 _ILLUSTRATED BY F. H. TOWNSEND_
 7         1260 <NA>
 8         1260 London
 9         1260 SERVICE & PATON
10         1260 5 HENRIETTA STREET
# i 20,991 more rows
```

We are interested in only those lines that have content, so we remove those empty lines that are just there for spacing. Then we can create counts of the number of e/Es in that line, for the first ten lines of each chapter. For instance, we can look at the first few lines and see that there are five e/Es in the first line and eight in the second.

```
jane_eyre_reduced <-
  jane_eyre |>
  filter(!is.na(text)) |> # Remove empty lines
  mutate(chapter = if_else(str_detect(text, "CHAPTER") == TRUE,
                           text,
                           NA_character_)) |> # Find start of chapter
  fill(chapter, .direction = "down") |>
  mutate(chapter_line = row_number(),
         .by = chapter) |> # Add line number to each chapter
  filter(!is.na(chapter),
         chapter_line %in% c(2:11)) |> # Remove "CHAPTER I" etc
  select(text, chapter) |>
```

```
    mutate(
      chapter = str_remove(chapter, "CHAPTER "),
      chapter = str_remove(chapter, "—CONCLUSION"),
      chapter = as.integer(as.roman(chapter))
    ) |> # Change chapters to integers
    mutate(count_e = str_count(text, "e|E"),
           word_count = str_count(text, "\\w+")
           # From: https://stackoverflow.com/a/38058033
           )
```

```
jane_eyre_reduced |>
  select(chapter, word_count, count_e, text) |>
  head()
```

```
# A tibble: 6 x 4
  chapter word_count count_e text
    <int>      <int>   <int> <chr>
1       1         13       5 There was no possibility of taking a walk that day~
2       1         11       8 wandering, indeed, in the leafless shrubbery an ho~
3       1         12       9 but since dinner (Mrs. Reed, when there was no com~
4       1         14       3 the cold winter wind had brought with it clouds so~
5       1         11       7 so penetrating, that further outdoor exercise was ~
6       1          1       1 question.
```

We can verify that the mean and variance of the number of e/Es is roughly similar by plotting all of the data (Figure 13.10). The mean, in pink, is 6.7, and the variance, in blue, is 6.2. While they are not entirely the same, they are similar. We include the diagonal in Figure 13.10b to help with thinking about the data. If the data were on the $y = x$ line, then on average there would be one e/E per word. Given the mass of points below that line expect that on average there is less than one per word.

```
mean_e <- mean(jane_eyre_reduced$count_e)
variance_e <- var(jane_eyre_reduced$count_e)

jane_eyre_reduced |>
  ggplot(aes(x = count_e)) +
  geom_histogram() +
  geom_vline(xintercept = mean_e,
             linetype = "dashed",
             color = "#C64191") +
  geom_vline(xintercept = variance_e,
             linetype = "dashed",
             color = "#0ABAB5") +
  theme_minimal() +
  labs(
    y = "Count",
    x = "Number of e's per line for first ten lines"
  )
```

```
jane_eyre_reduced |>
  ggplot(aes(x = word_count, y = count_e)) +
  geom_jitter(alpha = 0.5) +
  geom_abline(slope = 1, intercept = 0, linetype = "dashed") +
  theme_minimal() +
  labs(
    x = "Number of words in the line",
    y = "Number of e/Es in the line"
  )
```

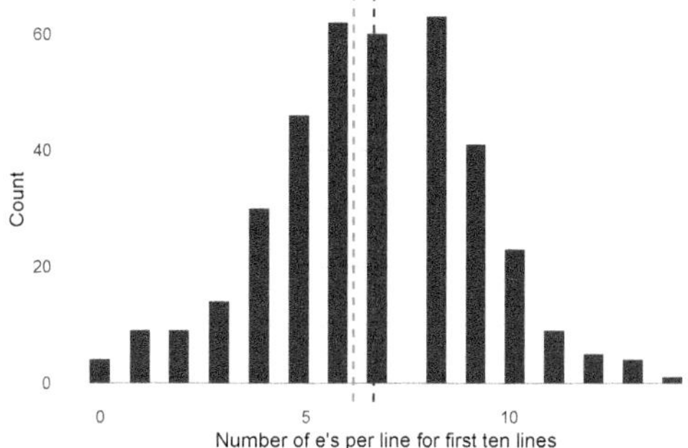

(a) Distribution of the number of e/Es

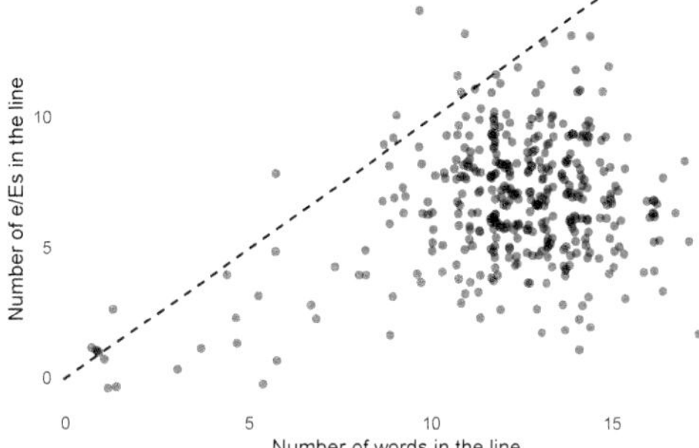

(b) Comparison of the number of e/Es in the line and the number of words in the line

Figure 13.10: Number of e/Es letters in the first ten lines of each chapter in Jane Eyre

We could consider the following model:

$$
\begin{aligned}
y_i|\lambda_i &\sim \text{Poisson}(\lambda_i) \\
\log(\lambda_i) &= \beta_0 + \beta_1 \times \text{Number of words}_i \\
\beta_0 &\sim \text{Normal}(0, 2.5) \\
\beta_1 &\sim \text{Normal}(0, 2.5)
\end{aligned}
$$

where y_i is the number of e/Es in the line and the explanatory variable is the number of words in the line. We could estimate the model using `stan_glm()`.

```
jane_e_counts <-
  stan_glm(
    count_e ~ word_count,
    data = jane_eyre_reduced,
    family = poisson(link = "log"),
    prior = normal(location = 0, scale = 2.5, autoscale = TRUE),
    prior_intercept = normal(location = 0, scale = 2.5, autoscale = TRUE),
    seed = 853
  )

saveRDS(
  jane_e_counts,
  file = "jane_e_counts.rds"
)
```

While we would normally be interested in the table of estimates, as we have seen that a few times now, rather than again creating a table of the estimates, we introduce `plot_cap()` from `marginaleffects`. We can use this to show the number of e/Es predicted by the model, for each line, based on the number of words in that line. Figure 13.11 makes it clear that we expect a positive relationship.

```
plot_predictions(jane_e_counts, condition = "word_count") +
  labs(x = "Number of words",
       y = "Average number of e/Es in the first 10 lines") +
  theme_classic()
```

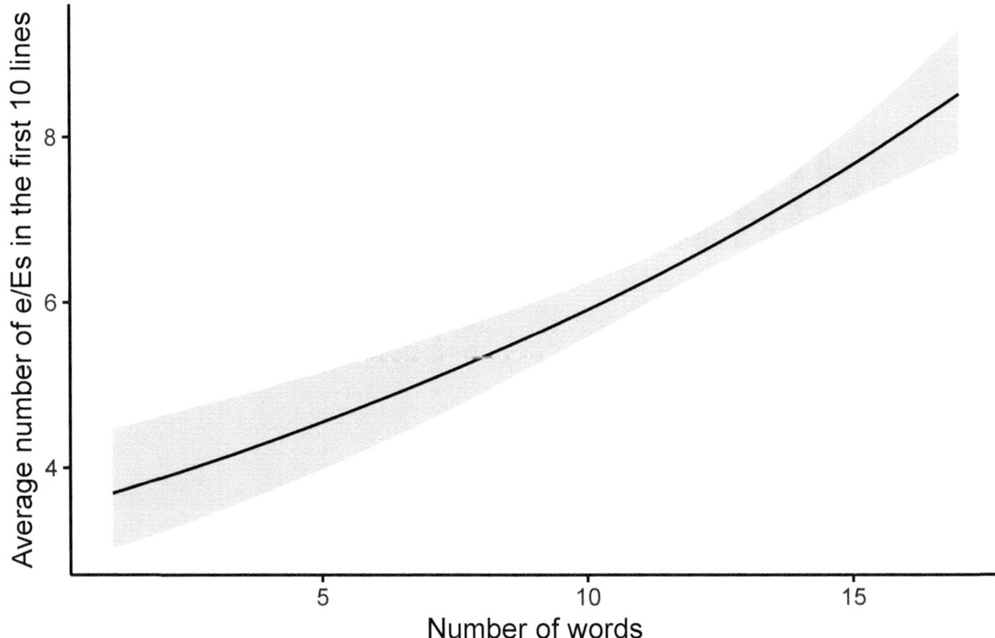

Figure 13.11: The predicted number of e/Es in each line based on the number of words

13.4 Negative binomial regression

One of the restrictions with Poisson regression is the assumption that the mean and the variance are the same. We can relax this assumption to allow over-dispersion by using a close variant, negative binomial regression.

Poisson and negative binomial models go hand in hand. It is often the case that we will end up fitting both, and then comparing them. For instance:

- Maher (1982) considers both in the context of results from the English Football League and discusses situations in which one may be considered more appropriate than the other.
- R. Smith (2002) considers the 2000 US presidential election and especially the issue of overdispersion in a Poisson analysis.
- Osgood (2000) compares them in the case of crime data.

13.4.1 Mortality in Alberta, Canada

Consider, somewhat morbidly, that every year each individual either dies or does not. From the perspective of a geographic area, we could gather data on the number of people who died each year, by their cause of death. The Canadian province of Alberta has made available[1] the number of deaths, by cause, since 2001, for the top 30 causes each year.

As always we first sketch our dataset and model. A quick sketch of what the dataset could look like is Figure 13.12a, and a quick sketch of our model is Figure 13.12b

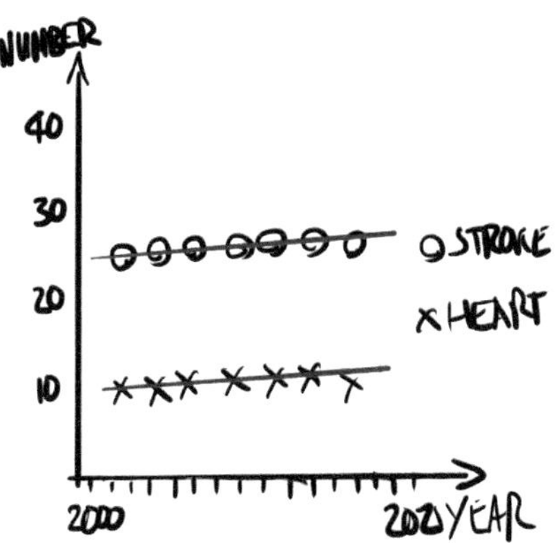

(a) Quick sketch of a dataset that could be used to examine cause of death in Alberta

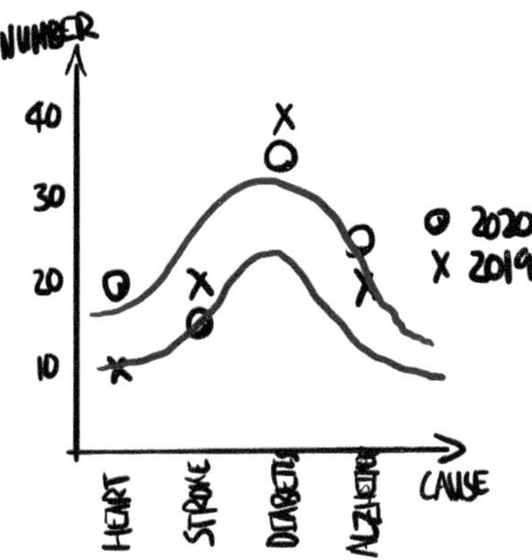

(b) Quick sketch of what we expect from the analysis of cause of death in Alberta before finalizing either the data or the analysis

Figure 13.12: Sketches of the expected dataset and analysis for cause of death in Alberta

We will simulate a dataset of cause of death distributed following the negative binomial distribution.

```
alberta_death_simulation <-
  tibble(
    cause = rep(x = c("Heart", "Stroke", "Diabetes"), times = 10),
    year = rep(x = 2016:2018, times = 10),
    deaths = rnbinom(n = 30, size = 20, prob = 0.1)
  )

alberta_death_simulation
```

```
# A tibble: 30 x 3
   cause     year deaths
   <chr>    <int>  <int>
 1 Heart     2016    160
 2 Stroke    2017    179
 3 Diabetes  2018    162
 4 Heart     2016    199
```

[1] https://open.alberta.ca/opendata/leading-causes-of-death

```
 5 Stroke     2017     206
 6 Diabetes   2018     222
 7 Heart      2016     222
 8 Stroke     2017     166
 9 Diabetes   2018     147
10 Heart      2016     151
# i 20 more rows
```

We can look at the distribution of these deaths, by year and cause (Figure 13.13). We have truncated the full cause of death because some are quite long. As some causes are not always in the top 30 each year, not all causes have the same number of occurrences.

```
alberta_cod <-
  read_csv(
    paste0("https://open.alberta.ca/dataset/03339dc5-fb51-4552-",
           "97c7-853688fc428d/resource/3e241965-fee3-400e-9652-",
           "07cfbf0c0bda/download/deaths-leading-causes.csv"),
    col_types = cols(
      `Calendar Year` = col_integer(),
      Cause = col_character(),
      Ranking = col_integer(),
      `Total Deaths` = col_integer()
    )
  ) |>
  clean_names() |>
  add_count(cause) |>
  mutate(cause = str_trunc(cause, 30))
```

If we were to look at the top-ten causes in 2021, we would notice a variety of interesting aspects (Table 13.6). For instance, we would expect that the most common causes would be present in all 21 years of our data. But we notice that the most common cause, "Other ill-defined and unknown causes of mortality", is only in three years. "COVID-19, virus identified", is only in two other years, as there were no known COVID deaths in Canada before 2020.

```
alberta_cod |>
  filter(
    calendar_year == 2021,
    ranking <= 10
  ) |>
  mutate(total_deaths = format(total_deaths, big.mark = ",")) |>
  kable(
    col.names = c("Year", "Cause", "Ranking", "Deaths", "Years"),
    align = c("l", "r", "r", "r", "r"),
    digits = 0, booktabs = TRUE, linesep = ""
  )
```

Table 13.6: Top-ten causes of death in Alberta in 2021

Year	Cause	Ranking	Deaths	Years
2021	Other ill-defined and unkno...	1	3,362	3
2021	Organic dementia	2	2,135	21
2021	COVID-19, virus identified	3	1,950	2
2021	All other forms of chronic ...	4	1,939	21
2021	Malignant neoplasms of trac...	5	1,552	21
2021	Acute myocardial infarction	6	1,075	21
2021	Other chronic obstructive p...	7	1,028	21
2021	Diabetes mellitus	8	728	21
2021	Stroke, not specified as he...	9	612	21
2021	Accidental poisoning by and...	10	604	9

For simplicity we restrict ourselves to the five most common causes of death in 2021 of those that have been present every year.

```
alberta_cod_top_five <-
  alberta_cod |>
  filter(
    calendar_year == 2021,
    n == 21
  ) |>
  slice_max(order_by = desc(ranking), n = 5) |>
  pull(cause)

alberta_cod <-
  alberta_cod |>
  filter(cause %in% alberta_cod_top_five)
```

```
alberta_cod |>
  ggplot(aes(x = calendar_year, y = total_deaths, color = cause)) +
  geom_line() +
  theme_minimal() +
  scale_color_brewer(palette = "Set1") +
  labs(x = "Year", y = "Annual number of deaths in Alberta") +
  facet_wrap(vars(cause), dir = "v", ncol = 1) +
  theme(legend.position = "none")
```

Table 13.7: Summary statistics of the number of yearly deaths, by cause, in Alberta, Canada

	Min	Mean	Max	SD	Var	N
total_deaths	280	1273	2135	427	182 378	105

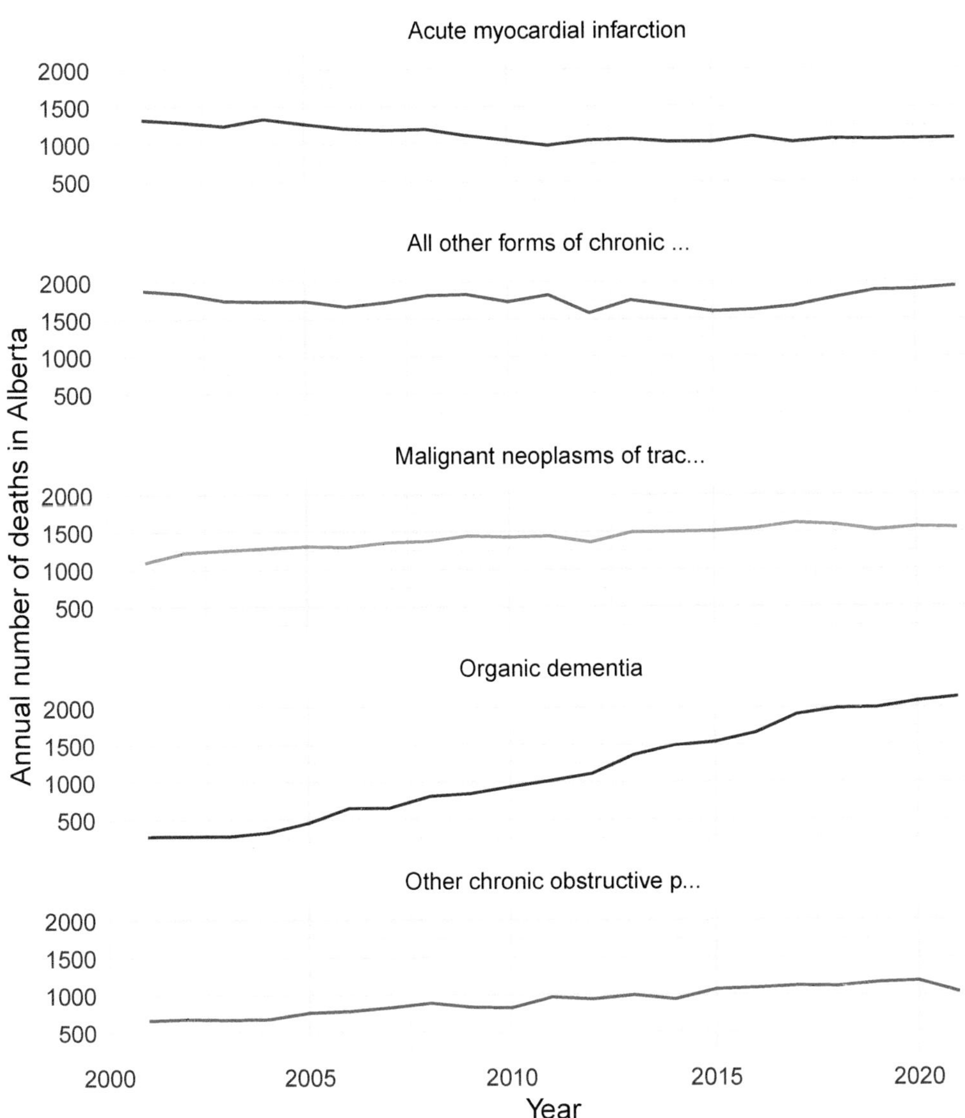

Figure 13.13: Annual number of deaths for the top-five causes in 2021, since 2001, for Alberta, Canada

One thing that we notice is that the mean, 1,273, is different to the variance, 182,378 (Table 13.7).

We can implement negative binomial regression when using `stan_glm()` by specifying the negative binomial distribution in "family". In this case, we run both Poisson and negative binomial.

```
cause_of_death_alberta_poisson <-
  stan_glm(
    total_deaths ~ cause,
    data = alberta_cod,
    family = poisson(link = "log"),
    seed = 853
  )

cause_of_death_alberta_neg_binomial <-
  stan_glm(
    total_deaths ~ cause,
    data = alberta_cod,
    family = neg_binomial_2(link = "log"),
    seed = 853
  )
```

We can compare our different models (Table 13.8).

```
coef_short_names <-
  c("causeAll other forms of chronic ischemic heart disease"
    = "causeAll other forms of...",
    "causeMalignant neoplasms of trachea, bronchus and lung"
    = "causeMalignant neoplas...",
    "causeOrganic dementia"
    = "causeOrganic dementia",
    "causeOther chronic obstructive pulmonary disease"
    = "causeOther chronic obst..."
    )

modelsummary(
  list(
    "Poisson" = cause_of_death_alberta_poisson,
    "Negative binomial" = cause_of_death_alberta_neg_binomial
  ),
  coef_map = coef_short_names
)
```

The estimates are similar. We could use posterior predictive checks, introduced in Section 12.4, to show that the negative binomial approach is a better choice for this circumstance (Figure 13.14).

```
pp_check(cause_of_death_alberta_poisson) +
  theme(legend.position = "bottom")

pp_check(cause_of_death_alberta_neg_binomial) +
  theme(legend.position = "bottom")
```

Finally, we can compare between the models using the resampling method leave-one-out

Table 13.8: Modeling the most prevalent cause of deaths in Alberta, 2001-2020

	Poisson	Negative binomial
causeAll other forms of...	0.442	0.439
		(0.104)
causeMalignant neoplas...	0.224	0.226
		(0.105)
causeOrganic dementia	0.001	0.002
		(0.107)
causeOther chronic obst...	−0.214	−0.217
		(0.104)
Num.Obs.	105	105
Log.Lik.	−5139.564	−771.297
ELPD	−5312.5	−775.8
ELPD s.e.	1099.1	10.0
LOOIC	10 625.0	1551.6
LOOIC s.e.	2198.3	20.0
WAIC	10 793.7	1551.6
RMSE	308.24	308.26

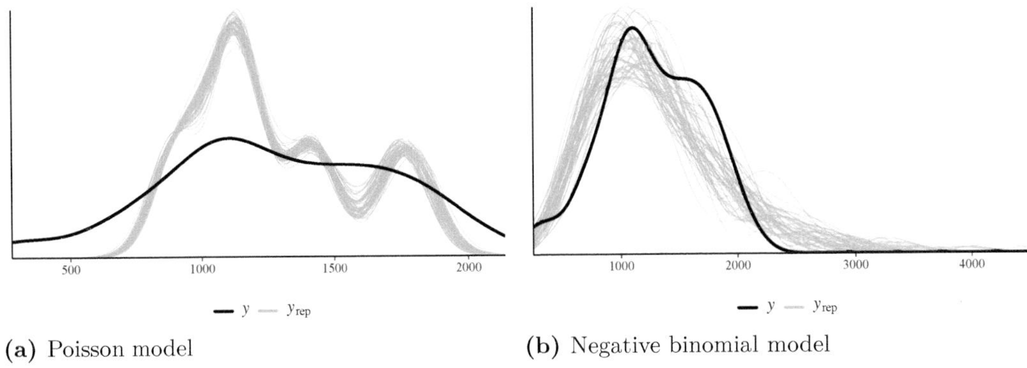

(a) Poisson model

(b) Negative binomial model

Figure 13.14: Comparing posterior prediction checks for Poisson and negative binomial models

(LOO) cross-validation (CV). This is a variant of cross-validation, where the size of each fold is one. That is to say, if there was a dataset with 100 observations, this LOO is equivalent to 100-fold cross validation. We can implement this in `rstanarm` with `loo()` for each model, and then compare between them with `loo_compare()` where the higher the better.[2]

We provide more information on cross-validation in the "Prediction" Online Appendix[3].

```
poisson <- loo(cause_of_death_alberta_poisson, cores = 2)
neg_binomial <- loo(cause_of_death_alberta_neg_binomial, cores = 2)
```

[2]By way of background, LOO-CV is not done by `loo()`, because it would be too computationally intensive. Instead an approximation is done which provides the expected log point wise predictive density (ELPD). The `rstanarm` vignettes provide more detail.

[3]https://tellingstorieswithdata.com/27-prediction.html

```
loo_compare(poisson, neg_binomial)
```

```
                                  elpd_diff se_diff
cause_of_death_alberta_neg_binomial     0.0       0.0
cause_of_death_alberta_poisson      -4536.7    1089.5
```

In this case we find that the negative binomial model is a better fit than the Poisson, because ELPD is larger.

13.5 Multilevel modeling

Multilevel modeling goes by a variety of names including "hierarchical", and "random effects". While there are sometimes small differences in meaning between disciplines, in general they refer to the same or at least similar ideas. The fundamental insight of multilevel modeling is that a lot of the time our observations are not completely independent of each other, and can instead be grouped. Accounting for that grouping when we model, can provide us with some useful information. For instance, there is a difference in the earnings of professional athletes depending on whether they compete in men's or women's events. If we were interested in trying to forecast the earnings of a particular athlete, based on their competition results, then knowing which type of competition the individual competed in would enable the model to make a better forecast.

> **i Shoulders of giants**
>
> Dr Fiona Steele is a Professor of Statistics at the London School of Economics (LSE). After earning a PhD in Statistics from University of Southampton in 1996, she was appointed as a Lecturer at the LSE, before moving to the University of London, and the University of Bristol where she was appointed a full professor in 2008. She returned to the LSE in 2013. One area of her research is multilevel modeling and applications in demography, education, family psychology, and health. For instance, Steele (2007) looks at multilevel models for longitudinal data, and Steele, Vignoles, and Jenkins (2007) uses a multilevel model to look at the relationship between school resources and pupil attainment. She was awarded the Royal Statistical Society Guy Medal in Bronze in 2008.

We distinguish between three settings:

1) Complete pooling, where we treat every observation as being from the same group, which is what we have been doing to this point.
2) No pooling, where we treat every group separately, which might happen if we were to run a separate regression for each group.
3) Partial pooling, where we allow group membership to have some influence.

For instance, consider we are interested in the relationship between GDP and inflation for each of the countries in the world. Complete pooling would have us put all the countries into the one group; no pooling would have us run separate regressions for each continent. We will now illustrate the partial pooling approach.

In general there are two ways to go about this:

1) enable varying intercepts, or
2) enable varying slopes.

In this book we consider only the first, but you should move onto Gelman, Hill, and Vehtari (2020), McElreath ([2015] 2020), and A. Johnson, Ott, and Dogucu (2022).

13.5.1 Simulated example: political support

Let us consider a situation in which the probability of support for a particular political party depends on an individual's gender, and the state that they live in.

$$
\begin{aligned}
y_i|\pi_i &\sim \text{Bern}(\pi_i) \\
\text{logit}(\pi_i) &= \beta_0 + \alpha^{\text{gender}}_{g[i]} + \alpha^{\text{state}}_{s[i]} \\
\beta_0 &\sim \text{Normal}(0, 2.5) \\
\alpha^{\text{gender}}_{g} &\sim \text{Normal}(0, 2.5) \text{ for } g = 1, 2 \\
\alpha^{\text{state}}_{s} &\sim \text{Normal}\left(0, \sigma^2_{\text{state}}\right) \text{ for } s = 1, 2, \dots, S \\
\sigma_{\text{state}} &\sim \text{Exponential}(1)
\end{aligned}
$$

where $\pi_i = \Pr(y_i = 1)$, there are two gender groups, because that is what is going to be available from the survey we will use in Chapter 15, and S is the total number of states. We include this in the function with "(1 | state)" within `stan_glmer()` from `rstanarm` (Goodrich et al. 2023). This term indicates that we are looking at a group effect by state, which means that the fitted model's intercept is allowed to vary according by state.

```
set.seed(853)

political_support <-
  tibble(
    state = sample(1:50, size = 1000, replace = TRUE),
    gender = sample(c(1, 2), size = 1000, replace = TRUE),
    noise = rnorm(n = 1000, mean = 0, sd = 10) |> round(),
    supports = if_else(state + gender + noise > 50, 1, 0)
  )

political_support
```

```
# A tibble: 1,000 x 4
  state gender noise supports
  <int>  <dbl> <dbl>    <dbl>
1     9      1    11        0
2    26      1     3        0
3    29      2     7        0
4    17      2    13        0
5    37      2    11        0
6    29      2     9        0
7    50      2     3        1
```

```
 8    20       2     3          0
 9    19       1    -1          0
10     3       2     7          0
# i 990 more rows
```

```
voter_preferences <-
  stan_glmer(
    supports ~ gender + (1 | state),
    data = political_support,
    family = binomial(link = "logit"),
    prior = normal(location = 0, scale = 2.5, autoscale = TRUE),
    prior_intercept = normal(location = 0, scale = 2.5, autoscale = TRUE),
    seed = 853
  )

saveRDS(
  voter_preferences,
  file = "voter_preferences.rds"
)
```

```
voter_preferences
```

```
stan_glmer
 family:       binomial [logit]
 formula:      supports ~ gender + (1 | state)
 observations: 1000
------
            Median MAD_SD
(Intercept) -4.4    0.7
gender       0.4    0.3

Error terms:
 Groups Name        Std.Dev.
 state  (Intercept) 2.5
Num. levels: state 50

------
* For help interpreting the printed output see ?print.stanreg
* For info on the priors used see ?prior_summary.stanreg
```

It is worth trying to look for opportunities to use a multilevel model when you come to a new modeling situation, especially one where inference is the primary concern. There is often some grouping that can be taken advantage of to provide the model with more information.

When we move to multilevel modeling, it is possible that some `rstanarm` models will result in a warning about "divergent transitions". For the purposes of getting a model working for this book, if there are just a handful of warnings and the Rhat values of the coefficients are all close to one (check this with `any(summary(change_this_to_the_model_name)[, "Rhat"] > 1.1)`), then just ignore it. If there are more than a handful, and/or any of the Rhats are not close to one, then add "adapt_delta = 0.99" as an argument to `stan_glmer()` and re-run the model (keeping in mind that it will take longer to run). If that does not fix the issue, then simplify the model by removing a variable. We will see an example in Chapter 15 when we apply MRP to the 2020 US election, where the "adapt_delta" strategy fixes the issue.

13.5.2 Austen, Brontë, Dickens, and Shakespeare

As an example of multilevel modeling, we consider data from Project Gutenberg on the length of books by four authors: Jane Austen, Charlotte Brontë, Charles Dickens, and William Shakespeare. We would expect that Austen, Brontë, and Dickens, as they wrote books, will have longer books than Shakespeare, as he wrote plays. But it is not clear what difference we should expect between the three book authors.

```
authors <- c("Austen, Jane", "Dickens, Charles",
             "Shakespeare, William", "Brontë, Charlotte")

# The document values for duplicates and letters that we do not want
dont_get_shakespeare <-
  c(2270, 4774, 5137, 9077, 10606, 12578, 22791, 23041, 23042, 23043,
    23044, 23045, 23046, 28334, 45128, 47518, 47715, 47960, 49007,
    49008, 49297, 50095, 50559)
dont_get_bronte <- c(31100, 42078)
dont_get_dickens <-
  c(25852, 25853, 25854, 30368, 32241, 35536, 37121, 40723, 42232, 43111,
    43207, 46675, 47529, 47530, 47531, 47534, 47535, 49927, 50334)

books <-
  gutenberg_works(
    author %in% authors,
    !gutenberg_id %in%
      c(dont_get_shakespeare, dont_get_bronte, dont_get_dickens)
    ) |>
  gutenberg_download(
    meta_fields = c("title", "author"),
    mirror = "https://gutenberg.pglaf.org/"
  )

write_csv(books, "books-austen_bronte_dickens_shakespeare.csv")
```

```
books <- read_csv(
  "books-austen_bronte_dickens_shakespeare.csv",
  col_types = cols(
    gutenberg_id = col_integer(),
    text = col_character(),
    title = col_character(),
    author = col_character()
  )
)
```

```
lines_by_author_work <-
  books |>
  summarise(number_of_lines = n(),
            .by = c(author, title))

lines_by_author_work
```

```
# A tibble: 125 x 3
   author            title                           number_of_lines
   <chr>             <chr>                                     <int>
 1 Austen, Jane      Emma                                      16488
 2 Austen, Jane      Lady Susan                                 2525
 3 Austen, Jane      Love and Freindship [sic]                  3401
 4 Austen, Jane      Mansfield Park                            15670
 5 Austen, Jane      Northanger Abbey                           7991
 6 Austen, Jane      Persuasion                                 8353
 7 Austen, Jane      Pride and Prejudice                       14199
 8 Austen, Jane      Sense and Sensibility                     12673
 9 Brontë, Charlotte Jane Eyre: An Autobiography               21001
10 Brontë, Charlotte Shirley                                   25520
# i 115 more rows
```

```
author_lines_rstanarm <-
  stan_glm(
    number_of_lines ~ author,
    data = lines_by_author_work,
    family = neg_binomial_2(link = "log"),
    prior = normal(location = 0, scale = 3, autoscale = TRUE),
    prior_intercept = normal(location = 0, scale = 3, autoscale = TRUE),
    seed = 853
  )

saveRDS(
  author_lines_rstanarm,
  file = "author_lines_rstanarm.rds"
)

author_lines_rstanarm_multilevel <-
  stan_glmer(
    number_of_lines ~ (1 | author),
    data = lines_by_author_work,
    family = neg_binomial_2(link = "log"),
    prior = normal(location = 0, scale = 3, autoscale = TRUE),
    prior_intercept = normal(location = 0, scale = 3, autoscale = TRUE),
    seed = 853
  )

saveRDS(
  author_lines_rstanarm_multilevel,
```

Table 13.9: Explaining whether Austen, Brontë, Dickens, or Shakespeare wrote a book based on the number of lines

	Neg binomial	Multilevel neg binomial
(Intercept)	9.245	8.980
	(0.342)	(0.371)
authorBrontë, Charlotte	0.686	
	(0.576)	
authorDickens, Charles	0.019	
	(0.364)	
authorShakespeare, William	−0.875	
	(0.361)	
Num.Obs.	125	125
ICC		1.0
Log.Lik.	−1234.105	−1234.124
ELPD	−1237.3	−1237.2
ELPD s.e.	11.5	11.5
LOOIC	2474.7	2474.4
LOOIC s.e.	23.1	23.1
WAIC	2474.6	2474.4
RMSE	8954.42	8984.71

```
  file = "author_lines_rstanarm_multilevel.rds"
)
```

```
modelsummary(
  list(
    "Neg binomial" = author_lines_rstanarm,
    "Multilevel neg binomial" = author_lines_rstanarm_multilevel
  )
)
```

Table 13.9 is a little empty for the multilevel model, and we often use graphs to avoid overwhelming the reader with numbers (we will see examples of this in Chapter 15). For instance, Figure 13.15 shows the distribution of draws for each of the four authors using `spread_draws()` from `tidybayes`.

```
author_lines_rstanarm_multilevel |>
  spread_draws(`(Intercept)`, b[, group]) |>
  mutate(condition_mean = `(Intercept)` + b) |>
  ggplot(aes(y = group, x = condition_mean)) +
  stat_halfeye() +
  theme_minimal()
```

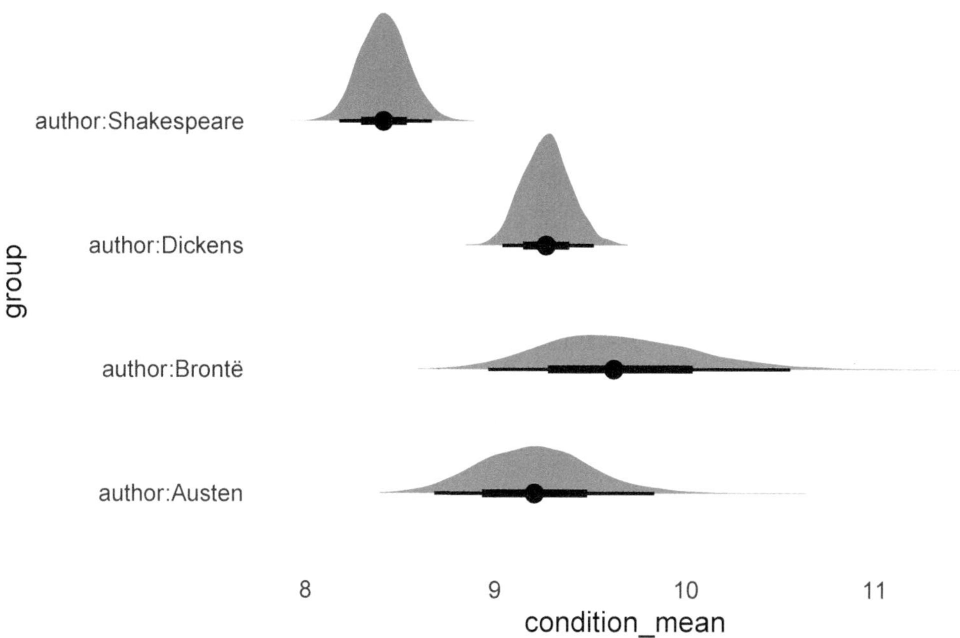

Figure 13.15: Examining the distribution of draws for each of the four authors

In this case, we see that we typically expect Brontë to write the longest books of the three book authors. Shakespeare, as expected, typically wrote works with the fewest lines.

13.6 Concluding remarks

In this chapter we have considered generalized linear models and introduced multilevel modeling. We built on the foundation established in Chapter 12 and provided some essentials for Bayesian model building. As mentioned in Chapter 12, this is enough to get started. Hopefully you are excited to learn more and to do that you should start with the modeling books recommended in Chapter 17.

Over the course of Chapter 12 and Chapter 13 we have covered a variety of approaches for Bayesian models. But we have not done everything for every model.

It is difficult to be definitive about what is "enough" because it is context specific, but the following checklist, drawn from concepts introduced across Chapter 12 and Chapter 13 would be sufficient for most purposes when you are getting started. In the model section of the paper, write out the model using equations and include a few paragraphs of text explaining the equations. Then justify the model choices, and briefly detail any alternatives that you considered. Finish with a sentence explaining how the model was fit, which in this case is likely to be with `rstanarm`, and that diagnostics are available in a cross-referenced appendix. In that appendix you should include: prior predictive checks, trace plots, Rhat plots, posterior distributions, and posterior predictive checks.

In the results section you should include a table of the estimates, built using `modelsummary`, and talk through them, likely with the help of `marginaleffects`. It may also be useful to include a graph of your results, especially if you are using a multilevel model, with the help of `tidybayes`. The model itself should be run in a separate R script. It should be preceded by tests of class and the number of observations. It should be followed by tests of the coefficients. These should be based on simulation. You should save the model in that R script using `saveRDS()`. In the Quarto document, you should read in that model using `readRDS()`.

13.7 Exercises

Scales

1. *(Plan)* Consider the following scenario: *A person is interested in the number of deaths, attributed to cancer, in Sydney, Australia. They collect data from the five largest hospitals, for the past 20 years.* Please sketch out what that dataset could look like and then sketch a graph that you could build to show all observations.
2. *(Simulate)* Please further consider the scenario described and simulate the situation, along with three predictor variables that are associated with the number of deaths, by cause. Please include at least ten tests based on the simulated data.
3. *(Acquire)* Please describe one possible source of such a dataset.
4. *(Explore)* Please use `ggplot2` to build the graph that you sketched. Then use `rstanarm` to build a model.
5. *(Communicate)* Please write two paragraphs about what you did.

Questions

1. When should we consider logistic regression (pick one)?
   a. Continuous outcome variable.
   b. Binary outcome variable.
   c. Count outcome variable.
2. We are interested in studying how voting intentions in the 2020 US presidential election vary by an individual's income. We set up a logistic regression model to study this relationship. In this study, one possible outcome variable would be (pick one)?
   a. Whether the respondent is a US citizen (yes/no)
   b. The respondent's personal income (high/low)
   c. Whether the respondent is going to vote for Biden (yes/no)
   d. Who the respondent voted for in 2016 (Trump/Clinton)
3. We are interested in studying how voting intentions in the 2020 US presidential election vary by an individual's income. We set up a logistic regression model to study this relationship. In this study, some possible predictor variables could be (select all that apply)?
   a. The race of the respondent (white/not white)
   b. The respondent's marital status (married/not)
   c. Whether the respondent is going to vote for Biden (yes/no)
4. The mean of a Poisson distribution is equal to its?
   a. Median.
   b. Standard deviation.
   c. Variance.

5. Please redo the `rstanarm` example of US elections but include additional variables. Which variable did you choose, and how did the performance of the model improve?
6. Please create the graph of the density of the Poisson distribution when $\lambda = 75$.
7. From Gelman, Hill, and Vehtari (2020), what is the offset in Poisson regression?
8. Redo the *Jane Eyre* example, but for "A/a".
9. The twentieth century British statistician George Box, famously said, "[s]ince all models are wrong the scientist must be alert to what is importantly wrong. It is inappropriate to be concerned about mice when there are tigers abroad." (Box 1976, 792). Discuss, with the help of examples and citations.

Tutorial

Please consider Maher (1982), R. Smith (2002), or N. Cohn (2016). Build a simplified version of their model. Obtain some recent relevant data, estimate the model, and discuss your choice between logistic, Poisson, and negative binomial regression.

Paper

At about this point the *Spadina* Paper in the "Papers" Online Appendix[4] would be appropriate.

[4]https://tellingstorieswithdata.com/23-assessment.html

Part VI

Applications

14

Causality from observational data

Prerequisites

- Read *Causal design patterns for data analysts*, (Riederer 2021)
  - This blog post provides an overview of different approaches for making causal claims from observational data.
- Read *BNT162b2 mRNA Covid-19 Vaccine in a Nationwide Mass Vaccination Setting*, (Dagan et al. 2021)
  - This paper compares causal conclusions drawn from observational data with those of a randomized trial.
- Read *The Effect: An Introduction to Research Design and Causality*, (Huntington-Klein 2021)
  - Focus on Chapters 18 "Difference-in-Differences", 19 "Instrumental Variables", and 20 "Regression Discontinuity", which provide an overview of three key approaches for making causal claims from observational data.
- Read *Understanding regression discontinuity designs as observational studies*, (Sekhon and Titiunik 2017)
  - Discusses some concerns with the use of regression discontinuity.

Key concepts and skills

- Running an experiment is not always possible, but we can use various approaches to nonetheless be able to speak to causality to some extent. The first step is to be clear about the relationships that we expect by building a directed acyclic graph (DAG).
- We need to be careful of common paradoxes including Simpson's paradox and Berkson's paradox, and be aware of both the potential and pitfalls of matching.
- We can use difference-in-differences when we have data on both treated and untreated units at both time periods. Regression discontinuity is useful when a group is either treated or not, but the two groups are very similar apart from the treatment. And instrumental variables is an approach used to estimate causality indirectly through another variable.
- In general, these approaches need to be used with humility and concern for weaknesses and assumptions, both those that we can test and those that we cannot.

Software and packages

- Base R (R Core Team 2023)
- `broom` (D. Robinson, Hayes, and Couch 2022)
- `broom.mixed` (Bolker and Robinson 2022)
- `estimatr` (G. Blair et al. 2021)
- `haven` (Wickham, Miller, and Smith 2023)
- `knitr` (Xie 2023)
- `MatchIt` (Ho et al. 2011)
- `modelsummary` (Arel-Bundock 2022)
- `palmerpenguins` (Horst, Presmanes Hill, and Gorman 2020)

- rdrobust (Calonico et al. 2021)
- rstanarm (Goodrich et al. 2023)
- scales (Wickham and Seidel 2022)
- tidyverse (Wickham et al. 2019)

```
library(broom)
library(broom.mixed)
library(estimatr)
library(haven)
library(knitr)
library(MatchIt)
library(modelsummary)
library(palmerpenguins)
library(rdrobust)
library(rstanarm)
library(scales)
library(tidyverse)
```

14.1 Introduction

Life is grand when we can conduct experiments to be able to speak to causality. But there are circumstances in which we cannot run an experiment, yet nonetheless want to be able to make causal claims. And data from outside experiments have value that experiments do not have. In this chapter we discuss the circumstances and methods that allow us to speak to causality using observational data. We use relatively simple methods, in sophisticated ways, drawing from statistics, but also a variety of social sciences, including economics and political science, as well as epidemiology.

For instance, Dagan et al. (2021) use observational data to confirm the effectiveness of the Pfizer-BioNTech vaccine. They discuss how one concern with using observational data in this way is confounding, which is where we are concerned that there is some variable that affects both the predictor and outcome variables and can lead to spurious relationships. Dagan et al. (2021) adjust for this by first making a list of potential confounders, such as age, sex, geographic location, and healthcare usage and then adjusting for each of them, by matching one-to-one between people that were vaccinated and those that were not. The experimental data guided the use of observational data, and the larger size of the latter enabled a focus on specific age-groups and extent of disease.

This chapter is about using observational data in sophisticated ways. How we can nonetheless be comfortable making causal statements, even when we cannot run A/B tests or RCTs. Indeed, in what circumstances may we prefer to not run those or to run observational-based approaches in addition to them. We cover three of the major methods: difference-in-differences, regression discontinuity, and instrumental variables.

14.2 Directed Acyclic Graphs

When we are discussing causality, it can help to be specific about what we mean. It is easy to get caught up in observational data and trick ourselves. We should think hard, and to use all the tools available to us. For instance, in that earlier example, Dagan et al. (2021) were able to use experimental data as a guide. Most of the time, we will not be so lucky as to have both experimental data and observational data available to us. One framework that can help with thinking hard about our data is the use of directed acyclic graphs (DAG). DAGs are a fancy name for a flow diagram and involve drawing arrows and lines between the variables to indicate the relationship between them.

To construct them we use Graphviz, which is an open-source package for graph visualization and is built into Quarto. The code needs to be wrapped in a "dot" chunk rather than "R", and the chunk options are set with "//|" instead of "#|". Alternatives that do not require this include the use of `DiagrammeR` (Iannone 2022) and `ggdag` (Barrett 2021b). We provide the whole chunk for the first DAG, but then, only provide the code for the others.

````
```{dot}
//| label: fig-dot-firstdag-pdf
//| fig-cap: "A causal relationship where x influences y"
//| fig-width: 2
digraph D {
  node [shape=plaintext, fontname = "helvetica"];

  {rank=same x y};

  x -> y;
}
```
````

Figure 14.1: A causal relationship where x influences y

In Figure 14.1, we are saying that we think x causes y.

14.2.1 Confounder

We could build another DAG where the situation is less clear. To make the examples a little easier to follow, we will switch to thinking about a hypothetical relationship between income and happiness, with consideration of variables that could affect that relationship. In this first one we consider the relationship between income and happiness, along with education (Figure 14.2).

```
digraph D {

  node [shape=plaintext, fontname = "helvetica"];

  a [label = "Income"];
  b [label = "Happiness"];
  c [label = "Education"];

  { rank=same a b};

  a->b;
  c->{a, b};
}
```

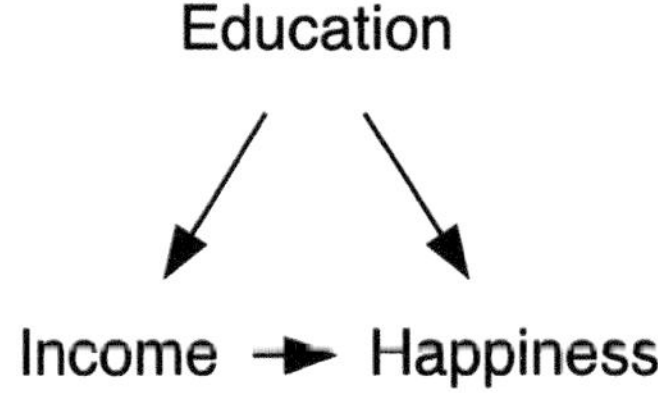

Figure 14.2: Education is a confounder that affects the relationship between income and happiness

In Figure 14.2, we think income causes happiness. But we also think that education causes happiness, and that education also causes income. That relationship is a "backdoor path", and failing to adjust for education in a regression could overstate the extent of the relationship, or even create a spurious relationship, between income and happiness in our analysis. That is, we may think that changes in income are causing changes in happiness, but it could be that education is changing them both. That variable, in this case, education, is called a "confounder".

Hernán and Robins (2023, 83) discuss an interesting case where a researcher was interested in whether one person looking up at the sky makes others look up at the sky also. There was a clear relationship between the responses of both people. But it was also the case that there was noise in the sky. It was unclear whether the second person looked up because the first person looked up, or they both looked up because of the noise. When using experimental data, randomization allows us to avoid this concern, but with observational data we cannot rely on that. It is also not the case that bigger data necessarily get around this problem for us. Instead, we should think carefully about the situation, and DAGs can help with that.

If there are confounders, but we are still interested in causal effects, then we need to adjust for them. One way is to include them in the regression. But the validity of this requires several assumptions. In particular, Gelman and Hill (2007, 169) warn that our estimate will only correspond to the average causal effect in the sample if we include all of the confounders and have the right model. Putting the second requirement to one side, and focusing only on the first, if we do not think about and observe a confounder, then it can be difficult to adjust for it. And this is an area where both domain expertise and theory can bring a lot to an analysis.

14.2.2 Mediator

In Figure 14.3 we again consider that income causes happiness. But, if income also causes children, and children also cause happiness, then we have a situation where it would be tricky to understand the effect of income on happiness.

```
digraph D {

  node [shape=plaintext, fontname = "helvetica"];

  a [label = "Income"];
  b [label = "Happiness"];
  c [label = "Children"];

  { rank=same a b};

  a->{b, c};
  c->b;
}
```

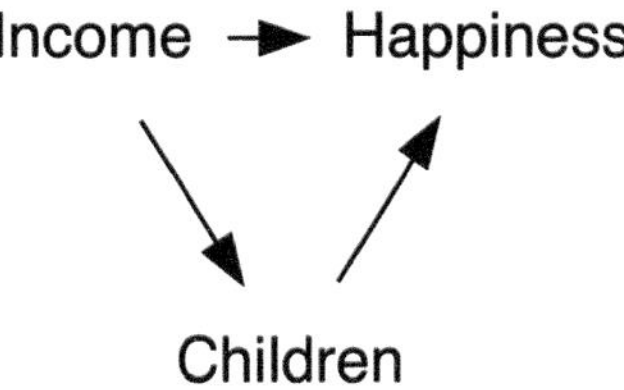

Figure 14.3: Children as a mediator between income and happiness

In Figure 14.3, children is called a "mediator" and we would not adjust for it if we were interested in the effect of income on happiness. If we were to adjust for it, then some of what we are attributing to income, would be due to children.

14.2.3 Collider

Finally, in Figure 14.4 we have yet another similar situation, where we think that income causes happiness. But this time both income and happiness also cause exercise. For instance, if you have more money, then it may be easier to exercise, but also it may be easier to exercise if you are happier.

```
digraph D {
```

```
    node [shape=plaintext, fontname = "helvetica"];

    a [label = "Income"];
    b [label = "Happiness"];
    c [label = "Exercise"];

    { rank=same a b};

    a->{b c};
    b->c;
  }
```

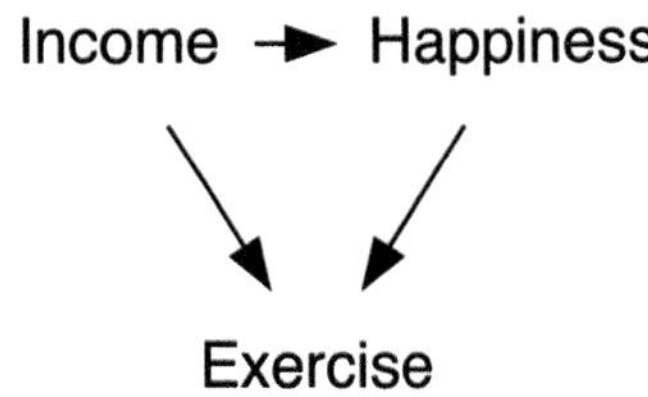

Figure 14.4: Exercise as a collider affecting the relationship between income and happiness

In this case, exercise is called a "collider" and if we were to condition on it, then we would create a misleading relationship. Income influences exercise, but a person's happiness also affects this. Exercise is a collider because both the predictor and outcome variable of interest influence it.

We will be clear about this: we must create the DAG ourselves, in the same way that we must put together the model ourselves. There is nothing that will create it for us. This means that we need to think carefully about the situation. Because it is one thing to see something in the DAG and then do something about it, but it is another to not even know that it is there. McElreath ([2015] 2020, 180) describes these as haunted DAGs. DAGs are helpful, but they are just a tool to help us think deeply about our situation.

When we are building models, it can be tempting to include as many predictor variables as possible. DAGs show clearly why we need to be more thoughtful. For instance, if a variable is a confounder, then we would want to adjust for it, whereas if a variable was a collider then we would not. We can never know the truth, and we are informed by aspects such as theory, what we are interested in, research design, limitations of the data, or our own limitations as researchers, to name a few. Knowing the limits is as important as reporting the model. Data and models with flaws are still useful, if you acknowledge those flaws. The work of thinking about a situation is never done, and relies on others, which is why we need to make all our work as reproducible as possible.

14.3 Two common paradoxes

There are two situations where data can trick us that are so common that we will explicitly go through them. These are:

1) Simpson's paradox, and
2) Berkson's paradox.

14.3.1 Simpson's paradox

Simpson's paradox occurs when we estimate some relationship for subsets of our data, but a different relationship when we consider the entire dataset (Simpson 1951). It is a particular case of the ecological fallacy, which is when we try to make claims about individuals, based on their group. For instance, it may be that there is a positive relationship between undergraduate grades and performance in graduate school in two departments when considering each department individually. But if undergraduate grades tended to be higher in one department than another while graduate school performance tended to be opposite, we may find a negative relationship between undergraduate grades and performance in graduate school. We can simulate some data to show this more clearly (Figure 14.5).

```
set.seed(853)

number_in_each <- 1000

department_one <-
  tibble(
    undergrad = runif(n = number_in_each, min = 0.7, max = 0.9),
    noise = rnorm(n = number_in_each, 0, sd = 0.1),
    grad = undergrad + noise,
    type = "Department 1"
  )

department_two <-
  tibble(
    undergrad = runif(n = number_in_each, min = 0.6, max = 0.8),
    noise = rnorm(n = number_in_each, 0, sd = 0.1),
    grad = undergrad + noise + 0.3,
    type = "Department 2"
  )

both_departments <- rbind(department_one, department_two)

both_departments
```

```
# A tibble: 2,000 x 4
   undergrad   noise  grad type
       <dbl>   <dbl> <dbl> <chr>
 1     0.772 -0.0566 0.715 Department 1
```

```
2        0.724 -0.0312 0.693 Department 1
3        0.797  0.0770 0.874 Department 1
4        0.763 -0.0664 0.697 Department 1
5        0.707  0.0717 0.779 Department 1
6        0.781 -0.0165 0.764 Department 1
7        0.726 -0.104  0.623 Department 1
8        0.749  0.0527 0.801 Department 1
9        0.732 -0.0471 0.684 Department 1
10       0.738  0.0552 0.793 Department 1
# i 1,990 more rows
```

```
both_departments |>
  ggplot(aes(x = undergrad, y = grad)) +
  geom_point(aes(color = type), alpha = 0.1) +
  geom_smooth(aes(color = type), method = "lm", formula = "y ~ x") +
  geom_smooth(method = "lm", formula = "y ~ x", color = "black") +
  labs(
    x = "Undergraduate results",
    y = "Graduate results",
    color = "Department"
  ) +
  theme_minimal() +
  scale_color_brewer(palette = "Set1") +
  theme(legend.position = "bottom")
```

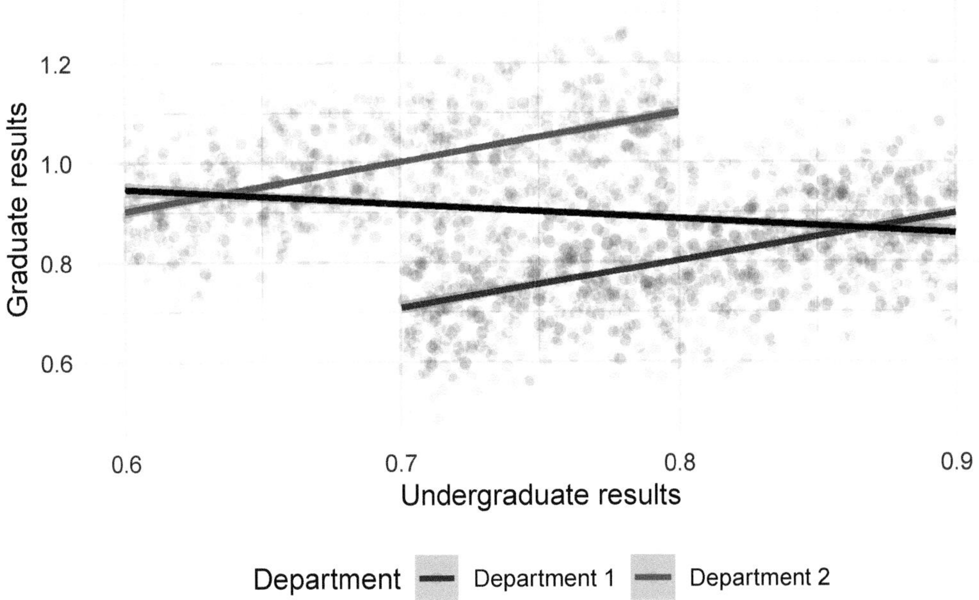

Figure 14.5: Illustration of simulated data that shows Simpson's paradox

Simpson's paradox is often illustrated using real-world data from University of California, Berkeley, on graduate admissions (Bickel, Hammel, and O'Connell 1975). This paper was mentioned in Chapter 4 as having one of the greatest sub-titles ever published. Hernán, Clayton, and Keiding (2011) create DAGs that further illuminate the relationship and the cause of the paradox.

More recently, as mentioned in its documentation, the "penguins" dataset from `palmerpenguins` provides an example of Simpson's paradox, using real-world data on the relationship between body mass and bill depth in different species of penguins (Figure 14.6). The overall negative trend occurs because Gentoo penguins tend to be heavier but with shorter bills compared to Adelie and Chinstrap penguins.

```
penguins |>
  ggplot(aes(x = body_mass_g, y = bill_depth_mm)) +
  geom_point(aes(color = species), alpha = 0.1) +
  geom_smooth(aes(color = species), method = "lm", formula = "y ~ x") +
  geom_smooth(
    method = "lm",
    formula = "y ~ x",
    color = "black"
  ) +
  labs(
    x = "Body mass (grams)",
    y = "Bill depth (millimeters)",
    color = "Species"
  ) +
  theme_minimal() +
  scale_color_brewer(palette = "Set1") +
  theme(legend.position = "bottom")
```

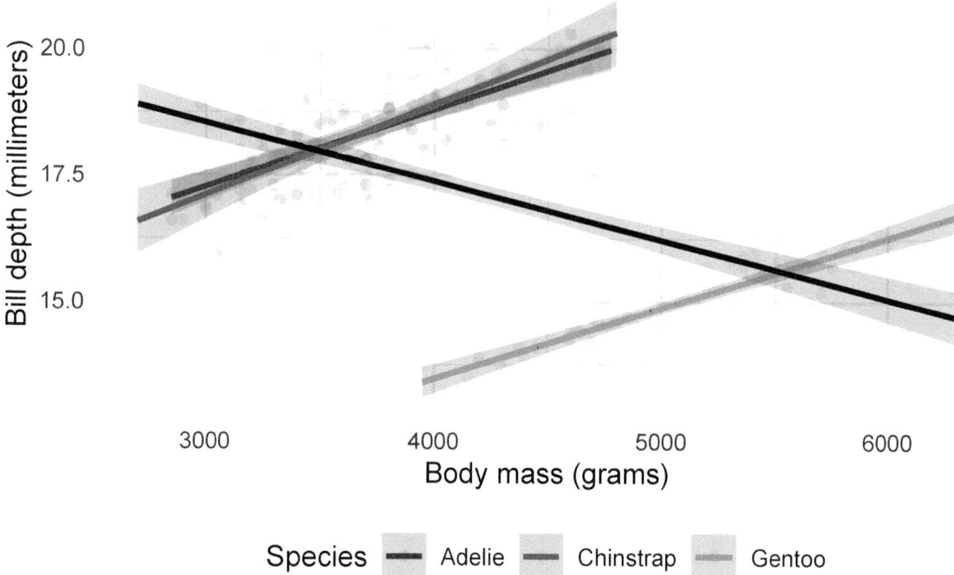

Figure 14.6: Illustration of Simpson's paradox in a dataset of penguin bill depth compared with their body mass

14.3.2 Berkson's paradox

Berkson's paradox occurs when we estimate some relationship based on the dataset that we have, but because the dataset is so selected, the relationship is different in a more general dataset (Berkson 1946). For instance, if we have a dataset of professional cyclists then we might find there is no relationship between their VO2 max and their chance of winning a bike race (Coyle et al. 1988; Podlogar, Leo, and Spragg 2022). But if we had a dataset of the general population then we might find a relationship between these two variables. The professional dataset has just been so selected that the relationship disappears; one cannot become a professional cyclist unless one has a good enough VO2 max, but among professional cyclists everyone has a good enough VO2 max. Again, we can simulate some data to show this more clearly (Figure 14.7).

```
set.seed(853)

num_pros <- 100
num_public <- 1000

professionals <- tibble(
  VO2 = runif(num_pros, 0.7, 0.9),
  chance_of_winning = runif(num_pros, 0.7, 0.9),
  type = "Professionals"
)

general_public <- tibble(
  VO2 = runif(num_public, 0.6, 0.8),
  chance_of_winning = VO2 + rnorm(num_public, 0, 0.03) + 0.1,
  type = "Public"
)

professionals_and_public <- bind_rows(professionals, general_public)
```

```
professionals_and_public |>
  ggplot(aes(x = VO2, y = chance_of_winning)) +
  geom_point(aes(color = type), alpha = 0.1) +
  geom_smooth(aes(color = type), method = "lm", formula = "y ~ x") +
  geom_smooth(method = "lm", formula = "y ~ x", color = "black") +
  labs(
    x = "VO2 max",
    y = "Chance of winning a bike race",
    color = "Type"
  ) +
  theme_minimal() +
  scale_color_brewer(palette = "Set1") +
  theme(legend.position = "bottom")
```

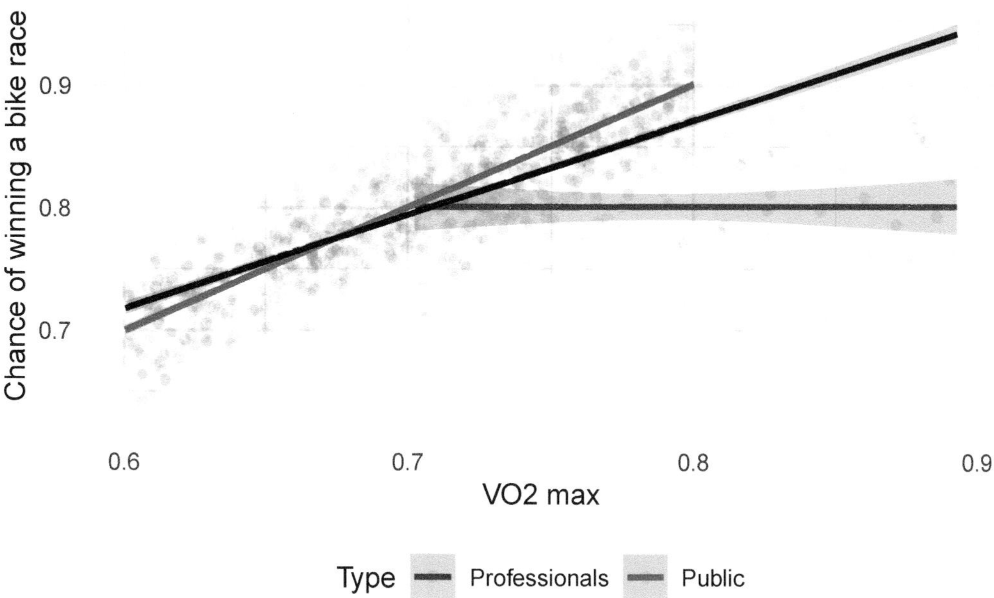

Figure 14.7: Illustration of simulated data that shows Berkson's paradox

14.4 Difference-in-differences

The ideal situation of being able to conduct an experiment is rarely possible. Can we reasonably expect that Netflix would allow us to change prices? And even if they did once, would they let us do it again, and again, and again? Further, rarely can we explicitly create treatment and control groups. Finally, experiments can be expensive or unethical. Instead, we need to make do with what we have. Rather than our counterfactual coming to us through randomization, and hence us knowing that the two are the same but for the treatment, we try to identify groups that were similar but for the treatment, and hence any differences can be attributed to the treatment.

With observational data, sometimes there are differences between our two groups before we treat. Provided those pre-treatment differences satisfy assumptions that essentially amount to the differences being both consistent, and that we expect that consistency to continue in the absence of the treatment—the "parallel trends" assumption—then we can look to any difference in the differences as the effect of the treatment. One of the aspects of difference-in-differences analysis is that we can do it using relatively straight forward methods, for instance John Tang (2015). Linear regression with a binary variable is enough to get started and do a convincing job.

Consider wanting to know the effect of a new tennis racket on serve speed. One way to test this would be to measure the difference between, say, Roger Federer's serve speed without the tennis racket and the serve speed of an enthusiastic amateur, let us call them Ville, with the tennis racket. Yes, we would find a difference, but would we know how much to attribute to the tennis racket? Another way would be to consider the difference between Ville's serve speed without the new tennis racket and Ville's serve speed with the new tennis racket. But what if serves were just getting faster naturally over time? Instead, we combine the two approaches to look at the difference in the differences.

We begin by measuring Federer's serve speed and compare it to Ville's serve speed, both without the new racket. We then measure Federer's serve speed again, and measure Ville's serve speed with the new racket. That difference in the differences would then be the estimate of the effect of the new racket. There are a few key questions we must ask to see if this analysis is appropriate:

1) Is there something else that may have affected only Ville, and not Federer that could affect Ville's serve speed?
2) Is it likely that Federer and Ville have the same trajectory of serve speed improvement? This is the "parallel trends" assumption, and it dominates many discussions of difference-in-differences analysis.
3) Finally, is it likely that the variance of our serve speeds of Federer and Ville are the same?

Despite these requirements, difference-in-differences is a powerful approach because we do not need the treatment and control group to be the same before the treatment. We just need to have a good idea of how they differed.

14.4.1 Simulated example: tennis serve speed

To be more specific about the situation, we simulate data. We will simulate a situation in which there is initially a difference of one between the serve speeds of the different people, and then after a new tennis racket, there is a difference of six. We can use a graph to illustrate the situation (Figure 14.8).

```
set.seed(853)

simulated_diff_in_diff <-
  tibble(
    person = rep(c(1:1000), times = 2),
    time = c(rep(0, times = 1000), rep(1, times = 1000)),
    treat_group = rep(sample(x = 0:1, size = 1000, replace = TRUE ), times = 2)
    ) |>
  mutate(
    treat_group = as.factor(treat_group),
    time = as.factor(time)
  )

simulated_diff_in_diff <-
  simulated_diff_in_diff |>
  rowwise() |>
  mutate(
    serve_speed = case_when(
      time == 0 & treat_group == 0 ~ rnorm(n = 1, mean = 5, sd = 1),
      time == 1 & treat_group == 0 ~ rnorm(n = 1, mean = 6, sd = 1),
      time == 0 & treat_group == 1 ~ rnorm(n = 1, mean = 8, sd = 1),
      time == 1 & treat_group == 1 ~ rnorm(n = 1, mean = 14, sd = 1)
```

```
    )
  )

simulated_diff_in_diff
```

```
# A tibble: 2,000 x 4
# Rowwise:
   person time  treat_group serve_speed
    <int> <fct> <fct>             <dbl>
 1      1 0     0                  4.43
 2      2 0     1                  6.96
 3      3 0     1                  7.77
 4      4 0     0                  5.31
 5      5 0     0                  4.09
 6      6 0     0                  4.85
 7      7 0     0                  6.43
 8      8 0     0                  5.77
 9      9 0     1                  6.13
10     10 0     1                  7.32
# i 1,990 more rows
```

```
simulated_diff_in_diff |>
  ggplot(aes(x = time, y = serve_speed, color = treat_group)) +
  geom_point(alpha = 0.2) +
  geom_line(aes(group = person), alpha = 0.1) +
  theme_minimal() +
  labs(x = "Time period", y = "Serve speed", color = "Person got a new racket") +
  scale_color_brewer(palette = "Set1") +
  theme(legend.position = "bottom")
```

We can obtain our estimate manually, by looking at the average difference of the differences. When we do that, we find that we estimate the effect of the new tennis racket to be 5.06, which is similar to what we simulated.

```
ave_diff <-
  simulated_diff_in_diff |>
  pivot_wider(
    names_from = time,
    values_from = serve_speed,
    names_prefix = "time_"
  ) |>
  mutate(difference = time_1 - time_0) |>
  # Average difference between old and new racket serve speed within groups
  summarise(average_difference = mean(difference),
            .by = treat_group)

# Difference between the average differences of each group
ave_diff$average_difference[2] - ave_diff$average_difference[1]
```

```
[1] 5.058414
```

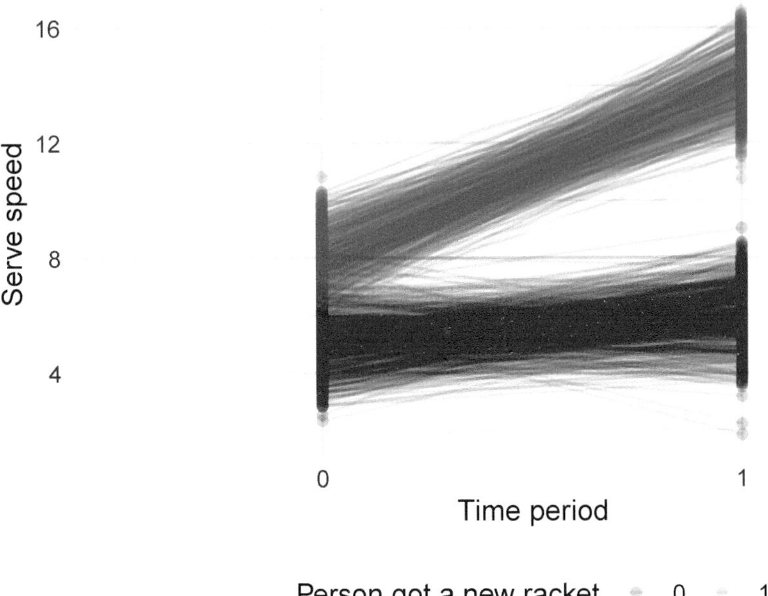

Figure 14.8: Illustration of simulated data that shows a difference before and after getting a new tennis racket

And we can use linear regression to get the same result. The model we are interested in is:

$$Y_{i,t} = \beta_0 + \beta_1 \times \text{Treatment}_i + \beta_2 \times \text{Time}_t + \beta_3 \times (\text{Treatment} \times \text{Time})_{i,t} + \epsilon_{i,t}$$

While we should include the separate aspects as well, it is the estimate of the interaction that we are interested in. In this case it is β_3. And we find that our estimated effect is 5.06 (Table 14.1).

```
diff_in_diff_example_regression <-
  stan_glm(
    formula = serve_speed ~ treat_group * time,
    data = simulated_diff_in_diff,
    family = gaussian(),
    prior = normal(location = 0, scale = 2.5, autoscale = TRUE),
    prior_intercept = normal(0, 2.5, autoscale = TRUE),
    prior_aux = exponential(rate = 1, autoscale = TRUE),
    seed = 853
  )

saveRDS(
  diff_in_diff_example_regression,
  file = "diff_in_diff_example_regression.rds"
)
```

Table 14.1: Illustration of simulated data that shows a difference before and after getting a new tennis racket

	(1)
(Intercept)	4.971
treatment_group1	3.035
time1	1.006
treatment_group1 × time1	5.057
Num.Obs.	2000
R2	0.927
R2 Adj.	0.927
Log.Lik.	−2802.166
ELPD	−2806.3
ELPD s.e.	32.1
LOOIC	5612.5
LOOIC s.e.	64.2
WAIC	5612.5
RMSE	0.98

```
diff_in_diff_example_regression <-
  readRDS(file = "diff_in_diff_example_regression.rds")
```

```
modelsummary(
  diff_in_diff_example_regression
)
```

14.4.2 Assumptions

If we want to use difference-in-differences, then we need to satisfy the assumptions. There were three that were touched on earlier, but here we will focus on the "parallel trends" assumption. The parallel trends assumption haunts everything to do with difference-in-differences analysis because we can never prove it; we can just be convinced of it, and try to convince others.

To see why we can never prove it, consider an example in which we want to know the effect of a new stadium on a professional sports team's wins/loses. To do this we consider two professional basketball teams: the Golden State Warriors and the Toronto Raptors. The Warriors changed stadiums at the start of the 2019-20 season, while the Raptors did not, so we will consider four time periods: the 2016-17 season, 2017-18 season, 2018-19 season, and finally we will compare the performance with the one after they moved, so the 2019-20 season. The Raptors here act as our counterfactual. This means that we assume the relationship between the Warriors and the Raptors, in the absence of a new stadium, would have continued to change in a consistent way. But the fundamental problem of causal inference means that we can never know that for certain. We must present sufficient evidence to assuage any concerns that a reader may have.

There are four main threats to validity when we use difference-in-differences, and we need to address all of them (Cunningham 2021, 272–77):

1. Non-parallel trends. The treatment and control groups may be based on differences. As such it can be difficult to convincingly argue for parallel trends. In this case, maybe try to find another factor to consider in your model that may adjust for some of that. This may require triple-differenced approaches. For instance, in the earlier example, we could perhaps add the San Francisco 49ers, a football team, as they are in the same broad geographic area as the Warriors. Or maybe rethink the analysis to see if we can make a different control group. Adding additional earlier time periods may help but may introduce more issues, which we touch on in the third point.
2. Compositional differences. This is a concern when working with repeated cross-sections. What if the composition of those cross-sections change? For instance, if we are working at an app that is rapidly growing, and we want to look at the effect of some change. In our initial cross-section, we may have mostly young people, but in a subsequent cross-section, we may have more older people as the demographics of the app usage change. Hence our results may just be an age-effect, not an effect of the change that we are interested in.
3. Long-term effects compared with reliability. As we discussed in Chapter 8, there is a trade-off between the length of the analysis that we run. As we run the analysis for longer there is more opportunity for other factors to affect the results. There is also increased chance for someone who was not treated to be treated. But, on the other hand, it can be difficult to convincingly argue that short-term results will continue in the long term.
4. Functional form dependence. This is less of an issue when the outcomes are similar, but if they are different then functional form may be responsible for some aspects of the results.

14.4.3 French newspaper prices between 1960 and 1974

In this case study we introduce Angelucci and Cagé (2019). They are interested in understanding the effect of the introduction of television on French newspapers. We will replicate one of the main findings.

The business model of newspapers has been challenged by the internet and many local newspapers have closed. This issue is not new. When television was introduced, there were similar concerns. Angelucci and Cagé (2019) use the introduction of television advertising in France, announced in 1967, to examine the effect of decreased advertising revenue on newspapers. They create a dataset of French newspapers from 1960 to 1974 and then use difference-in-differences to examine the effect of the reduction in advertising revenues on newspapers' content and prices. The change that they focus on is the introduction of television advertising, which they argue affected national newspapers more than local newspapers. They find that this change results in both less journalism content in the newspapers and lower newspaper prices. Focusing on this change, and analyzing it using difference-in-differences, is important because it allows us to disentangle a few competing effects. For instance, did newspapers become redundant because they could no longer charge high prices for their advertisements, or because consumers preferred to get their news from the television?

We can get free access to the data[1] that underpins Angelucci and Cagé (2019) after registration. The dataset is in the Stata data format, ".dta", which we can read with `read_dta()` from `haven`. The file that we are interested in is "Angelucci_Cage_AEJMicro_dataset.dta", which is the "dta" folder.

[1] https://www.openicpsr.org/openicpsr/project/116438/version/V1/view

```
newspapers <- read_dta("Angelucci_Cage_AEJMicro_dataset.dta")
```

There are 1,196 observations in the dataset and 52 variables. Angelucci and Cagé (2019) are interested in the 1960-1974 time period which has around 100 newspapers. There are 14 national newspapers at the beginning of the period and 12 at the end. The key period is 1967, when the French government announced it would allow advertising on television. Angelucci and Cagé (2019) argue that national newspapers were affected by this change, but local newspapers were not. The national newspapers are the treatment group and the local newspapers are the control group.

We focus just on the headline difference-in-differences result and construct summary statistics.

```
newspapers <-
  newspapers |>
  select(
    year, id_news, after_national, local, national, ra_cst, ps_cst, qtotal
    ) |>
  mutate(ra_cst_div_qtotal = ra_cst / qtotal,
         across(c(id_news, after_national, local, national), as.factor),
         year = as.integer(year))

newspapers
```

```
# A tibble: 1,196 x 9
    year id_news after_national local national    ra_cst ps_cst  qtotal
   <int> <fct>   <fct>          <fct> <fct>        <dbl>  <dbl>   <dbl>
 1  1960 1       0              1     0         52890272   2.29  94478.
 2  1961 1       0              1     0         56601060   2.20  96289.
 3  1962 1       0              1     0         64840752   2.13  97313.
 4  1963 1       0              1     0         70582944   2.43 101068.
 5  1964 1       0              1     0         74977888   2.35 102103.
 6  1965 1       0              1     0         74438248   2.29 105169.
 7  1966 1       0              1     0         81383000   2.31 126235.
 8  1967 1       0              1     0         80263152   2.88 128667.
 9  1968 1       0              1     0         87165704   3.45 131824.
10  1969 1       0              1     0        102596384   3.28 132417.
# i 1,186 more rows
# i 1 more variable: ra_cst_div_qtotal <dbl>
```

We are interested in what happened from 1967 onward, especially in terms of advertising revenue, and whether that was different for national, compared with local newspapers (Figure 14.9). We use `scales` to adjust the y-axis.

```
newspapers |>
  mutate(type = if_else(local == 1, "Local", "National")) |>
  ggplot(aes(x = year, y = ra_cst)) +
  geom_point(alpha = 0.5) +
  scale_y_continuous(
    labels = dollar_format(
```

```
      prefix = "$",
      suffix = "M",
      scale = 0.000001)) +
  labs(x = "Year", y = "Advertising revenue") +
  facet_wrap(vars(type), nrow = 2) +
  theme_minimal() +
  geom_vline(xintercept = 1966.5, linetype = "dashed")
```

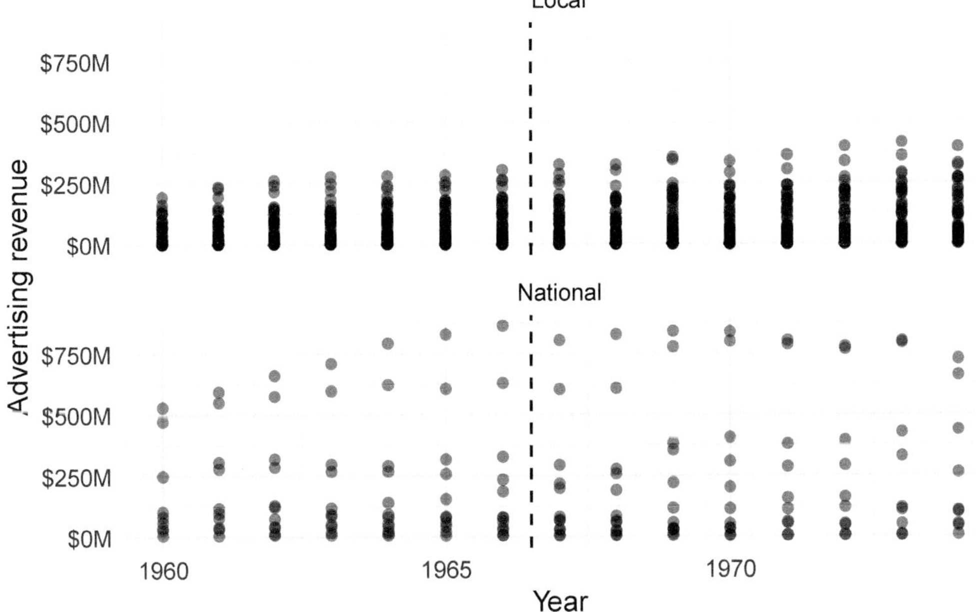

Figure 14.9: Revenue of French newspapers (1960-1974), by whether they were local or national

The model that we are interested in estimating is:

$$\ln(y_{n,t}) = \beta_0 + \beta_1 \times (\text{National binary} \times 1967 \text{ onward binary}) + \lambda_n + \gamma_t + \epsilon$$

It is the β_1 coefficient that we are especially interested in. We estimate the models using `stan_glm()`.

```
ad_revenue <-
  stan_glm(
    formula = log(ra_cst) ~ after_national + id_news + year,
    data = newspapers,
    family = gaussian(),
    prior = normal(location = 0, scale = 2.5, autoscale = TRUE),
    prior_intercept = normal(0, 2.5, autoscale = TRUE),
    prior_aux = exponential(rate = 1, autoscale = TRUE),
    seed = 853
  )
```

```
saveRDS(
  ad_revenue,
  file = "ad_revenue.rds"
)

ad_revenue_div_circulation <-
  stan_glm(
    formula = log(ra_cst_div_qtotal) ~ after_national + id_news + year,
    data = newspapers,
    family = gaussian(),
    prior = normal(location = 0, scale = 2.5, autoscale = TRUE),
    prior_intercept = normal(0, 2.5, autoscale = TRUE),
    prior_aux = exponential(rate = 1, autoscale = TRUE),
    seed = 853
  )

saveRDS(
  ad_revenue_div_circulation,
  file = "ad_revenue_div_circulation.rds"
)

# Consumer side
subscription_price <-
  stan_glm(
    formula = log(ps_cst) ~ after_national + id_news + year,
    data = newspapers,
    family = gaussian(),
    prior = normal(location = 0, scale = 2.5, autoscale = TRUE),
    prior_intercept = normal(0, 2.5, autoscale = TRUE),
    prior_aux = exponential(rate = 1, autoscale = TRUE),
    seed = 853
  )

saveRDS(
  subscription_price,
  file = "subscription_price.rds"
)
```

```
ad_revenue <-
  readRDS(file = "ad_revenue.rds")

ad_revenue_div_circulation <-
  readRDS(file = "ad_revenue_div_circulation")

subscription_price <-
  readRDS(file = "subscription_price.rds")
```

Looking at the advertising-side variables, such as revenue and prices, in Table 14.2 we find consistently negative coefficients.

Table 14.2: Effect of changed television advertising laws on revenue of French newspapers (1960-1974)

	Ad revenue	Ad revenue over circulation	Subscription price
Year	0.05	0.04	0.05
After change	−0.23	−0.15	−0.04
Num.Obs.	1052	1048	1044
R2	0.984	0.896	0.868
R2 Adj.	0.983	0.886	0.852
Log.Lik.	336.539	441.471	875.559
ELPD	257.4	362.3	793.5
ELPD s.e.	34.4	45.6	24.3
LOOIC	−514.8	−724.6	−1586.9
LOOIC s.e.	68.9	91.2	48.6
WAIC	−515.9	−725.5	−1588.9
RMSE	0.17	0.16	0.10

```
selected_variables <- c("year" = "Year", "after_national1" = "After change")

modelsummary(
  models = list(
    "Ad revenue" = ad_revenue,
    "Ad revenue over circulation" = ad_revenue_div_circulation,
    "Subscription price" = subscription_price
  ),
  fmt = 2,
  coef_map = selected_variables
)
```

We can replicate the main results of Angelucci and Cagé (2019) and find that in many cases there appears to be a difference from 1967 onward. Angelucci and Cagé (2019, 353–58) also include an excellent example of the discussion of interpretation, external validity, and robustness that is required for difference-in-differences models.

14.5 Propensity score matching

Difference-in-differences is a powerful analysis framework. But it can be tough to identify appropriate treatment and control groups. R. Alexander and Ward (2018) compare migrant brothers, where one brother had most of their education in a different country, and the other brother had most of their education in the United States. Given the data that are available, this match provides a reasonable treatment and control group. But other matches could have given different results, for instance friends or cousins.

We can only match based on observable variables. For instance, age-group or education. At two different times we compare smoking rates in 18-year-olds in one city with smoking rates in 18-year-olds in another city. This would be a coarse match because we know that there are many differences between 18-year-olds, even in terms of the variables that we commonly observe, say gender and education. One way to deal with this would be to create sub-groups: 18-year-old males with a high school education, etc. But then the sample sizes quickly become small. We also have the issue of how to deal with continuous variables. And is an 18-year-old really that different to a 19-year-old? Why not also compare with them?

One way to proceed is to consider a nearest neighbor approach, but there can be limited concern for uncertainty with this approach. There can also be an issue with having many variables because we end up with a high-dimension graph. This leads to propensity score matching. Here we explain the process of propensity score matching and a few of the concerns that are commonly brought up about it.

Propensity score matching involves assigning some probability—the "propensity score"—to each observation. We construct that probability based on the observation's values for the predictors without the treatment. That probability is our best guess at the probability of the observation being treated, regardless of whether it was actually treated. For instance, if 18-year-old males were treated but 19-year-old males were not, then, as there is not much difference between 18-year-old and 19-year-old males in general, our assigned probability would be similar. We then compare the outcomes of observations with similar propensity scores.

14.5.1 Simulated example: free shipping

One advantage of propensity score matching is that it allows us to easily consider many predictor variables at once, and it can be constructed using logistic regression. To be more specific we can simulate some data. We will pretend that we work for a large online retailer. We are going to treat some individuals with free shipping to see what happens to their average purchase.

```
set.seed(853)

sample_size <- 10000

purchase_data <-
  tibble(
    unique_person_id = 1:sample_size,
    age = sample(x = 18:100, size = sample_size, replace = TRUE),
    gender = sample(
      x = c("Female", "Male", "Other/decline"),
      size = sample_size,
      replace = TRUE,
      prob = c(0.49, 0.47, 0.02)
    ),
    income = rnorm(n = sample_size, mean = 60000, sd = 15000) |> round(0)
  )

purchase_data
```

```
# A tibble: 10,000 x 4
   unique_person_id   age gender income
              <int> <int> <chr>   <dbl>
```

```
 1              1    26 Male     68637
 2              2    81 Female   71486
 3              3    34 Male     75652
 4              4    46 Male     68068
 5              5   100 Female   73206
 6              6    20 Male     41872
 7              7    50 Female   75957
 8              8    36 Female   56566
 9              9    72 Male     54621
10             10    52 Female   40722
# i 9,990 more rows
```

Then we need to add some probability of being treated with free shipping. We will say that it depends on our predictors and that younger, higher-income, male individuals make this treatment more likely. We only know that because we simulated the situation. We would not know it if we were using actual data.

```
purchase_data <-
  purchase_data |>
  mutate(
    # change characteristics to bounded numbers
    age_num = rank(1 / age, ties.method = "random") %/% 3000,
    # force it between 0 and 3
    gender_num = case_when(
      gender == "Male" ~ 3,
      gender == "Female" ~ 2,
      gender == "Other/decline" ~ 1
    ),
    income_num = rank(income, ties.method = "random") %/% 3000
  ) |>
  mutate(
    sum_num = age_num + gender_num + income_num,
    softmax_prob = exp(sum_num) / exp(max(sum_num) + 0.5),
    free_shipping = rbinom(n = sample_size, size = 1, prob = softmax_prob)) |>
  select(-(age_num:softmax_prob))
```

Finally, we need to have some measure of a person's average spend. We will assume that this increases with income. We want those with free shipping to be slightly higher than those without.

```
purchase_data <-
  purchase_data |>
  mutate(
    noise = rnorm(n = nrow(purchase_data), mean = 5, sd = 2),
    spend = income / 1000 + noise,
    spend = if_else(free_shipping == 1, spend + 10, spend),
    spend = as.integer(spend)
    ) |>
  select(-noise) |>
  mutate(across(c(gender, free_shipping), as.factor))
```

Table 14.3: Difference in average spend by whether had free shipping

Received free shipping?	Average spend
No	64.44
Yes	86.71

```
purchase_data
```

```
# A tibble: 10,000 x 6
   unique_person_id   age gender income free_shipping spend
              <int> <int> <fct>   <dbl> <fct>         <int>
 1                1    26 Male    68637 0                72
 2                2    81 Female  71486 0                73
 3                3    34 Male    75652 0                80
 4                4    46 Male    68068 0                75
 5                5   100 Female  73206 0                78
 6                6    20 Male    41872 0                45
 7                7    50 Female  75957 0                78
 8                8    36 Female  56566 0                62
 9                9    72 Male    54621 0                55
10               10    52 Female  40722 0                47
# i 9,990 more rows
```

Naively we can see that there is a difference in the average spend between those with free shipping and those without (Table 14.3). But the fundamental concern is what would have the spend have been of those with free shipping if they have not had free shipping. Table 14.3 shows an average comparison but not everyone had the same chance of getting free shipping. So we question the validity of that use of an average comparison. Instead we use propensity score matching to "link" each observation that actually got free shipping with their most similar observation, based on the observable variables, that did not get free shipping.

```
purchase_data |>
  summarise(average_spend = round(mean(spend), 2), .by = free_shipping) |>
  mutate(free_shipping = if_else(free_shipping == 0, "No", "Yes")) |>
  kable(
    col.names = c("Received free shipping?", "Average spend"),
    booktabs = TRUE, linesep = ""
  )
```

We use `matchit()` from `MatchIt` to implement logistic regression and create matched groups. We then use `match.data()` to get the data of matches containing both all 254 people who were actually treated with free shipping and the untreated person who is considered as similar to them, based on propensity score, as possible. The result is a dataset of 508 observations.

```
matched_groups <-
  matchit(
  free_shipping ~ age + gender + income,
```

```
    data = purchase_data,
    method = "nearest",
    distance = "glm"
  )

  matched_groups
```

```
A matchit object
 - method: 1:1 nearest neighbor matching without replacement
 - distance: Propensity score
             - estimated with logistic regression
 - number of obs.: 10000 (original), 508 (matched)
 - target estimand: ATT
 - covariates: age, gender, income
```

```
  matched_dataset <- match.data(matched_groups)

  matched_dataset
```

```
# A tibble: 508 x 9
   unique_person_id   age gender       income free_shipping spend distance weights
              <int> <int> <fct>         <dbl> <fct>         <int>    <dbl>   <dbl>
 1               23    28 Female        65685 1                79  0.0334        1
 2               24    67 Male          71150 0                76  0.0220        1
 3               32    22 Female        86071 0                92  0.131         1
 4               48    66 Female       100105 0               108  0.0473        1
 5               59    25 Male          55548 1                68  0.0541        1
 6               82    66 Male          70721 0                75  0.0224        1
 7               83    58 Male          83443 0                88  0.0651        1
 8               87    46 Male          59073 1                73  0.0271        1
 9              119    89 Other/dec~    72284 0                74  0.00301       1
10              125    51 Female        81164 1                96  0.0303        1
# i 498 more rows
# i 1 more variable: subclass <fct>
```

Finally, we can estimate the effect of being treated on average spend using linear regression (Table 14.4). We are particularly interested in the coefficient associated with the treatment variable, in this case free shipping.

```
  propensity_score_regression <- lm(
    spend ~ age + gender + income + free_shipping,
    data = matched_dataset
  )

  modelsummary(propensity_score_regression)
```

In Table 14.4, which was based on only the matched sample, we find that the effect is what we simulated. That is, there is a difference of ten between the average spend of those who received free shipping and those that did not. That is in contrast to Table 14.3 which was based on the entire sample.

Table 14.4: Effect of being treated, using simulated data

	(1)
(Intercept)	3.862
	(0.506)
age	0.007
	(0.005)
genderMale	0.013
	(0.202)
genderOther/decline	−0.509
	(0.847)
income	0.001
	(0.000)
free_shipping1	10.073
	(0.180)
Num.Obs.	508
R2	0.983
R2 Adj.	0.983
AIC	2167.6
BIC	2197.2
Log.Lik.	−1076.811
F	5911.747
RMSE	2.02

We cover propensity score matching because it is widely used. But there are tradeoffs. Transparency is needed when it is being used (Greifer 2021). These concerns include (G. King and Nielsen 2019):

1. Unobservables. Propensity score matching cannot match on unobserved variables. This may be fine in a classroom setting, but in more realistic settings it will likely cause issues. It is difficult to understand why individuals that appear to be so similar, would have received different treatments, unless there is something unobserved that causes the difference. As propensity score matching cannot account for these, it is difficult to know which features are actually being brought together.
2. Modeling. The results of propensity score matching tend to be specific to the model that is used. As there is considerable flexibility as to which model is used, this enables researchers to pick through matches to find one that suits. Additionally, because the two regression steps (the matching and the analysis) are conducted separately, there is no propagation of uncertainty.

The fundamental problem of unobservables can never be shown to be inconsequential because that would require the unobserved data. Those who want to use propensity score matching, and other matching methods, need to be able to argue convincingly that it is appropriate. McKenzie (2021) presents a few cases where this is possible, for instance, when there are capacity limits. As is the common theme of this book, such cases will require focusing on the data and a deep understanding of the situation that produced it.

14.6 Regression discontinuity design

Regression discontinuity design (RDD) was established by Thistlethwaite and Campbell (1960) and is a popular way to get causality when there is a continuous variable with cut-offs that determine treatment. Is there a difference between a student who gets 79 per cent and a student who gets 80 per cent? Probably not much, but one may get a A-, while the other may get a B+. Seeing that on a transcript could affect who gets a job which could affect income. In this case the percentage is a "forcing variable" or "forcing function" and the cut-off for an A- is a "threshold". As the treatment is determined by the forcing variable we need to control for that variable. These seemingly arbitrary cut-offs can be seen all the time. Hence, there has been a great deal of work using RDD.

There is sometimes slightly different terminology used when it comes to RDD. For instance, Cunningham (2021) refers to the forcing function as a running variable. The exact terminology that is used does not matter provided we use it consistently.

14.6.1 Simulated example: income and grades

To be more specific about the situation, we simulate data. We will consider the relationship between income and grades, and simulate there to be a change if a student gets at least 80 (Figure 14.10).

```
set.seed(853)

num_observations <- 1000

rdd_example_data <- tibble(
  person = c(1:num_observations),
  mark = runif(num_observations, min = 78, max = 82),
  income = rnorm(num_observations, 10, 1)
)

## Make income more likely to be higher if mark at least 80
rdd_example_data <-
  rdd_example_data |>
  mutate(
    noise = rnorm(n = num_observations, mean = 2, sd = 1),
    income = if_else(mark >= 80, income + noise, income)
  )

rdd_example_data
```

```
# A tibble: 1,000 x 4
   person  mark income noise
    <int> <dbl>  <dbl> <dbl>
 1      1  79.4   9.43  1.87
 2      2  78.5   9.69  2.26
 3      3  79.9  10.8   1.14
 4      4  79.3   9.34  2.50
```

```
 5      5  78.1  10.7   2.21
 6      6  79.6   9.83  2.47
 7      7  78.5   8.96  4.22
 8      8  79.0  10.5   3.11
 9      9  78.6   9.53  0.671
10     10  78.8  10.6   2.46
# i 990 more rows
```

```
rdd_example_data |>
  ggplot(aes(
    x = mark,
    y = income
  )) +
  geom_point(alpha = 0.2) +
  geom_smooth(
    data = rdd_example_data |> filter(mark < 80),
    method = "lm",
    color = "black",
    formula = "y ~ x"
  ) +
  geom_smooth(
    data = rdd_example_data |> filter(mark >= 80),
    method = "lm",
    color = "black",
    formula = "y ~ x"
  ) +
  theme_minimal() +
  labs(
    x = "Mark",
    y = "Income ($)"
  )
```

We can use a binary variable with linear regression to estimate the effect of getting a mark over 80 on income. We expect the coefficient to be around two, which is what we simulated, and what we find (Table 14.5).

```
rdd_example_data <-
  rdd_example_data |>
  mutate(mark_80_and_over = if_else(mark < 80, 0, 1))

rdd_example <-
  stan_glm(
    formula = income ~ mark + mark_80_and_over,
    data = rdd_example_data,
    family = gaussian(),
    prior = normal(location = 0, scale = 2.5, autoscale = TRUE),
    prior_intercept = normal(0, 2.5, autoscale = TRUE),
    prior_aux = exponential(rate = 1, autoscale = TRUE),
    seed = 853
  )
```

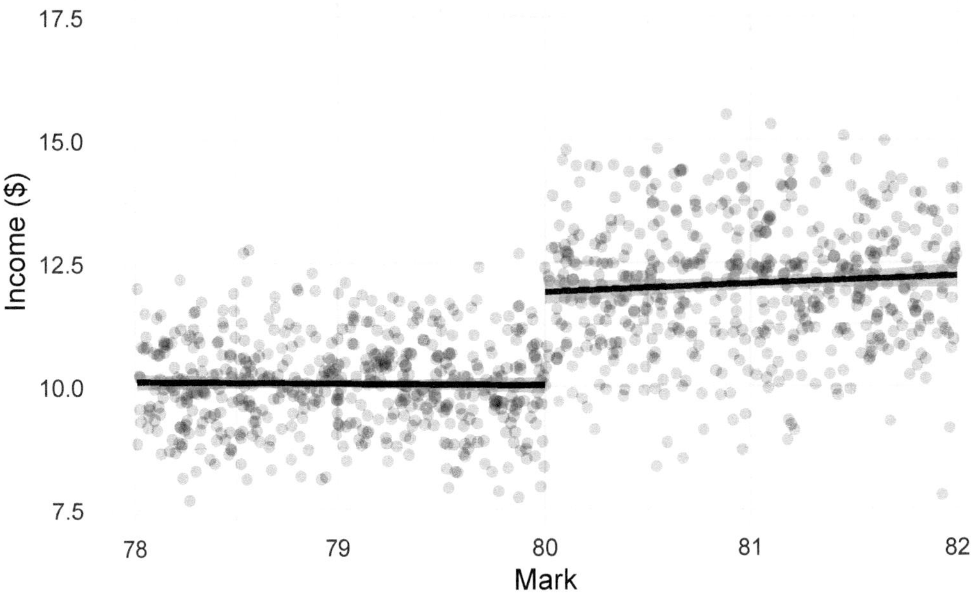

Figure 14.10: Illustration of simulated data that shows an effect on income from getting a mark that is 80, compared with 79

```
saveRDS(
  rdd_example,
  file = "rdd_example.rds"
)
```

```
rdd_example <-
  readRDS(file = "rdd_example.rds")
```

```
modelsummary(
  models = rdd_example,
  fmt = 2
)
```

There are various caveats to this estimate that we will discuss, but the essentials of RDD are here. Given an appropriate set-up, and model, RDD can compare favorably to randomized trials (Bloom, Bell, and Reiman 2020).

We could also implement RDD using `rdrobust`. The advantage of this approach is that many common extensions are easily available.

```
rdrobust(
  y = rdd_example_data$income,
  x = rdd_example_data$mark,
```

Table 14.5: Example of regression discontinuity with simulated data

	(1)
(Intercept)	5.22
mark	0.06
mark_80_and_over	1.89
Num.Obs.	1000
R2	0.417
R2 Adj.	0.415
Log.Lik.	−1591.847
ELPD	−1595.1
ELPD s.e.	25.4
LOOIC	3190.3
LOOIC s.e.	50.9
WAIC	3190.3
RMSE	1.19

```
    c = 80,
    h = 2,
    all = TRUE
  ) |>
    summary()
```

```
Sharp RD estimates using local polynomial regression.

Number of Obs.                 1000
BW type                      Manual
Kernel                   Triangular
VCE method                       NN

Number of Obs.                  497          503
Eff. Number of Obs.             497          503
Order est. (p)                    1            1
Order bias  (q)                   2            2
BW est. (h)                   2.000        2.000
BW bias (b)                   2.000        2.000
rho (h/b)                     1.000        1.000
Unique Obs.                     497          503

=============================================================================
        Method     Coef. Std. Err.         z     P>|z|      [ 95% C.I. ]
=============================================================================
  Conventional     1.913     0.161    11.876     0.000     [1.597 , 2.229]
Bias-Corrected     1.966     0.161    12.207     0.000     [1.650 , 2.282]
        Robust     1.966     0.232     8.461     0.000     [1.511 , 2.422]
=============================================================================
```

14.6.2 Assumptions

The key assumptions of RDD are (Cunningham 2021, 163):

1. The cut-off is specific, fixed, and known to all.
2. The forcing function is continuous.

The first assumption is largely about being unable to manipulate the cut-off, and ensures that the cut-off has meaning. The second assumption enables us to be confident that people on either side of the threshold are similar, apart from just happening to just fall on either side of the threshold.

When we discussed randomized control trials and A/B testing in Chapter 8 the randomized assignment of the treatment meant that the control and treatment groups were the same, but for the treatment. Then we moved to difference-in-differences, and we assumed that there was a common trend between the treated and control groups. We allowed that the groups could be different, but that we could "difference out" their differences. Finally, we considered matching, and we said that even if the control and treatment groups seemed different, we were able to match, to some extent, those who were treated with a group that were like them in all ways, apart from the fact that they were not treated.

In regression discontinuity we consider a slightly different setting. The two groups are completely different in terms of the forcing variable. They are on either side of the threshold. There is no overlap at all. But we know the threshold and believe that those on either side are essentially matched. Let us consider the 2019 NBA Eastern Conference Semifinals—Toronto and Philadelphia:

- Game 1: Raptors win 108-95;
- Game 2: 76ers win 94-89;
- Game 3: 76ers win 116-95;
- Game 4: Raptors win 101-96;
- Game 5: Raptors win 125-89;
- Game 6: 76ers win 112-101; and finally,
- Game 7: Raptors win 92-90, because of a ball that went in after bouncing on the rim four times.

Was there really that much difference between the teams?

The continuity assumption is important, but we cannot test this as it is based on a counterfactual. Instead, we need to convince people of it. Ways to do this include:

- Using a test/train set-up.
- Trying different specifications. We are especially concerned if results do not broadly persist with just linear or quadratic functions.
- Considering different subsets of the data.
- Considering different windows, which is the term we give to how far each side of the cutoff we examine.
- Being clear about uncertainty intervals, especially in graphs.
- Discuss and assuaging concerns about the possibility of omitted variables.

The threshold is also important. For instance, is there an actual shift or is there a non-linear relationship?

There are a variety of weaknesses of RDD, including:

- External validity may be difficult. For instance, when we think about the A-/B+ example, it is hard to see those generalizing to also B-/C+ students.
- The important responses are those that are close to the cut-off. This means that even if we have many A and B students, they do not help much. Hence, we need a lot of data or we may have concerns about our ability to support our claims (D. Green et al. 2009).
- As the researcher, we have a lot of freedom to implement different options. This means that open science best practice becomes vital.

To this point we have considered "sharp" RDD. That is, the threshold is strict. But, in reality, often the boundary is a little less strict. In a sharp RDD setting, if we know the value of the forcing function then we know the outcome. For instance, if a student gets a mark of 80 then we know that they got an A-, but if they got a mark of 79 then we know that they got a B+. But with fuzzy RDD it is only known with some probability.

We want as "sharp" an effect as possible, but if the thresholds are known, then they will be gamed. For instance, there is a lot of evidence that people run for certain marathon times, and we know that people aim for certain grades. Similarly, from the other side, it is a lot easier for an instructor to just give out As than it is to have to justify Bs. One way to look at this is to consider how "balanced" the sample is on either side of the threshold. We can do this using histograms with appropriate bins. For instance, think of the age-heaping that we found in the cleaned Kenyan census data in Chapter 9.

Another key factor for RDD is the possible effect of the decision around the choice of model. For instance, Figure 14.11 illustrates the difference between linear (Figure 14.11a) and polynomial (Figure 14.11b).

```
some_data <-
  tibble(
    outcome = rnorm(n = 100, mean = 1, sd = 1),
    running_variable = c(1:100),
    location = "before"
  )

some_more_data <-
  tibble(
    outcome = rnorm(n = 100, mean = 2, sd = 1),
    running_variable = c(101:200),
    location = "after"
  )

both <-
  rbind(some_data, some_more_data)

both |>
  ggplot(aes(x = running_variable, y = outcome, color = location)) +
  geom_point(alpha = 0.5) +
  geom_smooth(formula = y ~ x, method = "lm") +
  theme_minimal() +
  theme(legend.position = "bottom")

both |>
```

```
ggplot(aes(x = running_variable, y = outcome, color = location)) +
geom_point(alpha = 0.5) +
geom_smooth(formula = y ~ poly(x, 3), method = "lm") +
theme_minimal() +
theme(legend.position = "bottom")
```

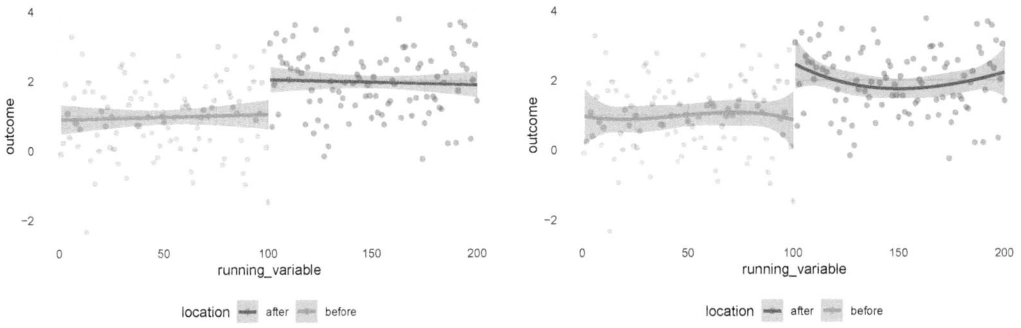

(a) Linear

(b) Polynomial

Figure 14.11: Comparing the result of considering the same situation with different functions

The result is that our estimate of the difference in outcome is dependent on the choice of model. We see this issue occur often in RDD (Gelman 2019) and it is especially recommended that higher order polynomials not be used, and instead the choice of models be either linear, quadratic, or some other smooth function (Gelman and Imbens 2019).

RDD is a popular approach, but meta-analysis suggests that standard errors are often inappropriately small and this could result in spurious results (Stommes, Aronow, and Sävje 2021). If you use RDD it is critical that you discuss the possibility of much wider standard errors than are reported by software packages, and what effect this would have on your conclusions.

14.6.3 Alcohol and crime in California

There are many opportunities to use regression discontinuity design. For instance, we often see it used in elections where one candidate barely wins. Caughey and Sekhon (2011) examine US House elections between 1942 and 2008 and showed that there is considerable difference between bare winners and bare losers. They highlight that one of the advantages of regression discontinuity is the fact that the assumptions can be tested. Another common use is when there is a somewhat arbitrary cut-off. For instance, in much of the USA the legal drinking age is 21. Carpenter and Dobkin (2015) consider the possible effect of alcohol on crime by comparing arrests and other records of those who are either side of 21 in California. They find those who are slightly over 21 are slightly more likely to be arrested than those slightly under 21. We will revisit Carpenter and Dobkin (2015) in the context of crime in California.

We can obtain their replication data (Carpenter and Dobkin 2014) from here[2]. Carpenter and Dobkin (2015) consider a large number of variables and construct a rate, and average

[2]https://dataverse.harvard.edu/dataset.xhtml?persistentId=doi:10.7910/DVN/27070

this rate over a fortnight, but for simplicity, we will just consider numbers for a few variables: assault, aggravated assault, DUI, and traffic violations (Figure 14.12).

```
carpenter_dobkin <-
  read_dta(
    "P01 Age Profile of Arrest Rates 1979-2006.dta"
  )


carpenter_dobkin_prepared <-
  carpenter_dobkin |>
  mutate(age = 21 + days_to_21 / 365) |>
  select(age, assault, aggravated_assault, dui, traffic_violations) |>
  pivot_longer(
    cols = c(assault, aggravated_assault, dui, traffic_violations),
    names_to = "arrested_for",
    values_to = "number"
  )

carpenter_dobkin_prepared |>
  mutate(
    arrested_for =
      case_when(
        arrested_for == "assault" ~ "Assault",
        arrested_for == "aggravated_assault" ~ "Aggravated assault",
        arrested_for == "dui" ~ "DUI",
        arrested_for == "traffic_violations" ~ "Traffic violations"
      )
  ) |>
  ggplot(aes(x = age, y = number)) +
  geom_point(alpha = 0.05) +
  facet_wrap(facets = vars(arrested_for), scales = "free_y") +
  theme_minimal()


carpenter_dobkin_aggravated_assault_only <-
  carpenter_dobkin_prepared |>
  filter(
    arrested_for == "aggravated_assault",
    abs(age - 21) < 2
  ) |>
  mutate(is_21_or_more = if_else(age < 21, 0, 1))


rdd_carpenter_dobkin <-
  stan_glm(
    formula = number ~ age + is_21_or_more,
    data = carpenter_dobkin_aggravated_assault_only,
    family = gaussian(),
    prior = normal(location = 0, scale = 2.5, autoscale = TRUE),
    prior_intercept = normal(0, 2.5, autoscale = TRUE),
```

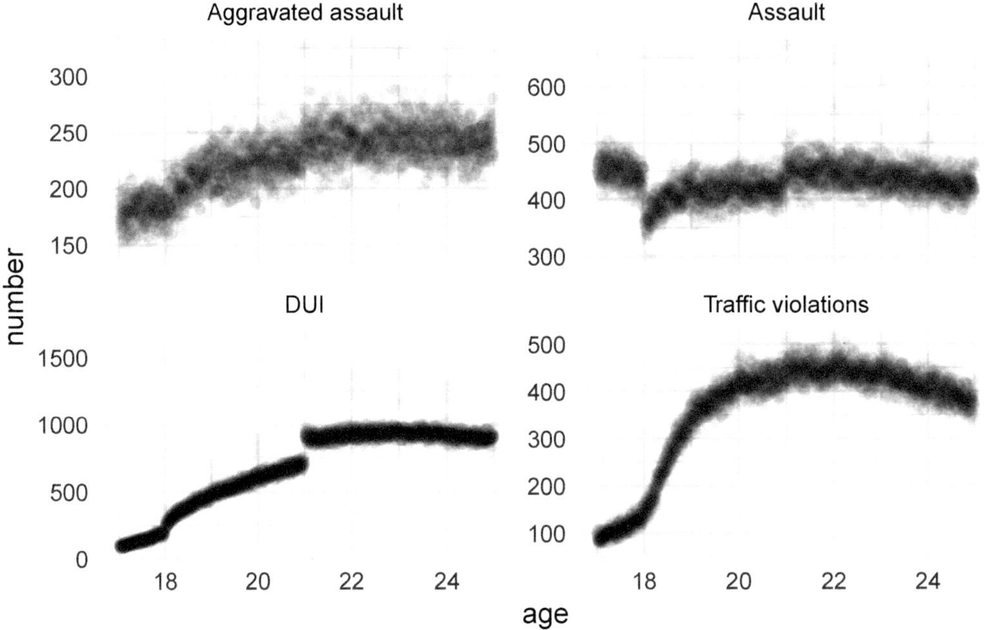

Figure 14.12: Comparing the number of arrests either side of turning 21 for selected reasons

```
    prior_aux = exponential(rate = 1, autoscale = TRUE),
    seed = 853
  )

saveRDS(
  rdd_example,
  file = "rdd_example.rds"
)


rdd_carpenter_dobkin <-
  readRDS(file = "rdd_carpenter_dobkin.rds")


modelsummary(
  models = rdd_carpenter_dobkin,
  fmt = 2
)
```

And the results are similar if we use `rdrobust`.

```
rdrobust(
  y = carpenter_dobkin_aggravated_assault_only$number,
  x = carpenter_dobkin_aggravated_assault_only$age,
  c = 21,
  h = 2,
```

Table 14.6: Examining the effect of alcohol on crime in California

	(1)
(Intercept)	145.54
age	3.87
is_21_or_more	13.24
Num.Obs.	1459
R2	0.299
R2 Adj.	0.297
Log.Lik.	−6153.757
ELPD	−6157.3
ELPD s.e.	32.9
LOOIC	12 314.6
LOOIC s.e.	65.7
WAIC	12 314.6
RMSE	16.42

```
    all = TRUE
  ) |>
    summary()
```

```
Sharp RD estimates using local polynomial regression.

Number of Obs.                 1459
BW type                      Manual
Kernel                   Triangular
VCE method                       NN

Number of Obs.                  729          730
Eff. Number of Obs.             729          730
Order est. (p)                    1            1
Order bias  (q)                   2            2
BW est. (h)                   2.000        2.000
BW bias (b)                   2.000        2.000
rho (h/b)                     1.000        1.000
Unique Obs.                     729          730

=============================================================================
        Method     Coef. Std. Err.         z     P>|z|      [ 95% C.I. ]
=============================================================================
  Conventional    14.126     1.918     7.364     0.000    [10.366 , 17.886]
Bias-Corrected    16.708     1.918     8.709     0.000    [12.948 , 20.468]
        Robust    16.708     2.879     5.804     0.000    [11.066 , 22.350]
=============================================================================
```

14.7 Instrumental variables

Instrumental variables (IV) is an approach that can be handy when we have some type of treatment and control going on, but we have a lot of correlation with other variables and we possibly do not have a variable that actually measures what we are interested in. Adjusting for observables will not be enough to create a good estimate. Instead we find some variable—the eponymous instrumental variable—that is:

1. correlated with the treatment variable, but
2. not correlated with the outcome.

This solves our problem because the only way the instrumental variable can have an effect is through the treatment variable, and so we can adjust our understanding of the effect of the treatment variable appropriately. The trade-off is that instrumental variables must satisfy a bunch of different assumptions, and that, frankly, they are difficult to identify *ex ante*. Nonetheless, when we are able to use them, they are a powerful tool for speaking about causality.

The canonical instrumental variables example is smoking. These days we know that smoking causes cancer. But because smoking is correlated with a lot of other variables, for instance, education, it could be that it was actually education that causes cancer. RCTs may be possible, but they are likely to be troublesome in terms of speed and ethics, and so instead we look for some other variable that is correlated with smoking, but not, in and of itself, with lung cancer. In this case, we look to tax rates, and other policy responses, on cigarettes. As the tax rates on cigarettes are correlated with the number of cigarettes that are smoked, but not correlated with lung cancer, other than through their impact on cigarette smoking, through them we can assess the effect of cigarettes smoked on lung cancer.

To implement instrumental variables we first regress tax rates on cigarette smoking to get some coefficient on the instrumental variable, and then (in a separate regression) regress tax rates on lung cancer to again, get some coefficient on the instrumental variable. Our estimate is then the ratio of these coefficients, which is described as a "Wald estimate" (Gelman and Hill 2007, 219).

Sometimes instrumental variables are used in the context of random allocation of treatment, such as the Oregon Health Insurance Experiment introduced in Chapter 8. Recall the issue was that a lottery was used to select individuals who were allocated to apply for health insurance, but there was nothing forcing them to do this. Our approach would then be to consider the relationship between being selected and taking up health insurance, and then between various health outcomes and taking up insurance. Our instrumental variable estimate, which would be the ratio, would estimate only those that took up health insurance because they were selected.

Following the language of Gelman and Hill (2007, 216), when we use instrumental variables we make a variety of assumptions including:

- Ignorability of the instrument.
- Correlation between the instrumental variable and the treatment variable.
- Monotonicity.
- Exclusion restriction.

As an aside, the history of instrumental variables is intriguing, and Stock and Trebbi (2003), via Cunningham (2021), provide a brief overview. The method was first published in Wright

(1928). This is a book about the effect of tariffs on animal and vegetable oil. Why might instrumental variables be important in a book about tariffs on animal and vegetable oil? The fundamental problem is that the effect of tariffs depends on both supply and demand. But we only know prices and quantities, so we do not know what is driving the effect. We can use instrumental variables to pin down causality. The intriguing aspect is that the instrumental variables discussion is only in "Appendix B" of that book. It would seem odd to relegate a major statistical break through to an appendix. Further, Philip G. Wright, the book's author, had a son Sewall Wright, who had considerable expertise in statistics and the specific method used in "Appendix B". Hence the mystery of "Appendix B": did Philip or Sewall write it? Cunningham (2021), Stock and Trebbi (2003), and Angrist and Krueger (2001) all go into more detail, but on balance feel that it is likely that Philip authored the work.

14.7.1 Simulated example: health status, smoking, and tax rates

Let us generate some data. We will explore a simulation related to the canonical example of health status, smoking, and tax rates. We are looking to explain how healthy someone is based on the amount they smoke, via the tax rate on smoking. We are going to generate different tax rates by provinces. The tax rate on cigarettes is now similar across the Canadian provinces but that this is fairly recent. Let us assume Alberta had a low tax, and Nova Scotia had a high tax.

We are simulating data for illustrative purposes, so we need to impose the answer that we want. When you actually use instrumental variables you will be reversing the process.

```
set.seed(853)

num_observations <- 10000

iv_example_data <- tibble(
  person = c(1:num_observations),
  smoker =
    sample(x = c(0:1), size = num_observations, replace = TRUE)
  )
```

Now we need to relate the number of cigarettes that someone smoked to their health. We will model health status as a draw from the Normal distribution, with either a high or low mean depending on whether the person smokes.

```
iv_example_data <-
  iv_example_data |>
  mutate(health = if_else(
    smoker == 0,
    rnorm(n = n(), mean = 1, sd = 1),
    rnorm(n = n(), mean = 0, sd = 1)
  ))
```

Now we need a relationship between cigarettes and the province (because in this illustration, the provinces have different tax rates).

```
iv_example_data <- iv_example_data |>
  mutate(
    province = case_when(
      smoker == 0 ~ sample(
        c("Nova Scotia", "Alberta"),
        size = n(),
        replace = TRUE,
        prob = c(1/2, 1/2)
      ),
      smoker == 1 ~ sample(
        c("Nova Scotia", "Alberta"),
        size = n(),
        replace = TRUE,
        prob = c(1/4, 3/4)
      )
    ),
    tax = case_when(province == "Alberta" ~ 0.3,
                    province == "Nova Scotia" ~ 0.5,
                    TRUE ~ 9999999
                    )
    )

iv_example_data
```

```
# A tibble: 10,000 x 5
   person smoker  health province      tax
    <int>  <int>   <dbl> <chr>       <dbl>
 1      1      0  1.11   Alberta       0.3
 2      2      1 -0.0831 Alberta       0.3
 3      3      1 -0.0363 Alberta       0.3
 4      4      0  2.48   Alberta       0.3
 5      5      0  0.617  Nova Scotia   0.5
 6      6      0  0.748  Alberta       0.3
 7      7      0  0.499  Alberta       0.3
 8      8      0  1.05   Nova Scotia   0.5
 9      9      1  0.113  Alberta       0.3
10     10      1 -0.0105 Alberta       0.3
# i 9,990 more rows
```

Now we can look at our data.

```
iv_example_data |>
  mutate(smoker = as_factor(smoker)) |>
  ggplot(aes(x = health, fill = smoker)) +
  geom_histogram(position = "dodge", binwidth = 0.2) +
  theme_minimal() +
  labs(
    x = "Health rating",
    y = "Number of people",
    fill = "Smoker"
```

```
  ) +
  scale_fill_brewer(palette = "Set1") +
  facet_wrap(vars(province))
```

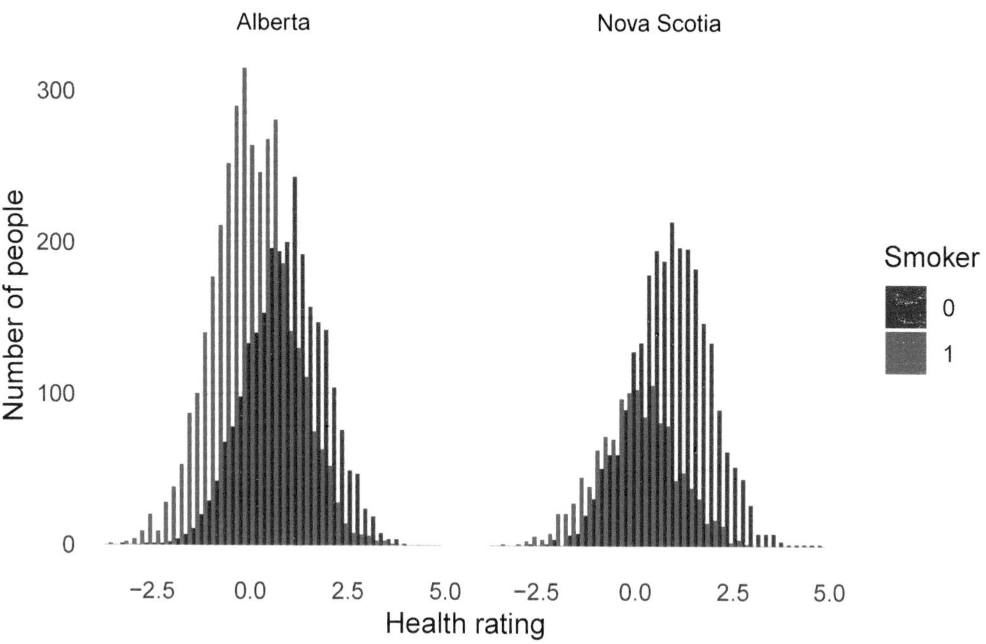

Finally, we can use the tax rate as an instrumental variable to estimate the effect of smoking on health.

```
health_on_tax <- lm(health ~ tax, data = iv_example_data)
smoker_on_tax <- lm(smoker ~ tax, data = iv_example_data)

tibble(
  coefficient = c("health ~ tax", "smoker ~ tax", "ratio"),
  value = c(
    coef(health_on_tax)["tax"],
    coef(smoker_on_tax)["tax"],
    coef(health_on_tax)["tax"] / coef(smoker_on_tax)["tax"]
  )
)
```

```
# A tibble: 3 x 2
  coefficient   value
  <chr>         <dbl>
1 health ~ tax  1.24
2 smoker ~ tax -1.27
3 ratio        -0.980
```

By understanding the effect of tax rates on both smoking and health, we find that if you smoke then your health is likely to be worse than if you do not smoke.

Table 14.7: Instrumental variable example using simulated data

	(1)
(Intercept)	0.977
	(0.041)
smoker	−0.980
	(0.081)
Num.Obs.	10 000
R2	0.201
R2 Adj.	0.201
AIC	28 342.1
BIC	28 363.7
RMSE	1.00

We can use `iv_robust()` from `estimatr` to estimate IV (Table 14.7). One nice reason for doing this is that it can help to keep everything organized and adjust the standard errors.

```
iv_robust(health ~ smoker | tax, data = iv_example_data) |>
  modelsummary()
```

14.7.2 Assumptions

The set-up of instrumental variables is described in Figure 14.13, which shows education as a confounder between income and happiness. A tax rebate likely only affects income, not education, and could be used as an instrumental variable.

```
digraph D {

  node [shape=plaintext, fontname = "helvetica"];
  a [label = "Income"]
  b [label = "Happiness"]
  c [label = "Education"]
  d [label = "Tax rebate"]
  { rank=same a b};

  a->b
  c->a
  c->b
  d->a
}
```

As discussed earlier, there are a variety of assumptions that are made when using instrumental variables. The two most important are:

1. Exclusion Restriction. This assumption is that the instrumental variable only affects the outcome variable through the predictor variable of interest.
2. Relevance. There must actually be a relationship between the instrumental variable and the predictor variable.

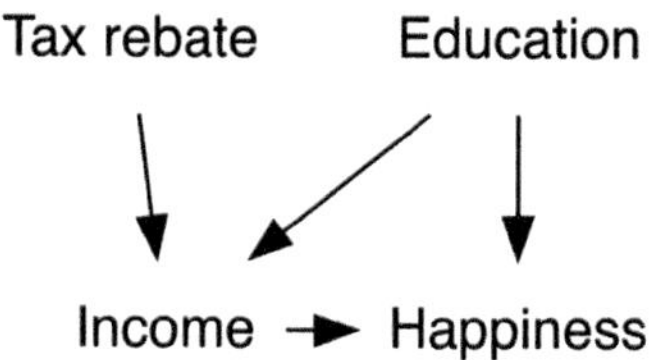

Figure 14.13: Education as a confounder for the relationship between income and happiness with tax rebate as an instrumental variable

There is typically a trade-off between these two. There are plenty of variables that satisfy one, precisely because they do not satisfy the other. Cunningham (2021, 211) describes how one test of a good instrument is if people are initially confused before you explain it to them, only to think it obvious in hindsight.

Relevance can be tested using regression and other tests for correlation. The exclusion restriction cannot be tested. We need to present evidence and convincing arguments. The difficult aspect is that the instrument needs to seem irrelevant because that is the implication of the exclusion restriction (Cunningham 2021, 225).

Instrumental variables is a useful approach because one can obtain causal estimates even without explicit randomization. Finding instrumental variables used to be a bit of a white whale, especially in academia. But there has been increased use of IV approaches downstream of A/B tests (Taddy 2019, 162).

For a long time, the canonical instrumental variable was rainfall, or more generally, the weather. However, the issue is that if the instrumental variable is correlated with other, potentially unobserved, variables, then they could be correlated with the variable of interest. This is a similar criticism to that above of propensity score matching. Mellon (2023) found a large number of variables have been linked to weather in instrumental variable papers. It would seem that the likelihood of incorrectly estimated effects in some of them is quite high.

When considering an instrumental variable approach, you should spend considerable amounts of time on both of these assumptions. Mellon (2023) shows that we are especially concerned that this particular tax rebate only affects income and no other variable, which could itself be linked with our variables of interest. Approaches based on instrumental variables provide extensive freedom for the researcher, and Brodeur, Cook, and Heyes (2020) find they are more associated with p-hacking and selection reporting compared with RCTs and RDD. As with multiple-imputation, and propensity score matching, we recommend caution when using IV, and that it is never naively turned to. Indeed, Betz, Cook, and Hollenbach (2018) go further and say that spatial instruments are rarely valid.

14.8 Exercises

Scales

1. *(Plan)* Consider the following scenario: *Two children will both look when an ambulance passes, but only the older one will look if a street car passes, and only the younger one will look when a bike passes.* Please sketch out what that dataset could look like and then sketch a graph that you could build to show all observations.
2. *(Simulate)* Please further consider the scenario described and simulate the situation. Please include at least ten tests based on the simulated data.
3. *(Acquire)* Please describe a possible source of such a dataset.
4. *(Explore)* Please use `ggplot2` to build the graph that you sketched. Then use `rstanarm` to build a model.
5. *(Communicate)* Please write two paragraphs about what you did.

Questions

1. What is the key assumption when using difference-in-differences?
2. Please read Varner and Sankin (2020) and discuss: i) two statistical aspects; and ii) two ethical aspects.
3. Please go to the GitHub page[3] related to Varner and Sankin (2020). Please list two points about what is good, and another two points about what could be improved.
4. What are the fundamental features of regression discontinuity design and what are the conditions that are needed in order for regression discontinuity design to be able to be used?
5. What are some threats to the validity of regression discontinuity design estimates?
6. According to Meng (2021) "Data science can persuade via..." (pick all that apply):
   a. the careful establishment of evidence from fair-minded and high-quality data collection
   b. processing and analysis
   c. the honest interpretation and communication of findings
   d. large sample sizes
7. According to Riederer (2021) if we have "disjoint treated and untreated groups partitioned by a sharp cut-off" then which method should we use to measure the local treatment effect at the juncture between groups (pick one)?
   a. regression discontinuity
   b. matching
   c. difference-in-differences
   d. event study methods
8. What does causal inference require according to Riederer (2021) (pick all that apply)?
   a. data management
   b. domain knowledge
   c. probabilistic reasoning

[3]https://github.com/the-markup/investigation-allstates-algorithm

9. Consider an Australian 30-39 year old male living in Toronto with two children and a PhD. Which of the following do you think they would match most closely with and why (please explain in a paragraph or two)?
   a. An Australian 30-39 year old male living in Toronto with one child and a bachelors degree
   b. A Canadian 30-39 year old male living in Toronto with one child and a PhD
   c. An Australian 30-39 year old male living in Ottawa with one child and a PhD
   d. A Canadian 18-29 year old male living in Toronto with one child and a PhD
10. What is propensity score matching? If you were matching people, then what are some of the features that you would like to match on? What sort of ethical questions does collecting and storing such information raise for you? (Please write at least one paragraph for each question.)
11. Draw a DAG illustrating the collider bias described by Bronner (2020).
12. Kahneman, Sibony, and Sunstein (2021) say "...while correlation does not imply causation, causation does imply correlation. Where there is a causal link, we should find a correlation". With reference to Cunningham (2021, chap. 1), are they right or wrong, and why?

Tutorial

You are interested in the characteristics of people's friendship groups and how those characteristics relate to individual-level outcomes, particularly economic measures.

You have access to individual-level data from a social media website, which contains information about social interactions (comments on posts, tags, etc) on the website, as well as a wide variety of individual-level characteristics.

1. While the social media website is very popular, not everyone in the population you are interested in has an account, and not everyone that has an account is active on the website. Given you are interested in economic measures, what are some possible issues with using these data to make inferences about the broader population?
2. The data do not contain information on individual-level income. But for around 20 per cent of the sample you have information on the "census block" of the individual. By way of background, a census block contains no more than 3,000 individuals. The median income of each census block is known. As such, you decide to estimate individual-level income as follows:
   a) Regress the median income of each census block on a series of individual level characteristics (such as age, education, marital status, gender, ...).
   b) Use these estimates to predict the income of individuals that do not have location information. Briefly discuss the advantages and disadvantages of this approach, particularly in how it could affect the study of income characteristics of friendship groups. Ensure that you address the ecological fallacy.
3. Understandably, the social media website will not allow the unfettered distribution of individual-level data. What are some ways in which you might nonetheless enhance the reproducibility of your work?

This should take at least two pages.

15

Multilevel regression with post-stratification

Prerequisites

- Read *Forecasting elections with non-representative polls*, (W. Wang et al. 2015)
  - Discusses the use of MRP on a biased sample drawn from the XBox platform.
- Read *Analyzing name changes after marriage using a non-representative survey*, (M. Alexander 2019c)
  - Implements MRP on a survey and provides detailed code and data.
- Read *Mister P helps us understand vaccine hesitancy*, (E. Green 2020)
  - Another worked example of MRP with available code and data.
- Watch *Statistical Models of Election Outcomes*, (Gelman 2020)
  - Discussion of building models for elections.
- Listen to *Episode 248: Are Democrats being irrational? (David Shor)*, (Galef 2020)
  - Focus on the first half which discusses the use of data in politics, with lessons that are broadly applicable.

Key concepts and skills

- Multilevel regression with post-stratification (MRP) takes a sample, usually a large poll, and uses that to train a model. Then that trained model is applied to a post-stratification dataset, typically a census or other larger sample.
- We use models because we are interested in answering questions that our data alone cannot answer. For instance, we may want to know what is going on in every political district, but it would be too expensive to appropriately poll every district. If we had perfect data, we would not need a model.
- Models allow us to answer some questions, but the trade-off is that we answer them with uncertainty. In the MRP set-up, our model borrows information from areas where we know a lot and uses that in areas where we know little. The degree to which this is appropriate is one aspect we would always like to know more about. One of the main difficulties with MRP is obtaining access to the required datasets.
- The fundamental assumption of MRP is that the relationship between predictors, like gender, age-group, district, etc, and the outcome, for instance, "who are you going to vote for?", are steady between the sample and the post-stratification dataset. One key question when considering MRP estimates is: "To what extent does that assumption hold?"
- As always, transparency is critical and there should be little reason that data preparation and modeling code cannot be made public alongside the model results even if the survey data cannot. This enables scrutiny from independent experts and enhances the credibility of MRP estimates.

Software and packages

- Base R (R Core Team 2023)
- `arrow` (Richardson et al. 2023)

- `broom.mixed` (Bolker and Robinson 2022)
- `gutenbergr` (Johnston and Robinson 2022)
- `haven` (Wickham, Miller, and Smith 2023)
- `knitr` (Xie 2023)
- `labelled` (Larmarange 2023)
- `modelsummary` (Arel-Bundock 2022)
- `rstanarm` (Goodrich et al. 2023)
- `tidybayes` (Kay 2022)
- `tidyverse` (Wickham et al. 2019)

```
library(arrow)
library(broom.mixed)
library(gutenbergr)
library(haven)
library(knitr)
library(labelled)
library(modelsummary)
library(rstanarm)
library(tidybayes)
library(tidyverse)
```

15.1 Introduction

> [The Presidential election of] 2016 was the largest analytics failure in US political history.
>
> David Shor, 13 August 2020

Multilevel regression with post-stratification (MRP) is a popular way to adjust non-representative surveys to analyze opinion and other responses. It uses a regression model to relate individual-level survey responses to various characteristics and then rebuilds the sample to better match the population. In this way MRP can not only allow a better understanding of responses, but also allow us to analyze data that may otherwise be unusable. However, it can be a challenge to get started with MRP as the terminology may be unfamiliar, and the data requirements can be onerous.

Consider a biased survey. For instance, perhaps we conducted a survey about computer preferences at an academic conference, so people with post-graduate degrees are likely over-represented. We are nonetheless interested in making claims about the broader population. Let us say that we found 37.5 per cent of respondents prefer Macs. One way forward is to just ignore the bias and conclude that "37.5 per cent of people prefer Macs". Another way is to adjust using information that we know. For instance, say 50 per cent of our respondents with a post-graduate degree prefer Macs, and of those without a post-graduate degree, 25 per cent prefer Macs. Then if we knew what proportion of the broader population had a post-graduate degree, say 10 per cent, then we could conduct re-weighting, or post-stratification, to create an estimate: $0.5 \times 0.1 + 0.25 \times 0.9 = 0.275$. Our estimate would be that 27.5 per cent of people prefer Macs. MRP is a third approach and uses a model to help do that re-weighting. Here we could use logistic regression to estimate the relationship between computer preferences and highest educational attainment in our survey. We then apply that relationship to a dataset that is representative, in terms of education, of our population. One advantage of this is that we can better account for uncertainty. In terms of a real-world example, Clinton, Lapinski, and Trussler (2022) find a substantial difference in telephone response rates between Democrats and Republicans in the 2020 US Presidential election and that when corrected this reduces average polling error.

MRP is a handy approach when dealing with survey data. Hanretty (2020) describes how we use MRP because the alternatives either do badly or are expensive. Essentially, MRP trains a model based on the survey, and then applies that trained model to another dataset. There are two main, related, advantages:

1) It can allow us to "re-weight" in a way that brings uncertainty front-of-mind and is not as hamstrung by small samples. The alternative way to deal with having a small sample is to either gather more data or throw it away.
2) It can allow us to use broad surveys to speak to subsets in a way that remains representative in certain aspects. For instance, say we gathered a sample that was representative of age, gender, and education across the country. If we were interested in state/provincial-specific estimates there is no guarantee that representativeness would hold at that disaggregated level.

From a practical perspective, it tends to be less expensive to collect non-probability samples and so there are benefits of being able to use these types of data. That said, MRP is not a magic bullet and the laws of statistics still apply. We will have larger uncertainty around our estimates than when using probability samples and they will still be subject to all the usual biases. It is an exciting area of research in both academia and industry.

The workflow that we need for MRP is straight forward, but the details and decisions that have to be made at each step can become overwhelming. The point to keep in mind is that we are trying to create a relationship between two datasets using a statistical model, and so we need to establish similarity between the two datasets in terms of their variables and levels. The steps are:

1) gather and prepare the survey dataset, thinking about what is needed for coherence with the post-stratification dataset;
2) gather and prepare the post-stratification dataset thinking about what is needed for coherence with the survey dataset;
3) model the variable of interest from the survey using predictors and levels that are available in both the survey and the post-stratification datasets;
4) apply the model to the post-stratification data.

One famous MRP example is W. Wang et al. (2015). They used data from the Xbox gaming platform to forecast the 2012 US Presidential Election. W. Wang et al. (2015) were able to implement an opt-in poll through the Xbox gaming platform during the 45 days leading up to the 2012 US presidential election, which was between Barack Obama and Mitt Romney. Each day there were three to five questions, including voter intention: "If the election were held today, who would you vote for?". Respondents were allowed to answer at most once per day. And first-time respondents were asked to provide information about themselves, including their sex, race, age, education, state, party ID, political ideology, and who they voted for in the 2008 presidential election.

> **i Shoulders of giants**
>
> Dr Andrew Gelman is Higgins Professor of Statistics and Political Science at Columbia University. After earning a PhD in Statistics from Harvard University in 1990, he was appointed as an assistant professor at the University of California, Berkeley, and then moved to Columbia in 1996, where he was promoted to full professor in 2000. His research focuses on statistics, social sciences, and their intersection. For instance, W. Wang et al. (2015) showed that biased surveys can still have value. He was the principal investigator for Stan, a probabilistic programming language, that is widely used for Bayesian modeling. And he has written many books, with *Data Analysis Using Regression and Multilevel/Hierarchical Models* (Gelman and Hill 2007) and *Bayesian Data Analysis* (Gelman et al. [1995] 2014) having been especially influential on a generation of researchers. He was appointed a Fellow of the American Statistical Association in 1998 and awarded the COPSS Presidents' Award in 2003.

In total, 750,148 interviews were conducted, with 345,858 unique respondents, over 30,000 of whom completed five or more polls. As may be expected, young men dominate the Xbox population: 18-to-29-year-olds comprise 65 per cent of the Xbox dataset, compared to 19 per cent in the exit poll; and men make up 93 per cent of the Xbox sample but only 47 per cent of the electorate.

The details do not matter, but essentially they model how likely a respondent is to vote for Obama, given various information such as state, education, sex, etc. Having a trained model that considers the effect of these various predictors on support for the candidates, they now post-stratify, where each of these "cell-level estimates are weighted by the proportion of the electorate in each cell and aggregated to the appropriate level (i.e., state or national)."

They need cross-tabulated population data which counts the number of people in each combination of variables. In general, the census would have worked, or one of the other large surveys available in the US, such as the ACS, which we introduced in Chapter 6. The difficulty is that the variables need to be available on a cross-tabulated basis. As such, they use exit polls, although these are not as widely available in other countries.

They make state-specific estimates by post-stratifying to the features of each state. And they similarly examine demographic-differences. Finally, they convert their estimates into electoral college estimates.

In general, MRP is a good way to accomplish specific aims, but it is not without trade-offs. If we have a good quality survey, then it may be a way to speak to disaggregated aspects of it. Or if we are concerned about uncertainty then it is a good way to think about that. If we have a biased survey, then it is a great place to start, but it is not a panacea. There is plenty of scope for exciting work from a variety of approaches. For instance, from a more statistical perspective, there is a lot of work to do in terms of thinking through how survey design and modeling approaches interact and the extent to which we are underestimating uncertainty. It is also interesting to think through the implications of small samples and uncertainty in the post-stratification dataset. There is an awful lot to do in terms of thinking through what the appropriate model is to use, and how do we even evaluate what "appropriate" means here, for instance, based on Si (2020). More generally, we have little idea of the conditions under which we will have the stable preferences and relationships that are required for MRP to be accurate. A great deal of work is needed to understand how this relates to uncertainty in survey design, for instance, based on Lauderdale et al. (2020) or Ghitza and Gelman (2020).

In this chapter, we begin with simulating a situation in which we pretend that we know the features of the population. We then consider the US 2020 presidential election.

15.2 Simulated example: coffee or tea?

15.2.1 Construct a population and biased sample

To get started we will harken back to the tea-tasting experiment in Chapter 8 and simulate a population about whether someone prefers coffee or tea. We will then take a biased sample in favor of tea, and use MRP get those population-level preferences back. We will have two explanatory variables. Age-group will be either "young" or "old", and nationality will be either "United States" or "England". The simulation will impose an increased chance of preferring tea of the individual is English and/or old. Everything in our population will be roughly balanced, (that is half and half between each of the variables). But our survey will skew older and English. To be clear, in this example we will "know" the "true" features of the population, but this is not something that occurs when we use real data—it is just to help you understand what is happening in MRP.

```
set.seed(853)

pop_size <- 1000000

sim_population <-
  tibble(
    age = rbinom(n = pop_size, size = 1, prob = 0.5),
    nationality = rbinom(n = pop_size, size = 1, prob = 0.5),
    probability = (age + nationality + 0.1) / 2.2, # prevent certainty
    prefers_tea = rbinom(n = pop_size, 1, prob = probability)
  )

sim_population
```

```
# A tibble: 1,000,000 x 4
    age nationality probability prefers_tea
  <int>       <int>       <dbl>       <int>
1     0           1      0.5              0
2     0           0      0.0455           0
3     0           1      0.5              1
4     0           0      0.0455           0
5     0           0      0.0455           0
6     0           0      0.0455           0
7     0           1      0.5              0
8     0           0      0.0455           0
```

Table 15.1: Preference for tea, by age and nationality

Age	Nationality	Prefers tea	Number
0	0	0	238,568
0	0	1	11,319
0	1	0	125,371
0	1	1	124,730
1	0	0	125,438
1	0	1	124,723
1	1	0	11,421
1	1	1	238,430

```
 9     0           1      0.5          1
10     0           0      0.0455       0
# i 999,990 more rows
```

We can see that the counts, by group, are fairly similar (Table 15.1).

```
sim_population |>
  count(age, nationality, prefers_tea) |>
  kable(
    col.names = c("Age", "Nationality", "Prefers tea", "Number"),
    format.args = list(big.mark = ","),
    booktabs = TRUE,
    linesep = ""
    )
```

On average, 50 per cent of the population prefers tea, but this preference depends on the population sub-groups.

Now we want to pretend that we have some survey that has a biased sample. We will allow that it over-samples older respondents and English respondents. We are interested in looking at what proportion of our biased sample prefers tea to coffee, and expect, by construction, that it will lean toward tea.

```
set.seed(853)

tea_sample <-
  sim_population |>
  slice_sample(n = 1000, weight_by = probability)
```

```
tea_sample |>
  count(age, nationality, prefers_tea) |>
  kable(
    col.names = c("Age", "Nationality", "Prefers tea", "Number"),
    format.args = list(big.mark = ","),
    booktabs = TRUE,
    linesep = ""
    )
```

Table 15.2: Biased sample of preferences for tea, by age and nationality, oversampling those who like tea

Age	Nationality	Prefers tea	Number
0	0	0	18
0	0	1	3
0	1	0	119
0	1	1	128
1	0	0	133
1	0	1	126
1	1	0	25
1	1	1	448

It is clear that our sample has a different average tea preference than the overall population (Table 15.2).

15.2.2 Model the sample

We now train a model based on the biased survey. We explain tea preferences based on age and national origin. There is nothing that says you have to use a multilevel model, but a lot of situations will have circumstances such that it is not likely to do any worse. To be clear, this means that although we have individual-level data, there is some grouping of the individuals that we will take advantage of.

$$
\begin{aligned}
y_i|\pi_i &\sim \text{Bern}(\pi_i) \\
\text{logit}(\pi_i) &= \beta_0 + \alpha^{\text{age}}_{a[i]} + \alpha^{\text{nat}}_{n[i]} \\
\alpha_0 &\sim \text{Normal}(0, 2.5) \\
\alpha^{\text{age}}_{a} &\sim \text{Normal}\left(0, \sigma^2_{\text{age}}\right) \text{ for } a = 1, 2, \dots, A \\
\alpha^{\text{nat}}_{n} &\sim \text{Normal}\left(0, \sigma^2_{\text{nat}}\right) \text{ for } n = 1, 2, \dots, N \\
\sigma_{\text{age}} &\sim \text{Exponential}(1) \\
\sigma_{\text{nat}} &\sim \text{Exponential}(1)
\end{aligned}
$$

where y_i is the tea preference of the respondent, $\pi_i = \Pr(y_i = 1)$, and α^{age} and α^{nat} are the effect of age and national origin, respectively. The $a[i]$ and $n[i]$ refer to which age-group and nationality, respectively, the respondent belongs to. A and N are the total number of age-groups and nationalities, respectively. We will estimate the model with `stan_glm()`.

```
tea_preference_model <-
  stan_glmer(
    prefers_tea ~ (1 | age) + (1 | nationality),
    data = tea_sample,
    family = binomial(link = "logit"),
    prior = normal(location = 0, scale = 0.5, autoscale = TRUE),
    prior_intercept = normal(location = 0, scale = 0.5, autoscale = TRUE),
    seed = 853
  )
```

Table 15.3: Model trained on biased sample that oversamples a preference for tea

	Tea preferences
(Intercept)	0.001
Sigma[age × (Intercept),(Intercept)]	2.171
Sigma[nationality × (Intercept),(Intercept)]	2.337
Num.Obs.	1000
R2	0.261
R2 Marg.	0.000
ICC	0.7
Log.Lik.	−457.970
ELPD	−461.0
ELPD s.e.	16.2
LOOIC	921.9
LOOIC s.e.	32.4
WAIC	921.9
RMSE	0.39

```
saveRDS(
  tea_preference_model,
  file = "tea_preference_model.rds"
)
```

```
tea_preference_model <-
  readRDS(file = "tea_preference_model.rds")
```

```
modelsummary(
  list(
    "Tea preferences" = tea_preference_model
  )
)
```

Figure 15.1 shows the distribution of draws for each of the different groups.

```
tea_preference_model |>
  spread_draws(`(Intercept)`, b[, group]) |>
  mutate(condition_mean = `(Intercept)` + b) |>
  ggplot(aes(y = group, x = condition_mean)) +
  stat_halfeye() +
  theme_minimal()
```

15.2.3 Post-stratification dataset

Now we will use a post-stratification dataset to get some estimates of the number in each cell. We typically use a larger dataset that may more closely reflect the population. In

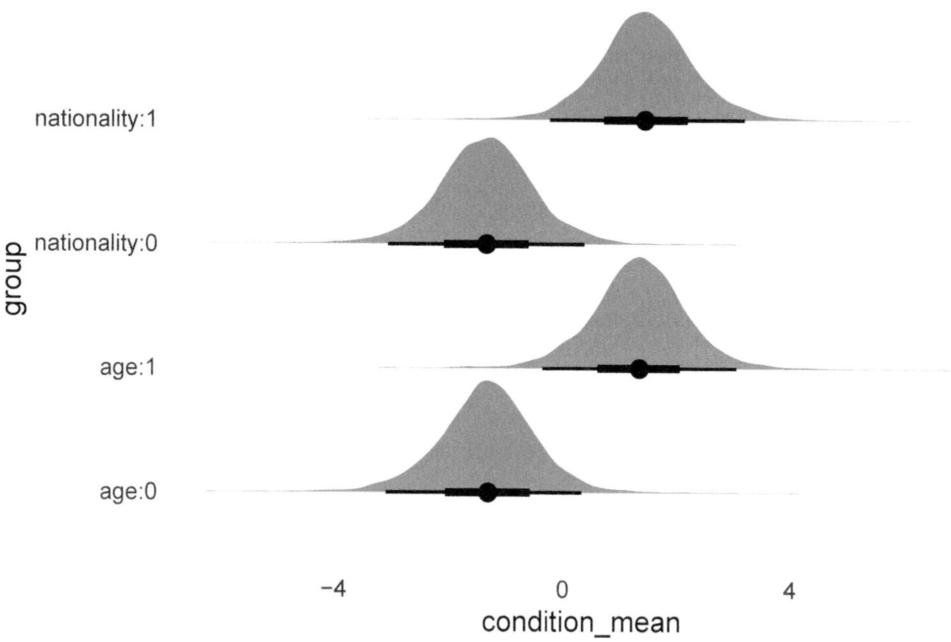

Figure 15.1: Examining the distribution of draws for each of the groups

the US a popular choice is the American Community Survey (ACS) which we covered in Chapter 6, while in other countries we typically use the census.

In this simulated example, we could use the population as our post-stratification dataset. The issue is that at one million observations it is unwieldy, so we take a 10,000 person sample from it. We also remove the tea preferences variable because that is what we are pretending we do not know.

```
set.seed(853)

tea_poststrat_dataset <-
  sim_population |>
  slice_sample(n = 10000) |>
  select(-prefers_tea)

tea_poststrat_dataset
```

```
# A tibble: 10,000 x 3
     age nationality probability
   <int>       <int>       <dbl>
 1     0           1      0.5
 2     0           1      0.5
 3     0           1      0.5
 4     0           1      0.5
 5     1           0      0.5
 6     1           0      0.5
 7     0           0      0.0455
```

```
8     1           0        0.5
9     1           0        0.5
10    1           0        0.5
# i 9,990 more rows
```

This is an idealized example where we assume individual-level data in our post-stratification dataset. In that world we can apply our model to each individual.

```
predicted_tea_preference <-
  tea_preference_model |>
  add_epred_draws(newdata = tea_poststrat_dataset,
                                      value = "preference") |>
  ungroup() |>
  summarise(
    average_preference = mean(preference),
    lower = quantile(preference, 0.025),
    upper = quantile(preference, 0.975),
    .by = c(age, nationality, .row)
  )

predicted_tea_preference |>
  count(age, nationality, average_preference)
```

```
# A tibble: 4 x 4
    age nationality average_preference     n
  <int>       <int>              <dbl> <int>
1     0           0             0.0657  2416
2     0           1             0.528   2505
3     1           0             0.496   2544
4     1           1             0.941   2535
```

Table 15.4 compares the MRP estimates, with the raw estimates from the biased sample. In this case, because we know the truth, we can also compare them to the known truth, but that is not something we can do normally.

```
comparison <- tibble(
  Type = c("Truth", "Biased sample", "MRP estimate"),
  Estimate = c(
    mean(sim_population$prefers_tea),
    mean(tea_sample$prefers_tea),
    mean(predicted_tea_preference$average_preference)
  )
)

comparison |>
  kable(digits = 2,
    booktabs = TRUE,
    linesep = "")
```

In this case, the MRP approach has done a good job of taking a biased sample and resulting in an estimate of tea preferences that did reflect the truth.

Table 15.4: MRP estimates compared with the truth and the biased sample

Type	Estimate
Truth	0.50
Biased sample	0.70
MRP estimate	0.51

15.3 Forecasting the 2020 United States election

Presidential elections in the United States have many features that are unique to the United States, but the model that we are going to build here will be generalizable to a variety of settings. We will use survey data from the Democracy Fund Voter Study Group introduced in Chapter 8. They conducted polling in the lead-up to the US election and make this publicly available after registration. We will use IPUMS, introduced in Chapter 6, to access the 2019 American Community Survey (ACS) as a post-stratification dataset. We will use state, age-group, gender, and education as explanatory variables.

15.3.1 Survey data

We will use the Democracy Fund Voter Study Group Nationscape survey dataset. One tricky aspect of MRP is ensuring consistency between the survey dataset and the post-stratification dataset. In this case, after reading in the dataset that we cleaned up in Chapter 8 we need to do some work to make the variables consistent.

```
nationscape_data <-
  read_csv(file = "nationscape_data.csv")
```

```
nationscape_data
```

```
# A tibble: 5,200 x 5
   gender state vote_biden age_group education_level
 * <chr>  <chr>      <dbl> <chr>     <chr>
 1 female WI             0 45-59     Post sec +
 2 female VA             0 45-59     Post sec +
 3 female TX             0 60+       High school or less
 4 female WA             0 45-59     High school or less
 5 female MA             1 18-29     Some post sec
 6 female TX             1 30-44     Some post sec
 7 female CA             0 60+       Some post sec
 8 female NC             0 45-59     Post sec +
 9 female MD             0 60+       Post sec +
10 female FL             1 45-59     Some post sec
# i 5,190 more rows
```

```
# Format state names to match IPUMS
states_names_and_abbrevs <-
  tibble(stateicp = state.name, state = state.abb)

nationscape_data <-
  nationscape_data |>
  left_join(states_names_and_abbrevs, by = "state")

rm(states_names_and_abbrevs)

# Make lowercase to match IPUMS data
nationscape_data <-
  nationscape_data |>
  mutate(stateicp = tolower(stateicp))

# Replace NAs with DC
nationscape_data$stateicp <-
  replace_na(nationscape_data$stateicp, "district of columbia")

# Tidy the class
nationscape_data <-
  nationscape_data |>
  mutate(across(c(gender, stateicp, education_level, age_group),
                as_factor))
```

Finally, we save the prepared dataset as a parquet file.

```
write_parquet(x = nationscape_data,
              sink = "nationscape_data_cleaned.parquet")
```

15.3.2 Post-stratification data

We have many options for a dataset to post-stratify by and there are various considerations. We are after a dataset that is good quality (however that is to be defined), and likely larger. From a strictly data perspective, the best choice would probably be something like the Cooperative Election Study (CES), as used in Chapter 12, but it is only publicly released after the election, which limits the reasonableness of using it for forecasting the election. W. Wang et al. (2015) use exit poll data, but again that is only available after the election.

We will use the 2019 American Community Survey (ACS) dataset that we gathered in Chapter 6.

```
poststrat_data
```

```
# A tibble: 407,354 x 4
  gender age_group education_level      stateicp
* <fct>  <fct>     <fct>                <fct>
1 male   60+       High school or less alabama
2 male   60+       Some post sec        alabama
```

```
 3 male   18-29     High school or less alabama
 4 female 18-29     Some post sec       alabama
 5 male   30-44     Some post sec       alabama
 6 female 18-29     High school or less alabama
 7 female 60+       High school or less alabama
 8 female 18-29     Some post sec       alabama
 9 male   60+       High school or less alabama
10 male   45-59     High school or less alabama
# i 407,344 more rows
```

This dataset is on an individual level. We will create counts of each sub-cell, and then proportions by state.

```
poststrat_data_cells <-
  poststrat_data |>
  count(stateicp, gender, age_group, education_level)
```

And finally we add proportions for each of these cells.

```
poststrat_data_cells <-
  poststrat_data_cells |>
  mutate(prop = n / sum(n),
         .by = stateicp)

poststrat_data_cells
```

```
# A tibble: 1,627 x 6
   stateicp    gender age_group education_level         n    prop
   <fct>       <fct>  <fct>     <fct>               <int>   <dbl>
 1 connecticut male   18-29     High school or less   194 0.0419
 2 connecticut male   18-29     Some post sec         128 0.0276
 3 connecticut male   18-29     Post sec +             72 0.0156
 4 connecticut male   18-29     Grad degree            14 0.00302
 5 connecticut male   30-44     High school or less   132 0.0285
 6 connecticut male   30-44     Some post sec          93 0.0201
 7 connecticut male   30-44     Post sec +            147 0.0317
 8 connecticut male   30-44     Grad degree            88 0.0190
 9 connecticut male   45-59     High school or less   187 0.0404
10 connecticut male   45-59     Some post sec          88 0.0190
# i 1,617 more rows
```

15.3.3 Model the sample

We are going to use logistic regression to estimate a model where the binary of support for Biden versus Trump is explained by gender, age-group, education, and state.

$$
\begin{aligned}
y_i|\pi_i &\sim \text{Bern}(\pi_i) \\
\text{logit}(\pi_i) &= \beta_0 + \alpha^{\text{gender}}_{g[i]} + \alpha^{\text{age}}_{a[i]} + \alpha^{\text{state}}_{s[i]} + \alpha^{\text{edu}}_{e[i]} \\
\beta_0 &\sim \text{Normal}(0, 2.5) \\
\alpha^{\text{gender}}_{g} &\sim \text{Normal}(0, 2.5) \text{ for } g = 1, 2 \\
\alpha^{\text{age}}_{a} &\sim \text{Normal}\left(0, \sigma^2_{\text{age}}\right) \text{ for } a = 1, 2, \dots, A \\
\alpha^{\text{state}}_{s} &\sim \text{Normal}\left(0, \sigma^2_{\text{state}}\right) \text{ for } s = 1, 2, \dots, S \\
\alpha^{\text{edu}}_{e} &\sim \text{Normal}\left(0, \sigma^2_{\text{edu}}\right) \text{ for } e = 1, 2, \dots, E \\
\sigma_{\text{gender}} &\sim \text{Exponential}(1) \\
\sigma_{\text{state}} &\sim \text{Exponential}(1) \\
\sigma_{\text{edu}} &\sim \text{Exponential}(1)
\end{aligned}
$$

where y_i is whether a respondent supports Biden and $\pi_i = \Pr(y = 1)$. Then α^{gender}, α^{age}, α^{state}, and α^{edu} are the effect of gender, age, state, and education, respectively. The $g[i]$, $a[i]$, $s[i]$, and $e[i]$ refer to which gender, age-group, state, and education level, respectively, the respondent belongs to. A, S, and E are the total number of age-groups, states, and education levels, respectively.

After reading in the data that we cleaned earlier, following Kennedy and Gabry (2020) we use `stan_glmer()` from `rstanarm` to estimate the model.

```
nationscape_data <-
  read_parquet(file = "nationscape_data_cleaned.parquet")


us_election_model <-
  stan_glmer(
    vote_biden ~ gender + (1|age_group) + (1|stateicp) + (1|education_level),
    data = nationscape_data,
    family = binomial(link = "logit"),
    prior = normal(location = 0, scale = 2.5, autoscale = TRUE),
    prior_intercept = normal(location = 0, scale = 2.5, autoscale = TRUE),
    cores = 4,
    adapt_delta = 0.99,
    seed = 853
  )


saveRDS(
  us_election_model,
  file = "us_election_model_mrp.rds"
)
```

This model will take about 15 minutes to run, so you should be careful to save it afterwards with `saveRDS()`. And you can load it with `readRDS()`.

Table 15.5: Estimating a model of choice between Biden and Trump in the 2020 US election

	(1)
(Intercept)	0.373
gendermale	−0.542
Sigma[stateicp × (Intercept),(Intercept)]	0.081
Sigma[education_level × (Intercept),(Intercept)]	0.036
Sigma[age_group × (Intercept),(Intercept)]	0.241
Num.Obs.	5200
R2	0.056
R2 Marg.	0.018
ICC	0.2
Log.Lik.	−3434.075
ELPD	−3468.0
ELPD s.e.	16.2
LOOIC	6936.1
LOOIC s.e.	32.4
WAIC	6936.0
RMSE	0.48

```
us_election_model <-
  readRDS(file = "us_election_model_mrp.rds")
```

We might be interested to look at the coefficient estimates (Table 15.5).

```
modelsummary(
  us_election_model
)
```

Figure 15.2 shows the distribution of draws for age groups, and education. We plot some selected states separately for reasons of space (Figure 15.3).

```
us_election_model |>
  spread_draws(`(Intercept)`, b[, group]) |>
  mutate(condition_mean = `(Intercept)` + b) |>
  separate(col = group,
           into = c("type", "instance"),
           sep = ":", remove = FALSE) |>
  filter(type != "stateicp") |>
  ggplot(aes(y = group, x = condition_mean)) +
  stat_halfeye() +
  theme_minimal()
```

```
us_election_model |>
  spread_draws(`(Intercept)`, b[, group]) |>
  mutate(condition_mean = `(Intercept)` + b) |>
```

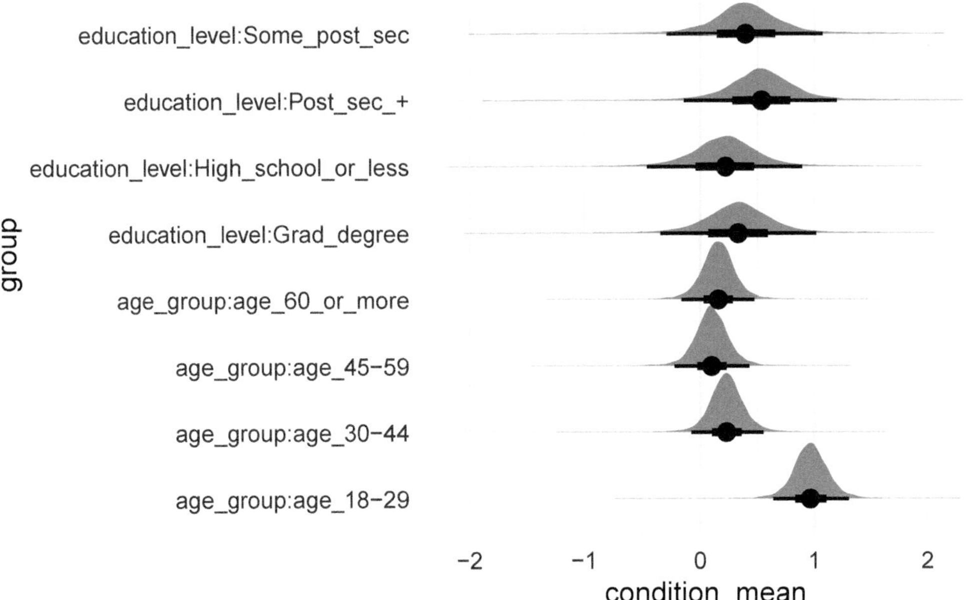

Figure 15.2: Examining the distribution of draws for each of the groups

```
  separate(col = group, into = c("type", "instance"), sep = ":", remove = FALSE) |>
  filter(type == "stateicp") |>
  filter(instance %in%
           c("california", "florida", "michigan", "new_york", "pennsylvania",
             "vermont", "west_virginia", "wisconsin")
         ) |>
  ggplot(aes(y = group, x = condition_mean)) +
  stat_halfeye() +
  theme_minimal()
```

15.3.4 Post-stratify

We now post-stratify according to the population proportions calculated previously, and calculate credible intervals for each state as well.

```
biden_support_by_state <-
  us_election_model |>
  add_epred_draws(newdata = poststrat_data_cells) |>
  rename(support_biden_predict = .epred) |>
  mutate(support_biden_predict_prop = support_biden_predict * prop) |>
  ungroup() |>
  summarise(support_biden_predict = sum(support_biden_predict_prop),
            .by = c(stateicp, .draw)) |>
  summarise(
    mean = mean(support_biden_predict),
```

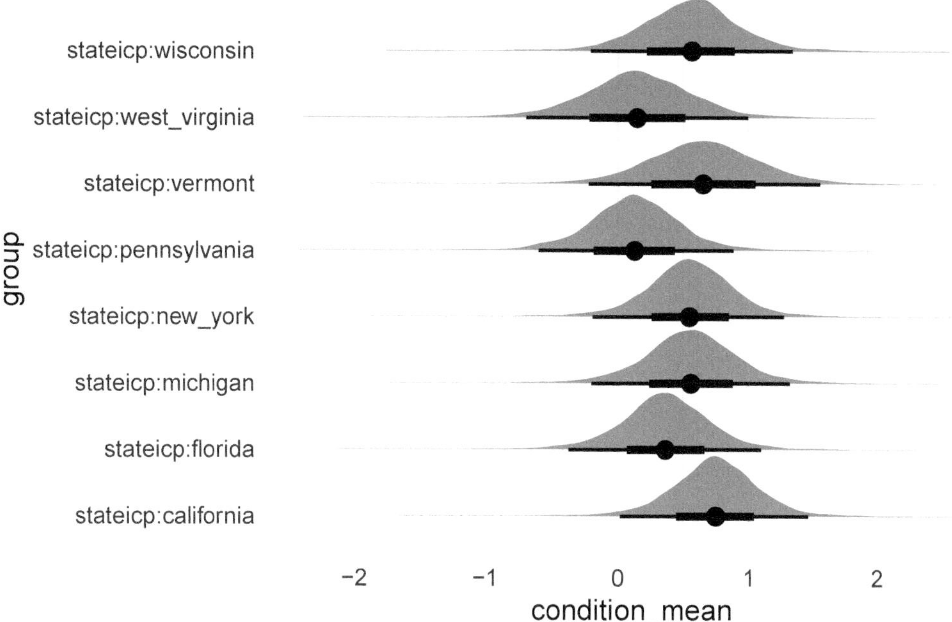

Figure 15.3: Examining the distribution of draws for selected states

```
    lower = quantile(support_biden_predict, 0.025),
    upper = quantile(support_biden_predict, 0.975),
    .by = stateicp
  )

head(biden_support_by_state)
```

```
# A tibble: 6 x 4
  stateicp       mean lower upper
  <fct>         <dbl> <dbl> <dbl>
1 connecticut   0.624 0.284 0.884
2 maine         0.535 0.211 0.840
3 massachusetts 0.623 0.292 0.884
4 new hampshire 0.531 0.201 0.834
5 rhode island  0.540 0.206 0.841
6 vermont       0.582 0.256 0.872
```

And we can have a look at our estimates graphically (Figure 15.4).

```
biden_support_by_state |>
  ggplot(aes(y = mean, x = fct_reorder(stateicp, mean),
             color = "MRP estimate")) +
  geom_point() +
  geom_errorbar(aes(ymin = lower, ymax = upper), width = 0) +
  geom_point(
    data = nationscape_data |>
```

```
      summarise(n = n(),
                .by = c(stateicp, vote_biden)) |>
      mutate(prop = n / sum(n),
             .by = stateicp) |>
      filter(vote_biden == 1),
    aes(y = prop, x = stateicp, color = "Nationscape raw data")
    ) +
  geom_hline(yintercept = 0.5, linetype = "dashed") +
  labs(
    x = "State",
    y = "Estimated proportion support for Biden",
    color = "Source"
  ) +
  theme_classic() +
  scale_color_brewer(palette = "Set1") +
  coord_flip() +
  theme(legend.position = "bottom")
```

The Nationscape dataset is a high-quality survey. But it was weighted to major census region—the West, the Midwest, the Northeast, and the South—rather than state, which could be one reason we see a difference between the MRP estimates and the raw data.

15.4 Exercises

Scales

1. *(Plan)* Consider the following scenario: *Support for a political party is a binary (yes/no), and is related to age-group, gender, income group, and highest education.* Please sketch out what that dataset could look like and then sketch a graph that you could build to show all observations.
2. *(Simulate)* Please further consider the scenario described and simulate the situation. Please include at least ten tests based on the simulated data.
3. *(Acquire)* Please describe one possible source of such a dataset.
4. *(Explore)* Please use `ggplot2` to build the graph that you sketched. Use `rstanarm` to estimate a model.
5. *(Communicate)* Please write two paragraphs about what you did.

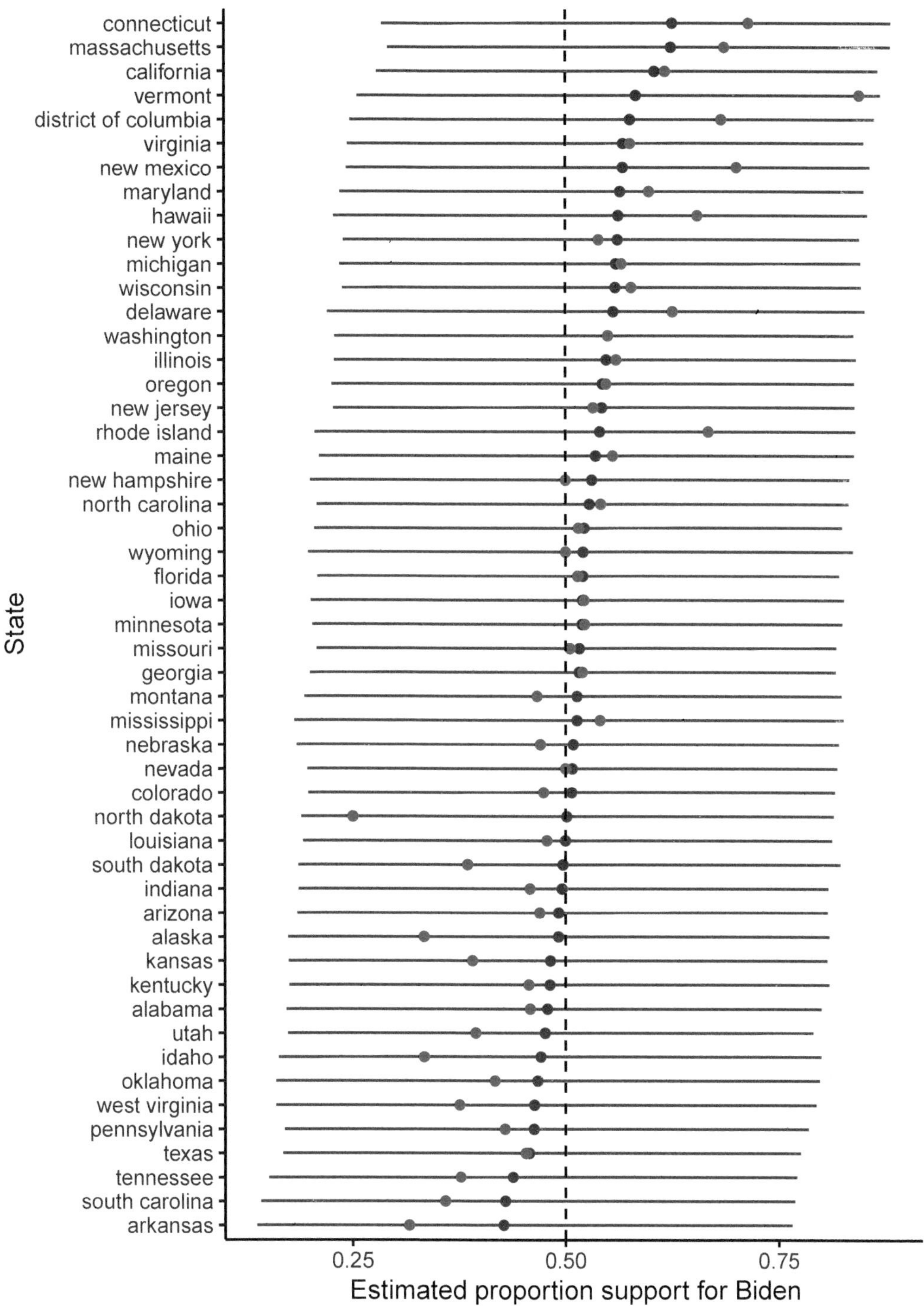

Figure 15.4: Comparing the MRP estimates with the Nationscape raw data

Questions

1. Please explain what MRP is, and the strengths and weaknesses, being sure to explain any technical terms that you use (write at least three paragraphs).
2. What are three aspects that you like about W. Wang et al. (2015)? What are three aspects that do you not? To what extent is it possible to reproduce the paper?
3. With respect to W. Wang et al. (2015), what is a weakness of MRP (pick one)?
   a. Detailed data requirement.
   b. Allows use of biased data.
   c. Expensive to conduct.
4. With respect to W. Wang et al. (2015), what is concerning about the Xbox sample (pick one)?
   a. Non-representative.
   b. Small sample size.
   c. Multiple responses from the same respondent.
5. We are interested in studying how voting intentions in the 2020 US presidential election vary by an individual's income. We set up a logistic regression model to study this relationship. In this study, what are some possible predictors (select all that apply)?
   a. Whether the respondent is registered to vote (yes/no).
   b. Whether the respondent is going to vote for Biden (yes/no).
   c. The race of the respondent (white/not white).
   d. The respondent's marital status (married/not).
6. Please think about N. Cohn (2016). Why is this type of exercise not carried out more? Why do you think that different groups, even with the same background and level of quantitative sophistication, could have such different estimates even when they use the same data?
7. We train a model based on a survey, and then post-stratify it using the ACS dataset. What are some of the practical considerations that we may have to contend with when doing this?
8. Consider a situation in which you have a survey dataset with these age-groups: 18-29; 30-44; 45-60; and 60+. And a post-stratification dataset with these age-groups: 18-34; 35-49; 50-64; and 65+. Please write about the approach you would take to bringing these together.

Tutorial

In a similar manner to Ghitza and Gelman (2020) pretend you have access to a US voter file record from a private company. You train a model on the 2020 US Cooperative Election Study, and post-stratify it, on an individual basis, based on that voter file.

a. Put together a datasheet for the voter file dataset following Gebru et al. (2021)? As a reminder, datasheets accompany datasets and document "motivation, composition, collection process, recommended uses," among other aspects.
b. Create a model card for your model, following M. Mitchell et al. (2019)? As a reminder, model cards are deliberately straight forward one- or two-page documents that report aspects such as: model details; intended use; metrics; training data; ethical considerations; as well as caveats and recommendations (M. Mitchell et al. 2019).

c. Discuss three ethical aspects around the features that you are using in your model? [Please write a paragraph or two for each point.]
d. Detail the protections that you would put in place in terms of the dataset, the model, and the predictions?

Paper

At about this point the *Spofforth* Paper in the "Papers" Online Appendix[1] would be appropriate.

[1] https://tellingstorieswithdata.com/23-assessment.html

16

Text as data

Prerequisites

- Read *Text as data: An overview*, (Benoit 2020)
  - This chapter provides an overview of using text as data.
- Read *Supervised Machine Learning for Text Analysis in R*, (Hvitfeldt and Silge 2021)
  - Focus on Chapters 6 "Regression", and 7 "Classification", which implements linear and generalized linear models using text as data.
- Read *The Naked Truth: How the names of 6,816 complexion products can reveal bias in beauty*, (Amaka and Thomas 2021)
  - Analysis of text on make-up products.

Key concepts and skills

- Understanding text as a source of data that we can analyze enables many interesting questions to be considered.
- Text cleaning and preparation are especially critical because of the large number of possible outcomes. There are many decisions that need to be made at this stage, which have important effects later in the analysis.
- One way to consider a text dataset is to look at which words distinguish particular documents.
- Another is to consider which topics are contained in a document.

Software and packages

- Base R (R Core Team 2023)
- `astrologer` (Gelfand 2022a) (this package is not on CRAN, so install it with: `devtools::install_github("sharlagelfand/astrologer")`)
- `beepr` (Bååth 2018)
- `fs` (Hester, Wickham, and Csárdi 2021)
- `gutenbergr` (Johnston and Robinson 2022)
- `quanteda` (Benoit et al. 2018)
- `stm` (Roberts, Stewart, and Tingley 2019)
- `tidytext` (Silge and Robinson 2016)
- `tidyverse` (Wickham et al. 2019)

```
library(astrologer)
library(beepr)
library(fs)
library(gutenbergr)
library(quanteda)
library(stm)
library(tidytext)
```

```
library(tidyverse)
```

16.1 Introduction

Text is all around us. In many cases, text is the earliest type of data that we are exposed to. Increases in computational power, the development of new methods, and the enormous availability of text, mean that there has been a great deal of interest in using text as data. Using text as data provides opportunities for unique analyses. For instance:

- text analysis of state-run newspapers in African countries can identify manipulation by governments (Hassan 2022);
- the text from UK daily newspapers can be used to generate better forecasts of GDP and inflation (Kalamara et al. 2022), and similarly, *The New York Times* can be used to create an uncertainty index which correlates with US economic activity (Alexopoulos and Cohen 2015);
- the analysis of notes in Electronic Health Records (EHR) can improve the efficiency of disease prediction (Gronsbell et al. 2019); and
- analysis of US congressional records indicates just how often women legislators are interrupted by men (M. Miller and Sutherland 2022).

Earlier approaches to the analysis of text tend to convert words into numbers, divorced of context. They could then be analyzed using traditional approaches, such as variants of logistic regression. More recent methods try to take advantage of the structure inherent in text, which can bring additional meaning. The difference is perhaps like a child who can group similar colors, compared with a child who knows what objects are; although both crocodiles and trees are green, and you can do something with that knowledge, it is useful to know that a crocodile could eat you while a tree probably would not.

Text can be considered an unwieldy, yet similar, version of the datasets that we have used throughout this book. The main difference is that we will typically begin with wide data, where each variable is a word, or token more generally. Often each entry is then a count. We would then typically transform this into rather long data, with one variable of words and another of the counts. Considering text as data naturally requires some abstraction from its context. But this should not be entirely separated as this can perpetuate historical inequities. For instance, Koenecke et al. (2020) find that automated speech recognition systems perform much worse for Black compared with White speakers, and Davidson, Bhattacharya, and Weber (2019) find that tweets that use Black American English, which is a specifically defined technical term, are classified at hate speech at higher rates than similar tweets in Standard American English, which again is a technical term.

One exciting aspect of text data is that it is typically not generated for the purposes of our analysis. The trade-off is that we typically must do a bunch more work to get it into a form that we can work with. There are a lot of decisions to be made in the data cleaning and preparation stages.

The larger size of text datasets means that it is especially important to simulate, and start small, when it comes to their analysis. Using text as data is exciting because of the quantity and variety of text that is available to us. But in general, dealing with text datasets is messy. There is a lot of cleaning and preparation that is typically required. Often, text datasets are large. As such having a reproducible workflow in place and then clearly communicating your findings, becomes critical. Nonetheless, it is an exciting area.

In this chapter we first consider preparing text datasets. We then consider Term Frequency-Inverse Document Frequency (TF-IDF) and topic models.

16.2 Text cleaning and preparation

Text modeling is an exciting area of research. But, and this is true more generally, the cleaning and preparation aspect is often at least as difficult as the modeling. We will cover some essentials and provide a foundation that can be built on.

The first step is to get some data. We discussed data gathering in Chapter 7 and mentioned in passing many sources including:

- Using *Inside Airbnb*, which provides text from reviews.
- Project Gutenberg which provides the text from out-of-copyright books.
- Scraping Wikipedia or other websites.

The workhorse packages that we need for text cleaning and preparation are `stringr`, which is part of the `tidyverse`, and `quanteda`.

For illustrative purposes we construct a corpus of the first sentence or two, from three books: *Beloved* by Toni Morrison, *The Last Samurai* by Helen DeWitt, and *Jane Eyre* by Charlotte Brontë.

```
last_samurai <-"My father's father was a Methodist minister."

beloved <- "124 was spiteful. Full of Baby's venom."

jane_eyre <- "There was no possibility of taking a walk that day."

bookshelf <-
  tibble(
    book = c("Last Samurai", "Beloved", "Jane Eyre"),
    first_sentence = c(last_samurai, beloved, jane_eyre)
  )

bookshelf
```

```
# A tibble: 3 x 2
  book         first_sentence
  <chr>        <chr>
1 Last Samurai My father's father was a Methodist minister.
2 Beloved      124 was spiteful. Full of Baby's venom.
3 Jane Eyre    There was no possibility of taking a walk that day.
```

We typically want to construct a document-feature matrix, which has documents in each observation, words in each column, and a count for each combination, along with associated metadata. For instance, if our corpus was the text from Airbnb reviews, then each document may be a review, and typical features could include: "The", "Airbnb", "was", "great". Notice here that the sentence has been split into different words. We typically talk of "tokens" to generalize away from words, because of the variety of aspects we may be interested in, but words are commonly used.

```
books_corpus <-
  corpus(bookshelf,
         docid_field = "book",
         text_field = "first_sentence")

books_corpus
```

```
Corpus consisting of 3 documents.
Last Samurai :
"My father's father was a Methodist minister."

Beloved :
"124 was spiteful. Full of Baby's venom."

Jane Eyre :
"There was no possibility of taking a walk that day."
```

We use the tokens in the corpus to construct a document-feature matrix (DFM) using `dfm()` from `quanteda` (Benoit et al. 2018).

```
books_dfm <-
  books_corpus |>
  tokens() |>
  dfm()

books_dfm
```

```
Document-feature matrix of: 3 documents, 21 features (57.14% sparse)
              features
docs            my father's father was a methodist minister . 124 spiteful
  Last Samurai  1        1      1   1 1         1        1 1   0        0
  Beloved       0        0      0   1 0         0        0 2   1        1
  Jane Eyre     0        0      0   1 1         0        0 1   0        0
[ reached max_nfeat ... 11 more features ]
```

We now consider some of the many decisions that need to be made as part of this process. There is no definitive right or wrong answer. Instead, we make those decisions based on what we will be using the dataset for.

16.2.1 Stop words

Stop words are words such as "the", "and", and "a". For a long time stop words were not thought to convey much meaning, and there were concerns around memory-constrained computation. A common step of preparing a text dataset was to remove stop words. We now know that stop words can have a great deal of meaning (Schofield, Magnusson, and Mimno 2017). The decision to remove them is a nuanced one that depends on circumstances.

We can get a list of stop words using `stopwords()` from `quanteda`.

```
stopwords(source = "snowball")[1:10]
```

```
 [1] "i"         "me"        "my"        "myself"    "we"        "our"
 [7] "ours"      "ourselves" "you"       "your"
```

We could then look for all instances of words in that list and crudely remove them with `str_replace_all()`.

```
stop_word_list <-
  paste(stopwords(source = "snowball"), collapse = " | ")

bookshelf |>
  mutate(no_stops = str_replace_all(
    string = first_sentence,
    pattern = stop_word_list,
    replacement = " ")
  ) |>
  select(no_stops, first_sentence)
```

```
# A tibble: 3 x 2
  no_stops                                 first_sentence
  <chr>                                    <chr>
1 My father's father a Methodist minister. My father's father was a Methodist m~
2 124 spiteful. Full Baby's venom.         124 was spiteful. Full of Baby's ven~
3 There no possibility taking walk day.    There was no possibility of taking a~
```

There are many different lists of stop words that have been put together by others. For instance, `stopwords()` can use lists including: "snowball", "stopwords-iso", "smart", "marimo", "ancient", and "nltk". More generally, if we decide to use stop words then we often need to augment such lists with project-specific words. We can do this by creating a count of individual words in the corpus, and then sorting by the most common and adding those to the stop words list as appropriate.

```
stop_word_list_updated <-
  paste(
    "Methodist |",
    "spiteful |",
    "possibility |",
    stop_word_list,
    collapse = " | "
  )

bookshelf |>
  mutate(no_stops = str_replace_all(
    string = first_sentence,
    pattern = stop_word_list_updated,
    replacement = " ")
  ) |>
  select(no_stops)
```

```
# A tibble: 3 x 1
  no_stops
  <chr>
1 My father's father a  minister.
2 124 spiteful. Full Baby's venom.
3 There no of taking walk day.
```

We can integrate the removal of stop words into our construction of the DFM with `dfm_remove()` from `quanteda`.

```
books_dfm |>
  dfm_remove(stopwords(source = "snowball"))
```

```
Document-feature matrix of: 3 documents, 14 features (61.90% sparse) and 0 docvars.
              features
docs            father's father methodist minister . 124 spiteful full baby's
  Last Samurai         1      1         1        1 1   0        0    0      0
  Beloved              0      0         0        0 2   1        1    1      1
  Jane Eyre            0      0         0        0 1   0        0    0      0
              features
docs            venom
  Last Samurai      0
  Beloved           1
  Jane Eyre         0
[ reached max_nfeat ... 4 more features ]
```

When we remove stop words we artificially adjust our dataset. Sometimes there may be a good reason to do that. But it must not be done unthinkingly. For instance, in Chapter 6 and Chapter 10 we discussed how sometimes datasets may need to be censored, truncated, or manipulated in other similar ways, to preserve the privacy of respondents. It is possible that the integration of the removal of stop words as a default step in natural language processing was due to computational power, which may have been more limited when these methods were developed. In any case, Jurafsky and Martin ([2000] 2023, 62) conclude that removing stop words does not improve performance for text classification. Relatedly, Schofield, Magnusson, and Mimno (2017) find that inference from topic models is not improved by the removal of anything other than the most frequent words. If stop words are to be removed, then they recommend doing this after topics are constructed.

16.2.2 Case, numbers, and punctuation

There are times when all we care about is the word, not the case or punctuation. For instance, if the text corpus was particularly messy or the existence of particular words was informative. We trade-off the loss of information for the benefit of making things simpler. We can convert to lower case with `str_to_lower()`, and use `str_replace_all()` to remove punctuation with "[:punct:]", and numbers with "[:digit:]".

```
bookshelf |>
  mutate(lower_sentence = str_to_lower(string = first_sentence)) |>
  select(lower_sentence)
```

```
# A tibble: 3 x 1
```

```
  lower_sentence
  <chr>
1 my father's father was a methodist minister.
2 124 was spiteful. full of baby's venom.
3 there was no possibility of taking a walk that day.
```

```
bookshelf |>
  mutate(no_punctuation_numbers = str_replace_all(
    string = first_sentence,
    pattern = "[:punct:]|[:digit:]",
    replacement = " "
  )) |>
  select(no_punctuation_numbers)
```

```
# A tibble: 3 x 1
  no_punctuation_numbers
  <chr>
1 "My father s father was a Methodist minister "
2 "    was spiteful  Full of Baby s venom "
3 "There was no possibility of taking a walk that day "
```

As an aside, we can remove letters, numbers, and punctuation with "[:graph:]" in `str_replace_all()`. While this is rarely needed in textbook examples, it is especially useful with real datasets, because they will typically have a small number of unexpected symbols that we need to identify and then remove. We use it to remove everything that we are used to, leaving only that which we are not.

More generally, we can use arguments in `tokens()` from `quanteda()` to do this.

```
books_corpus |>
  tokens(remove_numbers = TRUE, remove_punct = TRUE)
```

```
Tokens consisting of 3 documents.
Last Samurai :
[1] "My"         "father's"  "father"     "was"        "a"          "Methodist"
[7] "minister"

Beloved :
[1] "was"       "spiteful" "Full"     "of"         "Baby's"    "venom"

Jane Eyre :
 [1] "There"        "was"          "no"           "possibility" "of"
 [6] "taking"       "a"            "walk"         "that"         "day"
```

16.2.3 Typos and uncommon words

Then we need to decide what to do about typos and other minor issues. Every real-world text has typos. Sometimes these should clearly be fixed. But if they are made in a systematic way, for instance, a certain writer always makes the same mistakes, then they could have value if we were interested in grouping by the writer. The use of OCR will introduce common issues as well, as was seen in Chapter 7. For instance, "the" is commonly incorrectly recognized as "thc".

We could fix typos in the same way that we fixed stop words, i.e. with lists of corrections. When it comes to uncommon words, we can build this into our document-feature matrix creation with `dfm_trim()`. For instance, we could use "min_termfreq = 2" to remove any word that does not occur at least twice, or "min_docfreq = 0.05" to remove any word that is not in at least five per cent of documents or "max_docfreq = 0.90" to remove any word that is in at least 90 per cent of documents.

```
books_corpus |>
  tokens(remove_numbers = TRUE, remove_punct = TRUE) |>
  dfm(tolower = TRUE) |>
  dfm_trim(min_termfreq = 2)
```

```
Document-feature matrix of: 3 documents, 3 features (22.22% sparse) and 0 docvars.
               features
docs             was a of
  Last Samurai     1 1  0
  Beloved          1 0  1
  Jane Eyre        1 1  1
```

16.2.4 Tuples

A tuple is an ordered list of elements. In the context of text it is a series of words. If the tuple comprises two words, then we term this a "bi-gram", three words is a "tri-gram", etc. These are an issue when it comes to text cleaning and preparation because we often separate terms based on a space. This would result in an inappropriate separation.

This is a clear issue when it comes to place names. For instance, consider "British Columbia", "New Hampshire", "United Kingdom", and "Port Hedland". One way forward is to create a list of such places and then use `str_replace_all()` to add an underscore, for instance, "British_Columbia", "New_Hampshire", "United_Kingdom", and "Port_Hedland". Another option is to use `tokens_compound()` from `quanteda`.

```
some_places <- c("British Columbia",
                 "New Hampshire",
                 "United Kingdom",
                 "Port Hedland")
a_sentence <-
c("Vancouver is in British Columbia and New Hampshire is not")

tokens(a_sentence) |>
  tokens_compound(pattern = phrase(some_places))
```

```
Tokens consisting of 1 document.
text1 :
[1] "Vancouver"         "is"               "in"                "British_Columbia"
[5] "and"               "New_Hampshire"    "is"                "not"
```

In that case, we knew what the tuples were. But it might be that we were not sure what the common tuples were in the corpus. We could use `tokens_ngrams()` to identify them. We could ask for, say, all bi-grams in an excerpt from *Jane Eyre*. We showed how to download the text of this book from Project Gutenberg in Chapter 13 and so here we load the local version that we saved earlier.

```
jane_eyre <- read_csv(
  "jane_eyre.csv",
  col_types = cols(
    gutenberg_id = col_integer(),
    text = col_character()
  )
)

jane_eyre
```

```
# A tibble: 21,001 x 2
   gutenberg_id text
          <int> <chr>
 1         1260 JANE EYRE
 2         1260 AN AUTOBIOGRAPHY
 3         1260 <NA>
 4         1260 by Charlotte Brontë
 5         1260 <NA>
 6         1260 _ILLUSTRATED BY F. H. TOWNSEND_
 7         1260 <NA>
 8         1260 London
 9         1260 SERVICE & PATON
10         1260 5 HENRIETTA STREET
# i 20,991 more rows
```

As there are many blank lines we will remove them.

```
jane_eyre <-
  jane_eyre |>
  filter(!is.na(text))


jane_eyre_text <- tibble(
  book = "Jane Eyre",
  text = paste(jane_eyre$text, collapse = " ") |>
    str_replace_all(pattern = "[:punct:]",
                    replacement = " ") |>
    str_replace_all(pattern = stop_word_list,
                    replacement = " ")
)

jane_eyre_corpus <-
  corpus(jane_eyre_text, docid_field = "book", text_field = "text")
ngrams <- tokens_ngrams(tokens(jane_eyre_corpus), n = 2)
ngram_counts <-
  tibble(ngrams = unlist(ngrams)) |>
  count(ngrams, sort = TRUE)
```

```
head(ngram_counts)
```

```
# A tibble: 6 x 2
  ngrams            n
  <chr>         <int>
1 I_not           344
2 Mr_Rochester    332
3 I_thought       136
4 St_John         132
5 don_t           126
6 I_saw           122
```

Having identified some common bi-grams, we could add them to the list to be changed. This example includes names like "Mr Rochester" and "St John" which would need to remain together for analysis.

16.2.5 Stemming and lemmatizing

Stemming and lemmatizing words is another common approach for reducing the dimensionality of a text dataset. Stemming means to remove the last part of the word, in the expectation that this will result in more general words. For instance, "Canadians", "Canadian", and "Canada" all stem to "Canad". Lemmatizing is similar, but is more involved. It means changing words, not just on their spelling, but on their canonical form (Grimmer, Roberts, and Stewart 2022, 54). For instance, "Canadians", "Canadian", "Canucks", and "Canuck" may all be changed to "Canada".

We can do this with `dfm_wordstem()`. We notice, that, say, "minister", has been changed to "minist".

```
char_wordstem(c("Canadians", "Canadian", "Canada"))
```

```
[1] "Canadian" "Canadian" "Canada"
```

```
books_corpus |>
  tokens(remove_numbers = TRUE, remove_punct = TRUE) |>
  dfm(tolower = TRUE) |>
  dfm_wordstem()
```

```
Document-feature matrix of: 3 documents, 18 features (59.26% sparse) and 0 docvars.
              features
docs           my father was a methodist minist spite full of babi
  Last Samurai  1      2   1 1         1      1     0    0  0    0
  Beloved       0      0   1 0         0      0     1    1  1    1
  Jane Eyre     0      0   1 1         0      0     0    0  1    0
[ reached max_nfeat ... 8 more features ]
```

While this is a common step in using text as data, Schofield et al. (2017) find that in the context of topic modeling, which we cover later, stemming has little effect and there is little need to do it.

16.2.6 Duplication

Duplication is a major concern with text datasets because of their size. For instance, Bandy and Vincent (2021) showed that around 30 per cent of the data were inappropriately duplicated in the BookCorpus dataset, and Schofield, Thompson, and Mimno (2017) show that this is a major concern and could substantially affect results. However, it can be a subtle and difficult to diagnose problem. For instance, in Chapter 13 when we considered counts of page numbers for various authors in the context of Poisson regression, we could easily have accidentally included each Shakespeare entry twice because not only are there entries for each play, but also many anthologies that contained all of them. Careful consideration of our dataset identified the issue, but that would be difficult at scale.

16.3 Term Frequency-Inverse Document Frequency (TF-IDF)

16.3.1 Distinguishing horoscopes

Install and load `astrologer`, which is a dataset of horoscopes to explore a real dataset.

We can then access the "horoscopes" dataset.

```
horoscopes
```

```
# A tibble: 1,272 x 4
   startdate  zodiacsign  horoscope                                          url
   <date>     <fct>       <chr>                                              <chr>
 1 2015-01-05 Aries       Considering the fact that this past week (espec~ http~
 2 2015-01-05 Taurus      It's time Taurus. You aren't one to be rushed a~ http~
 3 2015-01-05 Gemini      Soon it will be time to review what you know, t~ http~
 4 2015-01-05 Cancer      Feeling  feelings and being full of flavorful s~ http~
 5 2015-01-05 Leo         Look, listen, watch, meditate and engage in pra~ http~
 6 2015-01-05 Virgo       Last week's astrology is still reverberating th~ http~
 7 2015-01-05 Libra       Get out your markers and your glue sticks. Get ~ http~
 8 2015-01-05 Scorpio     Time to pay extra attention to the needs of you~ http~
 9 2015-01-05 Sagittarius Everything right now is about how you say it, h~ http~
10 2015-01-05 Capricorn   The full moon on January 4th/5th was a healthy ~ http~
# i 1,262 more rows
```

There are four variables: "startdate", "zodiacsign", "horoscope", and "url" (note that URL is out-of-date because the website has been updated, for instance, the first one refers to here[1]). We are interested in the words that are used to distinguish the horoscope of each zodiac sign.

```
horoscopes |>
  count(zodiacsign)
```

```
# A tibble: 12 x 2
   zodiacsign      n
```

[1] https://chaninicholas.com/horoscopes-week-january-5th/

```
   <fct>        <int>
 1 Aries          106
 2 Taurus         106
 3 Gemini         106
 4 Cancer         106
 5 Leo            106
 6 Virgo          106
 7 Libra          106
 8 Scorpio        106
 9 Sagittarius    106
10 Capricorn      106
11 Aquarius       106
12 Pisces         106
```

There are 106 horoscopes for each zodiac sign. In this example we first tokenize by word, and then create counts based on zodiac sign only, not date. We use `tidytext` because it is used extensively in Hvitfeldt and Silge (2021).

```
horoscopes_by_word <-
  horoscopes |>
  select(-startdate,-url) |>
  unnest_tokens(output = word,
                input = horoscope,
                token = "words")

horoscopes_counts_by_word <-
  horoscopes_by_word |>
  count(zodiacsign, word, sort = TRUE)

horoscopes_counts_by_word
```

```
# A tibble: 41,850 x 3
   zodiacsign  word      n
   <fct>       <chr> <int>
 1 Cancer      to     1440
 2 Sagittarius to     1377
 3 Aquarius    to     1357
 4 Aries       to     1335
 5 Pisces      to     1313
 6 Leo         to     1302
 7 Libra       to     1270
 8 Sagittarius you    1264
 9 Virgo       to     1262
10 Scorpio     to     1260
# i 41,840 more rows
```

We can see that the most popular words appear to be similar for the different zodiacs. At this point, we could use the data in a variety of ways.

We might be interested to know which words characterize each group—that is to say, which words are commonly used only in each group. We can do that by first looking at a word's term frequency (TF), which is how many times a word is used in the horoscopes for each zodiac sign. The issue is that there are a lot of words that are commonly used regardless of context. As such, we may also like to look at the inverse document frequency (IDF) in which we "penalize" words that occur in the horoscopes for many zodiac signs. A word that occurs in the horoscopes of many zodiac signs would have a lower IDF than a word that only occurs in the horoscopes of one. The term frequency–inverse document frequency (tf-idf) is then the product of these.

We can create this value using `bind_tf_idf()` from `tidytext`. It will create new variables for each of these measures.

```
horoscopes_counts_by_word_tf_idf <-
  horoscopes_counts_by_word |>
  bind_tf_idf(
    term = word,
    document = zodiacsign,
    n = n
  ) |>
  arrange(-tf_idf)

horoscopes_counts_by_word_tf_idf
```

```
# A tibble: 41,850 x 6
   zodiacsign  word             n       tf   idf   tf_idf
   <fct>       <chr>        <int>    <dbl> <dbl>    <dbl>
 1 Capricorn   goat             6 0.000236  2.48 0.000585
 2 Pisces      pisces          14 0.000531  1.10 0.000584
 3 Sagittarius sagittarius     10 0.000357  1.39 0.000495
 4 Cancer      cancer          10 0.000348  1.39 0.000483
 5 Gemini      gemini           7 0.000263  1.79 0.000472
 6 Taurus      bulls            5 0.000188  2.48 0.000467
 7 Aries       warns            5 0.000186  2.48 0.000463
 8 Cancer      organize         7 0.000244  1.79 0.000437
 9 Cancer      overwork         5 0.000174  2.48 0.000433
10 Taurus      let's           10 0.000376  1.10 0.000413
# i 41,840 more rows
```

In Table 16.1 we look at the words that distinguish the horoscopes of each zodiac sign. The first thing to notice is that some of them have their own zodiac sign. On the one hand, there is an argument for removing this, but on the other hand, the fact that it does not happen for all of them is perhaps informative of the nature of the horoscopes for each sign.

```
horoscopes_counts_by_word_tf_idf |>
  slice(1:5,
        .by = zodiacsign) |>
  select(zodiacsign, word) |>
  summarise(all = paste0(word, collapse = "; "),
            .by = zodiacsign) |>
  knitr::kable(col.names = c("Zodiac sign",
                             "Most common words unique to that sign"))
```

Table 16.1: Most common words in horoscopes that are unique to a particular zodiac sign

Zodiac sign	Most common words unique to that sign
Capricorn	goat; capricorn; capricorns; signify; neighborhood
Pisces	pisces; wasted; missteps; node; shoes
Sagittarius	sagittarius; rolodex; distorted; coat; reinvest
Cancer	cancer; organize; overwork; procrastinate; scuttle
Gemini	gemini; mood; output; admit; faces
Taurus	bulls; let's; painfully; virgin; taurus
Aries	warns; vesta; aries; fearful; chase
Virgo	digesting; trace; liberate; someone's; final
Libra	proof; inevitably; recognizable; reference; disguise
Scorpio	skate; advocate; knots; bottle; meditating
Aquarius	saves; consult; yearnings; sexy; athene
Leo	trines; blessed; regrets; leo; agree

16.4 Topic models

Topic models are useful when we have many statements and we want to create groups based on which sentences that use similar words. We consider those groups of similar words to define topics. One way to get consistent estimates of the topics of each statement is to use topic models. While there are many variants, one way is to use the latent Dirichlet allocation (LDA) method of Blei, Ng, and Jordan (2003), as implemented by `stm`. For clarity, in the context of this chapter, LDA refers to latent Dirichlet allocation and not Linear Discriminant Analysis, although this is another common subject associated with the acronym LDA.

The key assumption behind the LDA method is that for each statement, a document, is made by a person who decides the topics they would like to talk about in that document, and who then chooses words, terms, that are appropriate to those topics. A topic could be thought of as a collection of terms, and a document as a collection of topics. The topics are not specified *ex ante*; they are an outcome of the method. Terms are not necessarily unique to a particular topic, and a document could be about more than one topic. This provides more flexibility than other approaches such as a strict word count method. The goal is to have the words found in documents group themselves to define topics.

LDA considers each statement to be a result of a process where a person first chooses the topics they want to speak about. After choosing the topics, the person then chooses appropriate words to use for each of those topics. More generally, the LDA topic model works by considering each document as having been generated by some probability distribution over topics. For instance, if there were five topics and two documents, then the first document may be comprised mostly of the first few topics; the other document may be mostly about the final few topics (Figure 16.1).

Similarly, each topic could be considered a probability distribution over terms. To choose the terms used in each document the speaker picks terms from each topic in the appropriate proportion. For instance, if there were ten terms, then one topic could be defined by giving more weight to terms related to immigration; and some other topic may give more weight to terms related to the economy (Figure 16.2).

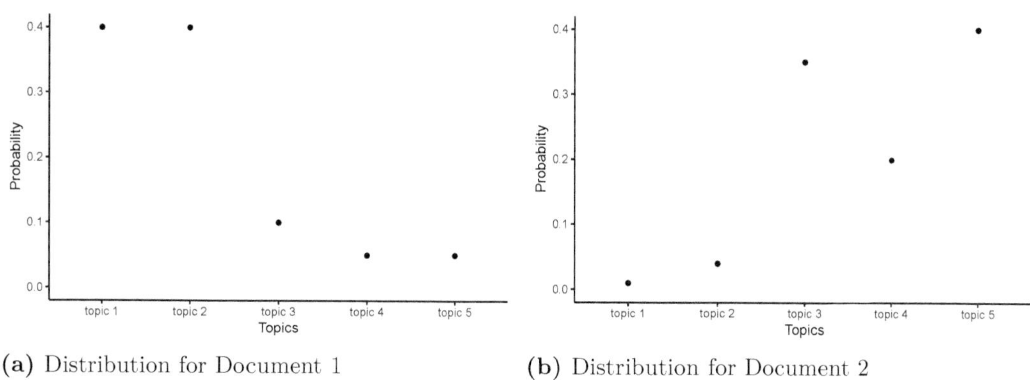

(a) Distribution for Document 1 **(b)** Distribution for Document 2

Figure 16.1: Probability distributions over topics

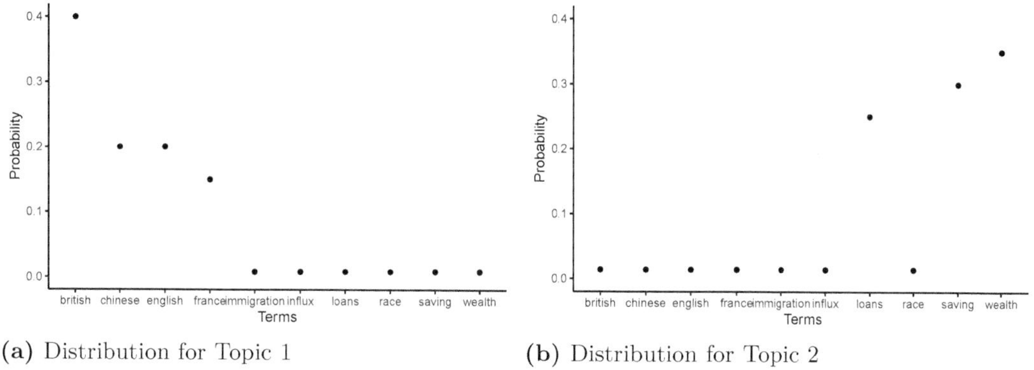

(a) Distribution for Topic 1 **(b)** Distribution for Topic 2

Figure 16.2: Probability distributions over terms

By way of background, the Dirichlet distribution is a variation of the beta distribution that is commonly used as a prior for categorical and multinomial variables. If there are just two categories, then the Dirichlet and the beta distributions are the same. In the special case of a symmetric Dirichlet distribution, $\eta = 1$, it is equivalent to a uniform distribution. If $\eta < 1$, then the distribution is sparse and concentrated on a smaller number of the values, and this number decreases as η decreases. A hyperparameter, in this usage, is a parameter of a prior distribution.

After the documents are created, they are all that we can analyze. The term usage in each document is observed, but the topics are hidden, or "latent". We do not know the topics of each document, nor how terms defined the topics. That is, we do not know the probability distributions of Figure 16.1 or Figure 16.2. In a sense we are trying to reverse the document generation process—we have the terms, and we would like to discover the topics.

If we observe the terms in each document, then we can obtain estimates of the topics (Steyvers and Griffiths 2006). The outcomes of the LDA process are probability distributions. It is these distributions that define the topics. Each term will be given a probability of being a member of a particular topic, and each document will be given a probability of being about a particular topic.

The initial practical step when implementing LDA given a corpus of documents is usually to remove stop words. Although, as mentioned earlier, this is not necessary, and may be better done after the groups are created. We often also remove punctuation and capitalization. We then construct our document-feature matrix using `dfm()` from `quanteda`.

After the dataset is ready, `stm` can be used to implement LDA and approximate the posterior. The process attempts to find a topic for a particular term in a particular document, given the topics of all other terms for all other documents. Broadly, it does this by first assigning every term in every document to a random topic, specified by Dirichlet priors. It then selects a particular term in a particular document and assigns it to a new topic based on the conditional distribution where the topics for all other terms in all documents are taken as given (Grün and Hornik 2011, 6). Once this has been estimated, then estimates for the distribution of words into topics and topics into documents can be backed out.

The conditional distribution assigns topics depending on how often a term has been assigned to that topic previously, and how common the topic is in that document (Steyvers and Griffiths 2006). The initial random allocation of topics means that the results of early passes through the corpus of document are poor, but given enough time the algorithm converges to an appropriate estimate.

The choice of the number of topics, k, affects the results, and must be specified *a priori*. If there is a strong reason for a particular number, then this can be used. Otherwise, one way to choose an appropriate number is to use a test and training set process. Essentially, this means running the process on a variety of possible values for k and then picking an appropriate value that performs well.

One weakness of the LDA method is that it considers a "bag of words" where the order of those words does not matter (Blei 2012). It is possible to extend the model to reduce the impact of the bag-of-words assumption and add conditionality to word order. Additionally, alternatives to the Dirichlet distribution can be used to extend the model to allow for correlation.

16.4.1 What is talked about in the Canadian parliament?

Following the example of the British, the written record of what is said in the Canadian parliament is called "Hansard". It is not completely verbatim, but is very close. It is available in CSV format from LiPaD[2], which was constructed by Beelen et al. (2017).

We are interested in what was talked about in the Canadian parliament in 2018. To get started we can download the entire corpus from here[3], and then discard all of the years apart from 2018. If the datasets are in a folder called "2018", we can use `read_csv()` to read and combine all the CSVs.

```
files_of_interest <-
  dir_ls(path = "2018/", glob = "*.csv", recurse = 2)

hansard_canada_2018 <-
  read_csv(
    files_of_interest,
    col_types = cols(
      basepk = col_integer(),
      speechdate = col_date(),
      speechtext = col_character(),
```

[2]https://www.lipad.ca

[3]https://www.lipad.ca/data/

```
      speakerparty = col_character(),
      speakerriding = col_character(),
      speakername = col_character()
    ),
    col_select =
      c(basepk, speechdate, speechtext, speakername, speakerparty,
        speakerriding)) |>
  filter(!is.na(speakername))

hansard_canada_2018
```

```
# A tibble: 33,105 x 6
    basepk speechdate speechtext           speakername speakerparty speakerriding
     <int> <date>     <chr>                <chr>       <chr>        <chr>
 1 4732776 2018-01-29 "Mr. Speaker, I wo~ Julie Dabr~ Liberal      Toronto—Danf~
 2 4732777 2018-01-29 "Mr. Speaker, I wa~ Matthew Du~ New Democra~ Beloeil—Cham~
 3 4732778 2018-01-29 "Mr. Speaker, I am~ Stephanie ~ Conservative Calgary Midn~
 4 4732779 2018-01-29 "Resuming debate.\~ Anthony Ro~ Liberal      Nipissing—Ti~
 5 4732780 2018-01-29 "Mr. Speaker, we a~ Alain Rayes Conservative Richmond—Art~
 6 4732781 2018-01-29 "The question is o~ Anthony Ro~ Liberal      Nipissing—Ti~
 7 4732782 2018-01-29 "Agreed.\n No."      Some hon. ~ <NA>         <NA>
 8 4732783 2018-01-29 "All those in favo~ Anthony Ro~ Liberal      Nipissing—Ti~
 9 4732784 2018-01-29 "Yea."               Some hon. ~ <NA>         <NA>
10 4732785 2018-01-29 "All those opposed~ Anthony Ro~ Liberal      Nipissing—Ti~
# i 33,095 more rows
```

The use of `filter()` at the end is needed because sometimes aspects such as "directions" and similar non-speech aspects are included in the Hansard. For instance, if we do not include that `filter()` then the first line is "The House resumed from November 9, 2017, consideration of the motion." We can then construct a corpus.

```
hansard_canada_2018_corpus <-
  corpus(hansard_canada_2018,
         docid_field = "basepk",
         text_field = "speechtext")
```

```
Warning: NA is replaced by empty string
```

```
hansard_canada_2018_corpus
```

```
Corpus consisting of 33,105 documents and 4 docvars.
4732776 :
"Mr. Speaker, I would like to wish everyone in this place a h..."

4732777 :
"Mr. Speaker, I want to thank my colleague from Richmond—Arth..."

4732778 :
"Mr. Speaker, I am here today to discuss a motion that asks t..."
```

```
4732779 :
"Resuming debate. There being no further debate, the hon. mem..."

4732780 :
"Mr. Speaker, we are nearing the end of the discussion and de..."

4732781 :
"The question is on the motion. Is the pleasure of the House ..."

[ reached max_ndoc ... 33,099 more documents ]
```

We use the tokens in the corpus to construct a document-feature matrix. To make our life a little easier, computationally, we remove any word that does not occur at least twice, and any word that does not occur in at least two documents.

```
hansard_dfm <-
  hansard_canada_2018_corpus |>
  tokens(
    remove_punct = TRUE,
    remove_symbols = TRUE
  ) |>
  dfm() |>
  dfm_trim(min_termfreq = 2, min_docfreq = 2) |>
  dfm_remove(stopwords(source = "snowball"))

hansard_dfm
```

```
Document-feature matrix of: 33,105 documents, 29,595 features (99.77% sparse)
         features
docs      mr speaker like wish everyone place happy new year great
  4732776  1       1    2    1        1     4     2   3    5     1
  4732777  1       1    5    0        1     1     0   0    0     1
  4732778  1       1    2    0        0     1     0   0    4     1
  4732779  0       0    0    0        0     0     0   0    0     0
  4732780  1       1    4    0        1     1     0   0    2     0
  4732781  0       0    0    0        0     0     0   0    0     0
[ reached max_ndoc ... 33,099 more documents, reached max_nfeat ]
```

At this point we can use `stm()` from `stm` to implement a LDA model. We need to specify a document-feature matrix and the number of topics. Topic models are essentially just summaries. Instead of a document becoming a collection of words, they become a collection of topics with some probability associated with each topic. But because it is just providing a collection of words that tend to be used at similar times, rather than actual underlying meaning, we need to specify the number of topics that we are interested in. This decision will have a big impact, and we should consider a few different numbers.

```
hansard_topics <- stm(documents = hansard_dfm, K = 10)

beepr::beep()

write_rds(
```

```
    hansard_topics,
    file = "hansard_topics.rda"
  )
```

This will take some time, likely 15-30 minutes, so it is useful to save the model when it is done using `write_rds()`, and use `beep` to get a notification when it is done. We could then read the results back in with `read_rds()`.

```
hansard_topics <- read_rds(
  file = "hansard_topics.rda"
)
```

We can look at the words in each topic with `labelTopics()`.

```
labelTopics(hansard_topics)
```

16.5 Exercises

Scales

1. *(Plan)* Consider the following scenario: *You run a news website and are trying to understand whether to allow anonymous comments. You decide to do a A/B test, where we keep everything the same, but only allow anonymous comments on one version of the site. All you will have to decide is the text data that you obtain from the test.* Please sketch out what that dataset could look like and then sketch a graph that you could build to show all observations.
2. *(Simulate)* Please further consider the scenario described and simulate the situation. Please include at least ten tests based on the simulated data.
3. *(Acquire)* Please describe one possible source of such a dataset.
4. *(Explore)* Please use `ggplot2` to build the graph that you sketched. Use `rstanarm` to build a model.
5. *(Communicate)* Please write two paragraphs about what you did.

Questions

1. Which argument to `str_replace_all()` would remove punctuation?
   a. "[:punct:]"
   b. "[:digit:]"
   c. "[:alpha:]"
   d. "[:lower:]"
2. Change `stopwords(source = "snowball")[1:10]` to find the ninth stopword in the "nltk" list.
   a. "her"
   b. "my"
   c. "you"
   d. "i"

3. Which function from quanteda() will tokenize a corpus?
   a. `tokenizer()`
   b. `token()`
   c. `tokenize()`
   d. `tokens()`
4. Which argument to `dfm_trim()` should be used if we want to only include terms that occur at least twice? = 2)
   a. "min_wordfreq"
   b. "min_termfreq"
   c. "min_term_occur"
   d. "min_ occurrence"
5. What is your favorite example of a tri-gram?
6. What is the second-most common word used in the zodiac signs for Cancer?
   a. to
   b. your
   c. the
   d. you
7. What is the sixth-most common word used in the zodiac signs for Pisces, that is unique to that sign?
   a. shoes
   b. prayer
   c. fishes
   d. pisces
8. Re-run the Canadian topic model, but only including five topics. Looking at the words in each topic, how would you describe what each of them is about?

Tutorial

Please follow the code of Hvitfeldt and Silge (2021) in *Supervised Machine Learning for Text Analysis in R*, Chapter 5.2 "Understand word embeddings by finding them yourself", freely available here[4], to implement your own word embeddings for one year's worth of data from LiPaD[5].

[4]https://smltar.com/embeddings.html
[5]https://www.lipad.ca

17

Concluding remarks

Prerequisites

- Read *Five ways to fix statistics*, (Leek et al. 2017)
  - Reflections on ways to do data science better.
- Read *Ten computer codes that transformed science*, (Perkel 2021)
  - Discussion of innovations in computing that underpin data science.
- Read *Learning from Data Journeys*, (Leonelli 2020)
  - Broad discussion of the role of data in data science.
- Read *Truth, Proof, and Reproducibility: There's No Counter-Attack for the Codeless*, (Gray and Marwick 2019)
  - Emphasizes the importance of reproducibility in data science.
- Watch *Science as Amateur Software Development*, (McElreath 2020)
  - Details lessons from software development that are applicable to data science.

17.1 Concluding remarks

There is an old saying, something along the lines of "may you live in interesting times". Maybe every generation feels this way, but we sure do live in interesting times. In this book, we have covered some essential skills for telling stories with data. And this is just the start.

In less than a generation, data science has gone from something that barely existed, to a defining part of academia and industry. The extent and pace of this change has many implications for those learning data science. For instance, it may imply that one should not just make decisions that optimize for what data science looks like right now, but also what could happen. While that is a little difficult, that is also one of the things that makes data science so exciting. That might mean choices like:

- taking courses on fundamentals, not just fashionable applications;
- reading core texts, not just whatever is trending; and
- trying to be at the intersection of at least a few different areas, rather than hyper-specialized.

One of the most exciting times when you learn data science is realizing that you just love playing with data. A decade ago, this did not fit into any particular department or company. These days, it fits into almost any of them.

Data science needs to insist on diversity, both in terms of approaches and applications. It is increasingly the most important work in the world, and hegemonic approaches have no place. It is just such an exciting time to be enthusiastic about data and able to build things.

The central thesis of this book has been that a revolution is needed in data science, and we have proposed one view of what it could look like. This revolution builds on the long history of statistics, borrows heavily from computer science, and draws on other disciplines as needed, but is centered around reproducibility, workflows, and respect. When data science began it was nebulous and ill-defined. As it has matured, we now come to see it as able to stand on its own.

This book has been a reimagining of what data science is, and what it could be. In Chapter 1 we provided an informal definition of data science. We now revisit it. We consider data science to be the process of developing and applying a principled, tested, reproducible, end-to-end workflow that focuses on quantitative measures in and of themselves, and as a foundation to explore questions. We have known for a long-time what rigor looks like in mathematical and statistical theory: theorems are accompanied by proofs (Horton et al. 2022). And we increasingly know what rigor looks like in data science: claims that are accompanied by verified, tested, reproducible, code and data. Rigorous data science creates lasting understanding of the world.

17.2 Some outstanding issues

There are many issues that are outstanding as we think about data science. They are not the type of issues with a definitive answer. Instead, they are questions to be explored and played with. This work will move data science forward and, more importantly, help us tell better stories about the world. Here we detail some of them.

1. How do we write effective tests?

Computer science has built a thorough foundation around testing and the importance of unit and functional tests is broadly accepted. One of the innovations of this book has been to integrate testing throughout the data science workflow, but this, like the first iteration of anything, needs considerable improvement and development.

We need to thoroughly integrate testing through data science. But it is unclear what this should look like, how we should do it, and what is the end-state. What does it mean to have well-tested code in data science? Code coverage, which is a measure of the percentage of lines of code that have tests, is not especially meaningful in data science, but what should we use instead? What do tests look like in data science? How are they written? The extensive use of simulation in statistics, which data science has adopted, provides groundwork, but there is a significant amount of work and investment that is needed.

2. What is happening at the data cleaning and preparation stage?

We do not have a good understanding how much data cleaning and preparation is driving estimates. Huntington-Klein et al. (2021), and Breznau et al. (2022), among others, have begun this work. They show that hidden research decisions have a big effect on subsequent estimates, sometimes greater than the standard errors. Statistics provides a good understanding of how modeling affects estimates, but we need more investigation of the influence of the earlier stages of the data science workflow. More specifically, we need to look for key points of failure and understand the ways in which failure can happen.

This is especially concerning as we scale to larger datasets. For instance, ImageNet is a dataset of 14 million images, which were hand-annotated. The cost, in both time and money, makes it prohibitively difficult to go through every image to ensure the label is consistent with the needs of each user of the dataset. Yet without undertaking this it is difficult to have much faith in subsequent model forecasts, especially in non-obvious cases.

3. How do we create effective names?

One of the crowning achievements of biology is the binomial nomenclature. This is the formal systematic approach to names, established by Carolus Linnaeus, the eighteenth century physician (Morange 2016, 81). Each species is referred to by two words with Latin grammatical form: the first is its genus, and the second is an adjective to characterize the species. Ensuring standardized nomenclature is given active consideration in biology. For instance, the use of nomenclature committees by researchers is recommended (McCarthy et al. 2023). As discussed in Chapter 9, names are a large source of friction in data science, and a standardized approach is similarly needed in data science.

The reason this is so pressing is that it affects understanding, which impacts efficiency. The binomial nomenclature provides diagnostic information, not just a casual reference (Koerner 2000, 45). This is particularly the case when data science is conducted in a team, rather than just one individual. A thorough understanding of what makes an effective name and then infrastructure to encourage them would bring significant dividends.

4. What is the appropriate relationship for data science with the constituent parts?

We have described the origins of data science as being various disciplines. Moving forward we need to consider what role these constituent parts, especially statistics and computer science, should play. More generally, we also need to establish how data science relates to, and interacts with, econometrics, applied mathematics, and computational social science. These draw on data science to answer questions in their own discipline, but like statistics and computer science, they also contribute back to data science. For instance, applications of machine learning in computational social science need to focus on transparency, interpretability, uncertainty, and ethics, and this all advances the more theoretical machine learning research done in other disciplines (Wallach 2018).

We must be careful to continue to learn statistics from statisticians, computer science from computer scientists, etc. An example of the danger of not doing this is clear in the case of p-values, which we have not made much of in this book, but which dominate quantitative analysis even though statisticians have warned about their misapplication for decades. One issue with not learning statistics from statisticians is that statistical practice can become a recipe that is naively followed, because that is the easiest way to teach it, even though that is not how statisticians do statistics.

Data science must remain deeply connected to these disciplines. How we continue to ensure that data science has the best aspects, without also bringing bad practice, is an especially significant challenge. And this is not just technical, but also cultural (Meng 2021). It is particularly important to ensure that data science maintains an inclusive culture of excellence.

5. How do we teach data science?

We are beginning to have agreement on what the foundations of data science are. It involves developing comfort with: computational thinking, sampling, statistics, graphs, Git and GitHub, SQL, command line, cleaning messy data, a few languages including R and Python, ethics, and writing. But we have very little agreement on how best to teach it. Partly this is because data science instructors often come from different fields, but it is also partly a difference in resources and priorities.

Complicating matters is that given the demand for data science skills we cannot limit data science education to graduate students because undergraduate students need those skills when they enter the workforce. If data science is to be taught at the undergraduate level, then it needs to be robust enough to be taught in large classes. Developing teaching tools that scale is critical. For instance, GitHub Actions could be used to run checks of student code and suggest improvements without instructor involvement. However, it is especially difficult to scale case studies style classes, which students often find so useful. Substantial innovation is needed.

6. What does the relationship between industry and academia look like?

Considerable innovation in data science occurs in industry, but sometimes this knowledge cannot be shared, and when it can it tends to be done slowly. The term data science has been used in academia since the 1960s, but it is because of industry that it has become popular in the past decade or so (Irizarry 2020).

Bringing academia and industry together is both a key challenge for data science and one of the easiest to overlook. The nature of the problems faced in industry, for instance scoping the needs of a client, and operating at scale, are removed from typical academic concerns. There is a danger that academic research could be rendered moot unless academics establish and maintain one foot in industry, and enable industry to actively participate in academia. From the industry side, ensuring that best practice is quickly adopted can be challenging if there is no immediate payoff. Ensuring that industry experience is valued in academic hiring and grant evaluation would help, as would encouraging entrepreneurship in academia.

17.3 Next steps

This book has covered much ground, and while we are toward the end of it, as the butler Stevens is told in the novel *The Remains of the Day* by Kazuo Ishiguro:

> The evening's the best part of the day. You've done your day's work. Now you can put your feet up and enjoy it.
>
> Ishiguro (1989)

Chances are there are aspects that you want to explore further, building on the foundation that you have established. If so, then the book has accomplished its aim.

If you were new to data science at the start of this book, then the next step would be to backfill what we skipped over. Begin with *Data Science: A First Introduction* (Timbers, Campbell, and Lee 2022). After that go through *R for Data Science* (Wickham, Çetinkaya-Rundel, and Grolemund [2016] 2023). We used R in this book and only mentioned SQL and Python in passing, but it is important to develop comfort in these languages. Start with

SQL for Data Scientists (Teate 2022), *Python for Data Analysis* (McKinney [2011] 2022), and the free Replit "100 Days of Code" Python course[1].

Sampling is a critical, but easy to overlook, aspect of data science. It would be sensible to go through *Sampling: Design and Analysis* (Lohr [1999] 2022). To deepen your understanding of surveys and experiments, go next to *Field Experiments: Design, Analysis, and Interpretation* (Gerber and Green 2012) and *Trustworthy online controlled experiments* (Kohavi, Tang, and Xu 2020).

For developing better data visualization skills, begin by turning to *Data Sketches* (Bremer and Wu 2021) and *Data Visualization* (Healy 2018). After that, develop strong foundations, such as *The Grammar of Graphics* (L. Wilkinson 2005).

If you are interested to learn more about modeling, then the next steps are *Statistical Rethinking: A Bayesian Course with Examples in R and Stan* (McElreath [2015] 2020), which additionally has an excellent series of accompanying videos, *Bayes Rules! An Introduction to Bayesian Modeling with R* (A. Johnson, Ott, and Dogucu 2022), and *Regression and Other Stories* (Gelman, Hill, and Vehtari 2020). It would also be worthwhile to establish a foundation of probability with *All of Statistics* (Wasserman 2005).

There is only one next natural step if you are interested in machine learning and that is *An Introduction to Statistical Learning* (James et al. [2013] 2021) followed by *The Elements of Statistical Learning* (Friedman, Tibshirani, and Hastie 2009).

To learn more about causality start with the economics perspective by going through *Causal Inference: The Mixtape* (Cunningham 2021) and *The Effect: An Introduction to Research Design and Causality* (Huntington-Klein 2021). Then turn to the health sciences perspective by going through *What If* (Hernán and Robins 2023).

For text as data, start with *Text As Data* (Grimmer, Roberts, and Stewart 2022). Then turn to *Supervised Machine Learning for Text Analysis in R* (Hvitfeldt and Silge 2021).

In terms of ethics, there are a variety of books. We have covered many chapters of it, throughout this book, but going through *Data Feminism* (D'Ignazio and Klein 2020) end-to-end would be useful, as would *Atlas of AI* (Crawford 2021).

And finally, for writing, it would be best to turn inward. Force yourself to write every day for a month. Then do it again and again. You will get better. That said, there are some useful books, including *Working* (Caro 2019) and *On Writing: A Memoir of the Craft* (S. King 2000).

We often hear the phrase "let the data speak". Hopefully it is clear this never happens. All that we can do is to acknowledge that we are the ones using data to tell stories, and strive and seek to make them worthy.

> It was her voice that made
> The sky acutest at its vanishing.
> She measured to the hour its solitude.
> She was the single artificer of the world
> In which she sang. And when she sang, the sea,

[1] https://replit.com/learn/100-days-of-python

Whatever self it had, became the self
That was her song, for she was the maker.

Extract from "The Idea of Order at Key West", (Stevens 1934)

17.4 Exercises

Questions

1. What is data science?
2. Who does data affect, and what affects data?
3. Discuss the inclusion of "race" and/or "sexuality" in a model.
4. What makes a story more or less convincing?
5. What is the role of ethics when dealing with data?

References

Abadie, Alberto, Susan Athey, Guido Imbens, and Jeffrey Wooldridge. 2017. "When Should You Adjust Standard Errors for Clustering?" Working Paper 24003. Working Paper Series. National Bureau of Economic Research. https://doi.org/10.3386/w24003.

Abelson, Harold, and Gerald Jay Sussman. 1996. *Structure and Interpretation of Computer Programs*. Cambridge: The MIT Press.

Abeysooriya, Mandhri, Megan Soria, Mary Sravya Kasu, and Mark Ziemann. 2021. "Gene Name Errors: Lessons Not Learned." *PLOS Computational Biology* 17 (7): 1–13. https://doi.org/10.1371/journal.pcbi.1008984.

Acemoglu, Daron, Simon Johnson, and James Robinson. 2001. "The Colonial Origins of Comparative Development: An Empirical Investigation." *American Economic Review* 91 (5): 1369–1401. https://doi.org/10.1257/aer.91.5.1369.

Achen, Christopher. 1978. "Measuring Representation." *American Journal of Political Science* 22 (3): 475–510. https://doi.org/10.2307/2110458.

Akerlof, George. 1970. "The Market for 'Lemons': Quality Uncertainty and the Market Mechanism." *The Quarterly Journal of Economics* 84 (3): 488–500. https://doi.org/10.2307/1879431.

Alexander, Monica. 2019a. "Reproducibility in Demographic Research." https://www.monicaalexander.com/posts/2019-10-20-reproducibility/.

———. 2019b. "The Concentration and Uniqueness of Baby Names in Australia and the US," January. https://www.monicaalexander.com/posts/2019-20-01-babynames/.

———. 2019c. "Analyzing Name Changes After Marriage Using a Non-Representative Survey," August. https://www.monicaalexander.com/posts/2019-08-07-mrp/.

———. 2021. "Overcoming Barriers to Sharing Code." *YouTube*, February. https://youtu.be/yvM2C6aZ94k.

Alexander, Monica, and Leontine Alkema. 2022. "A Bayesian Cohort Component Projection Model to Estimate Women of Reproductive Age at the Subnational Level in Data-Sparse Settings." *Demography* 59 (5): 1713–37. https://doi.org/10.1215/00703370-10216406.

Alexander, Monica, Mathew Kiang, and Magali Barbieri. 2018. "Trends in Black and White Opioid Mortality in the United States, 1979–2015." *Epidemiology* 29 (5): 707–15. https://doi.org/10.1097/EDE.0000000000000858.

Alexander, Rohan, and Monica Alexander. 2021. "The Increased Effect of Elections and Changing Prime Ministers on Topics Discussed in the Australian Federal Parliament Between 1901 and 2018." https://doi.org/10.48550/arXiv.2111.09299.

Alexander, Rohan, and Paul Hodgetts. 2021. *AustralianPoliticians: Provides Datasets About Australian Politicians*. https://CRAN.R-project.org/package=AustralianPoliticians.

Alexander, Rohan, and A Mahfouz. 2021. *heapsofpapers: Easily Download Heaps of PDF and CSV Files*. https://CRAN.R-project.org/package=heapsofpapers.

Alexander, Rohan, and Zachary Ward. 2018. "Age at Arrival and Assimilation During the Age of Mass Migration." *The Journal of Economic History* 78 (3): 904–37. https://doi.org/10.1017/S0022050718000335.

Alexopoulos, Michelle, and Jon Cohen. 2015. "The power of print: Uncertainty shocks, markets, and the economy." *International Review of Economics & Finance* 40 (November): 8–28. https://doi.org/10.1016/j.iref.2015.02.002.

Allen, Jeff. 2021. *plumberDeploy: Plumber Deployment.* https://CRAN.R-project.org/package=plumberDeploy.

Alsan, Marcella, and Amy Finkelstein. 2021. "Beyond Causality: Additional Benefits of Randomized Controlled Trials for Improving Health Care Delivery." *The Milbank Quarterly* 99 (4): 864–81. https://doi.org/10.1111/1468-0009.12521.

Alsan, Marcella, and Marianne Wanamaker. 2018. "Tuskegee and the Health of Black Men." *The Quarterly Journal of Economics* 133 (1): 407–55. https://doi.org/10.1093/qje/qjx029.

Altman, Douglas, and Martin Bland. 1995. "Statistics notes: The normal distribution." *BMJ* 310 (6975): 298–98. https://doi.org/10.1136/bmj.310.6975.298.

Amaka, Ofunne, and Amber Thomas. 2021. "The Naked Truth: How the Names of 6,816 Complexion Products Can Reveal Bias in Beauty." *The Pudding*, March. https://pudding.cool/2021/03/foundation-names/.

American Medical Association and New York Academy of Medicine. 1848. *Code of Medical Ethics.* Academy of Medicine. https://hdl.handle.net/2027/chi.57108026.

Andersen, Robert, and David Armstrong. 2021. *Presenting Statistical Results Effectively.* London: Sage.

Anderson, Margo, and Stephen Fienberg. 1999. *Who Counts?: The Politics of Census-Taking in Contemporary America.* Russell Sage Foundation. http://www.jstor.org/stable/10.7758/9781610440059.

Andrews, David, and Agnes Herzberg. 2012. *Data: A Collection of Problems from Many Fields for the Student and Research Worker.* New York: Springer Science & Business Media.

Angelucci, Charles, and Julia Cagé. 2019. "Newspapers in Times of Low Advertising Revenues." *American Economic Journal: Microeconomics* 11 (3): 319–64. https://doi.org/10.1257/mic.20170306.

Angrist, Joshua, and Alan Krueger. 2001. "Instrumental Variables and the Search for Identification: From Supply and Demand to Natural Experiments." *Journal of Economic Perspectives* 15 (4): 69–85. https://doi.org/10.1257/jep.15.4.69.

Angrist, Joshua, and Jörn-Steffen Pischke. 2010. "The Credibility Revolution in Empirical Economics: How Better Research Design Is Taking the Con Out of Econometrics." *Journal of Economic Perspectives* 24 (2): 3–30. https://doi.org/10.1257/jep.24.2.3.

Annas, George. 2003. "HIPAA Regulations: A New Era of Medical-Record Privacy?" *New England Journal of Medicine* 348 (15): 1486–90. https://doi.org/10.1056/NEJMlim035027.

Ansolabehere, Stephen, Brian Schaffner, and Sam Luks. 2021. "Guide to the 2020 Cooperative Election Study." https://doi.org/10.7910/DVN/E9N6PH.

Aprameya, Lavanya. 2020. "Improving Duolingo, One Experiment at a Time." *Duolingo Blog*, January. https://blog.duolingo.com/improving-duolingo-one-experiment-at-a-time/.

Arel-Bundock, Vincent. 2021. *WDI: World Development Indicators and Other World Bank Data.* https://CRAN.R-project.org/package=WDI.

———. 2022. "modelsummary: Data and Model Summaries in R." *Journal of Statistical Software* 103 (1): 1–23. https://doi.org/10.18637/jss.v103.i01.

———. 2023. *marginaleffects: Predictions, Comparisons, Slopes, Marginal Means, and Hypothesis Tests.* https://vincentarelbundock.github.io/marginaleffects/.

Arel-Bundock, Vincent, Ryan Briggs, Hristos Doucouliagos, Marco Mendoza Aviña, and T. D. Stanley. 2022. "Quantitative Political Science Research Is Greatly Underpowered." https://osf.io/bzj9y/.

Armstrong, Zan. 2022. "Stop Aggregating Away the Signal in Your Data." *The Overflow*, March. https://stackoverflow.blog/2022/03/03/stop-aggregating-away-the-signal-in-your-data/.

Arnold, Jeffrey. 2021. *ggthemes: Extra Themes, Scales and Geoms for "ggplot2"*. https://CRAN.R-project.org/package=ggthemes.

Athey, Susan, and Guido Imbens. 2017a. "The Econometrics of Randomized Experiments." In *Handbook of Field Experiments*, 73–140. Elsevier. https://doi.org/10.1016/bs.hefe.2016.10.003.

———. 2017b. "The State of Applied Econometrics: Causality and Policy Evaluation." *Journal of Economic Perspectives* 31 (2): 3–32. https://doi.org/10.1257/jep.31.2.3.

Athey, Susan, Guido Imbens, Jonas Metzger, and Evan Munro. 2021. "Using Wasserstein Generative Adversarial Networks for the Design of Monte Carlo Simulations." *Journal of Econometrics*. https://doi.org/10.1016/j.jeconom.2020.09.013.

Au, Randy. 2020. "Data Cleaning IS Analysis, Not Grunt Work," September. https://counting.substack.com/p/data-cleaning-is-analysis-not-grunt.

———. 2022. "Celebrating Everyone Counting Things," February. https://counting.substack.com/p/celebrating-everyone-counting-things.

Bååth, Rasmus. 2018. *beepr: Easily Play Notification Sounds on any Platform*. https://CRAN.R-project.org/package=beepr.

Bache, Stefan Milton, and Hadley Wickham. 2022. *magrittr: A Forward-Pipe Operator for R*. https://CRAN.R-project.org/package=magrittr.

Backus, John. 1981. "The History of FORTRAN I, II, and III." In *History of Programming Languages*, edited by Richard Wexelblat, 25–74. Academic Press.

Bailey, Rosemary. 2008. *Design of Comparative Experiments*. Cambridge: Cambridge University Press. https://doi.org/10.1017/CBO9780511611483.

Baio, Gianluca, and Marta Blangiardo. 2010. "Bayesian Hierarchical Model for the Prediction of Football Results." *Journal of Applied Statistics* 37 (2): 253–64. https://doi.org/10.1080/02664760802684177.

Baker, Dominique. 2023. "Scams Will Not Save Us (Tuition Dollars)," February. http://www.dominiquebaker.com/blog/2023/2/16/scams-will-not-save-us-tuition-dollars.

Baker, Reg, Michael Brick, Nancy Bates, Mike Battaglia, Mick Couper, Jill Dever, Krista Gile, and Roger Tourangeau. 2013. "Summary Report of the AAPOR Task Force on Non-Probability Sampling." *Journal of Survey Statistics and Methodology* 1 (2): 90–143. https://doi.org/10.1093/jssam/smt008.

Bandy, Jack, and Nicholas Vincent. 2021. "Addressing 'Documentation Debt' in Machine Learning Research: A Retrospective Datasheet for BookCorpus." arXiv. https://doi.org/10.48550/arXiv.2105.05241.

Banerjee, Abhijit, and Esther Duflo. 2011. *Poor Economics: A Radical Rethinking of the Way to Fight Global Poverty*. New York: PublicAffairs.

Banerjee, Abhijit, Esther Duflo, Rachel Glennerster, and Cynthia Kinnan. 2015. "The Miracle of Microfinance? Evidence from a Randomized Evaluation." *American Economic Journal: Applied Economics* 7 (1): 22–53. https://doi.org/10.1257/app.20130533.

Banes, Graham, Emily Fountain, Alyssa Karklus, Robert Fulton, Lucinda Antonacci-Fulton, and Joanne Nelson. 2022. "Nine out of ten samples were mistakenly switched by The Orang-utan Genome Consortium." *Scientific Data* 9 (1). https://doi.org/10.1038/s41597-022-01602-0.

Barba, Lorena. 2018. "Terminologies for Reproducible Research." https://arxiv.org/abs/1802.03311.

Barrett, Malcolm. 2021a. *Data Science as an Atomic Habit.* https://malco.io/2021/01/04/data-science-as-an-atomic-habit/.

———. 2021b. *ggdag: Analyze and Create Elegant Directed Acyclic Graphs.* https://CRAN.R-project.org/package=ggdag.

Barron, Alexander, Jenny Huang, Rebecca Spang, and Simon DeDeo. 2018. "Individuals, Institutions, and Innovation in the Debates of the French Revolution." *Proceedings of the National Academy of Sciences* 115 (18): 4607–12. https://doi.org/10.1073/pnas.1717729115.

Baumer, Benjamin, Daniel Kaplan, and Nicholas Horton. 2021. *Modern Data Science With R.* 2nd ed. Chapman; Hall/CRC. https://mdsr-book.github.io/mdsr2e/.

Baumgartner, Jason, Savvas Zannettou, Brian Keegan, Megan Squire, and Jeremy Blackburn. 2020. "The Pushshift Reddit Dataset." arXiv. https://doi.org/10.48550/arxiv.2001.08435.

Baumgartner, Peter. 2021. "Ways I Use Testing as a Data Scientist," December. https://www.peterbaumgartner.com/blog/testing-for-data-science/.

Beaumont, Jean-Francois. 2020. "Are Probability Surveys Bound to Disappear for the Production of Official Statistics?" *Survey Methodology* 46 (1): 1–29.

Beauregard, Katrine, and Jill Sheppard. 2021. "Antiwomen but Proquota: Disaggregating Sexism and Support for Gender Quota Policies." *Political Psychology* 42 (2): 219–37. https://doi.org/10.1111/pops.12696.

Becker, Richard, Allan Wilks, Ray Brownrigg, Thomas Minka, and Alex Deckmyn. 2022. *maps: Draw Geographical Maps.* https://CRAN.R-project.org/package=maps.

Beelen, Kaspar, Timothy Alberdingk Thim, Christopher Cochrane, Kees Halvemaan, Graeme Hirst, Michael Kimmins, Sander Lijbrink, et al. 2017. "Digitization of the Canadian Parliamentary Debates." *Canadian Journal of Political Science* 50 (3): 849–64.

Bender, Emily, Timnit Gebru, Angelina McMillan-Major, and Shmargaret Shmitchell. 2021. "On the Dangers of Stochastic Parrots: Can Language Models Be Too Big?" In *Proceedings of the 2021 ACM Conference on Fairness, Accountability, and Transparency.* ACM. https://doi.org/10.1145/3442188.3445922.

Bengtsson, Henrik. 2021. "A Unifying Framework for Parallel and Distributed Processing in R using Futures." *The R Journal* 13 (2): 208–27. https://doi.org/10.32614/RJ-2021-048.

Benoit, Kenneth. 2020. "Text as Data: An Overview." In *The SAGE Handbook of Research Methods in Political Science and International Relations*, edited by Luigi Curini and Robert Franzese, 461–97. London: SAGE Publishing. https://doi.org/10.4135/9781526486387.n29.

Benoit, Kenneth, Kohei Watanabe, Haiyan Wang, Paul Nulty, Adam Obeng, Stefan Müller, and Akitaka Matsuo. 2018. "quanteda: An R package for the quantitative analysis of textual data." *Journal of Open Source Software* 3 (30): 774. https://doi.org/10.21105/joss.00774.

Bensinger, Greg. 2020. "Google Redraws the Borders on Maps Depending on Who's Looking." *The Washington Post*, February. https://www.washingtonpost.com/technology/2020/02/14/google-maps-political-borders/.

Berdine, Gilbert, Vincent Geloso, and Benjamin Powell. 2018. "Cuban Infant Mortality and Longevity: Health Care or Repression?" *Health Policy and Planning* 33 (6): 755–57. https://doi.org/10.1093/heapol/czy033.

Berkson, Joseph. 1946. "Limitations of the Application of Fourfold Table Analysis to Hospital Data." *Biometrics Bulletin* 2 (3): 47–53. https://doi.org/10.2307/3002000.

Berners-Lee, Timothy. 1989. "Information Management: A Proposal." https://www.w3.org/History/1989/proposal.html.

Berry, Donald. 1989. "Comment: Ethics and ECMO." *Statistical Science* 4 (4): 306–10. https://www.jstor.org/stable/2245830.

Bertrand, Marianne, and Sendhil Mullainathan. 2004. "Are Emily and Greg More Employable Than Lakisha and Jamal? A Field Experiment on Labor Market Discrimination." *American Economic Review* 94 (4): 991–1013. https://doi.org/10.1257/0002828042002561.

Bethlehem, R. A. I., J. Seidlitz, S. R. White, J. W. Vogel, K. M. Anderson, C. Adamson, S. Adler, et al. 2022. "Brain Charts for the Human Lifespan." *Nature* 604 (7906): 525–33. https://doi.org/10.1038/s41586-022-04554-y.

Betz, Timm, Scott Cook, and Florian Hollenbach. 2018. "On the Use and Abuse of Spatial Instruments." *Political Analysis* 26 (4): 474–79. https://doi.org/10.1017/pan.2018.10.

Bickel, Peter, Eugene Hammel, and William O'Connell. 1975. "Sex Bias in Graduate Admissions: Data from Berkeley: Measuring Bias Is Harder Than Is Usually Assumed, and the Evidence Is Sometimes Contrary to Expectation." *Science* 187 (4175): 398–404. https://doi.org/10.1126/science.187.4175.398.

Biderman, Stella, Kieran Bicheno, and Leo Gao. 2022. "Datasheet for the Pile." https://arxiv.org/abs/2201.07311.

Birkmeyer, John, Jonathan Finks, Amanda O'Reilly, Mary Oerline, Arthur Carlin, Andre Nunn, Justin Dimick, Mousumi Banerjee, and Nancy Birkmeyer. 2013. "Surgical Skill and Complication Rates After Bariatric Surgery." *New England Journal of Medicine* 369 (15): 1434–42. https://doi.org/10.1056/nejmsa1300625.

Blair, Ed, Seymour Sudman, Norman M Bradburn, and Carol Stocking. 1977. "How to Ask Questions about Drinking and Sex: Response Effects in Measuring Consumer Behavior." *Journal of Marketing Research* 14 (3): 316–21. https://doi.org/10.2307/3150769.

Blair, Graeme, Jasper Cooper, Alexander Coppock, and Macartan Humphreys. 2019. "Declaring and Diagnosing Research Designs." *American Political Science Review* 113 (3): 838–59. https://doi.org/10.1017/S0003055419000194.

Blair, Graeme, Jasper Cooper, Alexander Coppock, Macartan Humphreys, and Luke Sonnet. 2021. *estimatr: Fast Estimators for Design-Based Inference*. https://CRAN.R-project.org/package=estimatr.

Blair, James. 2019. *Democratizing R with Plumber APIs*. https://www.rstudio.com/resources/rstudioconf-2019/democratizing-r-with-plumber-apis/.

Bland, Martin, and Douglas Altman. 1986. "Statistical Methods for Assessing Agreement Between Two Methods of Clinical Measurement." *The Lancet* 327 (8476): 307–10. https://doi.org/10.1016/S0140-6736(86)90837-8.

Blei, David. 2012. "Probabilistic Topic Models." *Communications of the ACM* 55 (4): 77–84. https://doi.org/10.1145/2133806.2133826.

Blei, David, Andrew Ng, and Michael Jordan. 2003. "Latent Dirichlet Allocation." *Journal of Machine Learning Research* 3 (Jan): 993–1022. https://www.jmlr.org/papers/volume3/blei03a/blei03a.pdf.

Bloom, Howard, Andrew Bell, and Kayla Reiman. 2020. "Using Data from Randomized Trials to Assess the Likely Generalizability of Educational Treatment-Effect Estimates from Regression Discontinuity Designs." *Journal of Research on Educational Effectiveness* 13 (3): 488–517. https://doi.org/10.1080/19345747.2019.1634169.

Boland, Philip. 1984. "A Biographical Glimpse of William Sealy Gosset." *The American Statistician* 38 (3): 179–83. https://doi.org/10.2307/2683648.

Bolker, Ben, and David Robinson. 2022. *broom.mixed: Tidying Methods for Mixed Models*. https://CRAN.R-project.org/package=broom.mixed.

Bolton, Ruth, and Randall Chapman. 1986. "Searching for Positive Returns at the Track." *Management Science* 32 (August): 1040–60. https://doi.org/10.1287/mnsc.32.8.1040.

Bombieri, Giulia, Vincenzo Penteriani, Kamran Almasieh, Hüseyin Ambarlı, Mohammad Reza Ashrafzadeh, Chandan Surabhi Das, Nishith Dharaiya, et al. 2023. "A Worldwide

Perspective on Large Carnivore Attacks on Humans." *PLOS Biology* 21 (1): e3001946. https://doi.org/10.1371/journal.pbio.3001946.

Bor, Jacob, Atheendar Venkataramani, David Williams, and Alexander Tsai. 2018. "Police Killings and Their Spillover Effects on the Mental Health of Black Americans: A Population-Based, Quasi-Experimental Study." *The Lancet* 392 (10144): 302–10. https://doi.org/10.1016/s0140-6736(18)31130-9.

Borer, Elizabeth T., Eric W. Seabloom, Matthew B. Jones, and Mark Schildhauer. 2009. "Some Simple Guidelines for Effective Data Management." *Bulletin of the Ecological Society of America* 90 (2): 205–14. https://doi.org/10.1890/0012-9623-90.2.205.

Borghi, John, and Ana Van Gulick. 2022. "Promoting Open Science Through Research Data Management." *Harvard Data Science Review* 4 (3). https://doi.org/10.1162/99608f92.9497f68e.

Borkin, Michelle, Zoya Bylinskii, Nam Wook Kim, Constance May Bainbridge, Chelsea Yeh, Daniel Borkin, Hanspeter Pfister, and Aude Oliva. 2015. "Beyond Memorability: Visualization Recognition and Recall." *IEEE Transactions on Visualization and Computer Graphics* 22 (1): 519–28. https://doi.org/10.1109/TVCG.2015.2467732.

Bosch, Oriol, and Melanie Revilla. 2022. "When survey science met web tracking: Presenting an error framework for metered data." *Journal of the Royal Statistical Society: Series A (Statistics in Society)*, November, 1–29. https://doi.org/10.1111/rssa.12956.

Bouguen, Adrien, Yue Huang, Michael Kremer, and Edward Miguel. 2019. "Using Randomized Controlled Trials to Estimate Long-Run Impacts in Development Economics." *Annual Review of Economics* 11 (1): 523–61. https://doi.org/10.1146/annurev-economics-080218-030333.

Bouie, Jamelle. 2022. "We Still Can't See American Slavery for What It Was." *The New York Times*, January. https://www.nytimes.com/2022/01/28/opinion/slavery-voyages-data-sets.html.

Bowen, Claire McKay. 2022. *Protecting Your Privacy in a Data-Driven World*. 1st ed. Chapman; Hall/CRC. https://doi.org/10.1201/9781003122043.

Bowers, Jake, and Maarten Voors. 2016. "How to Improve Your Relationship with Your Future Self." *Revista de Ciencia Política* 36 (3): 829–48. https://doi.org/10.4067/S0718-090X2016000300011.

Bowley, Arthur Lyon. 1901. *Elements of Statistics*. London: P. S. King.

———. 1913. "Working-Class Households in Reading." *Journal of the Royal Statistical Society* 76 (7): 672–701. https://doi.org/10.2307/2339708.

Box, George E. P. 1976. "Science and Statistics." *Journal of the American Statistical Association* 71 (356): 791–99. https://doi.org/10.1080/01621459.1976.10480949.

Boykis, Vicki. 2019. "A Deep Dive on Python Type Hints," July. https://vickiboykis.com/2019/07/08/a-deep-dive-on-python-type-hints/.

Boysel, Sam, and Davis Vaughan. 2021. *fredr: An R Client for the "FRED" API*. https://CRAN.R-project.org/package=fredr.

Bradley, Valerie, Shiro Kuriwaki, Michael Isakov, Dino Sejdinovic, Xiao-Li Meng, and Seth Flaxman. 2021. "Unrepresentative Big Surveys Significantly Overestimated US Vaccine Uptake." *Nature* 600 (7890): 695–700. https://doi.org/10.1038/s41586-021-04198-4.

Braginsky, Mika. 2020. *wordbankr: Accessing the Wordbank Database*. https://CRAN.R-project.org/package=wordbankr.

Brandt, Allan. 1978. "Racism and Research: The Case of the Tuskegee Syphilis Study." *Hastings Center Report*, 21–29. https://doi.org/10.2307/3561468.

Breiman, Leo. 1994. "The 1991 Census Adjustment: Undercount or Bad Data?" *Statistical Science* 9 (4). https://doi.org/10.1214/ss/1177010259.

———. 2001. "Statistical Modeling: The Two Cultures." *Statistical Science* 16 (3): 199–231. https://doi.org/10.1214/ss/1009213726.

Bremer, Nadieh, and Shirley Wu. 2021. *Data Sketches.* A K Peters/CRC Press. https://doi.org/10.1201/9780429445019.

Brewer, Cynthia. 2015. *Designing Better Maps: A Guide for GIS Users.* 2nd ed.

Brewer, Ken. 2013. "Three Controversies in the History of Survey Sampling." *Survey Methodology* 39 (2): 249–63.

Breznau, Nate, Eike Mark Rinke, Alexander Wuttke, Hung HV Nguyen, Muna Adem, Jule Adriaans, Amalia Alvarez-Benjumea, et al. 2022. "Observing Many Researchers Using the Same Data and Hypothesis Reveals a Hidden Universe of Uncertainty." *Proceedings of the National Academy of Sciences* 119 (44): e2203150119. https://doi.org/10.1073/pnas.2203150119.

Briggs, Ryan. 2021. "Why Does Aid Not Target the Poorest?" *International Studies Quarterly* 65 (3): 739–52. https://doi.org/10.1093/isq/sqab035.

Brodeur, Abel, Nikolai Cook, and Anthony Heyes. 2020. "Methods Matter: p-Hacking and Publication Bias in Causal Analysis in Economics." *American Economic Review* 110 (11): 3634–60. https://doi.org/10.1257/aer.20190687.

Brokowski, Carolyn, and Mazhar Adli. 2019. "CRISPR Ethics: Moral Considerations for Applications of a Powerful Tool." *Journal of Molecular Biology* 431 (1): 88–101. https://doi.org/10.1016/j.jmb.2018.05.044.

Bronner, Laura. 2020. "Why Statistics Don't Capture the Full Extent of the Systemic Bias in Policing." *FiveThirtyEight*, June. https://fivethirtyeight.com/features/why-statistics-dont-capture-the-full-extent-of-the-systemic-bias-in-policing/.

———. 2021. "Quantitative Editing." *YouTube*, June. https://youtu.be/LI5m9RzJgWc.

Brontë, Charlotte. 1847. *Jane Eyre.* https://www.gutenberg.org/files/1260/1260-h/1260-h.htm.

———. 1857. *The Professor.* https://www.gutenberg.org/files/1028/1028-h/1028-h.htm.

Brook, Robert, John Ware, William Rogers, Emmett Keeler, Allyson Ross Davies, Cathy Sherbourne, George Goldberg, Kathleen Lohr, Patricia Camp, and Joseph Newhouse. 1984. "The Effect of Coinsurance on the Health of Adults: Results from the RAND Health Insurance Experiment." https://www.rand.org/pubs/reports/R3055.html.

Brown, Zack. 2018. "A Git Origin Story." *Linux Journal*, July. https://www.linuxjournal.com/content/git-origin-story.

Bryan, Jenny. 2015. "Naming Things." *Reproducible Science Workshop*, May. https://speakerdeck.com/jennybc/how-to-name-files.

———. 2018a. "Excuse Me, Do You Have a Moment to Talk about Version Control?" *The American Statistician* 72 (1): 20–27. https://doi.org/10.1080/00031305.2017.1399928.

———. 2018b. "Code Smells and Feels." *YouTube*, July. https://youtu.be/7oyiPBjLAWY.

———. 2020. *Happy Git and GitHub for the useR.* https://happygitwithr.com.

Bryan, Jenny, and Jim Hester. 2020. *What They Forgot to Teach You About R.* https://rstats.wtf/index.html.

Bryan, Jenny, Jim Hester, David Robinson, Hadley Wickham, and Christophe Dervieux. 2022. *reprex: Prepare Reproducible Example Code via the Clipboard.* https://CRAN.R-project.org/package=reprex.

Bryan, Jenny, and Hadley Wickham. 2021. *gh: GitHub API.* https://CRAN.R-project.org/package=gh.

Buckheit, Jonathan, and David Donoho. 1995. "Wavelab and Reproducible Research." In *Wavelets and Statistics*, 55–81. Springer. https://doi.org/10.1007/978-1-4612-2544-7_5.

Bueno de Mesquita, Ethan, and Anthony Fowler. 2021. *Thinking Clearly with Data: A Guide to Quantitative Reasoning and Analysis.* New Jersey: Princeton University Press.

Buhr, Ray. 2017. *Using R as a Production Machine Learning Language (Part I).* https://raybuhr.github.io/blog/posts/making-predictions-over-http/.

Buja, Andreas, Dianne Cook, and Deborah Swayne. 1996. "Interactive High-Dimensional Data Visualization." *Journal of Computational and Graphical Statistics* 5 (1): 78–99. https://doi.org/10.2307/1390754.

Buneman, Peter, Sanjeev Khanna, and Tan Wang-Chiew. 2001. "Why and Where: A Characterization of Data Provenance." In *Database Theory — ICDT 2001*, 316–30. Springer Berlin Heidelberg. https://doi.org/10.1007/3-540-44503-x_20.

Buolamwini, Joy, and Timnit Gebru. 2018. "Gender Shades: Intersectional Accuracy Disparities in Commercial Gender Classification." In *Conference on Fairness, Accountability and Transparency*, 77–91.

Burch, Tyler James. 2023. "2023 NHL Playoff Predictions," April. https://tylerjamesburch.com/blog/misc/nhl-predictions.

Burton, Jason, Nicole Cruz, and Ulrike Hahn. 2021. "Reconsidering Evidence of Moral Contagion in Online Social Networks." *Nature Human Behaviour* 5 (12): 1629–35. https://doi.org/10.1038/s41562-021-01133-5.

Bush, Vannevar. 1945. "As We May Think." *The Atlantic Monthly*, July. https://www.theatlantic.com/magazine/archive/1945/07/as-we-may-think/303881/.

Byrd, James Brian, Anna Greene, Deepashree Venkatesh Prasad, Xiaoqian Jiang, and Casey Greene. 2020. "Responsible, Practical Genomic Data Sharing That Accelerates Research." *Nature Reviews Genetics* 21 (10): 615–29. https://doi.org/10.1038/s41576-020-0257-5.

Cahill, Niamh, Michelle Weinberger, and Leontine Alkema. 2020. "What Increase in Modern Contraceptive Use Is Needed in FP2020 Countries to Reach 75% Demand Satisfied by 2030? An Assessment Using the Accelerated Transition Method and Family Planning Estimation Model." *Gates Open Research* 4. https://doi.org/10.12688/gatesopenres.13125.1.

Calonico, Sebastian, Matias Cattaneo, Max Farrell, and Rocio Titiunik. 2021. *rdrobust: Robust Data-Driven Statistical Inference in Regression-Discontinuity Designs*. https://CRAN.R-project.org/package=rdrobust.

Cambon, Jesse, and Christopher Belanger. 2021. "tidygeocoder: Geocoding Made Easy." Zenodo. https://doi.org/10.5281/zenodo.3981510.

Canty, Angelo, and B. D. Ripley. 2021. *boot: Bootstrap R (S-Plus) Functions*.

Cardoso, Tom. 2020. "Bias behind bars: A Globe investigation finds a prison system stacked against Black and Indigenous inmates." *The Globe and Mail*, October. https://www.theglobeandmail.com/canada/article-investigation-racial-bias-in-canadian-prison-risk-assessments/.

Carleton, Chris. 2021. "wccarleton/conflict-europe: Acce." Zenodo. https://doi.org/10.5281/zenodo.4550688.

Carleton, Chris, Dave Campbell, and Mark Collard. 2021. "A Reassessment of the Impact of Temperature Change on European Conflict During the Second Millennium CE Using a Bespoke Bayesian Time-Series Model." *Climatic Change* 165 (1): 1–16. https://doi.org/10.1007/s10584-021-03022-2.

Caro, Robert. 2019. *Working*. 1st ed. New York: Knopf.

Carpenter, Christopher, and Carlos Dobkin. 2014. "Replication data for: The Minimum Legal Drinking Age and Crime." https://doi.org/10.7910/DVN/27070.

———. 2015. "The Minimum Legal Drinking Age and Crime." *The Review of Economics and Statistics* 97 (2): 521–24. https://doi.org/10.1162/REST_a_00489.

Carroll, Lewis. 1871. *Through the Looking-Glass*. Macmillan. https://www.gutenberg.org/files/12/12-h/12-h.htm.

Castro, Marcia, Susie Gurzenda, Cassio Turra, Sun Kim, Theresa Andrasfay, and Noreen Goldman. 2023. "Research Note: COVID-19 Is Not an Independent Cause of Death." *Demography*, February. https://doi.org/10.1215/00703370-10575276.

Caughey, Devin, and Jasjeet Sekhon. 2011. "Elections and the Regression Discontinuity Design: Lessons from Close U.S. House Races, 1942–2008." *Political Analysis* 19 (4): 385–408. https://doi.org/10.1093/pan/mpr032.

Chamberlain, Scott, Hadley Wickham, Winston Chang, and Mauricio Vargas. 2022. *Analogsea: Interface to "Digital Ocean"*. https://CRAN.R-project.org/package=analogsea.

Chamberlin, Donald. 2012. "Early History of SQL." *IEEE Annals of the History of Computing* 34 (4): 78–82. https://doi.org/10.1109/mahc.2012.61.

Chambliss, Daniel. 1989. "The Mundanity of Excellence: An Ethnographic Report on Stratification and Olympic Swimmers." *Sociological Theory* 7 (1): 70–86. https://doi.org/10.2307/202063.

Chambru, Cédric, and Paul Maneuvrier-Hervieu. 2022. "Introducing HiSCoD: A new gateway for the study of historical social conflict." *Working Paper Series, Department of Economics, University of Zurich*. https://doi.org/10.5167/uzh-217109.

Chan, Duo. 2021. "Combining Statistical, Physical, and Historical Evidence to Improve Historical Sea-Surface Temperature Records." *Harvard Data Science Review* 3 (1). https://doi.org/10.1162/99608f92.edcee38f.

Chang, Winston, Joe Cheng, JJ Allaire, Carson Sievert, Barret Schloerke, Yihui Xie, Jeff Allen, Jonathan McPherson, Alan Dipert, and Barbara Borges. 2021. *shiny: Web Application Framework for R*. https://CRAN.R-project.org/package=shiny.

Chase, William. 2020. "The Glamour of Graphics." *RStudio Conference*, January. https://www.rstudio.com/resources/rstudioconf-2020/the-glamour-of-graphics/.

Chawla, Dalmeet Singh. 2020. "Critiqued Coronavirus Simulation Gets Thumbs up from Code-Checking Efforts." *Nature* 582: 323–24. https://doi.org/10.1038/d41586-020-01685-y.

Chellel, Kit. 2018. "The Gambler Who Cracked the Horse-Racing Code." *Bloomberg Businessweek*, May. https://www.bloomberg.com/news/features/2018-05-03/the-gambler-who-cracked-the-horse-racing-code.

Chen, Heng, Marie-Hélène Felt, and Christopher Henry. 2018. "2017 Methods-of-Payment Survey: Sample Calibration and Variance Estimation." Bank of Canada. https://doi.org/10.34989/tr-114.

Chen, Wei, Xilu Chen, Chang-Tai Hsieh, and Zheng Song. 2019. "A Forensic Examination of China's National Accounts." *Brookings Papers on Economic Activity*, 77–127. https://www.jstor.org/stable/26798817.

Chen, Weijun, Yan Qi, Yuwen Zhang, Christina B, Akos Lada, and Harivardan Jayaraman. 2022. "Notifications: Why Less Is More," December. https://medium.com/@AnalyticsAtMeta/notifications-why-less-is-more-how-facebook-has-been-increasing-both-user-satisfaction-and-app-9463f7325e7d.

Cheng, Joe, Bhaskar Karambelkar, and Yihui Xie. 2021. *leaflet: Create Interactive Web Maps with the JavaScript "Leaflet" Library*. https://CRAN.R-project.org/package=leaflet.

Cheriet, Mohamed, Nawwaf Kharma, Cheng-Lin Liu, and Ching Suen. 2007. *Character Recognition Systems: A Guide for Students and Practitioner*. Wiley.

Chouldechova, Alexandra, Diana Benavides-Prado, Oleksandr Fialko, and Rhema Vaithianathan. 2018. "A Case Study of Algorithm-Assisted Decision Making in Child Maltreatment Hotline Screening Decisions." In *Proceedings of the 1st Conference on Fairness, Accountability and Transparency*, edited by Sorelle Friedler and Christo Wilson, 81:134–48. Proceedings of Machine Learning Research. https://proceedings.mlr.press/v81/chouldechova18a.html.

Chrétien, Jean. 2007. *My Years as Prime Minister*. 1st ed. Toronto: Knopf Canada.

Christensen, Garret, Allan Dafoe, Edward Miguel, Don Moore, and Andrew Rose. 2019. "A Study of the Impact of Data Sharing on Article Citations Using Journal Policies as a Natural Experiment." *PLOS ONE* 14 (12): e0225883. https://doi.org/10.1371/journal.pone.0225883.

Christensen, Garret, Jeremy Freese, and Edward Miguel. 2019. *Transparent and Reproducible Social Science Research.* California: University of California Press.

Christian, Brian. 2012. "The A/B Test: Inside the Technology That's Changing the Rules of Business." *Wired*, April. https://www.wired.com/2012/04/ff-abtesting/.

Cirone, Alexandra, and Arthur Spirling. 2021. "Turning History into Data: Data Collection, Measurement, and Inference in HPE." *Journal of Historical Political Economy* 1 (1): 127–54. https://doi.org/10.1561/115.00000005.

City of Toronto. 2021. *2021 Street Needs Assessment.* https://www.toronto.ca/city-government/data-research-maps/research-reports/housing-and-homelessness-research-and-reports/.

Cleveland, William. (1985) 1994. *The Elements of Graphing Data.* 2nd ed. New Jersey: Hobart Press.

Clinton, Joshua, John Lapinski, and Marc Trussler. 2022. "Reluctant Republicans, Eager Democrats?" *Public Opinion Quarterly* 86 (2): 247–69. https://doi.org/10.1093/poq/nfac011.

Cohen, Glenn, and Michelle Mello. 2018. "HIPAA and Protecting Health Information in the 21st Century." *JAMA* 320 (3): 231. https://doi.org/10.1001/jama.2018.5630.

Cohen, Jason, Steven Teleki, and Eric Brown. 2006. *Best Kept Secrets of Peer Code Review.* Smart Bear Incorporated.

Cohn, Alain. 2019. "Data and code for: Civic Honesty Around the Globe." Harvard Dataverse. https://doi.org/10.7910/dvn/ykbodn.

Cohn, Alain, Michel André Maréchal, David Tannenbaum, and Christian Lukas Zünd. 2019a. "Civic Honesty Around the Globe." *Science* 365 (6448): 70–73. https://doi.org/10.1126/science.aau8712.

———. 2019b. "Supplementary Materials for: Civic Honesty Around the Globe." *Science* 365 (6448): 70–73.

Cohn, Nate. 2016. "We Gave Four Good Pollsters the Same Raw Data. They Had Four Different Results." *The New York Times*, September. https://www.nytimes.com/interactive/2016/09/20/upshot/the-error-the-polling-world-rarely-talks-about.html.

Collins, Annie, and Rohan Alexander. 2022. "Reproducibility of COVID-19 Pre-Prints." *Scientometrics* 127: 4655–73. https://doi.org/10.1007/s11192-022-04418-2.

Colombo, Tommaso, Holger Fröning, Pedro Javier Garcìa, and Wainer Vandelli. 2016. "Optimizing the Data-Collection Time of a Large-Scale Data-Acquisition System Through a Simulation Framework." *The Journal of Supercomputing* 72 (12): 4546–72. https://doi.org/10.1007/s11227-016-1764-1.

Comer, Benjamin P., and Jason R. Ingram. 2022. "Comparing Fatal Encounters, Mapping Police Violence, and Washington Post Fatal Police Shooting Data from 2015-2019: A Research Note." *Criminal Justice Review*, January, 073401682110710. https://doi.org/10.1177/07340168211071014.

Cook, Dianne, Nancy Reid, and Emi Tanaka. 2021. "The Foundation Is Available for Thinking about Data Visualization Inferentially." *Harvard Data Science Review* 3 (3). https://doi.org/10.1162/99608f92.8453435d.

Cooley, David. 2020. *mapdeck: Interactive Maps Using "Mapbox GL JS" and "Deck.gl".* https://CRAN.R-project.org/package=mapdeck.

Council of European Union. 2016. "General Data Protection Regulation 2016/679." https://eur-lex.europa.eu/eli/reg/2016/679/oj.

Cowen, Tyler. 2021. "Episode 132: Amia Srinivasan on Utopian Feminism." *Conversations with Tyler*, September. https://conversationswithtyler.com/episodes/amia-srinivasan/.

———. 2023. "Episode 168: Katherine Rundell on the Art of Words." *Conversations with Tyler*, January. https://conversationswithtyler.com/episodes/katherine-rundell/.

Cox, David. 2018. "In Gentle Praise of Significance Tests." *YouTube*, October. https://youtu.be/txLj%5FP9UlCQ.

Cox, David, and Nancy Reid. 1987. "Parameter Orthogonality and Approximate Conditional Inference." *Journal of the Royal Statistical Society: Series B (Methodological)* 49 (1): 1–18. https://doi.org/10.1111/j.2517-6161.1987.tb01422.x.

Cox, Murray. 2021. "Inside Airbnb—Toronto Data." http://insideairbnb.com/get-the-data.html.

Coyle, Edward, Andrew Coggan, Mari Hopper, and Thomas Walters. 1988. "Determinants of Endurance in Well-Trained Cyclists." *Journal of Applied Physiology* 64 (6): 2622–30. https://doi.org/10.1152/jappl.1988.64.6.2622.

Craiu, Radu. 2019. "The Hiring Gambit: In Search of the Twofer Data Scientist." *Harvard Data Science Review* 1 (1). https://doi.org/10.1162/99608f92.440445cb.

Cramer, Jan Salomon. 2003. "The Origins of Logistic Regression." *SSRN Electronic Journal*. https://doi.org/10.2139/ssrn.360300.

Crane, Nic. 2022. *Apache Arrow R Cookbook*. https://arrow.apache.org/cookbook/r/index.html.

Crawford, Kate. 2021. *Atlas of AI*. 1st ed. New Haven: Yale University Press.

Crosby, Alfred. 1997. *The Measure of Reality: Quantification in Western Europe, 1250-1600*. Cambridge: Cambridge University Press.

Csárdi, Gábor. 2022. *gitcreds: Query "git" Credentials from "R"*. https://CRAN.R-project.org/package=gitcreds.

Csárdi, Gábor, Jim Hester, Hadley Wickham, Winston Chang, Martin Morgan, and Dan Tenenbaum. 2021. *remotes: R Package Installation from Remote Repositories, Including "GitHub"*. https://CRAN.R-project.org/package=remotes.

Cummins, Neil. 2022. "The Hidden Wealth of English Dynasties, 1892–2016." *The Economic History Review* 75 (3): 667–702. https://doi.org/10.1111/ehr.13120.

Cunningham, Scott. 2021. *Causal Inference: The Mixtape*. 1st ed. New Haven: Yale Press. https://mixtape.scunning.com.

D'Ignazio, Catherine, and Lauren Klein. 2020. *Data Feminism*. Massachusetts: The MIT Press. https://data-feminism.mitpress.mit.edu.

da Silva, Natalia, Dianne Cook, and Eun-Kyung Lee. 2023. "Interactive graphics for visually diagnosing forest classifiers in R." *Computational Statistics*, January. https://doi.org/10.1007/s00180-023-01323-x.

Dagan, Noa, Noam Barda, Eldad Kepten, Oren Miron, Shay Perchik, Mark Katz, Miguel Hernán, Marc Lipsitch, Ben Reis, and Ran Balicer. 2021. "BNT162b2 mRNA Covid-19 Vaccine in a Nationwide Mass Vaccination Setting." *New England Journal of Medicine* 384 (15): 1412–23. https://doi.org/10.1056/NEJMoa2101765.

Daston, Lorraine. 2000. "Why Statistics Tend Not Only to Describe the World but to Change It." *London Review of Books* 22 (8). https://www.lrb.co.uk/the-paper/v22/n08/lorraine-daston/why-statistics-tend-not-only-to-describe-the-world-but-to-change-it.

Data and Justice Criminology Lab, Institute of Criminology and Criminal Justice, Carleton University; The Centre for Research & Innovation for Black Survivors of Homicide Victims (The CRIB), at the Factor-Inwentash Faculty of Social Work, University of Toronto; Canadian Civil Liberties Association; Ethics and Technology Lab, Queen's University. 2022. "Tracking (in)justice: A Living Data Set Tracking Canadian Police-Involved Deaths." https://trackinginjustice.ca.

Davidson, Thomas, Debasmita Bhattacharya, and Ingmar Weber. 2019. "Racial Bias in Hate Speech and Abusive Language Detection Datasets." In *Proceedings of the Third Workshop on Abusive Language Online*, 25–35.

Davies, Rhian, Steph Locke, and Lucy D'Agostino McGowan. 2022. *datasauRus: Datasets from the Datasaurus Dozen*. https://CRAN.R-project.org/package=datasauRus.

Davis, Darren. 1997. "Nonrandom Measurement Error and Race of Interviewer Effects Among African Americans." *The Public Opinion Quarterly* 61 (1): 183–207. https://doi.org/10.1086/297792.

Davison, A. C., and D. V. Hinkley. 1997. *Bootstrap Methods and Their Applications*. Cambridge: Cambridge University Press. http://statwww.epfl.ch/davison/BMA/.

De Jonge, Edwin, and Mark van der Loo. 2013. *An introduction to data cleaning with R*. Statistics Netherlands Heerlen. https://cran.r-project.org/doc/contrib/de%5FJonge+van%5Fder%5FLoo-Introduction%5Fto%5Fdata%5Fcleaning%5Fwith%5FR.pdf.

Dean, Natalie. 2022. "Tracking COVID-19 Infections: Time for Change." *Nature* 602 (7896): 185. https://doi.org/10.1038/d41586-022-00336-8.

Deaton, Angus. 2010. "Instruments, Randomization, and Learning about Development." *Journal of Economic Literature* 48 (2): 424–55. https://doi.org/10.1257/jel.48.2.424.

Denby, Lorraine, and Colin Mallows. 2009. "Variations on the Histogram." *Journal of Computational and Graphical Statistics* 18 (1): 21–31. https://doi.org/10.1198/jcgs.2009.0002.

DeWitt, Helen. 2000. *The Last Samurai*. 1st ed. United States: Talk Mirimax Books.

Dillman, Don, Jolene Smyth, and Leah Christian. (1978) 2014. *Internet, Phone, Mail, and Mixed-Mode Surveys: The Tailored Design Method*. 4th ed. Wiley.

Doggers, Peter. 2021. "Carlsen Wins Game 6, Longest World Chess Championship Game of All Time," December. https://www.chess.com/news/view/fide-world-chess-championship-2021-game-6.

Dolatsara, Hamidreza Ahady, Ying-Ju Chen, Robert Leonard, Fadel Megahed, and Allison Jones-Farmer. 2021. "Explaining Predictive Model Performance: An Experimental Study of Data Preparation and Model Choice." *Big Data*, October. https://doi.org/10.1089/big.2021.0067.

Doll, Richard, and Bradford Hill. 1950. "Smoking and Carcinoma of the Lung." *British Medical Journal* 2 (4682): 739–48. https://doi.org/10.1136/bmj.2.4682.739.

Druckman, James, and Donald Green. 2021. "A New Era of Experimental Political Science." In *Advances in Experimental Political Science*, 1–16. Cambridge: Cambridge University Press. https://doi.org/10.1017/9781108777919.002.

Du, Kai, Steven Huddart, and Xin Daniel Jiang. 2022. "Lost in Standardization: Effects of Financial Statement Database Discrepancies on Inference." *Journal of Accounting and Economics*, December, 101573. https://doi.org/10.1016/j.jacceco.2022.101573.

Duflo, Esther. 2020. "Field Experiments and the Practice of Policy." *American Economic Review* 110 (7): 1952–73. https://doi.org/10.1257/aer.110.7.1952.

Dwork, Cynthia, Frank McSherry, Kobbi Nissim, and Adam Smith. 2006. "Calibrating Noise to Sensitivity in Private Data Analysis." In *Theory of Cryptography Conference*, 265–84. Springer. https://doi.org/10.1007/11681878_14.

Dwork, Cynthia, and Aaron Roth. 2013. "The Algorithmic Foundations of Differential Privacy." *Foundations and Trends in Theoretical Computer Science* 9 (3-4): 211–407. https://doi.org/10.1561/0400000042.

Edelman, Murray, Liberty Vittert, and Xiao-Li Meng. 2021. "An Interview with Murray Edelman on the History of the Exit Poll." *Harvard Data Science Review* 3 (1). https://doi.org/10.1162/99608f92.3a25cd24.

Edgeworth, Francis Ysidro. 1885. "Methods of Statistics." *Journal of the Statistical Society of London*, 181–217.

Edwards, Jonathan. 2017. "PACE team response shows a disregard for the principles of science." *Journal of Health Psychology* 22 (9): 1155–58. https://doi.org/10.1177/1359105317700886.

Efron, Bradley, and Carl Morris. 1977. "Stein's Paradox in Statistics." *Scientific American* 236 (May): 119–27. https://doi.org/10.1038/scientificamerican0577-119.

Eghbal, Nadia. 2020. *Working in Public: The Making and Maintenance of Open Source Software.* California: Stripe Press.

Eisenstein, Michael. 2022. "Need Web Data? Here's How to Harvest Them." *Nature* 607: 200–201. https://doi.org/10.1038/d41586-022-01830-9.

Elliott, Michael, Brady West, Xinyu Zhang, and Stephanie Coffey. 2022. "The Anchoring Method: Estimation of Interviewer Effects in the Absence of Interpenetrated Sample Assignment." *Survey Methodology* 48 (1): 25–48. http://www.statcan.gc.ca/pub/12-001-x/2022001/article/00005-eng.htm.

Elson, Malte. 2018. "Question Wording and Item Formulation." https://doi.org/10.31234/osf.io/e4ktc.

Enns, Peter, and Jake Rothschild. 2022. "Do You Know Where Your Survey Data Come From?" May. https://medium.com/3streams/surveys-3ec95995dde2.

Farrugia, Patricia, Bradley Petrisor, Forough Farrokhyar, and Mohit Bhandari. 2010. "Research Questions, Hypotheses and Objectives." *Canadian Journal of Surgery* 53 (4): 278.

Finkelstein, Amy, Sarah Taubman, Bill Wright, Mira Bernstein, Jonathan Gruber, Joseph Newhouse, Heidi Allen, Katherine Baicker, and Oregon Health Study Group. 2012. "The Oregon Health Insurance Experiment: Evidence from the First Year." *The Quarterly Journal of Economics* 127 (3): 1057–1106. https://doi.org/10.1093/qje/qjs020.

Firke, Sam. 2023. *janitor: Simple Tools for Examining and Cleaning Dirty Data.* https://CRAN.R-project.org/package=janitor.

Fisher, Ronald. 1926. "The Arrangement of Field Experiments." *Journal of the Ministry of Agriculture*, 503–15. https://doi.org/10.23637/rothamsted.8v61q.

———. (1925) 1928. *Statistical Methods for Research Workers.* 2nd ed. London: Oliver; Boyd.

———. (1935) 1949. *The Design of Experiments.* 5th ed. London: Oliver; Boyd.

Fiske, Susan, and Shiro Kuriwaki. 2021. "Words to the Wise on Writing Scientific Papers," November. https://doi.org/10.31234/osf.io/n32qw.

Fitts, Alexis Sobel. 2014. "The King of Content: How Upworthy Aims to Alter the Web, and Could End up Altering the World." *Columbia Journalism Review* 53: 34–38. https://archives.cjr.org/feature/the%5Fking%5Fof%5Fcontent.php.

Flake, Jessica, and Eiko Fried. 2020. "Measurement Schmeasurement: Questionable Measurement Practices and How to Avoid Them." *Advances in Methods and Practices in Psychological Science* 3 (4): 456–65. https://doi.org/10.1177/2515245920952393.

Flynn, Michael. 2022. *troopdata: Tools for Analyzing Cross-National Military Deployment and Basing Data.* https://CRAN.R-project.org/package=troopdata.

Ford, Paul. 2015. "What Is Code?" *Bloomberg Businessweek*, June. https://www.bloomberg.com/graphics/2015-paul-ford-what-is-code/.

Forster, Edward Morgan. 1927. *Aspects of the Novel.* London: Edward Arnold.

Foster, Gordon. 1968. "Computers, Statistics and Planning: Systems or Chaos?" *Geary Lecture.* https://www.esri.ie/system/files/publications/GLS2.pdf.

Fourcade, Marion, and Kieran Healy. 2017. "Seeing Like a Market." *Socio-Economic Review* 15 (1): 9–29. https://doi.org/10.1093/ser/mww033.

Fowler, Martin, and Kent Beck. 2018. *Refactoring: Improving the Design of Existing Code.* 2nd ed. New York: Addison-Wesley Professional.

Fox, John, and Robert Andersen. 2006. "Effect Displays for Multinomial and Proportional-Odds Logit Models." *Sociological Methodology* 36 (1): 225–55. https://doi.org/10.1111/j.1467-9531.2006.00180.

Fox, John, Sanford Weisberg, and Brad Price. 2022. *carData: Companion to Applied Regression Data Sets.* https://CRAN.R-project.org/package=carData.

Franconeri, Steven, Lace Padilla, Priti Shah, Jeffrey Zacks, and Jessica Hullman. 2021. "The Science of Visual Data Communication: What Works." *Psychological Science in the Public Interest* 22 (3): 110–61. https://doi.org/10.1177/15291006211051956.

Frandell, Ashlee, Mary Feeney, Timothy Johnson, Eric Welch, Lesley Michalegko, and Heyjie Jung. 2021. "The Effects of Electronic Alert Letters for Internet Surveys of Academic Scientists." *Scientometrics* 126 (8): 7167–81. https://doi.org/10.1007/s11192-021-04029-3.

Franklin, Laura. 2005. "Exploratory Experiments." *Philosophy of Science* 72 (5): 888–99. https://doi.org/10.1086/508117.

Frei, Christoph, and Liam Welsh. 2022. "How the Closure of a U.S. Tax Loophole May Affect Investor Portfolios." *Journal of Risk and Financial Management* 15 (5): 209. https://doi.org/10.3390/jrfm15050209.

Frick, Hannah, Fanny Chow, Max Kuhn, Michael Mahoney, Julia Silge, and Hadley Wickham. 2022. *rsample: General Resampling Infrastructure.* https://CRAN.R-project.org/package=rsample.

Fried, Eiko, Jessica Flake, and Donald Robinaugh. 2022. "Revisiting the Theoretical and Methodological Foundations of Depression Measurement." *Nature Reviews Psychology* 1 (6): 358–68. https://doi.org/10.1038/s44159-022-00050-2.

Friedman, Jerome, Robert Tibshirani, and Trevor Hastie. 2009. *The Elements of Statistical Learning.* 2nd ed. Springer. https://hastie.su.domains/ElemStatLearn/.

Friendly, Michael. 2021. *HistData: Data Sets from the History of Statistics and Data Visualization.* https://CRAN.R-project.org/package=HistData.

Friendly, Michael, and Howard Wainer. 2021. *A History of Data Visualization and Graphic Communication.* 1st ed. Massachusetts: Harvard University Press.

Fry, Hannah. 2020. "Big Tech Is Testing You." *The New Yorker*, February, 61–65. https://www.newyorker.com/magazine/2020/03/02/big-tech-is-testing-you.

Fuller, Mark, and James Mosher. 1987. "Raptor Survey Techniques." In *Raptor Management Techniques Manual*, edited by Beth Pendleton, Brian Millsap, Keith Cline, and David Bird, 37–65. National Wildlife Federation. https://www.sandiegocounty.gov/content/dam/sdc/pds/ceqa/JVR/AdminRecord/IncorporatedByReference/Appendices/Appendix-D---Biological-Resources-Report/Fuller%20and%20Mosher%201987.pdf.

Funkhouser, Gray. 1937. "Historical Development of the Graphical Representation of Statistical Data." *Osiris* 3: 269–404. https://doi.org/10.1086/368480.

Gagolewski, Marek. 2022. "stringi: Fast and Portable Character String Processing in R." *Journal of Statistical Software* 103 (2): 1–59. https://doi.org/10.18637/jss.v103.i02.

Galef, Julia. 2020. "Episode 248: Are Democrats Being Irrational? (David Shor)." *Rationally Speaking*, December. http://rationallyspeakingpodcast.org/248-are-democrats-being-irrational-david-shor/.

Gao, Lucy, Jacob Bien, and Daniela Witten. 2022. "Selective Inference for Hierarchical Clustering." *Journal of the American Statistical Association*, October, 1–11. https://doi.org/10.1080/01621459.2022.2116331.

Gao, Zheng, Christian Bird, and Earl T. Barr. 2017. "To Type or Not to Type: Quantifying Detectable Bugs in JavaScript." In *2017 IEEE/ACM 39th International Conference on Software Engineering (ICSE).* IEEE. https://doi.org/10.1109/icse.2017.75.

Garfinkel, Irwin, Lee Rainwater, and Timothy Smeeding. 2006. "A Re-Examination of Welfare States and Inequality in Rich Nations: How in-Kind Transfers and Indirect

Taxes Change the Story." *Journal of Policy Analysis and Management* 25 (4): 897–919. https://doi.org/10.1002/pam.20213.

Gargiulo, Maria. 2022. "Statistical Biases, Measurement Challenges, and Recommendations for Studying Patterns of Femicide in Conflict." *Peace Review* 34 (2): 163–76. https://doi.org/10.1080/10402659.2022.2049002.

Garnier, Simon, Noam Ross, Robert Rudis, Antônio Camargo, Marco Sciaini, and Cédric Scherer. 2021. *viridis – Colorblind-Friendly Color Maps for R*. https://doi.org/10.5281/zenodo.4679424.

Gazeley, Ursula, Georges Reniers, Hallie Eilerts-Spinelli, Julio Romero Prieto, Momodou Jasseh, Sammy Khagayi, and Veronique Filippi. 2022. "Women's Risk of Death Beyond 42 Days Post Partum: A Pooled Analysis of Longitudinal Health and Demographic Surveillance System Data in Sub-Saharan Africa." *The Lancet Global Health* 10 (11): e1582–89. https://doi.org/10.1016/s2214-109x(22)00339-4.

Gebru, Timnit, Jamie Morgenstern, Briana Vecchione, Jennifer Wortman Vaughan, Hanna Wallach, Hal Daumé III, and Kate Crawford. 2021. "Datasheets for Datasets." *Communications of the ACM* 64 (12): 86–92. https://doi.org/10.1145/3458723.

Gelfand, Sharla. 2021. "Make a ReprEx... Please." *YouTube*, February. https://youtu.be/G5Nm-GpmrLw.

———. 2022a. *Astrologer: Chani Nicholas Weekly Horoscopes (2013-2017)*. http://github.com/sharlagelfand/astrologer.

———. 2022b. *opendatatoronto: Access the City of Toronto Open Data Portal*. https://CRAN.R-project.org/package=opendatatoronto.

Gelman, Andrew. 2016. "What has happened down here is the winds have changed," September. https://statmodeling.stat.columbia.edu/2016/09/21/what-has-happened-down-here-is-the-winds-have-changed/.

———. 2019. "Another Regression Discontinuity Disaster and What Can We Learn from It," June. https://statmodeling.stat.columbia.edu/2019/06/25/another-regression-discontinuity-disaster-and-what-can-we-learn-from-it/.

———. 2020. "Statistical Models of Election Outcomes." *YouTube*, August. https://youtu.be/7gjDnrbLQ4k.

Gelman, Andrew, John Carlin, Hal Stern, David Dunson, Aki Vehtari, and Donald Rubin. (1995) 2014. *Bayesian Data Analysis*. 3rd ed. Chapman; Hall/CRC.

Gelman, Andrew, Sharad Goel, Douglas Rivers, and David Rothschild. 2016. "The Mythical Swing Voter." *Quarterly Journal of Political Science* 11 (1): 103–30. https://doi.org/10.1561/100.00015031.

Gelman, Andrew, and Jennifer Hill. 2007. *Data Analysis Using Regression and Multilevel/Hierarchical Models*. 1st ed. Cambridge University Press.

Gelman, Andrew, Jennifer Hill, and Aki Vehtari. 2020. *Regression and Other Stories*. Cambridge University Press. https://avehtari.github.io/ROS-Examples/.

Gelman, Andrew, and Guido Imbens. 2019. "Why High-Order Polynomials Should Not Be Used in Regression Discontinuity Designs." *Journal of Business & Economic Statistics* 37 (3): 447–56. https://doi.org/10.1080/07350015.2017.1366909.

Gelman, Andrew, and Eric Loken. 2013. "The Garden of Forking Paths: Why Multiple Comparisons Can Be a Problem, Even When There Is No 'Fishing Expedition' or 'p-Hacking' and the Research Hypothesis Was Posited Ahead of Time." *Department of Statistics, Columbia University*. http://www.stat.columbia.edu/~gelman/research/unpublished/p%5Fhacking.pdf.

Gelman, Andrew, Greggor Mattson, and Daniel Simpson. 2018. "Gaydar and the Fallacy of Decontextualized Measurement." *Sociological Science* 5 (12): 270–80. https://doi.org/10.15195/v5.a12.

Gelman, Andrew, Cristian Pasarica, and Rahul Dodhia. 2002. "Let's Practice What We Preach: Turning Tables into Graphs." *The American Statistician* 56 (2): 121–30. https://doi.org/10.1198/000313002317572790.

Gelman, Andrew, and Aki Vehtari. 2021. "What Are the Most Important Statistical Ideas of the Past 50 Years?" *Journal of the American Statistical Association* 116 (536): 2087–97. https://doi.org/10.1080/01621459.2021.1938081.

———. 2023. *Learn Statistics: Hundreds of Stories, Activities, and Examples.*

Gelman, Andrew, Aki Vehtari, Daniel Simpson, Charles Margossian, Bob Carpenter, Yuling Yao, Lauren Kennedy, Jonah Gabry, Paul-Christian Bürkner, and Martin Modrák. 2020. "Bayesian Workflow." arXiv. https://doi.org/10.48550/arXiv.2011.01808.

Gentemann, Chelle Leigh, Chris Holdgraf, Ryan Abernathey, Daniel Crichton, James Colliander, Edward Joseph Kearns, Yuvi Panda, and Richard Signell. 2021. "Science Storms the Cloud." *AGU Advances* 2 (2). https://doi.org/10.1029/2020av000354.

Gerber, Alan, and Donald Green. 2012. *Field Experiments: Design, Analysis, and Interpretation.* New York: WW Norton.

Gerring, John. 2012. "Mere Description." *British Journal of Political Science* 42 (4): 721–46. https://doi.org/10.1017/s0007123412000130.

Gertler, Paul, Sebastian Martinez, Patrick Premand, Laura Rawlings, and Christel Vermeersch. 2016. *Impact Evaluation in Practice.* 2nd ed. The World Bank. https://doi.org/10.1596/978-1-4648-0779-4.

Geuenich, Michael, Jinyu Hou, Sunyun Lee, Shanza Ayub, Hartland Jackson, and Kieran Campbell. 2021a. "Automated Assignment of Cell Identity from Single-Cell Multiplexed Imaging and Proteomic Data." *Cell Systems* 12 (12): 1173–86. https://doi.org/10.1016/j.cels.2021.08.012.

———. 2021b. "Replication Materials: "Automated Assignment of Cell Identity from Single-Cell Multiplexed Imaging and Proteomic Data"." https://doi.org/10.5281/ZENODO.5156049.

Ghitza, Yair, and Andrew Gelman. 2020. "Voter Registration Databases and MRP: Toward the Use of Large-Scale Databases in Public Opinion Research." *Political Analysis* 28 (4): 507–31. https://doi.org/10.1017/pan.2020.3.

Gibney, Elizabeth. 2022. "The leap second's time is up: world votes to stop pausing clocks." *Nature* 612 (7938): 18–18. https://doi.org/10.1038/d41586-022-03783-5.

Gleick, James. 1990. "The Census: Why We Can't Count." *The New York Times*, July. https://www.nytimes.com/1990/07/15/magazine/the-census-why-we-can-t-count.html.

Godfrey, Ernest. 1918. "History and Development of Statistics in Canada." In *The History of Statistics–Their Development and Progress in Many Countries. New York: Macmillan*, edited by John Koren, 179–98. Macmillan Company of New York.

Goodman, Leo. 1961. "Snowball Sampling." *The Annals of Mathematical Statistics* 32 (1): 148–70. https://doi.org/10.1214/aoms/1177705148.

Goodrich, Ben, Jonah Gabry, Imad Ali, and Sam Brilleman. 2023. "rstanarm: Bayesian applied regression modeling via Stan." https://mc-stan.org/rstanarm.

Google. 2022. "What to Look for in a Code Review." Google Engineering Practices Documentation. https://google.github.io/eng-practices/review/reviewer/looking-for.html.

Gordon, Brett, Robert Moakler, and Florian Zettelmeyer. 2022. "Close Enough? A Large-Scale Exploration of Non-Experimental Approaches to Advertising Measurement." *Marketing Science*, November. https://doi.org/10.1287/mksc.2022.1413.

Gordon, Brett, Florian Zettelmeyer, Neha Bhargava, and Dan Chapsky. 2019. "A Comparison of Approaches to Advertising Measurement: Evidence from Big Field Experiments at Facebook." *Marketing Science* 38 (2): 193–225. https://doi.org/10.1287/mksc.2018.1135.

Graham, Paul. 2020. "How to Write Usefully," February. http://paulgraham.com/useful.html.

Gray, Charles T., and Ben Marwick. 2019. "Truth, Proof, and Reproducibility: There's No Counter-Attack for the Codeless." In *Communications in Computer and Information Science*, 111–29. Springer Singapore. https://doi.org/10.1007/978-981-15-1960-4_8.

Green, Donald, Terence Leong, Holger Kern, Alan Gerber, and Christopher Larimer. 2009. "Testing the Accuracy of Regression Discontinuity Analysis Using Experimental Benchmarks." *Political Analysis* 17 (4): 400–417. https://doi.org/10.1093/pan/mpp018.

Green, Eric. 2020. "Nivi Research: Mister P helps us understand vaccine hesitancy," December. https://research.nivi.io/posts/2020-12-08-mister-p-helps-us-understand-vaccine-hesitancy/.

Greenberg, Bernard, Abdel-Latif Abul-Ela, Walt Simmons, and Daniel Horvitz. 1969. "The Unrelated Question Randomized Response Model: Theoretical Framework." *Journal of the American Statistical Association* 64 (326): 520–39. https://doi.org/10.1080/01621459.1969.10500991.

Greenland, Sander, Stephen Senn, Kenneth Rothman, John Carlin, Charles Poole, Steven Goodman, and Douglas Altman. 2016. "Statistical Tests, P values, Confidence Intervals, and Power: A Guide to Misinterpretations." *European Journal of Epidemiology* 31 (4): 337–50. https://doi.org/10.1007/s10654-016-0149-3.

Greifer, Noah. 2021. "Why Do We Do Matching for Causal Inference Vs Regressing on Confounders?" *Cross Validated*, September. https://stats.stackexchange.com/q/544958.

Grimmer, Justin, Margaret Roberts, and Brandon Stewart. 2022. *Text As Data: A New Framework for Machine Learning and the Social Sciences*. New Jersey: Princeton University Press.

Grolemund, Garrett, and Hadley Wickham. 2011. "Dates and Times Made Easy with lubridate." *Journal of Statistical Software* 40 (3): 1–25. https://doi.org/10.18637/jss.v040.i03.

Gronsbell, Jessica, Jessica Minnier, Sheng Yu, Katherine Liao, and Tianxi Cai. 2019. "Automated Feature Selection of Predictors in Electronic Medical Records Data." *Biometrics* 75 (1): 268–77. https://doi.org/10.1111/biom.12987.

Groves, Robert. 2011. "Three Eras of Survey Research." *Public Opinion Quarterly* 75 (5): 861–71. https://doi.org/10.1093/poq/nfr057.

Groves, Robert, and Lars Lyberg. 2010. "Total Survey Error: Past, Present, and Future." *Public Opinion Quarterly* 74 (5): 849–79. https://doi.org/10.1093/poq/nfq065.

Grün, Bettina, and Kurt Hornik. 2011. "topicmodels: An R Package for Fitting Topic Models." *Journal of Statistical Software* 40 (13): 1–30. https://doi.org/10.18637/jss.v040.i13.

Gustafsson, Karl, and Linus Hagström. 2017. "What Is the Point? Teaching Graduate Students How to Construct Political Science Research Puzzles." *European Political Science* 17 (4): 634–48. https://doi.org/10.1057/s41304-017-0130-y.

Gutman, Robert. 1958. "Birth and Death Registration in Massachusetts: II. The Inauguration of a Modern System, 1800-1849." *The Milbank Memorial Fund Quarterly* 36 (4): 373–402.

Hackett, Robert. 2016. "Researchers Caused an Uproar By Publishing Data From 70,000 OkCupid Users." *Fortune*, May. https://fortune.com/2016/05/18/okcupid-data-research/.

Halberstam, David. 1972. *The Best and the Brightest*. 1st ed. New York: Random House.

Hamming, Richard. (1997) 2020. *The Art of Doing Science and Engineering*. 2nd ed. Stripe Press.

Hammond, Jennifer, Heidi Leister-Tebbe, Annie Gardner, Paula Abreu, Weihang Bao, Wayne Wisemandle, MaryLynn Baniecki, et al. 2022. "Oral Nirmatrelvir for High-Risk, Nonhospitalized Adults with Covid-19." *New England Journal of Medicine* 386 (15): 1397–1408. https://doi.org/10.1056/nejmoa2118542.

Hand, David. 2018. "Statistical Challenges of Administrative and Transaction Data." *Journal of the Royal Statistical Society: Series A (Statistics in Society)* 181 (3): 555–605. https://doi.org/10.1111/rssa.12315.

Handcock, Mark, and Krista Gile. 2011. "Comment: On the Concept of Snowball Sampling." *Sociological Methodology* 41 (1): 367–71. https://doi.org/10.1111/j.1467-9531.2011.01243.x.

Hangartner, Dominik, Daniel Kopp, and Michael Siegenthaler. 2021. "Monitoring Hiring Discrimination Through Online Recruitment Platforms." *Nature* 589 (7843): 572–76. https://doi.org/10.1038/s41586-020-03136-0.

Hanretty, Chris. 2020. "An Introduction to Multilevel Regression and Post-Stratification for Estimating Constituency Opinion." *Political Studies Review* 18 (4): 630–45. https://doi.org/10.1177/1478929919864773.

Hao, Karen. 2019. "This is How AI Bias Really Happens—And Why It's So Hard To Fix." *MIT Technology Review*, February. https://www.technologyreview.com/2019/02/04/137602/this-is-how-ai-bias-really-happensand-why-its-so-hard-to-fix/.

Hart, Edmund, Pauline Barmby, David LeBauer, François Michonneau, Sarah Mount, Patrick Mulrooney, Timothée Poisot, Kara Woo, Naupaka Zimmerman, and Jeffrey Hollister. 2016. "Ten Simple Rules for Digital Data Storage." *PLOS Computational Biology* 12 (10): e1005097. https://doi.org/10.1371/journal.pcbi.1005097.

Hartocollis, Anemona. 2022. "U.S. News Ranked Columbia No. 2, but a Math Professor Has His Doubts." *The New York Times*, March. https://www.nytimes.com/2022/03/17/us/columbia-university-rank.html.

Hassan, Mai. 2022. "New Insights on Africa's Autocratic Past." *African Affairs* 121 (483): 321–33. https://doi.org/10.1093/afraf/adac002.

Hastie, Trevor, and Robert Tibshirani. 1990. *Generalized Additive Models*. 1st ed. Boca Raton: Chapman; Hall/CRC.

Hawes, Michael. 2020. "Implementing Differential Privacy: Seven Lessons From the 2020 United States Census." *Harvard Data Science Review* 2 (2). https://doi.org/10.1162/99608f92.353c6f99.

Hayot, Eric. 2014. *The Elements of Academic Style*. New York: Columbia University Press.

Healy, Kieran. 2018. *Data Visualization*. New Jersey: Princeton University Press. https://socviz.co.

———. 2020. "The Kitchen Counter Observatory," May. https://kieranhealy.org/blog/archives/2020/05/21/the-kitchen-counter-observatory/.

———. 2022. "Unhappy in Its Own Way," July. https://kieranhealy.org/blog/archives/2022/07/22/unhappy-in-its-own-way/.

Heckathorn, Douglas. 1997. "Respondent-Driven Sampling: A New Approach to the Study of Hidden Populations." *Social Problems* 44 (2): 174–99. https://doi.org/10.2307/3096941.

Heil, Benjamin, Michael Hoffman, Florian Markowetz, Su-In Lee, Casey Greene, and Stephanie Hicks. 2021. "Reproducibility Standards for Machine Learning in the Life Sciences." *Nature Methods* 18 (10): 1132–35. https://doi.org/10.1038/s41592-021-01256-7.

Heller, Jean. 2022. "AP Exposes the Tuskegee Syphilis Study: The 50th Anniversary." *AP*, July. https://apnews.com/article/tuskegee-study-ap-story-investigation-syphilis-53403657e77d76f52df6c2e2892788c9.

Hermans, Felienne. 2017. "Peter Hilton on Naming." *IEEE Software* 34 (3): 117–20. https://doi.org/10.1109/MS.2017.81.

———. 2021. *The Programmer's Brain: What Every Programmer Needs to Know about Cognition*. 1st ed. New York: Simon; Schuster. https://www.manning.com/books/the-programmers-brain.

Hernán, Miguel, David Clayton, and Niels Keiding. 2011. "The Simpson's Paradox Unraveled." *International Journal of Epidemiology* 40 (3): 780–85. https://doi.org/10.1093/ije/dyr041.

Hernán, Miguel, and James Robins. 2023. *What If*. 1st ed. Boca Raton: Chapman & Hall/CRC. https://www.hsph.harvard.edu/miguel-hernan/causal-inference-book/.

Herndon, Thomas, Michael Ash, and Robert Pollin. 2014. "Does High Public Debt Consistently Stifle Economic Growth? A Critique of Reinhart and Rogoff." *Cambridge Journal of Economics* 38 (2): 257–79. https://doi.org/10.1093/cje/bet075.

Hester, Jim, Florent Angly, Russ Hyde, Michael Chirico, Kun Ren, Alexander Rosenstock, and Indrajeet Patil. 2022. *lintr: A "Linter" for R Code*. https://CRAN.R-project.org/package=lintr.

Hester, Jim, Hadley Wickham, and Gábor Csárdi. 2021. *fs: Cross-Platform File System Operations Based on "libuv"*. https://CRAN.R-project.org/package=fs.

Hill, Austin Bradford. 1965. "The Environment and Disease: Association or Causation?" *Proceedings of the Royal Society of Medicine* 58 (5): 295–300.

Hillel, Wayne. 2017. *How Do We Trust Our Science Code?* https://www.hillelwayne.com/how-do-we-trust-science-code/.

Ho, Daniel, Kosuke Imai, Gary King, and Elizabeth Stuart. 2011. "MatchIt: Nonparametric Preprocessing for Parametric Causal Inference." *Journal of Statistical Software* 42 (8): 1–28. https://doi.org/10.18637/jss.v042.i08.

Hodgetts, Paul. 2022. "The Negative Space of Data," March. https://hodgettsp.netlify.app/post/data-negativespace/.

Hofmeister, Johannes, Janet Siegmund, and Daniel Holt. 2017. "Shorter Identifier Names Take Longer to Comprehend." In *2017 IEEE 24th International Conference on Software Analysis, Evolution and Reengineering (SANER)*, 217–27. https://doi.org/10.1109/saner.2017.7884623.

Holland, Paul. 1986. "Statistics and Causal Inference." *Journal of the American Statistical Association* 81 (396): 945–60. https://doi.org/10.2307/2289064.

Holliday, Derek, Tyler Reny, Alex Rossell Hayes, Aaron Rudkin, Chris Tausanovitch, and Lynn Vavreck. 2021. "Democracy Fund + UCLA Nationscape Methodology and Representativeness Assessment."

Hopper, Nate. 2022. "The Thorny Problem of Keeping the Internet's Time." *The New Yorker*, September. https://www.newyorker.com/tech/annals-of-technology/the-thorny-problem-of-keeping-the-internets-time.

Horst, Allison Marie, Alison Presmanes Hill, and Kristen Gorman. 2020. *palmerpenguins: Palmer Archipelago (Antarctica) penguin data*. https://doi.org/10.5281/zenodo.3960218.

Horton, Nicholas, Rohan Alexander, Micaela Parker, Aneta Piekut, and Colin Rundel. 2022. "The Growing Importance of Reproducibility and Responsible Workflow in the Data Science and Statistics Curriculum." *Journal of Statistics and Data Science Education* 30 (3): 207–8. https://doi.org/10.1080/26939169.2022.2141001.

Horton, Nicholas, and Stuart Lipsitz. 2001. "Multiple Imputation in Practice." *The American Statistician* 55 (3): 244–54. https://doi.org/10.1198/000313001317098266.

Hotz, Joseph, Christopher Bollinger, Tatiana Komarova, Charles Manski, Robert Moffitt, Denis Nekipelov, Aaron Sojourner, and Bruce Spencer. 2022. "Balancing Data Privacy and Usability in the Federal Statistical System." *Proceedings of the National Academy of Sciences* 119 (31): 1–10. https://doi.org/10.1073/pnas.2104906119.

Howes, Adam. 2022. "Representing Uncertainty Using Significant Figures," April. https://athowes.github.io/posts/2022-04-24-representing-uncertainty-using-significant-figures/.

Hug, Lucia, Monica Alexander, Danzhen You, Leontine Alkema, and UN Inter-agency Group for Child. 2019. "National, Regional, and Global Levels and Trends in Neonatal Mortality Between 1990 and 2017, with Scenario-Based Projections to 2030: A Systematic Analysis." *Lancet Global Health* 7 (6): e710–20. https://doi.org/10.1016/S2214-109X(19)30163-9.

Hughes, Nicola, and Jill Rutter. 2016. "Ministers Reflect: Interview with Oliver Letwin," December. https://www.instituteforgovernment.org.uk/ministers-reflect/person/oliver-letwin/.

Hulley, Stephen, Steven Cummings, Warren Browner, Deborah Grady, and Thomas Newman. 2007. *Designing Clinical Research.* 3rd ed. Lippincott Williams & Wilkins.

Hullman, Jessica, and Andrew Gelman. 2021. "Designing for Interactive Exploratory Data Analysis Requires Theories of Graphical Inference." *Harvard Data Science Review* 3 (3). https://doi.org/10.1162/99608f92.3ab8a587.

Huntington-Klein, Nick. 2021. *The Effect: An Introduction to Research Design and Causality.* 1st ed. Chapman & Hall. https://theeffectbook.net.

———. 2022. "Library of Statistical Techniques." https://lost-stats.github.io.

Huntington-Klein, Nick, Andreu Arenas, Emily Beam, Marco Bertoni, Jeffrey Bloem, Pralhad Burli, Naibin Chen, et al. 2021. "The Influence of Hidden Researcher Decisions in Applied Microeconomics." *Economic Inquiry* 59: 944–60. https://doi.org/10.1111/ecin.12992.

Huyen, Chip. 2020. "Machine Learning Is Going Real-Time," December. https://huyenchip.com/2020/12/27/real-time-machine-learning.html.

Hvitfeldt, Emil, and Julia Silge. 2021. *Supervised Machine Learning for Text Analysis in R.* 1st ed. Chapman; Hall/CRC. https://doi.org/10.1201/9781003093459.

Hyman, Michael, Luca Sartore, and Linda J Young. 2021. "Capture-Recapture Estimation of Characteristics of U.S. Local Food Farms Using a Web-Scraped List Frame." *Journal of Survey Statistics and Methodology* 10 (4): 979–1004. https://doi.org/10.1093/jssam/smab008.

Hyndman, Rob, Timothy Hyndman, Charles Gray, Sayani Gupta, and Jacquie Tran. 2022. *cricketdata: International Cricket Data.* https://CRAN.R-project.org/package=cricketdata.

Iannone, Richard. 2022. *DiagrammeR: Graph/Network Visualization.* https://CRAN.R-project.org/package=DiagrammeR.

Iannone, Richard, Joe Cheng, Barret Schloerke, Ellis Hughes, Alexandra Lauer, and JooYoung Seo. 2022. *gt: Easily Create Presentation-Ready Display Tables.*

Iannone, Richard, and Mauricio Vargas. 2022. *pointblank: Data Validation and Organization of Metadata for Local and Remote Tables.* https://CRAN.R-project.org/package=pointblank.

International Organization Of Legal Metrology. 2007. *International Vocabulary of Metrology – Basic and General Concepts and Associated Terms.* 3rd ed. https://www.oiml.org/en/files/pdf%5Fv/v002-200-e07.pdf.

Ioannidis, John. 2005. "Why Most Published Research Findings Are False." *PLOS Medicine* 2 (8): e124. https://doi.org/10.1371/journal.pmed.0020124.

Irizarry, Rafael. 2020. "The Role of Academia in Data Science Education." *Harvard Data Science Review* 2 (1). https://doi.org/10.1162/99608f92.dd363929.

Irving, Damien, Kate Hertweck, Luke Johnston, Joel Ostblom, Charlotte Wickham, and Greg Wilson. 2021. *Research Software Engineering with Python.* Chapman; Hall/CRC.

Isaacson, Walter. 2011. *Steve Jobs.* 1st ed. Simon & Schuster.

Ishiguro, Kazuo. 1989. *The Remains of the Day.* 1st ed. Faber; Faber.

Izrailev, Sergei. 2022. *tictoc: Functions for Timing R Scripts, as Well as Implementations of "Stack" and "List" Structures.* https://CRAN.R-project.org/package=tictoc.

James, Gareth, Daniela Witten, Trevor Hastie, and Robert Tibshirani. (2013) 2021. *An Introduction to Statistical Learning with Applications in R.* 2nd ed. Springer. https://www.statlearning.com.

Jenkins, Jennifer, Steven Rich, Andrew Ba Tran, Paige Moody, Julie Tate, and Ted Mellnik. 2022. "How the Washington Post Examines Police Shootings in the United States." https://www.washingtonpost.com/investigations/2022/12/05/washington-post-fatal-police-shootings-methodology/.

Jet Propulsion Laboratory. 2009. "JPL Institutional Coding Standard for the C Programming Language." *Document Number D-60411*, March. https://web.archive.org/web/20111015064908/http://lars-lab.jpl.nasa.gov/JPL_Coding_Standard_C.pdf.

Johnson, Alicia, Miles Ott, and Mine Dogucu. 2022. *Bayes Rules! An Introduction to Bayesian Modeling with R.* 1st ed. Chapman; Hall/CRC. https://www.bayesrulesbook.com.

Johnson, Kaneesha. 2021. "Two Regimes of Prison Data Collection." *Harvard Data Science Review* 3 (3). https://doi.org/10.1162/99608f92.72825001.

Johnston, Myfanwy, and David Robinson. 2022. *gutenbergr: Download and Process Public Domain Works from Project Gutenberg.* https://CRAN.R-project.org/package=gutenbergr.

Jones, Arnold. 1953. "Census Records of the Later Roman Empire." *The Journal of Roman Studies* 43: 49–64. https://doi.org/10.2307/297781.

Jordan, Michael. 2004. "Graphical Models." *Statistical Science* 19 (1). https://doi.org/10.1214/088342304000000026.

———. 2019. "Artificial Intelligence–The Revolution Hasn't Happened Yet." *Harvard Data Science Review* 1 (1). https://doi.org/10.1162/99608f92.f06c6e61.

Joyner, Michael. 1991. "Modeling: Optimal Marathon Performance on the Basis of Physiological Factors." *Journal of Applied Physiology* 70 (2): 683–87. https://doi.org/10.1152/jappl.1991.70.2.683.

Jurafsky, Dan, and James Martin. (2000) 2023. *Speech and Language Processing.* 3rd ed. https://web.stanford.edu/~jurafsky/slp3/.

Kahan, Brennan, Suzie Cro, Fan Li, and Michael Harhay. 2023. "Eliminating Ambiguous Treatment Effects Using Estimands." *American Journal of Epidemiology*, February. https://doi.org/10.1093/aje/kwad036.

Kahan, Brennan, Fan Li, Andrew Copas, and Michael Harhay. 2022. "Estimands in Cluster-Randomized Trials: Choosing Analyses That Answer the Right Question." *International Journal of Epidemiology*, July. https://doi.org/10.1093/ije/dyac131.

Kahle, David, and Hadley Wickham. 2013. "ggmap: Spatial Visualization with ggplot2." *The R Journal* 5 (1): 144–61. http://journal.r-project.org/archive/2013-1/kahle-wickham.pdf.

Kahneman, Daniel, Olivier Sibony, and Cass Sunstein. 2021. *Noise: A Flaw in Human Judgment.* William Collins.

Kalamara, Eleni, Arthur Turrell, Chris Redl, George Kapetanios, and Sujit Kapadia. 2022. "Making text count: Economic forecasting using newspaper text." *Journal of Applied Econometrics* 37 (5): 896–919. https://doi.org/10.1002/jae.2907.

Kalgin, Alexander. 2014. "Implementation of Performance Management in Regional Government in Russia: Evidence of Data Manipulation." *Public Management Review* 18 (1): 110–38. https://doi.org/10.1080/14719037.2014.965271.

Kapoor, Sayash, and Arvind Narayanan. 2022. "Leakage and the Reproducibility Crisis in ML-Based Science." arXiv. https://doi.org/10.48550/ARXIV.2207.07048.

Karsten, Karl. 1923. *Charts and Graphs.* New York: Prentice-Hall.

Kasy, Maximilian, and Alexander Teytelboym. 2022. "Matching with Semi-Bandits." *The Econometrics Journal*, September. https://doi.org/10.1093/ectj/utac021.

Katz, Lindsay, and Rohan Alexander. 2023a. "Digitization of the Australian Parliamentary Debates, 1998-2022." arXiv. https://doi.org/10.48550/arXiv.2304.04561.

———. 2023b. "A new, comprehensive database of all proceedings of the Australian Parliamentary Debates (1998-2022)." Zenodo. https://doi.org/10.5281/zenodo.7799678.

Kay, Matthew. 2022. *tidybayes: Tidy Data and Geoms for Bayesian Models.* https://doi.org/10.5281/zenodo.1308151.

Kennedy, Lauren, and Jonah Gabry. 2020. "MRP with rstanarm," July. https://mc-stan.org/rstanarm/articles/mrp.html.

Kennedy, Lauren, and Andrew Gelman. 2021. "Know Your Population and Know Your Model: Using Model-Based Regression and Poststratification to Generalize Findings Beyond the Observed Sample." *Psychological Methods* 26 (5): 547–58. https://doi.org/10.1037/met0000362.

Kennedy, Lauren, Katharine Khanna, Daniel Simpson, Andrew Gelman, Yajun Jia, and Julien Teitler. 2022. "He, She, They: Using Sex and Gender in Survey Adjustment." https://arxiv.org/abs/2009.14401.

Kenny, Christopher T., Shiro Kuriwaki, Cory McCartan, Evan T. R. Rosenman, Tyler Simko, and Kosuke Imai. 2021. "The use of differential privacy for census data and its impact on redistricting: The case of the 2020 U.S. Census." *Science Advances* 7 (41). https://doi.org/10.1126/sciadv.abk3283.

———. 2022. "Comment: The Essential Role of Policy Evaluation for the 2020 Census Disclosure Avoidance System." *Harvard Data Science Review*. https://doi.org/10.48550/arXiv.2210.08383.

Keshav, Srinivasan. 2007. "How to Read a Paper." *ACM SIGCOMM Computer Communication Review* 37 (3): 83–84. https://doi.org/10.1145/1273445.1273458.

Keyes, Os. 2019. "Counting the Countless." *Real Life*. https://reallifemag.com/counting-the-countless/.

Kharecha, Pushker, and James Hansen. 2013. "Prevented Mortality and Greenhouse Gas Emissions from Historical and Projected Nuclear Power." *Environmental Science & Technology* 47 (9): 4889–95. https://doi.org/10.1021/es3051197.

Kiang, Mathew, Alexander Tsai, Monica Alexander, David Rehkopf, and Sanjay Basu. 2021. "Racial/Ethnic Disparities in Opioid-Related Mortality in the USA, 1999–2019: The Extreme Case of Washington DC." *Journal of Urban Health* 98 (5): 589–95. https://doi.org/10.1007/s11524-021-00573-8.

King, Gary. 2006. "Publication, Publication." *PS: Political Science & Politics* 39 (1): 119–25. https://doi.org/10.1017/S1049096506060252.

King, Gary, and Richard Nielsen. 2019. "Why Propensity Scores Should Not Be Used for Matching." *Political Analysis* 27 (4): 435–54. https://doi.org/10.1017/pan.2019.11.

King, Stephen. 2000. *On Writing: A Memoir of the Craft*. 1st ed. Scribner.

Kirkegaard, Emil, and Julius Bjerrekær. 2016. "The OKCupid Dataset: A Very Large Public Dataset of Dating Site Users." *Open Differential Psychology*, 1–10. https://doi.org/10.26775/ODP.2016.11.03.

Kish, Leslie. 1959. "Some Statistical Problems in Research Design." *American Sociological Review* 24 (3): 328–38. https://doi.org/10.2307/2089381.

Kleiber, Christian, and Achim Zeileis. 2008. *Applied Econometrics with R*. New York: Springer-Verlag. https://CRAN.R-project.org/package=AER.

Knuth, Donald. 1984. "Literate Programming." *The Computer Journal* 27 (2): 97–111. https://doi.org/10.1093/comjnl/27.2.97.

———. 1998. *Art of Computer Programming, Volume 2: Seminumerical Algorithms*. 2nd ed.

Knutson, Victoria, Serge Aleshin-Guendel, Ariel Karlinsky, William Msemburi, and Jon Wakefield. 2022. "Estimating Global and Country-Specific Excess Mortality During the COVID-19 Pandemic," May. https://cdn.who.int/media/docs/default-source/world-health-data-platform/covid-19-excessmortality/covid-methods-paper-revision.pdf.

Koenecke, Allison, Andrew Nam, Emily Lake, Joe Nudell, Minnie Quartey, Zion Mengesha, Connor Toups, John Rickford, Dan Jurafsky, and Sharad Goel. 2020. "Racial Disparities in Automated Speech Recognition." *Proceedings of the National Academy of Sciences* 117 (14): 7684–89. https://doi.org/10.1073/pnas.1915768117.

Koenecke, Allison, and Hal Varian. 2020. "Synthetic Data Generation for Economists." https://arxiv.org/abs/2011.01374.

Koenker, Roger, and Achim Zeileis. 2009. "On Reproducible Econometric Research." *Journal of Applied Econometrics* 24 (5): 833–47. https://doi.org/10.1002/jae.1083.

Koerner, Lisbet. 2000. *Linnaeus: Nature and Nation.* Cambridge: Harvard University Press.

Kohavi, Ron, Alex Deng, Brian Frasca, Roger Longbotham, Toby Walker, and Ya Xu. 2012. "Trustworthy Online Controlled Experiments." In *Proceedings of the 18th ACM SIGKDD International Conference on Knowledge Discovery and Data Mining - KDD '12*, 1st ed. ACM Press. https://doi.org/10.1145/2339530.2339653.

Kohavi, Ron, Diane Tang, and Ya Xu. 2020. *Trustworthy Online Controlled Experiments: A Practical Guide to A/B Testing.* Cambridge University Press.

Koitsalu, Marie, Martin Eklund, Jan Adolfsson, Henrik Grönberg, and Yvonne Brandberg. 2018. "Effects of Pre-Notification, Invitation Length, Questionnaire Length and Reminder on Participation Rate: A Quasi-Randomised Controlled Trial." *BMC Medical Research Methodology* 18 (3): 1–5. https://doi.org/10.1186/s12874-017-0467-5.

Krantz, Sebastian. 2023. *collapse: Advanced and Fast Data Transformation.* https://CRAN.R-project.org/package=collapse.

Kuhn, Max. 2022. *tune: Tidy Tuning Tools.* https://CRAN.R-project.org/package=tune.

Kuhn, Max, and Hannah Frick. 2022. *poissonreg: Model Wrappers for Poisson Regression.* https://CRAN.R-project.org/package=poissonreg.

Kuhn, Max, and Davis Vaughan. 2022. *parsnip: A Common API to Modeling and Analysis Functions.* https://CRAN.R-project.org/package=parsnip.

Kuhn, Max, Davis Vaughan, and Emil Hvitfeldt. 2022. *yardstick: Tidy Characterizations of Model Performance.* https://CRAN.R-project.org/package=yardstick.

Kuhn, Max, and Hadley Wickham. 2020. *tidymodels: a collection of packages for modeling and machine learning using tidyverse principles.* https://www.tidymodels.org.

———. 2022. *recipes: Preprocessing and Feature Engineering Steps for Modeling.* https://CRAN.R-project.org/package=recipes.

Kuriwaki, Shiro, Will Beasley, and Thomas Leeper. 2023. *dataverse: R Client for Dataverse 4+ Repositories.*

Kuznets, Simon, Lillian Epstein, and Elizabeth Jenks. 1941. *National Income and Its Composition, 1919-1938.* National Bureau of Economic Research.

Lamott, Anne. 1994. *Bird by Bird: Some Instructions on Writing and Life.* Anchor Books.

Landau, William Michael. 2021. "The targets R Package: A Dynamic Make-Like Function-Oriented Pipeline Toolkit for Reproducibility and High-Performance Computing." *Journal of Open Source Software* 6 (57): 2959. https://doi.org/10.21105/joss.02959.

Lane, Nick. 2015. "The Unseen World: Reflections on Leeuwenhoek (1677) 'Concerning Little Animals'." *Philosophical Transactions of the Royal Society B: Biological Sciences* 370 (1666): 20140344. https://doi.org/10.1098/rstb.2014.0344.

Laouenan, Morgane, Palaash Bhargava, Jean-Benoît Eyméoud, Olivier Gergaud, Guillaume Plique, and Etienne Wasmer. 2022. "A Cross-Verified Database of Notable People, 3500BC–2018AD." *Scientific Data* 9 (290). https://doi.org/10.1038/s41597-022-01369-4.

Larmarange, Joseph. 2023. *labelled: Manipulating Labelled Data.* https://CRAN.R-project.org/package=labelled.

Latour, Bruno. 1996. "On Actor-Network Theory: A Few Clarifications." *Soziale Welt* 47 (4): 369–81. http://www.jstor.org/stable/40878163.

Lauderdale, Benjamin, Delia Bailey, Jack Blumenau, and Douglas Rivers. 2020. "Model-Based Pre-Election Polling for National and Sub-National Outcomes in the US and UK." *International Journal of Forecasting* 36 (2): 399–413. https://doi.org/10.1016/j.ijforecast.2019.05.012.

Leek, Jeff, Blakeley McShane, Andrew Gelman, David Colquhoun, Michèle Nuijten, and Steven Goodman. 2017. "Five Ways to Fix Statistics." *Nature* 551 (7682): 557–59. https://doi.org/10.1038/d41586-017-07522-z.

Leek, Jeff, and Roger Peng. 2020. "Advanced Data Science 2020." http://jtleek.com/ads2020/index.html.

Leonelli, Sabina. 2020. "Learning from Data Journeys." In *Data Journeys in the Sciences*, 1–24. Springer International Publishing. https://doi.org/10.1007/978-3-030-37177-7_1.

Leos-Barajas, Vianey, Theoni Photopoulou, Roland Langrock, Toby Patterson, Yuuki Watanabe, Megan Murgatroyd, and Yannis Papastamatiou. 2016. "Analysis of Animal Accelerometer Data Using Hidden Markov Models." *Methods in Ecology and Evolution* 8 (2): 161–73. https://doi.org/10.1111/2041-210x.12657.

Letterman, Clark. 2021. "Q&A: How Pew Research Center surveyed nearly 30,000 people in India," July. https://medium.com/pew-research-center-decoded/q-a-how-pew-research-center-surveyed-nearly-30-000-people-in-india-7c778f6d650e.

Levay, Kevin, Jeremy Freese, and James Druckman. 2016. "The Demographic and Political Composition of Mechanical Turk Samples." *SAGE Open* 6 (1): 1–17. https://doi.org/10.1177/2158244016636433.

Levine, Judah, Patrizia Tavella, and Martin Milton. 2022. "Towards a Consensus on a Continuous Coordinated Universal Time." *Metrologia* 60 (1): 014001. https://doi.org/10.1088/1681-7575/ac9da5.

Lewis, Crystal. 2023. *Data Management in Large-Scale Education Research.* https://datamgmtinedresearch.com/index.html.

Lichand, Guilherme, and Sharon Wolf. 2022. "Measuring Child Labor: Whom Should Be Asked, and Why It Matters," March. https://doi.org/10.21203/rs.3.rs-1474562/v1.

Light, Richard, Judith Singer, and John Willett. 1990. *By Design: Planning Research on Higher Education*. 1st ed. Cambridge: Harvard University Press.

Lima, Renato de, Oliver Phillips, Alvaro Duque, Sebastian Tello, Stuart Davies, Alexandre Adalardo de Oliveira, Sandra Muller, et al. 2022. "Making Forest Data Fair and Open." *Nature Ecology & Evolution* 6 (April): 656–58. https://doi.org/10.1038/s41559-022-01738-7.

Lin, Herbert. 2014. "A Proposal to Reduce Government Overclassification of Information Related to National Security." *Journal of National Security Law and Policy* 7: 443–63.

Lin, Sarah, Ibraheem Ali, and Greg Wilson. 2021. "Ten Quick Tips for Making Things Findable." *PLOS Computational Biology* 16 (12): 1–10. https://doi.org/10.1371/journal.pcbi.1008469.

Lips, Hilary. 2020. *Sex and Gender: An Introduction.* 7th ed. Illinois: Waveland Press.

Little, Roderick, and Roger Lewis. 2021. "Estimands, Estimators, and Estimates." *JAMA* 326 (10): 967. https://doi.org/10.1001/jama.2021.2886.

Liu, Emily, Lenny Bronner, and Jeremy Bowers. 2022. "What the Washington Post Elections Engineering Team Had to Learn about Election Data." *Washington Post Engineering*, April. https://washpost.engineering/what-the-washington-post-elections-engineering-team-had-to-learn-about-election-data-a41603daf9ca.

Lockheed Martin. 2005. "Joint Strike Fighter Air Vehicle C++ Coding Standards For The System Development And Demonstration Program." *Document Number 2RDU00001 Rev C*, December. https://www.stroustrup.com/JSF-AV-rules.pdf.

Lohr, Sharon. (1999) 2022. *Sampling: Design and Analysis.* 3rd ed. Chapman; Hall/CRC.

Loken, Meredith, and Hilary Matfess. 2023. "Introducing the Women's Activities in Armed Rebellion (WAAR) Project, 1946-2015." *Journal of Peace Research.*

Lovelace, Robin, Jakub Nowosad, and Jannes Muenchow. 2019. *Geocomputation with R.* 1st ed. Chapman; Hall/CRC. https://geocompr.robinlovelace.net.

Lucas, Jack, Reed Merrill, Kelly Blidook, Sandra Breux, Laura Conrad, Gabriel Eidelman, Royce Koop, et al. 2020. "Canadian Municipal Elections Database." Scholars Portal Dataverse. https://doi.org/10.5683/sp2/4mzjpq.

Lucas, Robert. 1978. "Asset Prices in an Exchange Economy." *Econometrica* 46 (6): 1429–45. https://doi.org/10.2307/1913837.

Luebke, David Martin, and Sybil Milton. 1994. "Locating the Victim: An Overview of Census-Taking, Tabulation Technology, and Persecution in Nazi Germany." *IEEE Annals of the History of Computing* 16 (3): 25–39. https://doi.org/10.1109/MAHC.1994.298418.

Lumley, Thomas. 2020. "survey: analysis of complex survey samples." https://cran.r-project.org/web/packages/survey/index.html.

Lundberg, Ian, Rebecca Johnson, and Brandon Stewart. 2021. "What Is Your Estimand? Defining the Target Quantity Connects Statistical Evidence to Theory." *American Sociological Review* 86 (3): 532–65. https://doi.org/10.1177/00031224211004187.

Luscombe, Alex, Kevin Dick, and Kevin Walby. 2021. "Algorithmic Thinking in the Public Interest: Navigating Technical, Legal, and Ethical Hurdles to Web Scraping in the Social Sciences." *Quality & Quantity* 56 (3): 1–22. https://doi.org/10.1007/s11135-021-01164-0.

Luscombe, Alex, Jamie Duncan, and Kevin Walby. 2022. "Jumpstarting the Justice Disciplines: A Computational-Qualitative Approach to Collecting and Analyzing Text and Image Data in Criminology and Criminal Justice Studies." *Journal of Criminal Justice Education* 33 (2): 151–71. https://doi.org/10.1080/10511253.2022.2027477.

Luscombe, Alex, and Alexander McClelland. 2020. "Policing the Pandemic: Tracking the Policing of Covid-19 Across Canada," April. https://doi.org/10.31235/osf.io/9pn27.

Lyman, Frank. 1981. "The Responsive Classroom Discussion: The Inclusion of All Students." *Mainstreaming Digest* 109: 109–13.

MacDorman, Marian, and Eugene Declercq. 2018. "The Failure of United States Maternal Mortality Reporting and Its Impact on Women's Lives." *Birth* 45 (2): 105–8. https://doi.org/1111/birt.12333.

Maher, Michael. 1982. "Modelling Association Football Scores." *Statistica Neerlandica* 36 (3): 109–18. https://doi.org/10.1111/j.1467-9574.1982.tb00782.x.

Maier, Maximilian, František Bartoš, Tom Stanley, David Shanks, Adam Harris, and Eric-Jan Wagenmakers. 2022. "No Evidence for Nudging After Adjusting for Publication Bias." *Proceedings of the National Academy of Sciences* 119 (31): e2200300119. https://doi.org/10.1073/pnas.2200300119.

Mammoliti, Anthony, Petr Smirnov, Minoru Nakano, Zhaleh Safikhani, Christopher Eeles, Heewon Seo, Sisira Kadambat Nair, et al. 2021. "Orchestrating and Sharing Large Multimodal Data for Transparent and Reproducible Research." *Nature Communications* 12 (1). https://doi.org/10.1038/s41467-021-25974-w.

Manski, Charles. 2022. "Inference with Imputed Data: The Allure of Making Stuff Up." arXiv. https://doi.org/10.48550/arXiv.2205.07388.

Marchese, David. 2022. "Her Discovery Changed the World. How Does She Think We Should Use It?" *The New York Times*, August. https://www.nytimes.com/interactive/2022/08/15/magazine/jennifer-doudna-crispr-interview.html.

Martin, Charles, and Ben Popper. 2021. "Don't Push That Button: Exploring the Software That Flies SpaceX Rockets and Starships." *The Overflow*, December. https://stackoverflow.blog/2021/12/27/dont-push-that-button-exploring-the-software-that-flies-spacex-starships/.

Martínez, Luis. 2022. "How Much Should We Trust the Dictator's GDP Growth Estimates?" *Journal of Political Economy* 130 (10): 2731–69. https://doi.org/10.1086/720458.

Matias, Nathan, Kevin Munger, Marianne Aubin Le Quere, and Charles Ebersole. 2021. "The Upworthy Research Archive, a time series of 32,487 experiments in U.S. media." *Scientific Data* 8 (1): 1–8. https://doi.org/10.1038/s41597-021-00934-7.

Mattson, Greggor. 2017. "Artificial Intelligence Discovers Gayface. Sigh." https://greggormattson.com/2017/09/09/artificial-intelligence-discovers-gayface/amp/.

McCarthy, Fiona M., Tamsin E. M. Jones, Anne E. Kwitek, Cynthia L. Smith, Peter D. Vize, Monte Westerfield, and Elspeth A. Bruford. 2023. "The Case for Standardizing

Gene Nomenclature in Vertebrates." *Nature* 614 (7948): E31–32. https://doi.org/10.1038/s41586-022-05633-w.

McClelland, Alexander. 2019. "'Lock This Whore up': Legal Violence and Flows of Information Precipitating Personal Violence Against People Criminalised for HIV-Related Crimes in Canada." *European Journal of Risk Regulation* 10 (1): 132–47. https://doi.org/10.1017/err.2019.20.

McElreath, Richard. (2015) 2020. *Statistical Rethinking: A Bayesian Course with Examples in R and Stan*. 2nd ed. Chapman; Hall/CRC.

———. 2020. "Science as Amateur Software Development." *YouTube*, September. https://youtu.be/zwRdO9%5FGGhY.

McIlroy, Doug, Ray Brownrigg, Thomas Minka, and Roger Bivand. 2023. *mapproj: Map Projections*. https://CRAN.R-project.org/package=mapproj.

McKenzie, David. 2021. "What Do You Need To Do To Make A Matching Estimator Convincing? Rhetorical vs Statistical Checks." *World Bank Blogs—Development Impact*, February. https://blogs.worldbank.org/impactevaluations/what-do-you-need-do-make-matching-estimator-convincing-rhetorical-vs-statistical.

McKinney, Wes. (2011) 2022. *Python for Data Analysis*. 3rd ed. https://wesmckinney.com/book/.

McPhee, John. 2017. *Draft No. 4*. 1st ed. Farrar, Straus; Giroux.

McQuire, Scott. 2019. "One Map to Rule Them All? Google Maps as Digital Technical Object." *Communication and the Public* 4 (2): 150–65. https://doi.org/10.1177/2057047319850192.

Mellon, Jonathan. 2023. "Rain, Rain, Go Away: 195 Potential Exclusion-Restriction Violations for Studies Using Weather as an Instrumental Variable." SocArXiv. https://doi.org/10.31235/osf.io/9qj4f.

Meng, Xiao-Li. 1994. "Multiple-Imputation Inferences with Uncongenial Sources of Input." *Statistical Science* 9 (4): 538–58. https://doi.org/10.1214/ss/1177010269.

———. 2012. "You Want Me to Analyze Data i Don't Have? Are You Insane?" *Shanghai Archives of Psychiatry* 24 (5): 297–301. https://doi.org/10.3969/j.issn.1002-0829.2012.05.011.

———. 2018. "Statistical Paradises and Paradoxes in Big Data (i): Law of Large Populations, Big Data Paradox, and the 2016 US Presidential Election." *The Annals of Applied Statistics* 12 (2): 685–726. https://doi.org/10.1214/18-AOAS1161SF.

———. 2021. "What Are the Values of Data, Data Science, or Data Scientists?" *Harvard Data Science Review* 3 (1). https://doi.org/10.1162/99608f92.ee717cf7.

Merali, Zeeya. 2010. "Computational Science:... Error." *Nature* 467 (7317): 775–77. https://doi.org/10.1038/467775a.

Miceli, Milagros, Julian Posada, and Tianling Yang. 2022. "Studying up Machine Learning Data." *Proceedings of the ACM on Human-Computer Interaction* 6 (January): 1–14. https://doi.org/10.1145/3492853.

Michener, William. 2015. "Ten Simple Rules for Creating a Good Data Management Plan." *PLOS Computational Biology* 11 (10): e1004525. https://doi.org/10.1371/journal.pcbi.1004525.

Mill, James. 1817. *The History of British India*. 1st ed. https://books.google.ca/books?id=Orw_AAAAcAAJ.

Miller, Greg. 2014. "The Cartographer Who's Transforming Map Design." *Wired*, October. https://www.wired.com/2014/10/cindy-brewer-map-design/.

Miller, Michael, and Joseph Sutherland. 2022. "The Effect of Gender on Interruptions at Congressional Hearings." *American Political Science Review*, 1–19. https://doi.org/10.1017/S0003055422000260.

Mills, David L. 1991. "Internet Time Synchronization: The Network Time Protocol." *IEEE Transactions on Communications* 39 (10): 1482–93.

Mindell, David. 2008. *Digital Apollo: Human and Machine in Spaceflight*. 1st ed. New York: The MIT Press.

Mineault, Patrick, and The Good Research Code Handbook Community. 2021. "The Good Research Code Handbook." https://doi.org/10.5281/zenodo.5796873.

Minsky, Yaron. 2011. "OCaml for the masses." *Communications of the ACM* 54 (11): 53–58. https://doi.org/10.1145/2018396.2018413.

———. 2015. "Automated Trading and OCaml with Yaron Minsky." *Hackers — Software Engineering Daily*, November. https://softwareengineeringdaily.com/2015/11/09/automated-trading-and-ocaml-with-yaron-minsky/.

Mitchell, Alanna. 2022a. "Get Ready for the New, Improved Second." *The New York Times*, April. https://www.nytimes.com/2022/04/25/science/time-second-measurement.html.

———. 2022b. "Time Has Run Out for the Leap Second." *The New York Times*, November. https://www.nytimes.com/2022/11/14/science/time-leap-second.html.

Mitchell, Margaret, Simone Wu, Andrew Zaldivar, Parker Barnes, Lucy Vasserman, Ben Hutchinson, Elena Spitzer, Inioluwa Deborah Raji, and Timnit Gebru. 2019. "Model Cards for Model Reporting." *Proceedings of the Conference on Fairness, Accountability, and Transparency*, January. https://doi.org/10.1145/3287560.3287596.

Mitrovski, Alen, Xiaoyan Yang, and Matthew Wankiewicz. 2020. "Joe Biden Projected to Win Popular Vote in 2020 US Election." https://github.com/matthewwankiewicz/US_election_forecast.

Miyakawa, Tsuyoshi. 2020. "No Raw Data, No Science: Another Possible Source of the Reproducibility Crisis." *Molecular Brain* 13 (1): 1–6. https://doi.org/10.1186/s13041-020-0552-2.

Mok, Lillio, Samuel Way, Lucas Maystre, and Ashton Anderson. 2022. "The Dynamics of Exploration on Spotify." In *Proceedings of the International AAAI Conference on Web and Social Media*, 16:663–74. https://doi.org/10.1609/icwsm.v16i1.19324.

Molanphy, Chris. 2012. "100 & Single: Three Rules to Define the Term 'One-Hit Wonder' in 2012." *The Village Voice*, September. https://www.villagevoice.com/2012/09/10/100-single-three-rules-to-define-the-term-one-hit-wonder-in-2012/.

Morange, Michel. 2016. *A History of Biology*. New Jersey: Princeton University Press.

Moyer, Brian, and Abe Dunn. 2020. "Measuring the Gross Domestic Product (GDP): The Ultimate Data Science Project." *Harvard Data Science Review* 2 (1). https://doi.org/10.1162/99608f92.414caadb.

Müller, Kirill. 2020. *here: A Simpler Way to Find Your Files*. https://CRAN.R-project.org/package=here.

Müller, Kirill, Tobias Schieferdecker, and Patrick Schratz. 2019. *Visualization, Transformation and Reporting with the Tidyverse*. https://krlmlr.github.io/vistransrep/.

Müller, Kirill, and Lorenz Walthert. 2022. *styler: Non-Invasive Pretty Printing of R Code*. https://CRAN.R-project.org/package=styler.

Müller, Kirill, and Hadley Wickham. 2022. *tibble: Simple Data Frames*. https://CRAN.R-project.org/package=tibble.

Murphy, Heather. 2017. "Why Stanford Researchers Tried to Create a 'Gaydar' Machine." *The New York Times*, October. https://www.nytimes.com/2017/10/09/science/stanford-sexual-orientation-study.html.

Navarro, Danielle. 2022. "Binding Apache Arrow to R," January. https://blog.djnavarro.net/posts/2022-01-18%5Fbinding-arrow-to-r/.

Navarro, Danielle, Jonathan Keane, and Stephanie Hazlitt. 2022. "Larger-Than-Memory Data Workflows with Apache Arrow," June. https://arrow-user2022.netlify.app.

Nelder, John. 1999. "From Statistics to Statistical Science." *Journal of the Royal Statistical Society: Series D (The Statistician)* 48 (2): 257–69. https://doi.org/10.1111/1467-9884.00187.

Nelder, John, and Robert Wedderburn. 1972. "Generalized Linear Models." *Journal of the Royal Statistical Society: Series A (General)* 135 (3): 370–84. https://doi.org/10.2307/2344614.

Neufeld, Anna, and Daniela Witten. 2021. "Discussion of Breiman's "Two Cultures": From Two Cultures to One." *Observational Studies* 7 (1): 171–74. https://doi.org/10.1353/obs.2021.0004.

Neufeld, Michael. 2002. "Wernher von Braun, the SS, and Concentration Camp Labor: Questions of Moral, Political, and Criminal Responsibility." *German Studies Review* 25 (1): 57–78. https://doi.org/10.2307/1433245.

Neuwirth, Erich. 2022. *RColorBrewer: ColorBrewer Palettes*. https://CRAN.R-project.org/package=RColorBrewer.

Newman, Daniel. 2014. "Missing Data: Five Practical Guidelines." *Organizational Research Methods* 17 (4): 372–411. https://doi.org/10.1177/1094428114548590.

Neyman, Jerzy. 1934. "On the Two Different Aspects of the Representative Method: The Method of Stratified Sampling and the Method of Purposive Selection." *Journal of the Royal Statistical Society* 97 (4): 558–625. https://doi.org/10.2307/2342192.

Nix, Justin, and M. James Lozada. 2020. "Police Killings of Unarmed Black Americans: A Reassessment of Community Mental Health Spillover Effects," January. https://doi.org/10.31235/osf.io/ajz2q.

Nobles, Melissa. 2002. "Racial Categorization and Censuses." In *Census and Identity: The Politics of Race, Ethnicity, and Language in National Censuses*, edited by David Kertzer and Dominique Arel, 43–70. Cambridge: Cambridge University Press. https://doi.org/10.1017/CBO9780511606045.003.

Northcutt, Curtis, Anish Athalye, and Jonas Mueller. 2021. "Pervasive Label Errors in Test Sets Destabilize Machine Learning Benchmarks." https://doi.org/10.48550/arXiv.2103.14749.

Obermeyer, Ziad, Brian Powers, Christine Vogeli, and Sendhil Mullainathan. 2019. "Dissecting Racial Bias in an Algorithm Used to Manage the Health of Populations." *Science* 366 (6464): 447–53. https://doi.org/10.1126/science.aax2342.

Oberski, Daniel, and Frauke Kreuter. 2020. "Differential Privacy and Social Science: An Urgent Puzzle." *Harvard Data Science Review* 2 (1). https://doi.org/10.1162/99608f92.63a22079.

OECD. 2014. "The Essential Macroeconomic Aggregates." In *Understanding National Accounts*, 13–46. OECD. https://doi.org/10.1787/9789264214637-2-en.

———. 2022. *Quarterly GDP*. https://data.oecd.org/gdp/quarterly-gdp.htm.

Ooms, Jeroen. 2014. "The jsonlite Package: A Practical and Consistent Mapping Between JSON Data and R Objects." *arXiv:1403.2805 [Stat.CO]*. https://arxiv.org/abs/1403.2805.

———. 2022a. *openssl: Toolkit for Encryption, Signatures and Certificates Based on OpenSSL*. https://CRAN.R-project.org/package=openssl.

———. 2022b. *pdftools: Text Extraction, Rendering and Converting of PDF Documents*. https://CRAN.R-project.org/package=pdftools.

———. 2022c. *ssh: Secure Shell (SSH) Client for R*. https://CRAN.R-project.org/package=ssh.

———. 2022d. *tesseract: Open Source OCR Engine*. https://CRAN.R-project.org/package=tesseract.

Open Science Collaboration. 2015. "Estimating the Reproducibility of Psychological Science." *Science* 349 (6251): aac4716. https://doi.org/10.1126/science.aac4716.

Orwell, George. 1946. *Politics and the English Language*. https://www.orwellfoundation.com/the-orwell-foundation/orwell/essays-and-other-works/politics-and-the-english-language/.

Osborne, Jason. 2012. *Best Practices in Data Cleaning: A Complete Guide to Everything You Need to Do Before and After Collecting Your Data*. SAGE Publications.

Osgood, D. Wayne. 2000. "Poisson-Based Regression Analysis of Aggregate Crime Rates." *Journal of Quantitative Criminology* 16 (1): 21–43. https://doi.org/10.1023/a:1007521427059.

Palmer Station Antarctica LTER, and Gorman, Kristen. 2020. "Structural Size Measurements and Isotopic Signatures of Foraging Among Adult Male and Female Adélie Penguins (Pygoscelis Adeliae) Nesting Along the Palmer Archipelago Near Palmer Station, 2007-2009." https://doi.org/10.6073/PASTA/98B16D7D563F265CB52372C8CA99E60F.

Patki, Neha, Roy Wedge, and Kalyan Veeramachaneni. 2016. "The Synthetic Data Vault." In *2016 IEEE International Conference on Data Science and Advanced Analytics (DSAA)*, 399–410. https://doi.org/10.1109/DSAA.2016.49.

Paullada, Amandalynne, Inioluwa Deborah Raji, Emily Bender, Emily Denton, and Alex Hanna. 2021. "Data and Its (Dis)contents: A Survey of Dataset Development and Use in Machine Learning Research." *Patterns* 2 (11): 100336. https://doi.org/10.1016/j.patter.2021.100336.

Pavlik, Kaylin. 2019. "Understanding + Classifying Genres Using Spotify Audio Features." https://www.kaylinpavlik.com/classifying-songs-genres/.

Pedersen, Thomas Lin. 2022. *patchwork: The Composer of Plots*. https://CRAN.R-project.org/package=patchwork.

Perepolkin, Dmytro. 2022. *polite: Be Nice on the Web*. https://CRAN.R-project.org/package=polite.

Perkel, Jeffrey. 2021. "Ten Computer Codes That Transformed Science." *Nature* 589 (7842): 344–48. https://doi.org/10.1038/d41586-021-00075-2.

Phillips, Alban. 1958. "The Relation Between Unemployment and the Rate of Change of Money Wage Rates in the United Kingdom, 1861-1957." *Economica* 25 (100): 283–99. https://doi.org/10.1111/j.1468-0335.1958.tb00003.x.

Piller, Charles. 2022. "Blots on a Field?" *Science* 377 (6604): 358–63. https://doi.org/10.1126/science.ade0209.

Pineau, Joelle, Philippe Vincent-Lamarre, Koustuv Sinha, Vincent Larivière, Alina Beygelzimer, Florence d'Alché-Buc, Emily Fox, and Hugo Larochelle. 2021. "Improving Reproducibility in Machine Learning Research (a Report from the NeurIPS 2019 Reproducibility Program)." *Journal of Machine Learning Research* 22 (164): 1–20. http://jmlr.org/papers/v22/20-303.html.

Pitman, Jim. 1993. *Probability*. 1st ed. New York: Springer. https://doi.org/10.1007/978-1-4612-4374-8.

Plant, Anne, and Robert Hanisch. 2020. "Reproducibility in Science: A Metrology Perspective." *Harvard Data Science Review* 2 (4). https://doi.org/10.1162/99608f92.eb6ddee4.

Podlogar, Tim, Peter Leo, and James Spragg. 2022. "Using VO2max as a marker of training status in athletes—Can we do better?" *Journal of Applied Physiology* 133 (6): 144–47. https://doi.org/10.1152/japplphysiol.00723.2021.

Preece, Donald Arthur. 1981. "Distributions of Final Digits in Data." *The Statistician* 30 (1): 31. https://doi.org/10.2307/2987702.

Prévost, Jean-Guy, and Jean-Pierre Beaud. 2015. *Statistics, Public Debate and the State, 1800–1945: A Social, Political and Intellectual History of Numbers*. Routledge.

R Core Team. 2023. *R: A Language and Environment for Statistical Computing*. Vienna, Austria: R Foundation for Statistical Computing. https://www.R-project.org/.

R Special Interest Group on Databases (R-SIG-DB), Hadley Wickham, and Kirill Müller. 2022. *DBI: R Database Interface*. https://CRAN.R-project.org/package=DBI.

Radcliffe, Nicholas. 2023. *Test-Driven Data Analysis (Python TDDA library)*. https://tdda.readthedocs.io/en/latest/index.html.

Register, Yim. 2020a. "Introduction to Sampling and Randomization." *YouTube*, November. https://youtu.be/U272FFxG8LE.

———. 2020b. "Data Science Ethics in 6 Minutes." *YouTube*, December. https://youtu.be/mA4gypAiRYU.

Rehaag, Sean. 2023. "Supreme Court of Canada Bulk Decisions Dataset." *Refugee Law Laboratory*. https://refugeelab.ca/bulk-data/scc.

Reid, Nancy. 2003. "Asymptotics and the Theory of Inference." *The Annals of Statistics* 31 (6): 1695–1731. https://doi.org/10.1214/aos/1074290325.

Richardson, Neal, Ian Cook, Nic Crane, Dewey Dunnington, Romain François, Jonathan Keane, Dragoș Moldovan-Grünfeld, Jeroen Ooms, and Apache Arrow. 2023. *arrow: Integration to Apache Arrow*. https://CRAN.R-project.org/package=arrow.

Riederer, Emily. 2020. "Column Names as Contracts," September. https://emilyriederer.netlify.app/post/column-name-contracts/.

———. 2021. "Causal Design Patterns for Data Analysts," January. https://emilyriederer.netlify.app/post/causal-design-patterns/.

Riffe, Tim, Enrique Acosta, Enrique José Acosta, Diego Manuel Aburto, Anna Alburez-Gutierrez, Ainhoa Altová, Ugofilippo Alustiza, et al. 2021. "Data Resource Profile: COVerAGE-DB: A Global Demographic Database of COVID-19 Cases and Deaths." *International Journal of Epidemiology* 50 (2): 390–390f. https://doi.org/10.1093/ije/dyab027.

Riley, Richard, Tim Cole, Jon Deeks, Jamie Kirkham, Julie Morris, Rafael Perera, Angie Wade, and Gary Collins. 2022. "On the 12th Day of Christmas, a Statistician Sent to Me..." *BMJ*, December, e072883. https://doi.org/10.1136/bmj-2022-072883.

Rilke, Rainer Maria. (1929) 2014. *Letters to a Young Poet*. Penguin Classics.

Roberts, Margaret, Brandon Stewart, and Dustin Tingley. 2019. "stm: An R Package for Structural Topic Models." *Journal of Statistical Software* 91 (2): 1–40. https://doi.org/10.18637/jss.v091.i02.

Robinson, David, Alex Hayes, and Simon Couch. 2022. *broom: Convert Statistical Objects into Tidy Tibbles*. https://CRAN.R-project.org/package=broom.

Robinson, Emily, and Jacqueline Nolis. 2020. *Build a Career in Data Science*. Shelter Island: Manning Publications. https://livebook.manning.com/book/build-a-career-in-data-science.

Rockoff, Hugh. 2019. "On the Controversies Behind the Origins of the Federal Economic Statistics." *Journal of Economic Perspectives* 33 (1): 147–64. https://doi.org/10.1257/jep.33.1.147.

Romer, Paul. 2018. "Jupyter, Mathematica, and the Future of the Research Paper," April. https://paulromer.net/jupyter-mathematica-and-the-future-of-the-research-paper/.

Rose, Angela, Rebecca Grais, Denis Coulombier, and Helga Ritter. 2006. "A Comparison of Cluster and Systematic Sampling Methods for Measuring Crude Mortality." *Bulletin of the World Health Organization* 84: 290–96. https://doi.org/10.2471/blt.05.029181.

Rosenau, James N. 1999. "A Transformed Observer in a Transforming World." *Studia Diplomatica* 52 (1/2): 5–14. http://www.jstor.org/stable/44838096.

Ross, Casey. 2022. "How a Decades-Old Database Became a Hugely Profitable Dossier on the Health of 270 Million Americans." *Stat*, February. https://www.statnews.com/2022/02/01/ibm-watson-health-marketscan-data/.

Rubinstein, Benjamin, and Francesco Alda. 2017. "Pain-Free Random Differential Privacy with Sensitivity Sampling." In *34th International Conference on Machine Learning (ICML'2017)*.

Rudis, Bob. 2020. *hrbrthemes: Additional Themes, Theme Components and Utilities for "ggplot2"*. https://CRAN.R-project.org/package=hrbrthemes.

Ruggles, Steven, Catherine Fitch, Diana Magnuson, and Jonathan Schroeder. 2019. "Differential Privacy and Census Data: Implications for Social and Economic Research." *AEA Papers and Proceedings* 109 (May): 403–8. https://doi.org/10.1257/pandp.20191107.

Ruggles, Steven, Sarah Flood, Sophia Foster, Ronald Goeken, Jose Pacas, Megan Schouweiler, and Matthew Sobek. 2021. "IPUMS USA: Version 11.0." Minneapolis, MN: IPUMS. https://doi.org/10.18128/d010.v11.0.

Ryan, Philip. 2015. "Keeping a Lab Notebook." *YouTube*, May. https://youtu.be/-MAIuaOL64I.

Sadowski, Caitlin, Emma Söderberg, Luke Church, Michal Sipko, and Alberto Bacchelli. 2018. "Modern Code Review: A Case Study at Google." In *Proceedings of the 40th International Conference on Software Engineering: Software Engineering in Practice*, 181–90. ICSE-SEIP '18. New York, NY, USA: Association for Computing Machinery. https://doi.org/10.1145/3183519.3183525.

Sakshaug, Joseph, Ting Yan, and Roger Tourangeau. 2010. "Nonresponse Error, Measurement Error, and Mode of Data Collection: Tradeoffs in a Multi-Mode Survey of Sensitive and Non-Sensitive Items." *Public Opinion Quarterly* 74 (5): 907–33. https://doi.org/10.1093/poq/nfq057.

Salganik, Matthew. 2018. *Bit by Bit: Social Research in the Digital Age*. New Jersey: Princeton University Press.

Salganik, Matthew, Peter Sheridan Dodds, and Duncan Watts. 2006. "Experimental Study of Inequality and Unpredictability in an Artificial Cultural Market." *Science* 311 (5762): 854–56. https://doi.org/10.1126/science.1121066.

Salganik, Matthew, and Douglas Heckathorn. 2004. "Sampling and Estimation in Hidden Populations Using Respondent-Driven Sampling." *Sociological Methodology* 34 (1): 193–240. https://doi.org/10.1111/j.0081-1750.2004.00152.x.

Sambasivan, Nithya, Shivani Kapania, Hannah Highfill, Diana Akrong, Praveen Paritosh, and Lora Aroyo. 2021. "'Everyone Wants to Do the Model Work, Not the Data Work': Data Cascades in High-Stakes AI." In *Proceedings of the 2021 CHI Conference on Human Factors in Computing Systems*. ACM. https://doi.org/10.1145/3411764.3445518.

Samuel, Arthur. 1959. "Some Studies in Machine Learning Using the Game of Checkers." *IBM Journal of Research and Development* 3 (3): 210–29. https://doi.org/10.1147/rd.33.0210.

Saulnier, Lucile, Siddharth Karamcheti, Hugo Laurençon, Léo Tronchon, Thomas Wang, Victor Sanh, Amanpreet Singh, et al. 2022. "Putting Ethical Principles at the Core of the Research Lifecycle." https://huggingface.co/blog/ethical-charter-multimodal.

Savage, Van, and Pamela Yeh. 2019. "Novelist Cormac McCarthy's Tips on How to Write a Great Science Paper." *Nature* 574 (7778): 441–42. https://doi.org/10.1038/d41586-019-02918-5.

Schaffner, Brian, Stephen Ansolabehere, and Sam Luks. 2021. "Cooperative Election Study Common Content, 2020." Harvard Dataverse. https://doi.org/10.7910/DVN/E9N6PH.

Schloerke, Barret, and Jeff Allen. 2022. *plumber: An API Generator for R*. https://CRAN.R-project.org/package=plumber.

Schmertmann, Carl. 2022. "UN API Test," July. https://bonecave.schmert.net/un-api-example.html.

Schofield, Alexandra, Måns Magnusson, and David Mimno. 2017. "Pulling Out the Stops: Rethinking Stopword Removal for Topic Models." In *Proceedings of the 15th Conference of the European Chapter of the Association for Computational Linguistics: Volume 2, Short Papers*, 432–36. Valencia, Spain: Association for Computational Linguistics. https://aclanthology.org/E17-2069.

Schofield, Alexandra, Måns Magnusson, Laure Thompson, and David Mimno. 2017. "Understanding Text Pre-Processing for Latent Dirichlet Allocation." In *ACL Workshop for Women in NLP (WiNLP)*. https://www.cs.cornell.edu/~xanda/winlp2017.pdf.

Schofield, Alexandra, Laure Thompson, and David Mimno. 2017. "Quantifying the Effects of Text Duplication on Semantic Models." In *Proceedings of the 2017 Conference on Empirical Methods in Natural Language Processing*, 2737–47. Copenhagen, Denmark: Association for Computational Linguistics. https://doi.org/10.18653/v1/D17-1290.

Scott, James. 1998. *Seeing Like a State*. Yale University Press.

Sekhon, Jasjeet, and Rocío Titiunik. 2017. "Understanding Regression Discontinuity Designs as Observational Studies." *Observational Studies* 3 (2): 174–82. https://doi.org/10.1353/obs.2017.0005.

Sen, Amartya. 1980. "Description as Choice." *Oxford Economic Papers* 32 (3): 353–69. https://doi.org/10.1093/oxfordjournals.oep.a041484.

Shankar, Shreya, Rolando Garcia, Joseph Hellerstein, and Aditya Parameswaran. 2022. "Operationalizing Machine Learning: An Interview Study." arXiv. https://doi.org/10.48550/ARXIV.2209.09125.

Si, Yajuan. 2020. "On the Use of Auxiliary Variables in Multilevel Regression and Poststratification." https://arxiv.org/abs/2011.00360.

Sides, John, Lynn Vavreck, and Christopher Warshaw. 2021. "The Effect of Television Advertising in United States Elections." *American Political Science Review*, 1–17. https://doi.org/10.1017/s000305542100112x.

Silberzahn, Raphael, Eric Uhlmann, Daniel Martin, Pasquale Anselmi, Frederik Aust, Eli Awtrey, Štěpán Bahník, et al. 2018. "Many Analysts, One Data Set: Making Transparent How Variations in Analytic Choices Affect Results." *Advances in Methods and Practices in Psychological Science* 1 (3): 337–56. https://doi.org/10.1177/2515245917747646.

Silge, Julia, and David Robinson. 2016. "tidytext: Text Mining and Analysis Using Tidy Data Principles in R." *The Journal of Open Source Software* 1 (3). https://doi.org/10.21105/joss.00037.

Silver, Nate. 2020. "We Fixed an Issue with How Our Primary Forecast Was Calculating Candidates' Demographic Strengths." *FiveThirtyEight*, February. https://fivethirtyeight.com/features/we-fixed-a-mistake-in-how-our-primary-forecast-was-calculating-candidates-demographic-strengths/.

Simonsohn, Uri. 2013. "Just Post It: The Lesson from Two Cases of Fabricated Data Detected by Statistics Alone." *Psychological Science* 24 (10): 1875–88. https://doi.org/10.1177/0956797613480366.

Simpson, Edward. 1951. "The Interpretation of Interaction in Contingency Tables." *Journal of the Royal Statistical Society: Series B (Methodological)* 13 (2): 238–41. https://doi.org/10.1111/j.2517-6161.1951.tb00088.x.

Smith, Jessie, Saleema Amershi, Solon Barocas, Hanna Wallach, and Jennifer Wortman Vaughan. 2022. "REAL ML: Recognizing, Exploring, and Articulating Limitations of Machine Learning Research." *2022 ACM Conference on Fairness, Accountability, and Transparency (FAccT '22)*. https://doi.org/10.1145/3531146.3533122.

Smith, Matthew. 2018. "Should Milk Go in a Cup of Tea First or Last?" July. https://yougov.co.uk/topics/consumer/articles-reports/2018/07/30/should-milk-go-cup-tea-first-or-last.

Smith, Richard. 2002. "A Statistical Assessment of Buchanan's Vote in Palm Beach County." *Statistical Science* 17 (4): 441–57. https://doi.org/10.1214/ss/1049993203.

Sobek, Matthew, and Steven Ruggles. 1999. "The IPUMS Project: An Update." *Historical Methods: A Journal of Quantitative and Interdisciplinary History* 32 (3): 102–10. https://doi.org/10.1080/01615449909598930.

Somers, James. 2015. "Toolkits for the Mind." *MIT Technology Review*, April. https://www.technologyreview.com/2015/04/02/168469/toolkits-for-the-mind/.

———. 2017. "Torching the Modern-Day Library of Alexandria." *The Atlantic*, April. https://www.theatlantic.com/technology/archive/2017/04/the-tragedy-of-google-books/523320/.

———. 2018. "The Scientific Paper Is Obsolete." *The Atlantic*, April. https://www.theatlantic.com/science/archive/2018/04/the-scientific-paper-is-obsolete/556676/.

Spear, Mary Eleanor. 1952. *Charting Statistics.* https://archive.org/details/ChartingStatistics_201801/.

Sprint, Gina, and Jason Conci. 2019. "Mining GitHub Classroom Commit Behavior in Elective and Introductory Computer Science Courses." *Journal of Computing Sciences in Colleges* 35 (1): 76–84.

Staicu, Ana-Maria. 2017. "Interview with Nancy Reid." *International Statistical Review* 85 (3): 381–403. https://doi.org/10.1111/insr.12237.

Staniak, Mateusz, and Przemysław Biecek. 2019. "The Landscape of R Packages for Automated Exploratory Data Analysis." *The R Journal* 11 (2): 347–69. https://doi.org/10.32614/RJ-2019-033.

Stantcheva, Stefanie. 2023. "How to Run Surveys: A Guide to Creating Your Own Identifying Variation and Revealing the Invisible." *Annual Review of Economics.* https://scholar.harvard.edu/files/stantcheva/files/How_to_run_surveys_Stantcheva.pdf.

Statistics Canada. 2017. "Guide to the Census of Population, 2016." Statistics Canada. https://www12.statcan.gc.ca/census-recensement/2016/ref/98-304/98-304-x2016001-eng.pdf.

———. 2020. "Sex at Birth and Gender: Technical Report on Changes for the 2021 Census." Statistics Canada. https://www12.statcan.gc.ca/census-recensement/2021/ref/98-20-0002/982000022020002-eng.pdf.

Steckel, Richard. 1991. "The Quality of Census Data for Historical Inquiry: A Research Agenda." *Social Science History* 15 (4): 579–99. https://doi.org/10.2307/1171470.

Steele, Fiona. 2007. "Multilevel Models for Longitudinal Data." *Journal of the Royal Statistical Society Series A: Statistics in Society* 171 (1): 5–19. https://doi.org/10.1111/j.1467-985x.2007.00509.x.

Steele, Fiona, Anna Vignoles, and Andrew Jenkins. 2007. "The Effect of School Resources on Pupil Attainment: A Multilevel Simultaneous Equation Modelling Approach." *Journal of the Royal Statistical Society Series A: Statistics in Society* 170 (3): 801–24. https://doi.org/10.1111/j.1467-985x.2007.00476.x.

Stevens, Wallace. 1934. *The Idea of Order at Key West.* https://www.poetryfoundation.org/poems/43431/the-idea-of-order-at-key-west.

Steyvers, Mark, and Tom Griffiths. 2006. "Probabilistic Topic Models." In *Latent Semantic Analysis: A Road to Meaning*, edited by T. Landauer, D McNamara, S. Dennis, and W. Kintsch. https://cocosci.princeton.edu/tom/papers/SteyversGriffiths.pdf.

Stigler, Stephen. 1978. "Francis Ysidro Edgeworth, Statistician." *Journal of the Royal Statistical Society. Series A (General)* 141 (3): 287–322. https://doi.org/10.2307/2344804.

———. 1986. *The History of Statistics.* Massachusetts: Belknap Harvard.

Stock, James, and Francesco Trebbi. 2003. "Retrospectives: Who Invented Instrumental Variable Regression?" *Journal of Economic Perspectives* 17 (3): 177–94. https://doi.org/10.1257/089533003769204416.

Stolberg, Michael. 2006. "Inventing the Randomized Double-Blind Trial: The Nuremberg Salt Test of 1835." *Journal of the Royal Society of Medicine* 99 (12): 642–43. https://doi.org/10.1177/014107680609901216.

Stoler, Ann Laura. 2002. "Colonial Archives and the Arts of Governance." *Archival Science* 2 (March): 87–109. https://doi.org/10.1007/bf02435632.

Stolley, Paul. 1991. "When Genius Errs: R. A. Fisher and the Lung Cancer Controversy." *American Journal of Epidemiology* 133 (5): 416–25. https://doi.org/10.1093/oxfordjournals.aje.a115904.

Stommes, Drew, P. M. Aronow, and Fredrik Sävje. 2021. "On the Reliability of Published Findings Using the Regression Discontinuity Design in Political Science." arXiv. https://doi.org/10.48550/ARXIV.2109.14526.

Student. 1908. "The Probable Error of a Mean." *Biometrika* 6 (1): 1–25. https://doi.org/10.2307/2331554.

Sunstein, Cass, and Lucia Reisch. 2017. *The Economics of Nudge*. Routledge.

Suriyakumar, Vinith, Nicolas Papernot, Anna Goldenberg, and Marzyeh Ghassemi. 2021. "Chasing Your Long Tails." In *Proceedings of the 2021 ACM Conference on Fairness, Accountability, and Transparency*. https://doi.org/10.1145/3442188.3445934.

Swain, Larry. 1985. "Basic Principles of Questionnaire Design." *Survey Methodology* 11 (2): 161–70.

Sylvester, Christine, Anastasia Ershova, Aleksandra Khokhlova, Nikoleta Yordanova, and Zachary Greene. 2023. "ParlEE plenary speeches V2 data set: Annotated full-text of 15.1 million sentence-level plenary speeches of six EU legislative chambers." *Harvard Dataverse*. https://doi.org/10.7910/DVN/VOPK0E.

Szaszi, Barnabas, Anthony Higney, Aaron Charlton, Andrew Gelman, Ignazio Ziano, Balazs Aczel, Daniel Goldstein, David Yeager, and Elizabeth Tipton. 2022. "No Reason to Expect Large and Consistent Effects of Nudge Interventions." *Proceedings of the National Academy of Sciences* 119 (31): e2200732119. https://doi.org/10.1073/pnas.2200732119.

Taddy, Matt. 2019. *Business Data Science*. 1st ed. McGraw Hill.

Taflaga, Marija, and Matthew Kerby. 2019. "Who Does What Work in a Ministerial Office: Politically Appointed Staff and the Descriptive Representation of Women in Australian Political Offices, 1979–2010." *Political Studies* 68 (2): 463–85. https://doi.org/10.1177/0032321719853459.

Tal, Eran. 2020. "Measurement in Science." In *The Stanford Encyclopedia of Philosophy*, edited by Edward Zalta, Fall 2020. https://plato.stanford.edu/archives/fall2020/entries/measurement-science/; Metaphysics Research Lab, Stanford University.

Tang, John. 2015. "Pollution havens and the trade in toxic chemicals: Evidence from U.S. trade flows." *Ecological Economics* 112 (April): 150–60. https://doi.org/10.1016/j.ecolecon.2015.02.022.

Tang, Jun, Aleksandra Korolova, Xiaolong Bai, Xueqiang Wang, and Xiaofeng Wang. 2017. "Privacy Loss in Apple's Implementation of Differential Privacy on MacOS 10.12." arXiv. https://doi.org/10.48550/arXiv.1709.02753.

Tausanovitch, Chris, and Lynn Vavreck. 2021. "Democracy Fund + UCLA Nationscape Project." https://www.voterstudygroup.org/data/nationscape.

Taylor, Adam. 2015. "New Zealand Says No to Jedis." *The Washington Post*, September. https://www.washingtonpost.com/news/worldviews/wp/2015/09/29/new-zealand-says-no-to-jedis/.

Teate, Renée. 2022. *SQL for Data Scientists*. Wiley.

The Economist. 2013. "Johnson: Those Six Little Rules: George Orwell on Writing," July. https://www.economist.com/prospero/2013/07/29/johnson-those-six-little-rules.

———. 2022a. "What Spotify Data Show about the Decline of English," January. https://www.economist.com/interactives/graphic-detail/2022/01/29/what-spotify-data-show-about-the-decline-of-english.

———. 2022b. "Will Emmanuel Macron Win a Second Term?" April. https://www.economist.com/interactive/france-2022/forecast.

———. 2022c. "France's Presidential Election: The Second Round in Detail," April. https://www.economist.com/interactive/france-2022/results-round-two.

The Washington Post. 2023. "Fatal Force Database." https://github.com/washingtonpost/data-police-shootings.

The White House. 2023. "Recommendations on the Best Practices for the Collection of Sexual Orientation and Gender Identity Data on Federal Statistical Survey," January. https://www.whitehouse.gov/wp-content/uploads/2023/01/SOGI-Best-Practices.pdf.

Thieme, Nick. 2018. "R Generation." *Significance* 15 (4): 14–19. https://doi.org/10.1111/j.1740-9713.2018.01169.x.

Thistlethwaite, Donald, and Donald Campbell. 1960. "Regression-Discontinuity Analysis: An Alternative to the Ex Post Facto Experiment." *Journal of Educational Psychology* 51 (6): 309–17. https://doi.org/10.1037/h0044319.

Thompson, Charlie, Daniel Antal, Josiah Parry, Donal Phipps, and Tom Wolff. 2022. *spotifyr: R Wrapper for the "Spotify" Web API.* https://CRAN.R-project.org/package=spotifyr.

Thomson-DeVeaux, Amelia, Laura Bronner, and Damini Sharma. 2021. "Cities Spend Millions On Police Misconduct Every Year. Here's Why It's So Difficult to Hold Departments Accountable." *FiveThirtyEight*, February. https://fivethirtyeight.com/features/why-statistics-dont-capture-the-full-extent-of-the-systemic-bias-in-policing/.

Thornhill, John. 2021. "Lunch with the FT: Mathematician Hannah Fry." *Financial Times*, July. https://www.ft.com/content/a5e33e5a-99b9-4bbc-948f-8a527c7675c3.

Tierney, Nicholas, Di Cook, Miles McBain, and Colin Fay. 2021. *naniar: Data Structures, Summaries, and Visualisations for Missing Data.* https://CRAN.R-project.org/package=naniar.

Tierney, Nicholas, and Karthik Ram. 2020. "A Realistic Guide to Making Data Available Alongside Code to Improve Reproducibility." https://arxiv.org/abs/2002.11626.

———. 2021. "Common-Sense Approaches to Sharing Tabular Data Alongside Publication." *Patterns* 2 (12): 100368. https://doi.org/10.1016/j.patter.2021.100368.

Timbers, Tiffany. 2020. *canlang: Canadian Census language data.* https://ttimbers.github.io/canlang/.

Timbers, Tiffany, Trevor Campbell, and Melissa Lee. 2022. *Data Science: A First Introduction.* Chapman; Hall/CRC. https://datasciencebook.ca.

Tolley, Erin, and Mireille Paquet. 2021. "Gender, Municipal Party Politics, and Montreal's First Woman Mayor." *Canadian Journal of Urban Research* 30 (1): 40–52. https://cjur.uwinnipeg.ca/index.php/cjur/article/view/323.

Tourangeau, Roger, Lance Rips, and Kenneth Rasinski. 2000. *The Psychology of Survey Response.* 1st ed. Cambridge University Press. https://doi.org/10.1017/CBO9780511819322.003.

Trisovic, Ana, Matthew Lau, Thomas Pasquier, and Mercè Crosas. 2022. "A Large-Scale Study on Research Code Quality and Execution." *Scientific Data* 9 (1). https://doi.org/10.1038/s41597-022-01143-6.

Tukey, John. 1962. "The Future of Data Analysis." *The Annals of Mathematical Statistics* 33 (1): 1–67. https://doi.org/10.1214/aoms/1177704711.

———. 1977. *Exploratory Data Analysis.*

Turcotte, Alexi, Aviral Goel, Filip Křikava, and Jan Vitek. 2020. "Designing Types for r, Empirically." *Proceedings of the ACM on Programming Languages* 4 (OOPSLA): 1–25. https://doi.org/10.1145/3428249.

UN IGME. 2021. "Levels and Trends in Child Mortality, 2021." https://childmortality.org/wp-content/uploads/2021/12/UNICEF-2021-Child-Mortality-Report.pdf.

Urban, Steve, Rangarajan Sreenivasan, and Vineet Kannan. 2016. "It's All A/Bout Testing: The Netflix Experimentation Platform." *Netflix Technology Blog*, April. https://netflixtechblog.com/its-all-a-bout-testing-the-netflix-experimentation-platform-4e1ca458c15.

Ushey, Kevin. 2022. *renv: Project Environments*. https://CRAN.R-project.org/package=renv.

van Buuren, Stef, and Karin Groothuis-Oudshoorn. 2011. "mice: Multivariate Imputation by Chained Equations in R." *Journal of Statistical Software* 45 (3): 1–67. https://doi.org/10.18637/jss.v045.i03.

Van den Broeck, Jan, Solveig Argeseanu Cunningham, Roger Eeckels, and Kobus Herbst. 2005. "Data Cleaning: Detecting, Diagnosing, and Editing Data Abnormalities." *PLOS Medicine* 2 (10): e267. https://doi.org/10.1371/journal.pmed.0020267.

van der Loo, Mark. 2022. *The Data Validation Cookbook*. https://data-cleaning.github.io/validate/.

van der Loo, Mark, and Edwin De Jonge. 2021. "Data Validation Infrastructure for R." *Journal of Statistical Software* 97 (10): 1–33. https://doi.org/10.18637/jss.v097.i10.

Vanderplas, Susan, Dianne Cook, and Heike Hofmann. 2020. "Testing Statistical Charts: What Makes a Good Graph?" *Annual Review of Statistics and Its Application* 7: 61–88. https://doi.org/10.1146/annurev-statistics-031219-041252.

Vanhoenacker, Mark. 2015. *Skyfaring: A Journey with a Pilot*. 1st ed. Alfred A. Knopf.

Varin, Cristiano, Nancy Reid, and David Firth. 2011. "An Overview of Composite Likelihood Methods." *Statistica Sinica*, 5–42. https://www.jstor.org/stable/24309261.

Varner, Maddy, and Aaron Sankin. 2020. "Suckers List: How Allstate's Secret Auto Insurance Algorithm Squeezes Big Spenders." *The Markup*, February. https://themarkup.org/allstates-algorithm/2020/02/25/car-insurance-suckers-list.

Vavreck, Lynn, and Chris Tausanovitch. 2021. "Democracy Fund + UCLA Nationscape Project User Guide." https://www.voterstudygroup.org/data/nationscape.

Vickers, Andrew, and Emily Vertosick. 2016. "An Empirical Study of Race Times in Recreational Endurance Runners." *BMC Sports Science, Medicine and Rehabilitation* 8 (1). https://doi.org/10.1186/s13102-016-0052-y.

Vidoni, Melina. 2021. "Evaluating Unit Testing Practices in R Packages." In *2021 IEEE/ACM 43rd International Conference on Software Engineering (ICSE)*, 1523–34. https://doi.org/10.1109/ICSE43902.2021.00136.

von Bergmann, Jens, Dmitry Shkolnik, and Aaron Jacobs. 2021. *cancensus: R package to access, retrieve, and work with Canadian Census data and geography*. https://mountainmath.github.io/cancensus/.

Walby, Kevin, and Alex Luscombe. 2019. *Freedom of Information and Social Science Research Design*. Routledge.

Walker, Kyle. 2022. *Analyzing US Census Data*. Chapman; Hall/CRC. https://walker-data.com/census-r/index.html.

Walker, Kyle, and Matt Herman. 2022. *tidycensus: Load US Census Boundary and Attribute Data as "tidyverse" and "sf"-Ready Data Frames*. https://CRAN.R-project.org/package=tidycensus.

Wallach, Hanna. 2018. "Computational Social Science $\neq$ Computer Science + Social Data." *Communications of the ACM* 61 (3): 42–44. https://doi.org/10.1145/3132698.

Wan, Mengting, and Julian J. McAuley. 2018. "Item Recommendation on Monotonic Behavior Chains." In *Proceedings of the 12th ACM Conference on Recommender Systems, RecSys 2018, Vancouver, BC, Canada, October 2-7, 2018*, edited by Sole Pera, Michael D. Ekstrand, Xavier Amatriain, and John O'Donovan, 86–94. ACM. https://doi.org/10.1145/3240323.3240369.

Wan, Mengting, Rishabh Misra, Ndapa Nakashole, and Julian J. McAuley. 2019. "Fine Grained Spoiler Detection from Large-Scale Review Corpora." In *Proceedings of the 57th*

Conference of the Association for Computational Linguistics, ACL 2019, Florence, Italy, July 28- August 2, 2019, Volume 1: Long Papers, edited by Anna Korhonen, David R. Traum, and Lluís Màrquez, 2605–10. Association for Computational Linguistics. https://doi.org/10.18653/v1/p19-1248.

Wang, Wei, David Rothschild, Sharad Goel, and Andrew Gelman. 2015. "Forecasting Elections with Non-Representative Polls." *International Journal of Forecasting* 31 (3): 980–91. https://doi.org/10.1016/j.ijforecast.2014.06.001.

Wang, Yilun, and Michal Kosinski. 2018. "Deep Neural Networks Are More Accurate Than Humans at Detecting Sexual Orientation from Facial Images." *Journal of Personality and Social Psychology* 114 (2): 246–57. https://doi.org/10.1037/pspa0000098.

Wardrop, Robert. 1995. "Simpson's Paradox and the Hot Hand in Basketball." *The American Statistician* 49 (1): 24–28. https://doi.org/10.2307/2684806.

Ware, James. 1989. "Investigating Therapies of Potentially Great Benefit: ECMO." *Statistical Science* 4 (4): 298–306. https://doi.org/10.1214/ss/1177012384.

Wasserman, Larry. 2005. *All of Statistics.* Springer.

Wei, LJ, and S Durham. 1978. "The Randomized Play-the-Winner Rule in Medical Trials." *Journal of the American Statistical Association* 73 (364): 840–43. https://doi.org/10.2307/2286290.

Weinberg, Gerald. 1971. *The Psychology of Computer Programming.* New York: Van Nostrand Reinhold Company.

Weissgerber, Tracey, Natasa Milic, Stacey Winham, and Vesna Garovic. 2015. "Beyond Bar and Line Graphs: Time for a New Data Presentation Paradigm." *PLoS Biology* 13 (4): e1002128. https://doi.org/10.1371/journal.pbio.1002128.

Whitby, Andrew. 2020. *The Sum of the People.* New York: Basic Books.

Whitelaw, James. 1805. *An Essay on the Population of Dublin. Being the Result of an Actual Survey Taken in 1798, with Great Care and Precision, and Arranged in a Manner Entirely New.* Graisberry; Campbell.

Wicherts, Jelte, Marjan Bakker, and Dylan Molenaar. 2011. "Willingness to Share Research Data Is Related to the Strength of the Evidence and the Quality of Reporting of Statistical Results." *PLOS ONE* 6 (11): e26828. https://doi.org/10.1371/journal.pone.0026828.

Wickham, Hadley. 2009. "Manipulating Data." In *ggplot2*, 157–75. Springer New York. https://doi.org/10.1007/978-0-387-98141-3_9.

———. 2010. "A Layered Grammar of Graphics." *Journal of Computational and Graphical Statistics* 19 (1): 3–28. https://doi.org/10.1198/jcgs.2009.07098.

———. 2011. "testthat: Get Started with Testing." *The R Journal* 3: 5–10. https://journal.r-project.org/archive/2011-1/RJournal%5F2011-1%5FWickham.pdf.

———. 2014. "Tidy Data." *Journal of Statistical Software* 59 (1): 1–23. https://doi.org/10.18637/jss.v059.i10.

———. 2016. *ggplot2: Elegant Graphics for Data Analysis.* Springer-Verlag New York. https://ggplot2.tidyverse.org.

———. 2017. *tidyverse: Easily Install and Load the "Tidyverse".* https://CRAN.R-project.org/package=tidyverse.

———. 2018. "Whole Game." *YouTube*, January. https://youtu.be/go5Au01Jrvs.

———. 2019. *Advanced R.* 2nd ed. Chapman; Hall/CRC. https://adv-r.hadley.nz.

———. 2020. *Tidyverse.* https://www.tidyverse.org/.

———. 2021a. *babynames: US Baby Names 1880-2017.* https://CRAN.R-project.org/package=babynames.

———. 2021b. *Mastering Shiny.* 1st ed. O'Reilly Media. https://mastering-shiny.org.

———. 2021c. *The Tidyverse Style Guide.* https://style.tidyverse.org/index.html.

———. 2022a. *R Packages.* 2nd ed. O'Reilly Media. https://r-pkgs.org.

———. 2022b. *rvest: Easily Harvest (Scrape) Web Pages.* https://CRAN.R-project.org/package=rvest.

———. 2022c. *stringr: Simple, Consistent Wrappers for Common String Operations*. https://CRAN.R-project.org/package=stringr.

———. 2023a. *forcats: Tools for Working with Categorical Variables (Factors)*. https://CRAN.R-project.org/package=forcats.

———. 2023b. *httr: Tools for Working with URLs and HTTP*. https://CRAN.R-project.org/package=httr.

Wickham, Hadley, Mara Averick, Jenny Bryan, Winston Chang, Lucy D'Agostino McGowan, Romain François, Garrett Grolemund, et al. 2019. "Welcome to the Tidyverse." *Journal of Open Source Software* 4 (43): 1686. https://doi.org/10.21105/joss.01686.

Wickham, Hadley, and Jennifer Bryan. 2023. *readxl: Read Excel Files*. https://CRAN.R-project.org/package=readxl.

Wickham, Hadley, Jennifer Bryan, and Malcolm Barrett. 2022. *usethis: Automate Package and Project Setup*. https://CRAN.R-project.org/package=usethis.

Wickham, Hadley, Mine Çetinkaya-Rundel, and Garrett Grolemund. (2016) 2023. *R for Data Science*. 2nd ed. O'Reilly Media. https://r4ds.hadley.nz.

Wickham, Hadley, Romain François, Lionel Henry, and Kirill Müller. 2022. *dplyr: A Grammar of Data Manipulation*. https://CRAN.R-project.org/package=dplyr.

Wickham, Hadley, Maximilian Girlich, and Edgar Ruiz. 2022. *dbplyr: A "dplyr" Back End for Databases*. https://CRAN.R-project.org/package=dbplyr.

Wickham, Hadley, and Lionel Henry. 2022. *purrr: Functional Programming Tools*. https://CRAN.R-project.org/package=purrr.

Wickham, Hadley, Jim Hester, and Jenny Bryan. 2022. *readr: Read Rectangular Text Data*. https://CRAN.R-project.org/package=readr.

Wickham, Hadley, Jim Hester, Winston Chang, and Jenny Bryan. 2022. *devtools: Tools to Make Developing R Packages Easier*. https://CRAN.R-project.org/package=devtools.

Wickham, Hadley, Jim Hester, and Jeroen Ooms. 2021. *xml2: Parse XML*. https://CRAN.R-project.org/package=xml2.

Wickham, Hadley, Evan Miller, and Danny Smith. 2023. *haven: Import and Export "SPSS" "Stata" and "SAS" Files*. https://CRAN.R-project.org/package=haven.

Wickham, Hadley, and Dana Seidel. 2022. *scales: Scale Functions for Visualization*. https://CRAN.R-project.org/package=scales.

Wickham, Hadley, and Lisa Stryjewski. 2011. "40 Years of Boxplots," November. https://vita.had.co.nz/papers/boxplots.pdf.

Wickham, Hadley, Davis Vaughan, and Maximilian Girlich. 2023. *tidyr: Tidy Messy Data*. https://CRAN.R-project.org/package=tidyr.

Wiessner, Polly. 2014. "Embers of Society: Firelight Talk Among the Ju/'hoansi Bushmen." *Proceedings of the National Academy of Sciences* 111 (39): 14027–35. https://doi.org/10.1073/pnas.1404212111.

Wilde, Oscar. 1891. *The Picture of Dorian Gray*. https://www.gutenberg.org/files/174/174-h/174-h.htm.

Wilford, John Noble. 1977. "Wernher von Braun, Rocket Pioneer, Dies." *The New York Times*, June. https://www.nytimes.com/1977/06/18/archives/wernher-von-braun-rocket-pioneer-dies-wernher-von-braun-pioneer-in.html.

Wilkinson, Leland. 2005. *The Grammar of Graphics*. 2nd ed. Springer.

Wilkinson, Mark, Michel Dumontier, IJsbrand Jan Aalbersberg, Gabrielle Appleton, Myles Axton, Arie Baak, Niklas Blomberg, et al. 2016. "The FAIR Guiding Principles for Scientific Data Management and Stewardship." *Scientific Data* 3 (1): 1–9. https://doi.org/10.1038/sdata.2016.18.

Wilson, Greg, Jenny Bryan, Karen Cranston, Justin Kitzes, Lex Nederbragt, and Tracy Teal. 2017. "Good Enough Practices in Scientific Computing." *PLOS Computational Biology* 13 (6): 1–20. https://doi.org/10.1371/journal.pcbi.1005510.

Wong, Julia Carrie. 2020. "One Year Inside Trump's Monumental Facebook Campaign." *The Guardian*, January. https://www.theguardian.com/us-news/2020/jan/28/donald-trump-facebook-ad-campaign-2020-election.

Wood, Simon. 2015. *Core Statistics*. Cambridge University Press. https://www.maths.ed.ac.uk//%7Eswood34/core-statistics.pdf.

World Health Organization. 2019. "Trends in Maternal Mortality 2000 to 2017: Estimates by WHO, UNICEF, UNFPA, World Bank Group and the United Nations Population Division." https://www.who.int/reproductivehealth/publications/maternal-mortality-2000-2017/en/.

Wright, Philip. 1928. *The Tariff on Animal and Vegetable Oils*. New York: Macmillan Company.

Wu, Changbao, and Mary Thompson. 2020. *Sampling Theory and Practice*. Springer.

Xie, Yihui. 2019. "TinyTeX: A lightweight, cross-platform, and easy-to-maintain LaTeX distribution based on TeX Live." *TUGboat*, no. 1: 30–32. https://tug.org/TUGboat/Contents/contents40-1.html.

———. 2023. *knitr: A General-Purpose Package for Dynamic Report Generation in R*. https://yihui.org/knitr/.

Xu, Ya. 2020. "Causal Inference Challenges in Industry: A Perspective from Experiences at LinkedIn." *YouTube*, July. https://youtu.be/OoKsLAvyIYA.

Yoshioka, Alan. 1998. "Use of Randomisation in the Medical Research Council's Clinical Trial of Streptomycin in Pulmonary Tuberculosis in the 1940s." *BMJ* 317 (7167): 1220–23. https://doi.org/10.1136/bmj.317.7167.1220.

Zhang, Ping, XunPeng Shi, YongPing Sun, Jingbo Cui, and Shuai Shao. 2019. "Have China's provinces achieved their targets of energy intensity reduction? Reassessment based on nighttime lighting data." *Energy Policy* 128 (May): 276–83. https://doi.org/10.1016/j.enpol.2019.01.014.

Zhang, Susan, Stephen Roller, Naman Goyal, Mikel Artetxe, Moya Chen, Shuohui Chen, Christopher Dewan, et al. 2022. "OPT: Open Pre-Trained Transformer Language Models." arXiv. https://doi.org/10.48550/arXiv.2205.01068.

Zimmer, Michael. 2018. "Addressing Conceptual Gaps in Big Data Research Ethics: An Application of Contextual Integrity." *Social Media + Society* 4 (2): 1–11. https://doi.org/10.1177/2056305118768300.

Zinsser, William. 1976. *On Writing Well*. New York: HarperCollins.

Zook, Matthew, Solon Barocas, danah boyd, Kate Crawford, Emily Keller, Seeta Peña Gangadharan, Alyssa Goodman, et al. 2017. "Ten Simple Rules for Responsible Big Data Research." *PLOS Computational Biology* 13 (3): e1005399. https://doi.org/10.1371/journal.pcbi.1005399.

Index

For Product Safety Concerns and Information please contact our EU representative GPSR@taylorandfrancis.com Taylor & Francis Verlag GmbH, Kaufingerstraße 24, 80331 München, Germany